Fuzzy Logic and Computational Intelligence

Fuzzy Logic and Computational Intelligence

Guest Editors

**Himansu Das
Mahendra Kumar Gourisaria**

Basel • Beijing • Wuhan • Barcelona • Belgrade • Novi Sad • Cluj • Manchester

Guest Editors

Himansu Das
School of Computer
Engineering
KIIT Deemed to be University
Bhubaneswar
India

Mahendra Kumar Gourisaria
School of Computer
Engineering
KIIT Deemed to be University
Bhubaneswar
India

Editorial Office
MDPI AG
Grosspeteranlage 5
4052 Basel, Switzerland

This is a reprint of the Special Issue, published open access by the journal *Mathematics* (ISSN 2227-7390), freely accessible at: https://www.mdpi.com/si/mathematics/Fuzzy_Log_CI.

For citation purposes, cite each article independently as indicated on the article page online and as indicated below:

Lastname, A.A.; Lastname, B.B. Article Title. *Journal Name* **Year**, *Volume Number*, Page Range.

ISBN 978-3-7258-3319-1 (Hbk)
ISBN 978-3-7258-3320-7 (PDF)
https://doi.org/10.3390/books978-3-7258-3320-7

© 2025 by the authors. Articles in this book are Open Access and distributed under the Creative Commons Attribution (CC BY) license. The book as a whole is distributed by MDPI under the terms and conditions of the Creative Commons Attribution-NonCommercial-NoDerivs (CC BY-NC-ND) license (https://creativecommons.org/licenses/by-nc-nd/4.0/).

Contents

About the Editors vii

Preface ix

Shilpa Suman, Dheeraj Kumar and Anil Kumar
Fuzzy Based Convolutional Noise Clustering Classifier to Handle the Noise and Heterogeneity in Image Classification
Reprinted from: *Mathematics* 2022, 10, 4056, https://doi.org/10.3390/math10214056 1

Sudheer Babu Punuri, Sanjay Kumar Kuanar, Manjur Kolhar, Tusar Kanti Mishra, Abdalla Alameen, Hitesh Mohapatra, Soumya Ranjan Mishra
Efficient Net-XGBoost: An Implementation for Facial Emotion Recognition Using Transfer Learning
Reprinted from: *Mathematics* 2023, 11, 776, https://doi.org/10.3390/math11030776 28

Narayan Nayak, Soumya Ranjan Das, Tapas Kumar Panigrahi, Himansu Das, Soumya Ranjan Nayak, Krishna Kant Singh, et al.
Overshoot Reduction Using Adaptive Neuro-Fuzzy Inference System for an Autonomous Underwater Vehicle
Reprinted from: *Mathematics* 2023, 11, 1868, https://doi.org/10.3390/math11081868 52

Himansu Das, Sanjay Prajapati, Mahendra Kumar Gourisaria, Radha Mohan Pattanayak, Abdalla Alameen and Manjur Kolhar
Feature Selection Using Golden Jackal Optimization for Software Fault Prediction
Reprinted from: *Mathematics* 2023, 11, 2438, https://doi.org/10.3390/math11112438 78

Sunil K. Panigrahi, Veena Goswami, Hemant K. Apat, Ganga B. Mund, Himansu Das and Rabindra K. Barik
PQ-Mist: Priority Queueing-Assisted Mist–Cloud–Fog System for Geospatial Web Service
Reprinted from: *Mathematics* 2023, 11, 3562, https://doi.org/10.3390/math11163562 106

Yung-Yue Chen and Ming-Zhen Ellis-Tiew
Autonomous Trajectory Tracking and Collision Avoidance Design for Unmanned Surface Vessels: A Nonlinear Fuzzy Approach
Reprinted from: *Mathematics* 2023, 11, 3632, https://doi.org/10.3390/math11173632 127

Hanan H. Sakr, Salem A. Alyami and Mohamed A. Abd Elgawad
Medical Diagnosis under Effective Bipolar-Valued Multi-Fuzzy Soft Settings
Reprinted from: *Mathematics* 2023, 11, 3747, https://doi.org/10.3390/math11173747 144

Surbhi Bhatia Khan, Mohammed Alojail and Moteeb Al Moteri
Advancing Disability Management in Information Systems: A Novel Approach through Bidirectional Federated Learning-Based Gradient Optimization
Reprinted from: *Mathematics* 2024, 12, 119, https://doi.org/10.3390/math12010119 173

Sergey Agayan, Shamil Bogoutdinov, Dmitriy Kamaev, Boris Dzeboev and Michael Dobrovolsky
Trends and Extremes in Time Series Based on Fuzzy Logic
Reprinted from: *Mathematics* 2024, 12, 284, https://doi.org/10.3390/math12020284 193

Antonios Kalampakas, Sovan Samanta, Jayanta Bera and Kinkar Chandra Das
A Fuzzy Logic Inference Model for the Evaluation of the Effect of Extrinsic Factors on the Transmission of Infectious Diseases
Reprinted from: *Mathematics* 2024, 12, 648, https://doi.org/10.3390/math12050648 226

Camelia Delcea, Ionuț Nica, Irina Georgescu, Nora Chiriță and Cristian Ciurea
Integrating Fuzzy MCDM Methods and ARDL Approach for Circular Economy Strategy Analysis in Romania
Reprinted from: *Mathematics* **2024**, *12*, 2997, https://doi.org/10.3390/math12192997 . . . . **244**

About the Editors

Himansu Das

Dr. Himansu Das works as an Associate Professor at the School of Computer Engineering, Kalinga Institute of Industrial Technology (KIIT) Deemed to be University, Bhubaneswar, India. He has published several research papers in various international journals and has presented at several conferences. He has also edited several books published by IGI Global, Springer, CRC press, and Elsevier. He has also served on many journals and conferences as an Editorial or Reviewer Board Member. He is proficient in the field of Computer Science Engineering and served as an organizing chair, a publicity chair, and acted as a member of the technical program committees of many national and international conferences. His research interests include Data Mining, Soft Computing, and Machine Learning. He has more than seventeen years of teaching and research experience in various engineering colleges and universities.

Mahendra Kumar Gourisaria

Dr. Mahendra Kumar Gourisaria received his Bachelor's degree in commerce with honours from Calcutta University. He completed an ICWAI (Intermediate) from the Institute of Cost and Works Accountants of India. He has completed a DNIIT from NIIT Sahid Nagar, Bhubaneswar. He obtained his Master's degree in computer application from Indira Gandhi National Open University, New Delhi, and his M. Tech. in Computer Science and Engineering from Biju Patnaik University of Technology, Rourkela. He completed his Ph.D. in CSE from the KIIT Deemed to be University, Bhubaneswar, Odisha. Presently, he is working as an Assistant Professor at the School of Computer Engineering, KIIT Deemed to be University, Bhubaneswar, Odisha. He has more than 22 years of experience in academia and 10 years of research experience. He has guided more than 120 B. Tech. students in their project work, as well as 7 M. Tech. theses. He has published more than 170 research works, including various book chapters, papers in international journals, and presentations at conferences of repute. He has also received a Research Achievement Award from London Metropolitan University (IUILA 2024). His Google Scholar citation rate is more than 2100, with an h-index of 23 and an i10-index of 54. He has also served as an organizing committee member for various conferences and workshops. He has chaired sessions at several international conferences and reviewed for a number of reputed publishers, such as Springer, Hindawi, etc., as well as many reputable conferences. His research interests include cloud computing, machine learning, deep learning, data mining, soft computing, and internet and web technology. He is a member of IEEE, IAENG, and UACEE, as well as a Life Member of ISTE, CSI, and ISCA.

Preface

The development of new technology in the twenty-fifth century has led to an alarming rate of data generation. Before judgments can be made, it is sometimes necessary to analyze and extract relevant information from the vast volume of created data. Analyzing data sensibly and learning from it is a difficult endeavor. Models based on machine learning can learn from data to simulate systems. However, because of unclear, inaccurate, and confusing data, these systems might not always produce improved outcomes. The development of computationally appropriate intelligent systems that can extract high-level knowledge from data is necessary to overcome these problems. This presents the fuzzy logic technique, which enhances system performance by gleaning high-level information from data. In order to create computationally high intelligent systems, machine learning models are used to learn this high-level extracted knowledge to analyze information in order to accomplish a specific objective or reach a decision.

The present reprint contains 11 articles accepted for publication among the 35 total manuscripts submitted to the Special Issue "Fuzzy Logic and Computational Intelligence" of the MDPI *Mathematics* journal. The 11 articles in this reprint, which were previously published in Volumes 10 (2022), 11 (2023), and 12 (2024) of the journal, cover a wide range of subjects related to the theory and applications of fuzzy sets, as well as their application in computational intelligence. These topics include, among others, elements from MCDM methods, inference models, multi-fuzzy soft settings, non-linear fuzzy approaches, adaptive neuro-fuzzy systems in field of federated learning, time series data analysis, feature engineering, mist–cloud–fog systems, facial emoticon recognition, and fuzzy-based convolutional noise classification. Experts who work in the fields of fuzzy sets, fuzzy systems, and fuzzy logic, as well as those who possess the necessary mathematical training and are eager to learn about the latest developments in fuzzy mathematics and fuzzy logic, are expected to find the reprint engaging and helpful.

As the Special Issue's Guest Editor, we would like to express our gratitude to the authors of the papers for their excellent contributions, the reviewers for their insightful criticism on how to make the submitted works better, and the MDPI publications' administrative team for helping us finish this project. The Special Issue's Managing Editor, Dr. Syna Mu, deserves special recognition for outstanding cooperation and helpful support.

Himansu Das and Mahendra Kumar Gourisaria
Guest Editors

Article

Fuzzy Based Convolutional Noise Clustering Classifier to Handle the Noise and Heterogeneity in Image Classification

Shilpa Suman [1,*], Dheeraj Kumar [1] and Anil Kumar [2]

1. Remote Sensing and GIS Laboratory, IIT (ISM), Dhanbad 826004, India
2. PRSD Department, IIRS, Dehradun 248001, India
* Correspondence: suman.shilpa077@gmail.com

Abstract: Conventional Noise Clustering (NC) algorithms do not consider any spatial information in the image. In this study, three algorithms have been presented, Noise Local Information *c*-means (NLICM) and Adaptive Noise Local Information *c*-Means (ADNLICM), which use NC as the base classifier, and Noise Clustering with constraints (NC_S), which incorporates spatial information into the objective function of the NC classifier. These algorithms enhance the performance of classification by minimizing the effect of noise and outliers. The algorithms were tested on two study areas, Haridwar (Uttarakhand) and Banasthali (Rajasthan) in India. All three algorithms were examined using different parameters (distance measures, fuzziness factor, and δ). An analysis determined that the ADNLICM algorithm with Bray–Curtis distance measures, fuzziness factor $m = 1.1$, and $\delta = 10^6$, outperformed the other algorithm and achieved 91.53% overall accuracy. The optimized algorithm returned the lowest variance and RMSE for both study areas, demonstrating that the optimized algorithm works for different satellite images. The optimized technique can be used to categorize images with noisy pixels and heterogeneity for various applications, such as mapping, change detection, area estimation, feature recognition, and classification.

Keywords: remote sensing; NLICM; ADNLICM; NC_S; fuzziness factor; distance measures

MSC: 62H30; 94D05

1. Introduction

Image classification plays a vital role in remote sensing research because classification results are primary for many applications. To improve classification accuracy, many researchers and practitioners have introduced novel classification approaches and techniques [1]. Image classification is mainly done either as hard or soft classification. In hard classification techniques, one pixel belongs to a single class, which is impossible for a real scenario. An image may contain mixed pixels in a real scenario, which means one pixel may have multiple and partial class membership values. Fuzzy clustering algorithms are mainly designed to handle mixed pixels. Fuzzy *c*-means (FCM) [2], Possibilistic *c*-means (PCM) [3], and Noise Clustering (NC) [4] are the primary classifiers used for mixed pixel classification. FCM is a clustering method that allows one sample of data to assign a membership degree function to two or more clusters [5]. FCM is the first and most powerful method used in image classification. FCM was first developed in 1973 by Dunn [6] and further modified by Bezdek (1981). It is based on the minimization of an objective function and has been used for clustering, feature analysis, and target recognition. Pixel-based classification algorithms allot a pixel to a region based on similarities of spectral signature [7]. FCM does not consider information about the immediate neighborhood pixel, so it does not fully utilize the spatial information characteristics [8,9]. Ahmed et al. proposed Fuzzy *c*-means with constraints (FCM_S) [9]; in this algorithm, FCM combined with spatial information permits the labels in a pixel's immediate neighborhood to affect its labeling. However, FCM_S is limited to single feature inputs [10]. To overcome the problem of FCM_S, [11] introduced the Fuzzy Local Information c-Means (FLICM) algorithm. A new factor was added to FLICM, incorporating both local- and gray-level information to control the neighborhood pixel effect and preserve the image details. Further, Zhang et al. proposed the Adaptive Fuzzy Local Information c-Means (ADFLICM) [12] algorithm to overcome the limitation of the FLICM algorithm. Zheng et al. proposed the generalized hierarchical fuzzy c-means algorithm [13] to solve the issue which comes from the outliers and Euclidean distance measures. Ding et al. proposed Kernel-based fuzzy c-means [14] to improve the clustering performance. Guo et al. designed an FCM-based framework to enhance the performance of noisy image segmentation by applying the filter [15]. Xu et al. suggested an intuitionistic fuzzy c-means (IFCM) algorithm that handles the uncertainty but does not correctly handle the noise [16]. To make IFCM handle the noise Verma et al. proposed improved intuitionistic fuzzy c-means (IIFCM) [17].

Some previous studies used contextual information using local convolutional techniques with FCM and PCM as base classifiers. In the current study, we have similarly used NC as a base classifier to incorporate contextual information in local convolutional methods to produce our three proposed algorithms, Noise Local Information c-Means (NLICM), Adaptive Noise Local Information c-Means (ADNLICM), and Noise Clustering with constraints (NC_S). The proposed algorithms may be utilized to prepare land-use land cover maps, which will be useful in agricultural mapping, hazard mapping, and other fields where a highly accurate LULC map is required [18–21]. FLICM, ADFLICM, FCM_S, Possibilistic c-means with constraints (PCM_S), Possibilistic Local Information c-Means (PLICM), Adaptive Possibilistic Local Information c-Means (ADPLICM) [22], Modified Possibilistic c-Means with constraints (MPCM-S) [23] are able to handle the noisy pixel problem; however, these were not tested for handling heterogeneity and different distance measures. Heterogeneity handling has now become an essential step in the classification process. To overcome this problem, this paper introduces three novel algorithms NLICM, ADNLICM, and NC_S, which are inspired by the FLICM, ADFLICM, and FCM_S algorithms, respectively. The FCM_S, FLICM, and ADFLICM algorithms are, in turn, based on the FCM algorithm, and the FCM algorithm is sensitive to noisy data and outliers [24]. To resolve the problem of this limitation of FCM, Dave and Sen (1993) introduced the Noise Clustering (NC) algorithm, which uses a new parameter delta (δ), known as "noise distance".

The aim of this paper was to design and analyze NC-based local convolutional algorithms concerning different parameters to classify the satellite images, which handle the noisy and heterogeneous pixels. This paper proposed three NC-based algorithms, NLICM, ADNLICM, and NC_S, for handling noisy pixels and heterogeneity. These algorithms were first analyzed concerning different distance measures and important parameters (δ, m) of NC-based classifiers to obtain the best values by comparing the overall accuracy obtained by (FERM). Secondly, to check the performance of the algorithms, first, the variance was calculated to show that the optimized algorithm handles the heterogeneity correctly, and second, different degrees of random noise (1, 3, 5, 7, and 9%) were inserted in images of two sites (Haridwar and Banasthali) and the images classified by the optimized algorithm to confirm that the algorithm is suitable for handling noisy pixels. The paper is organized into four sections. Section 1 provides the background of the problem, a discussion of the different algorithms, and the aim of this study. Section 2 describes the Materials (study area and algorithms) and Methodology used in this paper. Section 3 explain the obtained results and their discussion. Finally, Section 4 summarizes the conclusions of the study.

2. Materials and Methods

2.1. Mathematical Concept of Classifiers

This section explains the mathematical principles behind the NC classifier's use of spectral pixel-based information as well as the additional spatial local information added via the convolution approach. The algorithms Noise Local Information c-Means (NLICM),

Adaptive Noise Local Information c-Means (ADNLICM), and Noise Clustering with Constraints (NC_S) have added local spatial information.

2.1.1. NC Classifier

The idea of Noise Clustering was suggested to handle the noise in a given dataset [25]. In this approach, noise is defined as a separate class and denoted by a parameter that consists of a constant distance, known as noise distance (δ), from all the data points. This algorithm is derived from the standard K-means algorithm. NC is generally used for building FCM and related robust algorithms. The NC algorithm is obtained using the following steps.

1. Assign the means for each class and the value of the fuzziness factor (m).
2. Compute the noise distance (δ) using Equation (1).

$$\delta^2 = \lambda \left[\frac{\sum_{k=1}^{C-1} \sum_{i=1}^{N} \|x_i - v_k\|^2}{n(c-1)} \right] \quad (1)$$

3. Calculate the membership value (u_{ki}) and mean cluster center (v_k) from Equation (2) and Equation (3), respectively;

$$u_{ki} = \frac{1}{\sum_{j=1}^{C} \left[\frac{\|x_i - v_k\|^2}{\|x_i - v_j\|^2} \right]^{\frac{1}{m-1}} + \left[\frac{\|x_i - v_k\|^2}{\delta^2} \right]^{\frac{1}{m-1}}} \quad (2)$$

$$v_k = \frac{\sum_{k=1}^{N} (u_{ki})^m x_i}{\sum_{k=1}^{N} (u_{ki})^m} \quad (3)$$

4. Assign the final class to each pixel.

$$J_m = \sum_{i=1}^{N} \sum_{k=1}^{C} u_{ki}^m \|x_i - v_k\|^2 + \sum_{i=1}^{N} \delta^2 \left(1 - \sum_{k=1}^{C} u_{ki} \right)^m \quad (4)$$

Here, m = fuzziness factor (consisting of real values > 1), u_{ki} = degree of membership of ith pixel for cluster k, x_i = i^{th} d-dimensional measured data, v_k = mean value (cluster center) of the kth class, v_j = mean value (cluster center) of the jth class, N = total no of a pixel in the image, C = number of classes, δ = noise distance, $\|x_i - v_k\|$ = distance between x_i and v_k, $\|x_j - v_k\|$ = distance between x_j and v_k and $\|x_i - v_j\|$ = distance between x_i and v_j, J_m define the objective function of the algorithms (NC, NLICM, ADNLICM, and NC_S), and λ represents the multiplier used to calculate δ from the average distances.

2.1.2. Noise Local Information c-Means (NLICM)

In this section, the NLICM algorithm is described. NLICM uses the neighborhood pixel to reduce the noisy pixel. It incorporates gray level and local spatial information into the objective function of the NC algorithm and the G_{ki} parameter, which was introduced by Krinidis and Chatzis (2010) in the FCM classifier. In this paper G_{ki} parameter is applied in the NC classifier, as the NC classifier handles noisy pixels better than the FCM classifier. The NLICM algorithm was obtained using the following steps.

1. Assign the no of cluster (c) and fuzziness factor (m).
2. Compute the δ parameter from Equation (1) and fuzzy factor (G_{ki}) from Equation (5).

$$G_{ki} = \sum_{\substack{i \neq j \\ j \in N_i}} \frac{1}{\|x_i - v_j\| + 1} (1 - u_{kj})^m \|x_j - v_k\|^2 \tag{5}$$

3. Compute a new cluster applying Equation (6).

$$v_k = \frac{\sum_{k=1}^{N} (u_{ki})^m x_i}{\sum_{k=1}^{N} (u_{ki})^m} \tag{6}$$

4. Calculate the value of membership (Equation (7)).

$$u_{ki} = \frac{1}{\sum_{j=1}^{C} \left[\frac{\|x_i - v_k\|^2}{\|x_i - v_j\|^2} + G_{ki} \right]^{\frac{1}{m-1}} + \left[\frac{\|x_i - v_k\|^2}{\delta^2} + G_{ki} \right]^{\frac{1}{m-1}}} \tag{7}$$

5. Assign the final class to each pixel.

The objective functions of NLICM, as mentioned in Equation (8), after applying G_{ki} function in the objective function of NC can be calculated from:

$$J_m = \sum_{i=1}^{N} \sum_{k=1}^{C} \left[u_{ki}^m \|x_i - v_k\|^2 + \sum_{i=1}^{N} \delta^2 \left(1 - \sum_{k=1}^{C} u_{ki} \right)^m + G_{ki} \right] \tag{8}$$

2.1.3. Adaptive Noise Local Information c-Means (ADNLICM)

This algorithm incorporates a local similarity measure in the image as well as a pixel spatial attraction model between pixels. According to Zhang et al. (2017), the local similarity measure in ADFLICM is based on the pixel spatial attraction model, which adaptively determines the weighting components for nearby pixels, similar to the way we used it for the NC- based fuzzy classifier on image feature enhancement. The objective function of ADNLICM is given in Equation (13). It uses local similarity measures (S_{ir}). The ADNLICM algorithm was obtained using the following steps.

1. For each class, assign mean values.
2. Assign the local window size, the fuzziness factor (m), and the no of class (c).
3. Determine the noise distance (δ) using Equation (1) and the local similarity measure S_{ir} using Equations (9) and (10).

$$S_{ir} = \begin{Bmatrix} SA_{ir}, i^1 r \\ 0, i = r \end{Bmatrix} \tag{9}$$

$$SA_{ir}(k) = \frac{u_{ki} \times u_{kr}}{D_{ir}} \tag{10}$$

Here, r^{th} = pixel is the neighborhood pixel that falls into N_i, SA_{ir} = pixel spatial attraction, and D_{ir} = spatial distance between i and r pixel.

4. Generate the final membership (u_{ki}) and cluster mean (v_k) matrix using Equation (11) and Equation (12), respectively.

$$u_{ki} = \cfrac{1}{\sum_{j=1}^{C} \left(\cfrac{\|x_i - v_k\|^2 + \sum_{i=1}^{N} \delta^2 \left(1 - \sum_{k=1}^{C} u_{ki}\right)^m + \frac{1}{N_r} \sum_{\substack{r \in N_i \\ r \neq i}} (1 - S_{ir}) \|x_r - v_k\|^2}{\|x_i - v_j\|^2 + \sum_{i=1}^{N} \delta^2 \left(1 - \sum_{k=1}^{C} u_{ki}\right)^m + \frac{1}{N_r} \sum_{\substack{r \in N_i \\ r \neq i}} (1 - S_{ir}) \|x_r - v_k\|^2} \right)^{\frac{1}{m-1}}} \qquad (11)$$

$$v_k = \cfrac{\sum_{i=1}^{N} u_{ki}^m \left(x_i + \frac{1}{N_R} \sum_{\substack{r \in N_i \\ r \neq i}} (1 - S_{ir}) \times x_r \right)}{1 + \frac{1}{N_R} \sum_{\substack{r \in N_i \\ r \neq i}} (1 - S_{ir}) \times \sum_{i=1}^{N} u_{ki}^m} \qquad (12)$$

5. Assign each pixel to a final class.

ADNLICM integrates local spatial- and gray-level information into NC's objective function. The objective function of ADNLICM is shown in Equation (13).

$$J_m = \sum_{i=1}^{N} \sum_{k=1}^{C} u_{ki}^m \times \left[\|x_i - v_k\|^2 + \sum_{i=1}^{N} \delta^2 \left(1 - \sum_{k=1}^{C} u_{ki} \right)^m + \frac{1}{N_r} \sum_{\substack{r \in N_i \\ r \neq i}} (1 - S_{ir}) \|x_r - v_k\|^2 \right] \qquad (13)$$

The objective function in Equation (13) was minimized to provide the membership function (Equation (11)).

2.1.4. Noise Clustering with Constraints (NC_S)

The NC_S algorithm is motivated by Fuzzy Clustering with Constraints (FCM_S) which was proposed by Ahmed et al. [26]. FCM_S introduces a new term into the standard FCM algorithm. This new term permits pixel labeling to be impacted by neighborhood labels. This paper used a new term in the NC classifier in place of the FCM classifier to handle the noise and heterogeneity. The computation steps for this algorithm are as follows.

1. Assign the means for each class and the fuzziness factor (m).
2. Compute the noise distance (δ) using Equation (1).
3. The computation of the membership partition matrix (u_{ki}) and the cluster centers are performed as follows (v_k) from Equation (14) and Equation (15), respectively;

$$u_{ki} = \cfrac{\left(\cfrac{\|x_i - v_k\|^2}{\delta^2} + \cfrac{a}{N_r} \sum_{r \in N_i} \cfrac{\|x_r - v_k\|^2}{\delta^2} \right)^{\frac{1}{m-1}}}{\sum_{j=1}^{C} \left(\cfrac{\|x_i - v_j\|^2}{\delta^2} + \cfrac{a}{N_r} \sum_{r \in N_i} \cfrac{\|x_r - v_j\|^2}{\delta^2} \right)} \qquad (14)$$

$$v_k = \cfrac{\sum_{i=1}^{N} u_{ki}^m \left(x_i + \cfrac{a}{N_R} \sum_{r \in N_i} x_r \right)}{(1 + a) \sum_{i=1}^{N} u_{ki}^m} \qquad (15)$$

Here, $\frac{1}{N_R \sum_{r \in N_i} x_r}$ = edge of the average value of the gray level over the x_i within a window, N_R = cardinality, a = parameter (control the effect of the neighbor term), and x_r = represent the neighbor of x_i.

4. Assign the final class to each pixel.

The NC_S algorithm objective function is derived as Equation (16).

$$J_m = \sum_{i=1}^{N} \sum_{k=1}^{C} u_{ki}^m \|x_i - v_k\|^2 + \sum_{i=1}^{N} \delta^2 \left(1 - \sum_{k=1}^{C} u_{ki}\right)^m + \frac{a}{N_R} \sum_{i=1}^{N} \sum_{k=1}^{C} u_{ki}^m \sum_{r \in N_i} \|x_i - v_k\|^2 \quad (16)$$

2.2. Mathematical Formula of Similarity and Dissimilarity Measures

Two similarity metrics, Cosine, and Correlation, and eight dissimilarity measures, including Bray–Curtis, Canberra, Chessboard, Euclidean, Manhattan, Mean Absolute Difference, Median Absolute Difference, and Normalized Square Euclidean, have been utilized. Different measures of similarity and dissimilarity were investigated in fuzzy classifiers as distance criteria to be constructed to identify to which class unknown vectors belong. In this study, the most widely used distance metrics across several applications were chosen for investigation. The various distance measures were utilized to test and evaluate the models and to see how they affected the fuzzy classifier algorithm that was the subject of this study. All the dissimilarity and similarity measures' mathematical expressions are given below. Here, c is the mean value, b is the number of bands, and x and v are the vector pixels. The different distance measures described in [27] are used in this study.

2.2.1. Bray–Curtis

The Bray–Curtis [28] dissimilarity is used to determine the connection between environmental sciences, ecology, and related fields. Bray–Curtis distance has the convenient property of having a value between 0 and 1. The same coordinate is represented by zero Bray–Curtis. The equation for Bray–Curtis is given in Equation (17). Figure 1 illustrates how Bray–Curtis distance works.

$$D(x,y) = \frac{\sum_{i=1}^{N} |x_i - y_i|}{\sum_{i=1}^{N} |x_i + y_i|} \quad (17)$$

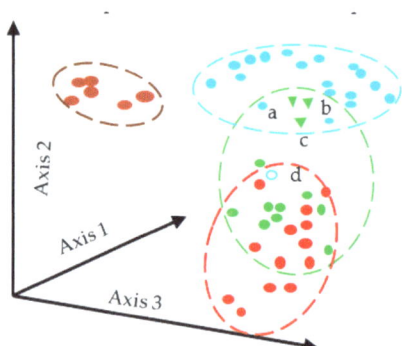

Figure 1. Schematic Diagram of Bray–Curtis Distance Measures, a–d represents the sampling point.

Here N represents the no of data points, and y is the sample.

2.2.2. Canberra

The Canberra [29] measure is mainly applied to positive values. It analyses the total amount of fractional discrepancies between two objects' coordinates. It has been employed to compare ranked lists and for intrusion detection in computer security. The equation for Canberra distance measures is given in Equation (18).

$$D(x_j, v_i) = \frac{|x_{j1} - v_{i1}|}{|x_{j1}| + |v_{i1}|} + \frac{|x_{j2} - v_{i2}|}{|x_{j2}| + |v_{i2}|} + \ldots\ldots\ldots \frac{|x_{jb} - v_{ib}|}{|x_{jb}| + |v_{ib}|} \tag{18}$$

2.2.3. Chessboard

Chessboard [30] distance measures operate as a vector space to determine the greatest distance along two vectors between any two coordinate dimensions. It is also referred to as the Chebyshev distance. Equation (19) provides the formula for the distance on a chessboard. The concept of chessboard distance is shown in Figure 2.

$$D(x_j, v_i) = \text{Max}\left[|x_{j1} - v_{i1}|, |x_{j2} - v_{i2}|, \ldots\ldots, |x_{jb} - v_{ib}|\right] \tag{19}$$

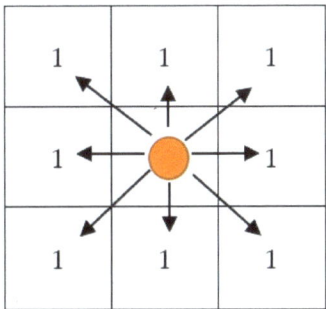

Figure 2. Schematic Diagram of Chessboard Distance Measures.

2.2.4. Correlation

Correlation [31] similarity is a calculation that determines the correlation between two vectors. The Pearson-r correlation is used to determine how similar the two vectors are. With a perfect positive correlation at +1 and a perfect negative correlation at −1, its value ranges from −1 to +1, with 0 representing no correlation. Equation (20) contains the correlation's mathematical formula. Figure 3 depicts the correlation distance idea.

$$D(x_j, v_i) = 1 - \frac{\left[\left\{x_{j1} + \frac{1}{b}(-x_{j1} - x_{j2} - \ldots - x_{jb})\right\}\left\{v_{i1} + \frac{1}{b}(-v_{i1} - v_{i2} - \ldots - v_{ib})\right\} + \ldots + \left\{x_{jb} + \frac{1}{b}(-x_{j1} - x_{j2} - \ldots - x_{jb})\right\}\left\{v_{ib} + \frac{1}{b}(-v_{i1} - v_{i2} - \ldots - v_{ib})\right\}\right]}{\sqrt{\left|\left[x_{j1} + \frac{1}{b}(-x_{j1} \ldots - x_{jb})\right]^2\right| + \ldots + \left|\left[x_{j1} + \frac{1}{b}(-x_{j1} \ldots - x_{jb})\right]^2\right|} \sqrt{\left|\left[v_{i1} + \frac{1}{b}(-v_{i1} \ldots - v_{ib})\right]^2\right| + \ldots + \left|\left[v_{ib} + \frac{1}{b}(-v_{i1} \ldots - v_{ib})\right]^2\right|}} \tag{20}$$

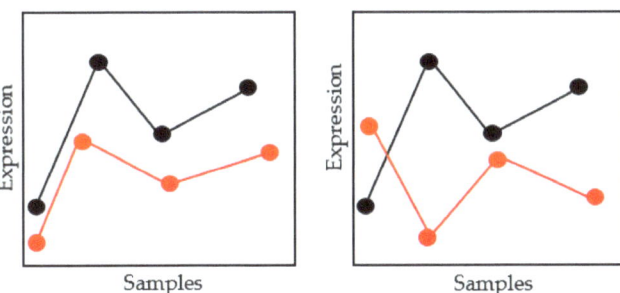

Figure 3. Schematic Diagram of Correlation Distance Measures.

2.2.5. Cosine

Cosine [32] similarity measurements compute the cosine of an angle along two vectors in an inner product space. They provide the distance between two vectors as measured. Equation (21) contains the mathematical equation for Cosine similarity. Figure 4 depicts the cosine distance approach.

$$D(x_j, v_i) = 1 - \frac{x_{j1}v_{i1} + x_{j2}v_{i2} + \ldots + x_{jb}v_{ib}}{\sqrt{|x_{j1}|^2 + \ldots + |x_{jb}|^2}\sqrt{|v_{i1}|^2 + \ldots + |v_{ib}|^2}} \quad (21)$$

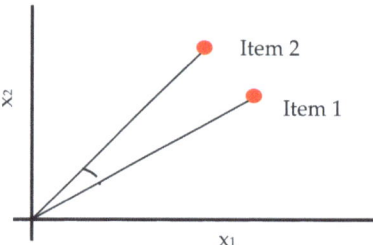

Figure 4. Schematic Diagram of Cosine Distance Measures.

2.2.6. Euclidean

Two points in Euclidean space are separated by the Euclidean distance [30]. It computes the square root of the value difference between parallel data points as the sum of squares. Equation (22) contains the equation for Euclidean distance measures.

$$D(x, y) = \sqrt{\sum_{i=1}^{N} |x_i - y_i|^2} \quad (22)$$

2.2.7. Manhattan

Images are compared using the Manhattan distance measures [33]. Manhattan distance is the product of the parallel element differences between any two data points. A small deviation from Euclidean distance is the Manhattan distance, which has a different formula for determining the separation between two data points. The Manhattan distance measures equation is given in Equation (23). The concepts of Euclidean and Manhattan distance are shown in Figure 5.

$$D(x_j, v_i) = |x_{j1} - v_{i1}| + |x_{j2} - v_{i2}| + \ldots + |x_{jb} - v_{ib}| \quad (23)$$

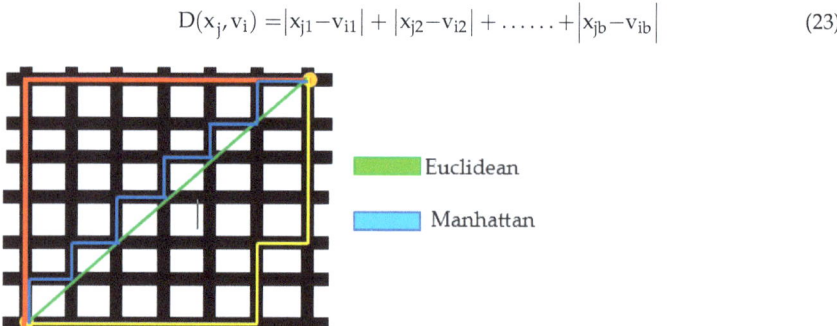

Figure 5. Schematic Diagram of Euclidean and Manhattan Distance Measures.

2.2.8. Mean Absolute Difference

A statistical technique for depression is the Mean Absolute Difference [34]. It is determined by multiplying the total number of bands by the absolute difference between two things with similar locations in the same location and the variable between those two items. Equation (24) contains the formula for the Mean Absolute Difference in distance measurements. Figure 6 illustrates the idea of mean absolute difference distance.

$$D(x_j, v_i) = \frac{1}{b}\left[\left|x_{j1}-v_{i1}\right| + \left|x_{j2}-v_{i2}\right| + \ldots\ldots + \left|x_{jb}-v_{ib}\right|\right] \qquad (24)$$

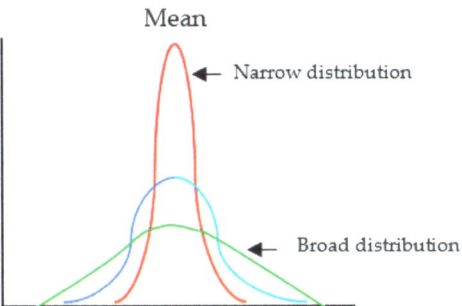

Figure 6. Schematic Diagram of Mean Absolute Difference Distance Measures.

2.2.9. Median Absolute Difference

To lessen the impact of impulsive noise on the derived measures, the median absolute difference (MAD) [35] may be used instead of the mean absolute difference. Mathematically generally, MAD is defined as finding the difference in the absolute brightness of the comparable pixels in two images before taking the data's median. Equation (25) contains the equation for MAD distance measurements. Figure 7 illustrates the idea of median absolute difference distance.

$$D(x_j, v_i) = \text{Median}\left[\left|x_{j1}-v_{i1}\right|, \left|x_{j2}-v_{i2}\right|, \ldots\ldots, \left|x_{jb}-v_{ib}\right|\right] \qquad (25)$$

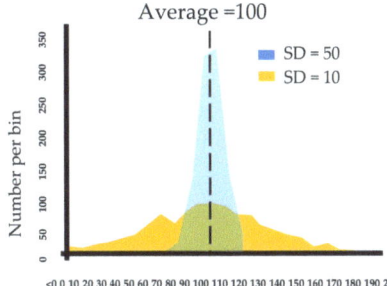

Figure 7. Schematic diagram of Median Absolute Difference Distance Measures.

2.2.10. Normalized Square Euclidean

The NSE distance between two vectors can be calculated using Normalized Square Euclidean (NSE) [33]. Before computing, the sum of the squared difference between the pixels of two images, the intensities of the pixels must first be normalized. Equation (26) contains the equation for NSE distance measurements.

$$D(x_j, v_i) = \frac{\left|\left\{x_{j1}+\frac{1}{b}(-x_{j1}-x_{j2}-\ldots-x_{jb})-v_{i1}+\frac{1}{b}(v_{i1}+v_{i2}+\ldots+v_{ib})\right\}^2\right| + \ldots + \left|\left\{x_{jb}+\frac{1}{b}(-x_{j1}-x_{j2}-\ldots-x_{jb})-v_{ib}+\frac{1}{b}(v_{i1}+v_{i2}+\ldots+v_{ib})\right\}^2\right|}{2\left[\left|\left\{x_{j1}+\frac{1}{b}(-x_{j1}-x_{j2}-\ldots x_{jb})\right\}^2\right| + \ldots + \left|\left\{x_{jb}+\frac{1}{b}(-x_{j1}-x_{j2}-\ldots x_{jb})\right\}^2\right| + \left|\left\{v_{i1}+\frac{1}{b}(-v_{i1}-v_{i2}-\ldots v_{ib})\right\}^2\right| + \ldots + \left|\left\{v_{ib}+\frac{1}{b}(-v_{i1}-v_{i2}-\ldots v_{ib})\right\}^2\right|\right]} \qquad (26)$$

2.3. Study Area and Dataset Used

This research work tested the NC algorithm and its versions in two study areas (site 1 and site 2). As shown in Figure 8, the first site considered was Haridwar (Uttarakhand). Site 1 was used to determine the optimized algorithm. The latitudes and longitudes covered by the first site are from 29°49′14″ to 29°52′21″ and 78°9′17″ to 78°13′4″, respectively. The coverage area is 5.92 km, east to west, and 5.95 km, north to south. Land-use diversity was the prime reason to choose this area; it helped examine and experiment with the convolutional method. The area includes water, wheat, dense forest, eucalyptus, grassland, and riverine sand. Landsat-8 and Formosat-2 satellite data were used in this study area; Table 1 shows the sensors' specifications of Landsat-8, Formosat-2, and Sentinel-2 satellites.

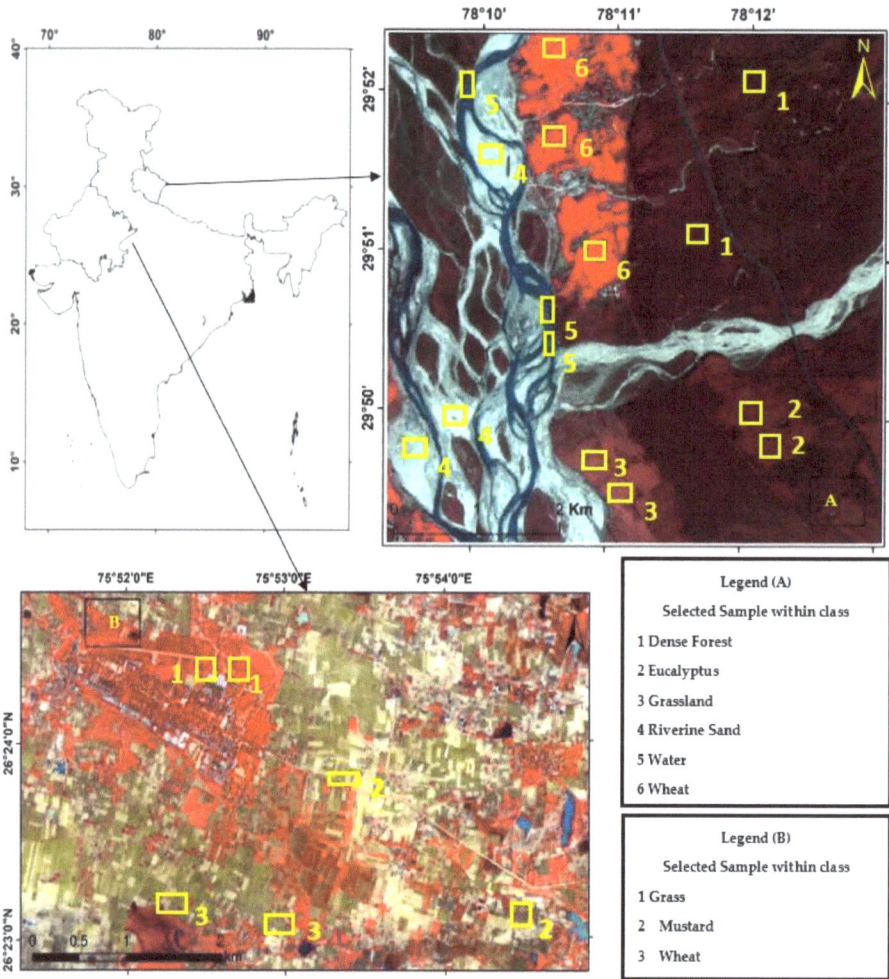

Figure 8. Study Areas (**A**) Haridwar (Uttarakhand) (**B**) Banasthali (Rajasthan).

Table 1. Specification of Landsat-8, Formosat-2, and Sentinel-2 [36,37].

Characteristics	Landsat-8	Formosat-2	Sentinel 2
Spatial Resolution (m)	30 m	8 m	10 m
Spectral Resolution	8 bands	4 bands	13 bands
Revisit Period	Repeat every 16 days	Daily	Repeat every 5 days

The area surrounding Banasthali Vidyapith (Rajasthan) was selected as the second site area (Figure 8). This study area was used to classify the homogeneous classes by applying the optimized algorithm. The coverage area is situated in the northeastern region of Rajasthan, between latitudes 26°23′ and 26°24′ North and longitudes 75°51′ and 75°54′ East.

2.4. Methodology Adopted

Figure 9 shows the methodology and process flow adopted for this research work. This study's primary focus has been on studying the conventional NC and proposed convolutional (NLICM, ADNLICM, and NC_S) classifiers. In addition, the influence of the delta (δ) and fuzziness factors, and various distance measures, on the proposed algorithm were studied using the two study areas (Haridwar and Banasthali). All algorithms were implemented in the JAVA environment through an in-house tool called SMIC (Sub-pixel Multi-spectral Image Classifier) [38]. The methodology was derived by the following steps.

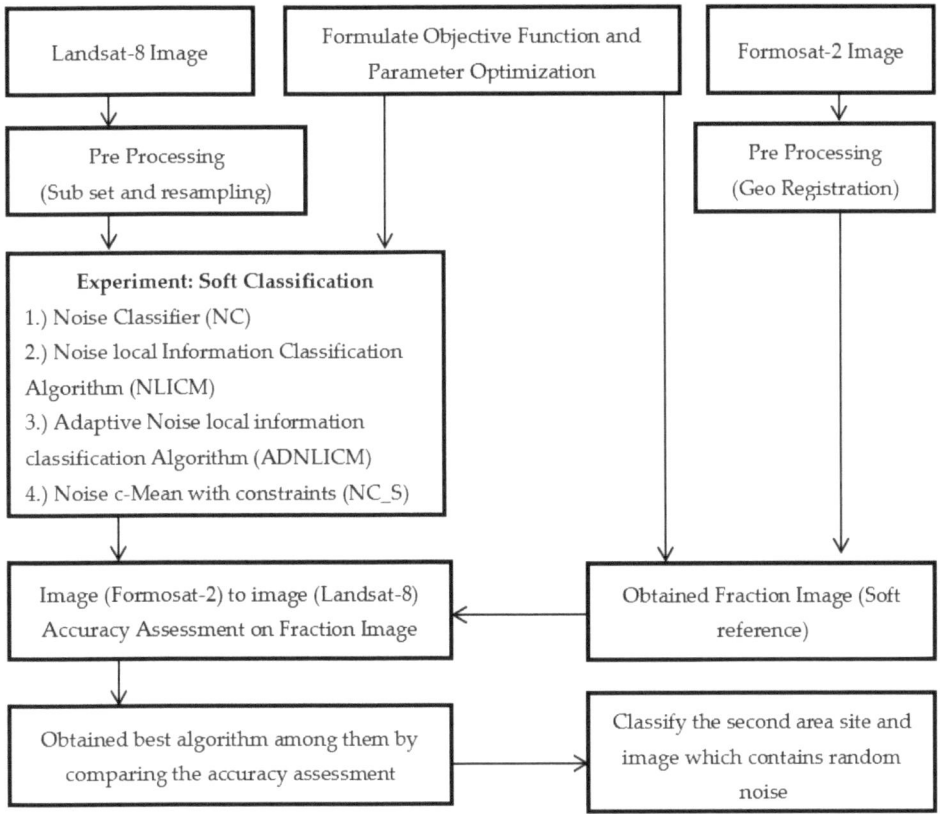

Figure 9. Flow diagram of Adopted Methodology.

Step 1: Classify the image by NC classifier and local conventional NLICM, ADNLICM, and NC_S using NC as the base classifier employing various delta (δ), distance measures, and fuzziness factor parameters.

Step 2: Calculate the overall accuracy of the obtained classified image to determine the optimized parameters for the algorithm.

Step 3: Calculate the overall accuracy and compare all algorithms to find the best algorithm.

Step 4: Use the optimal proposed algorithm and NC classifier to classify the image with 1% (density = 0.01), 3% (density = 0.03), 5% (density = 0.05), 7% (density = 0.07), and 9% (density = 0.09), pepper and salt-and-pepper random noise to show that the proposed algorithms handle the noise correctly.

Step 5: Calculate the variance of the obtained optimal proposed algorithm and NC classifier to show that the proposed algorithm is better able to handle the heterogeneity than the NC classifier.

Step 6: Use the optimal proposed algorithm and NC classifier to classify the second study area (site 2) with (1, 3, 5, 7, and 9%) pepper and salt-and-pepper noise or without random noise to show that the proposed algorithm can also handle noise and heterogeneity with different images.

3. Results and Discussion

The result and discussion section are divided into five experiments. In the First Experiment, the optimized algorithm with respect to OA for the NC and NC base local convolutional classifier (NLICM, ADNLICM, and NC_S) is obtained while applying different parameters such as various distance measures, delta (δ), and fuzziness factor (m). The distance measures tested consist of Bray–Curtis, Canberra, Chessboard, Correlation, Cosine, Manhattan, Mean Absolute Difference, Median Absolute Difference, and Normalized Square Euclidean. Values of δ in the range 10^4 to 10^{13}, with an interval of multiple of 10, and m values (1.1-3) with a period of 0.2, were considered. In the second experiment, the optimized algorithms were used to classify the Landsat-8 image containing 1%, 3%, 5%, 7%, or 9% pepper, and salt-and-pepper random noise.

In the third experiment, the NC and proposed algorithms were used to classify the Landsat-8 classes (Dense Forest, Eucalyptus, Grassland, Riverine Sand, Water, and Wheat) and calculate the OA and variance to confirm that the ADNLICM algorithm handles random heterogeneity better than the other algorithms. The fourth and fifth experiments are the same as the second and third, respectively, with a Sentinel-2 image used in place of the Landsat-8 image to show that the proposed algorithm also works on other satellite data and maps the homogeneous class (Mustard, Wheat, and Grassland) correctly.

3.1. Experiment 1: Compute the Optimized Algorithms

In this section, OA is computed using the FERM technique to obtain the optimized NC, NLICM, ADNLICM, and NC_S algorithms with respect to different distance measures and parameters. The best algorithm will be selected by comparison.

Figure 10 shows the different weighting components and overall accuracy for the NC classifier with various delta (δ), m, and distance measures. For $\delta = 10^4$, Canberra distance measures delivered the highest OA (80.48%) at m = 1.1 (Figure 10a). At $\delta = 10^5$, Mean Absolute Difference distance measures gave the best OA (77.22%) at m = 1.1 (Figure 10b). At $\delta = 10^6$, Bray–Curtis distance measures, gave the highest OA (77.72%) at m = 1.1 (Figure 10c). At $\delta = 10^7$, Bray–Curtis distance measures produced the highest OA (77.81%) at m = 1.1 (Figure 10d). At $\delta = 10^8$, Canberra distance measures produced the highest OA (82.55%) at m = 1.1 (Figure 10e). At $\delta = 10^9$, Mean Absolute Difference distance measures result in the highest OA (78.46%) at m = 1.1 (Figure 10f). At $\delta = 10^{10}$, Mean Absolute Difference distance measures delivered the highest OA (77.75%) at m = 1.1 (Figure 10d). At $\delta = 10^{11}$, Bray–Curtis distance measures, gave the highest OA (77.35%) at m = 1.1 (Figure 10g). At $\delta = 10^{12}$, Canberra distance measures gave the highest OA (81.33%) at m = 1.1 (Figure 10h).

At $\delta = 10^{13}$, Mean Absolute Difference distance measures produced the most increased OA (78.30%) at m = 1.1 (Figure 10i).

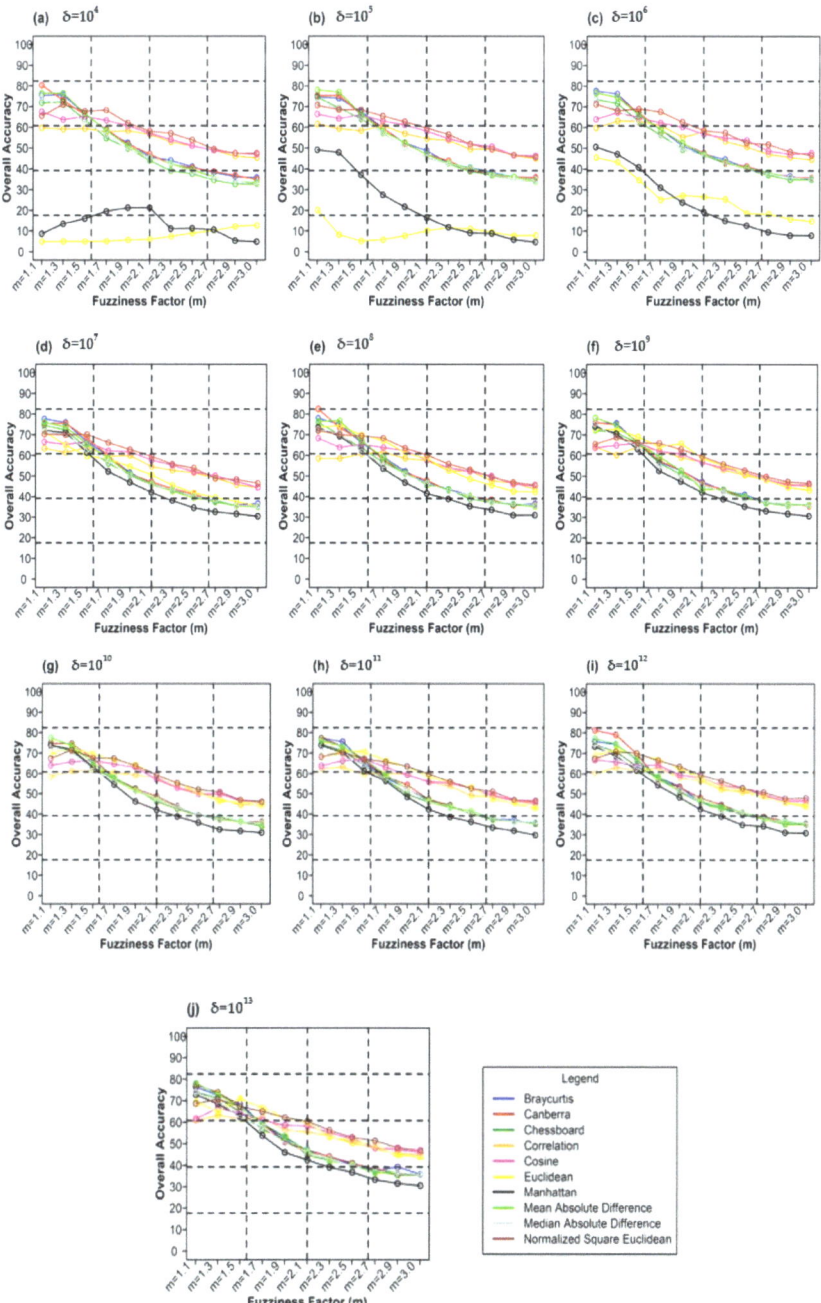

Figure 10. Comparison of overall accuracy in NC classifier for applying different distance measures, m (1.1–3.0), and (**a**–**j**) for site 1 (Haridwar).

Figure 11 plots different weighting components and overall accuracy for various delta (δ) and distance measures for the NLICM classifier. At $\delta = 10^4$, Canberra distance measures gave the highest OA (86.91%) at m = 1.1 (Figure 11a). For $\delta = 10^5$, Bray–Curtis distance measures gave the highest OA (86.40%) at m = 1.1 (Figure 11b). For $\delta = 10^6$, Canberra distance measures gave the highest OA (87.38%) at m = 1.1 (Figure 11c). At 10^7, Mean Absolute Difference distance measures produced the highest OA (87.80%) at m = 1.1 (Figure 11d). For $\delta = 10^8$, Canberra distance measures gave the highest OA (88.75%) at m = 1.1 (Figure 11e). At $\delta = 10^9$, the highest OA (89.50%) at m = 1.1 was achieved by Bray–Curtis distance measures (Figure 11f). At $\delta = 10^{10}$, Manhattan distance measures delivered the highest OA (88.45%) at m = 1.1 (Figure 11g). At $\delta = 10^{11}$, Manhattan distance measures gave the highest OA (88.35%) at m = 1.1 (Figure 11h). For $\delta = 10^{12}$, Euclidean distance measures gave the highest OA (88.47%) at m = 1.3 (Figure 11i). At $\delta = 10^{13}$, Canberra distance measures delivered the highest OA (87.40%) at m = 1.1 (Figure 11j).

Figure 12 shows plots of the different weighting components and overall accuracy for various delta (δ) and distance measures for the ADNLICM classifier. For $\delta = 10^4$, Mean Absolute Difference distance measures produced the highest OA (88.93%) at m = 1.1 Figure 12a). At $\delta = 10^5$, Bray–Curtis distance measures gave the highest OA (89.45%) at m = 1.3 (Figure 12b). At $\delta = 10^6$ Bray–Curtis distance measures delivered the highest OA (91.53%) at m = 1.1 (Figure 12c). At $\delta = 10^7$, Mean Absolute Difference distance measures gave the highest OA (90.22%) at m = 1.3 (Figure 12d). At $\delta = 10^8$ Mean Absolute Difference distance measures, produced the most increased OA (89.47%) at m = 1.3 (Figure 12e). For $\delta = 10^9$, Manhattan distance measures made the most increased OA (90.22%) at m = 1.3 (Figure 12f). At $\delta = 10^{10}$, Mean Absolute Difference distance measures gave the highest OA (89.50%) at m = 1.3 (Figure 12g). At $\delta = 10^{11}$, Mean Absolute Difference distance measures gave the highest OA (89.33%) at m = 1.1 (Figure 12h). At $\delta = 10^{12}$, Bray–Curtis distance measures delivered the highest OA (88.90%) at m = 1.3 (Figure 12i). For $\delta = 10^{13}$, Manhattan distance measures gave the highest OA (89.94 %) at m = 1.3 (Figure 12j).

Figure 13 shows plots between different weighting components and overall accuracy for various delta (δ) and distance measures for the NC_S classifier. For $\delta = 10^4$, Canberra distance measures gave the highest OA (87.70%) at m = 1.1 (Figure 13a). At $\delta = 10^5$ Manhattan distance measures gave the highest OA (89.02%) at m = 1.1 (Figure 13b). At $\delta = 10^6$, Bray–Curtis distance measures delivered the highest OA (89.36%) at m = 1.1 (Figure 13c). At $\delta = 10^7$, Canberra distance measures gave the highest OA (89.43%) at m = 1.1 (Figure 13d). For $\delta = 10^8$, Manhattan distance measures produced the highest OA (89.99%) at m = 1.1 (Figure 13e). At $\delta = 10^9$, Bray–Curtis distance measures gave the highest OA (90.01%) at m = 1.1 (Figure 13f). At $\delta = 10^{10}$, Bray–Curtis distance measures delivered the highest OA (89.14%) at m = 1.1 (Figure 13g). At $\delta = 10^{11}$, Mean Absolute Difference distance measures produced the best OA (87.95%) at m = 1.1 (Figure 13g). For $\delta = 10^{12}$, Euclidean distance measures gave the best OA (88.00%) at m = 1.3 (Figure 13h). At $\delta = 10^{13}$, Manhattan distance measures gave the highest OA (89.28%) at m = 1.1 (Figure 13i).

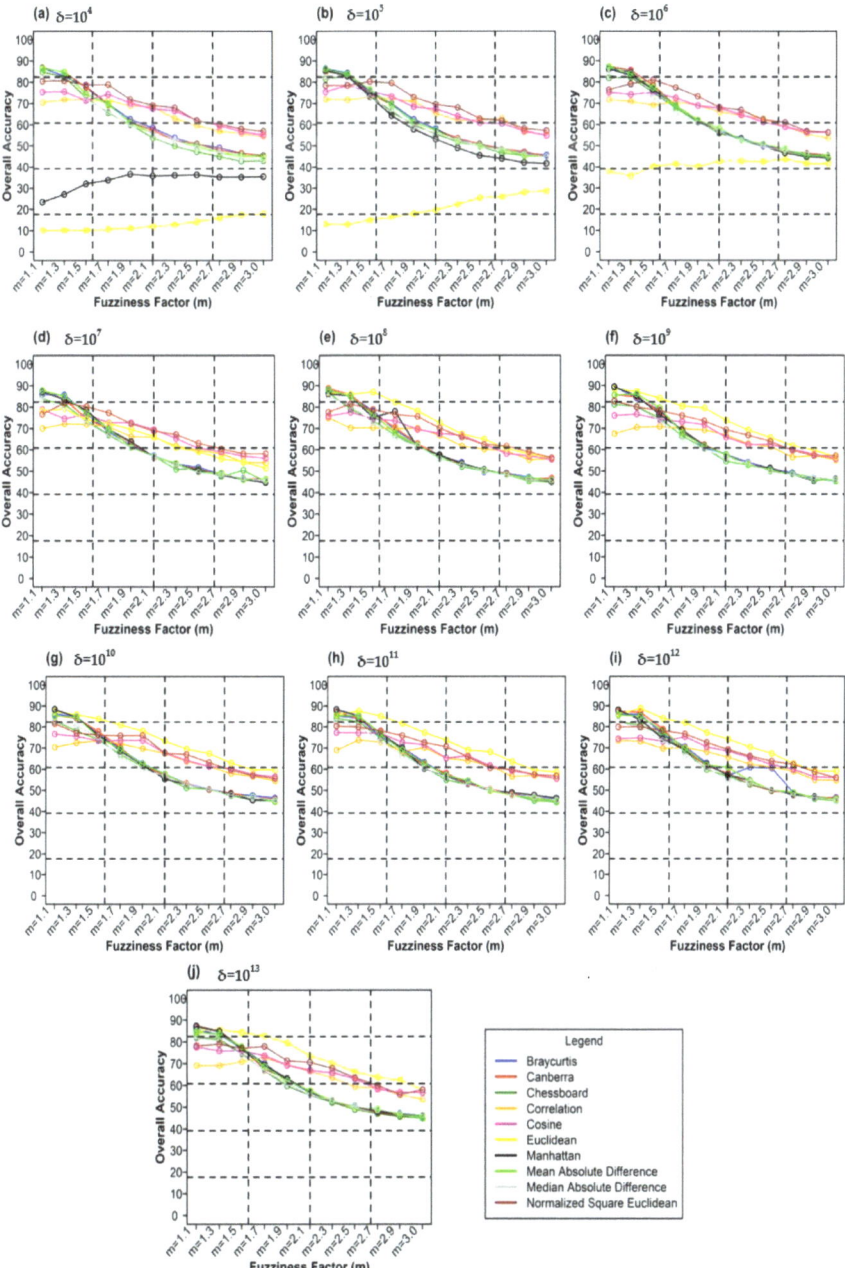

Figure 11. Comparison of overall accuracy in NLICM classifier for applying different distance measures, m (1.1–3.0), and (**a**–**j**) for site 1 (Haridwar).

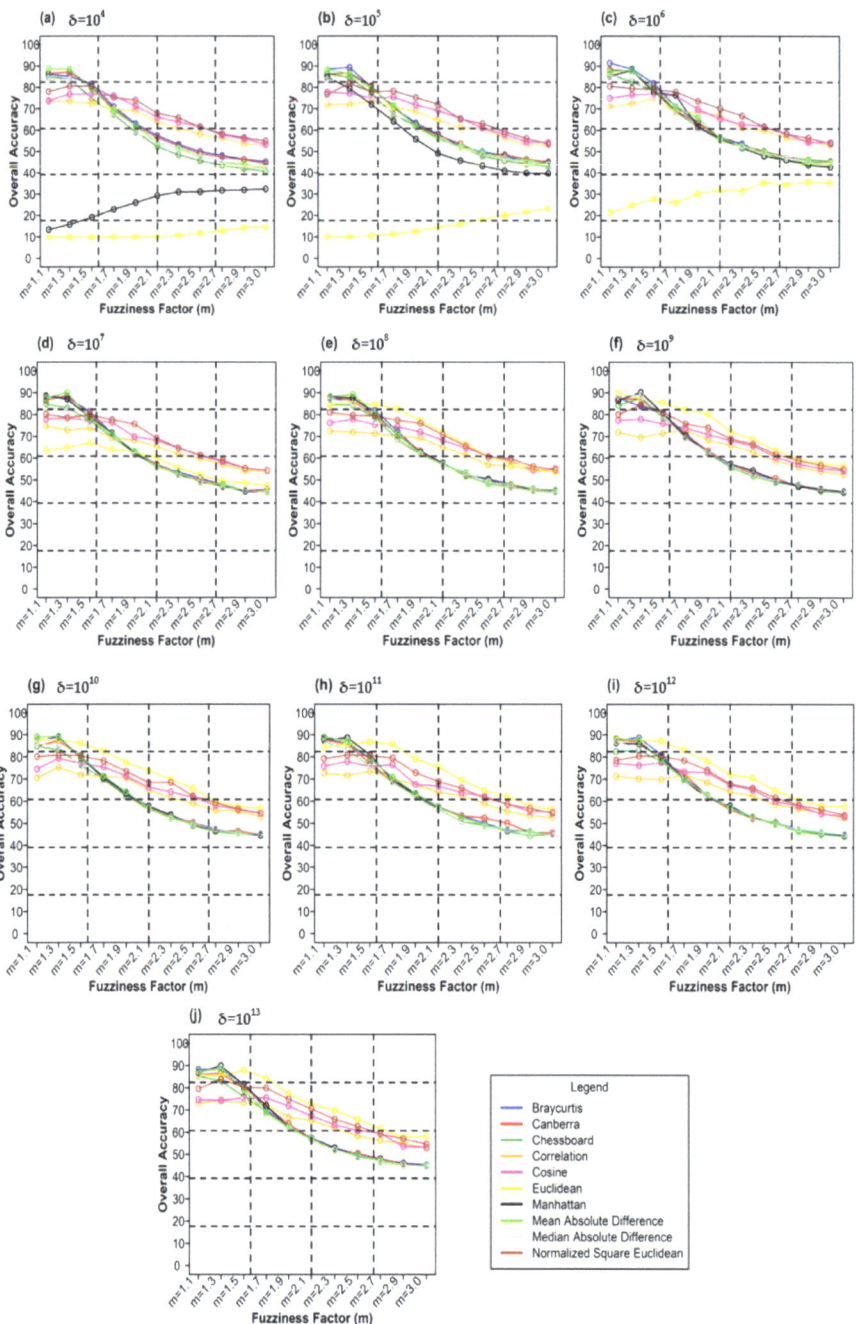

Figure 12. Comparison of overall accuracy in ADNLICM classifier for applying different distance measures, m (1.1–3.0), and (**a**–**j**) for site 1 (Haridwar).

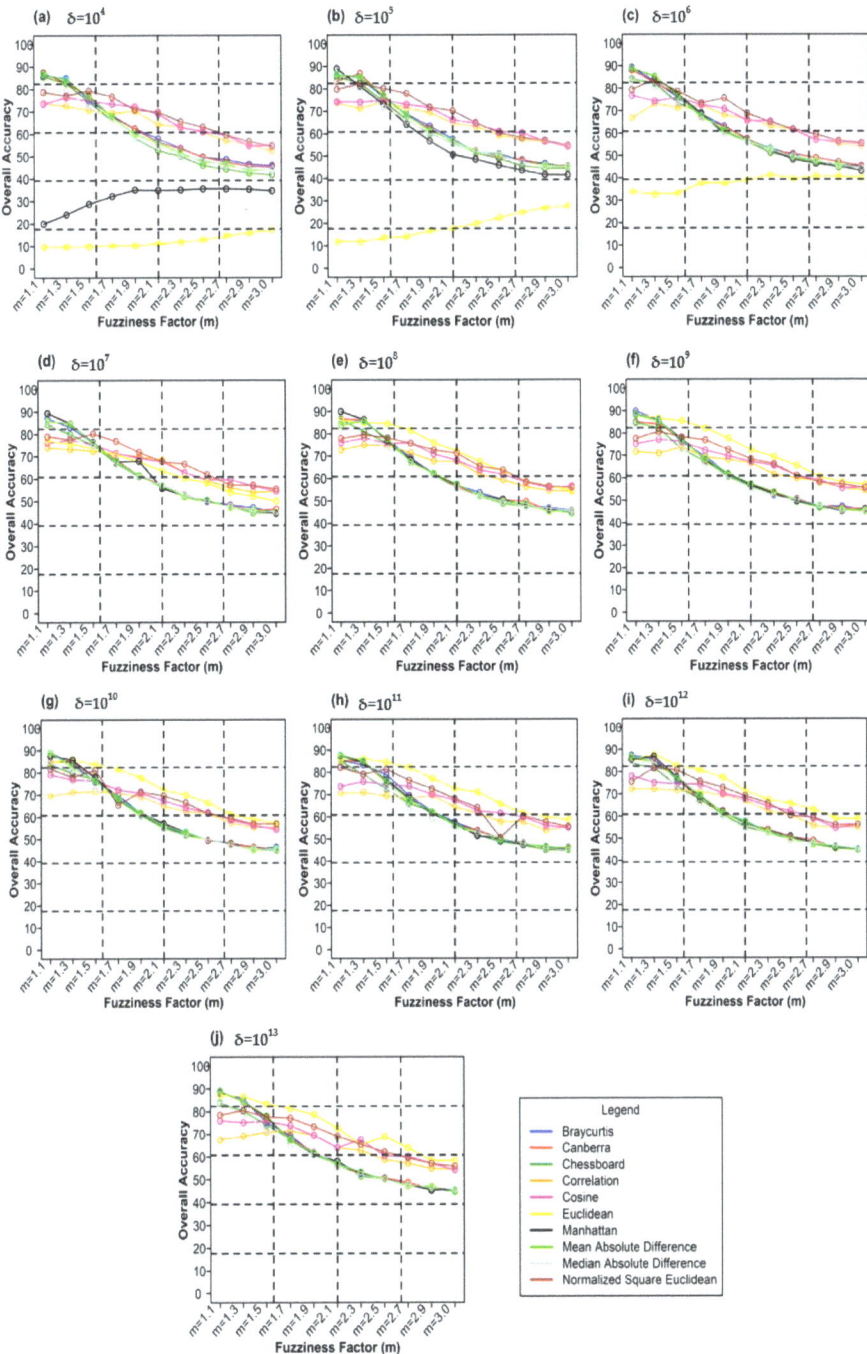

Figure 13. Comparison of overall accuracy in NC_S classifier for applying different distance measures, m (1.1–3.0), and (**a**–**j**) for site 1 (Haridwar).

For the NC, NLICM, ADNLICM, and NC_S classifiers, Tables 2–5 show the Kappa and RMSE calculated for the maximum overall accuracy (Shown in Figures 10–13) observed with regard to various parameters.

Table 2. Kappa and RMSE determined for the highest overall accuracy of the NC classifier by applying different parameters for site 1 (Haridwar).

Delta(δ)	m	Distance Measures	FERM(OA) in %	Kappa	RMSE
10^4	1.1	Canberra	80.48	0.758	0.218
10^5	1.1	Mean Absolute Difference	77.22	0.727	0.243
10^6	1.1	Bray–Curtis	77.72	0.732	0.242
10^7	1.1	Bray–Curtis	77.81	0.733	0.242
10^8	1.1	Canberra	82.55	0.777	0.204
10^9	1.1	Mean Absolute Difference	78.46	0.739	0.238
10^{10}	1.1	Mean Absolute Difference	77.75	0.732	0.242
10^{11}	1.1	Bray–Curtis	77.35	0.728	0.244
10^{12}	1.1	Canberra	81.33	0.766	0.209
10^{13}	1.1	Mean Absolute Difference	78.30	0.737	0.232

Table 3. Kappa and RMSE determined for the highest overall accuracy of the NLICM classifier by applying different parameters for site 1 (Haridwar).

Delta(δ)	m	Distance Measures	FERM(OA) in %	Kappa	RMSE
10^4	1.1	Canberra	86.91	0.818	0.175
10^5	1.1	Bray–Curtis	86.40	0.814	0.174
10^6	1.1	Canberra	87.38	0.823	0.172
10^7	1.1	Mean Absolute Difference	87.80	0.827	0.171
10^8	1.1	Canberra	88.75	0.836	0.169
10^9	1.1	Bray–Curtis	89.50	0.843	0.161
10^{10}	1.1	Manhattan	88.45	0.833	0.170
10^{11}	1.1	Manhattan	88.35	0.832	0.169
10^{12}	1.3	Euclidean	88.87	0.837	0.165
10^{13}	1.1	Canberra	87.40	0.823	0.171

Table 4. Kappa and RMSE determined for the highest overall accuracy of the ADNLICM classifier by applying different parameters for site 1 (Haridwar).

Delta(δ)	m	Distance Measures	FERM(OA) in %	Kappa	RMSE
10^4	1.1	Mean Absolute Difference	88.93	0.837	0.161
10^5	1.3	Bray–Curtis	89.45	0.843	0.163
10^6	1.1	Bray–Curtis	91.53	0.862	0.136
10^7	1.3	Mean Absolute Difference	90.22	0.850	0.148
10^8	1.3	Mean Absolute Difference	89.47	0.843	0.164
10^9	1.3	Manhattan	90.20	0.850	0.146
10^{10}	1.3	Mean Absolute Difference	89.50	0.843	0.164
10^{11}	1.1	Mean Absolute Difference	89.33	0.841	0.162
10^{12}	1.3	Bray–Curtis	88.90	0.837	0.171
10^{13}	1.3	Manhattan	89.94	0.847	0.165

Table 5. Kappa and RMSE determined for the highest overall accuracy of the NC_S classifier by applying different parameters for site 1 (Haridwar).

Delta(δ)	m	Distance Measures	FERM(OA) in %	Kappa	RMSE
10^4	1.1	Canberra	87.70	0.826	0.171
10^5	1.1	Manhattan	89.02	0.838	0.162
10^6	1.1	Bray–Curtis	89.36	0.842	0.162
10^7	1.1	Canberra	89.43	0.842	0.162
10^8	1.1	Manhattan	89.99	0.847	0.158
10^9	1.1	Bray–Curtis	90.01	0.848	0.157
10^{10}	1.1	Bray–Curtis	89.14	0.839	0.161
10^{11}	1.1	Mean Absolute Difference	87.95	0.828	0.173
10^{12}	1.3	Euclidean	88.00	0.829	0.169
10^{13}	1.1	Manhattan	89.28	0.841	0.164

3.2. Experiment 2: Classification in the Presence of Noise in the Haridwar Study Area Site

This experiment evaluated the effects of adding 1%, 3%, 5%, 7%, and 9% random noise in the form of pepper and salt-and-pepper to Landsat-8 images. The original image with 1%, 3%, 5%, 7%, and 9% additional pepper and salt-and-pepper noise is shown in Tables 6 and 7, respectively. The difference between the original classified image and the noisy classified image is used to calculate the RMSE and FERM. Kappa is also calculated. To calculate FERM and RMSE, Formosat-2 images were utilized as the reference image. RMSE, FERM, and kappa results show (Table 8) that the ADNLICM classifier performs better than the other classifiers.

Table 6. Landsat-8 original and dense forest classified class image with respect to different random pepper noise (for site 1 (Haridwar)).

	Original Image	NC Classifier	ADNLICM Classifier	NC_S Classifier	NLICM Classifier
Inserted 1% random noise					
Inserted 3% random noise					
Inserted 5% random noise					

Table 6. *Cont.*

	Original Image	NC Classifier	ADNLICM Classifier	NC_S Classifier	NLICM Classifier
Inserted 7% random noise					
Inserted 9% random noise					

Table 7. Landsat-8 original and dense forest classified class image with respect to different random salt-and-pepper noise (for site 1 (Haridwar)).

	Original Image	NC Classifier	ADNLICM Classifier	NC_S Classifier	NLICM Classifier
Inserted 1% random noise					
Inserted 3% random noise					
Inserted 5% random noise					
Inserted 7% random noise					

Table 7. *Cont.*

	Original Image	NC Classifier	ADNLICM Classifier	NC_S Classifier	NLICM Classifier
Inserted 9% random noise					

Table 8. RMSE, FERM, and Kappa of the algorithms concerning different random noise (pepper and salt-and-pepper noise) for site 1 (Haridwar).

Random Noise	NC			NLICM			NC_S			ADNLICM		
	RMSE	FERM	Kappa	RMSE	FERM	Kappa	RMSE	FERM	Kappa	RMSE	FERM	Kappa
Without noise	0.204	82.55	0.777	0.161	89.50	0.843	0.157	90.01	0.848	0.136	91.53	0.862
1%	0.210	79.05	0.763	0.171	88.02	0.829	0.161	89.03	0.839	0.160	89.14	0.840
3%	0.212	78.13	0.745	0.180	87.56	0.825	0.162	89.02	0.838	0.162	88.88	0.837
5%	0.214	77.89	0.743	0.184	86.22	0.812	0.164	87.12	0.821	0.163	88.05	0.829
7%	0.217	76.81	0.733	0.188	85.49	0.805	0.168	86.01	0.810	0.165	88.00	0.828
9%	0.219	75.04	0.716	0.193	83.42	0.786	0.172	85.48	0.805	0.167	87.89	0.828

Tables 6 and 7 show the Landsat-8 image consisting of 1%, 3%, 5%, 7%, and 9% random pepper and salt-and-pepper noise in the original image and classified image of dense forest with NC, NLICM, NC_S, and ADNLICM algorithm, respectively.

Table 8 shows the calculated Root Mean Square Error (RMSE), FERM (Fuzzy Error Matrix), and Kappa value of the NC, NLICM, NC_S, and ADNLICM algorithms for the Dense Forest classified class with 1%, 3%, 5%, 7%, and 9% random pepper and salt-and-pepper noise. Pepper and salt-and-pepper noise give almost the same result. This result shows that the ADNLICM algorithm obtained a lower value for RMSE, FERM, and Kappa than the other algorithms. Thus, we conclude that the ADNLICM algorithm performs better in the presence of noise than the other algorithms.

3.3. Experiment 3: Classification Outputs of Haridwar Study Area Site to Calculate Variance and SSE

Table 9 shows the classified outputs of the NC, NLICM, NC_S, and ADNLICM algorithms. The green patches show the classified classes of dense forest, eucalyptus, grassland, sand, water, and wheat.

Table 10 shows the variance within the class for the NC, NLICM, NC_S, and ADNLICM algorithms. It was observed that the ADNLICM classifier provides the least variance value for all six classes. This result shows that the ADNLICM classification algorithm handles heterogeneity correctly.

Next, we calculated the variance (Table 10) and Sum of Square Errors (SSE) (Table 11) of the classified outcomes of the Haridwar study area site using the proposed technique. Lower variance values demonstrate an algorithm's ability to handle heterogeneity well. In contrast, lower SSE values reveal which algorithm performs the best clustering validation.

Mathematics **2022**, *10*, 4056

Table 9. Classified classes for each algorithm for site 1 (Haridwar).

	NC Classifier	ADNLICM Classifier	NLICM Classifier	NC_S Classifier
Dense Forest				
Eucalyptus				
Grassland				
Riverine Sand				
Water				
Wheat				

Table 10. Variance within the class for each algorithm for site 1 (Haridwar).

	Dense Forest	Eucalyptus	Grassland	Riverine Sand	Water	Wheat
NLICM	0.040	0.250	0.058	0.029	0.003	0.029
ADNLICM	0.010	0.090	0.038	0.010	0.004	0.004
NC_S	0.029	0.188	0.040	0.010	0.004	0.029
NC	0.052	0.255	0.062	0.031	0.005	0.031

Table 11. SSE values for the proposed algorithms for site 1 (Haridwar).

	Dense Forest	Eucalyptus	Grassland	Riverine Sand	Water	Wheat
NLICM	3.960	24.75	5.742	2.871	0.342	2.871
ADNLICM	0.990	8.910	3.762	0.990	0.039	0.039
NC_S	2.871	18.59	3.960	0.990	0.039	0.990

Table 11 shows SSE, used to show the cluster validity of the proposed algorithm, values. This cluster validity method comes under the relative approach. Table 12 again shows that the ADNLICM algorithm performed better than the other algorithms.

Table 12. Sentinel-2 original and hard classified image for site 2 (Banasthali).

Random Noise	Original Image	NLICM Classifier	ADNLICM Classifier	NC_S Classifier
Inserted 1% random noise				
Inserted 3% random noise				
Inserted 5% random noise				
Inserted 7% random noise				
Inserted 9% random noise				

3.4. Experiment 4: Classification in the Presence of Noise in the Banasthali Study Area Site

This experiment assessed the impacts of 1%, 3%, 5%, 7%, and 9% pepper and salt-and-pepper-style random noise added to Sentinel-2 Landsat-8 images. Table 12 shows the Sentinel-2 image containing 1%, 3%, 5%, 7%, and 9% random pepper noise in the original image and hard classified image of the Sentinel-2 image shown after applying NLICM, NC_S, and ADNLICM algorithm.

The RMSE was calculated using the difference between the original classified image and the noisy classified image. FERM and Kappa were also calculated. To calculate FERM and RMSE, Sentinel-2 images were classified as hard and ERDAS Imagine Software was used. RMSE, FERM, and kappa result shows (Table 8) which classifier performs better compared to other classifiers.

Table 13 shows the evaluated overall accuracy (FERM), RMSE, and Kappa of the NC, NLICM, NC_S, and ADNLICM algorithms for hard classified images with 1%, 3%, 5%, 7%, and 9% random pepper noise. This result shows that the ADNLICM algorithm performed better than the other algorithms. Thus, it has been concluded that the ADNLICM algorithm performs better in the presence of noise than the other algorithms.

Table 13. RMSE, FERM, and Kappa for each algorithm with different random noise (pepper) for site 2 (Banasthali).

Random Noise	NC			NLICM			NC_S			ADNLICM		
	RMSE	FERM	Kappa	RMSE	FERM	Kappa	RMSE	FERM	Kappa	RMSE	FERM	Kappa
Without noise	0.151	89.12	0.853	0.144	93.25	0.871	0.150	91.23	0.872	0.149	92.48	0.910
1%	0.152	88.33	0.831	0.151	92.33	0.865	0.151	90.44	0.851	0.151	91.33	0.849
3%	0.157	86.72	0.811	0.153	90.67	0.854	0.152	88.56	0.834	0.153	89.45	0.838
5%	0.159	82.45	0.772	0.157	87.21	0.821	0.156	87.58	0.824	0.154	88.47	0.834
7%	0.161	80.12	0.742	0.154	86.45	0.814	0.157	86.47	0.808	0.155	87.26	0.813
9%	0.163	77.97	0.712	0.153	85.00	0.789	0.143	85.22	0.798	0.156	86.81	0.815

3.5. Experiment 5: Classification Outputs of Banasthali Study Area Site to Calculate Variance

Table 14 shows the classified outputs of the NLICM, NC_S, and ADNLICM algorithms, to compare classified results and calculate the variance value. The green patches show the classified classes of Grass, Mustard, and Wheat.

Table 14. Classified classes for site 1 (Haridwar).

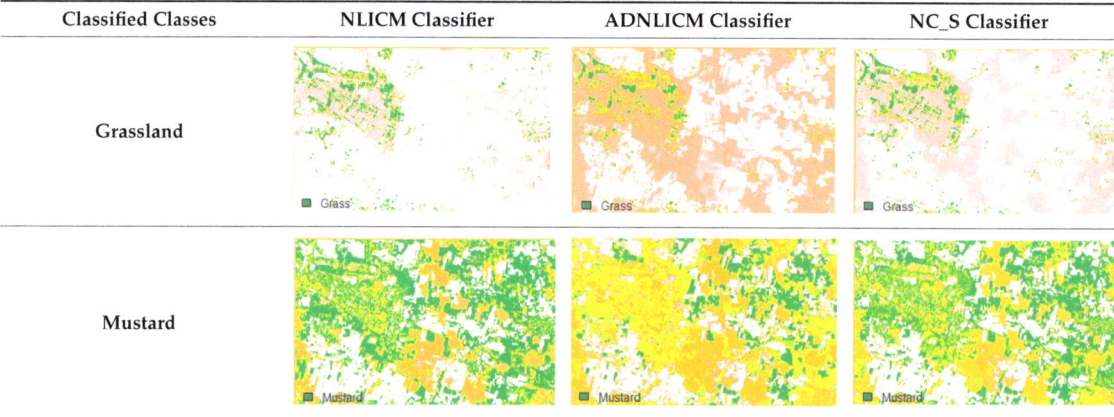

Table 14. Cont.

Classified Classes	NLICM Classifier	ADNLICM Classifier	NC_S Classifier
Wheat			

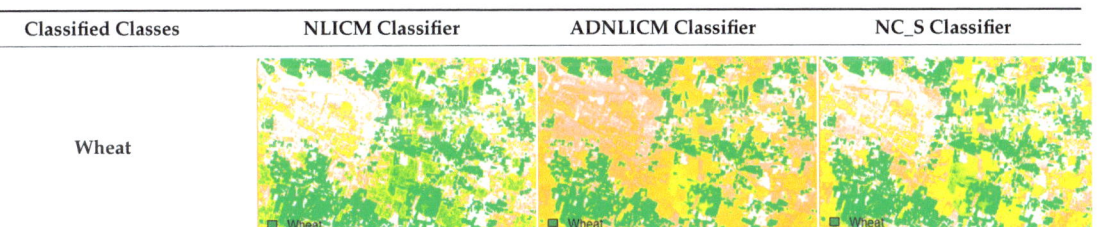

This experiment calculates the variance (Table 15) for the Banasthali study Area site. Lower variance values show the robustness of an algorithm to heterogeneity.

Table 15. Variance within the classes for the given algorithms for site 2 (Banasthali).

Variance within Class	Grassland	Mustard	Wheat
NLICM	7.78	15.32	14.36
ADNLICM	3.36	4.2	8.5
NC_S	5.44	12.3	12.19

Table 15 shows the variance within the classes for the NC, NLICM, NC_S, and ADNLICM algorithms; it was seen that the ADNLICM classifier provides the least variance value for all three classes. This result shows that the ADNLICM classification algorithm handles heterogeneity well.

3.6. Discussion in Comparison with Other Studies

The present study focused on local convolutional information methods. Previous studies on this method used FCM and PCM-based classifiers, while the present study is based on NC classifiers. A comparison of maximum OA obtained in previous studies and the present work is shown in Table 16. The optimized algorithm achieved from this study was comparable with the other studies in terms of overall accuracy.

Table 16. Comparison of OA with different studies.

Algorithms	Overall Accuracy
FLICM [27]	80.31%
PLICM [39]	86.37%
ADPLICM [22]	86.48%
MPCM_S [40]	78.94%
MRF (DA) [41]	82.06%
ADNLICM	91.53%

The Markov Random Field (MRF (DA)) [41] approach requires optimization of the global energy function, which is very sensitive to handle, which ADNLICM does not require. The FLICM [27], ADPLICM [22], MPCM_S [40], and PLICM [39] algorithms studied the handling of noisy pixels utilizing FC and PCM as the base classifier. Whereas, in this research work, local convolution methods have been added to the NC classifier, resulting in increased OA. The ADNLICM algorithm provides good classification results in terms of noisy pixels and heterogeneity and provides the highest Overall Accuracy of 91.53%. All the compared studies were performed on the same Landsat-8 dataset and resolution; hence a logical comparison was performed in this study, and it is inferred from the analysis that the proposed algorithm improved the overall accuracy.

4. Conclusions

The conventional Noise Clustering (NC) algorithm does not incorporate spatial information. This research examined three novel NC-based algorithms, NLICM, ADNLICM, and NC_S, that consider spatial information to better handle noise and heterogeneity. This paper concentrated on obtaining an optimized algorithm concerning different parameters (distance measures, m, and δ). The optimum overall accuracy for the ADNLICM algorithm was found to be 91.53% for Bray–Curtis distance measures, fuzziness factor at (m) = 1.1, and δ = 10^6. The proposed algorithms with NC-based classifier tested using 1%, 3%, 6%, and 9% random noise (pepper, and salt-and-pepper) achieve the lowest value of RMSE, FERM, and kappa for the Dense Forest class using the ADNLICM algorithm, which shows that the proposed method handles noise effectively. For the optimized ADNLICM algorithm, the variance is also lower compared to the other classifiers. Further, in this research, the optimized ADNLICM algorithm was validated using the sentinel-2 data in terms of RMSE, kappa, and variance for handling noise and heterogeneity, respectively.

The previous work performed for the study area used FCM- and PCM-based classifiers; in this study, the NC classifier was used, which performs better than FCM and PCM in handling noise and heterogeneity. Previous works mainly studied two or three distance measures to calculate the accuracy; in this work, 10 different distance measures and parameters were utilized to calculate the accuracy; and it was found that overall accuracy improved substantially. The proposed algorithm preserves the boundaries of the different feature classes. The techniques may be used for various applications, including mapping, change detection, area estimation, feature recognition, and classification while handling noisy/isolated pixels.

Author Contributions: Conceptualization, S.S., A.K. and D.K.; methodology, S.S. and A.K.; software, S.S. and A.K.; validation, A.K., S.S. and D.K.; formal analysis, S.S.; writing—original draft preparation, S.S.; writing—review and editing, A.K. and D.K.; visualization, S.S.; supervision, A.K. and D.K. All authors have read and agreed to the published version of the manuscript.

Funding: This research received no external funding.

Data Availability Statement: Not applicable.

Conflicts of Interest: The authors declare no conflict of interest.

References

1. Lillesand, T.; Kiefer, R.W.; Chipman, J. *Remote Sensing and Image Interpretation*; John Wiley & Sons: Hobokan, NJ, USA, 2014.
2. Bezdek, J.C.; Ehrlich, R.; Full, W. FCM: The fuzzy c-means clustering algorithm. *Comput. Geosci.* **1984**, *10*, 191–203. [CrossRef]
3. Krishnapuram, R.; Keller, J. A possibilistic approach to clustering. *IEEE Trans. Fuzzy Syst.* **1993**, *1*, 98–110. [CrossRef]
4. Dave, R.; Sen, S. *Noise Clustering Algorithm Revisited*; IEEE: Piscataway, NZ, USA, 1997; pp. 199–204.
5. Dagher, I.; Issa, S. Subband effect of the wavelet fuzzy C-means features in texture classification. *Image Vis. Comput.* **2012**, *30*, 896–905. [CrossRef]
6. Dunn, J.C. A Fuzzy Relative of the ISODATA Process and Its Use in Detecting Compact Well-Separated Clusters. *J. Cybern.* **1973**, *3*, 32–57. [CrossRef]
7. Chakraborty, D.; Singh, S.; Dutta, D. Segmentation and classification of high spatial resolution images based on Hölder exponents and variance. *Geo-Spatial Inf. Sci.* **2017**, *20*, 39–45. [CrossRef]
8. Yu, J.; Guo, P.; Chen, P.; Zhang, Z.; Ruan, W. Remote sensing image classification based on improved fuzzy c-means. *Geo-spatial Inf. Sci.* **2008**, *11*, 90–94. [CrossRef]
9. Ahmed, M.; Yamany, S.; Farag, A.; Moriarty, T. *Bias Field Estimation and Adaptive Segmentation of MRI Data Using a Modified Fuzzy C-Means Algorithm*; IEEE: Piscataway, NZ, USA, 2003; pp. 1250–1255.
10. Chuang, K.-S.; Tzeng, H.-L.; Chen, S.; Wu, J.; Chen, T.-J. Fuzzy c-Means clustering with spatial information for image segmentation. *Comput. Med. Imaging Graph.* **2006**, *30*, 9–15. [CrossRef]
11. Krinidis, S.; Chatzis, V. A Robust Fuzzy Local Information C-Means Clustering Algorithm. *IEEE Trans. Image Process.* **2010**, *19*, 1328–1337. [CrossRef]
12. Zhang, H.; Wang, Q.; Shi, W.; Hao, M. A Novel Adaptive Fuzzy Local Information C-Means Clustering Algorithm for Remotely Sensed Imagery Classification. *IEEE Trans. Geosci. Remote Sens.* **2017**, *55*, 5057–5068. [CrossRef]
13. Zheng, Y.H.; Jeon, B.; Xu, D.H.; Wu, Q.M.J.; Zhang, H. Image segmentation by generalized hierarchical fuzzy C-means algorithm. *J. Intell. Fuzzy Syst.* **2015**, *28*, 961–973. [CrossRef]

14. Ding, Y.; Fu, X. Kernel-Based fuzzy *c*-Means clustering algorithm based on genetic algorithm. *Neurocomputing* **2016**, *188*, 233–238. [CrossRef]
15. Guo, L.; Chen, L.; Chen, C.P.; Zhou, J. Integrating guided filter into fuzzy clustering for noisy image segmentation. *Digit. Signal Process.* **2018**, *83*, 235–248. [CrossRef]
16. Xu, Z.; Wu, J. Intuitionistic fuzzy C-means clustering algorithms. *J. Syst. Eng. Electron.* **2010**, *21*, 580–590. [CrossRef]
17. Verma, H.; Agrawal, R.; Sharan, A. An improved intuitionistic fuzzy *c*-means clustering algorithm incorporating local information for brain image segmentation. *Appl. Soft Comput.* **2016**, *46*, 543–557. [CrossRef]
18. Rawat, A.; Kumar, D.; Chatterjee, R.S.; Kumar, H. A GIS-based liquefaction susceptibility mapping utilising the morphotectonic analysis to highlight potential hazard zones in the East Ganga plain. *Environ. Earth Sci.* **2022**, *81*, 1–16. [CrossRef]
19. Rawat, A.; Kumar, D.; Chatterjee, R.S.; Kumar, H. Reconstruction of liquefaction damage scenario in Northern Bihar during 1934 and 1988 earthquake using geospatial methods. *Geomatics Nat. Hazards Risk* **2022**, *13*, 2560–2578. [CrossRef]
20. Zhang, D.; Pan, F.; Diao, Q.; Feng, X.; Li, W.; Wang, J. Seeding Crop Detection Framework Using Prototypical Network Method in UAV Images. *Agriculture* **2021**, *12*, 26. [CrossRef]
21. Pant, N.; Dubey, R.K.; Bhatt, A.; Rai, S.P.; Semwal, P.; Mishra, S. Soil erosion and flood hazard zonation using morphometric and morphotectonic parameters in Upper Alaknanda river basin. *Nat. Hazards* **2020**, *103*, 3263–3301. [CrossRef]
22. Singh, A.; Kumar, A.; Upadhyay, P. A novel approach to incorporate local information in Possibilistic *c*-Means algorithm for an optical remote sensing imagery. *Egypt. J. Remote Sens. Space Sci.* **2020**, *24*, 1–11. [CrossRef]
23. Wu, X.H.; Zhou, J.J. Modified possibilistic clustering model based on kernel methods. *J. Shanghai Univ.* **2008**, *12*, 136–140. [CrossRef]
24. Zhao, F. Fuzzy clustering algorithms with self-tuning non-local spatial information for image segmentation. *Neurocomputing* **2013**, *106*, 115–125. [CrossRef]
25. Dave, R.; Krishnapuram, R. Robust clustering methods: A unified view. *IEEE Trans. Fuzzy Syst.* **1997**, *5*, 270–293. [CrossRef]
26. Ahmed, M.; Yamany, S.; Mohamed, N.; Farag, A.; Moriarty, T. A modified fuzzy *c*-means algorithm for bias field estimation and segmentation of MRI data. *IEEE Trans. Med. Imaging* **2002**, *21*, 193–199. [CrossRef]
27. Suman, S.; Kumar, D.; Kumar, A. Study the Effect of Convolutional Local Information-Based Fuzzy *c*-Means Classifiers with Different Distance Measures. *J. Indian Soc. Remote Sens.* **2021**, *49*, 1561–1568. [CrossRef]
28. Bray, J.R.; Curtis, J.T. An Ordination of the Upland Forest Communities of Southern Wisconsin. *Ecol. Monogr.* **1957**, *27*, 325–349. [CrossRef]
29. Agarwal, S.; Burges, C.; Crammer, K. Advances in Ranking. In Proceedings of the Twenty-Third Annual Conference on Neural Information Processing Systems, Whistler, BC, USA; 2009; pp. 1–81.
30. Baccour, L.; John, R.I. Experimental analysis of crisp similarity and distance measures. In Proceedings of the 2014 6th International Conference of Soft Computing and Pattern Recognition (SoCPaR), Tunis, Tunisia, 11–14 August 2014; IEEE: Piscataway, NZ, USA, 2014; pp. 96–100.
31. Székely, G.J.; Rizzo, M.L.; Bakirov, N.K. Measuring and testing dependence by correlation of distances. *Ann. Stat.* **2007**, *35*, 2769–2794. [CrossRef]
32. Senoussaoui, M.; Kenny, P.; Stafylakis, T.; Dumouchel, P. A Study of the Cosine Distance-Based Mean Shift for Telephone Speech Diarization. *IEEE/ACM Trans. Audio Speech Lang. Process.* **2013**, *22*, 217–227. [CrossRef]
33. Hasnat, A.; Halder, S.; Bhattacharjee, D.; Nasipuri, M.; Basu, D.K. *Comparative Study of Distance Metrics for Finding Skin Color Similarity of Two Color Facial Images*; ACER: New Taipei City, Taiwan, 2013; pp. 99–108.
34. Vassiliadis, S.; Hakkennes, E.; Wong, J.; Pechanek, G. The sum-Absolute-Difference motion estimation accelerator. In Proceedings of the 24th EUROMICRO Conference (Cat. No. 98EX204), Vasteras, Sweden, 27 August 1998; IEEE: Piscataway, NZ, USA, 2002.
35. Scollar, I.; Huang, T.; Weidner, B. Image enhancement using the median and the interquartile distance. In Proceedings of the 2018 IEEE International Conference on Multimedia and Expo (ICME), Boston, MA, USA, 14–16 April 1983; IEEE: Piscataway, NZ, USA, 1984.
36. Nandan, R.; Kamboj, A.; Kumar, A.; Kumar, S.; Reddy, K.V. Formosat-2 with Landsat-8 Temporal -Multispectral Data for Wheat Crop Identification using Hypertangent Kernel based Possibilistic classifier. *J. Geomat.* **2016**, *10*, 89–95.
37. Khamdamov, R.; Saliev, E.; Rakhmanov, K. Classification of crops by multispectral satellite images of sentinel 2 based on the analysis of vegetation signatures. *J. Phys. Conf. Ser.* **2020**, *1441*, 012143. [CrossRef]
38. Kumar, A.; Upadhyay, P. *Fuzzy Machine Learning Algorithms for Remote Sensing Image Classification*; CRC Press: Boca Raton, FL, USA, 2020.
39. Suman, S.; Kumar, A.; Kumar, D.; Soni, A. Augmenting possibilistic *c*-means classifier to handle noise and within class heterogeneity in classification. *J. Appl. Remote Sens.* **2021**, *15*, 1–17. [CrossRef]
40. Singh, A.; Kumar, A.; Upadhyay, P. Modified possibilistic *c*-means with constraints (MPCM-S) approach for incorporating the local information in a remote sensing image classification. *Remote Sens. Appl. Soc. Environ.* **2020**, *18*, 100319. [CrossRef]
41. Suman, S.; Kumar, D.; Kumar, A. Study the Effect of MRF Model on Fuzzy c Means Classifiers with Different Parameters and Distance Measures. *J. Indian Soc. Remote Sens.* **2022**, *50*, 1177–1189. [CrossRef]

Article

Efficient Net-XGBoost: An Implementation for Facial Emotion Recognition Using Transfer Learning

Sudheer Babu Punuri [1], Sanjay Kumar Kuanar [1], Manjur Kolhar [2,*], Tusar Kanti Mishra [3,*], Abdalla Alameen [4], Hitesh Mohapatra [5] and Soumya Ranjan Mishra [5]

1 CSE Department, GIET University, Gunupur 765022, Odisha, India
2 Department of Computer Science, College of Arts and Science, Prince Sattam Bin Abdulaziz University, Al-Kharj 16278, Saudi Arabia
3 School of Computer Science and Engineering, Vellore Institute of Technology, Vellore 632014, Tamil Nadu, India
4 Computer Science Department, Prince Sattam Bin Abdul Aziz University, Al-Kharj 16278, Saudi Arabia
5 School of Computer Engineering, KIIT (Deemed to Be) University, Bhubaneswar 751024, Odisha, India
* Correspondence: m.kolhar@psau.edu.sa (M.K.); tusar.k.mishra@gmail.com (T.K.M.)

Citation: Punuri, S.B.; Kuanar, S.K.; Kolhar, M.; Mishra, T.K.; Alameen, A.; Mohapatra, H.; Mishra, S.R. Efficient Net-XGBoost: An Implementation for Facial Emotion Recognition Using Transfer Learning. *Mathematics* **2023**, *11*, 776. https://doi.org/10.3390/math11030776

Academic Editor: Giancarlo Consolo

Received: 29 December 2022
Revised: 14 January 2023
Accepted: 29 January 2023
Published: 3 February 2023

Copyright: © 2023 by the authors. Licensee MDPI, Basel, Switzerland. This article is an open access article distributed under the terms and conditions of the Creative Commons Attribution (CC BY) license (https://creativecommons.org/licenses/by/4.0/).

Abstract: Researchers are interested in Facial Emotion Recognition (FER) because it could be useful in many ways and has promising applications. The main task of FER is to identify and recognize the original facial expressions of users from digital inputs. Feature extraction and emotion recognition make up the majority of the traditional FER. Deep Neural Networks, specifically Convolutional Neural Network (CNN), are popular and highly used in FER due to their inherent image feature extraction process. This work presents a novel method dubbed as EfficientNet-XGBoost that is based on Transfer Learning (TL) technique. EfficientNet-XGBoost is basically a cascading of the EfficientNet and the XGBoost techniques along with certain enhancements by experimentation that reflects the novelty of the work. To ensure faster learning of the network and to overcome the vanishing gradient problem, our model incorporates fully connected layers of global average pooling, dropout and dense. EfficientNet is fine-tuned by replacing the upper dense layer(s) and cascading the XGBoost classifier making it suitable for FER. Feature map visualization is carried out that reveals the reduction in the size of feature vectors. The proposed method is well-validated on benchmark datasets such as CK+, KDEF, JAFFE, and FER2013. To overcome the issue of data imbalance, in some of the datasets namely CK+ and FER2013, we augmented data artificially through geometric transformation techniques. The proposed method is implemented individually on these datasets and corresponding results are recorded for performance analysis. The performance is computed with the help of several metrics like precision, recall and F1 measure. Comparative analysis with competent schemes are carried out on the same sample data sets separately. Irrespective of the nature of the datasets, the proposed scheme outperforms the rest with overall rates of accuracy being 100%, 98% and 98% for the first three datasets respectively. However, for the FER2013 datasets, efficiency is less promisingly observed in support of the proposed work.

Keywords: facial emotion recognition; transfer learning; deep learning; EfficientNet; XGBoost

MSC: 68T07

1. Introduction

Facial Emotion Recognition (FER) techniques are used to identify facial expressions that convey emotions on human faces. Different types of emotions exist, some of which might not be apparent to the human eye. Hence, with proper tools, any indications preceding or following can be related to identifying the recognition [1]. In the field of FER, there are seven universal facial expressions namely: anger, fear, disgust, happiness, sadness, surprise, and neutral. Emotion extraction from facial expressions is a topic of active research in psychology, psychiatry, and mental health at present. The automatic detection of emotions from facial expressions has many uses, including smart living, health care, HCI (human-computer interaction), HBI (human-robot interaction), and modern augmented reality [2]. Researchers keep looking into FER because it has so many uses.

The main goal of FER is to match different facial expressions with different emotional states. In the classical FER, the two most important steps are "feature extraction" and "emotion recognition". Prior to feature extraction, all images need to be preprocessed, which includes finding faces, cropping, resizing, and normalising. Standard techniques which includes notable methods such as discrete wavelet transform and histogram of oriented gradients (HOG) [3] are suitably used for feature extraction. Finally, neural networks (NN) and other machine learning techniques are used to classify emotions based on the features that were extracted.

Deep neural networks (DNNs), especially convolutional neural networks (CNNs), are popular among researchers working on FER. This is because of the inherent feature extraction and recognition integration architectures [4–6]. However, the current FER approaches reported by CNN still have some challenges. The very low difference in facial expressions due to different emotional states makes the task challenging. Further, substantial intra-class variance and low inter-class variation [7] along with changes in facial position have also posed several challenges. Challenges also persist in emotion recognition under naturalistic situations like occlusion and pose variation [8], which can dramatically alter facial appearance. This is where we try to identify an opportunity for research. Advances in computer vision [9] has lead to high-quality emotion recognition under controlled conditions and consistent environments.

Nowadays, the applications of deep learning, particularly CNN, make it possible to extract numerous features and learn from them. A CNN with several hidden layers requires difficult training and performs poorly in practice. In order to improve accuracy, deep CNN architecture can be pre-trained using a variety of models and methodologies. EfficientNet [10], DenseNet-161 [1], Inception-v3, Resnet-50, and VGG-16 [1] are the most popular pre-trained DCNN models; however, training a large model takes a huge dataset and intensive computing power.

Advanced computer vision research, is also able to solve the problem of unlabeled data, in medical image analysis. Moreover, there is no guarantee of large datasets for training. Ref. [11]'s work has solved the problem of unlabeled data and developed an estimation method for hard cases. As the volume of the dataset grows, we require high computing power. This situation is resource hunger. GPUs are a must for computing large datasets. For efficiently Using GPUs, we need to accelerate. Mengyang Zhao et al. [12] contribute a novel method for GPU acceleration by a method fast mean shift algorithm, which increases speed by up to 7–10 times. Face recognition has a wide range of applications. Capturing devices may produce 2D images, but there is a need for 3D images for more spatial information. Jin, B [13] have introduced the D+GAN method for the translation of image-to-image with facial conditions.

Training a deep learning model from scratch requires a lot of processing power and takes a long time. As a result, rather than reinventing the wheel, a Deep Convolutional Neural Network (DCNN) trained on another task and fine-tuned can be used. This approach is called "Transfer Learning" (TL) [14]. The conditions required for applying transfer learning are data type consistency and similarity in the problem domain. In our study EfficientNet [10], already pre-trained on a large dataset of imagenet is used for the task of FER. CNN's are scaled up to achieve better accuracy in the task of classification on most benchmark datasets. But convolutional techniques of model scaling are done randomly. Some models are scaled depth-wise and others width-wise. Random scaling requires manual tuning and requires many person-hours. EfficientNet on the other hand, uses a method called "compound co-efficient" to scale models in a simple but effective way. After extraction of features using pre-trained DCNN models, efficient classification models can be employed for the task of emotion recognition. XGBoost [15] is an algorithm under the category of supervised learning. This algorithm runs on both single and distributed systems for classifying the input samples. In case of large data sets, XGBoost does efficient memory management keeping the limitations of the RAM size and supports cross validation. It also has a wide range of regularizations, which helps with the reduction of overfitting. Through auto tree pruning it avoids decision tree growth after a certain limit internally. This motivates us to take-up XGBoost as a classifier in our research pipeline. This study's key contribution can be summed up as follows:

(i)   To implement a robust FER technique utilising the power of Transfer Learning through EfficientNet-XGBoost model.
(ii) Adding fully connected layers to the model for fine tuning for attaining high accuracy.
(iii) Analyze the proposed method's proficiency by comparing its accuracy in recognising emotions to that of other methods currently in use.

2. Related Work

In recent times, several techniques have been proposed in the context of FER. According to conventional methods, facial features are extracted first, and emotions are then classified using those features. On the other hand, the FER job is done by current deep-learning models that combine both steps into a single computational process.

In the domain of artificial intelligence (AI) domain, automatic FER has become a challenging task, mostly in its subdomain of Machine Learning (ML). FER was implemented using different traditional algorithms like K-Nearest Neighbor (KNN), neural networks, etc. during the origin of FER. The methods like wavelet energy feature (WEF) and Fisher's linear discriminants (FLD) were the first methods used for feature extraction, and the KNN method is used for classifying the classes of emotions. Feng et al. [16] extracted the Local Binary Patterns (LBP) histograms from images at different locations, summed all these patterns, and then classified the emotion using a linear programming (LP) technique. Lee et al. [1] improved the wavelet transform for 2D, named contourlet transform (CT), in order to extract features from images and used boosting algorithms for classifying emotions. Support vector machine (SVM) is used by various models for classification of emotions for the extracted features using different techniques. Liew adn Yairi [17] have done a comparative study considering SVM and several other methods, which include Gabor, Haar, and LBP. Two years ago, researchers found various classification algorithms for their suggested geometry-based feature extraction, including logistic regression, LDA (linear discriminate analysis), examples include KNN, naive Bayes, SVM, and classification and regression trees. Goodfellow et al. [3] FER2013 dataset is used to construct a model on FER, although it could only reach 57.7% accuracy using the Histogram of Oriented Gradients (HOG) feature extractor and SVM. This is much worse accuracy than the baseline. The primary drawback of these conventional methods is that they only consider the frontal views of FER as features.

A new approach for FER is deep learning in machine learning, and so far there are several CNN-based models introduced in the literature. The integration of deep belief network (DBN) and neural network (NN) was proposed by Zhao and Shi [18], where DBN is used for feature extraction and the neural network is used for classifying emotions. At first, some models used a standard CNN architecture with two convolutional-pooling layers to look at the images of facial expressions of emotion that they had collected for FER. Mollahosseini et al. [19] introduced a bigger model with 4-inception and 2-convolutional-pooling layers. Pons and Masipcite [4] developed an ensemble of 72 CNNs, where each CNN is trained on different filter sizes in convolutional layers and a different number of neurons in fully connected layers. The [5] model also employs an ensemble of 100 CNNs, whereas the previous model utilised a predetermined number of CNNs. When all of the FER datasets were benchmarked, CNN-based deep learning models had the highest accuracy. However, unlike HOG or LBP, existing models implement the recognition process as a whole. Image classification applications were used by combining CNN model using KNN or the SVM classifier, which attained slightly higher accuracy than CNN models.

Jabid et al. [6] and Shima and Omori [20] fine-tuned the algorithm and improved better accuracy on the dataset JAFFE by 90.1% and 95.3% respectively. With 35,887 images, the FER-2013 dataset is the most challenging one. Saeed et al. [21] achieved a baseline accuracy of 68 percent.

Xiao Sun and Man Lv [22] created a model with hybrid features that combine SIFT and deep learning features using a CNN model with different levels of extraction. Ref. [23] proposed a multilevel Haar wavelet-based approach. By using the Viola-Jones cascade, object detector components like eyes, mouths, and eyebrows are extracted. Kuan Li and Yi Jin [24] proposed a cropping and rotation method which makes the model easy to train only on the useful features. C. Shi, CTan et al. [25] proposed a model that effectively extracts features by modifying the structure of a single CNN model based on a Multi-Branch Cross-Connection (MBCC-CNN). M. Aouayeb et al. [26] developed a model with Squeeze and Excitation with Vision Transformer which overcomes the disadvantages of regular CNN models. Shervin et al. [2] implemented an approach using attentional convolutional networks by focusing only on the significant parts of the face images. SL Happy et al. [27] developed a model, by identifying facial patches that are active in particular emotions, thus these features are classified. [28] The authors created an automatic FER by identifying the best feature descriptor using the Facial Landmarks descriptor and classifying with Support Vector Machine (SVM). Due to ambiguity facial gestures, less-informative facial images, and subjectivity of annotators, it is enormously hard to annotate a qualitative large-scale facial expression dataset. These uncertainties pose a significant obstacle of FER in large-scale in the era of deep learning. The work of the researcher [29] proposes a simple yet effective SelfCure Network (SCN) that efficiently suppresses uncertainties and prevents deep neural networks from overfitting uncertain facial images.

Training a large neural model such as deep convolutional neural network is difficult due to the network's numerous parameters. It is common knowledge that a large network is required to train large amounts of data. If trained with too little or insufficient data, overfitting is inevitable. In some research works, it has become a combustion task arrange sufficient sample set to train on deep convolutional neural network. However, in cases where a huge amount of data is not available, transfer learning [14,30] solves the issue. No doubt, transfer learning is a concept used to represent the knowledge learned from different tasks which has the same applications. In the literature review, it was identified that the TL method worked better when both the tasks were similar. It has been investigated that TL achieved good accuracy on the task different from training, which is the motivation of this work.

3. Materials and Methods

3.1. Deep Learning Using Transfer Learning

Reusing a model that has already been trained to solve a new issue is called transfer learning. Transfer learning has a number of advantages, but its major ones are reducing training time, improving neural network performance, and not requiring a lot of data. To the pre-trained model (EfficientNet), fully connected layers, namely global average pooling, dropout, and dense layer, are added. Lastly, to the pre-trained model, we added XGBoost for the classification.

FER is also done through pre-trained deep neural frameworks using appropriate Transfer Learning. Mahendran [30] has the learning process in frameworks such as CNN. The visualization reveals preliminary features from input images from the first layer. The next layer identifies the complex features like texture or shape. So the same mechanism goes on towards identifying the complex features. Transfer learning is primarily advantageous because it is difficult to train a DCNN from scratch. Instead of reinventing the wheel, we will use the pre-trained weights and fine-tune the model for FER. Employing TL for FER provides promising results as well.

A DCNN model (EFficientNet) pre-trained with a large dataset with 1000 classes (e.g., ImageNet) is well suited for FER. Figure 1 shows the general architecture of transfer learning. Here, the foundation of the convolutional is similar to that of pre-trained DCNN by excluding the classification stage. The existing classifier part in the model is replaced by newly added fully connected layers and a classifier. Overall, the module consists of a Convolutional Base to extract feature extraction, fully connected layers for fine-tuning the model, and an XGBoost Classifier.

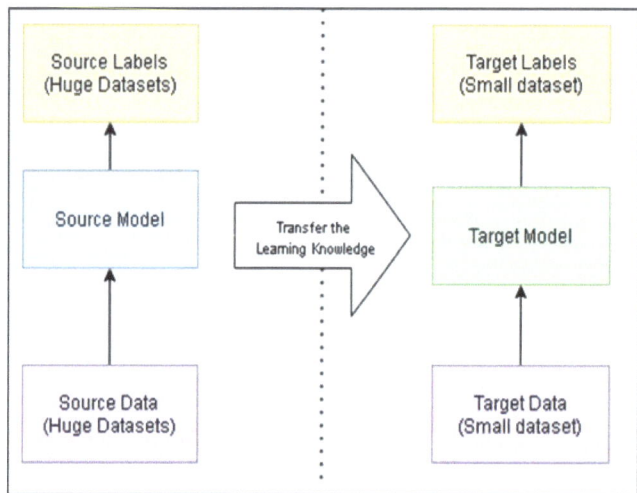

Figure 1. Idea of Transfer Learning (TL).

EfficientNets is a collection of models (named as EfficientNet-B0 to B7). They are derived by compound scaling up the baseline network EfficientNet-B0. The benefit of EfficientNets manifests itself in two ways. First, it offers high accuracy. Second, it enhances the performance of the model by reducing the dimensionality and floating-point computational cost. Compounding scaling is used to produce various versions of EfficientNet. Compound Scaling refers to the utilization of a weighted scale containing three interconnected hyper-parameters of the model (stated in Equation (1)), namely depth d, width w and resolution r defined as:

$$depth : d = A^\phi, width : w = B^\phi, resolution : r = \Gamma^\phi \quad (1)$$

where A, B and Γ are the constants that defines the resolution of the network.

Initially, the compound coefficient $\varnothing$ is set to 1, which defines the base compound configuration, EfficientNetB0. The same configuration is used in the grid search, for optimizing the co-efficients A, B and Γ such that:

$$A * B^2 * \Gamma^2 \approx 2 \quad (2)$$

where $A \geq 1, B \geq 1, \Gamma \geq 1$

We achieved the optimal values for A, B and Γ as 1.2, 1.1 and 1.15 respectively, under the constraints stated in of (2). If we change the value of $\varnothing$ in Equation (1), the scaled versions of EfficientNet-B1 to B7 will be achieved. EfficientNet-B0 baseline architecture is used for feature extraction. The EfficientNet-B0 architecture consists of mainly 3 modules, the Stem, the Blocks and the Head.

Stem: Stem has a convolutional Layer, (3 × 3) with kernel size, Batch normalization Layer, and a Swish activation. These 3 are integrated.

Blocks: Blocks consist of several Mobile inverted bottleneck convolutions (MBConv) Figure 2. MBConv has different versions. In MBConvX, X denotes the expansion ratio.

Basically, MBConv1 and MBConv6 is used in EfficientNet. MBConv1 and MBConv6 description is given below.

$$MBConv1 \leftarrow DwC + BN + Swish + SE + Conv + BN \quad (3)$$

$$MBConv6 \leftarrow Conv + BN + Swish + DwC + BN + Swish + SE + Conv + BN \quad (4)$$

where
DwC—DepthWise Convolution
BN—Batch Normalisation
SE—Squeeze Excitation.
Swish—an activation.

The no. of layers in blocks are MBConv1, k3 × 3, MBConv6, k3 × 3 repeated twice, MBConv6, k5 × 5 is repeated twice, MBConv6, k3 × 3 is repeated thrice, MBConv6, k3 × 3 is repeated thrice, MBConv6, k5 × 5 is repeated thrice, MBConv6, k5 × 5 is repeated 4 times, MBConv6, k3 × 3, total 16 blocks exists.

Head: Head is a layer consisting of Convolution, Batch Normalization, Swish, Pooling, Dropout and Fully Connected layers. Head is represented as follows:

$$Head \leftarrow Conv + BN + Swish \quad (5)$$

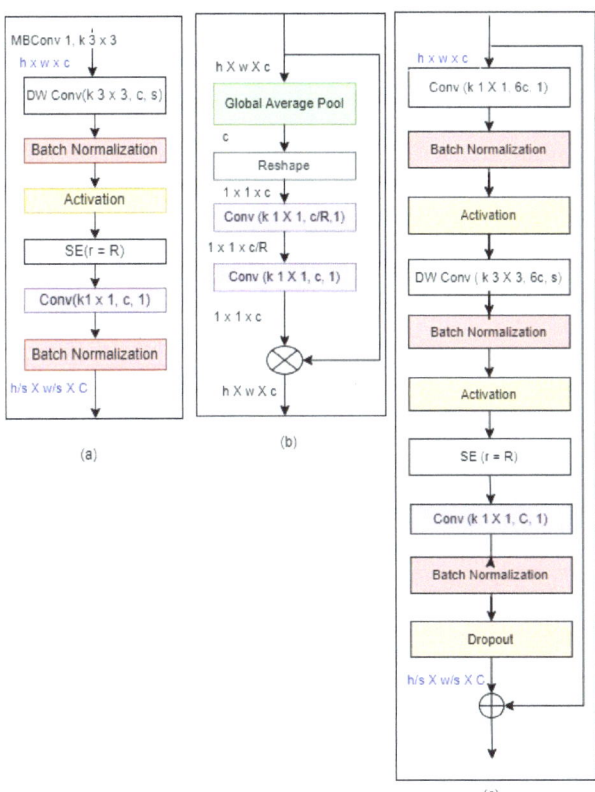

Figure 2. EfficientNet Blocks: (**a**–**c**) are the 3 basic building blocks. h, w, and c are input with respect to height, width, and channel for all the MBConv blocks. The Output channel for the two blocks is denoted by C.

The detailed EfficietNet Architecture is represented in Table 1. A Note to remember is that MBConv6, k5 × 5 and MBConv6, k3 × 3 but only the difference is that MBConv6, k5 × 5 is applied to a kernel size of 5 × 5.

Table 1. Outline of the EfficientNet-B0 baseline network layers.

Stage	Operator	Resolution	Output Features	Layers
1	Conv 3 × 3	224 × 224	32	1
2	MBConv1, k3 × 3	112 × 112	16	1
3	MBConv6, k3 × 3	112 × 112	24	2
4	MBConv6, k5 × 5	56 × 56	40	2
5	MBConv6, k3 × 3	28 × 28	80	3
6	MBConv6, k5 × 5	14 × 14	112	3
7	MBConv6, k5 × 5	14 × 15	192	4
8	MBConv6, k3 × 3	7 × 7	320	1
9	Conv 1 × 1 & Pooling & FC	7 × 7	1280	1

3.2. Fully Connected Layer

This module consists of 3 layers Global Average Pooling, Dropout layer and Dense Layer.

Global Average Pooling: Global Average Pooling layers replace fully connected layers in traditional CNNs. In the final layer, the goal is for generating the feature sets corresponding to respective classification levels. We take the average of each feature map instead of designing a complete connected layers above the feature maps. The basic advantage of global average pooling is that it is very similar to the structure of convolutional structure by enforcing the relation between corresponding feature maps with respect to classes. Another advantage is to avoid over-fitting, as there are zero parameters to optimize in global average pooling. Global Average Pooling does something different. Average pooling is applied on. It uses average pooling on the spatial dimensions until each is one and leaves the other dimensions alone. Global Average Pooling layer does transformation of (N_1, N_2, N_3), feature set of size $(1, N_3)$ and feature map where (N_1, N_2) corresponds to image dimension, and N_3 being the count of filters used.

Dropout: While using DCNN, co-adaptation is the drawback when training a model. This indicated that the neuron are very dependent on other neurons. They influence each other considerably and are not independent enough regarding their inputs. It is very common to find in some situation that some neurons have a predictive capacity that is more significant than others. These kind of state can be avoided and the weights must be distributed to prevent over-fitting. There are various regularization methods which can be applied for regulating co-adaptation and high predictive capacity of of some neurons. To resolve this problem Dropout can be used. Depending on whether the model is DCNN, or a CNN or a Recurrent Neural Network (RNN) different dropout methods can be used. Here in our work we have used standard dropout method. The modeling of dropout layer on a neuron mathematically represented as follows:

$$f(\kappa, \rho) = \begin{cases} \kappa & \text{if } \kappa = 1 \\ 1 - \rho & \text{if } \kappa = 0 \end{cases} \qquad (6)$$

where:
κ denotes the desired results.
ρ is the probability of the real-valued representations.
If $\rho = 1$ the neuron holding a real value is de-activated else activated.

The next layer we have is dense layer. In the neural network, a dense layer deeply connects to its next layer. Each of the neuron links to every neuron of its next layer. The neuron in this dense layer represents the neuron's matrix-vector multiplications. Every neuron in the dense layer unit receives output from each neuron in the preceding layers in the model. The dense layer units perform matrix-vector cross product. In product, the row vector of the output from the previous layers is identical to the column vector of the dense layer. The major hyper parameters to tune in this layer are units and activation function. The very basic and necessary parameter in dense layer is units. In dense layer, size is defined by units which is always greater than 1. Activation function aids in transforming the input values to neurons. Basically it produces non-linearity into the network where relationship of input and output values are learnt.

3.3. XGBoost

eXtreme Gradient Boosting (XGBoost) [15] algorithm is one of the best algorithm in Machine Learning (ML) developed by Chen and Guestrin. XGBoost can be considered as both a classifier and regressor in the framework of scikit-learn. The XGBoost model for classification is called XGBClassifier which is used in this study. We can create and fit to our training dataset. The beauty of XGBoost is its scalability, which drives fast learning through parallel and distributed computing and provides memory usage efficiently. XGBoost is a distributed gradient boosting library that has been developed to be highly versatile and portable. The objective function (loss function and regularization) is represented as follows:

$$F^t \approx \sum_{j=1}^{T}[(\sum_{i \epsilon I_j} g_i)w_j + \frac{1}{2}(\sum_{i \epsilon I_j} h_i + \lambda)w_j^2] + = \rho T \qquad (7)$$

F—Objective Function
g_i—Mean Square Error first derivative.
w—Score Vectors on leaves.
h_i—Mean Square Error second derivative.
λ—Penality
T—Number of leaves.
ρ—Leaf's Complexity
I_j—Leaf node j data samples.

The beauty of XGBoost motivated and produced the best results in our work.

4. Proposed Work

The proposed work consists of 3 modules. First the EfficientNet Module, Fully Connected Layer and Finally the XGBoost Classifier. Figure 3 illustrates the models block diagram. Images are given as input to the EfficientNet and processed for feature extraction.

4.1. Proposed Algorithm

The Algorithm for the EfficientNet-XGBoost is designed in this section. Algorithms 1 and 2 are the step wise refinements of MBConv1 and MBConv6 respectively. Algorithm 3 is the model step wise refinement, MBConv1 and MBConv functions are executed repeatedly as discussed in the model setup Section 3.1.

Algorithm 1 : MBConv1(K × K, B, S)

Require: $KKernelSize, B : OutputFeatureMaps, S : Stride, R : Reductionratio of SE, T : TotalImages\{X_1, X_2, \ldots X_T\}$

1: $dwc \Leftarrow DepthwiseConv(K \times K, M, S)$
2: $bn \Leftarrow BatchNomalization(dwc)$
3: $sw \Leftarrow Swish(bn)$
4: $e \Leftarrow SE(R = 4, sw)$
5: $conv \Leftarrow Conv(1 \times 1, B, 1, se)$
6: $bn \Leftarrow BatchNormalization(conv)$
7: return (h/s × w/s, B = bn)

Algorithm 2: MBConv6(K × K, B, S)

Require: Inputs: $K : KernelSize, B : OutputFeatureMaps, S : Stride$, R: Reduction ratio of SE, $T : TotalImages\{X_1, X_2, \ldots X_T\}$
1: $conv \Leftarrow Conv(1 \times 1, 6M, 1)$
2: $bn \Leftarrow BatchNomalization(dwc)$
3: $bn \Leftarrow BatchNormalization(bn)$
4: $sw \Leftarrow Swish(bn)$
5: $se \Leftarrow SE(R = 4, sw)$
6: $conv \Leftarrow Conv(1 \times 1, B, 1, se)$
7: $bn \Leftarrow BatchNormalization(conv)$
8: return (h/s × w/s, B = bn)

Algorithm 3: EFFICIENTNET-XGBOOST()

Ensure: weights $\Leftarrow Imagenetweights$
Ensure: biases $\Leftarrow ImagenetBias$
Ensure: input $\Leftarrow (48, 48, 3)$, T is total images.
1: begin:

```
for i in range(0, T) do
begin:
{  conv<-- Conv(3 x 3, image)
   bn <-- BatchNormalization(conv)
   sw <-- bn * sigmoid(bn)}
end;
```

2: $mbc1 \Leftarrow MBConv1(3 \times 3, B, S, sw)$ 16 rounds

```
for i in range(0, 2):
    mbc6 <-- MBConv6(3 x 3, B, S, mbc1)
for i in range(0, 2):
    mbc6 <-- MBConv6(5 x 5, B, S, mbc6)
for i in range(0, 3):
    mbc6 <-- MBConv6(3 x 3, B, S, mbc6)
for i in range(0, 6):
    mbc6 <-- MBConv6(5 x 5, B, S, mbc6)
```

3: $mbc6 \Leftarrow MBConv6(3 \times 3, B, S)(mbc6)$
4: $conv1 \Leftarrow Conv(1 \times 1, M, S)(mbc6)$ Fully Connected Layer
5: $pool \Leftarrow MaxPool2D(pool\_size = [1,1], padding = 'valid', S = 2)$
6: $d \Leftarrow Dropout(0.5, pool)$
7: $de \Leftarrow Dense(N = 1024, d)$

```
for i in [feature\_maps]:
  read i:
  begin
    { train\_y = train[$neurons=1024$]
      train\_x = train.drop[$neurons=1024$]
      dataset = xgboost.Dmatrix(train\_y, train\_x) }
    end:
```

8: PARAMS:$max\_depth = 7, eta = 0.2, num_classes = 7, objective = softmax$
9: $Xg \Leftarrow XGBOOST.train(params, dataset, num\_boost\_round = 200)$
10: $Yhat \Leftarrow Xg.predict(x\_test)$
11: $score \Leftarrow accuracy\_score(test\_y, Yhat)$
12: End;
13: $Output :: score$

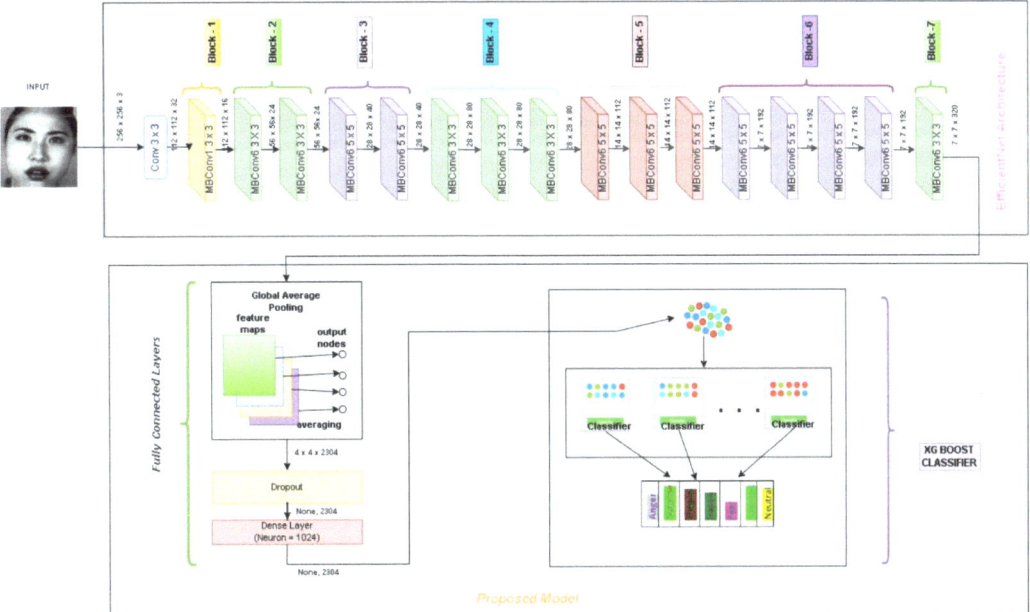

Figure 3. Proposed FER model based on Transfer Learning.

4.2. Experimental Setup

In our work, we are trying to use the EfficientNet by TL method to extract the features for the given input image, fine tune the model, and finally, classify it using the XGBoost classifier. The model is divided into 3 modules: EfficientNet, Fully Connected Layer, and XGBoost Classifier. First we try to preprocess the images, which is explained in Section 4.4, and then apply TL for feature extraction. EfficientNet is known for obtaining great precision with few parameters and FLOPS (Floating Point Operation Per Second). Traditional CNNs are involved in fine tuning manually. Fine tuning is done in 3 dimensions. There are three of them: the number of layers, the number of channels, and the image size. The compound scaling process is used by EfficientNet for scaling. The Swish function is used, and the following is the mathematical representation:

$$swish(x) = x * sigmoid(x) \qquad (8)$$

The image is of size (48 × 48) is given as input. Various phases of feature extraction are performed on the input image by the model. The model architecture consists of seven inverted residual blocks denoted by MBConv and two residual blocks denoted by Conv. In Table 1, detailed information about each layer of the EfficientNet-B0 baseline network is shown. Both MBConv1, k3 × 3, and MBConv6, k3 × 3, employ depthwise convolution, which combines the 3 × 3 kernel size with s as the stride size. Both of these blocks comprise batch normalization, activation, and convolution. They have a kernel size of 1 × 1. The classifier and expression predictor is XGBoost. XGBoost is replaced with softmax, for best performance and accuracy.

Model Training and Evaluation: The model execution for training and testing was performed on Google Colab Cloud Platform. Tensorflow 2.6 was used on Python 3.7, and the GPU was a Tesla P100-PCIE-16GB. The CPU is an Intel(R) Xeon(R) CPU running at 2.20 GHz. The researchers can reuse the weights learned and unfreeze some layers as per requirement to perform training, thanks to TL, helped for developing FER system. We have used Adam optimizer an adaptive learning rate method for training. The batch size considered is 32 with epochs ranging from 100–150. The parameters used are shown in Table 2.

Table 2. Parameters used during model training.

Parameter	Value
Epochs	100–150
Batch Size	32 or 64
Dropout Rate	0.001
Optimizer	Adam
Loss Function	Categorical Cross Entropy
Early Stop	Enabled

4.3. Datasets

To measure the performance of the proposed model, we have chosen 4 datasets for facial emotion. Table 3 shows the no of sample images in each category of different datasets.

Table 3. Image distribution of Datasets.

| S.No | Name of the Data Set | Emotions | | | | | | | No. of Images |
		Anger	Fear	Happy	Surprise	Disgust	Sadness	Neutral	
1	CK+48	75	207	249	77	84	135	NA	927
2	JAFFEE	30	30	30	30	30	30	30	180
3	KDEF	70	70	70	70	70	70	70	490
4	FER2013	5121	8989	4002	547	6077	4953	6198	35,887

4.3.1. CK+

The (CK+) [28] was published in the year 2010. CK+ is an extension of the Cohn-Kanada dataset is used in our research which contains 7 types of basic expressions. The images of this dataset are in size of 48 × 48. They are Anger, Disgust, Fear, Happiness, Sadness, Surprise with sample size of 135, 177, 75, 207, 84, 249 respectively. This makes it a total count to be 927 images. The dataset split for Training is 648, Validation is 139 and Testing is 140 images.

4.3.2. KDEF

In total, the Karolinska Directed Emotional Faces (KDEF) dataset [31] contains 490 images of human facial expressions. The images in this dataset are 256 × 256 in size. This dataset contains 7 emotion classes as mentioned similar to Section 4.3.1. Here the samples are distributed evenly, with 70 images of each type.

4.3.3. JAFFE

The JAFFE [26] dataset consists of 180 images of 6 basic classes. The images in this dataset are of size 120 × 120. The emotion classes are Sad, Disgust, Fear, Surprise, Anger and Happy with 30 images each.

4.3.4. FER2013

The FER2013 [28], very challenging dataset consists of 35,887 face image samples. 28,709 images for training and 3589 images for training and testing each. The images in this dataset are set to grayscale. The images are of size 48 × 48. The samples are categorized into 7 classes of emotions. 0—Anger, 1—Disgust, 2—Fear, 3—Happy, 4—Sad, 5—Surprised and 6—Neutral. We discovered some label errors in the test dataset during the experiment. This dataset's benchmark accuracy is only (65 + 5) percent, which is extremely difficult. Even so, most researchers continue to use this dataset to test their models. A snapshot of the samples is presented in Figure 4.

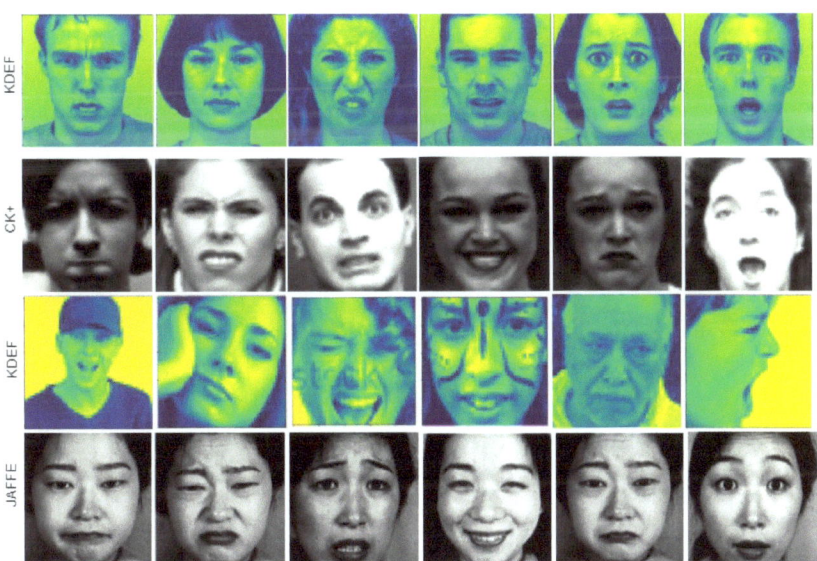

Figure 4. Sample Images of different datasets.

4.4. Data Pre-Processing

It is very natural that we need to process the image before training. Data sets namely KDEF and FER2013 are in Comma Separated Values .CSV format. CK+ dataset and JAFFE are in .jpg images. During the preprocessing phase, we reshaped the images into an acceptable format for the model. If we look at Table 3 for the FER2013 and CK+ datasets, we can see that all of the images in classes are not equal. Few classes have a larger sample size, while others have fewer samples. This is referred to as class-imbalance. To overcome this type of issue, we must include additional images into the classes with fewer samples. This is possible with the help of data-augmentation. Augmentation aids in increasing the size of the data set as Table 4. The more variation in the train data, the better the model learns. In this work, data is augmented is carried out artificially through geometric transformation techniques like translation, reflection, shearing, and other means [20]. The augmented image samples generated during the pre-processing phase are shown in Figure 5.

Table 4. Data Augmentation and Pre-Processing Parameter used in ImageDataGenerator of Keras.

Parameter	Value
Zoom	0.15
Width Shift	0.2
Range of Brightness	(0.6–1.2)
Shear	0.15
Height Shift	0.2
Fill Mode	Nearest

The dataset has three sections: train data, validate data, and test data. In our model, we used an 80/20 split to train the model and the remaining 20% to test the model's performance. To avoid performance errors, 10% of train data is split into validation data using parameter adjustment. After the model has been trained, test data is used to assess the model's performance. Figure 6 clearly represents splitting of data into Train, Test and Validation.

Figure 5. Samples of Augmented Images Generated.

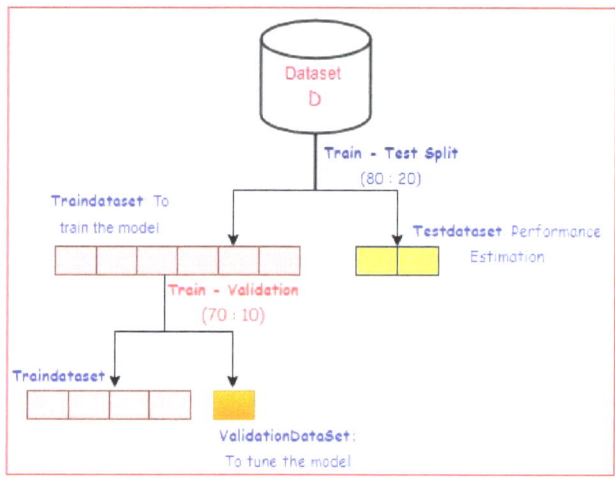

Figure 6. Dataset Split for Training, Validation and Testing.

A confusion matrix is used to evaluate a classification's performance. The confusion matrix (as shown in Figure 7) is calculated for finding the class's accuracy. It's represented as a matrix. The confusion matrix allows for a comparison of actual and predicted values. The confusion matrix for N-class classification is N × N. True Positive (TP), False Positive (FP), True Negative (TN), and False Negative (FN) are the four terms that make up the confusion matrix (FN). Representation of confusion matrix is shown in Figure 7.

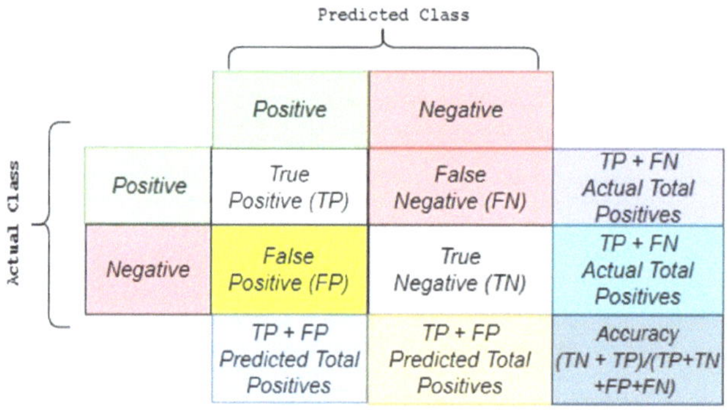

Figure 7. Confusion Matrix Overview.

Accuracy: Accuracy is calculated by dividing the total number of predicted values by the total number of predictions made by the model. The formula below represents accuracy.

$$Accuracy = \frac{TP + TN}{TP + FN + FP + TN} \tag{9}$$

Accuracy gives a false sense of prediction if the dataset is imbalanced.

Precision: Precision is the percentage of true positive predictions out of all positive predictions. Precision is denoted by the following equation:

$$Precision = \frac{TP}{TP + FP} \tag{10}$$

Recall: What proportion of the total positive is predicted to be positive? It's the same as TPR (True Positive Rate). The formula is represented as:

$$Recall = \frac{TP}{TP + FN} \tag{11}$$

F1-score: The harmonic mean of precision and recall is defined. It's a statistical metric for evaluating performance.

$$F1 - Score = 2 * \frac{Recall * Precision}{Recall + Precision} \tag{12}$$

ROC AUC: Receiver Operating Characteristics (ROC) is a graph that compares the true positive rate (on the y-axis) and false positive rate (on the x-axis) for every classification threshold that is conceivable. ROC-AUC stands for the area determined under the ROC curve.

$$ROC - AUC = \frac{1 + TP - FP}{2} \tag{13}$$

It represents the probability that a model ranks randomly positive observation higher than the randomly chosen negative observation, and thus it is a useful metric. We can see parameters used for XGBoost as Table 5.

Table 5. Parameters Used for XGBoost.

Parameter	Value
Max Depth	7
eta	0.2
Number of Classes	{6, 7} based on dataset
Objective	softmax, softprob
Eval_Metric	merror
alpha	default
gamma	default

5. Results and Discussion

In this section, confusion matrix analysis, classification performance analysis, accuracy, and feature maps of the proposed model EfficientNet-XGBoost are discussed clearly.

5.1. Training and Validation

The model is trained and validated with the training dataset. Loss must be reduced in order to fine-tune the model. The accuracy and loss corresponding to validation process are represented through a plot respectively in Figure 8. In Figure 8a, the plot related to training and validation accuracy is shown. The X-axis represents the count of epochs and the Y-axis represents the rate of accuracy, scaled from 0.3 to 1.0, where 0.3 is 30% and 1.0 is 100% accuracy, and Figure 8b is the plot for training and validation loss. The linear axis represents the count of epochs, and the vertical axis represents the measure of loss. These plots represent the model training and validation on the CK+ dataset. From Figure 8a, it is clearly observed that 100% accuracy is obtained on training and validation of the dataset. The accuracy measure corresponding to test samples is presented in the results section in the form of a confusion matrix.

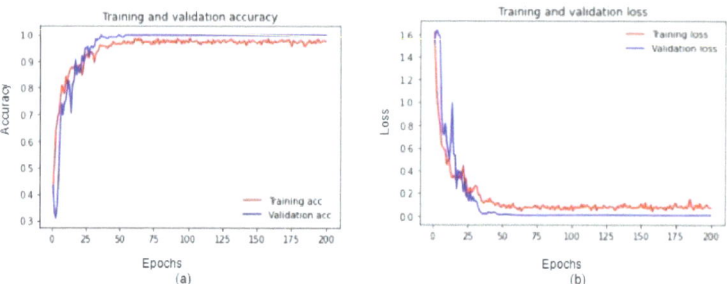

Figure 8. (**a**) Training & Validation accuracy on CK+ dataset (**b**) Training & Validation loss on CK+ dataset.

5.2. Analysis Using Confusion Matrix

The confusion matrix is primarily utilized for comparing the classifier outcomes with the actual class level. This helps in genuine evaluation of the classifier model. The confusion matrices in Figure 9 are derived from the datasets CK+, KDEF, FER2013, and JAFFE. As shown in Figure 9, each class's prediction accuracy is concentrated along the diagonal. Each of the confusion matrices has the predicted class and the true class. In contrast to Fer2013's data set, which has low classification accuracy, the CK+ data set's seven categories have high prediction accuracy. Fer2013 is a very large and challenging dataset which has class imbalance. Despite this, the most popular data set for facial expression recognition is Fer2013. The experiment also uses the Fer2013 dataset to compare outcomes with other approaches using the same parameters. If we look at the CK+ dataset, all the emotions are correctly identified, except that the emotion "fear" is classified as "surprise". Figure 9 also depicts the confusion matrix of the KDEF and JAFFE data sets. We can see from the confusion matrix results that the proposed method has good classification performance.

For the KDEF dataset also, if we observe the figure, 8 images are misclassified. 4 images of neutral emotions are classified as 1 happy and 3 surprise emotions. One image of a happy emotion and one image of anger are misclassified as surprise. There are clearly a lot of misclassified emotions in FER2013 dataset. This is due to the large size and very challenging dataset. For the JAFFE dataset, we have 4 misclassified emotions. One disgust image is identified as an angry image, one surprise image is identified as a disgust image, and finally, one surprise image is identified as sadness. This is due to the similarity expression in the dataset. Also, to train the model, we have a very small number of images per class.

5.3. Analysis of Classification Performance

Figures 10–13 shows the Precision, Recall, F1-Score, and Support of the proposed model EfficientNet-XGBoost on the CK+, KDEF, JAFFE, and FER2013 datasets. It is clearly observed that from Figures 10–12 all the evaluation shown for each emotion classes of CK+ dataset is very high. The FER2013 dataset is low. The reason for this is due to FER2013 dataset is very challenging dataset. These figures represent the classification performance of the model. The representation is in the form of bar plots. In the figures, X-Axis represents classes of emotions of 4 datasets. The CK+ and JAFFE datasets have six categories of emotions. The FER2013 and KDEF datasets each contain seven categories of emotions. Y-Axis represents the percentage of accuracy, scaling from 0.00 to 1.00 range. The order of the datasets represented in the plot is CK+, JAFFE, KDEF, and FER2013.

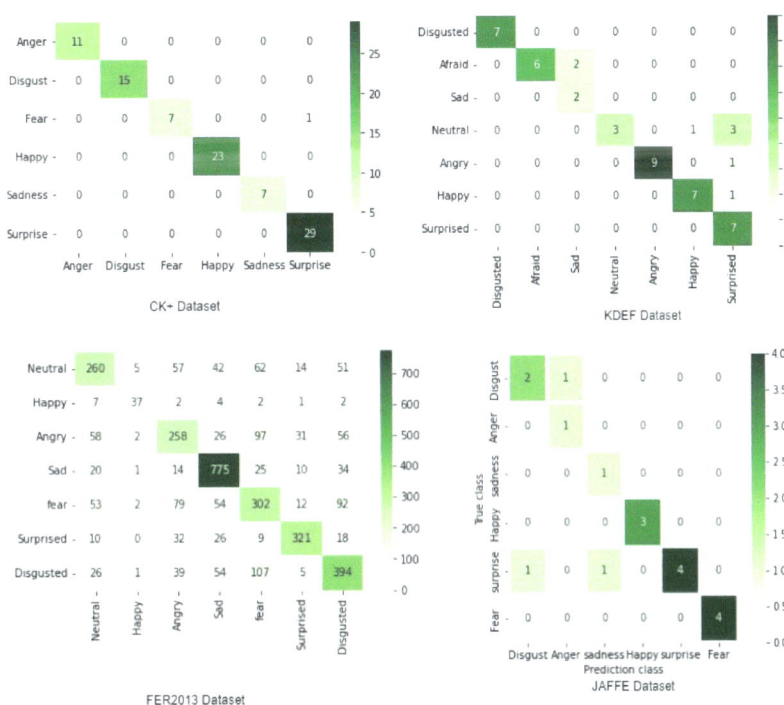

Figure 9. The Confusion matrix obtained by EfficientNet-XGBoost on CK+, JAFFE, KDEF and FER2013.

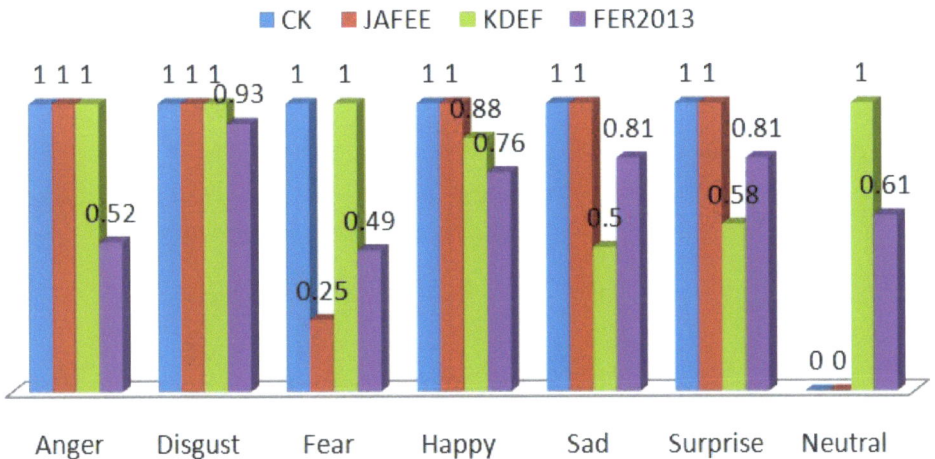

Figure 10. Precision for CK+, JAFFE, KDEF and FER2013 datasets.

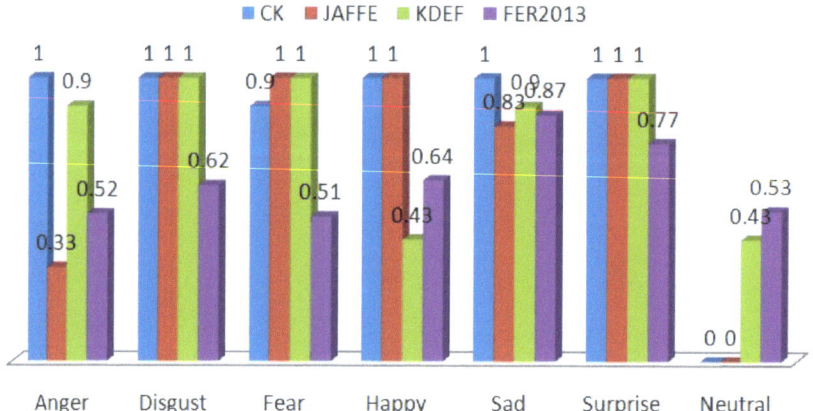

Figure 11. Recall for CK+, JAFFE, KDEF and FER2013 datasets.

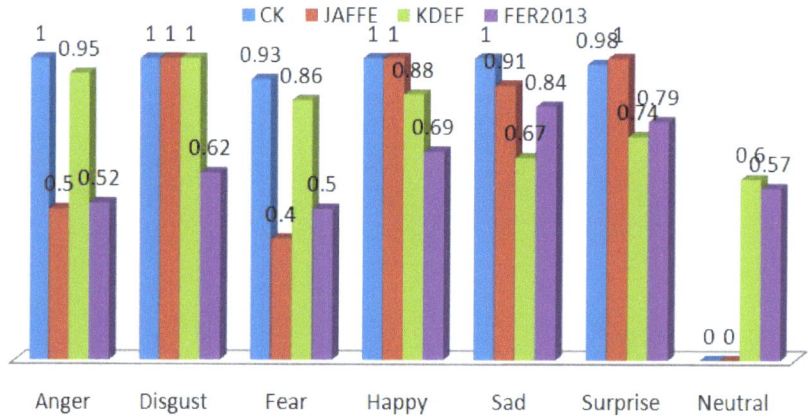

Figure 12. F1-Score for CK+, JAFFE, KDEF and FER2013.

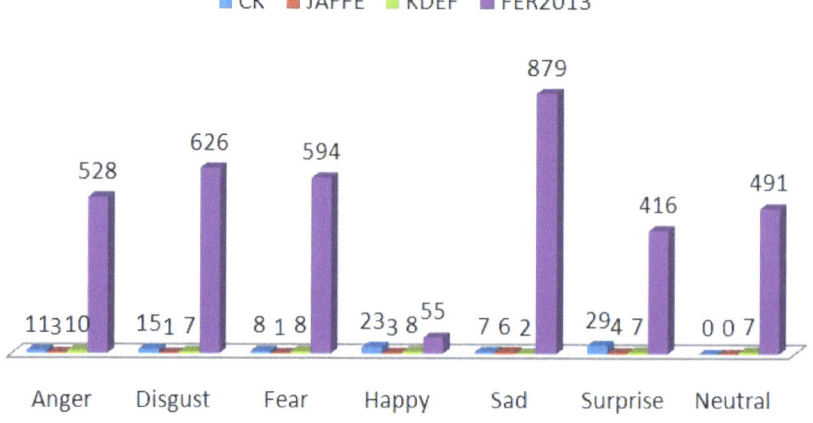

Figure 13. Support for CK+, JAFFE, KDEF and FER2013.

Precision is shown in Figure 10. The bar plot show emotions on the X-Axis. It is very clear that for Anger, Disgust, Fear, Happy, Sad and Surprise shows 1, which indicates that these emotions achieved 100% precision measure for CK+, JAFFE and KDEF dataset. For the datasets CK+ and JAFFE the expression NEUTRAL is not available. Hence marked as zero.

Recall is shown in Figure 11, anger, fear, happy, sad and surprise emotions for CK+, JAFFE and KDEF achieved 100%. Fear emotion is 90%. for CK+ dataset, this is due to class imbalance. It has only 75 sample in the dataset. A very less sample for the model to train. Recall in Anger class of JAFFE dataset is 33%. The reason behind this is the images are very similar to fear emotion. This is the challenge in this dataset. The F1-Score for the model is calculated. It is shown in Figure 12. From figure, we can see that the best results for CK+ and KDEF datasets are very close to 100% for anger, disgust, fear, happiness, sadness, and surprise. Support for the datasets CK+, JAFFE, KDEF, and FER2013 is shown in Figure 13. The number of samples of the true prediction that fall into each class of target values can be used to determine support. The structural weakness in the scores represents the imbalanace state of the training data. Low value of support, leads either for stratified sampling or rebalancing.

5.4. Feature Maps

Verification of the feature extraction can be done by visualising the feature sets for the images in different layers. The major objective to visualize a feature set corresponding to particular input image is to gain some understanding about the inherent characteristics. The proposed model thus, gains further insights of the inputs. Perhaps it detects some parts that we desire to extract. It is very interesting to directly examine the features like colors and edges, which are known as low-level features, and high level features like shapes and objects. In our model, it's easy to see that the eyes, nose, and lips are all there.

Feature maps for the images at random layers are shown in Figure 14. In Figure 14 we see that the features extracted by each layer from the face's most significant features.

Figure 14. Feature Maps of few layers.

5.5. Receiver Operating Characteristic

The area under the curve (AUC) values and receiver operating characteristic (ROC) curves were computed in order to further assess the results of each expression's recognition.

It is a curve of probability that plots the True Positive Rate (TPR) over False Positive Rate (FPR) at different threshold values and essentially separates the signal from the noise. The ROC for the CK+ dataset is shown in Figure 15. X_axis represents the false positive rate and Y_axis represents the true positive rate. The colored curves indicate different classes. As shown in Figure 15 black curve which is far away from other curves and at the bottom represents fear emotion. Fear emotion is falsely predicted as a surprise (Figure 9) emotion of the cK+ dataset. The accuracy of the Fear class is less when compared with other emotions.

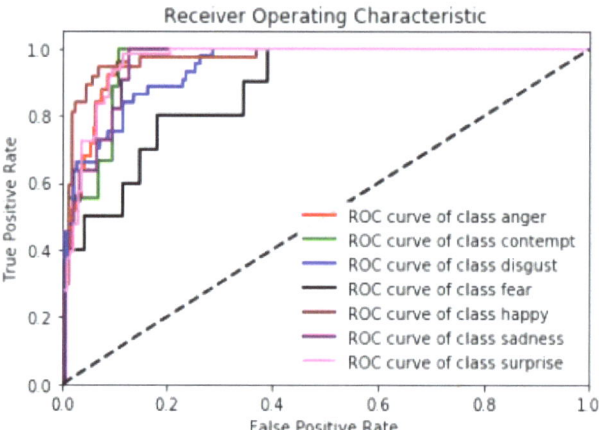

Figure 15. ROC of CK+ Dataset.

5.6. Comparison of Results with Other Works

This section presents an investigation on the efficacy of the stated model on benchmark datasets. EfficientNet-XGBoost, the developed model, is entirely based on the transfer learning technique. Because EfficientNet is the foundation of the proposed model, it is thoroughly tested to determine how well it works. Table 6 represents the results for the accuracy in training, validation, and test images experimented with the base model EfficientNet. The dataset was split into 80% and 20% for training and testing data. We have experienced that feature extraction was done efficiently by this model. Here, the softmax layer helps in classifying emotions. We replace this softmax layer with the machine learning algorithm XGBoost to improve accuracy. The proposed EfficientNet-XGBoost method can efficiently extract image features and enhance the accuracy of facial expression recognition.

Table 6. Base model EfficientNet experimental results on CK+, FER2013, JAFFE and KDEF dataset (LR: learning Rate, Val-Loss: Validation Loss).

S.No	Dataset	LR	Val-Loss	Accuracy (%)		
				Train	Validation	Test
1.	CK+	2.499×10^{-4}	0.1368	94.35	95.714	94.41
2.	FER2013	0.145	-	90.35	61.44	61.54
3.	JAFFE	-	0.7315	98.44	98.44	97.67
4.	KDEF	-	0.4512	96.54	94.15	93.74

Suitable simulations are carried out on the same train/test split using notable methods from the literature. To fully validate the proposed method's effectiveness, for comparison under the same conditions, 20 related expression recognition techniques are chosen. Tables 7–10 shows the accuracy of other models compared with our model EfficientNet-XGBoost on CK+, JAFFE, KDEF and FER2013 datasets respectively.

A weighted mixture deep neural network (WMDNN) [32] was proposed and tested on the CK+ dataset with 97.02% accuracy. SIFT-CNN, a hybrid model proposed by X. Sun and M. Lv [33], has a 94.82 percent accuracy. In [23] AdaBoost was used to segment the face's largest geometric component, and multistage Haar wavelet was used to extract the features of the components. AdaBoost, on the other hand, is sensitive to abnormal samples, which will result in higher weights in the iterative process and thus affect segmentation performance. In the meantime, using the Haar wavelet base will result in inefficient feature extraction. The recognition accuracy of this model for the CK+ data sets is 90.48 percent. This model has a very low recognition accuracy when compared to other methods. A region-aware sub-net (RASnet) [34] learns binary masks for locating expression-related critical regions with coarse-to-fine granularity levels, whereas an expression recognition sub-net (ERSnet) with a multiple attention (MA) block learns comprehensive discriminate features. This model achieved 96.28% accuracy.

Among the models [33,34] in the above comparison, two have used traditional methods for mining expression recognition. Shi, Cuiping, et al. [25] created a CNN model based on a residual network. Before extracting the features from the expression images, this model first preprocesses the input images. The accuracy of feature extraction is increased to 98.48 percent after being extracted by various network branches and then fused together, which is higher than other methods but lower than our accuracy.

From Table 7 our model EfficientNet-XGBoost has achieved 100% accuracy when compared with other models. This was achieved with epoch of 150 on dataset CK+.

Table 8 shows the accuracies of the KDEF dataset with other models. [28] identifies the features through the Facial Landmarks descriptor and the Center of Gravity descriptor. On KDEF, these features are classified by Support Vector Machine (SVM) with an accuracy of 90.80% which is the lowest accuracy among the comparisons. The stacked Convolutional Auto-Encoder (SCAE) [28] model is proposed and used random weights for training the images. Random weights will take many person-hours. Convolution layers and a recurrent neural network (RNN) are the two components of the network architecture that Jain et al. [31] proposed. The combined model extracts relationships within facial images, and by using the recurrent network, the temporal dependencies that exist in the images can be taken into account during classification.

Table 7. Accuracy of CK+ Dataset.

Model Name	Accuracy (%)
E. et al., B. Yang, J. Cao, and B. Yang [32]	97.02%
X. Sun and M. Lv [33]	94.82%
M. Goyani and N. Patel [23]	98.73%
Gan, Y., Chen, J., Yang, Z., and Xu, L. [34]	94.51%
K. Li et al. [24]	97.54%
WMCNN-LSTM [35]	97.50%
N. Sun, Q. Li, et al. [22]	98.38%
MBCC-CNN [25]	98.48%
EfficientNet-XGBoost (Proposed Model)	100%

Table 8. Accuracy of KDEF Dataset.

Model Name	Accuracy (%)
Alshami el al [28]	90.80%
Ruiz-Garcia et al [18]	92.52%
Jain et al. [31]	94.91
EfficientNet-XGBoost (Proposed)	98.44%

Table 9. Accuracy of JAFFE Dataset.

Model Name	Accuracy (%)
Aouayeb M, Hamidouche W et al. [26]	94.83%
E. al, B. Yang, J. Cao, and B. Yang [32]	92.2%
Minaee S, Minaei M, Abdolrashidi A [2]	92.8%
Happy SL [27]	91.8%
Alshame al at. [28]	91.90%
Zhao and Zhang [35]	90.95%
EfficientNet-XGBoost (Proposed)	98.3%

The accuracy of our model using the JAFFE dataset is compared with other works in Table 9. For the FER task, [26] proposes a model called the Vision Transformer in conjunction with a Squeeze and Excitation (SE) block. with an accuracy of 94.83% which is a bit low compared to our work. Vision transformers require large datasets, whereas JAFFE only has a small number of samples. image distribution of JAFFE is shown in Table 3. The JAFFE dataset has only 180 images, but they are equally distributed with all 7 classes of emotions. The paper [2] proposes a deep learning strategy based on an attentional convolutional network, which is capable of focusing on key facial features such as the nose, eyes, lips, and cheeks. The accuracy of [14] is 92.8%. The proposed models' accuracy using the JAFFE dataset would be high if the number of samples were greater. This attention was drawn during experimentation.

Table 10. Accuracy of FER2013 Dataset.

Model Name	Accuracy (%)
VGG-19	70.80%
EfficientNet-B0	70.80%
GoogleNet	71.97%
ResNet34	72.42%
Inception V3	72.72 %
Bam - ResNet 50	73.12%
DenseNet121	73.16%
ResNet152	73.16%
EfficientNet-XGBoost (Proposed)	72.54%

The model's test results for each class are compared to other works. The overall accuracy of the model is directly proportional to the accuracy of the individual classes. Figure 16 shows the accuracy achieved by our model and others on individual classes of emotions. X_axis denotes the works and Y_axis denotes accuracy. It is observed from Figure 16 that our proposed work achieves 100% accuracy for each emotion class except Fear. Six basic facial emotion classes are depicted in the figure. Though, some researchers have also included Neutral as one of the emotions. The proposed model, EfficientNet-XGBoost, has shown the best performance on the CK+ dataset. The JAFFE dataset and KDEF dataset contain frontal images. The FER2013 dataset is a challenging dataset with 35,887 sample images, which did not produce high accuracy but was equal to the benchmark accuracy. The major issue with this dataset is the class imbalance. Proper augmentation needs to be done by producing synthetic images rather than augmenting them using geographic features.

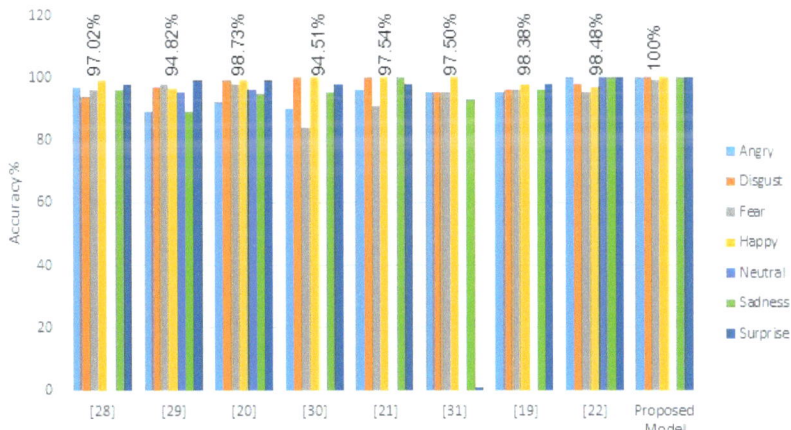

Figure 16. Class accuracy of the model compared with other works.

6. Conclusions and Future Scope

An efficient scheme with a state-of-the-art transfer learning mechanism has been presented suitably for facial emotion recognition. The scheme is dubbed as EfficientNet-XGBoost. Novelty of the scheme is exhibited with certain combination of pre-trained EfficientNet architecture, fully connected layers, XGBoost classifier, and custom fine-tuning of parameters. Input facial images are suitably pre-processed and the task of feature extraction is carried out through using the custom model. The feature points are extracted through various networks. To average the feature maps, the global average pooling is applied and the final feature set is fed to XGBoost Classifier which recognizes the class labels for distinct emotions. Four distinct datasets are used to validate the scheme. The experimental results for the dataset CK+ shows outstanding performance at an overall rate of accuracy of 100%. Further, the proposed model can recognize expressions accurately with low latency. An overall rate of accuracy of 98% is observed on datasets like JAFFE and KDEF. In FER2013, although the sample distribution is imbalanced, augmentation through geometric transformation techniques has led to reach a benchmark accuracy of 72.54%. In support of our claim, a comparative analysis of our results with other works on existing datasets is presented. The future scope of the work would be to mitigate the issue of increasing its efficiency for imbalanced sample sets. Exploring the use of custom GAN (generative adversarial networks) could be a wise consideration towards the recognition of facial expressions from the imbalanced datasets.

Author Contributions: Conceptualization, S.B.P., S.K.K., T.K.M., H.M. and S.R.M.; Methodology, S.B.P., T.K.M., A.A. and H.M.; Software, S.B.P., S.K.K., T.K.M., A.A., H.M. and S.R.M.; Validation, S.B.P., S.K.K., T.K.M., A.A. and H.M.; Formal analysis, S.B.P., S.K.K., T.K.M. and A.A.; Investigation, S.B.P., S.K.K. and T.K.M.; Resources, S.B.P., S.K.K. and H.M.; Data curation, S.B.P., T.K.M., H.M. and S.R.M.; Writing—original draft, S.B.P., S.K.K., T.K.M., A.A., H.M. and S.R.M.; Writing—review and editing, S.B.P., S.K.K., T.K.M., H.M. and S.R.M.; Visualization, S.B.P., S.K.K. and H.M.; Supervision, S.B.P., S.K.K., M.K. and H.M.; Project administration, S.B.P., S.K.K., M.K. and H.M.; Funding acquisition, M.K. All authors have read and agreed to the published version of the manuscript.

Funding: This research received no external funding.

Data Availability Statement: Not applicable.

Conflicts of Interest: The authors declare no conflict of interest. No financial support has been received from any agency for the proposed work.

References

1. Akhand, M.; Roy, S.; Siddique, N.; Kamal, M.A.S.; Shimamura, T. Facial emotion recognition using transfer learning in the deep CNN. *Electronics* **2021**, *10*, 1036. [CrossRef]
2. Minaee, S.; Minaei, M.; Abdolrashidi, A. Deep-emotion: Facial expression recognition using attentional convolutional network. *Sensors* **2021**, *21*, 3046. [CrossRef] [PubMed]
3. Goodfellow, I.J.; Erhan, D.; Carrier, P.L.; Courville, A.; Mirza, M.; Hamner, B.; Cukierski, W.; Tang, Y.; Thaler, D.; Lee, D.H.; et al. Challenges in representation learning: A report on three machine learning contests. In Proceedings of the International Conference on Neural Information Processing, Daegu, Republic of Korea, 3–7 November 2013; Springer: Berlin/Heidelberg, Germany, 2013; pp. 117–124.
4. Pons, G.; Masip, D. Supervised committee of convolutional neural networks in automated facial expression analysis. *IEEE Trans. Affect. Comput.* **2017**, *9*, 343–350. [CrossRef]
5. Wen, G.; Hou, Z.; Li, H.; Li, D.; Jiang, L.; Xun, E. Ensemble of deep neural networks with probability-based fusion for facial expression recognition. *Cogn. Comput.* **2017**, *9*, 597–610. [CrossRef]
6. Jabid, T.; Kabir, M.H.; Chae, O. Robust facial expression recognition based on local directional pattern. *ETRI J.* **2010**, *32*, 784–794. [CrossRef]
7. Mahendran, A.; Vedaldi, A. Visualizing deep convolutional neural networks using natural pre-images. *Int. J. Comput. Vis.* **2016**, *120*, 233–255. [CrossRef]
8. Wang, K.; Peng, X.; Yang, J.; Meng, D.; Qiao, Y. Region attention networks for pose and occlusion robust facial expression recognition. *IEEE Trans. Image Process.* **2020**, *29*, 4057–4069. [CrossRef]
9. Simonyan, K.; Vedaldi, A.; Zisserman, A. Learning local feature descriptors using convex optimisation. *IEEE Trans. Pattern Anal. Mach. Intell.* **2014**, *36*, 1573–1585. [CrossRef]
10. Tan, M.; Le, Q. Efficientnet: Rethinking model scaling for convolutional neural networks. In Proceedings of the International Conference on Machine Learning, PMLR, Long Beach, CA, USA, 9–15 June 2019; pp. 6105–6114.
11. Yao, T.; Qu, C.; Liu, Q.; Deng, R.; Tian, Y.; Xu, J.; Jha, A.; Bao, S.; Zhao, M.; Fogo, A.B.; et al. Compound figure separation of biomedical images with side loss. In *Deep Generative Models, and Data Augmentation, Labelling, and Imperfections*; Springer: Berlin/Heidelberg, Germany, 2021; pp. 173–183.
12. Zhao, M.; Jha, A.; Liu, Q.; Millis, B.A.; Mahadevan-Jansen, A.; Lu, L.; Landman, B.A.; Tyska, M.J.; Huo, Y. Faster Mean-shift: GPU-accelerated clustering for cosine embedding-based cell segmentation and tracking. *Med. Image Anal.* **2021**, *71*, 102048. [CrossRef]
13. Jin, B.; Cruz, L.; Gonçalves, N. Pseudo RGB-D Face Recognition. *IEEE Sens. J.* **2022**, *22*, 21780–21794. [CrossRef]
14. Yosinski, J.; Clune, J.; Bengio, Y.; Lipson, H. How transferable are features in deep neural networks? *Adv. Neural Inf. Process. Syst.* **2014**, *27*, 3320–3328.
15. Chen, T.; Guestrin, C. Xgboost: A scalable tree boosting system. In Proceedings of the 22nd ACM Sigkdd International Conference on Knowledge Discovery and Data Mining, San Francisco, CA, USA, 13–17 August 2016; pp. 785–794.
16. Feng, X.; Pietikäinen, M.; Hadid, A. Facial expression recognition based on local binary patterns. *Pattern Recognit. Image Anal.* **2007**, *17*, 592–598. [CrossRef]
17. Liew, C.F.; Yairi, T. Facial expression recognition and analysis: A comparison study of feature descriptors. *IPSJ Trans. Comput. Vis. Appl.* **2015**, *7*, 104–120. [CrossRef]
18. Zhao, X.; Shi, X.; Zhang, S. Facial expression recognition via deep learning. *IETE Tech. Rev.* **2015**, *32*, 347–355. [CrossRef]
19. Mollahosseini, A.; Chan, D.; Mahoor, M.H. Going deeper in facial expression recognition using deep neural networks. In Proceedings of the 2016 IEEE Winter Conference on Applications of Computer Vision (WACV), Lake Placid, NY, USA, 7–10 March 2016; IEEE: Piscataway, NJ, USA, 2016; pp. 1–10.
20. Shima, Y.; Omori, Y. Image augmentation for classifying facial expression images by using deep neural network pre-trained with object image database. In Proceedings of the 3rd International Conference on Robotics, Control and Automation, Chengdu, China, 19–22 July 2018; pp. 140–146.
21. Saeed, S.; Baber, J.; Bakhtyar, M.; Ullah, I.; Sheikh, N.; Dad, I.; Sanjrani, A.A. Empirical evaluation of svm for facial expression recognition. *Int. J. Adv. Comput. Sci. Appl.* **2018**, *9*. [CrossRef]
22. Sun, N.; Li, Q.; Huan, R.; Liu, J.; Han, G. Deep spatial-temporal feature fusion for facial expression recognition in static images. *Pattern Recognit. Lett.* **2019**, *119*, 49–61. [CrossRef]
23. Goyani, M.M.; Patel, N.M. Multi-level haar wavelet based facial expression recognition using logistic regression. *Int. J. Next Gener. Comput.* **2018**, *10*, 131–151. [CrossRef]
24. Li, K.; Jin, Y.; Akram, M.W.; Han, R.; Chen, J. Facial expression recognition with convolutional neural networks via a new face cropping and rotation strategy. *Vis. Comput.* **2020**, *36*, 391–404. [CrossRef]
25. Shi, C.; Tan, C.; Wang, L. A facial expression recognition method based on a multibranch cross-connection convolutional neural network. *IEEE Access* **2021**, *9*, 39255–39274. [CrossRef]
26. Aouayeb, M.; Hamidouche, W.; Soladie, C.; Kpalma, K.; Seguier, R. Learning vision transformer with squeeze and excitation for facial expression recognition. *arXiv* **2021**, arXiv:2107.03107.
27. Happy, S.; Routray, A. Automatic facial expression recognition using features of salient facial patches. *IEEE Trans. Affect. Comput.* **2014**, *6*, 1–12. [CrossRef]

28. Alshamsi, H.; Kepuska, V.M.H. Real time automated facial expression recognition app development on smart phones. In Proceedings of the 8th IEEE Annual Information Technology, Electronics and Mobile Communication Conference (IEMCON), Vancouver, BC, Canada, 3–5 October 2017; pp. 384–392.
29. Wang, K.; Peng, X.; Yang, J.; Lu, S.; Qiao, Y. Suppressing uncertainties for large-scale facial expression recognition. In Proceedings of the IEEE/CVF Conference on Computer Vision and Pattern Recognition, Seattle, WA, USA, 13–19 June 2020; pp. 6897–6906.
30. Oquab, M.; Bottou, L.; Laptev, I.; Sivic, J. Learning and transferring mid-level image representations using convolutional neural networks. In Proceedings of the IEEE Conference on Computer Vision and Pattern Recognition, Columbus, OH, USA, 23–28 June 2014; pp. 1717–1724.
31. Jain, N.; Kumar, S.; Kumar, A.; Shamsolmoali, P.; Zareapoor, M. Hybrid deep neural networks for face emotion recognition. *Pattern Recognit. Lett.* **2018**, *115*, 101–106. [CrossRef]
32. Yang, B.; Cao, J.; Ni, R.; Zhang, Y. Facial expression recognition using weighted mixture deep neural network based on double-channel facial images. *IEEE Access* **2017**, *6*, 4630–4640. [CrossRef]
33. Sun, X.; Lv, M. Facial expression recognition based on a hybrid model combining deep and shallow features. *Cogn. Comput.* **2019**, *11*, 587–597. [CrossRef]
34. Gan, Y.; Chen, J.; Yang, Z.; Xu, L. Multiple attention network for facial expression recognition. *IEEE Access* **2020**, *8*, 7383–7393. [CrossRef]
35. Zhang, H.; Huang, B.; Tian, G. Facial expression recognition based on deep convolution long short-term memory networks of double-channel weighted mixture. *Pattern Recognit. Lett.* **2020**, *131*, 128–134. [CrossRef]

Disclaimer/Publisher's Note: The statements, opinions and data contained in all publications are solely those of the individual author(s) and contributor(s) and not of MDPI and/or the editor(s). MDPI and/or the editor(s) disclaim responsibility for any injury to people or property resulting from any ideas, methods, instructions or products referred to in the content.

Article

Overshoot Reduction Using Adaptive Neuro-Fuzzy Inference System for an Autonomous Underwater Vehicle

Narayan Nayak [1], Soumya Ranjan Das [2], Tapas Kumar Panigrahi [2], Himansu Das [3], Soumya Ranjan Nayak [3], Krishna Kant Singh [4,*], S. S. Askar [5] and Mohamed Abouhawwash [6,7]

[1] Department of Electronics and Instrumentation Engineering, Silicon Institute of Technology, Bhubaneswar 751024, India
[2] Department of Electrical Engineering, Parala Maharaja Engineering College, Berhampur 761003, India
[3] School of Computer Engineering, KIIT Deemed to Be University, Bhubaneswar 751024, India
[4] Department of CSE, ASET, Amity University Uttar Pradesh, Noida 201313, India
[5] Department of Statistics and Operations Research, College of Science, King Saud University, P.O. Box 2455, Riyadh 11451, Saudi Arabia
[6] Department of Computational Mathematics, Science and Engineering (CMSE), College of Engineering, Michigan State University, East Lansing, MI 48824, USA
[7] Department of Mathematics, Faculty of Science, Mansoura University, Mansoura 35516, Egypt
* Correspondence: krishnaiitr2011@gmail.com

Abstract: In this paper, an adaptive depth and heading control of an autonomous underwater vehicle using the concept of an adaptive neuro-fuzzy inference system (ANFIS) is designed. The autonomous underwater vehicle dynamics have six degrees of freedom, which are highly nonlinear and time-varying. It is affected by environmental effects such as ocean currents and tidal waves. Due to nonlinear dynamics designing, a stable controller in an autonomous underwater vehicle is a difficult end to achieve. Fuzzy logic and neural network control blocks make up the proposed control design to control the depth and heading angle of autonomous underwater vehicle. The neural network is trained using the back-propagation algorithm. In the presence of noise and parameter variation, the proposed adaptive controller's performance is compared with that of the self-tuning fuzzy-PID and fuzzy logic controller. Simulations are conducted to obtain the performance of both controller models in terms of overshoot, and the rise time and the result of the proposed adaptive controller exhibit superior control performance and can eliminate the effect of uncertainty.

Keywords: adaptive neuro-fuzzy inference system; autonomous underwater vehicle; fuzzy logic controller; neural network; self-tuning fuzzy-PID

MSC: 68T05; 68U01; 68W50

1. Introduction

Over the past decade, the ocean space has gained importance in the global scenario for its competitive potential in military and economic applications. In this context, the autonomous underwater vehicle [1–3] has proven to be the most effective object for underwater activities such as inspection of oil industry pipelines, target search, seabed surface reconstruction, military operation, and so on. The researchers consider it a great challenge to design the controller of the autonomous underwater vehicle because of its eminent nature of dynamism and nonlinearity due to ocean currents, an uncertainty parameter, external disturbances, hydrodynamic forces, etc. The estimated autonomous underwater vehicle parameters have more uncertainty and variation; therefore, the designed controller must be robust and adaptive. Due to nonlinearity, time-varying dynamic characteristics, and disturbances of sea waves and currents, linear and nonlinear control techniques have been developed. Linear controllers such as PID control techniques cannot offer better performance because the dynamic characteristics of an autonomous underwater vehicle are quite complex. The design of an autonomous underwater vehicle's control system takes into account many factors: stability, robustness, and the ability to change parameters, which itself requires adaptive capability due to sensor noise, disturbances caused by sea currents and waves, and changes in autonomous underwater vehicle dynamics. There are many controller models of autonomous underwater vehicles that have been proposed, including linear controllers such as PID [4], linear quadratic regulators, and linear quadratic Gaussian [5,6]. These controllers have produced better performance when the autonomous underwater vehicle is operating as a linear model. Similarly, some other linear techniques such as linear matrix inequality are used as solutions for fifth-order systems [7]. It determines the global optimal solution numerically effectively and consistently. It can be used to examine the dynamics system for heading and depth plane high-precision control of an autonomous underwater vehicle's stability [8]. However, linear matrix is feasible for lower-order systems, but for higher-order systems, results become complicated. Due to some uncertainty parameters, the autonomous underwater vehicle faces unexpected errors during underwater motion. The nonlinearity of the system prevents the linear controller from achieving a better outcome. Some of the adaptive techniques such as fuzzy logic controller [9–12], sliding mode controller [13–15], model predictive controller [16,17], adaptive controllers [18–26], neural network [27–29], and intelligent robust control method [30,31] are widely used for the overshoot reduction for an autonomous underwater vehicle. Further, some authors have addressed techniques that are based on machine learning, such as semi-supervised and supervised learning [32], deep learning [33], and reinforcement learning [34,35], which are employed in autonomous underwater vehicles for better depth control, heading control, and tracking of the desired path. Though the model has time-varying and uncertain parameters, the adaptive controller, which is a nonlinear type used in the autonomous underwater vehicle model, achieves better performance. The controller can adapt itself to the turbulence of wave, current, and changes in weight of the autonomous underwater vehicle. The neural network has some loopholes that hinder the scope of its improvement and has a slow convergence rate with more training time, which is not applicable to fit into many systems. The system should produce a fast response with less overshoot and undershoot than the classical neural network, which cannot accomplish the above requirements. Sliding mode controllers produce chattering on actuators, but it is an appropriate controller design solution for a nonlinear system. By converting the sign function to a saturation function and combining fuzzy logic, the chattering effect can be minimized.

Further, the PID controller is taken for comparison with the proposed techniques. Although PID is a conventional controller still in industrial control, PID control is the most commonly used. PID controller has the advantages of simple structure, good stability, reliable operation, and convenient adjustment and does not need the prerequisite of an accurate system model. When we cannot obtain accurate and precise system modeling, PID control technology is the most appropriate. However, when the controlled object is in complex underwater environment, and the system is nonlinear, the control effect of the PID control method is limited, and it is difficult to meet the precision requirements of the system. To overcome the problems with PID, it is required to tune the parameters of the PID controller. Initially, fuzzy–PID controller or self-tuning fuzzy PID controller (STFPID) is chosen for tuning the PID parameters. However, it is found that the factors of more settling time, more overshoot, and slow response are the demerits of the self-tuning fuzzy-PID controller. To reduce these issues, the authors have taken ANFIS because of its zero percent of steady-state error, superior set point tracking against parameter and external disruption, and reliability.

The main contributions of this paper are highlighted as follows:

(a) In this work, the autonomous underwater vehicle is considered to be the most effective object for underwater activities such as inspection of oil industry pipelines, target search, seabed surface reconstruction, military operation, etc.;

(b) It is a challenging issue to design the controller of the autonomous underwater vehicle because of its eminent nature of dynamism and nonlinearity characteristics;

(c) Therefore, it is required to adapt a technique that must be robust and adaptive, and also, it is necessary to rationally optimize the space motion model of autonomous underwater vehicle so that it can adapt to the complex and have high reliability;

(d) Various linear and nonlinear control techniques have been developed to handle non-linearity, time-varying dynamic characteristics, and disturbances of sea waves and currents;

(e) The PID control techniques cannot offer better performance because the dynamic characteristics of an autonomous underwater vehicle are quite complex;

(f) Self-tuning fuzzy-PID is then considered for the operation of autonomous underwater vehicles. However, the performance is weak in terms of settling time, more overshoot, and slow response. Moreover, acceptable overshoot and oscillations appear because of the consideration of reducing the complexity and difficulty of the controller design process;

(g) In the presence of various uncertain factors, the system with the ANFIS method can adapt to the complex environment and unknown ocean current interference so that the control effect of the controller can remain consistent and has good robustness. The ANFIS controller performed better than other control techniques when hydrodynamic constraints varied.

The performance of the proposed models was compared with other soft computing techniques and was assessed by MATLAB/Simulink.

The rest of the paper is organized as follows: In Section 2, the autonomous underwater vehicle's mathematical model design is described. In Section 3, the controlling strategies are discussed. Section 4 presents the results of the analysis and simulation study, and Section 5 presents the conclusion.

2. Mathematical Model Design of Autonomous Underwater Vehicle

The autonomous underwater vehicle equation can be designed by considering the following elements: kinematic motion in geometric aspects and rigid body dynamics, which represent the inertia matrix of autonomous underwater vehicle and moments of force caused by the motion of autonomous underwater vehicle. The autonomous underwater vehicle kinematics and dynamics are represented in vector form and explained in Equations (1)–(5). The general movement of the autonomous underwater vehicle in six degrees of freedom is shown in Figure 1, and Table 1 represents six degrees of freedom motions.

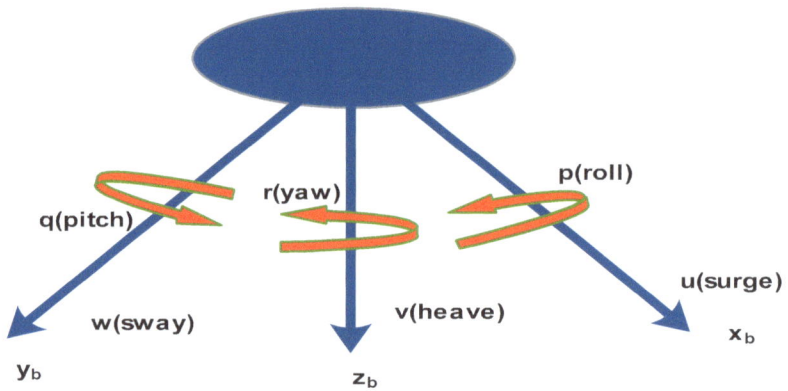

Figure 1. Motion parameters of the autonomous underwater vehicle.

Table 1. Six degrees of freedom motions.

Degrees of Freedom	Motion	Position and Angle	Linear and Angular Velocities	Force and Moment
1	Surge (x-axis motion)	x	u	X
2	Sway (y-axis motion)	y	v	Y
3	Heave (z-axis motion)	z	w	Z
4	Roll (x-axis rotation)	Φ	p	K
5	Pitch (y-axis rotation)	θ	q	M
6	Yaw (z-axis rotation)	Ψ	r	N

Assume the autonomous underwater vehicle's body is fixed frame, earth is reference frame, and it can be depicted by the following vectors:

$$\eta_1 = [xyz]^T \tag{1}$$

$$\eta_2 = [\phi\theta\psi]^T \tag{2}$$

where η_1, η_2 are position and orientation vectors.

$$v_1 = [uv\omega]^T \tag{3}$$

$$v_2 = [pqr]^T \tag{4}$$

$$\tau_1 = [XYZ]^T \text{ and } \tau_2 = [MNP]^T \tag{5}$$

The translational and rotational velocities are v_1 and v_2, and τ_2, τ_2 are the total force and moment of the autonomous underwater vehicle in the forward direction, respectively.

The linear velocities during movement of the autonomous underwater vehicle are explained in Equation (6).

$$\begin{bmatrix} \frac{dx}{dt} \\ \frac{dy}{dt} \\ \frac{dy}{dt} \end{bmatrix} = J_1(\eta_2) * \begin{bmatrix} u \\ v \\ w \end{bmatrix} \tag{6}$$

where $J_1(\eta_2)$ is represented in Equation (7).

$$J_1(\eta_2) = \begin{bmatrix} C\Psi C\theta & -S\Psi C\phi + C\Psi S\theta S\phi & S\Psi S\phi + C\Psi S\theta S\phi \\ S\Psi C\theta & C\Psi C\theta + S\Psi S\theta S\phi & -C\Psi S\phi + S\Psi S\theta C\phi \\ -S\theta & C\theta S\phi & C\theta S\phi \end{bmatrix} \tag{7}$$

where C stands for Cos, and S stands for Sin.

The angular velocity of the autonomous underwater vehicle is shown in Equation (8).

$$\begin{bmatrix} \dot{\phi} \\ \dot{\theta} \\ \dot{\psi} \end{bmatrix} = J_2(\eta_2) \begin{bmatrix} p \\ q \\ r \end{bmatrix} \tag{8}$$

where $J_2(\eta_2)$ is represented in Equation (9).

$$J_2(\eta_2) = \begin{bmatrix} 1 & \sin\phi\tan\theta & \cos\phi\tan\theta \\ 0 & \cos\phi & -\sin\phi \\ 0 & \frac{\sin\phi}{\cos\theta} & \frac{\cos\phi}{\cos\theta} \end{bmatrix} \tag{9}$$

The parameters J_1, J_2 are obtained from [1,2].

The autonomous underwater vehicle in six degrees of freedom with a fixed body coordinate [1–3] system is presented in Equations (10)–(15).

$$M\left[\frac{du}{dt} - vr + wp - x_g(q^2 + r^2) + y_g\left(pq - \frac{dr}{dt}\right) + z_g\left(pr + \frac{dq}{dt}\right)\right] = \sum X_{ext} \quad (10)$$

$$M\left[\frac{dv}{dt} - wp + ur - y_g(r^2 + p^2) + z_g\left(pr - \frac{dp}{dt}\right) + x_g\left(qp + \frac{dr}{dt}\right)\right] = \sum Y_{ext} \quad (11)$$

$$M\left[\frac{dw}{dt} - uq + vp - z_g(p^2 + q^2) + x_g\left(rp - \frac{dq}{dt}\right) + y_g\left(rq + c\frac{dp}{dt}\right)\right] = \sum Z_{ext} \quad (12)$$

$$I_{xx}\frac{dp}{dt} + (I_{zz} - I_{yy})qr + M\left[y_g\left(\frac{dw}{dt} - uq + vp\right) - z_g\left(\frac{dv}{dt} - wp + ur\right)\right] = \sum K_{ext} \quad (13)$$

$$I_{yy}\frac{dq}{dt} + (I_{xx} - I_{zz})rp + M\left[z_g\left(\frac{du}{dt} - vr + wq\right) - x_g\left(\frac{dw}{dt} - uq + vp\right)\right] = \sum M_{ext} \quad (14)$$

$$I_{zz}\frac{dr}{dt} + (I_{yy} - I_{xx})pq + M\left[x_g\left(\frac{dv}{dt} - wp + ur\right) - y_g\left(\frac{du}{dt} - vr + wp\right)\right] = \sum N_{ext} \quad (15)$$

where the mass of the autonomous underwater vehicle is M.

The nonlinear equations for hydrostatic force and movement are presented in Equations (16)–(20).

$$Y_{HS} = -(W - D)\sin\phi\cos\theta \quad (16)$$

$$Z_{HS} = -(W - D)\cos\phi\cos\theta \quad (17)$$

$$K_{HS} = -(y_g W - y_b D)\cos\phi\cos\theta - (z_g W - z_b D)\sin\phi\cos\theta \quad (18)$$

$$M_{HS} = -(z_g W - z_b D)\sin\theta - (x_g W - x_b D)\cos\phi\cos\theta \quad (19)$$

$$N_{HS} = -(x_g W - x_b D)\cos\theta\sin\phi - (y_g W - y_b D)\sin\theta \quad (20)$$

After separating the acceleration terms, the kinematics and dynamics equation of the autonomous underwater vehicle can be represented in the form of a matrix, which is derived in (21) and (22).

$$\begin{bmatrix} M - X_{\dot{u}} & 0 & 0 & 0 & Mz_g & -My_g \\ 0 & M - Y_{\dot{v}} & 0 & -Mz_g & 0 & Mx_g - Y_{\dot{r}} \\ 0 & 0 & M - Z_{\dot{w}} & My_g & -Mx_g - Z_{\dot{q}} & 0 \\ 0 & -Mz_g & My_g & I_{xx} - K_{\dot{p}} & 0 & 0 \\ Mz_g & 0 & -Mx_g - M_{\dot{w}} & 0 & I_{yy} - M_{\dot{q}} & 0 \\ -My_g & Mx_g - N_{\dot{v}} & 0 & 0 & 0 & I_{zz} - N_{\dot{r}} \end{bmatrix} \begin{bmatrix} \dot{u} \\ \dot{v} \\ \dot{w} \\ \dot{p} \\ \dot{q} \\ \dot{r} \end{bmatrix} = \begin{bmatrix} \sum X \\ \sum Y \\ \sum Z \\ \sum K \\ \sum M \\ \sum N \end{bmatrix} \quad (21)$$

This implies the following:

$$\begin{bmatrix}\dot{u}\\\dot{v}\\\dot{w}\\\dot{p}\\\dot{q}\\\dot{r}\end{bmatrix} = \begin{bmatrix} M-X_{\dot{u}} & 0 & 0 & 0 & Mz_g & -My_g \\ 0 & M-Y_{\dot{v}} & 0 & -Mz_g & 0 & Mx_g-Y_{\dot{r}} \\ 0 & 0 & M-Z_{\dot{w}} & My_g & -Mx_g-Z_{\dot{q}} & 0 \\ 0 & -Mz_g & My_g & I_{xx}-K_{\dot{p}} & 0 & 0 \\ Mz_g & 0 & -Mx_g-M_{\dot{w}} & 0 & I_{yy}-M_{\dot{q}} & 0 \\ -My_g & Mx_g-N_{\dot{v}} & 0 & 0 & 0 & I_{zz}-N_{\dot{r}} \end{bmatrix}^{-1} \begin{bmatrix}\sum X\\\sum Y\\\sum Z\\\sum K\\\sum M\\\sum N\end{bmatrix} \quad (22)$$

Equation (22) is derived from the autonomous underwater vehicle kinematics and dynamics equation. It is required to derive the inverse for finding the state space equation of heading and depth plane of the autonomous underwater vehicle.

2.1. Heading Plane Model

The angle ψ measured from the inertial-x axis and the vehicle's yaw (angular) velocity, r, together describe the orientation of the object. When the autonomous underwater vehicle is moving, consider the body's relative surge velocity, u; sway velocity, v; and yaw rate as well as earth-frame-referenced positions x, y, and yaw angle to determine the autonomous underwater vehicle's heading plane model. In other words, $W = p = q = z = \phi = \theta = 0$. All other body-relative velocity and earth-frame-position parameters are taken to be zero. To obtain the force and moments necessary for the desired vehicle motion and to correct the yaw angle (ψ) caused by disturbances, the heading controller should provide the proper rudder angle (δ_r) described in Figure 2.

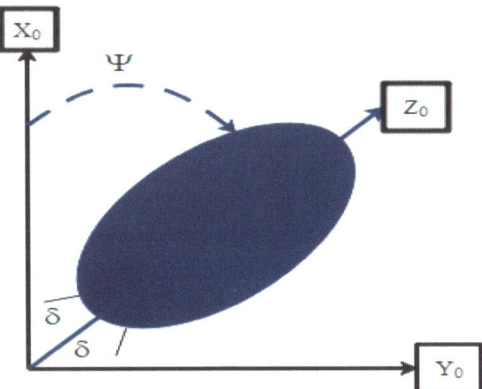

Figure 2. Heading plane motion of the autonomous underwater vehicle.

The nonlinear equation stated in the preceding equations is used to derive the autonomous underwater vehicle's static and dynamic coefficients. To simplify all of the equations, modify the aforementioned formulae, and assume that there are no hydrostatic forces in any of the three axes (x, y, or z). Since u = U, the axial drag is given by X u = X u/u × 2U. Heave velocity and pitch rate must both be zero for the autonomous underwater vehicle's cross-flow drag to be linearized. All added masses and cross-flow-added mass terms should be kept when solving the following equations, but other cross terms need to be changed. Similar to this, all terms in the X, Y, and N axes are added together to calculate body lift coefficients, moments, and forces. The value of the linearized coefficients and inertia along all axes are calculated as shown in Tables 2 and 3.

Table 2. Value of linearized coefficient.

Parameter	Value	Units	Description
$X_{\dot{u}}$	−0.58	kg	Mass (added)
Z_w	−46.003	kg·m/s	Combined term
Z_q	−6.534	kg·m/s	Combined term
$Z_{\dot{w}}$	−23.899	kg	Mass (added)
$Z_{\dot{q}}$	1.9986	kg·m	Mass (added)
Z_{δ_s}	−39.04	kg·m/s²	Fin lift
M_w	20.026	kg·m/s	Combined term
M_θ	−3.49236	kg·m²/s²	Hydrostatic force
M_q	−6.002	kg·m²/s	Combined term
$M_{\dot{w}}$	3.12	kg·m	Mass (added)
$M_{\dot{q}}$	−3.022	kg·m²	Mass (added)
M_{δ_s}	−16.07	kg·m²/s²	Fin lift

Table 3. Autonomous underwater vehicle's inertia value along various axes.

Inertia	Value	Units
I_{xx}	0.05398	kg·m²
I_{yy}	1.2697	kg·m²
I_{zz}	1.2799	kg·m²

Thus, the autonomous underwater vehicle's kinematics can be described as [1,2] and represented by Equations (23)–(25). On the other hand, Equations (26)–(28) show the autonomous underwater vehicle's dynamics.

$$\dot{x} = U\mathrm{Sin}\psi + u\mathrm{Cos}\psi \tag{23}$$

$$\dot{y} = V\mathrm{Cos}\psi - u\mathrm{Sin}\psi \tag{24}$$

$$\dot{\psi} = r \tag{25}$$

The total force in the x-axis is as follows:

$$X = M\left[\dot{u} - U_r - x_g r^2\right] \tag{26}$$

The total force in the y-axis is as follows:

$$Y = M\left[\dot{v} + x_g \dot{r} + U_r\right] \tag{27}$$

The total moments in the z-axis are as follows:

$$N = I_{zz}\dot{r} + M\left[x_g \dot{v} + x_g U_r\right] \tag{28}$$

The reduced linearized form equation of motion in a heading plane model of autonomous underwater vehicles is presented in Equations (30)–(32).

$$\dot{U} - [Mx_g + Y_{\dot{r}}]\dot{r} \quad -Y_v v - [MU + Y_r]r$$
$$= Y_{\delta_r}\delta_r - [Mx_g + N_{\dot{v}}]\dot{v} + [I_{zz} - N_{\dot{r}}]\dot{r} - N_v v + [Mx_g U - N_r]r \tag{29}$$
$$= N_{\delta_r}\delta_r$$

$$\dot{y} = u + U\psi \tag{30}$$

$$\dot{\psi} = r \tag{31}$$

Considering that Y is very small, the state space is given by Equation (32).

$$\begin{bmatrix} (M-Y_{\dot{v}}) & Y_{\dot{r}} & 0 \\ N_{\dot{v}} & (I_{zz}-N_{\dot{r}}) & 0 \\ 0 & 0 & 1 \end{bmatrix} \begin{bmatrix} \dot{v} \\ \dot{r} \\ \dot{\psi} \end{bmatrix} - \begin{bmatrix} -Y_v & -(Y_r-MU) & 0 \\ -N_v & -N_r & 0 \\ 0 & 1 & 0 \end{bmatrix} \begin{bmatrix} v \\ r \\ \psi \end{bmatrix} = \begin{bmatrix} Y_{\delta_r} \\ N_{\delta_r} \\ 0 \end{bmatrix} \delta_r \quad (32)$$

Applying all the parameter values from Tables 2 and 3 in Equation (32), Equation (33) includes the state space equation for the heading plane of the autonomous underwater vehicle.

$$\begin{bmatrix} \dot{v} \\ \dot{r} \\ \dot{\psi} \end{bmatrix} = \begin{bmatrix} -3.236 & -1.015 & 0 \\ 5.838 & 1.636 & 0 \\ 0 & 1 & 0 \end{bmatrix} \begin{bmatrix} v \\ r \\ \psi \end{bmatrix} + \begin{bmatrix} 1.21 \\ -5.156 \\ 0 \end{bmatrix} \delta_r \quad (33)$$

The heading plane control loop depicted in Figure 3 states that the inner control loop governs the autonomous underwater vehicle's rudder angle, while the outer control loop governs the heading angle.

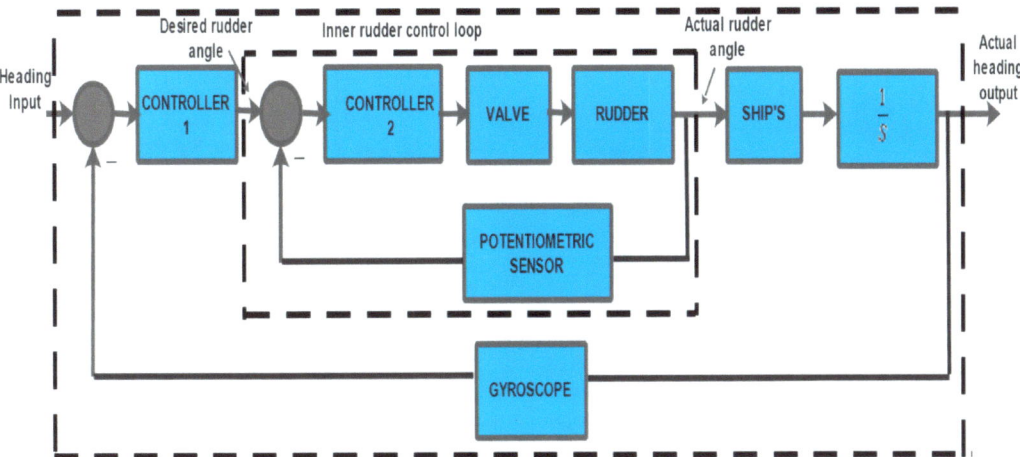

Figure 3. Control loop of heading plane.

The control law is created in a way that forces the autonomous underwater vehicle to travel in the fixed direction that is desired and to stay there. The orientation of the rudder in the inner control loop is the control input that helps the autonomous underwater vehicle stay pointed in the right direction. However, the rudder's ability to move is physically constrained. The autonomous underwater vehicle's unbalance may result from high yaw rates, which can also cause roll and sway motion. As a result, the rudder angle of the autonomous underwater vehicle completely determines how the outer control loop measures the heading angle. Therefore, while navigating an autonomous underwater vehicle, restrictions must be placed on rudder orientation and yaw rate.

2.2. Depth Plane Control

The depth plane model of the autonomous underwater vehicle is shown in Figure 4. Here, body is fixed, and earth is taken as reference.

The depth plane control of the autonomous underwater vehicle uses two control loops. The pitch angle and depth of the autonomous underwater vehicle system are controlled by the inner and outer control loops, respectively, which are described in Figure 5. The current autonomous underwater vehicle assumes the pitch angle (θ) is zero, forward speed is nearly constant, and wind wave is ignored.

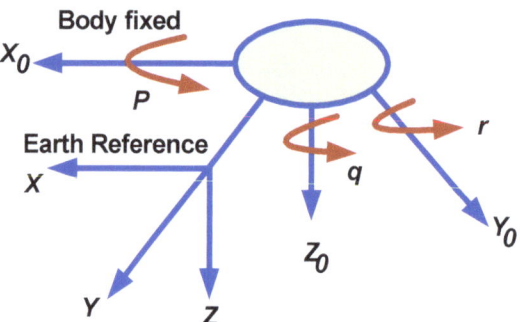

Figure 4. Autonomous underwater vehicle's depth plane motion.

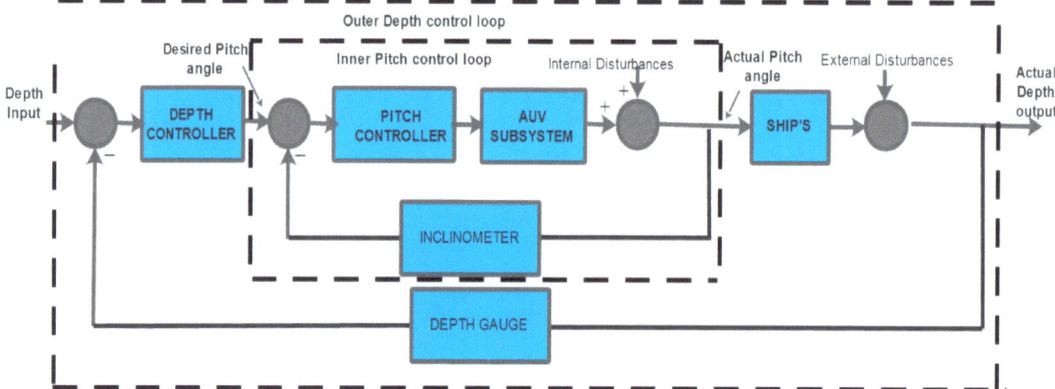

Figure 5. Block diagram of autonomous underwater vehicle's depth plane control.

The individual components of depth plane motion of the autonomous underwater vehicle are simplified [3] in Equation (34).

$$\left(Mx_G + Z_{\dot{q}}\right)\dot{q} - (Mu_i + Z_q)q + Z_W W + \dot{W} = Z_{\delta_s}\delta_s \\ \left(I_{yy} - M\dot{q}\right)\dot{q} - (Mx_G u_i - M_q)q - M_w W - (Mx_G + M_{\dot{w}})\dot{W} - M_\theta = M_{\delta_s}\delta_s \tag{34}$$

$$\dot{\theta} = q$$

and

$$\dot{Z} = W - u_i\theta$$

The standard diving equation of the depth plane motion of the autonomous underwater vehicle is simplified in Equation (35).

$$\begin{bmatrix} Mx_G - M_{\dot{w}} & I_y - M_q & 0 \\ 0 & 0 & 1 \\ 0 & 0 & 0 \end{bmatrix} * \begin{bmatrix} \dot{q} \\ \dot{\theta} \\ \dot{z} \end{bmatrix} + \begin{bmatrix} -M_{\dot{w}} & Mx_G u_i - M_q & BG_z W \\ 0 & -1 & 0 \\ -1 & 0 & u_i \end{bmatrix} * \begin{bmatrix} q \\ \theta \\ z \end{bmatrix} = \begin{bmatrix} M_\delta \\ 0 \\ 0 \end{bmatrix} \delta_s \tag{35}$$

Similarly, by putting all the parameter data from Tables 1 and 2 in Equation (35), the depth plane system is described by state space Equation (36).

$$\begin{bmatrix} \dot{q} \\ \dot{\theta} \\ \dot{z} \end{bmatrix} = \begin{bmatrix} -0.9 & -0.2021 & 0 \\ 1 & 0 & 0 \\ 0 & -1.25 & 0 \end{bmatrix} \begin{bmatrix} q \\ \theta \\ z \end{bmatrix} + \begin{bmatrix} -4.399 \\ 0 \\ 0 \end{bmatrix} \delta_s \tag{36}$$

3. Controlling Techniques

In this section, different controlling techniques such as fuzzy logic controller, self-tuning fuzzy-PID, and ANFIS are implemented. The working principles and simulation design of these controllers are same for both heading plane and depth plane control.

3.1. Fuzzy Logic Controller

The dynamics of an autonomous underwater vehicle are uncertain, and the heading plane and depth plane trajectory control involves several uncertainties. FLC is one of the soft computing techniques used for simulating the complex systems. The interesting characteristic of the controller is the usage of linguistic variables that are closer to human thoughts. The four primary components of the controller are explained briefly, and the overall structure is shown in Figure 6.

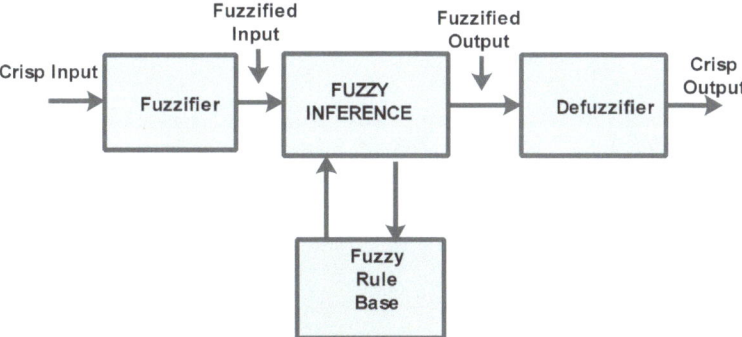

Figure 6. Schematic for a fuzzy logic controller.

In order to successfully track the desired depth and heading for the autonomous underwater vehicle, FLC accepts the error and derivative error and generates the appropriate input. The crisp value is transformed into a fuzzy set during fuzzification. The FLC receives two control variables as input: ΔE (error) and ΔDE (derivative error). Figures 7 and 8 depict the two input variables ER and DE represented as seven triangular membership functions, and Figure 9 depicts the output variable (out) as nine triangular membership function.

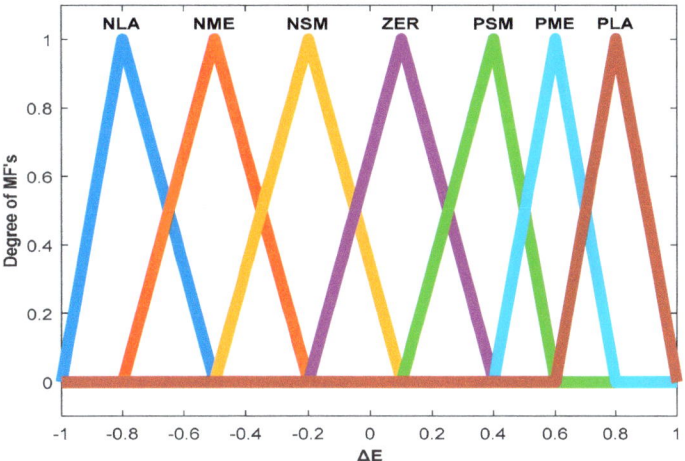

Figure 7. Input variable MFs of error (ΔE).

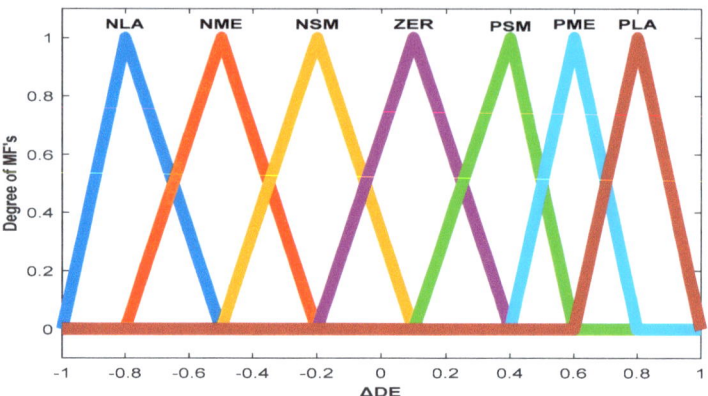

Figure 8. Input variable MFs of change in error (ΔDE).

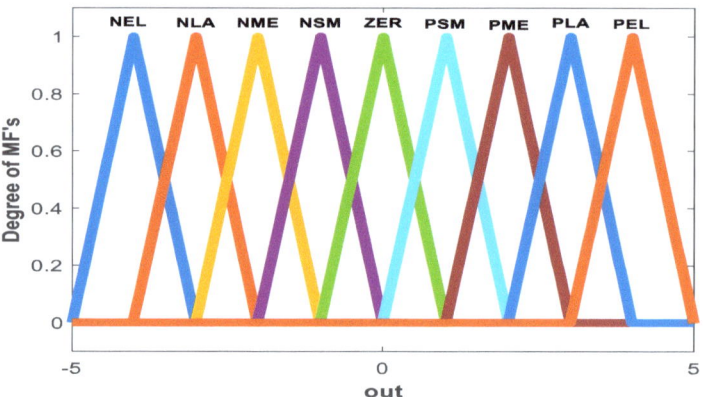

Figure 9. Output variable MFs.

Each input variable, such as ΔE and ΔDE, has seven triangular MFs; therefore, 49 fuzzy rules are prepared for FLC, as shown in Table 4. The MFs for input variables are defined as negative large (NLA), negative medium (NME), negative small (NSM), zero (ZER), positive small (PSM), positive medium (PME), and positive large (PLA). The MFs for out variable are defined as negative extra-large (NEL), positive extra-large (PEL), negative large (NLA), negative medium (NME), negative small (NSM), zero (ZER), positive small (PSM), positive medium (PME), and positive large (PLA).

Table 4. Fuzzy rule of error (ΔE) and change in error (ΔDE).

ΔDE \ ΔE	NLA	NME	NSM	ZER	PSM	PME	PLA
NLA	NEL	NME	NME	NLA	NME	NME	ZER
NME	NLA	NLA	NME	NME	NSM	ZER	PME
NSM	NME	NME	NME	NSM	ZER	PSM	PME
ZER	NLA	NME	NSM	ZER	PSM	PME	PLA
PSM	NME	NSM	ZER	PSM	PME	PLA	PLA
PME	NME	ZER	PSM	PME	PLA	PLA	PLA
PLA	ZER	PSM	PME	PLA	PLA	PLA	PEL

The fuzzy inference is based on max-min principle, where there are two fuzzy variables with triangular MFs, and follows with given rule. Mathematically, it can be represented using Equation (37).

$$\mu_r(x,y) = \min[\mu_A(x_1,y_1), \mu_B(x_1,y_1)] \tag{37}$$

$\mu_A(x_1,y_1)$ and $\mu_B(x_1,y_1)$ are MFs of two input fuzzy variables, and $\mu_r(x,y)$ is the fuzzy resultant composite MF of output fuzzy variables.

Defuzzification method is used to obtain crisp output from the fuzzy set. There are different kinds of defuzzification methods used to find the crisp output, such as centroid, mean of maxima, and center of sums. Output is found from the composite fuzzy set, and it is achieved by centroid method, which is followed in this paper.

The autonomous underwater vehicle follows a third-order system for the measurement of depth, which results in very slow system response. In order to make the time of response very fast, the FLC is combined with phase lag compensator, where the time-response characteristics produce satisfactory results during effective depth trajectory tracking.

3.2. Self-Tuning Fuzzy-PID

Many researchers are doing research work on hybrid intelligent algorithms, especially using the fuzzy logic concept. The self-tuning fuzzy-PID controller is designed as the fuzzy inference system tunes the PID parameters (K_P, K_I, KD), which depend on fuzzy rules. The self-tuning fuzzy-PID structure is given in Figure 10.

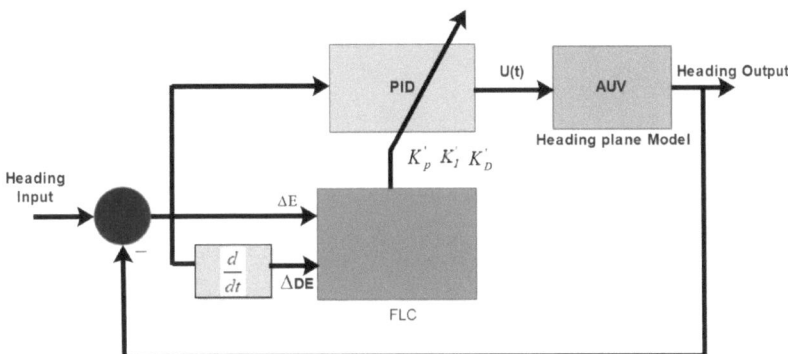

Figure 10. Block diagram of self-tuning fuzzy-PID.

Error (ER) and change in error (DE) are the input of FLC, and outputs are PID tuning parameters such as K'_P, K'_I, K'_D. The tuned PID parameters are given in Equations (38)–(40).

$$K_{Pnew} = K_{Pold} + K'_P \tag{38}$$

$$K_{Dnew} = K_{Dold} + K'_D \tag{39}$$

$$K_{Inew} = K_{Iold} + K'_I \tag{40}$$

Based on the knowledge of error and change in error, a number of rules are assigned to tune the PID parameters (K'_P, K'_I, K'_D). Figure 11 depicts the self-tuning fuzzy-PID's two-input and three-output fuzzy inference system.

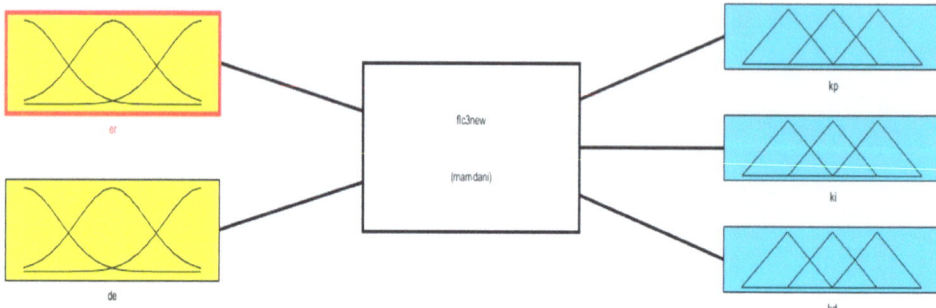

Figure 11. Two-input and three-output fuzzy inference system.

After tuning PID parameters [10], the controller output is represented using Equation (41).

$$U(t) = (K_P + K'_P K_I + K'_I \int E(t)dt + (K_D + K'_D)\frac{\partial E(t)}{\partial t} \quad (41)$$

The triangle MFs with seven linguistic variables are considered for each input variables ER (error) and change in error (DE).

$$\Delta E = \{NEL, NME, NSM, ZER, PSM, PME, PEL\}$$

$$\Delta DE = \{NLA, NME, NSM, ZER, PSM, PME, PLA\}$$

Similarly, the MFs of output $K'_P, K'_I,$ and K'_D are also described with seven linguistic variables and are assigned as follows:

$$K'_P = \{PLA, PME, PSM, ZER, NSM, NME, NLA\}$$
$$K'_I = \{PLA, PME, PSM, ZER, NSM, NME, NLA\}$$
$$K'_D = \{PLA, PME, PSM, ZER, NSM, NME, NLA\}$$

Fuzy rules are dsigned to get greater accuraccy of the autonomous underwater vehicle system and also depends on practical knowledge experience of the designer.

The designing of fuzzy rules of the self-tuning fuzzy-PID controller is as follows:

1. If the deviation error is greater, the K_P value should be viewed as being larger, the K_D value should be smaller, and the K_I value should be as small as possible;
2. Where deviation error is medium (intermediate), K_P should be small to reduce the percentage of overshoot;
3. Where deviation error is small, $K_P \& K_I$ should be larger value to improve the stability, and K_D is mentioned.

3.3. ANFIS Controller

ANFIS is a five-layered feed-forward neural network model. The ANFIS is a unique blend of a fuzzy inference system and learning algorithm of an artificial neural network. ANFIS initiates with a prior well-constructed framework. The neural system needs a pair of information, such as input and output data, for training purpose. As it is linguistically structured, the intermediate results can be implemented through a first-order Sugeno fuzzy system, which has more computational efficiency and flexibility. ANFIS trains the paired data set of the target, and taking into consideration the best response of the system, the objective can be obtained. By its very nature, FLC has proven a bit complex in developing membership functions and yielding fuzzy rules, so in most of the cases, the rules are designed in a randomized way. To avoid the above demerits, the globally applicable control model, i.e., ANFIS, was developed. The schematics of the ANFIS structure are briefly explained in Figure 12.

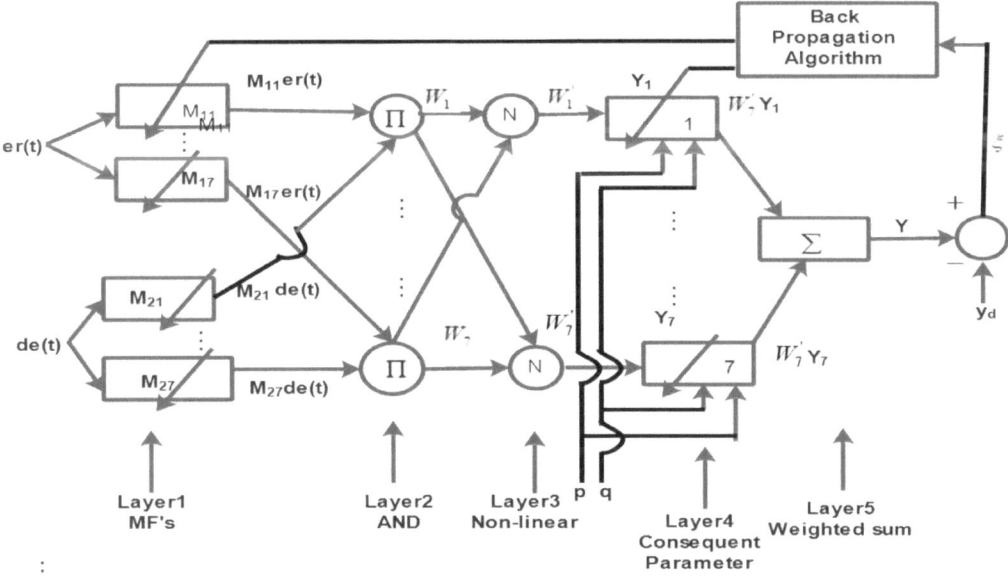

Figure 12. Block diagram of ANFIS controller techniques.

The two inputs of ANFIS controller are $er(t)$ and $de(t)$.

$$er(t) Z_r - Z_d \text{ and } det = \frac{er(t)_k - er(t)_{k-1}}{T} \times 100$$

where Z_r is the reference depth, Z_d is the desired depth, and T is the sampling time. There are seven Gaussian-type fuzzy rules of the proposed Sugeno fuzzy model. The output of singleton membership function is defined using Equation (42).

$$y_i = m_{1i} er(t) + m_{2i}\, de(t) + r_i \tag{42}$$

where m_{1i}, m_{2i}, and r_i are the training parameters.

Layer1: All nodes in this layer of fuzzification are adaptable nodes. A gradient descent algorithm is used to optimize the input MFs such as error (ΔE) and derivative error (ΔDE). The output of this layer is represented using Equations (43) and (44).

$$O_i^1 = \mu_{1i}(er(t)), i = 1, 2, \ldots .7 \tag{43}$$

$$O_i^1 = \mu_{1i}(de(t)), i = 1, 2, \ldots .7 \tag{44}$$

μ_{1i} and μ_{2i} are the Gaussian-type MFs, as shown in Figure 13.

Layer2: This layer evaluates the rule's firing power for the two inputs, and it is a fixed node represented by π, operated with fuzzy AND operator.

$$W_i O_i^2 = \mu_{1i}(er(t)) \cdot \mu_{2i}(de(t)), i = 1, 2, \ldots .7 \tag{45}$$

Layer3: As a fixed node, this layer is denoted by the letter N. The weight is calculated in every node. There are ith number of weights with the firing strength of the rule. The normalized firing strength is calculated as $\overline{W_1}$.

$$\overline{W_1} = \frac{w_i}{\sum_{i=1}^{7} W_i} \tag{46}$$

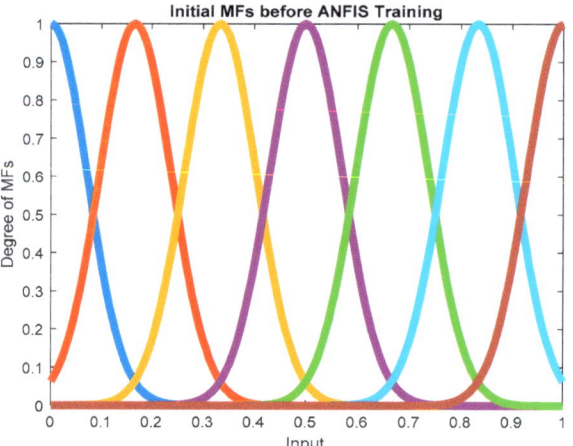

Figure 13. Initial MFs before ANFIS training.

Layer4: Each and every node in this layer is an adaptive node, and the output of this node comprises normalized firing strength ($\overline{W_l}$) and consequent parameter (y_i).

$$O_i^4 = \overline{W_l} \cdot y_i \tag{47}$$

where

$$y_i = m_{1i}er(t) + m_{2i}de(t) + r_i, \; i = 1, 2, \ldots 7 \tag{48}$$

Layer 5: Each and every node in this layer is a fixed node and represented by a symbol (Σ). The overall ANFIS output is calculated as the overall addition of incoming signals to this node.

$$O_i^5 = \frac{\sum_{i=1}^{7} W_i y_i}{\sum_{i=1}^{7} W_i} = \sum_{i=1}^{7} \overline{W}_i y_i \tag{49}$$

ANFIS Controller Training

The proposed ANFIS controller [36,37] is designed with the back-propagation algorithm and reduces error by least square method. This algorithm has salient features such as fast convergence rate and less complexity in computation. For the weight updating, the steepest descent gradient algorithm is used. The cost function of the adaptive system is defined as follows:

$$E = \frac{1}{2} \sum_{l=1}^{n} (y_{d_l} - y_l)^2 \tag{50}$$

where, the desired output is y_d, and y is what the ANFIS model actually produces. Therefore, for the proposed ANFIS model, the cost function is redefined as follows:

$$E = \frac{1}{2} \sum_{l=1}^{n} (Z_{d_l} - Z_l)^2 = \frac{1}{2} e^2 \tag{51}$$

where, Z_d is the desired depth response, and Z is the estimated depth output of the autonomous underwater vehicle. As per the back-propagation adaptive algorithm, the updated parameters can be evaluated as follows:

$$p_i(k+1) = p(k) - \eta \, \nabla_p E(k) \tag{52}$$

$$q_i(k+1) = q(k) - \eta \, \nabla_q E(k) \tag{53}$$

$$w(k+1) = w(k) - \eta \nabla E(k) \tag{54}$$

where p, q are input parameters; w is the weight; and η is the fixed learning rate.

$\nabla p_i E(k)$, $\nabla q_i E(k)$, and $\nabla w_i E(k)$ are the gradient of cost function E corresponding to parameters (p_i, q_i, w_i) that are described in the equation below.

$$\nabla p_i E(k) = \frac{\partial E}{\partial e} \cdot \frac{\partial e}{\partial Z} \cdot \frac{\partial Z}{\partial y} \cdot \frac{\partial y}{\partial O_i^1} \cdot \frac{\partial O_i^1}{\partial p_i} \tag{55}$$

$$\nabla q_i E(k) = \frac{\partial E}{\partial e} \cdot \frac{\partial e}{\partial Z} \cdot \frac{\partial Z}{\partial y} \cdot \frac{\partial y}{\partial O_i^1} \cdot \frac{\partial O_i^1}{\partial q_i} \tag{56}$$

$$\nabla w_i E(k) = \frac{\partial E}{\partial e} \cdot \frac{\partial e}{\partial Z} \cdot \frac{\partial Z}{\partial y} \cdot \frac{\partial y}{\partial w_i} \tag{57}$$

The differential terms of the above equations are briefly described and mentioned below.

$$\frac{\partial E}{\partial e} = Zd - Z, \frac{\partial e}{\partial Z} = -1 \text{ and } \frac{\partial Z}{\partial y} = k, \text{Constant} \tag{58}$$

The value of k is considered greater than zero.

$$\frac{\partial y}{\partial O_i^1} = \frac{y(k)}{\sum_{i=1}^n W_i(k)} \tag{59}$$

$$\frac{\partial O_i^1}{\partial p_i} = \frac{2}{p(k)} \tag{60}$$

$$\frac{\partial O_i^1}{\partial q_i} = \frac{1 - O_i^1(k)}{q_i(k)} \tag{61}$$

$$\frac{\partial y}{\partial w_i} = \frac{y_i(k)}{\sum_{i=1}^n O_i^1(k)} \tag{62}$$

As the error propagates in a backward manner for the back-propagation algorithm, so the shape of Gaussian MFs is modified after training. The MFs before and after training are given in Figures 13 and 14, respectively.

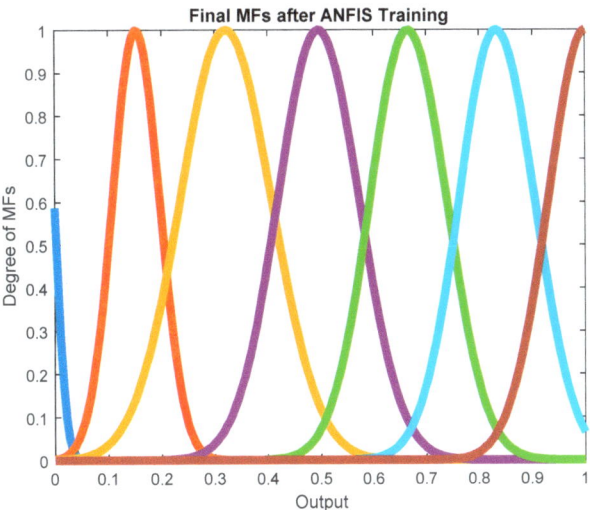

Figure 14. Final MFs after ANFIS training.

The error curves start to decrease and follow the gradient algorithm where minimized Rmse is 0.140414 for depth control, which is shown in Figure 15. Similarly, the Rmse value of heading plane control is 0.09912, as shown in Figure 16.

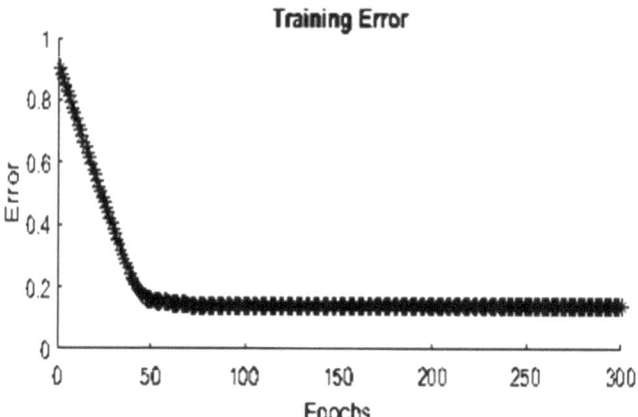

Figure 15. Training error curve of proposed ANFIS control for depth plane.

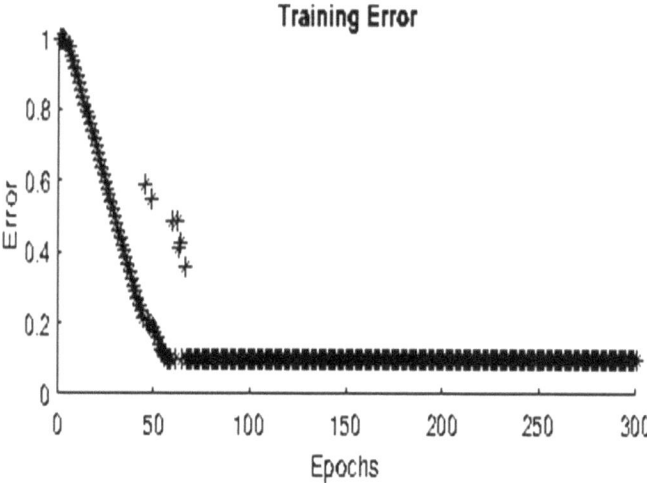

Figure 16. Training error curve of proposed ANFIS control for heading plane.

After training the input data, the five-layer Simulink structure of the ANFIS model is obtained, and it is shown in Figure 17. To better understand the implementation process of the ANFIS model, it is briefly explained in the flow chart illustrated in Figure 18. Initially, the depth plane parameters are considered as input training data, and each input is defined with MFs. In next step, the number of epochs and percentage of training data are described for training the model. After, the successful training yields the best FIS and training results of ANFIS model, which is mentioned in third step. In the final step, compliance of the input parameter for the prediction and prediction result is attained, which is compared with evaluated result of the depth controller parameter.

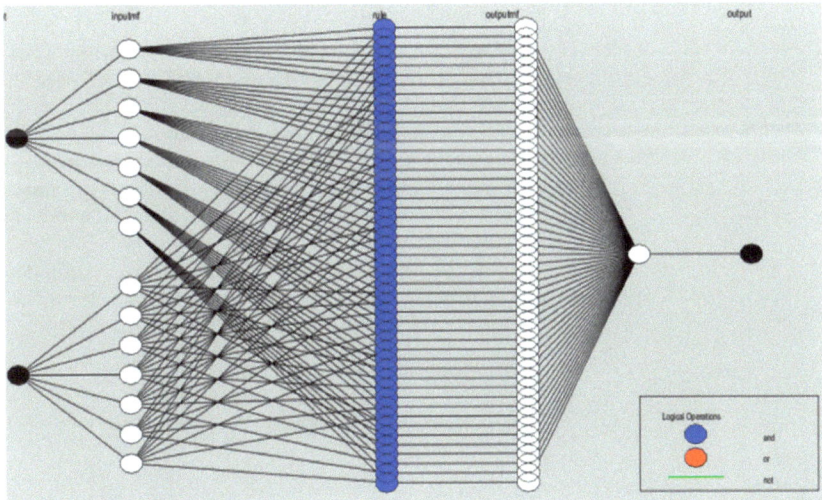

Figure 17. ANFIS Simulink structure.

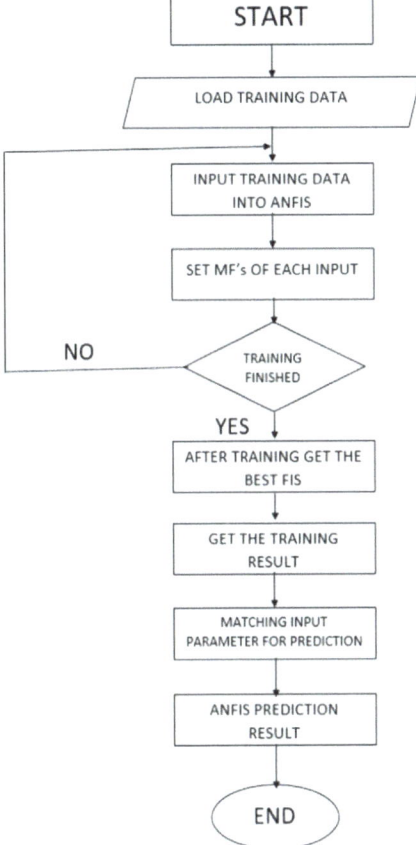

Figure 18. Flow chart of ANFIS control technique.

4. Simulation Results

This section explains an example of how the suggested ANFIS controller techniques performed for the autonomous underwater vehicle in depth and heading planes. Using the MATLAB/Simulink tool, the behavior of the autonomous underwater vehicle's mathematical model is simulated, and the effectiveness of the ANFIS is evaluated in comparison to traditional PID, FLC, and self-tuning fuzzy-PID controller techniques. Figures 19 and 20 show, respectively, a brief explanation of the step response result analysis of the heading and depth plane controls. To start, the heading and depth planes of the autonomous underwater vehicle are controlled using the conventional PID controller gains that are obtained from online PID tuning separately. This controller provides satisfactory performance but produces large overshoot and more settling time, as shown in Tables 5 and 6.

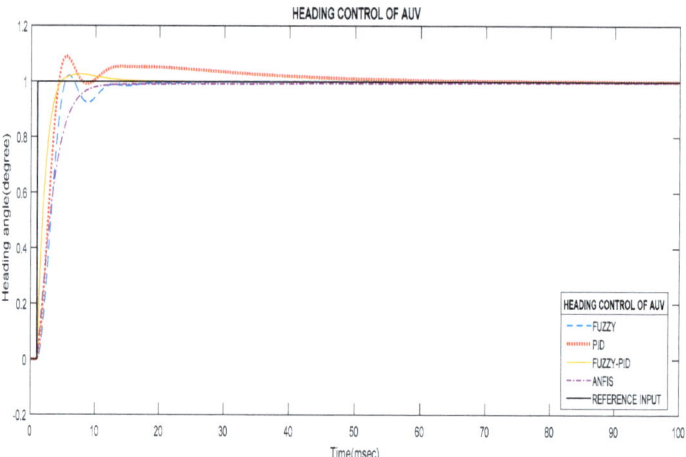

Figure 19. Step response curve of heading plane control by FLC, PID, self-tuning fuzzy-PID, and ANFIS control techniques.

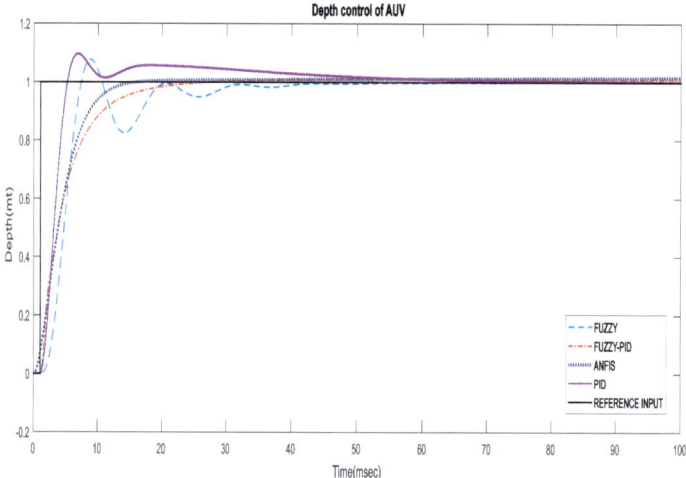

Figure 20. Time-response curve of depth plane control by FLC, PID, fuzzy-PID, and ANFIS control techniques.

Table 5. Time-response characteristics comparison of heading plane control.

Time Response	FLC	STFPID	ANFIS	PID
T_r (ms)	246.7	211.05	318.89	217.93
T_s (ms)	749.8	705.0058	703.76	1446.4
%Overshoot	2.0971	2.57	0	8.87

Table 6. Time-response characteristics comparison of depth control.

Time Response	FLC	STFPID	ANFIS	PID
T_r (ms)	92.56	254.29	248.69	117.75
T_s (ms)	677.063	553.22	429.35	955.6
%Overshoot	7.65	0.0228	0	9.46

The autonomous underwater vehicle system, which is a third-order system, was compensated with a lag compensator, which significantly improved the system's time-response performance. The Mamadani FLC was introduced to produce better timing. The disturbances were added at the input side of the system, but the controller gives it good load rejection capability, allowing it to achieve the desired response and readily stabilizing the system. The self-tuning fuzzy-PID controller is a hybrid technique, and the old (K_P, K_I, and K_D) parameters need to be designed before simulation of the FPID model. The nonlinear equation of the controller output is able to control both autonomous underwater vehicle systems with the desired time response. The proposed ANFIS model does a better job of controlling the parameters of the nonlinear mathematical autonomous underwater vehicle model, resulting in a more accurate and faster response. Since ANFIS combines fuzzy logic and neural networks, it provides accuracy to non-linear systems such as autonomous underwater vehicles. Without exclusively relying on expert knowledge sufficient for a fuzzy logic model, the ANFIS model can be trained. The proposed model benefits from having both linguistic and numerical knowledge. The ANFIS controller outperforms the PID, FLC, and self-tuning fuzzy-PID controllers according to their responses. As a result, the proposed system offers significantly improved functionality in terms of flexibility, consistency, ability to adapt, and capacity for quick learning. The time-response characteristics in terms of rise time, settling time, and overshoot comparison of the heading and depth planes of the autonomous underwater vehicle are shown in Tables 5 and 6, respectively. The overshoot of the proposed ANFIS controller for both control operations is almost zero in comparison to that of other controller techniques. Similarly, this controller produces better speed response with a minimum settling time.

In this paper, the tracking performance of a heading controller with multi-step, square, and ramp inputs is examined. The autonomous underwater vehicle successfully tracks the desired heading with various inputs applied to the model, as shown in Figures 21–23. The performance of PID and FLC in terms of overshoot and settling time is very poor, but the performance is much better with the ANFIS. Figures 24 and 25 show the time-response performance, as represented on the bar chart of the heading and depth planes, respectively.

Owing to its minimal oscillation, better speed, and accurate steady state response, the proposed ANFIS controller's data are referred to as referential target input, and the other controllers such as ANFIS, FLC, and self-tuning fuzzy-PID are considered as input data for NN optimization. The MATLAB neural network tool is used for the optimization of controller response. Up until the network reaches the reference target, the NN is trained. The output is correctly predicted by the training network based on the target data. As a result, it can be said that the NN effectively models and predicts the autonomous underwater vehicle's heading angle. The derivative of the loss function is taken into account when using the gradient descent algorithm in this case, and the expected value of the target can be expressed as a weighted sum of the functions. The results related to the training, validation, testing, and regression of self-tuning fuzzy-PID, ANFIS, and FLC controllers are described in Figures 26–28, respectively. The regression value of the

ANFIS controller is comparatively high compared to that of other controllers. The overall regression values of all controllers are represented as a clustered cone bar graph and shown in Figure 29. In comparison to FLC and self-tuning fuzzy-PID controllers, it was found that the autonomous underwater vehicle system based on the ANFIS controller significantly reduces overshoot with essentially no loss of accuracy.

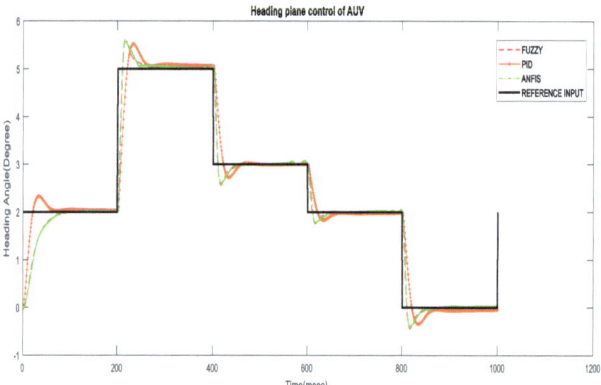

Figure 21. Multi-step response of heading plane control.

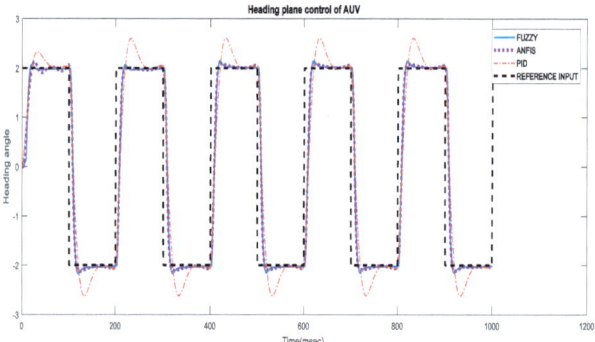

Figure 22. Square wave response of heading plane control.

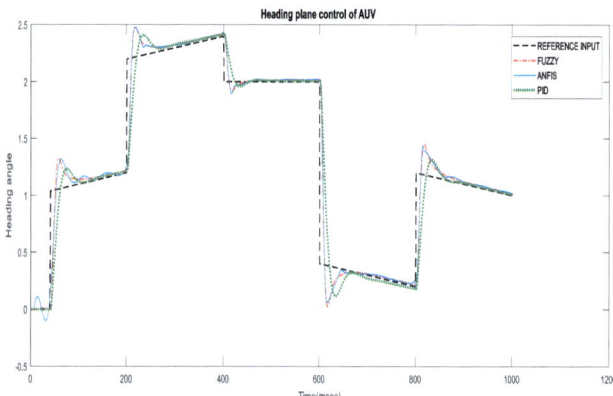

Figure 23. Ramp response of heading plane control.

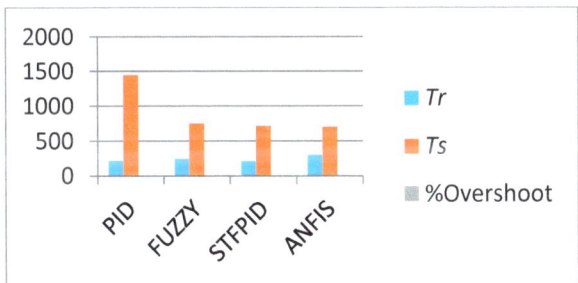

Figure 24. Bar chart of the heading plane control.

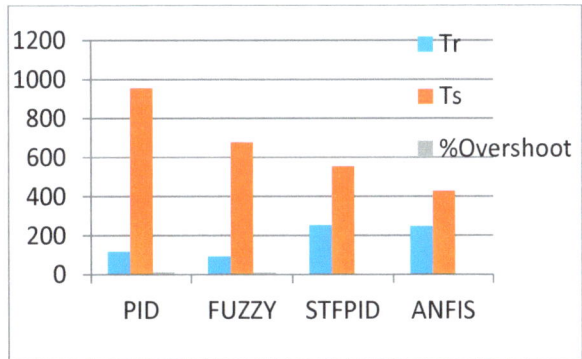

Figure 25. Bar chart of the depth plane control.

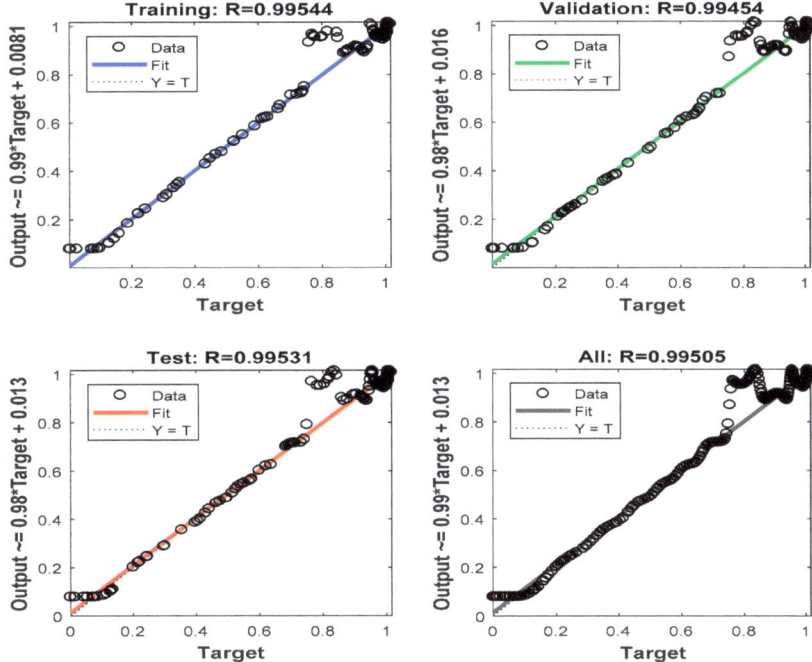

Figure 26. Results of fuzzy after NN optimization.

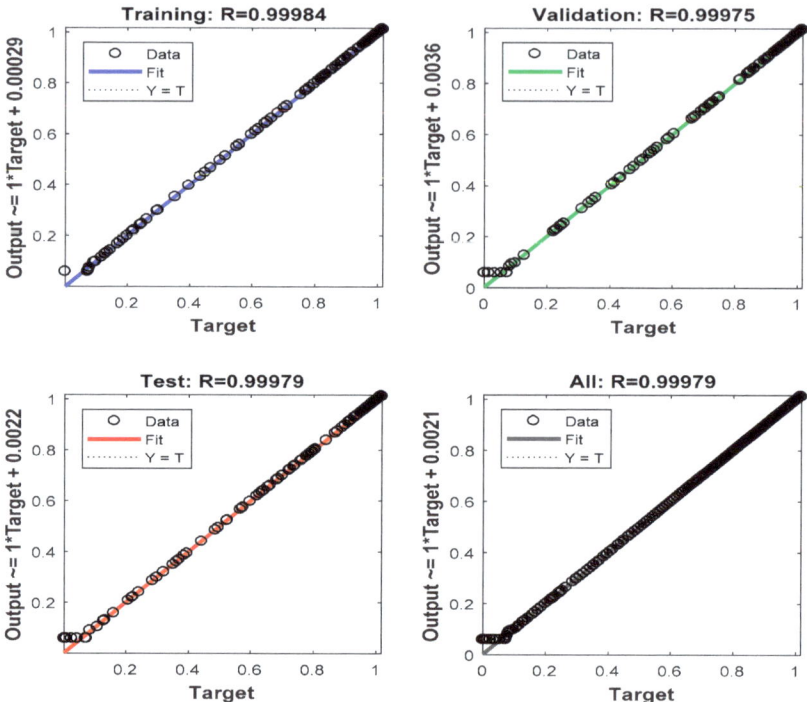

Figure 27. Results of self-tuning fuzzy-PID after NN optimization.

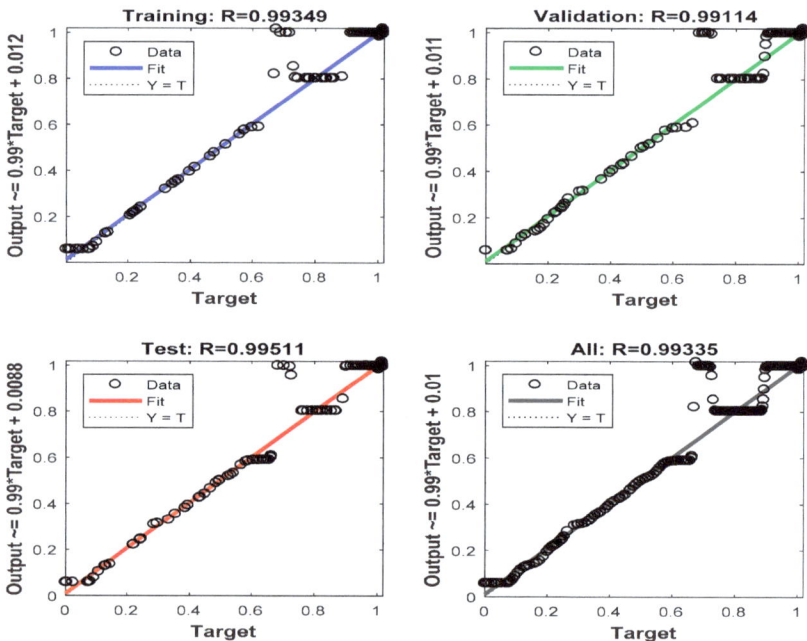

Figure 28. Results of PID after NN optimization.

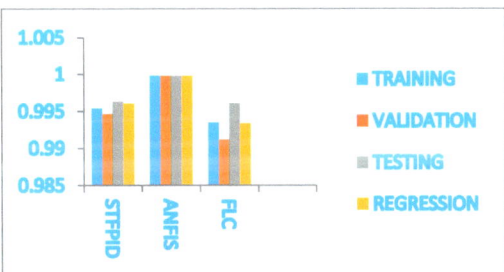

Figure 29. Clustered cone bar graph of various controllers.

5. Conclusions

The self-tuning fuzzy logic controller has the advantages of quick response, excellent anti-interference ability, and more, according to experiments and simulations. The PID controller has the largest steady-state error, while the fuzzy-based controller has a slightly longer average rising time than the others. While the autonomous underwater vehicle is controlled for both heading and depth, the steady-state error of the STFLC gradually decreases, and the response gets closer to the desired value. The time-response performance in controlling both heading and depth significantly improved with the use of the designed ANFIS controller model, which was the subject of this study. The ANFIS's gradient error-based self-learning mechanism is capable of handling the nonlinearities and uncertainties present in underwater motion both in terms of depth and heading plane. Accurate heading angle determination for underwater vehicles towards targets is possible by using the ANFIS approach in a variety of ways. The effectiveness of an underwater vehicle during different path movements can be demonstrated by simulation results. The proposed ANFIS controller has a quick response, less overshoot, minimal error, and better heading and depth-tracking capability than the traditional PID, FLC, and self-tuning fuzzy-PID controller models.

Author Contributions: Conceptualization, N.N.; Methodology, N.N., K.K.S. and M.A.; Software, T.K.P., H.D. and S.S.A.; Validation, T.K.P.; Formal analysis, S.R.D. and T.K.P.; Investigation, S.R.N.; Resources, S.R.N.; Data curation, H.D.; Writing—original draft, N.N., M.A.; Writing—review & editing, S.R.D. and K.K.S.; Funding acquisition, S.S.A. All authors have read and agreed to the published version of the manuscript.

Funding: This project is funded by King Saud University, Riyadh, Saudi Arabia. Researchers Supporting Project number (RSP2023R167), King Saud University, Riyadh, Saudi Arabia.

Data Availability Statement: Data will be made available on request.

Acknowledgments: Researchers Supporting Project number (RSP2023R167), King Saud University, Riyadh, Saudi Arabia.

Conflicts of Interest: The authors declare that they have no competing interest.

References

1. Fossen, T.I. *Guidance and Control of Ocean Vehicles*; Wiley: Hoboken, NY, USA, 1994.
2. Fossen, T.I. Maritime Control Systems—Guidance, Navigation and Control of Ships, Rigs and Underwater Vehicles. In *Marine Cybernetics*; Springer: Trondheim, Norway, 2002.
3. Fossen, T.I. *Handbook of Marine Craft Hydrodynamics and Motion Control*; Norwegian University of Science and Technology: Trondheim, Norway, 2011.
4. Huang, H.; Zhang, C.; Ding, W.; Zhu, X.; Sun, G.; Wang, H. Design of the Depth Controller for a Floating Ocean Seismograph. *J. Mar. Sci. Eng.* **2020**, *8*, 166. [CrossRef]
5. Tchilian, R.S.; Rafikova, E.; Gafurov, S.A.; Rafikov, M. Optimal control of an underwater glider vehicle. *Procedia Eng.* **2017**, *176*, 732–740. [CrossRef]
6. Srivastava, A.; Tripathy, A.K.; Prasad, M.P.R. Comparative Analysis on Depth Control of an Underwater Vehicle. In Proceedings of the Innovations in Power and Advanced Computing Technologies, Vellore, India, 22–23 March 2019; pp. 1–5.

7. Liu, C.; Yue, X.; Shi, K.; Sun, Z. *Spacecraft Attitude Control: A Linear Matrix Inequality Approach*; Elsevier: Amsterdam, The Netherlands, 2022.
8. Liu, C.; Shi, K.; Yue, X.; Sun, Z. Inertia-free saturated output feedback attitude stabilization for uncertain spacecraft. *Int. J. Robust Nonlinear Control* **2020**, *30*, 5101–5121. [CrossRef]
9. Zhao, T.; Chen, Y.; Dian, S.; Guo, R.; Li, S. General type-2 fuzzy gain scheduling PID controller with application to powerline inspection robots. *Int. J. Fuzzy Syst.* **2020**, *22*, 181–200. [CrossRef]
10. Huo, X.; Ge, T.; Wang, X. Horizontal path-following control for deep-sea work-class ROVs based on a fuzzy logic system. *Ships Offshore Struct.* **2018**, *13*, 637–648. [CrossRef]
11. Xiang, X.; Yu, C.; Lapierre, L.; Zhang, J.; Zhang, Q. Survey on Fuzzy-Logic-Based Guidance and Control of Marine Surface Vehicles and Underwater Vehicles. *Int. J. Fuzzy Syst.* **2018**, *20*, 572–586. [CrossRef]
12. Zadeh, L.A. Fuzzy sets. *Inf. Control* **1965**, *8*, 338–353. [CrossRef]
13. Chu, Z.; Xiang, X.; Zhu, D.; Luo, C.; Xie, D. Adaptive Fuzzy Sliding Mode Diving Control for Autonomous Underwater Vehicle with Input Constraint. *Int. J. Fuzzy Syst.* **2018**, *20*, 1460–1469. [CrossRef]
14. Londhe, P.S.; Patre, B.M. Adaptive fuzzy sliding mode control for robust trajectory tracking control of an autonomous underwater vehicle. *Intell. Serv. Robot.* **2019**, *12*, 87–102. [CrossRef]
15. Londhe, P.S.; Dhadekar, D.D.; Patre, B.M.; Waghmare, L.M. Uncertainty and disturbance estimator based sliding mode control of an autonomous underwater vehicle. *Int. J. Dyn. Control* **2017**, *5*, 1122–1138. [CrossRef]
16. Yao, F.; Yang, C.; Liu, X.; Zhang, M. Experimental Evaluation on Depth Control Using Improved Model Predictive Control for Autonomous Underwater Vehicle (AUVs). *Sensors* **2018**, *18*, 2321. [CrossRef] [PubMed]
17. Sudirman, R.M.; Effend, R. Model Predictive Control of Autonomous Underwater Vehicles Based on Horizon Optimization. *JAREE-J. Adv. Res. Electr. Eng.* **2020**, *4*, 107884. [CrossRef]
18. Makavita, C.D.; Jayasinghe, S.G.; Nguyen, H.D.; Ranmuthugala, D. Experimental Study of Command Governor Adaptive Control for Unmanned Underwater Vehicles. *IEEE Trans. Control Syst. Technol.* **2019**, *27*, 332–345. [CrossRef]
19. Chen, Y.; Wang, K.; Chen, W. Adaptive fuzzy depth control with trajectory feedforward compensator for autonomous underwater vehicles. *Adv. Mech. Eng.* **2019**, *11*, 1687814019838172. [CrossRef]
20. Guerreroa, J.; Torresa, J.; Creuzeb, V.; Chemorib, A. Trajectory tracking for autonomous underwater vehicle: An adaptive approach. *Ocean Eng.* **2019**, *172*, 511–522. [CrossRef]
21. Wang, N.; Sun, J.C.; Er, M.J. Tracking-error-based universal adaptive fuzzy control for output tracking of nonlinear systems with completely unknown dynamics. *IEEE Trans. Fuzzy Syst.* **2018**, *26*, 869–883. [CrossRef]
22. Zheng, Z.; Huang, Y.; Xie, L.; Zhu, B. Adaptive trajectory tracking control of a fully actuated surface vessel with asymmetrically constrained input and output. *IEEE Trans. Control Syst. Technol.* **2017**, *97*, 83–91. [CrossRef]
23. Makavita, C.D.; Jayasinghe, S.G.; Nguyen, H.D.; Ranmuthugala, D. Experimental Study of a Command Governor Adaptive Depth Controller for an Unmanned Underwater Vehicle. *Appl. Ocean Res.* **2019**, *86*, 61–72. [CrossRef]
24. Manzanilla, A.; Castillo, P.; Lozano, R. Nonlinear algorithm with adaptive properties to stabilize an underwater vehicle real-time experiments. *IFAC* **2017**, *50*, 6857–6862. [CrossRef]
25. Wang, N.; Qian, C.; Sun, J.C.; Liu, Y.C. Adaptive robust finite time trajectory tracking control of fully actuated marine surface vehicles. *IEEE Trans. Control Syst. Technol.* **2016**, *24*, 1454–1462. [CrossRef]
26. Hassaneina, O.; Anavattib, S.G.; Shimc, H.; Ray, T. Model-based adaptive control system for autonomous underwater vehicles. *Ocean Eng.* **2016**, *127*, 58–69. [CrossRef]
27. Cui, R.; Yang, C.; Li, Y.; Sharma, S. Adaptive Neural Network Control of AUVs With Control Input Nonlinearities Using Reinforcement Learning. *IEEE Trans. Syst. Man Cybern. Syst.* **2017**, *47*, 1019–1029. [CrossRef]
28. Geranmehr, B.; Vafaee, K. Hybrid Adaptive Neural Network AUV Controller Design with Sliding Mode Robust Term. *IJMT* **2017**, *72*, 49–55. [CrossRef]
29. Alvarado, R.H.; Valdovinos, L.G.G.; Jiménez, T.S.; Espinosa, A.G.; Navarro, F.F. Neural Network-Based Self-Tuning PID Control for Underwater Vehicles. *Sensors* **2016**, *16*, 1429. [CrossRef]
30. Huang, H.; Zhang, G.; Qing, H.; Zhou, Z. Autonomous underwater vehicle precise motion control for target following with model uncertainty. *Int. J. Adv. Robot. Syst.* **2017**, *14*, 1729881417719808.
31. Xiang, X.; Yu, C.; Zhang, Q. Robust fuzzy 3D path following for autonomous underwater vehicle subject to uncertainties. *Comput. Oper. Res.* **2017**, *84*, 165–177. [CrossRef]
32. Jin, P.; Wang, B.; Li, L.; Chao, P.; Xie, F. Semi-supervised underwater acoustic source localization based on residual convolutional auto encoder. *EURASIP J. Adv. Signal Process.* **2022**, *2022*, 107. [CrossRef]
33. Ma, H.; Mu, X.; He, B. Adaptive Navigation Algorithm with Deep Learning for Autonomous Underwater Vehicle. *Sensors* **2021**, *21*, 6406. [CrossRef]
34. Wu, H.; Song, S.; You, K.; Wu, C. Depth control of model-free AUVs via reinforcement learning. *IEEE Trans. Syst. Man Cybern. Syst.* **2018**, *49*, 2499–2510. [CrossRef]
35. Duan, K.; Fong, S.; Chen, C.P. 2022. Reinforcement learning based model-free optimized trajectory tracking strategy design for an AUV. *Neurocomputing* **2022**, *469*, 289–297. [CrossRef]

36. Parhi, D.R.; Kundu, S. Reactive Navigation of Underwater Mobile Robot Using ANFIS Approach in a Manifold Manner. *Int. J. Autom. Comput.* **2017**, *14*, 307–320.
37. Nayak, N.; Das, P.; Das, S.R. Heading plane control of an autonomous underwater vehicle: A novel fuzzy and model reference adaptive control approach. In Proceedings of the 2020 Third International Conference on Advances in Electronics, Computers and Communications (ICAECC), Bengaluru, India, 11–12 December 2020; pp. 1–5.

Disclaimer/Publisher's Note: The statements, opinions and data contained in all publications are solely those of the individual author(s) and contributor(s) and not of MDPI and/or the editor(s). MDPI and/or the editor(s) disclaim responsibility for any injury to people or property resulting from any ideas, methods, instructions or products referred to in the content.

Article

Feature Selection Using Golden Jackal Optimization for Software Fault Prediction

Himansu Das [1,*], Sanjay Prajapati [1], Mahendra Kumar Gourisaria [1], Radha Mohan Pattanayak [2], Abdalla Alameen [3] and Manjur Kolhar [4]

1. School of Computer Engineering, KIIT Deemed to be University, Bhubaneswar 751024, Odisha, India; mkgourisariafcs@kiit.ac.in (M.K.G.)
2. School of Computer Science & Engineering, VIT-AP University, Amaravati 522237, Andhra Pradesh, India
3. Computer Science Department, Prince Sattam Bin Abdulaziz University, Al-Kharj 16278, Saudi Arabia
4. Department of Computer Science, College of Arts and Science, Prince Sattam Bin Abdulaziz University, Al-Kharj 16278, Saudi Arabia
* Correspondence: himanshufcs@kiit.ac.in

Abstract: A program's bug, fault, or mistake that results in unintended results is known as a software defect or fault. Software flaws are programming errors due to mistakes in the requirements, architecture, or source code. Finding and fixing bugs as soon as they arise is a crucial goal of software development that can be achieved in various ways. So, selecting a handful of optimal subsets of features from any dataset is a prime approach. Indirectly, the classification performance can be improved through the selection of features. A novel approach to feature selection (FS) has been developed, which incorporates the Golden Jackal Optimization (GJO) algorithm, a meta-heuristic optimization technique that draws on the hunting tactics of golden jackals. Combining this algorithm with four classifiers, namely K-Nearest Neighbor, Decision Tree, Quadrative Discriminant Analysis, and Naive Bayes, will aid in selecting a subset of relevant features from software fault prediction datasets. To evaluate the accuracy of this algorithm, we will compare its performance with other feature selection methods such as FSDE (Differential Evolution), FSPSO (Particle Swarm Optimization), FSGA (Genetic Algorithm), and FSACO (Ant Colony Optimization). The result that we got from FSGJO is great for almost all the cases. For many of the results, FSGJO has given higher classification accuracy. By utilizing the Friedman and Holm tests, to determine statistical significance, the suggested strategy has been verified and found to be superior to prior methods in selecting an optimal set of attributes.

Keywords: software fault prediction; software defect prediction; feature selection; classification algorithms; golden jackal optimization

MSC: 65D18; 65D19; 68M07

1. Introduction

Software's flaws can harm its reliability and quality, necessitating more maintenance and an effort to rectify it. While testing results can aid software development teams in detecting bugs, testing complete software modules is costly and time-consuming. The performance of various software development tasks by individuals can lead to the emergence of multiple software bugs over time, ultimately resulting in user dissatisfaction. Therefore, early identification of software flaws is one of the primary research areas of interest. Software fault prediction [1,2] is the process of spotting potential flaws or defects in software before they happen using data analysis and machine learning methods. This can aid developers in effectively identifying and resolving potential problems, producing software that is of higher quality and contains fewer flaws. There are several approaches to predicting software faults, such as statistical and machine learning methods [3,4]. These techniques involve analyzing data from past software projects to identify patterns and trends that may indicate potential faults. The data used for this analysis may include testing and debugging logs, source code, and other relevant information. Commonly utilized methods for predicting software faults include DT [5,6], SVM [7], Neural Networks [8], LR [9], and many more. These techniques involve analyzing data to identify patterns and trends indicating potential flaws or bugs. In addition to machine learning techniques, code analysis and testing are employed to predict software faults. These methods involve scrutinizing the software code for potential issues and performing various tests to detect and rectify bugs. Predicting software failures is a vital aspect of software development that can enhance the quality and reliability of software. By effectively identifying and resolving potential issues, developers can reduce the probability of bugs and improve the overall user experience.

In the field of machine learning, one of the critical tasks is Feature Selection (FS) [10,11]. The process entails determining the most significant features that can improve the precision of predictive models. Several methods are available for FS, each with advantages and limitations. We can say FS is a crucial stage in software fault prediction that aids in locating the most important predictors of software faults. Feature selection is required when the available dataset is extensive and includes many features or variables, making it challenging to analyze and interpret the findings accurately. The most crucial characteristics should be chosen to simplify the analysis and increase the precision of the software fault prediction model. For FS in software fault detection, various methods are employed. One of the methods used for FS is the filter method [12]. These methods employ statistical properties such as correlation with the target variable or variance to select features. Some examples of filter methods include chi-square [12] and ANOVA [12,13]. Wrapper methods [14], on the other hand, evaluate subsets of features by training and testing a predictive model on each subgroup. Recursive feature elimination [15] and forward/backward selection [16] are examples of wrapper methods. Embedded methods [17,18] combine feature selection with model training. Lasso [19] and ridge regression [20] are two examples of embedded methods used to identify the essential elements for prediction. The ridge penalty reduces the regression coefficient estimate, but not precisely to zero. For this reason, the incapability of ridge regression to perform variable selection has long been a source of criticism. As a result, penalized regression techniques like elastic-net, adaptive elastic-net, and adaptive-lasso are more beneficial for variable selection. Meanwhile, dimensionality reduction methods aim to reduce the number of features while retaining the most relevant information for prediction. Some examples of dimensionality reduction methods include Principal Component Analysis (PCA) [21] and t-SNE (neighbor encoding) [22]. It should be emphasized that the selection of the method depends on the specific problem at hand. Therefore, trying multiple ways and comparing their performance is often beneficial to select the best one for a specific situation. Feature selection plays a crucial role in software fault prediction by identifying the most significant variables or features that influence the likelihood of software faults.

Researchers have used many different types of FS algorithms. Evolutionary-based algorithms [23] and swarm-based algorithms [24] have been used for the feature selection approaches. This study's primary objective is to enhance classification accuracy while minimizing errors. The Genetic Algorithm (GA) [25] utilizes a computational technique that is guided by natural selection and genetic evolution in living organisms. This method involves utilizing a group of potential solutions, using genetic techniques such as selection, crossover, and mutation to create new possible solutions, and assessing their efficacy based on a specified function. Particle Swarm Optimization (PSO) [26,27] emulates the movement of a set of particles exploring a search space with multiple dimensions, where each particle embodies a prospective solution to the problem. Through continuous evaluation of each particle's fitness, the algorithm adjusts their position and velocity by considering individual and group experiences. Its ultimate goal is to find the most optimal solution. DE (Differential Evolution) [28] is an optimization algorithm that operates on a population of candidate solutions using a set of operators, including mutation, crossover, and selection, to converge toward the optimal solution. It uses a difference vector to create new solutions and iteratively improves them by comparing their fitness with the current population. Ant Colony Optimization (ACO) [29] is a metaheuristic optimization algorithm that simulates the foraging behavior of ants to find the optimal solution in a search space. The algorithm uses pheromone trails deposited by ants to guide the search toward the optimal solution. Any algorithm's performance depends on how the user sets its parameter values and utilizes them to find the answer, resulting in its output.

Generally, feature selection is a common task in machine learning. The goal is to identify the most relevant subset of features (i.e., input variables) that are most informative for a given prediction task. The process of feature selection involves an optimization problem that seeks to identify the ideal set of features that maximizes the performance of the model while minimizing its complexity. The objective of the paper is to apply effective FS methods to uncover a subset of features that produces a precise and easy-to-interpret model. The objective of feature selection is to improve the quality and usability of the machine learning model for real-world applications.

The main contribution here is it presents a new feature selection method called feature selection using Golden Jackal Optimization (FSGJO) [30]. Golden Jackal Optimization (GJO) in FS aids in identifying the appropriate set of features. GJO mimics the hunting behavior of golden jackals, known for their cooperative hunting strategy and ability to adapt to changing environments. The algorithm consists of a population of candidate solutions, called jackals, that move around the search space for the ideal solution. The advantage of GJO is its ability to handle complex, high-dimensional optimization problems with multiple objectives. GJO is less likely to get stuck in local optima, which can be a problem for other optimization algorithms because GJO uses a combination of exploratory and exploitative search strategies, which allows it to escape local optima and continue searching for better solutions. The efficacy of the newly developed algorithm has been evaluated against several other feature selection (FS) algorithms, including FSGA, FSDE, FSPSO, and FSACO. Thus, it will be an effective method for feature selection. The new algorithm FSGJO and other FS methods have been used on classification models such as KNN, DT, NB, and QDA to check which model is giving the best accuracy output. The results of the new algorithm were compared with other FS methods for their significance. Software developers can enhance the precision and efficiency of their software fault prediction models by carefully selecting the most appropriate features.

The arrangement of this paper is as follows: in Section 2, the literature on feature selection algorithms is explored, while Section 3 introduces the GJO algorithm, and Section 4 explains the FSGJO approach. Section 5 details the experimental results and analysis, followed by a statistical analysis in Section 6. Finally, the conclusion is presented in Section 7.

2. Literature Review

Software fault prediction methods involve analyzing software code, metrics, or historical data to detect possible faults that may occur during the development process or after the software has been released. These techniques can help developers proactively identify and fix potential defects before they become significant issues. After software development, software testing [31] is conducted to ensure that the software meets the defined requirements and to detect and resolve any defects or problems that may have been overlooked during the development phase. In summary, software fault prediction is typically performed during development, while software testing is performed after the software has been developed. Both techniques are essential for ensuring high-quality software meets user requirements. In software fault prediction (SFP), classification [32–37] is a commonly used technique to predict whether a particular module or component of software contains a fault or defect.

Sonali and Divya [38] introduced a model, known as the Linear Twin Support Vector Machine (LSTSVM), to predict defective software modules. The model incorporates feature selection techniques and was evaluated on four datasets—CM1, PC1, KC1, and KC2. The study reported encouraging outcomes on the latter three datasets. Turabieh et al., in 2019 [39], took a dataset from the Promise repository which was iteratively subjected to three wrapper feature selection (FS) algorithms—(BPSO), (BGA), and (BACO)—which were applied iteratively, and received results with an average of 0.8358 over all datasets. Ezgi and Selma [40] proposed a hybrid approach using an artificial bee colony and differential evolution, which helps to select a relevant set of features without reducing accuracy. Ibrahim et al. conducted a study in 2017 [41] where they utilized the BSA for feature selection and Random Forest as a classifier on PC1, PC2, PC3, and PC4, which resulted in practical outcomes. In the study [42], the authors employed PSO as a feature selection method and the bagging technique as a classifier. They used eleven classifiers and nine samples from the NASA repository. Except for SVM, their future work, all classifier performances improved after comparing the findings with their methodology. On some of the well-known NASA datasets, authors in [43] combined the Centroid Bat Approach (CBA-SVM) and Support Vector Machine (SVM) methods, contrasted the outcomes with those of other ways, and discovered that their strategy was producing promising results. The authors in [44] employed the bagging technique with the GA and PSO metaheuristic methods to enhance performance. They discovered that the results of the two algorithms were comparable, but the combination with bagging exhibited superior outcomes. Authors in [45] used four datasets, namely PC1, PC2, PC3, and PC4, and tested with a correlation-based feature selection technique with five classifiers. Finally, they found out that CFS with RF has the best performance. There are many different FS algorithms, such as the electric field algorithm [46], Jaya Algorithm [47], RHSFOS [48], FSBWO [49], and many more, that can be tested on the software fault prediction datasets. The author in [50] has done feature selection using the firefly algorithm with SVM, KNN, and NB classifiers achieving better classification accuracy with FS.

The FS approaches have various parameters that control the coming accuracy. So, tuning all those parameters is necessary, and for every problem, it will be different.

3. Summary of Golden Jackal Optimization Algorithm

The Golden Jackal Optimization (GJO) algorithm is a meta-heuristic optimization technique that draws ideas from the hunting pattern of golden jackals. This algorithm aims to emulate the hunting strategy of these opportunistic predators, known for their adaptability to diverse environments. By doing so, GJO seeks to solve optimization problems efficiently and effectively.

The primary stages of hunting for a golden jackal pair are outlined below:
1. Locating the prey and advancing towards it.
2. Trapping the prey and agitating it.
3. Attacking and capturing the prey.

Like other meta-heuristics, the GJO is a population-based technique that initiates with a randomized distribution of the first solution across the search space, as shown in Equation (1).

$$X_0 = X_{min} + rand * X_{max} - X_{min} \tag{1}$$

where X_{min} is lower bound, and X_{max} is upper bound, and $rand$ is a function whose value range between 0 to 1.

The initial matrix Prey (X_{prey}) is represented in Equation (2) which is generated during initialization, where the top two fittest members are a pair of jackals.

$$X_{prey} = \begin{bmatrix} X_{1,1} & X_{1,2} & \cdots & X_{1,q} \\ X_{2,1} & X_{2,2} & \cdots & X_{2,q} \\ \vdots & \vdots & \vdots & \vdots \\ X_{p,1} & X_{p,2} & \cdots & X_{p,q} \end{bmatrix} \tag{2}$$

As shown in Equation (2), it involves p preys and q variables. The position (location) of each prey represents the parameters of a particular solution. As part of the optimization procedure, a fitness function is utilized to assess the appropriateness of each prey. As described in Equation (3), the fitness values of all prey are gathered in a matrix, where the F matrix holds the fitness values of every prey. $X_{p,q}$ represents the value of the p_{th} dimension of the q_{th} prey. The optimization involves p preys, and the objective function is denoted by F. In the hunting patterns of golden jackals, the male jackal is considered the most suitable prey, followed by the female jackal as the second fittest. The positions of the prey are acquired by the jackal pair accordingly.

$$\begin{bmatrix} f(X_{1,1}; X_{1,2}; \cdots X_{1,q}) \\ f(X_{2,1}; X_{2,2}; \cdots X_{2,q}) \\ \vdots \\ f(X_{P,1}; X_{P,2}; \cdots X_{p,q}) \end{bmatrix} \qquad (3)$$

Due to their inherent nature, jackals are adept at identifying and pursuing prey, but at times the prey may prove elusive and manage to evade them. As a result, the jackals must resort to exploring alternative prey, and this is referred to as the exploration stage. The male jackal is responsible for leading the hunt, with the female jackal following in pursuit. The updated position of the male jackal is shown in Equations (4) and (5), where i corresponds to the current iteration. The prey's position vector is denoted by X_{prey}. X_{FM} represents the location of the female jackal, and X_M represents the location of the male jackal. The revised position of male jackal is symbolized as X_1, and the revised position of female jackal is symbolized as X_2 with respect to the prey. The energy the prey uses to evade is represented by e and is determined using Equation (6).

$$X_1 = X_M(i) - e|X_M(i) - s1 * X_{prey}(i)| \qquad (4)$$

$$X_2 = X_{FM}(i) - e|X_{FM}(i) - s1 * X_{prey}(i)| \qquad (5)$$

$$e = e_0 * e_1 \qquad (6)$$

where e_0 denotes the initial energy and e_1 indicates the decreasing energy of the prey.

$$e_0 = 2 * r - 1 \qquad (7)$$

$$e_1 = c_1 * \left(1 - \frac{i}{I}\right) \qquad (8)$$

The variable of Equations (7) and (8) includes r as a random integer whose value ranges between (0,1) and c_1 represents a constant value set at 1.5. The I signifies the max number of iterations and current iteration is denoted by i. Additionally, the value of e_1 is gradually reduced in a linear manner from 1.5 to 0 over the course of the iterations.

Equations (4) and (5) involve the calculation of the distance between the jackal and prey, represented as $X(i) - s1 * X_{prey}(i)$. Depending on the evading energy of the prey, this distance is either added or subtracted from the current position of the jackal. The two equations utilize a vector $s1$, which consists of a set of random numbers that adhere to the Levy distribution and signify the Levy movement. To simulate the movement of the prey in a Levy fashion, the equation multiplies the vector $s1$ with the Prey vector, as shown in Equation (9).

$$s1 = 0.05 * LF(x) \qquad (9)$$

The levy flight function, denoted by $LF(x)$, is computed in Equations (10) and (11), where v ranges between 0 to 1 and δ is generally set to 1.5.

$$LF(x) = \frac{0.05 * \sigma_u}{v^{\frac{1}{\delta}}} \tag{10}$$

$$\sigma_u = \left[\frac{\Gamma(1+\delta) * \sin\left(\frac{\pi\delta}{2}\right)}{\Gamma\left(\frac{1+\delta}{2}\right) * \delta * 2^{\frac{\delta-1}{2}}}\right]^{\frac{1}{\delta}} \tag{11}$$

Finally, the Equation (12) shows the updated positions of the jackals are obtained by averaging the results of Equations (4) and (5).

$$X(i+1) = \frac{X_1(i) + X_2(i)}{2} \tag{12}$$

In a mathematical model, the cooperative hunting behavior of a male jackal and female jackal is represented in Equations (13) and (14), respectively, where i denotes the current iteration, X_{prey} refers to the position vector of the prey, and $X_M(i)$ refers to the location of the male jackal, and $X_{FM}(i)$ refers to the location of female jackal. $X_1(i)$ represents the revised positions of the male jackal, and $X_2(i)$ represent the revised positions of female jackal with respect to the prey. The position updates of the jackals are determined by Equations (6) and (12), which are utilized to compute the evading energy of the prey. To avoid getting stuck in local optima and encourage exploration, Equations (13) and (14) incorporate the function $s1$. The use of Equation (9) to compute $s1$ is aimed at overcoming any sluggishness towards local optima, especially in the later iterations. This factor is akin to the obstacles that jackals face while pursuing prey in their natural habitat. During the exploitation stage, $s1$ serves the purpose of addressing these obstacles.

$$X_1(i) = X_M(i) - e|s1 * X_M(i) - X_{prey}(i)| \tag{13}$$

$$X_2(i) = X_{FM}(i) - e|s1 * X_{FM}(i) - X_{prey}(i)| \tag{14}$$

To sum up, the GJO algorithm starts by creating a random prey population as a potential solution. During each iteration of the algorithm, the jackals work together to anticipate the potential location of their prey. Every individual in the population adjusts the distance between the jackal pairs according to the specified criterion. The parameter e_1 is decreased from 1.5 to 0 over time to balance exploration and exploitation. If e exceeds 1, the golden jackal pairs move farther from the prey. In contrast, if e is less than 1, the teams move closer to the prey to increase the chances of capturing it.

4. Feature Selection Using Golden Jackal Optimization

Feature selection refers to picking a smaller relevant subset of predictor variables from a larger dataset, aiming to enhance the accuracy of machine learning models, decrease computational expenses, and reduce the chances of overfitting. Put differently, it is a method of determining the essential features with the highest impact on the target variable. Naturally, selecting parts for classification is difficult; therefore, FSGJO uses GJO optimization to select a relevant subset of features. Using FSGJO, there is an increase in classification accuracy. Below is an explanation of the various phases of FSGJO.

4.1. Initialization

GJO is a population-based approach, similar to various other metaheuristics; the search space is uniformly explored starting from an initial or first solution. The initial solution is shown in Equation (15), where X_{min} is lower bound, X_{max} is upper bound, and $rand()$ is a function whose value range between 0 to 1.

$$X_{initial} = X_{min} + rand() \cdot (X_{max} - X_{min}) \tag{15}$$

Suppose there are p preys and q variable; then, an individual can be represented as shown in Equation (16), where $1 \leq i \leq p$ is the index of each prey. However, the population of the prey is directly represented by a $p \times q$ matrix such that, $X_{prey} = (x_{ij})_{p \times q}$ as shown in Equation (17), where $i = 1, 2, 3, \ldots, p$, $j = 1, 2, 3, \ldots, q$, and a row represents an individual prey, and a column represents a dimension (variable). X_{prey} is the initial matrix of prey generated during initialization, where the top two fittest members are a pair of jackals (male jackal and female jackal, respectively).

$$X_i = x_{i1} + x_{i2} + x_{i3} + \cdots + x_{iq} \tag{16}$$

$$X_{prey} = X_{ij} = \begin{bmatrix} X_{1,1} & X_{1,2} & \cdots & X_{1,q} \\ X_{2,1} & X_{2,2} & \cdots & X_{2,q} \\ \vdots & \vdots & \vdots & \vdots \\ X_{p,1} & X_{p,2} & \cdots & X_{p,q} \end{bmatrix} \tag{17}$$

The optimization process involves p preys and q variables. The position of each prey represents the parameters of a particular solution. In order to assess the performance of each candidate solution during the optimization process, a fitness function (also known as objective function) is utilized, and the output values of this function for all solutions are stored in a matrix as shown in Equation (18), where, $i = 1, 2, 3, \ldots, p$, $j = 1, 2, 3, \ldots, q$, and fitness values of each prey are stored in a matrix called F_{ij}, where the notation $X_{p,q}$ refers the value of the p_{th} prey on the q_{th} dimension. The optimization involves p preys, and the objective function is denoted by F_{ij}. The male and female jackals acquire the positions of the fittest and second fittest prey, respectively, and these are known as the male jackal and female jackal prey positions.

$$F_{ij} = \begin{bmatrix} f(X_{1,1}; X_{1,2}; \cdots X_{1,q}) \\ f(X_{2,1}; X_{2,2}; \cdots X_{2,q}) \\ \vdots \\ f(X_{P,1}; X_{P,2}; \cdots X_{p,q}) \end{bmatrix} \tag{18}$$

4.2. Exploration Phase

In GJO, exploration is achieved by simulating the movement of a golden jackal pack searching for food in an unknown territory. Each jackal (solution) moves randomly within a specific range to explore the search space. This behavior helps prevent the algorithm from being trapped in local optima and facilitates discovering new solutions. Although, occasionally, the prey cannot be easily grabbed and manages to escape, it is in the nature of the jackal to be able to perceive and track it. Thus, if the prey is not easily caught, the jackals enter the exploration stage, searching for other potential targets. During hunting, the female jackal follows behind while the male jackal takes the lead. The updated position of male jackal is shown in Equations (19) and (20), where variable X_{prey} refers to the location vector of the prey, X_M is the location of the male jackal, and X_{FM} is the location of the female jackal. Variable i represents the current iteration. X_a is the revised positions of the male jackal (X_M), and X_b indicates the revised positions of the female jackal (X_{FM}) in relation to prey. The calculation of the prey's evading energy, E_p, involves Equation (21), wherein the initial energy of the prey can be represented by E_{p0}, while E_{p1} signifies the reduction of its energy.

$$X_a = X_M(i) - E_p |X_M(i) - s1 * X_{prey}(i)| \tag{19}$$

$$X_b = X_{FM}(i) - E_p |X_{FM}(i) - s1 * X_{prey}(i)| \qquad (20)$$

$$E_p = E_{p0} * E_{p1} \qquad (21)$$

E_{p0} is calculated using Equation (22), and E_{p1} is calculated using Equation (23), where r, that is a random number between 0 and 1, as well as a constant value denoted as c_1 that is equal to 1.5. Additionally, the maximum number of iterations is represented by I, while i indicates the current iteration number. The decreasing energy of the prey is denoted by the variable E_{p1}. During the iterative process, this value decreases linearly from 1.5 to 0, indicating the gradual depletion of the prey's energy.

$$E_{p0} = 2 * r - 1 \qquad (22)$$

$$E_{p1} = c_1 * \left(1 - \frac{i}{I}\right) \qquad (23)$$

Equations (19) and (20) are used to calculate the distance between the jackal and its prey as $X(i) - s1 * X_{prey}(i)$. The energy level of the prey controls the jackal's movement, which shifts its location either higher or lower depending on how far it is from the prey. The vector $s1$ employed in Equations (19) and (20) is a series of random numbers that complies with the Levy distribution, which is a specific type of probability distribution. This distribution is utilized to emulate the Levy movement, and it is multiplied by the Prey vector to determine the movement of the prey in a Levy fashion. The calculation of $s1$ shown in Equation (24).

$$s1 = 0.05 * LF(x) \qquad (24)$$

The Levy Flight function (LF) is a mathematical function that simulates random movements in a search space. It is commonly used in optimization algorithms as it is used here. The process involves generating random numbers from the Levy distribution and using them to update the position of the search agent. The Levy distribution is a probability distribution with heavy tails, allowing for occasional large movements. This property is helpful in optimization because it enables search agents to explore distant areas of the search space that would be difficult to reach with small, incremental movements. LF can be calculated using Equation (25), where u, v u, v are a normal distribution function with a standard deviation of σ_u and σ_v such that $u = normal(0, \sigma_u^2)$ and $v = normal(0, \sigma_v^2)$. σ_u is calculated using the Equation (26).

$$LF(x) = \frac{0.05 * u}{v^{\frac{1}{\delta}}} \qquad (25)$$

$$\sigma_u = \left[\frac{(1+\delta) * \sin\left(\frac{\pi \delta}{2}\right)}{\frac{1+\delta}{2} * \delta * 2^{\frac{\delta-1}{2}}}\right]^{\frac{1}{\delta}} \qquad (26)$$

Equation (27) illustrates the position update of the male jackal and female jackal, which involves the averages Equations (19) and (20).

$$X(i+1) = \frac{X_a(i) + X_b(i)}{2} \qquad (27)$$

4.3. Exploitation Phase

The simulation imitates the hunting behaviors of a dominant male golden jackal that takes the lead and guides the pack towards the food source to exploit the prey. The harassment of the prey by the jackals gradually reduces its ability to evade, enabling the male and female jackal pair to surround the prey discovered earlier. After being contained, the jackals pounce on their target and devour it. In a mathematical model, the cooperative hunting behavior of jackals is represented in Equations (28) and (29), where i indicates the current iteration of the simulation. X_{prey} is the location vector of the prey, while $X_M(i)$ represents the location of the male jackal and $X_{FM}(i)$ represents the location of female jackal. $X_a(i)$ represents the revised location of the male jackal, and $X_b(i)$ represents the revised positions of the female jackal with respect to the prey. Equation (21) is employed to compute the evading energy of the prey, denoted as E_p. Equation (27) is then utilized to revise the positions of the jackals. In the exploitation phase, the function $s1$ is utilized in Equations (28) and (29) to promote exploration and prevent the algorithm from becoming trapped in local optima. Equation (24) is used to calculate $s1$, which helps to overcome sluggishness towards local optima, particularly in the final iterations. This element represents obstacles that hinder the jackals from moving towards the prey, such as those encountered in natural chasing paths. The function of $s1$ during the exploitation stage is to address these obstacles and facilitate the jackals' movement towards the prey.

$$X_a(i) = X_M(i) - E_p \big| s1 * X_M(i) - X_{prey}(i) \big| \tag{28}$$

$$X_b(i) = X_{FM}(i) - E_p \big| s1 * X_{FM}(i) - X_{prey}(i) \big| \tag{29}$$

4.4. Fitness and Transfer Function

Before computing fitness and updating it, the continuous values of the position matrix (X_{prey}) are converted into binary values using a transfer function. A sigmoid transfer function is used in this study, as shown in Equation (30). The reason for using this S-shaped transfer function is that it allows for a smooth and continuous transition from real-valued positions to binary values, which can help to avoid premature convergence and improve the search performance of the optimization algorithm.

$$TF = \frac{1}{1 + e^{-X}} \tag{30}$$

In this equation, X represents the position value in the position matrix (X_{prey}) before being converted to binary. The sigmoid function maps the continuous value of X to a value having 0 and 1, which can then be used to determine the corresponding binary value. The purpose of this conversion is to ensure that the position values are binary and can be used to calculate the fitness value of the prey.

The fitness in this context refers to the prediction error of a machine learning (ML) classifier. It is determined by comparing the actual output of the classifier with its estimated output. To train the classifier, a 0.2 data split size is used, meaning that 20% of the data is held out for testing while the remaining 80% is used for training. The fitness is calculated using the Equation (31), where k is a value that ranges from 1 to m (the number of testing observations) and $Err(k)$ is the prediction error for the kth observation. The summation is divided by m to obtain an average prediction error.

$$fitness = \sum_{i=1}^{m} \frac{Err(k)}{m} \tag{31}$$

The algorithm maintains two variables for the updating of fitness; the variables *MaleJackalscore* and *FemaleJackalscore* represent the fitness scores of the best male and female jackals found so far during the optimization process. *fitness* can be assumed as old fitness; *MaleJackalscore* and *FemaleJackalscore* can be assumed as new fitness. If the *fitness* of a jackal is lower than the current *MaleJackalscore*, it means that the jackal has a better *fitness* than the current male jackal, and thus, its position and score will replace the current male jackal's position and score. On the other hand, if the *fitness* of a jackal is higher than the *MaleJackalscore* but lower than the *FemaleJackalscore*, it means that the jackal has a better fitness than the current female jackal, but not better than the male jackal.

In this case, its position and score will replace the current female jackal's position and score. After the fitness calculation, the fitness stored as shown in Equation (32), where the fitness array is denoted as f_i, which consists of p elements $f_1, f_2, f_3, \ldots, f_p$.

$$f_i = (f_1, f_2, f_3, \ldots, f_p) \tag{32}$$

In each iteration of the algorithm, a random value between -1 and 1 is assigned to the initial energy E_{p0}. The value of E_{p0} is an indicator of the prey's physical strength, where a decrease from 0 to -1 indicates a decline in the prey's strength. An elevation from 0 to 1 denotes a boost in the prey's strength, whereas a decrease in E_p is observed during the iterative process, as shown in Figure 1. If the magnitude of E_p is greater than 1, it means that the jackal pairs are searching for prey in different areas, which suggests that the algorithm is in an exploration phase. On the other hand, if the magnitude of E_p is less than 1, the algorithm switches to an exploitation phase and starts attacking the prey (Algorithms 1).

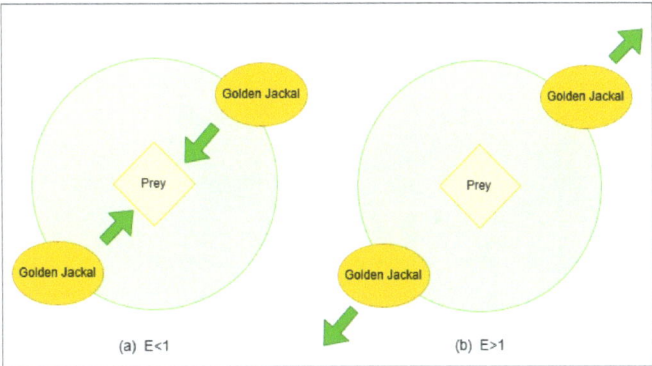

Figure 1. Searching and Attacking.

Algorithms 1 FSGJO

1. Initialize prey population randomly, $X_i = (i = 1, 2, \ldots, P)$
2. while ($i < I$)
3.   Let, Male Jackal Position be X_a
4.   Let, Female Jackal Position be X_b
5.   Determine the preys' fitness value
6.   if ($fitness < MaleJackalscore$)
7. $MaleJackalscore = fitness$
8.   if ($fitness > MaleJackalscore$ and $fitness < FemaleJackalscore$)
9. $FemaleJackalscore = fitness$
10.   for (each prey)
11.   Using Equations (21)–(23) update the evading energy E_p)
12.   Using Equations (24) and (25) Update $s1$
13.   if ($E \geq 1$) (Exploration phase)
14.   Using Equations (19), (20) and (27) Update the prey position
15.   if ($E < 1$) (Exploration phase)
16.   Using Equations (27)–(29) Update the prey position
17.   Update Jackal Position, $X(i) = \frac{X_a + X_b}{2}$
18.   Using transfer function to convert continuous values of X_i i.e., position, in binary values using Equation (30)
19.   end for
20. $i++$
21. end while
22. Return Male Jackal Position X_a

The FSGJO algorithm is an optimization algorithm in metaheuristic form that works on the hunting pattern of golden jackals. After randomly initializing a population of prey, the algorithm proceeds to search for the ideal solution through a series of iterations. The algorithm employs the idea of jackals, wherein the male jackal denotes the best solution found thus far, while the female jackal represents the second-best solution. The algorithm updates the position and evading energy of each prey based on certain equations and then performs an exploration or exploitation phase depending on the value of the evading energy. The algorithm updates the jackal position by taking the average of the male and female positions. Then it converts the continuous values of the prey positions into binary values using a transfer function. The algorithm continues for a specified repetitions and returns the male jackal position, representing the best solution found by the algorithm. The detailed explanation of FSGJO algorithm is presented in Algorithms 1. A flowchart depicting it is shown in Figure 2.

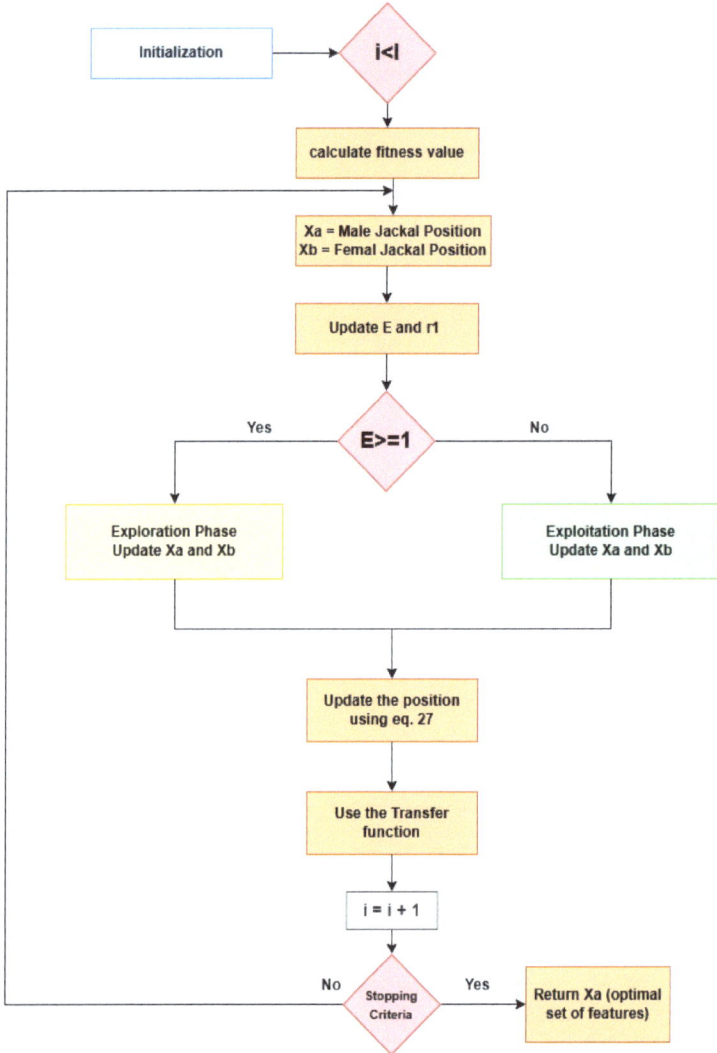

Figure 2. Flowchart for FSGJO.

5. Results

This section provides information on the datasets utilized in the experiment, the experimental setup, and the analysis of the obtained results.

5.1. Datasets

Most of these datasets are publicly available and have been used in various software engineering and machine learning research studies. Some of these are commonly used benchmark datasets, and their sources can be found in multiple academic publications or online repositories. The PROMISE repository provides a collection of datasets for various software engineering tasks, including software fault prediction. These datasets are primarily meant for research purposes and are frequently employed to assess the efficacy of different software fault prediction models. The datasets in the PROMISE repository are sourced from various software projects and programming languages. Each dataset usually contains additional metrics and features that characterize the analyzed software, along with details on the occurrence or non-occurrence of faults in the software. Some examples of the metrics and features that are in these datasets are:

- LOC (Lines of Code): This metric measures the number of lines of code in the software being analyzed.
- Cyclomatic Complexity: This metric measures the complexity of the software's control flow and can help identify potential trouble spots.
- Code Churn: This metric measures the software's change over time and can help identify modules or components that may be more prone to faults.
- Code Coverage: This metric measures the extent to which the software's code has been tested and can help identify code areas that may be more likely to contain faults.
- Halstead's Complexity Measures: These metrics measure various aspects of the complexity of the software's code, such as the number of distinct operators and operands, and can help identify potential trouble spots.

Each dataset in the PROMISE repository typically includes a description of the software project, as well as information on the available metrics and features. The datasets may also include information about the presence or absence of faults in the software, such as the number of bugs that were discovered during testing or the number of incidents that were reported by users. Researchers can use these datasets to train and test different software fault prediction models. To assess the efficacy of diverse software fault prediction approaches and discover scopes for further enhancement, researchers can analyze the performance of various models on a common dataset. Here, 12 datasets from the PROMISE repository by NASA have been used. The datasets are KC1, PC5, MC1, JM1, PC1, MW1, PC2, KC3, PC4, CM1, and MC2. Table 1 provides the specifics of the datasets.

Table 1. Detail of the datasets.

S. No.	Datasets	Number of Instances	Number of Features
1	MC1	1988	39
2	MC2	125	40
3	MW1	253	38
4	PC1	705	38
5	PC2	745	37
6	PC3	1077	38
7	PC4	1287	38
8	PC5	1711	39
9	CM1	327	38
10	KC1	1183	22
11	KC3	194	40
12	CM1	327	38

In dimensionality reduction, there are some issues with the dataset such as correlation and collinearity. Correlation is a statistical measure that describes the strength and direction of a relationship between two variables. Correlation can be used to explore the relationship between any two quantitative variables. Feature selection can be used to deal with the correlation problem in data analysis and modeling. Feature selection is a technique that aims to select a subset of the most important features from a set of features in a dataset. By selecting only the most important features, we can reduce the impact of correlated variables and improve the performance of our models. The algorithms such as FSGE, FSPSO, FSDE, and FSACO and the proposed FSGJO algorithm used in the manuscript can effectively deal with correlation and other complex dependencies between features. Table 2 shows the correlation data for different datasets. It ranges from −1 to +1, where −1 indicates a perfect negative correlation (as one variable increases, the other decreases), +1 indicates a perfect positive correlation (as one variable increases, the other also increases), and 0 indicates no correlation between the variables.

Table 2. Correlation Data for different Datasets.

Sr. No.	Datasets	Avg Mean	Avg Min	Avg Std	Avg (25%)	Avg (50%)	Avg (75%)	Max
1	PC1	0.378607	−0.33978	0.333734	0.13995	0.472284	0.584182	1
2	PC2	0.406	−0.334	0.361	0.147	0.539	0.627	1
3	PC3	0.28585	−0.32153	0.299	0.122	0.287	0.449	1
4	PC4	0.28585	−0.3215	0.299	0.122	0.287	0.449	1
5	PC5	0.309287	−0.25837	0.318001	0.107005	0.337127	0.505981	1
6	JM1	0.523668	−0.26472	0.297546	0.434064	0.58751	0.695541	1
7	KC1	0.602172	−0.31984	0.311581	0.583292	0.694918	0.7534	1
8	KC3	0.401659	−0.49557	0.381206	0.125805	0.540514	0.642491	1
9	MW1	0.3446	−0.438	0.3462	0.0564	0.4107	0.5741	1
10	MC1	0.329962	−0.2981	0.34041	0.08559	0.42838	0.55244	1
11	MC2	0.422839	−0.36885	0.364055	0.262204	0.565452	0.643115	1
12	CM1	0.447366	−0.39526	0.34699	0.22507	0.57133	0.64822	1

For example, the first row of Table 2 shows the correlation data for the dataset named "PC1". The average correlation value for this dataset is 0.378607, indicating a moderate positive correlation between the variables. The minimum correlation value is −0.33978, indicating some negative correlation between the variables, and the maximum correlation value is 1, indicating a perfect positive correlation between the variables. The standard deviation of correlation values for this dataset is 0.333734, indicating that the correlation values vary widely in the dataset. The value in the max column is 1, which suggests that at least one pair of variables has a perfect correlation. Similarly, each row in the table shows the correlation data for a different dataset. The correlation values can help identify patterns in the data, such as strong positive or negative correlations, weak correlations, or no correlations. This information can be useful for statistical analysis, such as identifying which variables are most strongly related to each other, or for modeling, such as using the correlation data to make predictions or develop models. Overall, the correlation data in this table provides valuable information about the relationships between variables in different datasets, which can help researchers and analysts gain insights into the data and make informed decisions based on the results.

Collinearity is a problem that occurs when two or more features in a dataset are highly correlated. In the context of feature selection, collinearity can make it difficult to identify the most important features. This is because the coefficient estimates for all of the correlated features may be large, even if only one of the features is truly independent. There are a number of ways to deal with collinearity. One way is to use a correlation matrix to identify correlated features. The correlation matrix for dataset MC1 and JM1 is shown in Figures 3 and 4, respectively. Once you have identified correlated features, you can use feature selection to remove them from the dataset. There are a number of different feature selection methods available. Feature selection can be a useful tool for dealing with collinearity. By removing correlated features from the dataset, you can improve the stability of the coefficient estimates and the accuracy of the model, as we have used the different feature selection methods such as FSGA, FSPSO, FSDE, and FSACO and the newly proposed FSGJO which does the work efficiently.

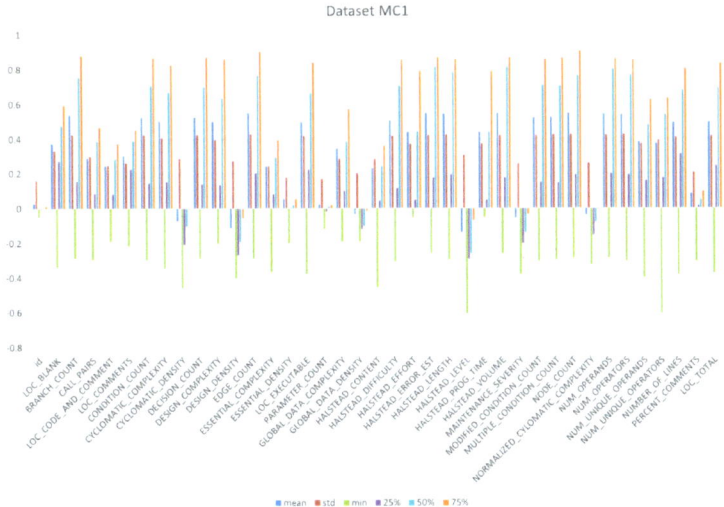

Figure 3. Correlation Matrix graph for MC1 Dataset.

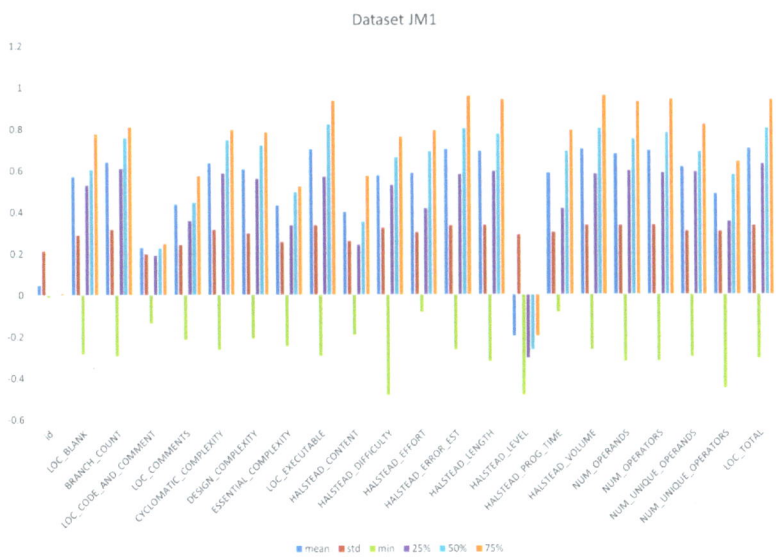

Figure 4. Correlation Matrix graph for JM1 Dataset.

5.2. Experimental Condition

In the context of the study, the trial was conducted using VS Code and the 3.9.12 version of Python. The laptop utilized for the experiment was equipped with an AMD Ryzen 75,000 series processor, a clock speed of 1.80 GHz, 16 GB of RAM, and AMD Radeon graphics. The parameters of the experiment such as β were set to 1.5; population size was set to 30, and the maximum iteration was set to 200.

5.3. Experimental Analysis

To predict software faults, 12 different datasets that were used are listed in Table 2. The classifiers employed for the experiments are DT, KNN, NB, and QDA. Then, randomly split the datasets into training and testing sets, maintaining a ratio of 80:20, respectively. To maintain the consistency of each algorithm's performance, we conducted 10 runs of the experiments. The average accuracy results obtained from FSGJO and the other FS models are presented in Table 3.

Table 3. Comparison between different FS Algorithms.

S. No.	Datasets	Classifier	Without FS (%)	FSGA (%)	FSPSO (%)	FSDE (%)	FSACO (%)	FSGJO (%)
1	PC1	KNN	89.36	93.67	90.08	93.4	93.71	94.42
		DT	88.66	95.01	92.05	95.02	93.79	95.03
		NB	87.32	91.12	89.56	90.46	92.26	92.67
		QDA	86.25	93.62	89.27	93.84	92.19	94.32
	No. of features selected		38	19.1	16.2	18.9	10.8	13
2	PC2	KNN	96.46	97.66	97.54	97.34	97.09	98.65
		DT	95.23	98.41	96.15	98.11	97.52	98.65
		NB	93.26	96.89	95.48	96.13	97.23	96.98
		QDA	97.23	98.85	97.83	97.83	98.21	97.98
	No. of features selected		37	14.7	15.2	17.1	10.7	11
3	PC3	KNN	82.14	86.43	84.67	85.39	86.17	87.03
		DT	78.07	86.93	82.19	86.73	84.34	87.03
		NB	68.89	86.58	80.38	86.18	87.8	87.3
		QDA	62.4	86.54	83.83	86.67	86.09	87.5
	No. of features selected		38	16.6	13.5	17.2	11.6	11.4
4	PC4	KNN	84.05	90.18	86.36	87.06	91.61	90.69
		DT	91.9	93.52	92.64	93.52	92.4	93.02
		NB	86.28	91.95	89.1	91.47	91.04	91.86
		QDA	47.76	91.28	86.89	92.84	91.28	93.41
	No. of features selected		38	17.6	14.4	18.6	14.2	14.6
5	PC5	KNN	67.6	75.36	71.8	75.36	76.58	78.42
		DT	72.95	77.37	73.35	77.18	75.61	77.84
		NB	70.45	71.75	70.28	71.64	72.91	72.99
		QDA	69.93	72.75	70.85	72.29	71.1	73.46
	No. of features selected		39	18.4	15.7	19.3	14.8	17
6	JM1	DT	73.53	77.81	75.6	76.63	79.62	78.16
		KNN	69.49	78.63	72.49	73.39	79.59	79.6
		NB	78.01	79.84	79.15	79.62	79.89	79.89
		QDA	75.85	79.71	79.04	79.82	79.78	79.82
	No. of features selected		22	4.9	8.9	10.3	3	6
7	KC1	KNN	69.26	76.46	76.46	76.33	77.59	78.05
		DT	72.51	77.6	73.21	76.3	76.48	77.79
		NB	74.62	77.32	76.21	77.32	77.47	77.63
		QDA	74.62	78.01	76.92	77.39	77.58	78.48

Table 3. Cont.

S. No.	Datasets	Classifier	Without FS (%)	FSGA (%)	FSPSO (%)	FSDE (%)	FSACO (%)	FSGJO (%)
	No. of features selected		22	8.2	8.3	9.4	4.5	8
8	KC3	KNN	74.63	79.89	76.51	79.32	86.29	82.05
		DT	76.29	89.54	81.3	87.96	85.31	89.74
		NB	66.76	76.29	71.45	76.51	79.39	76.92
		QDA	76.29	86.29	79.47	87.96	86.15	89.74
	No. of features selected		40	17.7	16.9	18.8	8.9	16.6
9	CM1	KNN	75.67	86.28	83.43	85.03	87.24	89.39
		DT	80.03	89.07	83.28	88.49	87.37	89.39
		NB	77.37	83.34	81.97	83.28	84.45	84.46
		QDA	83.21	88.84	83.79	88.84	88.81	90.9
	No. of features selected		38	18.2	14.5	17.8	12.1	15.8
10	MC1	KNN	96.37	97.63	97.46	97.48	98.10	97.73
		DT	97.64	98.47	98.39	98.57	98.24	98.74
		NB	95.64	97.61	96.21	97.62	97.64	97.73
		QDA	97.39	97.64	97.39	97.64	97.64	97.73
	No. of features selected		39	19.2	12.4	19.2	13.4	13.2
11	MC2	KNN	75	87.46	79	85.12	89.12	92
		DT	68	90.78	75.21	89.26	85	89.26
		NB	93	95.56	92.71	93.12	95	96
		QDA	83	95.12	88.34	95.12	95.12	96
	No. of features selected		40	18.4	17.2	18.4	7.2	8
12	MW1	KNN	78.34	87.35	84.61	85.56	86.57	88.27
		DT	74.41	87.74	82.64	87.15	85.19	85.29
		NB	76.37	83.42	78.78	82.25	87.16	88.27
		QDA	80.49	88.52	84.21	86.56	90.29	92.14
	No. of features selected		38	13.5	12.9	17.2	8.7	7.8

The performance of the novel FSGJO algorithm is evaluated against various FS techniques, including FSPSO, FSGA, FSACO, and FSDE, using a set of 12 datasets obtained from NASA's open repository. Table 3 provides the performance comparison of various feature selection techniques on different datasets using different classifiers. The table represents the average classification accuracy of various classifiers applied to different datasets with and without feature selection. In addition, the table also presents the mean number of features chosen by each FS technique. The classifiers were tested on various datasets using diverse feature selection methods mentioned previously. From the results, FSGJO has performed well in most of the datasets except for a few of the datasets. For the PC4 dataset, the highest accuracy has been achieved by the FSGA model, but the difference between the accuracy of both the FSGJO and FSGA models is very minor. For the MC1 and MC2 datasets, the average accuracy of FSGA, FSDE, and FSPSO for the QDA classifier is the same. Similarly, for other datasets the accuracy of models is somewhat the same and somewhat different, less or more with each other. However, for the majority of the cases FSGJO has greater average accuracy.

The fitness error plot of the four classifiers—DT, KNN, NB, and QDA—is shown in Figures 5–8, respectively. It includes the error plots of each FS model—FSGA, FSPSO, FSDE, FSACO, and FSGJO. Each figure contains the plots for all the 12 datasets. From the error plot, it can be seen that for many times the plot for FSGJO is lower, but for some it coincides with other FS models, and for some it is above the other. In Figure 5 (DT classifier), the fitness plots of FSGA and FSGJO coincide with each other at 165 iterations in the PC3 dataset. It is similar for FSACO and FSGJO in the MW1 dataset after 145 iterations. In the KNN classifier, the coincidences of the error plot occur in CM1 and PC2 between

FSACO, FSDE, and FSGJO after 50 and 150 iterations, respectively. In the NB classifier, the coincidences of the error plot occur in the KC3 dataset between FSACO and FSDE, in the MC2 and MC1 dataset between FSACO and FSGJO, and in the PC3 dataset between FSACO and FSGJO for some number of iterations. Lastly, in the QDA classifier, the coincidences of the error plot occurred in MC1 datasets for all classifiers in the MC2 dataset between FSACO, FSDE, and FSGJO. For the rest of the other datasets and classifiers, the error plot of FSGJO is less than the others which shows that FSGJO performs better than the other models.

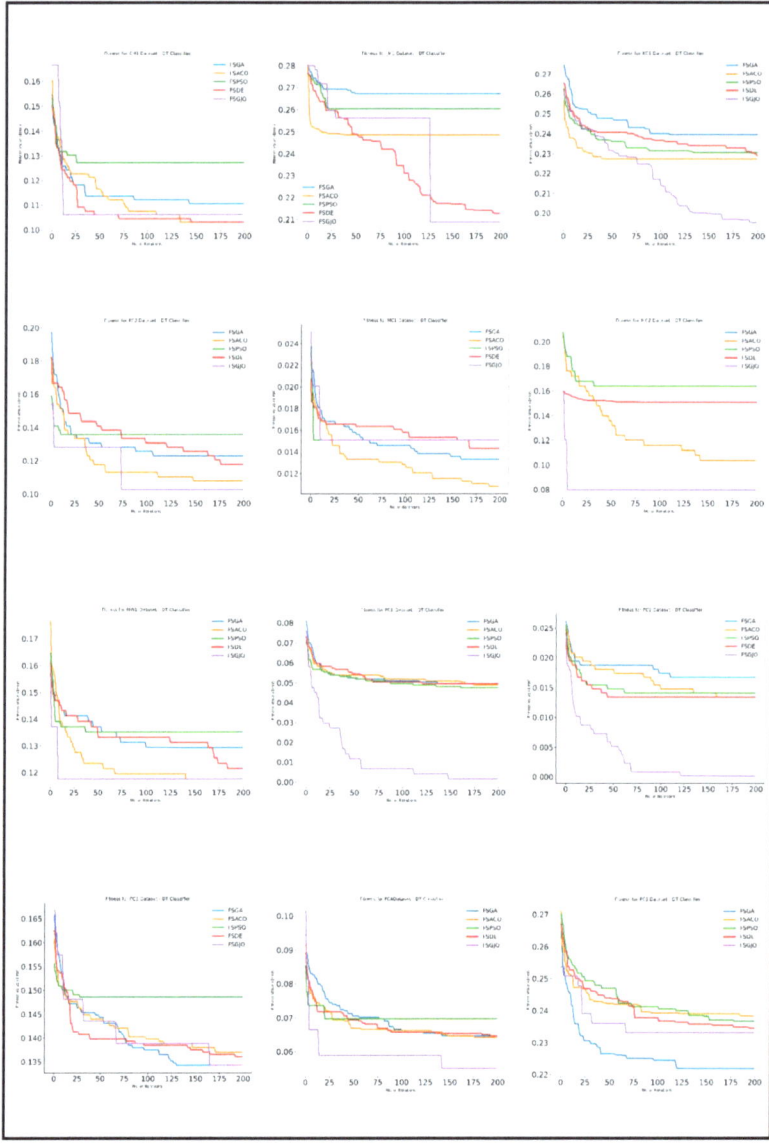

Figure 5. Fitness Error Plot for DT.

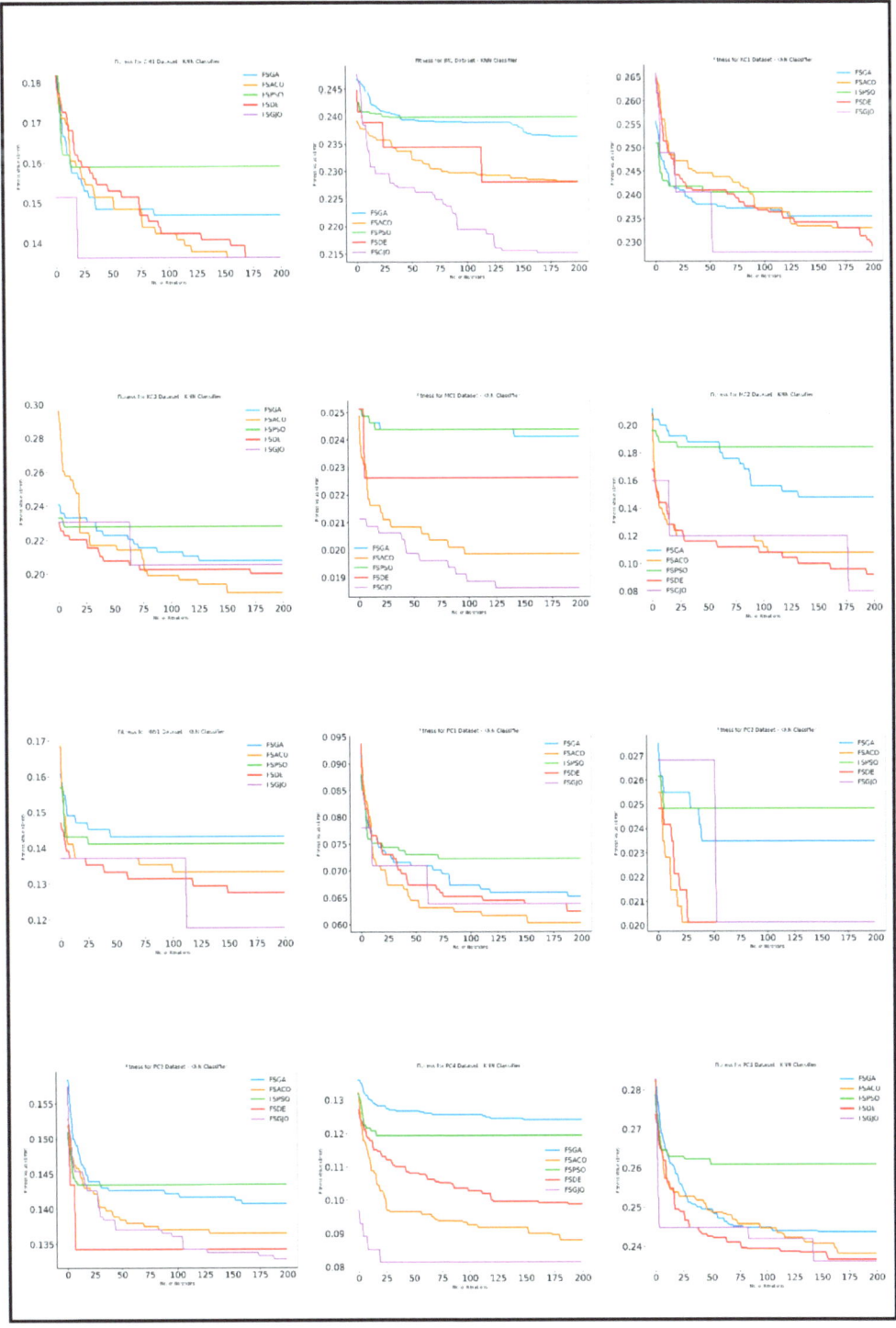

Figure 6. Fitness Error Plot for KNN.

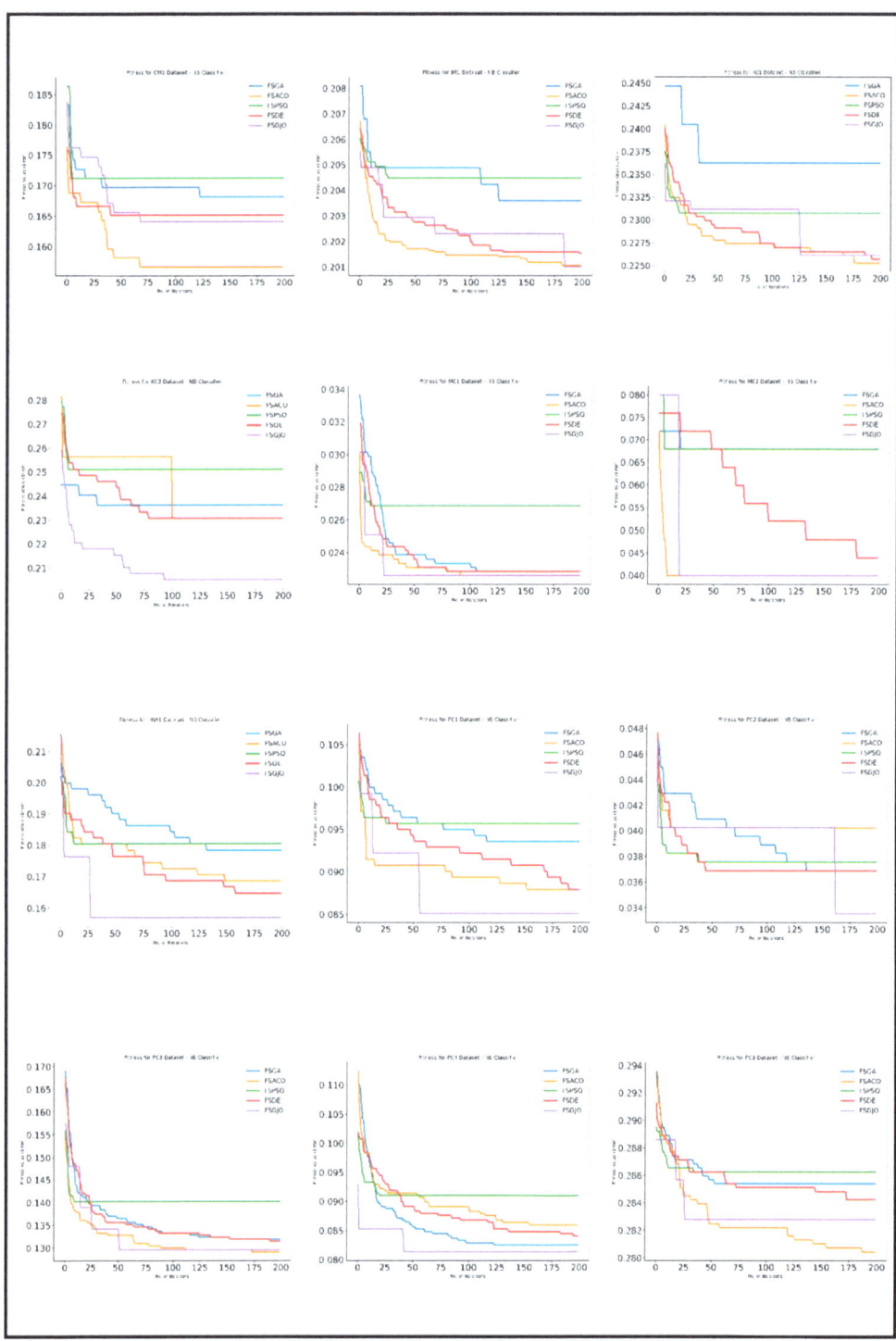

Figure 7. Fitness Error Plot for NB.

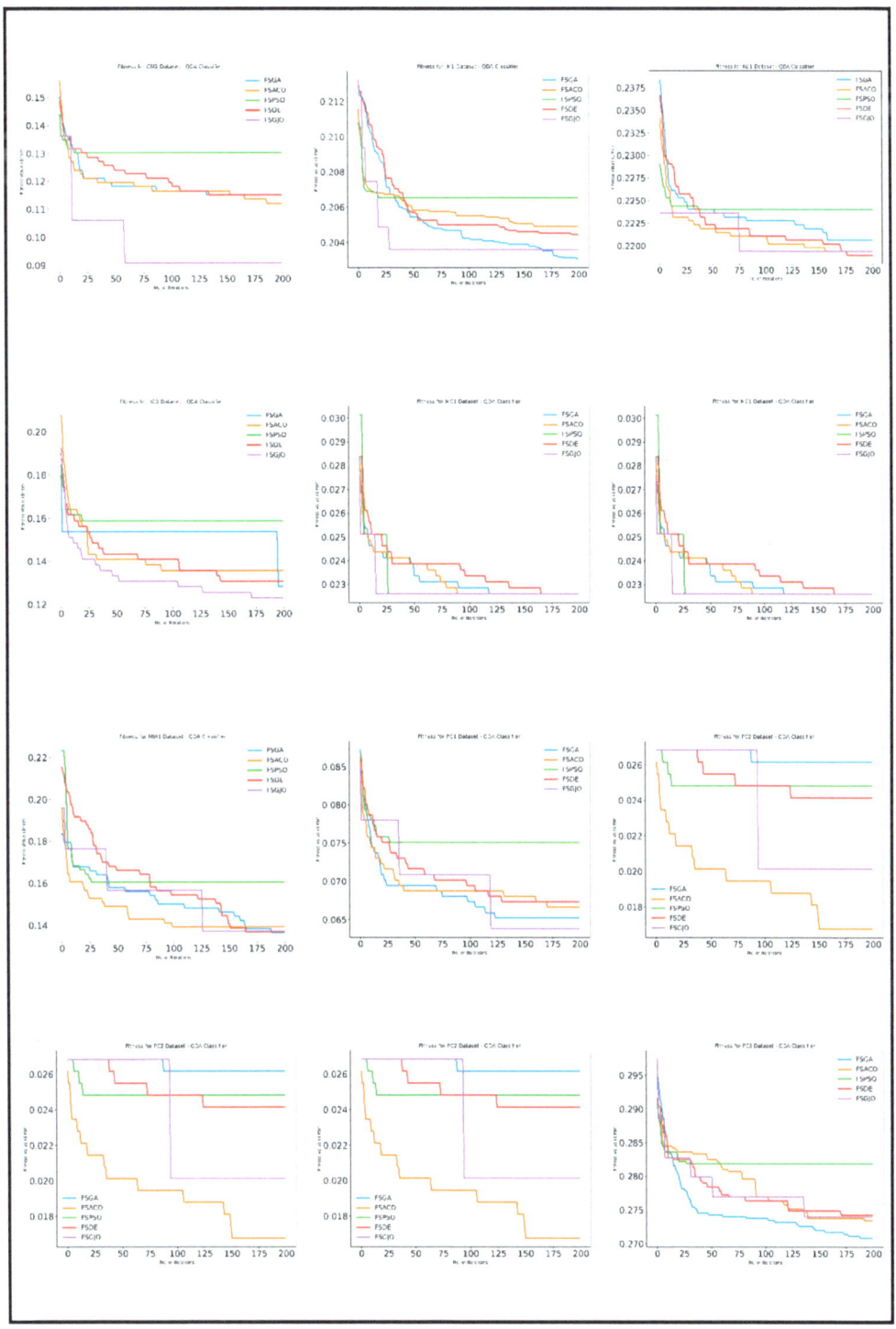

Figure 8. Fitness Error Plot for QDA.

The parameters utilized in various FS models are listed in Table 4. The algorithms utilized in the study employ different parameters. The number of populations is set to 30 for all models, and the max number of iterations is 200. The value of δ is 1.5 in GJO. To specify the parameters for ACO, the values of alpha, beta, and rho are set to 1, 0.1, and 0.2, respectively. In GA, the mutation rate (MR) utilized is 0.01, and the crossover rate (CR) is 0.8. The utilization of 0.9 as the crossover rate (CR) and 0.8 as the scaling factor (SF) is common in Differential Evolution (DE). The initial weights W_{min} and W_{max} in PSO are set to 0.4 and 0.9, respectively.

Table 4. Parameters used in different FS models.

Parameters	GA	PSO	DE	ACO	GJO
No. of iterations	200	200	200	200	200
Population Size	30	30	30	30	30
W_{max}	-	0.9	-	-	-
W_{min}	-	0.4	-	-	-
SF	-	-	0.8	-	-
c1	-	2	-	-	-
CR	0.8	-	0.9	-	-
MR	0.01	-	-	-	-
c2	-	2	-	-	-
α (alpha)	-	-	-	1	-
β (beta)	-	-	-	0.1	-
ρ (rho)	-	-	-	0.2	-
δ	-	-	-	-	1.5

6. Statistical Analysis

Statistical analysis [51] is an important component of machine learning (ML), as it helps to make sense of data by identifying patterns and relationships. By using the same parameters, the proposed model can be compared with other models in terms of their performance. Some common statistical techniques used in ML include regression analysis, cluster analysis, principal component analysis (PCA), hypothesis testing, and Bayesian analysis. Overall, statistical analysis is an essential tool for understanding and making sense of data in machine learning. In statistical hypothesis testing, there are two main types of tests: parametric (using parameters) and nonparametric (using a hypothesis). Parametric statistical testing is a type of statistical analysis that assumes that the data being analyzed follows a particular probability distribution, most commonly the normal distribution. This assumption allows for the use of a range of statistical tests that are more powerful than their non-parametric counterparts. The use of parametric tests requires that several assumptions are met, including the assumptions of normality, homogeneity of variance, and independence of observations. When conducting a parametric test, it is crucial to ensure that the assumptions are met, as any violations of these assumptions can lead to inaccurate outcomes and conclusions that are not valid. Therefore, it is imperative to verify these assumptions beforehand and to consider utilizing non-parametric tests if they are not met. Non-parametric statistical testing is a form of statistical analysis that does not rely on a particular probability distribution assumption for the data being analyzed. Instead, non-parametric tests are based on the ranks or orderings of the data, making them more robust to violations of assumptions and more widely applicable than parametric tests. Non-parametric tests do not require assumptions of normality, homogeneity of variance, or independence of observations, making them more versatile than parametric tests. However, they may be less powerful than parametric tests when the assumptions of the parametric tests are met. Selecting an appropriate statistical test that is tailored to the research question and the characteristics of the data being analyzed is crucial. Here, the Friedman test has been used, which is a non-parametric statistical test that is used to compare three or more related groups.

The Friedman test is utilized to determine if there are any noteworthy disparities between groups by comparing their average ranks. The test's null hypothesis suggests that there are no differences between the groups, while the alternative hypothesis proposes that at least one group displays a significant difference from the others. The test statistic used in the Friedman test is based on the chi-squared distribution, and the significance level is determined using the appropriate critical values from the chi-squared distribution table. In cases where the computed test statistic is higher than the critical value, the null hypothesis is refuted, signifying a significant distinction between the groups. One important consideration when using the Friedman test is that it is an omnibus test, meaning that it only determines whether there is a significant difference between the groups as a whole. Additional tests, such as post hoc analyses, may be necessary to identify the particular groups that exhibit significant differences from one another.

In hypothesis testing, the null hypothesis (H_0) postulates that there is no significant disparity between the models, whereas the alternative hypothesis (H_1) proposes the contrary. When the p-value is less than the significance level, it means there is a difference between two or more models, and we can reject the null hypothesis. The Friedman test assigns a rank to each model based on its classification performance in the experiment. The models are ranked from the one with the lowest number to the one with the highest number, with the highest rank assigned to the one with the lowest number and the lowest rank assigned to the one with the highest number. Table 5 presents the results of evaluating various models (FSACO, FSDE, FSGA, FSGJO, FSPSO, and Without FS) with different classifiers (KNN, DT, NB, and QDA), showing the $AvgRankModels$ calculated with Equation (33). Table 5 presents the $AvgRankDatasets$ obtained by evaluating the mean of all ranks for each associated model (Without FS, FSGA, FSPSO, FSDE, FSACO, and FSGJO) across all datasets using Equation (34). The computation of $AvgRankDatasets$ involves adding up the ranks of all classification models used and dividing the sum by the total number of models. In Table 6, we report the average ranks of the feature selection (FS) models employed in our experiment. To calculate the average rank performance of a group of models and datasets, add up the mean rank of each one and divide by the total number of models.

$$AvgRankModels = \frac{total\ sum\ of\ rank\ of\ different\ classifiers}{total\ no.\ of\ classifiers} \tag{33}$$

$$AvgRankDatasets = \frac{AvgRankModels}{total\ no.\ of\ datasets} \tag{34}$$

Table 5. FS Algorithm ranks for 12 datasets using the Friedman Test.

S. No.	Datasets	Classifier	Without FS (%)	FSGA (%)	FSPSO (%)	FSDE (%)	FSACO (%)	FSGJO (%)
1	PC1	KNN	89.36 (6)	93.67 (3)	90.08 (5)	93.4 (4)	93.71 (2)	94.42 (1)
		DT	88.66 (6)	95.01 (3)	92.05 (5)	95.02 (2)	93.79 (4)	95.03 (1)
		NB	87.32 (6)	91.12 (3)	89.56 (5)	90.46 (4)	92.26 (2)	92.67 (1)
		QDA	86.25 (6)	93.62 (3)	89.27 (5)	93.84 (2)	92.19 (4)	94.32 (1)
	Avg. Rank of Models		6	3	5	3	3	1
2	PC2	KNN	96.46 (6)	97.66 (2)	97.54 (3)	97.34 (4)	97.09 (5)	98.65 (1)
		DT	95.23 (6)	98.41 (2)	96.15 (5)	98.11 (3)	97.52 (4)	98.65 (1)
		NB	93.26 (6)	96.89 (3)	95.48 (5)	96.13 (4)	97.23 (1)	96.98 (2)
		QDA	97.23 (5)	98.85 (2)	97.83 (4)	97.83 (4)	98.21 (3)	97.98 (1)
	Avg. Rank of Models		5.75	2.25	4.25	3.75	3.25	1.25

Table 5. Cont.

S. No.	Datasets	Classifier	Without FS (%)	FSGA (%)	FSPSO (%)	FSDE (%)	FSACO (%)	FSGJO (%)
3	PC3	KNN	82.14 (6)	86.43 (2)	84.67 (5)	85.39 (4)	86.17 (3)	87.03 (1)
		DT	78.07 (6)	86.93 (2)	82.19 (5)	86.73 (3)	84.34 (4)	87.03 (1)
		NB	68.89 (6)	86.58 (3)	80.38 (5)	86.18 (4)	87.8 (2)	87.3 (1)
		QDA	62.4 (6)	86.54 (3)	83.83 (5)	86.67 (2)	86.09 (4)	87.5 (1)
	Avg. Rank of Models		6	2.50	5	3.25	3.25	1
4	PC4	KNN	84.05 (6)	90.18 (3)	86.36 (5)	87.06 (4)	91.61 (1)	90.69 (2)
		DT	91.90 (5)	93.52 (1)	92.63 (3)	93.52 (1)	92.40 (4)	93.02 (2)
		NB	86.28 (6)	91.95 (1)	89.10 (5)	91.47 (3)	91.04 (4)	91.86 (2)
		QDA	47.76 (5)	91.28 (3)	86.89 (4)	92.84 (2)	91.28 (3)	93.41 (1)
	Avg. Rank of Models		5.50	2	4.25	2.50	3	1.75
5	PC5	KNN	67.6 (5)	75.36 (3)	71.80 (4)	75.36 (3)	76.58 (2)	78.42 (1)
		DT	72.95 (6)	77.37 (2)	73.35 (5)	77.18 (3)	75.61 (4)	77.84 (1)
		NB	70.45 (6)	71.75 (3)	70.28 (5)	71.64 (4)	72.91 (2)	72.99 (1)
		QDA	69.93 (6)	72.75 (2)	70.85 (5)	72.29 (3)	71.10 (4)	73.46 (1)
	Avg. Rank of Models		5.75	2.50	4.75	3.25	3	1
6	JM1	DT	73.53 (6)	77.81 (3)	75.60 (5)	76.63 (4)	79.62 (1)	78.16 (2)
		KNN	69.49 (6)	78.63 (3)	72.49 (5)	73.39 (4)	79.59 (2)	79.60 (1)
		NB	78.01 (5)	79.84 (2)	79.15 (4)	79.62 (3)	79.89 (1)	79.89 (1)
		QDA	75.85 (5)	79.71 (3)	79.04 (4)	79.82 (1)	79.78 (2)	79.82 (1)
	Avg. Rank of Models		5.50	2.75	4.50	3	1.50	1.25
7	KC1	KNN	69.26 (5)	76.46 (3)	76.46 (3)	76.33 (4)	77.59 (2)	78.05 (1)
		DT	72.51 (6)	77.60 (2)	73.21 (5)	76.30 (4)	76.48 (3)	77.79 (1)
		NB	74.62 (5)	77.32 (3)	76.21 (4)	77.32 (3)	77.47 (2)	77.63 (1)
		QDA	74.62 (6)	78.01 (2)	76.92 (5)	77.39 (4)	77.58 (3)	78.48 (1)
	Avg. Rank of Models		5.50	2.50	4.25	3.75	2.50	1
8	KC3	KNN	74.63 (6)	79.89 (3)	76.51 (5)	79.32 (4)	86.29 (1)	82.05 (2)
		DT	76.29 (6)	89.54 (2)	81.30 (5)	87.96 (3)	85.31 (4)	89.74 (1)
		NB	66.76 (6)	76.29 (5)	71.45 (4)	76.51 (2)	79.39 (3)	76.92 (1)
		QDA	76.29 (6)	86.29 (3)	79.47 (5)	87.96 (2)	86.15 (4)	89.74 (1)
	Avg. Rank of Models		6	3.25	4.75	2.75	3	1.25
9	CM1	KNN	75.67 (6)	86.28 (3)	83.43 (5)	85.03 (4)	87.24 (2)	89.39 (1)
		DT	80.03 (6)	89.07 (2)	83.28 (5)	88.49 (3)	87.37 (4)	89.39 (1)
		NB	77.37 (6)	83.34 (3)	81.97 (5)	83.28 (4)	84.45 (2)	84.46 (1)
		QDA	83.21 (5)	88.84 (2)	83.79 (4)	88.84 (2)	88.81 (3)	90.90 (1)
	Avg. Rank of Models		5.75	2.50	4.75	3.25	2.75	1
10	MC1	KNN	96.37 (6)	97.63 (3)	97.46 (5)	97.48 (4)	98.10 (1)	97.73 (2)
		DT	97.64 (2)	98.47 (4)	98.39 (5)	98.57 (3)	98.24 (6)	98.74 (1)
		NB	95.64 (6)	97.61 (4)	96.21 (5)	97.62 (3)	97.64 (2)	97.73 (1)
		QDA	97.39 (3)	97.64 (2)	97.39 (3)	97.64 (2)	97.64 (2)	97.73 (1)
	Avg. Rank of Models		4.25	3.25	4.50	3.00	2.75	1.25
11	MC2	KNN	75 (6)	87.46 (3)	79 (5)	85.12 (4)	89.12 (2)	92 (1)
		DT	68 (5)	90.78 (1)	75.21 (4)	89.26 (2)	85 (3)	89.26 (2)
		NB	93 (6)	95.56 (2)	92.71 (5)	93.12 (4)	95 (3)	96 (1)
		QDA	83 (4)	95.12 (2)	88.34 (3)	95.12 (2)	95.12 (2)	96 (1)
	Avg. Rank of Models		5.25	2.00	4.25	3.00	2.50	1.25
12	MW1	KNN	78.34 (6)	87.35 (2)	84.61 (5)	85.56 (4)	86.57 (3)	88.27 (1)
		DT	74.41 (6)	87.74 (1)	82.64 (5)	87.15 (2)	85.19 (4)	85.29 (3)
		NB	76.37 (6)	83.42 (3)	78.78 (5)	82.25 (4)	87.16 (2)	88.27 (1)
		QDA	80.49 (6)	88.52 (3)	84.21 (4)	86.56 (4)	90.29 (2)	92.14 (1)
	Avg. Rank of Models		6.00	2.25	4.75	3.50	2.75	1.50

Table 6. FS models Avg. Rank.

S. No.	Datasets	Without FS	FSGA	FSPSO	FSDE	FSACO	FSGJO
1	PC1	6	3	5	3	3	1
2	PC2	5.75	2.25	4.25	3.75	3.25	1.25
3	PC3	6	2.50	5	3.25	3.25	1
4	PC4	5.50	2	4.25	2.50	3	1.75
5	PC5	5.75	2.50	4.75	3.25	3	1
6	JM1	5.50	2.75	4.50	3	1.50	1.25
7	KC1	5.50	2.50	4.25	3.75	2.50	1
8	KC3	6	3.25	4.75	2.75	3	1.25
9	CM1	5.75	2.50	4.75	3.25	2.75	1
10	MC1	4.25	3.25	4.50	3.00	2.75	1.25
11	MC2	5.25	2.00	4.25	3.00	2.50	1.25
12	MW1	6.00	2.25	4.75	3.50	2.75	1.50
Avg. Rank Datasets		5.60	2.56	4.58	3.17	2.77	1.21
		AR6	AR2	AR5	AR4	AR3	AR1

The computation of X_F^2 in Equation (35) involves utilizing the *AvgRankModels*, which is determined to be 15.93. The variables M and N are used to represent the number of datasets and models in the experiment, respectively. The resulting value for the Friedman statistic, F_F, is calculated as 3.98 based on Equation (36). The analysis in this instance is conducted using 12 datasets and 6 models. The critical value is calculated as 2.449 with $(6-1)$ and $(6-1) \times (12-1)$ degrees of freedom, and the significance level of α is 0.05.

$$X_F^2 = \frac{12 \times M}{N \times (N+1)} \times \left[\sum_j AR^2 - \frac{N \times (N+1)^2}{4} \right] \quad (35)$$

$$F_F = \frac{(M-1) \times X_F^2}{M \times (N-1) - X_F^2} \quad (36)$$

The density plot in Figure 9, with a degree of freedom of (5,55), shows the critical value of 2.269. The fact that the Friedman Statistics ($F_F = 3.98$) is higher than the critical value allows us to reject the null hypothesis (H_0). This implies that there is a noteworthy difference between at least two models.

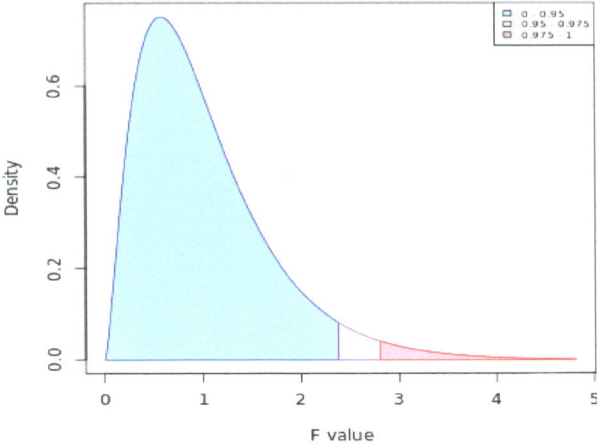

Figure 9. Density plot.

Upon rejecting the null hypothesis in the Friedman test, which implies the presence of variations among multiple models, it is standard practice to conduct a post hoc test to identify the specific models that exhibit significant differences. There are several post hoc tests that can be used, such as the Wilcoxon signed-rank test, the Holm–Bonferroni method, and the Nemenyi test. The choice of the post hoc test depends on the specific research question and the characteristics of the data. The main goal of the post hoc test is to provide more detailed information about the differences between the models and to identify which models are significantly better than others. Additionally, it has been shown to have more statistical power than other methods while maintaining an acceptable type I error rate. Controlling the Type I error rate is important in statistical inference because it helps ensure that the results drawn from the data are accurate and reliable. The Holm procedure [52–56] is a multiple comparison procedure that can be used as a post hoc test after conducting a statistical test like the Friedman test. It uses the p-value and z-value to evaluate the performance of each individual. The calculation of z is performed using Equation (37), and then the corresponding p-value is obtained from the normal distribution table.

$$z = \frac{AR_x - AR_y}{\sqrt{\frac{N \times (N+1)}{6 \times M}}} \tag{37}$$

The value of z in this context refers to the z-score value, which is calculated using a formula represented by Equation (37). In the formula, N and M represent the quantity of models and datasets used in the experiment, respectively. The average rank of the xth and y^{th} models is symbolized as AR_x and AR_y respectively. Table 7 shows the comparison of all the models using the z-value, p-value, and (α/N-i). The significance level used in the assessment is 0.05, denoted by α.

Table 7. Test results of Holm method.

		Holm Test		
Sr. No.	FS Models	z Value	p Value	Alpha/v-i
1	FSGJO:WFS	5.755497	0.00001	0.01
2	FSGJO:FSGA	1.77302	0.038114	0.0125
3	FSGJO:FSPSO	4.418912	0.00001	0.016667
4	FSGJO:DE	2.56406	0.005174	0.025
5	FSGJO:ACO	2.045793	0.020393	0.05

Table 7 displays the outcomes of a Holm test carried out on five FS (Feature Selection) models: FSGJO:WFS, FSGJO:FSGA, FSGJO:FSPSO, FSGJO:DE, and FSGJO:ACO. The table presents the alpha/v-I, the p-value, and the z-value for each model. The adjusted alpha level (α/N-i) was calculated based on their ranks and the number of models. The adjusted alpha level is the significance level adjusted for the multiple comparisons in the test. It is used to determine if a result is statistically significant after adjusting for the number of tests conducted. The table indicates that, for the most part, the p-values are lower than or equal to the adjusted alpha level (α/N-i), except for the FSGJO and FSGA models. These findings indicate that, with the exception of the FSGA model, the FSGJO model exhibits superior and statistically significant results compared to the other models. According to the table, the FSGJO model has noteworthy outcomes and performs better than the other models, except for the FSGA model. There is no statistical significance in the differences of performance among these models.

7. Conclusions

In this study, a novel method for feature selection called FSGJO is introduced, which employs metaheuristic optimization using the GJO algorithm to efficiently identify the optimal set of features. The FSGJO feature selection technique strives to choose the most significant features within the solution space, aiming to exclude redundant and irrelevant ones. This research assesses the efficiency of the FSGJO method on 12 different datasets using four classifiers (DT, KNN, NB, and QDA). The primary objective is to compare FSGJO's performance with that of existing feature selection models such as FSPSO, FSGA, FSDE, and FSACO, which have different benchmark dimensions. Statistical analysis using the Friedman test indicated that at least two models differed significantly from one another, and the null hypothesis was rejected, which led to the Holm test. Based on the results, it was found that FSGJO displayed a better performance compared to other methods for selecting features, both in relation to accurately classifying data and efficiently eliminating features that were not useful. The advantage of GJO is its ability to handle high-dimensional optimization problems with multiple objectives and avoid local optima by combining exploratory and exploitative search strategies. The only limitation of the proposed model is that its parameters must be adjusted according to the given problem. The proposed method can be applied to other fields such as medical data and gene data.

Author Contributions: Conceptualization, H.D. and S.P.; Methodology, H.D.; Software, S.P.; Validation, M.K.G.; Formal analysis, M.K.G.; Resources, A.A.; Visualization, R.M.P. and M.K. All authors have read and agreed to the published version of the manuscript.

Funding: This research received no external funding.

Data Availability Statement: The data used for this experiment are available in public repository (NASA software defects datasets from PROMISE). The detailed information about the data are provided in the result analysis section.

Conflicts of Interest: The authors declare no conflict of interest.

References

1. Catal, C. Software fault prediction: A literature review and current trends. *Expert Syst. Appl.* **2011**, *38*, 4626–4636. [CrossRef]
2. Kundu, A.; Dutta, P.; Ranjit, K.; Bidyadhar, S.; Gourisaria, M.K.; Das, H. Software Fault Prediction Using Machine Learning Models. In Proceedings of the 2022 OITS International Conference on Information Technology (OCIT), Bhubaneswar, India, 14–16 December 2022; IEEE: Manhattan, NY, USA, 2022; pp. 170–175.
3. Malhotra, R. Comparative analysis of statistical and machine learning methods for predicting faulty modules. *Appl. Soft Comput.* **2014**, *21*, 286–297. [CrossRef]
4. Gm, H.; Gourisaria, M.K.; Pandey, M.; Rautaray, S.S. A comprehensive survey and analysis of generative models in machine learning. *Comput. Sci. Rev.* **2020**, *38*, 100285. [CrossRef]
5. Rathore, S.S.; Kumar, S. A decision tree logic based recommendation system to select software fault prediction techniques. *Computing* **2017**, *99*, 255–285. [CrossRef]
6. Rathore, S.S.; Kumar, S. A Decision Tree Regression based Approach for the Number of Software Faults Prediction. *ACM SIGSOFT Softw. Eng. Notes* **2016**, *41*, 1–6. [CrossRef]
7. Singh, Y.; Kaur, A.; Malhotra, R. Software fault proneness prediction using support vector machines. In Proceedings of the World Congress on Engineering, London, UK, 1–3 July 2009; Volume 1, pp. 1–3.
8. Li, J.; He, P.; Zhu, J.; Lyu, M.R. Software defect prediction via convolutional neural network. In Proceedings of the 2017 IEEE International Conference on Software Quality, Reliability and Security (QRS), Prague, Czech Republic, 25–29 July 2017; IEEE: Manhattan, NY, USA, 2017; pp. 318–328.
9. Goyal, J.; Ranjan Sinha, R. Software defect-based prediction using logistic regression: Review and challenges. In Proceedings of the Second International Conference on Sustainable Technologies for Computational Intelligence: Proceedings of ICTSCI 2021, Dehradun, India, 22–23 May 2021; Springer: Singapore, 2022; pp. 233–248.
10. Chandrashekar, G.; Sahin, F. A survey on feature selection methods. *Comput. Electr. Eng.* **2014**, *40*, 16–28. [CrossRef]
11. Brezočnik, L.; Fister, I., Jr.; Podgorelec, V. Swarm intelligence algorithms for feature selection: A review. *Appl. Sci.* **2018**, *8*, 1521. [CrossRef]
12. Cherrington, M.; Thabtah, F.; Lu, J.; Xu, Q. Feature Selection: Filter Methods Performance Challenges. In Proceedings of the 2019 International Conference on Computer and Information Sciences (ICCIS), Sakaka, Saudi Arabia, 3–4 April 2019; pp. 1–4. [CrossRef]
13. Gayatri, N.; Nickolas, S.; Reddy, A.V. ANOVA discriminant analysis for features selected through decision tree induction method. In *Global Trends in Computing and Communication Systems*; Springer: Berlin/Heidelberg, Germany, 2012; pp. 61–70.
14. Chen, G.; Chen, J. A novel wrapper method for feature selection and its applications. *Neurocomputing* **2015**, *159*, 219–226. [CrossRef]

15. Zeng, X.; Chen, Y.W.; Tao, C. Feature selection using recursive feature elimination for handwritten digit recognition. In Proceedings of the 2009 Fifth International Conference on Intelligent Information Hiding and Multimedia Signal Processing, Kyoto, Japan, 12–14 September 2009; IEEE: Manhattan, NY, USA, 2009; pp. 1205–1208.
16. Borboudakis, G.; Tsamardinos, I. Forward-backward selection with early dropping. *J. Mach. Learn. Res.* **2019**, *20*, 276–314.
17. Lal, T.N.; Chapelle, O.; Weston, J.; Elisseeff, A. Embedded methods. In *Feature Extraction: Foundations and Applications*; Springer: Berlin/Heidelberg, Germany, 2006; pp. 137–165.
18. Chen, C.-W.; Tsai, Y.-H.; Chang, F.-R.; Lin, W.-C. Ensemble feature selection in medical datasets: Combining filter, wrapper, and embedded feature selection results. *Expert Syst.* **2020**, *37*, e12553. [CrossRef]
19. Muthukrishnan, R.; Rohini, R. LASSO: A feature selection technique in predictive modeling for machine learning. In Proceedings of the 2016 IEEE International Conference on Advances in Computer Applications (ICACA), Coimbatore, India, 24 October 2016; pp. 18–20. [CrossRef]
20. Paul, S.; Drineas, P. Feature Selection for Ridge Regression with Provable Guarantees. *Neural Comput.* **2016**, *28*, 716–742. [CrossRef] [PubMed]
21. Song, F.; Guo, Z.; Mei, D. Feature selection using principal component analysis. In Proceedings of the 2010 International Conference on System Science, Engineering Design and Manufacturing Informatization, Yichang, China, 12–14 November 2010; IEEE: Manhattan, NY, USA, 2010; Volume 1, pp. 27–30.
22. Belkina, A.C.; Ciccolella, C.O.; Anno, R.; Halpert, R.; Spidlen, J.; Snyder-Cappione, J.E. Automated optimized parameters for T-distributed stochastic neighbor embedding improve visualization and analysis of large datasets. *Nat. Commun.* **2019**, *10*, 5415. [CrossRef] [PubMed]
23. Malhotra, R.; Pritam, N.; Singh, Y. On the applicability of evolutionary computation for software defect prediction. In Proceedings of the 2014 International Conference on Advances in Computing, Communications and Informatics (ICACCI), Delhi, India, 24–27 September 2014; pp. 2249–2257. [CrossRef]
24. Ab Wahab, M.N.; Nefti-Meziani, S.; Atyabi, A. A Comprehensive Review of Swarm Optimization Algorithms. *PLoS ONE* **2015**, *10*, e0122827. [CrossRef] [PubMed]
25. Prajapati, S.; Das, H.; Gourisaria, M.K. Feature selection using genetic algorithm for microarray data classification. In Proceedings of the 2022 OPJU International Technology Conference on Emerging Technologies for Sustainable Development (OTCON), Raigarh, India, 8–10 February 2022.
26. Du, K.L.; Swamy MN, S.; Du, K.L.; Swamy, M.N.S. Particle swarm optimization. In *Search and Optimization by Metaheuristics: Techniques and Algorithms Inspired by Nature*; Springer: Berlin/Heidelberg, Germany, 2016; pp. 153–173.
27. Brezočnik, L.; Podgorelec, V. Applying weighted particle swarm optimization to imbalanced data in software defect prediction. In *New Technologies, Development and Application 4*; Springer International Publishing: Manhattan, NY, USA, 2019; pp. 289–296.
28. Das, S.; Suganthan, P.N. Differential Evolution: A Survey of the State-of-the-Art. *IEEE Trans. Evol. Comput.* **2010**, *15*, 4–31. [CrossRef]
29. Prajapati, S.; Das, H.; Gourisaria, M.K. Feature Selection using Ant Colony Optimization for Microarray Data Classification. In Proceedings of the 2023 6th International Conference on Information Systems and Computer Networks (ISCON), Mathura, India, 3–4 March 2023; pp. 1–6.
30. Chopra, N.; Ansari, M.M. Golden jackal optimization: A novel nature-inspired optimizer for engineering applications. *Expert Syst. Appl.* **2022**, *198*, 116924. [CrossRef]
31. Prasad, D. *Automated Software Testing: Foundations Applications Challenges*; Jena, A.K., Das, H., Mohapatra, D.P., Eds.; Springer: Berlin/Heidelberg, Germany, 2020; pp. 1–165.
32. Das, H.; Gourisaria, M.K.; Sah, B.K.; Bilgaiyan, S.; Badajena, J.C.; Pattanayak, R.M. E-Healthcare System for Disease Detection Based on Medical Image Classification Using, C.N.N. In *Empirical Research for Futuristic E-Commerce Systems: Foundations and Applications*; IGI Global: Hershey, PA, USA; pp. 213–230.
33. Prajapati, S.; Das, H.; Gourisaria, M.K. Microarray data classification using machine learning algorithms. In Proceedings of the 2022 OPJU International Technology Conference on Emerging Technologies for Sustainable Development (OTCON), Raigarh, India, 8–10 February 2022.
34. Das, H.; Naik, B.; Behera, H.; Jaiswal, S.; Mahato, P.; Rout, M. Biomedical data analysis using neuro-fuzzy model with post-feature reduction. *J. King Saud Univ. Comput. Inf. Sci.* **2020**, *34*, 2540–2550. [CrossRef]
35. Das, H.; Naik, B.; Behera, H.S. Medical disease analysis using neuro-fuzzy with feature extraction model for classification. *Inform. Med. Unlocked* **2020**, *18*, 100288. [CrossRef]
36. Das, H.; Naik, B.; Behera, H.S. An experimental analysis of machine learning classification algorithms on biomedical data. In Proceedings of the 2nd International Conference on Communication, Devices and Computing, Haldia, India, 14–15 March 2020; Springer: Singapore, 2020; pp. 525–539.
37. Saha, I.; Gourisaria, M.K.; Harshvardhan, G.M. Classification System for Prediction of Chronic Kidney Disease Using Data Mining Techniques. In *Advances in Data and Information Sciences: Proceedings of ICDIS 2021*; Springer: Singapore, 2022; pp. 429–443.
38. Agarwal, S.; Tomar, D. A Feature Selection Based Model for Software Defect Prediction. *Int. J. Adv. Sci. Technol.* **2014**, *65*, 39–58. [CrossRef]
39. Turabieh, H.; Mafarja, M.; Li, X. Iterated feature selection algorithms with layered recurrent neural network for software fault prediction. *Expert Syst. Appl.* **2019**, *122*, 27–42. [CrossRef]

40. Zorarpacı, E.; Özel, S.A. A hybrid approach of differential evolution and artificial bee colony for feature selection. *Expert Syst. Appl.* **2016**, *62*, 91–103. [CrossRef]
41. Ibrahim, D.R.; Ghnemat, R.; Hudaib, A. Software defect prediction using feature selection and random forest algorithm. In Proceedings of the 2017 International Conference on New Trends in Computing Sciences (ICTCS), Amman, Jordan, 11–13 October 2017; IEEE: Manhattan, NY, USA, 2017; pp. 252–257.
42. Wahono, R.S.; Suryana, N. Combining Particle Swarm Optimization based Feature Selection and Bagging Technique for Software Defect Prediction. *Int. J. Softw. Eng. Its Appl.* **2013**, *7*, 153–166. [CrossRef]
43. Rong, X.; Li, F.; Cui, Z. A model for software defect prediction using support vector machine based on CBA. *Int. J. Intell. Syst. Technol. Appl.* **2016**, *15*, 19–34. [CrossRef]
44. Wahono, R.S.; Suryana, N.; Ahmad, S. Metaheuristic Optimization based Feature Selection for Software Defect Prediction. *J. Softw.* **2014**, *9*, 1324–1333. [CrossRef]
45. Jacob, S.G. Improved Random Forest Algorithm for Software Defect Prediction through Data Mining Techniques. *Int. J. Comput. Appl.* **2015**, *117*, 18–22.
46. Das, H.; Naik, B.; Behera, H.S. Optimal Selection of Features Using Artificial Electric Field Algorithm for Classification. *Arab. J. Sci. Eng.* **2021**, *46*, 8355–8369. [CrossRef]
47. Das, H.; Naik, B.; Behera, H. A Jaya algorithm based wrapper method for optimal feature selection in supervised classification. *J. King Saud Univ. Comput. Inf. Sci.* **2020**, *34*, 3851–3863. [CrossRef]
48. Padhi, B.K.; Chakravarty, S.; Naik, B.; Pattanayak, R.M.; Das, H. RHSOFS: Feature Selection Using the Rock Hyrax Swarm Optimization Algorithm for Credit Card Fraud Detection System. *Sensors* **2022**, *22*, 9321. [CrossRef]
49. Dutta, H.; Gourisaria, M.K.; Das, H. Wrapper Based Feature Selection Approach Using Black Widow Optimization Algorithm for Data Classification. In *Computational Intelligence in Pattern Recognition: Proceedings of CIPR 2022*; Springer Nature: Singapore, 2022; pp. 487–496.
50. Anbu, M.; Mala, G.S.A. Feature selection using firefly algorithm in software defect prediction. *Clust. Comput.* **2019**, *22*, 10925–10934. [CrossRef]
51. Demšar, J. Statistical comparisons of classifers over multiple data sets. *J. Mach. Learn. Res.* **2006**, *7*, 1–30.
52. Friedman, M. The use of ranks to avoid the assumption of normality implicit in the analysis of variance. *J. Am. Stat. Assoc.* **1937**, *32*, 675–701. [CrossRef]
53. Friedman, M. A comparison of alternative tests of signifcance for the problem of m rankings. *Ann. Math. Stat.* **1940**, *11*, 86–92. [CrossRef]
54. Iman, R.L.; Davenport, J.M. Approximations of the critical region of the fbietkan statistic. *Commun. Stat. Theory Methods* **1980**, *9*, 571–595. [CrossRef]
55. García, S.; Fernández, A.; Luengo, J.; Herrera, F. Advanced nonparametric tests for multiple comparisons in the design of experiments in computational intelligence and data mining: Experimental analysis of power. *Inf. Sci.* **2010**, *180*, 2044–2064. [CrossRef]
56. Luengo, J.; García, S.; Herrera, F. A study on the use of statistical tests for experimentation with neural networks: Analysis of parametric test conditions and non-parametric tests. *Expert Syst. Appl.* **2009**, *36*, 7798–7808. [CrossRef]

Disclaimer/Publisher's Note: The statements, opinions and data contained in all publications are solely those of the individual author(s) and contributor(s) and not of MDPI and/or the editor(s). MDPI and/or the editor(s) disclaim responsibility for any injury to people or property resulting from any ideas, methods, instructions or products referred to in the content.

Article

PQ-Mist: Priority Queueing-Assisted Mist–Cloud–Fog System for Geospatial Web Service

Sunil K. Panigrahi [1], Veena Goswami [2], Hemant K. Apat [2], Ganga B. Mund [1], Himansu Das [1,*] and Rabindra K. Barik [2,*]

[1] School of Computer Engineering, Kalinga Institute of Industrial Technology, Bhubaneswar 751024, India; ctcsunil@gmail.com (S.K.P.); mund@kiit.ac.in (G.B.M.)
[2] School of Computer Applications, Kalinga Institute of Industrial Technology, Bhubaneswar 751024, India; veena@kiit.ac.in (V.G.); hemant.fca@kiit.ac.in (H.K.A.)
* Correspondence: das.himansu2007@gmail.com or himanshufcs@kiit.ac.in (H.D.); rabindra.mnnit@gmail.com or rabindrafca@kiit.ac.in (R.K.B.)

Citation: Panigrahi, S.K.; Goswami, V.; Apat, H.K.; Mund, G.B.; Das, H.; Barik, R.K. *PQ-Mist*: Priority Queueing-Assisted Mist–Cloud–Fog System for Geospatial Web Services. *Mathematics* **2023**, *11*, 3562. https://doi.org/10.3390/math11163562

Academic Editors: Steve Drekic and Vassilis C. Gerogiannis

Received: 30 June 2023
Revised: 17 July 2023
Accepted: 16 August 2023
Published: 17 August 2023

Copyright: © 2023 by the authors. Licensee MDPI, Basel, Switzerland. This article is an open access article distributed under the terms and conditions of the Creative Commons Attribution (CC BY) license (https:// creativecommons.org/licenses/by/ 4.0/).

Abstract: The IoT and cloud environment renders enormous quantities of geospatial information. Fog and mist computing is the scaling technology that handles geospatial data and sends it to the cloud storage system through fog/mist nodes. Installing a mist–cloud–fog system reduces latency and throughput. This mist–cloud–fog system has processed different types of geospatial web services, i.e., web coverage service (WCS), web processing services (WPS), web feature services (WFS), and web map services (WMS). There is an urgent requirement to increase the number of computer devices tailored to deliver high-priority jobs for processing these geospatial web services. This paper proposes a priority-queueing assisted mist–cloud–fog system for efficient resource allocation for high- and low-priority tasks. In this study, WFS is treated as high-priority service, whereas WMS is treated as low-priority service. This system dynamically allocates mist nodes and is determined by the load on the system. In addition to that, the assignment of tasks is determined by priority. Not only does this classify high-priority tasks and low-priority tasks, which helps reduce the amount of delay experienced by high-priority jobs, but it also dynamically allocates mist devices within the network depending on the computation load, which helps reduce the amount of power that is consumed by the network. The findings indicate that the proposed system can achieve a significantly lower delay for higher-priority jobs for more significant rates of task arrival when compared with other related schemes. In addition to this, it offers a technique that is both mathematical and analytical for investigating and assessing the performance of the proposed system. The QoS requirements for each device demand are factored into calculating the number of mist nodes deployed to satisfy those requirements.

Keywords: edge computing; cloud computing; geospatial data; fog computing; mist computing; priority queue; geospatial web services; WMS; WFS

MSC: 60K25; 60K30; 68M20

1. Introduction

The demand for cloud services has significantly expanded in recent years as more people have access to the technology required to run cloud computing. These days, off-device computation and storage are accomplished through the usage of cloud services [1,2]. The internet of things (IoT) and cloud environments generate an enormous number of geographical data. The harnessing technology that analyzes geospatial data and provides it to the cloud storage system via fog/mist nodes is referred to as fog and mist computing [3–5].

According to the report that was presented by [6,7], the size of the geospatial analytics market is projected to increase from USD 74.78 billion in 2023 to USD 148.91 billion at a

CAGR of 14.77% during the forecast period of 2023–2028. So, these statements motivate us to deliver geospatial services quickly and effectively.

As a result, cloud computing, fog computing, and mist computing are currently the most common forms of computing platforms. These forms of computing make virtualized and scalable resources available through web services. Consequently, both the difficulty of deploying and maintaining web applications and the quality of the environment in which computing takes place are improved [8,9]. Cloud applications and the service providers that support them are gaining popularity as a result of the unique features that they possess. These properties include ease of maintenance, resilience, and sustainability, all of which make it possible to schedule resources and maintain performance control. To improve service delivery for various geospatial data, cloud, fog, mist, and edge computing systems, they have been adopted by many authors [10,11]. However, adding an extra layer to the conventional mist computing system is inefficient for many geospatial IoT devices. We need to evaluate each layer experimentally and analytically to make it cost-efficient and improve system performance. Geospatial IoT devices still communicate directly with cloud services, allowing for more complex computations to be performed. Cloud computing has enabled robust geospatial computing systems to share geospatial data among various parties. This cloud architecture allows many users to access geospatial data through geospatial web services (GWS) [12,13].

In a mist–cloud–fog system, particularly for GWS, the computation jobs need to be correctly divided between the mist and fog nodes. This ensures that the mist, the fog devices, and the cloud can coordinate effectively and adequately. As a result, we use queuing theory for the performance study to examine this kind of resource allocation approach [10,11,14].

To enable online geospatial services, the open geospatial consortium (OGC) has recently published a set of specifications that are either an adaptation or an extension of the usual online service standards. Standardizing service interfaces and data models is possible with several well-known products such as WMS (web map service), WFS (web feature service), WCS (web coverage service), and CSW (catalogue service for the web). In the meantime, a web processing service (WPS) interface can be utilized to gain access to any environmental model or geospatial algorithm that is classified as a geoprocessing service [15–17].

The queuing model has seen extensive use for this kind of study since it may shed light on various QoS parameters, including the response time for the system, CPU utilization, mean throughput, and many more. Mist computing is used to provide improved QoS for high-priority tasks. However, due to the limited computing available on most devices, finishing some allotted work within a delay threshold is possible. This is one of the drawbacks of using mist computing. In [18], the authors suggested that the limited processing capabilities of mist devices place a ceiling on the number of task requests. As a result, we utilize a priority queueing strategy to maximize the high-priority task request rather than consider another low-priority task.

Thus, this study presents a priority-queuing assisted mist–cloud–fog system for geospatial applications to allocate resources to efficiently provide high- and low-priority tasks. WFS is given a high-priority status in this study, whereas WMS is given a low-priority status. This system determines how to dynamically allocate mist nodes in a way that is dependent on the load being placed on the system. The load defines how the system should allocate mist nodes.

1.1. Contributions

The present research paper is structured with the following contributions:

- It presents a description of geospatial computing paradigms, geospatial web services, and different performance evaluations strategies, with varieties of queueing approaches associated with edge, mist, fog, and cloud computing perspectives.

- It introduces the priority queueing-assisted mist–cloud–fog system for geospatal web services.
- It provides the analytical queueing approach along with performance analysis for the proposed system.
- It also carries the performance measurement and experimental results of the proposed system with the variability of arithmetic outcomes in graphs.

1.2. Organizations

The rest of the paper is organized as follows. Section 2 explains the related work. It details the geospatial computing paradigm, the geospatial web services, and the performance evaluations of various models used in different application domains. Section 3 presents a detailed description of the proposed priority queueing analytical approach for the mist–cloud–fog system for geospatial web services. Section 4 presents the experimental results and performance evaluation of the proposed model and the proposed model's performance measurement and experimental results, which are based on the variability of arithmetic outcomes in graphs. Section 5 draws the concluding remarks of the present research paper.

2. Related Work
2.1. Geospatial Computing Paradigms
2.1.1. Geospatial Edge Computing

The term "edge computing" refers to an advanced technology that transfers a module, data, or service from one internet hub to the subsequent hub. A customer who is either physically present or easily duped is close. The perimeter of this computing system is where the data are generated and handled. Through the utilization of this computing technology, edge devices are given the ability to interact with cloud platforms [16,19]. Before cloud platforms can be upgraded to leverage cloud services, the model must alter to sort information by velocity, volume, and variety. Edge computing equalizes data providers and consumers. Near-edge cloud computing jobs are carried out. This computing stores, distributes, caches, processes, and delivers data to clients. Because so many jobs are running on the edge computing network, the edge hubs need to be constructed to meet the requirements for data reliability, privacy, and data security [20]. In this edge computing design, the processing assets should be located close to the information sources. These advantages of cutting-edge standards outweigh those of the cloud framework. For example, mobile phones symbolize the transition between the cloud and the human body, whereas smart houses symbolize the transition between the cloud and the domestic sphere. The cloud-to-mobile edges comprise cloudlets and tiny data centers [1].

2.1.2. Geospatial Mist Computing

Mist computing offloads some computation to the cloud data center's network's edge, actuator devices, and sensors. Mist computing in embedded nodes' microcontrollers computed the network's edge [11,21,22]. Mist computing minimises latency and boosts autonomy. Cloud, fog, and mist computing are complementary because the fog layer's gateway can run computationally complex application tasks, while edge devices can run less intensive ones [23].

The user can access cloud data centre data. Mist computing provides varied services across computing nodes. Cisco invented fog and mist computing, which expands client–server architecture like edge. Geosptial mist computing has four layers: cloud, fog, mist, and edge [10,18].

2.1.3. Geospatial Fog Computing

Cisco invented fog computing in early 2012. This computing paradigm gives untrained users data center resources. It does not use cloud data centers for computing. Cloud servers make computation and data storage for convenient for customers, reducing latencies relative to transmission overheads. They provide a user interface similar to smart devices. Local processing offers data compression, faster throughput, and decreased latency. Smart cities, residences, and healthcare use fog computing [24–26].

Fog computing uses fog devices. Raspberry Pi and Intel Edison fog devices are cloud-to-user gateways. Geographic big data analysis and distribution require scalable and efficient geospatial fog computing systems. Fog computing minimizes latency and increases throughput for ignorant clients. Fog architecture stores geographical data near local devices instead of a cloud infrastructure data server [2,27,28].

A fog computing system processes customer requests and returns responses. Cloud computing supplies storage and analysis. All resource utilization components, including fog servers, respond to unequal demands. Inefficient resource management reduces QoS and increases energy usage [29–32]. Smart cities use fog computing to manage urban data. Fog computing can promote smart cities, urban business, industry, tourism, and transit management [30,33,34].

2.1.4. Geospatial Cloud Computing

The method of cloud computing deals with an enormous number of large data by dividing up the available computer resources among multiple locations in the cloud. The paradigm of cloud computing allows for the pooling of resources and the provision of services on demand. You are able to do data analysis and visualization with the help of this computing method [17,23,35].

A multi-tenant design is supported by geospatial cloud computing systems, and a single instance can serve several customers for processing, storage, and data transfer. Putting in place enhancements and additional software benefits the user. In cloud GIS architecture, geospatial web services are the essential component of the core functional feature. The discovery of app data and features is performed by a number of geospatial cloud computing solutions using geospatial web services. Because of this, they are utilized in the SOA infrastructure operations of enterprise organizations [35–37].

There are three client tiers available in a geospatial cloud computing system: thin, thick, and mobile. Mobile clients use mobile devices. Thin clients are those that function on web browsers, whereas thick clients are those that function on desktop or standalone systems. In order to connect to cloud servers, thick clients require an additional module or piece of software. On the application layer, servers are responsible for running geospatial web services. This facilitates communication between the many service providers and the end users. Within the application-tier, there is a separate dedicated server for every one of the application services (WPS, WCS, WMS, and WFS, respectively).

The Table 1 highlights the various aspects of geospatial computing paradigms by addressing the cloud, fog, mist, and edge computing paradigms for geospatial applications.

Table 1. Features of geospatial computing paradigms through cloud, fog, mist, and edge computing.

Features	Cloud	Fog	Mist	Edge
Mobility management	No	Yes	Yes	Yes
Computing resources	Yes	Yes	Yes	Yes
Virtualization mechanism	Yes	Yes	Yes	No
Scalability support	Yes	Yes	Yes	Yes
IoT uses	Yes	Yes	Yes	Yes
Large-scale storage	Yes	No	No	No
Real time applications	No	Yes	Yes	Yes
Inter-operability support	No	Yes	Yes	Yes
High energy consumption	Yes	No	No	No
Low latency	No	Yes	Yes	Yes
Location awareness	No	Yes	Yes	Yes
Standardized	Yes	Yes	No	No
Geographically distributed	No	Yes	Yes	Yes
Large-scale processing power	Yes	No	No	No

The geospatial mist–cloud–fog model is presented in Figure 1 with the integration of the geospatial edge, mist, fog, and cloud computing system.

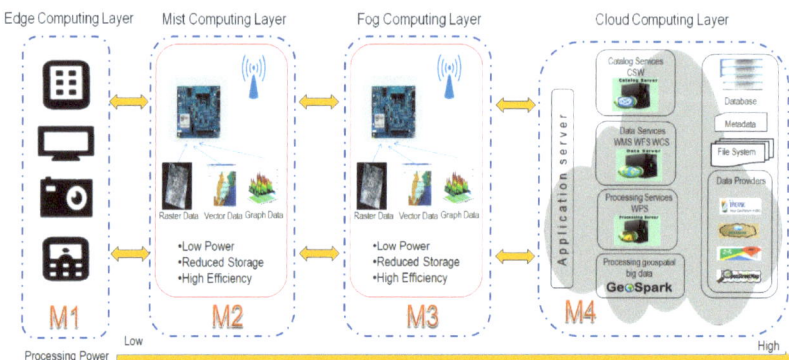

Figure 1. General mist–cloud–fog model for geospatial web services and geospatial data processing.

2.2. Geospatial Web Services

The development of a wide variety of web-based models by scientists is facilitated by geospatial web services (GWS). The development of technology based on cloud computing has opened the door to environmental modeling that is both quicker and more effective. There are public cloud, private cloud, and hybrid cloud products [2,36,38]. GWS caters to the requirements of environmental scientists developing and distributing their models in several ways to meet their needs. The phrase geoprocessing service describes any function or model for processing geospatial and associated data, whereas the term geospatial data service refers to geospatial services for collecting geospatial data. Both geospatial data and geoprocessing services can be derived from GWS in their own right [23,35,39].

Users can access, edit, and utilize hosted geospatial feature datasets through WFS. Distributed tools are used in WMS to produce and host both static and dynamic maps. Access to coverage data in practical formats for client-side rendering, as input into scientific models, and for usage by other clients is made available by a WCS. Users can use web processing services to run GIS calculations on geospatial data. WPS has standardized geospatial statistics methods and standardizes inputs and outputs for geospatial data within the geospatial cloud platform [40,41].

GWS alleviates the burden of tasks by utilizing the combined capacity of distributed services throughout the network. It is accomplished by using massive volumes of geographical data and functions flexibly [24,38].

Compared to the conventional method, in which each activity is carried out on an individual computer, this method facilitates greater remote participation, promotes collaboration, and enhances the repeatability of research.

Many web-based geospatial applications, also known as spatial data infrastructures (SDIs), have been built to utilize geospatial data, geoprocessing services, or both. When many GWSs are available online, researchers integrate various services to fulfill the requirements of more complicated applications. As a result, geospatial analysis and the deployment of GWS are both commonly carried out on the cloud (for example, on Amazon Web Services (AWS), Microsoft Azure, and Google Cloud) [2,41,42].

Specific cloud infrastructures and web services standards are typically created by integrating cloud, fog, and mist computing with diverse geographic applications.

2.3. Performance Evaluations Strategies

Many research works have been carried out where priority and non-priority queueing analytical methodologies have been employed to conduct performance assessments on computing-based systems based on edge, cloud, fog, and mist systems. This is to achieve the objective of conducting performance assessments. Table 2 compares different queuing mathematical and analytical approaches used by other researchers in the context of the various application services. It can be observed that most of the research works preferred different strategies to the norm.

Table 2. Review of various queuing approaches used in edge, cloud, fog, and mist systems.

		Various Queuing Approach					
Year	Author	Reference	Edge	Mist	Fog	Cloud	Approach
2011	Khazaei et al.	[43]	✗	✗	✗	✓	M/M/1
2011	Khazaei et al.	[43]	✗	✗	✗	✓	M/G/s
2012	Ellens et al.	[44]	✗	✗	✗	✓	M/M/c/N
2012	Do et al.	[45]	✗	✗	✗	✓	M/M/m/m
2013	Salah	[46]	✗	✗	✗	✓	M/M/1
2013	Pal and Hui	[47]	✗	✗	✗	✓	M/M/1
2014	Mohanty et al.	[48]	✓	✗	✗	✓	M/M/1
2014	Chiang et al.	[49]	✗	✗	✗	✓	M/M/c/N
2015	Evangelin and Vidhya	[50]	✗	✗	✗	✓	M/M/1
2015	Cheng et al.	[51]	✗	✗	✗	✓	M/M/1
2015	Bai et al.	[52]	✗	✗	✗	✓	M/M/c
2015	Kirsal et al.	[53]	✗	✗	✗	✓	M/M/c
2015	Guo et al.	[54]	✗	✗	✗	✓	M/M/1
2016	Akbari et al.	[55]	✗	✗	✗	✓	M/M/1
2017	Chang et al.	[56]	✗	✗	✗	✓	M/M/1
2017	Liu et al.	[57]	✗	✗	✓	✓	M/M/1
2017	El Kafhali and Salah	[30]	✗	✗	✓	✓	M/M/c
2017	Safvati and Sharzehei	[58]	✗	✗	✓	✓	M/M/1
2018	Tadakamalla et al.	[59]	✗	✗	✓	✗	M/M/1
2018	Sthapit et al.	[60]	✗	✗	✓	✗	M/M/c
2018	Chunxia and Shunfu	[61]	✗	✗	✓	✗	M/M/1
2018	Sophin et al.	[62]	✗	✗	✓	✗	M/M/c
2018	Vasconcelos	[63]	✗	✗	✓	✓	M/M/1
2019	Barik et al.	[2]	✗	✓	✗	✗	M/M/c
2019	Jafarnejad et al.	[64]	✓	✗	✓	✓	M/M/1
2019	Barik et al.	[23]	✗	✓	✓	✓	M/M/c
2019	Li et al.	[65]	✗	✓	✓	✗	M/M/1
2020	Kumar and Raja	[66]	✗	✗	✓	✓	M/M/1
2020	Xu et al.	[67]	✓	✗	✓	✓	M/M/1
2020	Patra et al.	[68]	✗	✓	✗	✗	M/M/1
2020	Bouanaka et al.	[21]	✗	✓	✓	✗	M/M/1
2021	Sedaghat et al.	[69]	✗	✗	✓	✓	M/M/1
2021	Sufyan and Banerjee	[70]	✗	✗	✓	✗	M/M/1
2021	Tadakamalla and Menasce	[71]	✗	✗	✓	✗	M/M/1
2021	Feitosa et al.	[72]	✗	✗	✓	✗	M/M/1
2021	Panigrahi et al.	[73]	✗	✓	✓	✗	M/M/1
2021	Behera et al.	[74]	✗	✗	✓	✗	M/M/c/N
2021	Hmissi and Ouni	[11]	✗	✓	✓	✗	M/M/1
2021	Dutta et al.	[22]	✗	✗	✓	✓	M/M/1
2021	Shahid et al.	[18]	✗	✓	✓	✗	M/M/1
2022	Mas et al.	[75]	✗	✗	✓	✓	M/M/1
2022	Rodrigues et al.	[76]	✗	✗	✓	✓	M/M/c/K
2022	Hamdi et al.	[77]	✗	✗	✓	✓	M/M/1
2022	Nikoui et al.	[5]	✗	✗	✓	✓	G/G/1
2022	Golkar et al.	[9]	✗	✗	✓	✓	Multi Queue Priority
2022	Maiti et al.	[76]	✗	✗	✓	✓	M/M/c
2023	Arefian et al.	[14]	✗	✓	✗	✓	M/M/1
2023	Hazra et al.	[78]	✗	✓	✗	✓	M/M/k
2023	Goswami et al.	[3]	✗	✓	✗	✓	M/M/c
2023	Yazdani et al.	[79]	✗	✓	✗	✓	M/M/1
2023	Saif et al.	[80]	✗	✓	✗	✓	M/M/1 and M/M/c
2023	Saif et al.	[81]	✗	✓	✗	✓	M/M/1 and M/M/c
2023	Mallick et al.	[13]	✗	✓	✗	✓	M/M/c

Many different networking fragments are available in an edge, mist, fog, and cloud computing platform, and each networking device operates according to the concept of "first come, first serve". The queueing model has become an important consideration in the system model to evaluate the effectiveness of cloud computing.

Muniir et al. [82] also demonstrated and detailed an integrated fog-assisted cloud architecture for IoT applications that improve performance, latency, scalability, and localized accuracy. To explore and analyze the performance of geospatial fog computing systems within the healthcare business, Barik et al. [2] developed a queuing mathematical and analytical technique. Barik et al. [23] developed a mathematical and analytical approach to queuing in order to explore and examine the performance of geospatial mist computing systems in the education and tourism industries.

Mukherjee et al. [4] took into account a high-priority queue and a low-priority queue in each fog node. These queues are filled with tasks that have directly arrived from the end-users and have been offloaded from the fog nodes. Each task's delay deadline determines which queue it is placed in. In addition, the Lyapunov drift algorithm was utilized for queue scheduling when the tasks in these two queues had stringent latency requirements.

Adhikari et al. [83] devised a plan for prioritizing the assignment of work by dividing it into three distinct groups according to the lengths of their respective due dates. In addition, they also established a rule-based task scheduling technique to discover an ideal sequence for the tasks and reduce the time spent waiting in the queue.

Bhushan and Ma [8] presented an analytical queuing model to implement priority-based job scheduling within a fog-cloud architecture. The model categorized the jobs into two groups to facilitate the implementation of the priority-based service offering. Class 1 refers to computing jobs with a higher priority and more sensitivity to delays. In contrast, Class 2 relates to computing tasks with lower priority and less sensitivity to delays.

He et al. [19] considered a scenario of cloud-assisted multi-access edge computing involving multiple mobile devices. It considered the mobile devices in question to be operating under an $M/G/1$ non-preemptive priority queueing model, with each edge server operating under an $M/G/m$ non-preemptive priority queueing model, and the cloud data center operating under an $M/G/\infty$ queueing model.

3. Proposed Model

This section presents the analytical queuing model for the mist–cloud–fog system by describing its four-tier network topology, as represented in Figure 2. The first tier is the bottom layer, the edge layer. It includes all IoT devices responsible for sensing a wide range of events and relaying the raw detected data to the upper layer immediately above them. It is predicated on the assumption that the total number of IoT devices remains constant and equal to X end customers. The access point connects IoT devices to the mist nodes, connecting them in wireless or cable connections. The access points receive that inbound traffic from end clients. These IoT device messages are gathered at the access points (positioned near the IoT devices) and then forwarded to the mist nodes for further processing. The mist computing layer is the next layer near the client layer. The mist computing layer comprises mist nodes that are clever enough to process, compute, and temporarily store the information that has been received and transmit any leftover requests or burdens to the fog tier for additional processing or storage. Each of these mist nodes connects to the fog gateway. They are in charge of transmitting data to and from the cloud via the fog gateway. The cloud layer is the uppermost tier. This layer comprises a large data center where virtual machines can process and store massive data.

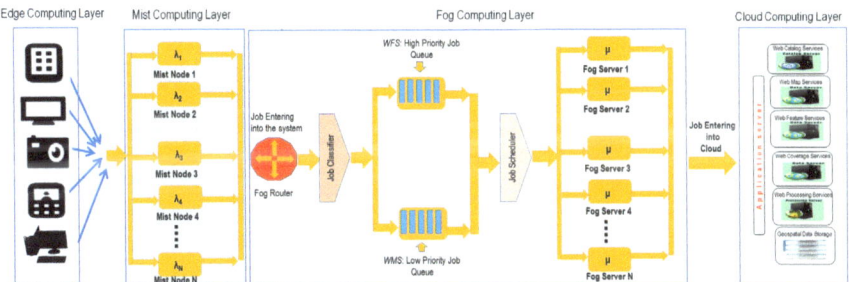

Figure 2. Proposed preemptive-resume priority queueing analytical approach.

Figure 3 describes the overall sequence diagram of the proposed architecture.

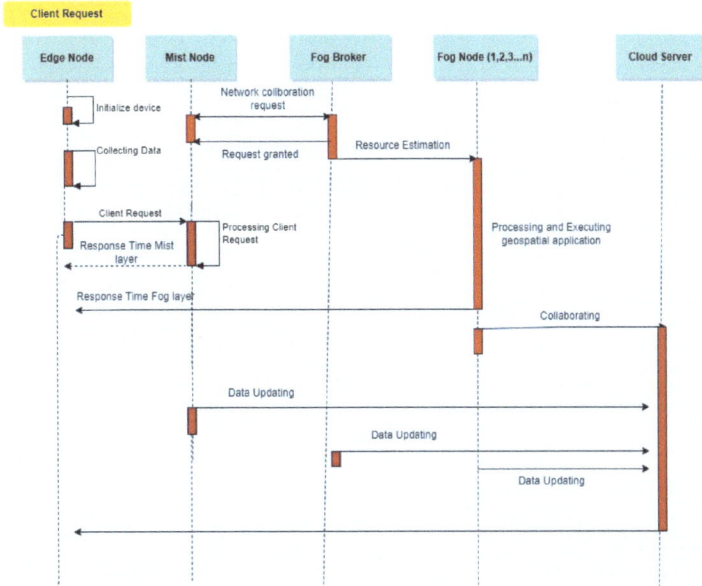

Figure 3. Sequence diagram of the proposed mist–cloud–fog system with preemptive-resume priority queueing approach.

Let us assume that tasks arrive as a Poisson process at a single exponential processor and that each job is assigned to one of the two priority classes upon arrival in the system. It is customary to number priority tasks so that small numbers correspond to higher priorities. Assume that the (Poisson) arrivals of the first or higher priority task have a mean arrival rate λ_h and those of the second or lower priority task have a mean arrival rate λ_ℓ. The total arrival rate is $\lambda = \lambda_h + \lambda_\ell$.

Queue disciplines that prioritize specific tasks are frequent in service systems. Priority can be based on elements such as the classification of tasks and the type of service. With the advent of cloud computing, a broad range of priority tasks were put in to improve system measures. Analyzing more variants entails much more complex underlying processes.

Here, we discuss the priority model of two-type as part of the $M/M//1$ set-up. To start, when considering the priority queues in the fog system, the following components need special attention:

- There is more than one class of tasks on the basis of their demands or significance to the system.

- The tasks of one class are more important than the other. When there are more than two classes, it is possible to organize them into a hierarchy of service priorities.
- The priority that agrees with a class of tasks may or may not be preemptive. If one task is prioritized in relation to another, the priority task will prevent the non-priority task from obtaining service.
- When service preemption is permitted, it can resume the service to the preempted task after the priority tasks are processed, from when the service was preempted or initiated from the start. They are disciplines of preventive recovery and preventive repetition, respectively.

Consider the preemptive-resume priority class for the $M/M/1$ queue. Tasks of type 1 are a higher priority for the service than tasks of type 2. By preemptive resume, we mean that a Class 1 task will be served immediately upon arrival if there are not already Class 1 tasks in the system. As a result, a Class 1 task may preempt a Class 2 task already on the service system. If a class 2 task is preemptive, it goes to the "top of the line" for Class 2 jobs, and when processed, the service is restarted, not repeated. Let the arrival and departure of the task take place according to Poisson and exponential distribution, respectively. The arrival and processing rates of the tasks of the two types are as follows: Type 1—arrival rate λ_h, processing rate μ_h; Type 2—arrival rate λ_ℓ, service rate μ_ℓ. Since the processing time of the task is exponentially distributed, the memory-less property of the processing-time distribution makes it easier to simplify the preemptive-resume analysis. Figure 4 depicts the flow chart of the proposed preemptive-resume priority queueing model for WFS and WMS.

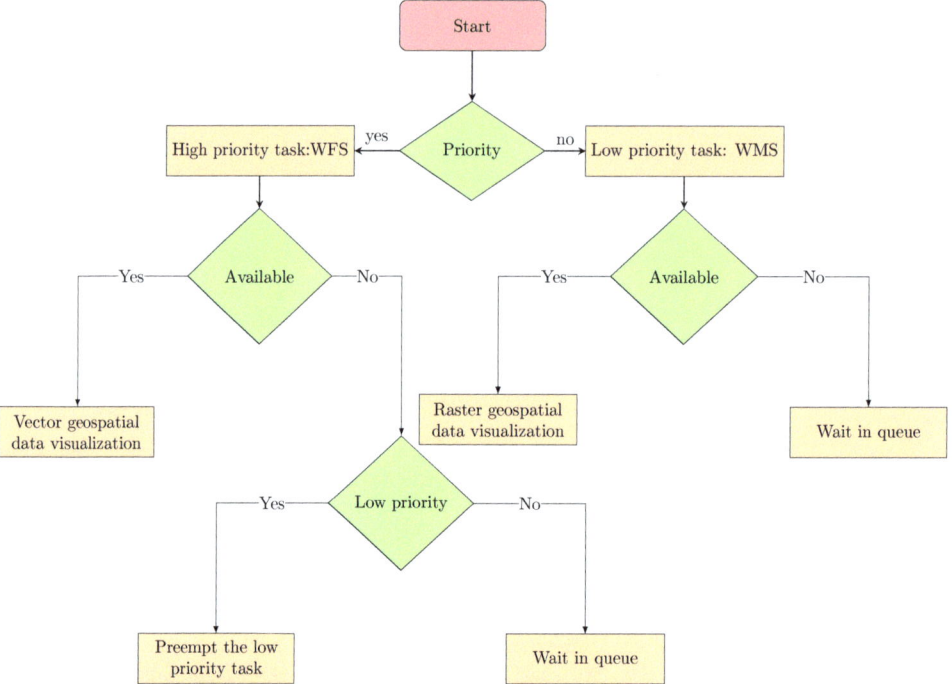

Figure 4. Flow chart of proposed preemptive-resume priority queueing model for WFS and WMS.

In the case of a preemptive priority scheme, system tasks are ranked in order of priority. The moment the high-priority task arrives, a low-priority task in the process is turned out from service immediately. The disrupted task is permitted back into service once the system has no higher-priority task. As we assume a preemptive resume policy, when the service resumes, it proceeds from where it was disrupted.

Let us assume $\pi(m,n)$ is the steady state of two types of tasks, where the number of high-priority and low-priority tasks are m and n, respectively. The common notations and their representations used across the paper are given in Table 3. We have the following equations in steady-state by applying flow out = flow in:

$$(\lambda_h + \lambda_\ell)\pi(0,0) = \mu_h \pi(1,0) + \mu_\ell \pi(0,1), \tag{1}$$
$$(\lambda_h + \lambda_\ell + \mu_h)\pi(m,0) = \lambda_h \pi(m-1,0) + \mu_h \pi(m+1,0),\ m \geq 1, \tag{2}$$
$$(\lambda_h + \lambda_\ell + \mu_\ell)\pi(0,n) = \lambda_\ell \pi(0,n-1) + \mu_h \pi(1,n) + \mu_\ell \pi(0,n+1),\ n \geq 1, \tag{3}$$
$$(\lambda_h + \lambda_\ell + \mu_h)\pi(m,n) = \lambda_h \pi(m-1,n) + \lambda_\ell \pi(m,n-1)$$
$$+ \mu_h \pi(m+1,n),\ m,n \geq 1. \tag{4}$$

Under equilibrium conditions ($\lambda_h < \mu_h$), the probability distribution for the number of tasks of type 1 in the system is

$$\pi(1,n) = \rho_h^n (1-\rho_h),\ n \geq 1$$

where $\rho_h = \lambda_h/\mu_h$. For the class 1 tasks, the class 2 tasks do not exist. Thus, we have

$$E(L_h) = \frac{\rho_h}{1-\rho_h}. \tag{5}$$

As the processing times of all tasks are exponentially distributed with the same mean, the complete tasks in the system do not depend on their processing. This number is, therefore, the same as in the system in which all tasks are completed in order of arrival. Hence,

$$E(L_\ell) = \frac{\rho_\ell}{1-\rho_h-\rho_\ell}\left[1 + \frac{\mu_\ell \rho_h}{\mu_h(1-\rho_h)}\right] \tag{6}$$

where $\rho_\ell = \lambda_\ell/\mu_\ell$.

$$E(L_h) + E(L_\ell) = \frac{\rho_h}{1-\rho_h} + \frac{\rho_\ell}{1-\rho_h-\rho_\ell}\left[1 + \frac{\mu_\ell \rho_h}{\mu_h(1-\rho_h)}\right]. \tag{7}$$

The mean number of low-priority tasks in the mist–fog system is

$$\sum_{n=0}^{\infty} n\, \pi(m,n) = \frac{\rho_\ell}{1-\rho_h-\rho_\ell}\left[1 + \frac{\mu_\ell \rho_h}{\mu_h(1-\rho_h)}\right].$$

The mean sojourn time of high-priority tasks in the mist–fog structure is

$$W_h = \frac{1}{\mu_h - \lambda_h} \tag{8}$$

and for low-priority tasks by

$$W_\ell = \frac{1}{\mu_\ell(1-\rho_h-\rho_\ell)}\left[1 + \frac{\mu_\ell \rho_h}{\mu_h(1-\rho_h)}\right]. \tag{9}$$

The average sojourn time in the queue of high-priority task class is given by

$$W_{q,h} = \frac{\rho_h}{\mu_h(1-\rho_h)} \tag{10}$$

The average sojourn time in the queue of low-priority task class is

$$W_{q,\ell} = \frac{1}{\mu_\ell(1 - \rho_h - \rho_\ell)} \left[\rho_h + \rho_\ell + \frac{\mu_\ell \rho_h}{\mu_h(1 - \rho_h)} \right]. \tag{11}$$

In steady-state, let $E(L_j)$ be the mean number of type-j jobs in the system. The $E(L_k)$ of the kth task class is generalized (Jaiswal 1968 [84]) and is given by

$$E(L_k) = \frac{\rho_k}{1 - \sum_{j=1}^{k-1} \rho_j} + \frac{\lambda_k \sum_{j=1}^{k}(\lambda_j/\mu_j^2)}{(1 - \sum_{j=1}^{k-1} \rho_j)(1 - \sum_{j=1}^{k-2} \rho_j)}. \tag{12}$$

Table 3. Notations used.

Notation	Representation
λ_h	High-priority task arrival rate
λ_ℓ	Low-priority task arrival rate
μ_h	Service rate of high-priority task
μ_ℓ	Service rate of low-priority task
λ	Total task arrival rate
μ	Service rate of total task
ρ	System utilization factor
$E(L_h)$	Average number of high-priority tasks in the system
$E(L_\ell)$	Average number of low-priority tasks in the system
W_h	Average sojourn time of high-priority tasks in the system
W_ℓ	Average sojourn time of low-priority tasks in the system
$W_{q,h}$	Average sojourn time in the queue of high-priority task class
$W_{q,\ell}$	Average sojourn time in the queue of low-priority task class
C_h	Cost of having a task of high-priority class
C_ℓ	Cost of having a task of low-priority class
$\Delta(F(\lambda))$	Expected total cost

Optimal Cost for Task of Priorities

Let us assume that the priorities are pre-assigned. To compare several potential priority tasks, we require the associated cost factors. The optimum allocation of tasks is that for which the total cost is a minimum. Consider that C_h is the cost of having a task of high-priority class, and C_ℓ is the cost of having a task of low-priority class. Here, $C_h, C_\ell \geq O$. Especially, if $C_h = C_\ell$ is equal, then we are looking for a priority allocation that minimizes the expected number of tasks in all classes. In the model discussed here, there are two classes of tasks, specified by arrival and processing rates (λ_i, μ_i) for $i = h, \ell$, and the priority allocation is high for $i = h$ and low for $i = \ell$. Then the expected total cost is

$$F(\lambda_\ell, \mu_\ell, C_\ell; \lambda_h, \mu_h, C_h) = C_\ell E(L_\ell) + C_h E(L_h), \tag{13}$$

Using (5) and (6) in (13), we find the cost function to be

$$\Delta(F(\lambda_\ell)) = F(\lambda_\ell, \mu_\ell, C_\ell; \lambda_h, \mu_h, C_h) = \frac{C_\ell \rho_\ell}{1 - \rho_h - \rho_\ell}\left[1 + \frac{\mu_\ell \rho_h}{\mu_h(1 - \rho_h)}\right] + \frac{C_h \rho_h}{1 - \rho_h}.$$

We alter this priority allocation to low for $i = h$ and high for $i = \ell$ and study the impact of this variation on the cost function (13). Therefore,

$$\Delta(F(\lambda_h)) = F(\lambda_h, \mu_h, C_h; \lambda_\ell, \mu_\ell, C_\ell) = \frac{C_h \rho_h}{1 - \rho_\ell - \rho_h}\left[1 + \frac{\mu_h \rho_\ell}{\mu_\ell(1 - \rho_\ell)}\right] + \frac{C_\ell \rho_\ell}{1 - \rho_\ell}.$$

After simplification, we have

$$\Delta(F(\lambda_\ell)) < \Delta(F(\lambda_h)),$$

this implies that the class h tasks should be allocated higher priority when

$$C_h \, \mu_h > C_\ell \, \mu_\ell.$$

The algorithm for finding optimal cost for task of priorities is described in Algorithm 1.

Algorithm 1 Algorithm for finding optimal cost for task of priorities
---
Input: $\lambda_h, \lambda_\ell, \mu_h, \mu_\ell, C_h, C_\ell$.
Output: $\Delta F(\lambda_h), \Delta F(\lambda_\ell)$,
1: **Initialize:**
2: $\rho_h = \frac{\lambda_h}{\mu_h} < 1, \rho_\ell = \frac{\lambda_\ell}{\mu_\ell} < 1$.
3: $C_h \leftarrow$ Cost of having a task of high-priority class.
4: $C_\ell \leftarrow$ Cost of having a task of low-priority class.
5: **Compute:**
6: $E(L_h) = \frac{\rho_h}{1-\rho_h}$;
7: $E(L_\ell) = \frac{\rho_\ell}{1-\rho_h-\rho_\ell}\left[1 + \frac{\mu_\ell \rho_h}{\mu_h(1-\rho_h)}\right]$;
8: $Z = \Delta(F(\lambda_i)) = C_h \, E(L_h) + C_\ell \, E(L_\ell)$;
9: **Compute:**
10: $\Delta(F(\lambda_\ell)) = \frac{C_\ell \rho_\ell}{1-\rho_h-\rho_\ell}\left[1 + \frac{\mu_\ell \rho_h}{\mu_h(1-\rho_h)}\right] + \frac{C_h \rho_h}{1-\rho_h}$;
11: $\Delta(F(\lambda_h)) = \frac{C_h \rho_h}{1-\rho_\ell-\rho_h}\left[1 + \frac{\mu_h \rho_\ell}{\mu_\ell(1-\rho_\ell)}\right] + \frac{C_\ell \rho_\ell}{1-\rho_\ell}$;
12: **return** Z
13: **exit**
---

4. Numerical Results

To illustrate the analytical results presented herein, some numerical results are illustrated in tables and figures. The calculations were made with double accuracy and performed in a 64-bit windows ten professional OS possessing Intel® Core i5 6200U processor @2:30 GHz and 8 GB DDR3 RAM manufacturer Dell utilizing MAPLE 22 software. We reported the numeric results to only the nearest four digits, but the results were very accurate.

Figure 5 depicts the impact of ρ on the average number of tasks in the system for two priority classes. We observe that in the mist–fog system, the average number of tasks rises with the increase in ρ, and even more so in priority class-2, which is the low-priority class. When there are two priority classes, as far as the higher-priority task is referred, the system performs just like a regular M/M/1 system. Figure 6 describes the impact of ρ on the mean number of tasks in the system for five priority classes. One can see that with an increase in ρ, the mean number of tasks in the system increases. The average number of tasks in the system is less in the case of priority class 1 than in other priority classes. In this case, the system outperforms when the value of ρ is lower.

Figure 7 plots the dependence of ρ on the average waiting time in the queue (W_q). Observe that the system W_q increases with an increase in ρ. For higher values of ρ, the variation in mean waiting time in the queue for both classes increases. The mean waiting time in the queue is less for the higher-priority task than for the low-priority task. However, the impact of the low-priority task is twofold: the queue time and the processing time. Figure 8 illustrates the influence of the mean waiting time in the queue (W_q) on the ρ. With an increase in ρ, we note an increasing trend in all priority classes. For priority class 1, W_q is almost static when ρ is more significant than 0.5. We note that the performance of various classes impacts the system's performance. For instance, the processing time and wait time are more in class 5 than in class 4. Thus, a hierarchy of priorities would arise if there were more classes of tasks.

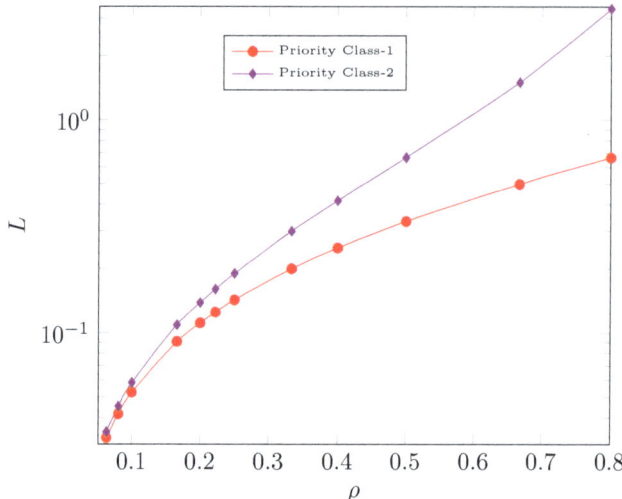

Figure 5. Impact of ρ on L with two priority classes.

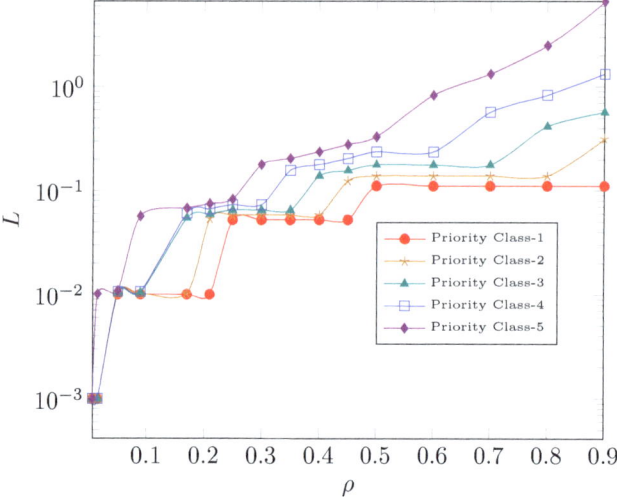

Figure 6. Impact of ρ on L with five priority classes.

Figures 9 and 10 show the impact of λ on server utilization % and the average waiting time in the mist–fog system (W), respectively. From Figure 9, we observe an increasing trend, with an increase in λ. But, with the rise of μ, we see a decreasing trend. Also, the server utilization % increases with the increase in arrival rate with a fixed service rate. Thus, we may carefully assume the arrival and service rate to ensure the balance of the server utilization of the system. From Figure 10, we note an increasing trend, with an increase in λ. For the small value of μ, the average waiting time rises monotonically. Moreover, with a fixed service rate, the average wait time increases with the increase in the arrival rate. To reduce the average wait time of the system, we can meticulously put in place the service and the arrival rate to achieve it.

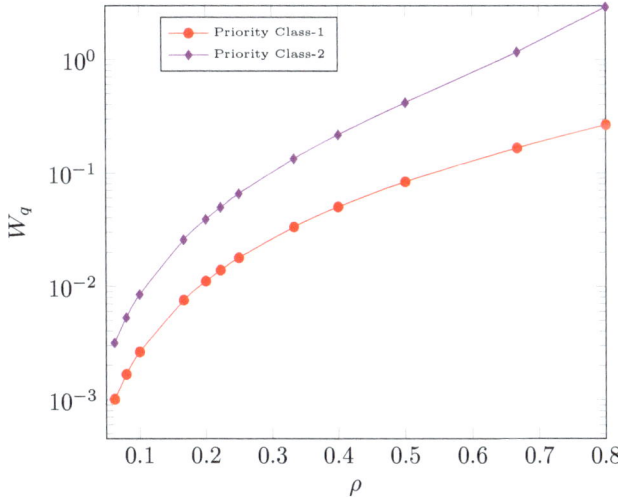

Figure 7. Impact of ρ on W_q with two priority classes.

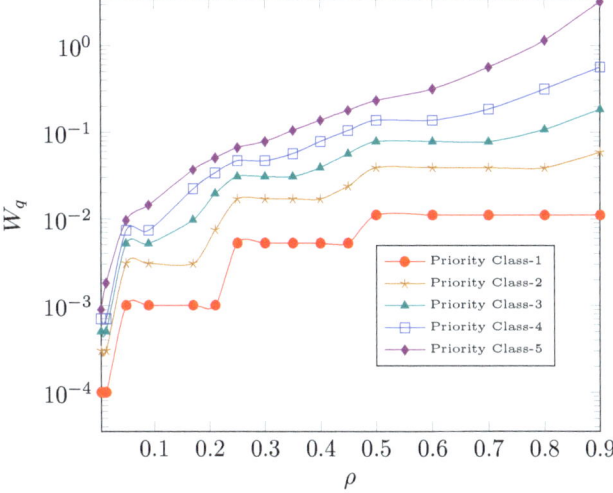

Figure 8. Impact of ρ on W_q with five priority classes.

Tables 4 and 5 present performance measures of the task allocation system of two priority class when $\mu_h = \mu_\ell$ and $\mu_h \neq \mu_\ell$, respectively. In Table 4, we vary λ_1 and assume other parameters as $\lambda_\ell = 5$ and $\mu_h = \mu_\ell = 10.9091$. Note that with the gain of λ_h, the performance indices increases. Comparing priority type 1 and type 2, observe that the mean number of tasks in the queue (system) and the average waiting time in the queue (system) is less in the case of priority class 1. In Table 6, we vary λ_h and assume other parameters as $\lambda_\ell = 5$, $\mu_h = 10.9091$, and $\mu_\ell = 10.9091$. We also compared the system when there was no priority task. The relevant results are presented in the second column of the tables as the overall result.

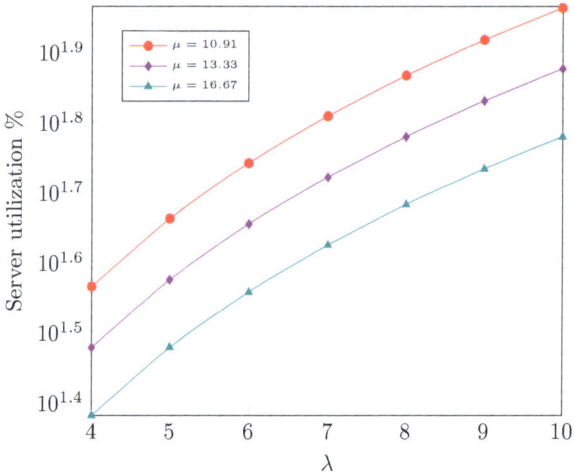

Figure 9. Effect of λ on percentage of server utilization.

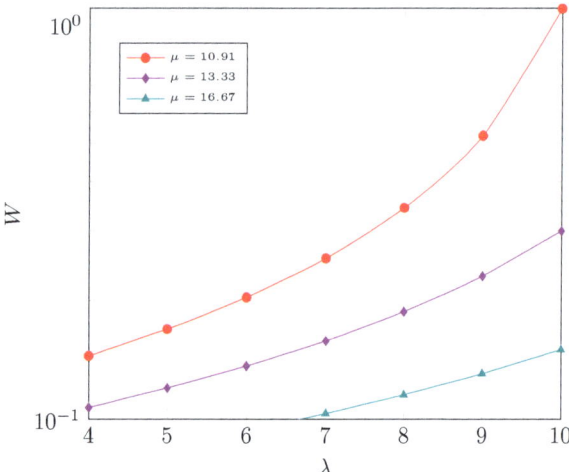

Figure 10. Effect of λ on W.

Table 4. Performance measures of two priority classes.

	$\lambda_\ell = 5, \mu_h = \mu_\ell = 10.9091$					
	$\lambda_h = 1$			$\lambda_h = 2$		
	Overall	Type-1	Type-2	Overall	Type-1	Type-2
L_s	1.222222	0.100917	1.121305	1.790698	0.22449	1.566208
L_q	0.672222	0.009251	0.662971	1.149031	0.041156	1.107875
W_s	0.203704	0.100917	0.224261	0.255814	0.112245	0.313242
W_q	0.112037	0.009251	0.132594	0.164147	0.020578	0.221575
	$\lambda_h = 3$			$\lambda_h = 4$		
	Overall	Type-1	Type-2	Overall	Type-1	Type-2
L_s	2.75	0.37931	2.37069	4.714286	0.578947	4.135338
L_q	2.016667	0.10431	1.912356	3.889286	0.212281	3.677005
W_s	0.34375	0.126437	0.474138	0.52381	0.144737	0.827068
W_q	0.252083	0.03477	0.382471	0.432143	0.05307	0.735401

Table 5. Performance measures of two priority classes when $\mu_h \neq \mu_\ell$.

| | $\lambda_\ell = 5, \mu_h = 10.9091, \mu_\ell = 12$ | | | | | |
| | $\lambda_h = 1$ | | | $\lambda_h = 2$ | | |
	Overall	Type-1	Type-2	Overall	Type-1	Type-2
L_s	0.165636	0.100917	0.064719	0.305812	0.224489	0.081322
L_q	0.023970	0.009251	0.014719	0.072478	0.041156	0.031322
W_s	0.103523	0.100917	0.107865	0.117619	0.112245	0.135537
W_q	0.014981	0.009251	0.024532	0.027876	0.020578	0.052203
	$\lambda_h = 3$			$\lambda_h = 4$		
	Overall	Type-1	Type-2	Overall	Type-1	Type-2
L_s	0.484291	0.37931	0.104981	0.719247	0.578947	0.140301
L_q	0.159291	0.10431	0.054981	0.302581	0.21228	0.090301
W_s	0.134525	0.126436	0.174968	0.156358	0.144737	0.233834
W_q	0.044247	0.03477	0.091635	0.065778	0.05307	0.150501

Table 6. Performance measures of five priority classes.

| | $\lambda_1 = 1, \lambda_2 = \lambda_3 = \lambda_4 = \lambda_5 = 2, \lambda = 5, \mu = 10, \rho = 0.9$ | | | | | |
	Overall	Type-1	Type-2	Type-3	Type-4	Type-5
L_s	9	0.111111	0.31746	0.571429	1.333333	6.666667
L_q	8.1	0.011111	0.11746	0.371429	1.133333	6.466667
W_s	1	0.111111	0.15873	0.285714	0.666667	3.333333
W_q	0.9	0.011111	0.05873	0.185714	0.566667	3.233333
	$\lambda_1 = 0.5, \lambda_2 = \lambda_3 = \lambda_4 = \lambda_5 = 1, \lambda = 5, \mu = 10, \rho = 0.45$					
	Overall	Type-1	Type-2	Type-3	Type-4	Type-5
L_s	0.818182	0.052632	0.123839	0.156863	0.205128	0.27972
L_q	0.368182	0.002632	0.023839	0.056863	0.105128	0.17972
W_s	0.181818	0.105263	0.123839	0.156863	0.205128	0.27972
W_q	0.081818	0.005263	0.023839	0.056863	0.105128	0.17972

Figures 11 and 12 demonstrate the impact of processing rate μ_h on total cost of low- and high-priority tasks when $\lambda_h = \lambda_\ell$ and $\lambda_h \neq \lambda_\ell$, respectively. One may note that the total cost decreases as μ_h increases in both cases. When $\lambda_h = \lambda_\ell$, the total cost of the low-priority task decreases more rapidly for higher values of μ_h in comparison to the high-priority task. But the result is just reversed in the case of $\lambda_h \neq \lambda_\ell$.

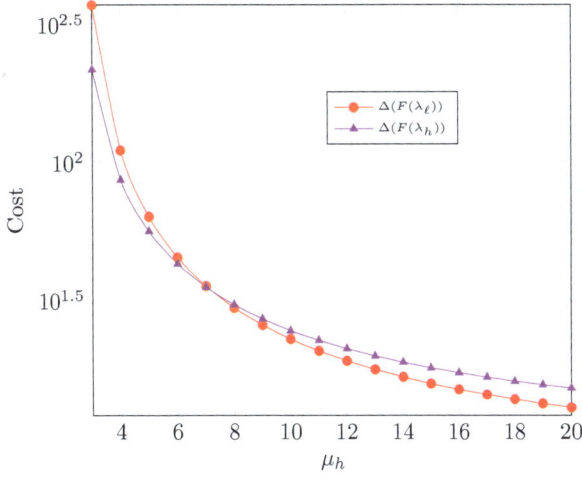

Figure 11. Cost function when $\lambda_h = \lambda_\ell$.

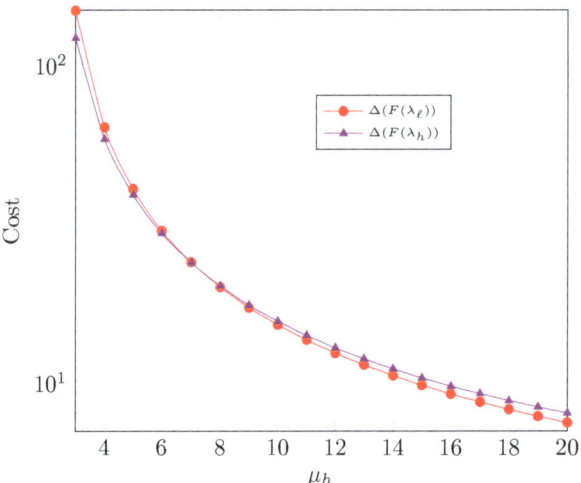

Figure 12. Cost function when $\lambda_h \neq \lambda_\ell$.

5. Concluding Remarks

In this article, the concepts of cloud computing, fog computing, and mist computing for geospatial web services, in particular WMS and WFS, are analyzed and explored. This paper proposed the preemptive-resume priority queueing strategy for the mist–cloud–fog system and associated components for improved data processing and analysis in geospatial web applications. Because of the mist and fog nodes, the number of geospatial data that need to be stored as well as processed is cut down, which results in transmission that is both efficient and has a lower latency and throughput. Additionally, a priority-based queuing strategy was presented in order to limit the dynamism of the suggested model and conduct analysis on it. Using the proper diagrams, the performance analysis, performance assessment, and performance measurement of the provided framework, in addition to the experimental results, have been discussed.

The proposed model is going to be put to the test in future application-oriented case studies, which will will include a wide range of parameters. The model that was suggested incorporates, among other things, specific data regarding the utilization of the CPU, the response time, the loss rate, the throughput, and the average number of jobs that were requested.

Author Contributions: Conceptualization, S.K.P., R.K.B. and V.G.; writing—review and editing, V.G., H.K.A. and R.K.B. ; Methodology, H.D. and G.B.M.; Software, S.K.P. and V.G.; Validation, G.B.M. and R.K.B.; Formal analysis, V.G. and G.B.M.; Resources, V.G. and H.K.A.; Visualization, S.K.P. and H.D. All authors have read and agreed to the published version of the manuscript

Funding: This research received no external funding.

Data Availability Statement: Not applicable.

Conflicts of Interest: The authors declare no conflict of interest.

References

1. Armstrong, M.P. High performance computing for geospatial applications: A retrospective view. In *High Performance Computing for Geospatial Applications*; Springer: Berlin/Heidelberg, Germany , 2020; pp. 9–25
2. Barik, R.K.; Dubey, H.; Mankodiya, K.; Sasane, S.A.; Misra, C. Geofog4health: A fog-based sdi framework for geospatial health big data analysis. *J. Ambient. Intell. Humaniz. Comput.* **2019**, *10*, 551–567. [CrossRef]
3. Goswami, V.; Sharma, B.; Patra, S.S.; Chowdhury, S.; Barik, R.K.; Dhaou, I.B. Iot-fog computing sustainable system for smart cities: A queueing-based approach. In Proceedings of the 2023 1st International Conference on Advanced Innovations in Smart Cities (ICAISC), Jeddah, Saudi Arabia, 23–25 January 2023; pp. 1–6.

4. Mukherjee, M.; Guo, M.; Lloret, J.; Iqbal, R.; Zhang, Q. Deadline-aware fair scheduling for offloaded tasks in fog computing with inter-fog dependency. *IEEE Commun. Lett.* **2019**, *24*, 307–311. [CrossRef]
5. Nikoui, T.S.; Rahmani, A.M.; Balador, A.; Javadi, H.H.S. Analytical model for task offloading in a fog computing system with batch-size-dependent service. *Comput. Commun.* **2022**, *190*, 201–215. [CrossRef]
6. Geobuiz 23: Global Geospatial Industry Market Size, Forecast, and Growth Trends Report. Available online: https://geospatialworld.net/consulting/reports/geobuiz/2023/index.html (accessed on 17 March 2023).
7. Geospatial Analytics Market Size & Share Analysis—Growth Trends & Forecasts (2023–2028). Available online: https://www.mordorintelligence.com/industry-reports/geospatial-analytics-market (accessed on 17 March 2023).
8. Bhushan, S.; Mat, M. Priority-queue based dynamic scaling for efficient resource allocation in fog computing. In Proceedings of the 2021 IEEE International Conference on Service Operations and Logistics, and Informatics (SOLI), Delhi, India, 2–4 December 2021; pp. 1–6.
9. Golkar, A.; Malekhosseini, R.; RahimiZadeh, K.; Yazdani, A.; Beheshti, A. A priority queue-based telemonitoring system for automatic diagnosis of heart diseases in integrated fog computing environments. *Health Inform. J.* **2022**, *28*, 14604582221137453. [CrossRef] [PubMed]
10. Barik, R.K.; Dubey, A.C.; Tripathi, A.; Pratik, T.; Sasane, S.; Lenka, R.K.; Dubey, H.; Mankodiya, K.; Kumar, V. Mist data: Leveraging mist computing for secure and scalable architecture for smart and connected health. *Procedia Comput. Sci.* **2018**, *125*, 647–653. [CrossRef]
11. Hmissi, F.; Ouni, S. An mqtt brokers distribution based on mist computing for real-time iot communications. *Res. Sq. preprint.* **2021**. [CrossRef]
12. Maiti, P.; Sahoo, B.; Turuk, A.K.; Kumar, A.; Choi, B.J. Internet of things applications placement to minimize latency in multi-tier fog computing framework. *ICT Express* **2022**, *8*, 166–173. [CrossRef]
13. Mallick, S.R.; Lenka, R.K.; Goswami, V.; Sharma, S.; Dalai, A.K.; Das, H.; Barik, R.K. Bcgeo: Blockchain-assisted geospatial web service for smart healthcare system. *IEEE Access* **2023**, *11*, 58610–58623. [CrossRef]
14. Arefian, Z.; Khayyambashi, M.R.; Movahhedinia, N. Delay reduction in mtc using sdn based offloading in fog computing. *PLoS ONE* **2023**, *18*, e0286483. [CrossRef]
15. Cai, P.; Jiang, Q. Gis spatial information sharing of smart city based on cloud computing. *Clust. Comput.* **2019**, *22*, 14435–14443. [CrossRef]
16. Das, J.; Ghosh, S.K.; Buyya, R. Geospatial edge-fog computing: A systematic review, taxonomy, and future directions. In *Mobile Edge Computing*; Springer: Berlin/Heidelberg, Germany, 2021; pp. 47–69.
17. Fareed, N.; Rehman, K. Integration of remote sensing and gis to extract plantation rows from a drone-based image point cloud digital surface model. *ISPRS Int. J. -Geo-Inf.* **2020**, *9*, 151. [CrossRef]
18. Shahid, H.; Shah, M.A.; Almogren, A.; Khattak, H.A.; Din, I.U.; Kumar, N.; Maple, C. Machine learning-based mist computing enabled internet of battlefield things. *ACM Trans. Internet Technol. (TOIT)* **2021**, *21*, 1–26. [CrossRef]
19. He, Z.; Xu, Y.; Liu, D.; Zhou, W.; Li, K. Energy-efficient computation offloading strategy with task priority in cloud assisted multi-access edge computing. *Future Gener. Comput. Syst.* **2023**, *148*, 298–313. [CrossRef]
20. Chavhan, S.; Gupta, D.; Gochhayat, S.P.; Khanna, A.; Shankar, K.; Rodrigues, J.J. Edge computing ai-iot integrated energy-efficient intelligent transportation system for smart cities. *ACM Trans. Internet Technol.* **2022**, *22*, 1–18. [CrossRef]
21. Bouanaka, C.; Laouir, A.E.; Medkour, R. Iedss: Efficient scheduling of emergency department resources based on fog computing. In Proceedings of the 2020 IEEE/ACS 17th International Conference on Computer Systems and Applications (AICCSA), Antalya, Turkey, 2–5 November 2020; pp. 1–6.
22. Dutta, A.; Misra, C.; Barik, R.K.; Mishra, S. Enhancing mist assisted cloud computing toward secure and scalable architecture for smart healthcare. In *Advances in Communication and Computational Technology*; Springer: Berlin/Heidelberg, Germany, 2021; pp. 1515–1526.
23. Barik, R.K.; Misra, C.; Lenka, R.K.; Dubey, H.; Mankodiya, K. Hybrid mist-cloud systems for large scale geospatial big data analytics and processing: Opportunities and challenges. *Arab. J. Geosci.* **2019**, *12*, 32. [CrossRef]
24. Das, J.; Mukherjee, A.; Ghosh, S.K.; Buyya, R. Spatio-fog: A green and timeliness-oriented fog computing model for geospatial query resolution. *Simul. Model. Pract. Theory* **2020**, *100*, 102043. [CrossRef]
25. Etemadi, M.; Ghobaei-Arani, M.; Shahidinejad, A. Resource provisioning for iot services in the fog computing environment: An autonomic approach. *Comput. Commun.* **2020**, *161*, 109–131. [CrossRef]
26. Silva, F.A.; Fé, I.; Gonçalves, G. Stochastic models for performance and cost analysis of a hybrid cloud and fog architecture. *J. Supercomput.* **2021**, *77*, 1537–1561. [CrossRef]
27. Sharma, S.; Saini, H. A novel four-tier architecture for delay aware scheduling and load balancing in fog environment. *Sustain. Comput. Inform. Syst.* **2019**, *24*, 100355. [CrossRef]
28. Wang, T.; Liang, Y.; Jia, W.; Arif, M.; Liu, A.; Xie, M. Coupling resource management based on fog computing in smart city systems. *J. Netw. Comput. Appl.* **2019**, *135*, 11–19. [CrossRef]
29. Alli, A.A.; Alam, M.M. Secoff-fciot: Machine learning based secure offloading in fog-cloud of things for smart city applications. *Internet Things* **2019**, *7*, 100070. [CrossRef]

30. El Kafhali, S.; Salah, K. Efficient and dynamic scaling of fog nodes for iot devices. *J. Supercomput.* **2017**, *73*, 5261–5284. [CrossRef]
31. El Kafhali, S.; Salah, K. Modeling and analysis of performance and energy consumption in cloud data centers. *Arab. J. Sci. Eng.* **2018**, *43*, 7789–7802. [CrossRef]
32. Zhang, C. Design and application of fog computing and internet of things service platform for smart city. *Future Gener. Comput. Syst.* **2020**, *112*, 630–640. [CrossRef]
33. Ghobaei-Arani, M.; Souri, A.; Rahmanian, A.A. Resource management approaches in fog computing: A comprehensive review. *J. Grid Comput.* **2019**, *18*, 1–42. [CrossRef]
34. Yousefpour, A.; Fung, C.; Nguyen, T.; Kadiyala, K.; Jalali, F.; Niakanlahiji, A.; Kong, J.; Jue, J.P. All one needs to know about fog computing and related edge computing paradigms: A complete survey. *J. Syst. Archit.* **2019**, *98*, 289–330. [CrossRef]
35. Evangelidis, K.; Ntouros, K.; Makridis, S.; Papatheodorou, C. Geospatial services in the cloud. *Comput. Geosci.* **2014**, *63*, 116–122. [CrossRef]
36. Barik, R.K. Cloudganga: Cloud computing based sdi model for ganga river basin management in india. In *Geospatial Intelligence: Concepts, Methodologies, Tools, and Applications*; IGI Global: Hershey, PA, USA, 2019; pp. 278–297.
37. Wieclaw, L.; Pasichnyk, V.; Kunanets, N.; Duda, O.; Matsiuk, O.; Falat, P. Cloud computing technologies in "smart city" projects. In Proceedings of the 2017 9th IEEE International Conference on Intelligent Data Acquisition and Advanced Computing Systems: Technology and Applications (IDAACS), Bucharest, Romania, 21–23 September 2017; Volume 1, pp. 339–342.
38. Liang, J.; Jin, F.; Zhang, X.; Wu, H. Ws4gee: Enhancing geospatial web services and geoprocessing workflows by integrating the google earth engine. *Environ. Model. Softw.* **2023**, *161*, 105636. [CrossRef]
39. AL Kharouf, R.A.; Alzoubaidi, A.R.; Jweihan, M. An integrated architectural framework for geoprocessing in cloud environment. *Spat. Inf. Res.* **2017**, *25*, 89–97. [CrossRef]
40. Barik, R.K.; Lenka, R.; Sahoo, S.; Das, B.; Pattnaik, J. Development of educational geospatial database for cloud sdi using open source gis. In *Progress in Advanced Computing and Intelligent Engineering*; Springer: Berlin/Heidelberg, Germany, 2018; pp. 685–695.
41. Goldberg, D.; Olivares, M.; Li, Z.; Klein, A.G. Maps & gis data libraries in the era of big data and cloud computing. *J. Map Geogr. Libr.* **2014**, *10*, 100–122.
42. Zhang, J.; Xu, L.; Zhang, Y.; Liu, G.; Zhao, L.; Wang, Y. An on-demand scalable model for geographic information system (gis) data processing in ancloud gis. *ISPRS Int. J. -Geo-Inf.* **2019**, *8*, 392. [CrossRef]
43. Khazaei, H.; Misic, J.; Misic, V.B. Performance analysis of cloud computing centers using M/G/m/m+ r queuing systems. *IEEE Trans. Parallel Distrib. Syst.* **2011**, *23*, 936–943. [CrossRef]
44. Ellens, W.; Akkerboom, J.; Litjens, R.; Van Den Berg, H. Performance of cloud computing centers with multiple priority classes. In Proceedings of the 2012 IEEE Fifth International Conference on Cloud Computing, Honolulu, HI, USA, 24–29 June 2012; pp. 245–252.
45. Do, C.T.; Tran, N.H.; VanNguyen, M.; Hong, C.S.; Lee, S. Social optimization strategy in unobserved queueing systems in cognitive radio networks. *IEEE Commun. Lett.* **2012**, *16*, 1944–1947. [CrossRef]
46. Salah, K. A queueing model to achieve proper elasticity for cloud cluster jobs. In Proceedings of the 2013 IEEE Sixth International Conference on Cloud Computing, Santa Clara, CA, USA, 28 June–3 July 2013; pp.755–761.
47. Pal, R.; Hui, P. Economic models for cloud service markets: Pricing and capacity planning. *Theor. Comput. Sci.* **2013**, *496*, 113–124. [CrossRef]
48. Mohanty, S.; Pattnaik, P.K.; Mund, G.B. A comparative approach to reduce the waiting time using queuing theory in cloud computing environment. *Int. J. Inf. Comput. Technol.* **2014**, *4*, 469–474.
49. Chiang, Y.J.; Ouyang, Y.C.; Hsu, C.H. Performance and cost-effectiveness analyses for cloud services based on rejected and impatient users. *IEEE Trans. Serv. Comput.* **2014**, *9*, 446–455. [CrossRef]
50. Evangelin, K.R; Vidhya, V. Performance measures of queuing models using cloud computing. *Asian J. Eng. Appl. Technol.* **2015**, *4*, 8–11. [CrossRef]
51. Cheng, C.; Li, J.; Wang, Y. An energy-saving task scheduling strategy based on vacation queuing theory in cloud computing. *Tsinghua Sci. Technol.* **2015**, *20*, 28–39. [CrossRef]
52. Bai, W.H.; Xi, J.Q.; Zhu, J.X.; Huang, S.W. Performance analysis of heterogeneous data centers in cloud computing using a complex queuing model. *Math. Probl. Eng.* **2015**, *2015*, 980645 . [CrossRef]
53. Kirsal, Y.; Ever, Y.K.; Mostarda, L.; Gemikonakli, O. Analytical modelling and performability analysis for cloud computing using queuing system. In Proceedings of the 2015 IEEE/ACM 8th International Conference on Utility and Cloud Computing (UCC), Limassol, Cyprus, 7–10 December 2015; pp. 643–647.
54. Guo, L.; Yan, T.; Zhao, S.; Jiang, C. Dynamic performance optimization for cloud computing using M/M/m queueing system. *J. Appl. Math.* **2014**, *2014*, 756592. [CrossRef]
55. Akbari, E.; Cung, F.; Patel, H.; Razaque, A.; Dalal, H.N. Incorporation of weighted linear prediction technique and M/M/1 queuing theory for improving energy efficiency of cloud computing datacenters. In Proceedings of the 2016 IEEE Long Island Systems, Applications and Technology Conference (LISAT), Farmingdale, NY, USA, 29 April 2016; pp. 1–5.

56. Chang, Z.; Zhou, Z.; Ristaniemi, T.; Niu, Z. Energy efficient optimization for computation offloading in fog computing system. In Proceedings of the GLOBECOM 2017–2017 IEEE Global Communications Conference, Singapore, 4–8 December 2017; pp. 1–6.
57. Liu, L.; Chang, Z.; Guo, X.; Mao, S.; Ristaniemi, T. Multiobjective optimization for computation offloading in fog computing. *IEEE Internet Things J.* **2017**, *5*, 283–294. [CrossRef]
58. Safvati, M.; Sharzehei, M. Analytical review on queuing theory in clouds environments. In Proceedings of the Third National Conference on New Approaches in Computer and Electrical Engineering Young Researchers and Elite Club , 2017. Available online: https://www.researchgate.net/publication/316438195_Analytical_Review_on_Queuing_Theory_in_Clouds_Enviroments (accessed on 17 March 2023).
59. Tadakamalla, U.; Menascé, D. Fogqn: An analytic model for fog/cloud computing. In Proceedings of the 2018 IEEE/ACM International Conference on Utility and Cloud Computing Companion (UCC Companion), Zurich, Switzerland, 17–20 December 2018; pp. 307–313
60. Sthapit, S.; Thompson, J.; Robertson, N.M.; Hopgood, J.R. Computational load balancing on the edge in absence of cloud and fog. *IEEE Trans. Mob. Comput.* **2018**, *18*, 1499–1512. [CrossRef]
61. Chunxia, Y.; Shunfu, J. An energy-saving strategy based on multi-server vacation queuing theory in cloud data center. *J. Supercomput.* **2018**, *74*, 6766–6784. [CrossRef]
62. Sopin, E.S.; Daraseliya, A.V.; Correia, L.M. Performance analysis of the offloading scheme in a fog computing system. In Proceedings of the 2018 10th International Congress on Ultra Modern Telecommunications and Control Systems and Workshops (ICUMT), Moscow, Russia, 5–9 November 2018; pp. 1–5.
63. Vasconcelos, D.R.D. Smart shadow-predictive computing resources allocation for smart devices in the mist computing environment. Ph.D. Dissertation, Universidade Federal Do Ceará, Fortaleza, Brazil, 2018.
64. Jafarnejad Ghomi, E.; Rahmani, A.M.; Qader, N.N. Applying queue theory for modeling of cloud computing: A systematic review. *Concurr. Comput. Pract. Exp.* **2019**, *31*, e5186. [CrossRef]
65. Li, G.; Yan, J.; Chen, L.; Wu, J.; Lin, Q.; Zhang, Y. Energy consumption optimization with a delay threshold in cloud-fog cooperation computing. *IEEE access* **2019**, *7*, 159688–159697. [CrossRef]
66. Kumar, M.S.; Raja, M.I. A queuing theory model for e-health cloud applications. *Int. J. Internet Technol. Secur. Trans.* **2020**, *10*, 585–600. [CrossRef]
67. Xu, R.; Wu, J.; Cheng, Y.; Liu, Z.; Lin, Y.; Xie, Y. Dynamic security exchange scheduling model for business workflow based on queuing theory in cloud computing. *Secur. Commun. Netw.* **2020**, *2020*, 8886640. [CrossRef]
68. Patra, S.; Amodi, S.A.; Goswami, V.; Barik, R. Profit maximization strategy with spot allocation quality guaranteed service in cloud environment. In Proceedings of the 2020 International Conference on Computer Science, Engineering and Applications (ICCSEA), Gunupur, India, 13–14 March 2020; pp. 1–6.
69. Sedaghat, S.; Jahangir, A.H. Rt-telsurg: Real time telesurgery using sdn, fog, and cloud as infrastructures. *IEEE Access* **2021**, *9*, 52238–52251. [CrossRef]
70. Sufyan, F.; Banerjee, A. Computation offloading for smart devices in fog-cloud queuing system. *IETE J. Res.* **2021**, *69*, 1509–1521. [CrossRef]
71. Tadakamalla, U.; Menasce, D.A. Autonomic resource management for fog computing. *IEEE Trans. Cloud Comput.* **2021**, *11*, 2334–2350. [CrossRef]
72. Feitosa, L.; Santos, L.; Gonçalves, G.; Nguyen, T.A.; Lee, J.W.; Silva, F.A. Internet of robotic things: A comparison of message routing strategies for cloud-fog computing layers using m/m/c/k queuing networks. In Proceedings of the 2021 IEEE International Conference on Systems, Man, and Cybernetics (SMC), Melbourne, Australia, 17–20 October 2021; pp. 2049–2054.
73. Panigrahi, S.K.; Barik, R.K.; Behera, S.; Barik, L.; Patra, S.S. Performability analysis of foggis model for geospatial web services. In Proceedings of the 2021 11th International Conference on Cloud Computing, Data Science & Engineering (Confluence), Noida, India, 28–29 January 2021; pp. 239–243.
74. Behera, S.; Al Amodi, S.; Patra, S.S.; Lenka, R.K.; Goje, N.S.; Barik, R.K. Profit maximization scheme in iot assisted mist computing healthcare environment using M/G/c/N queueing model. In Proceedings of the 2021 IEEE International Conference on Electronics, Computing and Communication Technologies (CONECCT), Bangalore, India, 9–11 July 2021; pp. 1–6.
75. Mas, L.; Vilaplana, J.; Mateo, J.; Solsona, F. A queuing theory model for fog computing. *J. Supercomput.* **2022**, *78*, 11138–11155. [CrossRef]
76. Rodrigues, L.; Rodrigues, J.J.; Serra, A.D.B.; Silva, F.A. A queueing-based model performance evaluation for internet of people supported by fog computing. *Future Internet* **2022**, *14*, 23. [CrossRef]
77. Hamdi, A.M.A.; Hussain, F.K.; Hussain, O.K. Task offloading in vehicular fog computing: State-of-the-art and open issues. *Future Gener. Comput. Syst.* **2022**, *133*, 201–212. [CrossRef]
78. Hazra, A.; Rana, P.; Adhikari, M.; Amgoth, T. Fog computing for next-generation internet of things: Fundamental, state-of-the-art and research challenges. *Comput. Sci. Rev.* **2023**, *48*, 100549. [CrossRef]
79. Yazdani, A.; Dashti, S.F.; Safdari, Y. A fog-assisted information model based on priority queue and clinical decision support systems. *Health Inform. J.* **2023**, *29*, 14604582231152792. [CrossRef] [PubMed]
80. Saif, F.A.; Latip, R.; Hanapi, Z.M.; Alrshah, M.A.; Shafinah, K. Workload allocation towards energy consumption-delay trade-off in cloud-fog computing using multi-objective npso algorithm. *IEEE Access* **2023**, *11*, 45393–45404. [CrossRef]

81. Saif, F.A.; Latip, R.; Hanapi, Z.M.; Shafinah, K. Multi-objective grey wolf optimizer algorithm for task scheduling in cloud-fog computing. *IEEE Access* **2023**, *11*, 20635–20646. [CrossRef]
82. Munir, A.; Kansakar, P.; Khan, S. Ifciot: Integrated fog cloud iot architectural paradigm for future iots. *arXiv* **2017**, arXiv:1701.08474.
83. Adhikari, M.; Mukherjee, M.; Srirama, S.N. Dpto: A deadline and priority-aware task offloading in fog computing framework leveraging multilevel feedback queueing. *IEEE Internet Things J.* **2019**, *7*, 5773–5782. [CrossRef]
84. Jaiswal, N.K. *Priority Queues*; Academic Press: New York, NY, USA, 1968; Volume 50.

Disclaimer/Publisher's Note: The statements, opinions and data contained in all publications are solely those of the individual author(s) and contributor(s) and not of MDPI and/or the editor(s). MDPI and/or the editor(s) disclaim responsibility for any injury to people or property resulting from any ideas, methods, instructions or products referred to in the content.

Article

Autonomous Trajectory Tracking and Collision Avoidance Design for Unmanned Surface Vessels: A Nonlinear Fuzzy Approach

Yung-Yue Chen * and Ming-Zhen Ellis-Tiew

Department of Systems and Naval Mechatronic Engineering, National Cheng Kung University, No. 1, University Road, Tainan 701, Taiwan; p16095016@gs.ncku.edu.tw
* Correspondence: yungyuchen@mail.ncku.edu.tw; Tel.: +886-91-218-6952

Abstract: An intelligent fuzzy-based control system that consists of several subsystems—a fuzzy collision evaluator, a fuzzy collision avoidance acting timing indicator, a collision-free trajectory generator, and a nonlinear adaptive fuzzy robust control law—is proposed for the collision-free condition and trajectory tracking of unmanned surface vessels (USVs). For the purpose of ensuring that controlled USVs are capable of executing tasks in an actual ocean environment that is full of randomly encountered ships under collision-free conditions, the real-time decision making and the desired trajectory arrangements of this proposed control system were developed by following the "Convention on the International Regulations for Preventing Collisions at Sea" (COLREGs). From the simulation results, several promising properties were demonstrated: (1) robustness with respect to modeling uncertainties and ocean environmental disturbances, (2) a precise trajectory tracking ability, and (3) sailing collision avoidance was shown by this proposed system for controlled USVs.

Keywords: intelligent unmanned surface vessel; fuzzy-based ship collision avoidance system; nonlinear fuzzy robust control law

MSC: 93B51

Citation: Chen, Y.-Y.; Ellis-Tiew, M.-Z. Autonomous Trajectory Tracking and Collision Avoidance Design for Unmanned Surface Vessels: A Nonlinear Fuzzy Approach. *Mathematics* **2023**, *11*, 3632. https://doi.org/10.3390/math11173632

Academic Editors: Himansu Das and Mahendra Kumar Gourisaria

Received: 25 June 2023
Revised: 16 July 2023
Accepted: 19 July 2023
Published: 22 August 2023

Copyright: © 2023 by the authors. Licensee MDPI, Basel, Switzerland. This article is an open access article distributed under the terms and conditions of the Creative Commons Attribution (CC BY) license (https:// creativecommons.org/licenses/by/ 4.0/).

1. Introduction

Shortages of crew and experienced seafarers have affected the shipping industry for years and are expected to worsen over the next couple of years due to the pandemic impacting training. Many experienced crews have also decided to leave the industry as they were stuck onboard vessels for months due to pandemic restrictions. Shipping companies have started to take the approach that intelligent unmanned surface vessels (USVs) are the future of marine industries [1]. They believe that intelligent unmanned surface vessels will not only solve the problem of seafarer shortages but also revolutionize the prospects of ship design and operations to reduce human error, expenses, and so on [1]. For the reasons above, the development of intelligent USVs has become a new trend for advanced ship designs because they possess the ability to execute given tasks, such as ocean military and research activities, without humans and to satisfy requirements due to the rapid growth in global trades. A race between major shipbuilding companies and research institutes for autonomous ship designs is already underway, and the related autonomous ships market is predicted to reach a value of USD 235.73 billion by 2028 according to Acute Market Reports [2]. The Korean shipbuilding company Hyundai Heavy Industries' Avikus seized the opportunity to complete the world's first transoceanic voyage on 2 June 2022 [3] with their new LNG carrier design, "the Prism Courage which equipped with level two autonomous navigation technology". It is worth mentioning that the Prism Courage sailed roughly 10,000 km using an autonomous navigation system, and this was almost half of the distance of the voyage. This application reveals that key technologies for well-developed intelligent unmanned surface vessels include collision risk evaluation, real-time planning of collision avoidance trajectories according to the COLREGs (Convention on the International Regulations for Preventing Collisions at Sea 1972), effective evasion decision making, and precise control methodology. Currently, most collision avoidance methods still focus on the developments of collision avoidance strategies without taking ship models and control laws into account via arranging several scenarios in waterways [4–6], and indeed, these methodologies cannot cover all sailing situations or control the trajectory tracking performances of ships. As mentioned above, these published results have excluded guidance systems and ship models even though they have developed collision-free methods following the COLREGs. In recent years, there has been an increase in the amount of studies discussing the integration of the COLREGs, decision-making functions, and guidance systems. These researchers demonstrated the concepts of combining static optimized collision avoidance paths with PI or PID linear controllers [7,8]. However, ship–ship dynamics were not considered in the design procedures; hence, they are only workable at certain operating conditions and are not applicable in real applications. Currently, these kinds of collision avoidance control designs are still the main trend. As for the literature that took ship–ship dynamics into consideration, simplified ship models were mostly adopted for designing the guidance systems of USVs and never included the effects of ocean disturbances (wave, current, and wind) and USVs' modeling uncertainties [9]. In 2021, one published study proposed a rare example of a collision avoidance control system that advanced the collision avoidance guidance system designs of USVs [10]. This paper proposed a smart collision avoidance control design that fulfilled the COLREGs and considered challenging ocean environmental disturbances simultaneously. The smart collision avoidance control system was designed by integrating a collision risk indicator, a collision avoidance acting timing indicator, and a velocity reduction generator based on fuzzy rules that accumulated experience from expert captains, an optimal collision-free trajectory generator based on an oscillatory particle swarm optimizer (OSC-PSO), which naturally requires a high computational cost due to iterative calculations, and a nonlinear optimal guidance system. One drawback: "This integrated control design reveals a weak immunity to ocean environmental disturbances and modeling uncertainties of USVs", was found after performing more simulations. To increase immunity to ocean environmental disturbances, model uncertainties of USVs, and reduce the computational cost, an intelligent fuzzy-based control system that integrates an intelligent collision avoidance system and a nonlinear adaptive fuzzy robust control law is proposed in this paper. The collision-free trajectory generator of the intelligent collision avoidance system, constructed using the cubic spline method, highly reduces the computational cost, and the cancellation and elimination abilities of the adaptive fuzzy approximator and the robust compensator overcome the effects of modeling uncertainties and ocean environmental disturbances. Based on this arrangement, the proposed intelligent fuzzy-based control system delivers more precise and robust abilities for USVs to sail in a challenging ocean environment. This paper is organized as follows: in Section 2, the intelligent collision avoidance system and nonlinear adaptive fuzzy robust control law are derived; in Section 3, the simulation results of the proposed method with respect to COLREGs' Rule 15—Crossing Situation is shown and discussed; and in the last section, the conclusions of this proposed design are stated.

2. Problem Description and Design Objective

In this investigation, the design target was to develop a control system that can intelligently make decisions to robustly guide the controlled USV to execute the given missions by following the COLREGs in an ocean environment that is full of random dynamical obstacles. The control design process for achieving this target is summarized as follows:

2.1. Intelligent Collision Avoidance Control System for USVs

As shown in Figure 1, the intelligent fuzzy control system, which integrates a fuzzy collision evaluator, a fuzzy collision avoidance acting timing indicator, a collision-free trajectory generator, and a nonlinear adaptive fuzzy robust control law, is illustrated. The procedure of this proposed control system, which can make decisions by obeying the COLREGs and precisely guide USVs to track arbitrary collision-free desired trajectories, can be summarized with the following four phases:

Phase 1: Related position and attitude acquisitions of the controlled USV and corresponding ships in the monitored area of the ocean.
Phase 2: Intelligent collision risk evaluation and collision avoidance decision making.
Phase 3: Real-time generation of a collision avoidance trajectory.
Phase 4: Robust and precise trajectory tracking executed by the controlled USV.

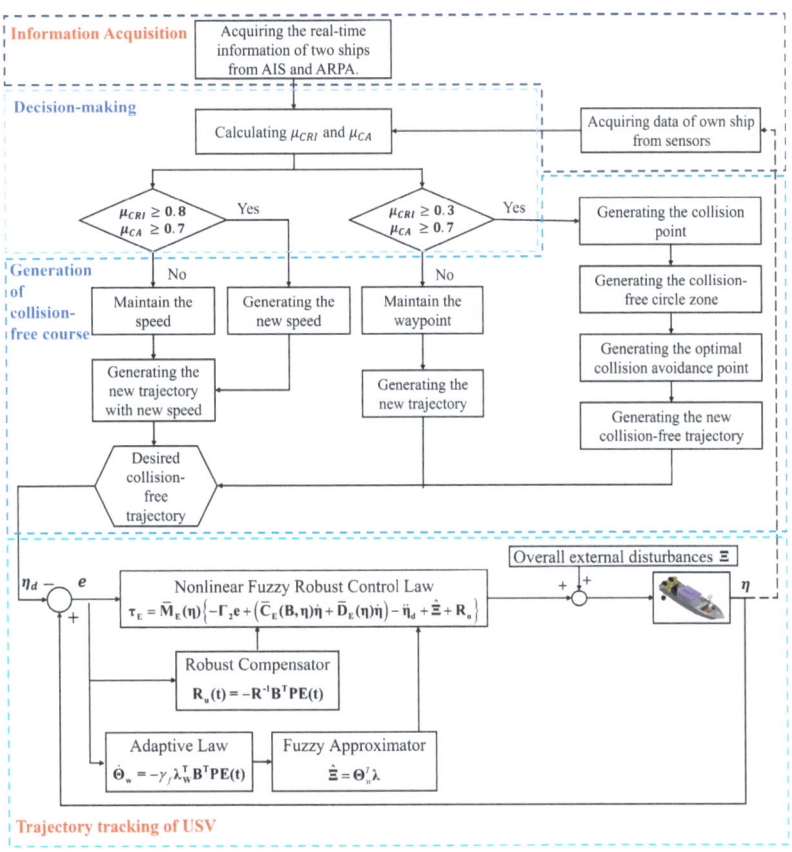

Figure 1. Details of the proposed collision avoidance control system for USVs.

The proposed control system has the function of collecting the positions, velocities, and heading angles of two encountered ships by using the automatic identification system (AIS) and automatic radar plotting aids (ARPA), respectively, for Phase 1. Using the measured data in Phase 1, real-time intelligent collision risk evaluations and collision avoidance decisions can be then calculated via the fuzzy collision evaluator and the fuzzy collision avoidance acting timing indicator in Phase 2. Collision-free trajectories are further generated based on the evaluation results from Phase 3. In Phase 4, the proposed nonlinear adaptive fuzzy robust control law plays a role in precisely guiding the USV to follow the collision-free trajectory generated in Phase 3. In Figure 1, $\mu_{CRI} \in [0, 1]$ is the evaluated index of the fuzzy collision evaluator, and $\mu_{CA} \in [0, 1]$ is the evaluated index of the fuzzy collision avoidance acting timing indicator. These two indices will be introduced in Section 2.3.

2.2. Governing Equations of USVs

As shown in Figure 2, a 3DOFs model (surge, sway, and yaw) was adopted for a controlled USV in this investigation.

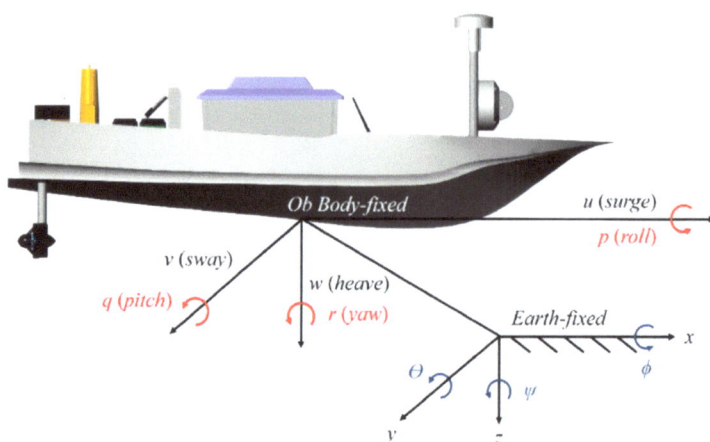

Figure 2. Motions of USV in body-fixed and earth frames.

Dynamics of the controlled USV in the body-fixed frame is formulated as [10]:

$$\mathbf{M_B \dot{B}} + \mathbf{C_B(B)B} + \mathbf{D_B(B)B} = \boldsymbol{\tau_B} + \boldsymbol{\tau_{dB}} \qquad (1)$$

where $\mathbf{B} = \begin{bmatrix} u & v & r \end{bmatrix}^T$ is the vector of velocities, u is the linear velocity in surge, v is the linear velocity in sway, and r is the angular velocity in yaw. Additionally, $\mathbf{M_B}$ is the mass and inertia matrix, $\mathbf{C_B(B)}$ is the Coriolis–centripetal matrix, $\mathbf{D_B(B)}$ is the hydrodynamic damping matrix, $\boldsymbol{\tau_B}$ is the control input, and $\boldsymbol{\tau_{dB}}$ is the ocean environmental disturbances.

The transformation between the body-fixed frame to the earth frame of the controlled USV is:

$$\dot{\boldsymbol{\eta}} = \mathbf{J}(\boldsymbol{\eta})\mathbf{B} \qquad (2)$$

where $\boldsymbol{\eta} = \begin{bmatrix} x & y & \psi \end{bmatrix}^T$ is the position of the controlled USV in the earth frame, and $\mathbf{J}(\boldsymbol{\eta})$ is the transformation matrix:

$$\mathbf{J}(\boldsymbol{\eta}) = \begin{bmatrix} \cos\psi & -\sin\psi & 0 \\ \sin\psi & \cos\psi & 0 \\ 0 & 0 & 1 \end{bmatrix} \qquad (3)$$

The equations of motion of the controlled USV in the earth frame can be presented as:

$$\mathbf{M_E}(\boldsymbol{\eta})\ddot{\boldsymbol{\eta}} + \mathbf{C_E}(\mathbf{B},\boldsymbol{\eta})\dot{\boldsymbol{\eta}} + \mathbf{D_E}(\boldsymbol{\eta})\dot{\boldsymbol{\eta}} = \boldsymbol{\tau_E} + \boldsymbol{\tau_{dE}} \qquad (4)$$

where $\mathbf{M_E}$ is the inertia mass in the earth frame, $\mathbf{C_E}$ is the Coriolis–centripetal matrix in the earth frame, $\mathbf{D_E}(\boldsymbol{\eta})$ is the damping matrix in the earth frame, $\boldsymbol{\tau_{dE}}$ is ocean environmental disturbance, and $\boldsymbol{\tau_E}$ is the control input.

The ocean environmental disturbance $\boldsymbol{\tau_{dE}}$ contains three sub-disturbances, which are the wave-induced disturbance $\boldsymbol{\tau_{wave}}$, wind-induced disturbance $\boldsymbol{\tau_{wind}}$, and ocean-current-induced disturbance $\boldsymbol{\tau_{current}}$:

$$\boldsymbol{\tau_{dE}} = \boldsymbol{\tau_{wave}} + \boldsymbol{\tau_{wind}} + \boldsymbol{\tau_{current}} \qquad (5)$$

The equations of motion of the controlled USV in the earth frame in Equation (4) will be used for the nonlinear fuzzy robust controller design, and the inertia mass $\mathbf{M_E}(\boldsymbol{\eta})$,

Coriolis and centripetal matrix $C_E(B,\eta)$, and damping matrix $D_E(\eta)$ can be expressed as nominal value terms $\overline{M_E}(\eta)$, $\overline{C_E}(B,\eta)$, $\overline{D_E}(\eta)$ and modeling uncertainties $\Delta M_E(\eta)$, $\Delta C_E(B,\eta)$, $\Delta D_E(\eta)$:

$$M_E(\eta) = \overline{M_E}(\eta) + \Delta M_E(\eta)$$
$$C_E(B,\eta) = \overline{C_E}(B,\eta) + \Delta C_E(B,\eta) \quad (6)$$
$$D_E(\eta) = \overline{D_E}(\eta) + \Delta D_E(\eta)$$

Substituting (6) into (4), the dynamics equation of the USV can be reformulated as:

$$\overline{M_E}(\eta)\ddot{\eta} + \overline{C_E}(B,\eta)\dot{\eta} + \overline{D_E}(\eta)\dot{\eta} = \tau_E + \Xi \quad (7)$$

where

$$\Xi = \tau_{dE} - \Delta M_E(\eta)\ddot{\eta} - \Delta C_E(B,\eta)\dot{\eta} - \Delta D_E(\eta)\dot{\eta} \quad (8)$$

with $\|\Delta M_E(\eta)\ddot{\eta}\| \leq \varepsilon_1$, $\|\Delta C_E(B,\eta)\dot{\eta}\| \leq \varepsilon_2$, and $\|\Delta D_E(\eta)\dot{\eta}\| \leq \varepsilon_3$ are bounded, and ε_1, ε_2, and ε_3 are finite and bounded values.

2.3. Generator of Collision-Free Trajectories

In the trajectory-tracking problem of USVs, a desired trajectory will be generated by interpolating a set of assigned waypoints if a collision-free condition is not demanded. However, the requirement of a collision-free condition must be met in practical sailing applications of USVs; hence, a real-time modified desired trajectory with no expected collisions should be arranged based on new sets of collision avoidance waypoints when a warning of a ship-to-ship collision occurs. In this investigation, a modification in generating sailing trajectories was adopted to create a collision avoidance trajectory for the controlled USV. A brief description of this modified trajectory generator is given below.

The conventional trajectory is made of multiple third-order polynomials, and two third-order polynomials can generate a continuous trajectory as follows:

$$x_d(\varpi) = a_4\varpi^3 + a_3\varpi^2 + a_2\varpi + a_1 \quad (9)$$

$$y_d(\varpi) = d_4\varpi^3 + d_3\varpi^2 + d_2\varpi + d_1 \quad (10)$$

where $(x_d(\varpi), y_d(\varpi))$ is the instantaneous position in the path, and $a_4, a_3, a_2, a_1, d_4, d_3, d_2,$ and d_1 are identifiable coefficients. The related calculations of these coefficients are omitted in this investigation and can be found within [10]. In [10], the suggestion for arranging the new modified collision-free trajectory was to reassign a set of waypoints that can create a collision-free trajectory and satisfy the COLREGs. To ensure the modified trajectory connects to the original trajectory smoothly, as displayed in Figure 3, the position, velocity, and acceleration in the connected point (first red circle of the red trajectory) between these two trajectories must be the same. Based on this modified trajectory generator, a real-time, collision-free trajectory (the blue trajectory) that is made of a new set of coefficients ($a_4, a_3, a_2, a_1, d_4, d_3, d_2,$ and d_1) can be obtained when the arbitrary collisions appear in the voyage of a controlled USV, and the state vector of this collision-free trajectory is defined as $\eta_d = \begin{bmatrix} x_d & y_d & \psi_d \end{bmatrix}^T$.

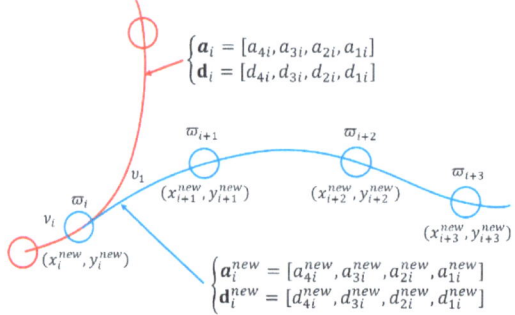

Figure 3. Schematic diagram of generating a collision-free trajectory.

2.3.1. Integrated Fuzzy-Based Control System

The proposed control system used for the purpose of decision making and guidance for the controlled USV was developed by integrating "a fuzzy decision maker" and "a robust fuzzy control law". In this proposed control system, the fuzzy decision maker, which is responsible for ship–ship collision evaluations and risk pre-warnings, consists of a fuzzy collision risk evaluator and a fuzzy collision avoidance acting timing indicator. As for the robust fuzzy control law, this part provides the precise trajectory tracking function to guide the USV to sail along the desired collision-free trajectory even under the effects of random ocean environmental disturbances and modeling uncertainties. Descriptions of this proposed control system will be given below.

2.3.2. Fuzzy Decision Maker

In this investigation, a fuzzy decision maker that mainly comprises a fuzzy collision risk evaluator with an evaluated index $\mu_{CRI} \in [0, 1]$ and a fuzzy collision avoidance acting timing indicator with an evaluated index $\mu_{CA} \in [0, 1]$ were built to assess the collision risk and the degree of residual time for the controlled USV capable of taking evasive action with respect to the surrounding sailing USVs. To more safely guide the controlled USV with a definite collision-free condition under the effects of ocean environmental disturbances and modeling uncertainties in practice, conservative arrangements for three risk-evaluating parameters of these indicators: DCPA, TCPA, and total length D, which takes lengths of the controlled USV (L_O) and target ship (L_T) into account, were made as shown in Figure 4. The detailed design procedure of this fuzzy decision maker can be found in the published study [10]. In this investigation, sets of ($\mu_{CRI} \geq 0.8$, $\mu_{CA} \geq 0.7$) and ($\mu_{CRI} \geq 0.3$, $\mu_{CA} \geq 0.7$) will be utilized as thresholds for triggering the functions of reducing the speed of the controlled USV and generating a new collision-free trajectory by referring to [10].

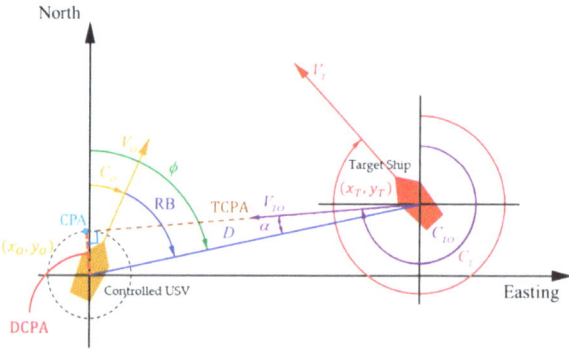

Figure 4. DCPA, TCPA, and total length D between two encountered USVs.

2.4. Robust Fuzzy Control Law Design

Another significant part of this proposed control system is the "robust fuzzy control law", which was designed with the aim of precisely guiding a controlled USV along a collision-free trajectory when random ships appear in the waterway. The design procedure of this robust fuzzy control law is derived below.

We defined the trajectory tracking error vector of the controlled USV with respect to arbitrary collision-free trajectories in the earth frame as follows:

$$e = \begin{bmatrix} \dot{\tilde{\eta}} \\ \tilde{\eta} \end{bmatrix} = \begin{bmatrix} \dot{\eta} - \dot{\eta}_d \\ \eta - \eta_d \end{bmatrix} \tag{11}$$

where $\eta_d = \begin{bmatrix} x_d & y_d & \psi_d \end{bmatrix}^T$ is the desired trajectory obtained by using the generator of collision-free trajectories.

Since $\ddot{\eta} = -\overline{\mathbf{M}_E(\eta)}^{-1}(\overline{\mathbf{C}_E(\mathbf{B},\eta)}\dot{\eta} + \overline{\mathbf{D}_E(\eta)}\dot{\eta}) + \overline{\mathbf{M}_E(\eta)}^{-1}\tau_E + \overline{\mathbf{M}_E(\eta)}^{-1}\Xi$ and the generated collision-free trajectory is at least double-differentiable, namely, $\eta_d \in C^2$, the trajectory tracking error dynamics can be formulated as:

$$\begin{aligned} \ddot{e} &= \ddot{\eta}_d - \ddot{\eta} \\ &= \ddot{\eta}_d - \overline{\mathbf{M}_E(\eta)}^{-1}(\overline{\mathbf{C}_E(\mathbf{B},\eta)}\dot{\eta} + \overline{\mathbf{D}_E(\eta)}\dot{\eta}) + \overline{\mathbf{M}_E(\eta)}^{-1}\tau_E + \overline{\mathbf{M}_E(\eta)}^{-1}\Xi \end{aligned} \tag{12}$$

Selecting a candidate control law τ_E as follows:

$$\tau_E = \overline{\mathbf{M}_E(\eta)}\{-\Gamma_2 e + (\overline{\mathbf{C}_E(\mathbf{B},\eta)}\dot{\eta} + \overline{\mathbf{D}_E(\eta)}\dot{\eta}) - \ddot{\eta}_d + \hat{\Xi} + \mathbf{R}_u\} \tag{13}$$

where $\mathbf{R}_u$ is the robust compensator that will be designed later developed for eliminating the residual overall disturbance, and $\hat{\Xi}$ is a fuzzy approximator of the overall disturbance. The disclosure results reveal that a well-developed fuzzy system can be utilized to be a universal approximator for approaching any nonlinear systems as precisely as possible in [11–13]. Based on the concept of [11–13], the proposed fuzzy approximator $\hat{\Xi}$ can be expressed as a regression form as below:

$$\hat{\Xi} = \Theta_w^{T*}\lambda_w \tag{14}$$

where $\Theta_w = \begin{bmatrix} \theta_{w1} & \theta_{w2} & \dots & \theta_{wM} \end{bmatrix}^T$ is the adjustable parameter vector, and $\lambda_w = \begin{bmatrix} \lambda_{w1} & \lambda_{w2} & \dots & \lambda_{wM} \end{bmatrix}^T$ is the fuzzy basis function, respectively. λ_{wi} is defined as:

$$\lambda_{wi}(x) = \frac{\Pi_{i=1}^n \mu_{\lambda_{wi}^{\updownarrow}}(x_i)}{\sum_{l=1}^M \left(\Pi_{i=1}^n \mu_{\lambda_{wi}^{\updownarrow}}(x_i) \right)} \tag{15}$$

where M is the rule number.

The optimal fuzzy approximation error can be further presented as:

$$\Delta \Xi = \Xi - \hat{\Xi}^* = \Xi - \Theta_w^{T*}\lambda_w \tag{16}$$

where $\Theta_w^* = \underset{\Theta_w}{\arg\min}\|\Xi - \Theta_w^T \lambda_w\|$.

Remark 1. *Theoretically speaking, by increasing the rule number M, the approximation error can be mitigated as far as possible. However, a trade-off between the accuracy of the fuzzy approximator and the computational effort should be made in practice.* ∎

Based on Equations (1), (13), (14), and (16), a matrix–vector form of the trajectory tracking error dynamics can be obtained:

$$\ddot{\mathbf{e}} + \mathbf{\Gamma}_1 \dot{\mathbf{e}} + \mathbf{\Gamma}_2 \mathbf{e} = \tilde{\mathbf{\Theta}}_w^T \lambda_w + \mathbf{R}_u + \overline{\mathbf{M}_E(\eta)}^{-1} \Delta \Xi \tag{17}$$

where $\tilde{\mathbf{\Theta}}_w = \mathbf{\Theta}_w^* - \mathbf{\Theta}_w$.

The trajectory tracking error dynamics in Equation (17) can be further expressed in an augmented form as

$$\begin{aligned}\dot{\mathbf{E}} &= \mathbf{AE} + \mathbf{BR}_u + \mathbf{B}\tilde{\mathbf{\Theta}}_w^T \lambda_w + \mathbf{Bd} \\ &= \begin{bmatrix} 0 & 1 \\ -\mathbf{\Gamma}_1 & -\mathbf{\Gamma}_2 \end{bmatrix} \mathbf{E} + \begin{bmatrix} 0 \\ 1 \end{bmatrix} \mathbf{R}_u + \begin{bmatrix} 0 \\ 1 \end{bmatrix} \tilde{\mathbf{\Theta}}_w^T \lambda_w + \begin{bmatrix} 0 \\ 1 \end{bmatrix} \mathbf{d}\end{aligned} \tag{18}$$

where

$$\mathbf{E} = \begin{bmatrix} \mathbf{e} & \dot{\mathbf{e}} \end{bmatrix}^T,$$

$$\mathbf{d} = \overline{\mathbf{M}_E(\eta)}^{-1} \Delta \Xi,$$

$$\mathbf{\Gamma}_1 = \begin{bmatrix} \alpha_1 & 0 & 0 \\ 0 & \alpha_2 & 0 \\ 0 & 0 & \alpha_3 \end{bmatrix},$$

and

$$\mathbf{\Gamma}_2 = \begin{bmatrix} \alpha_4 & 0 & 0 \\ 0 & \alpha_5 & 0 \\ 0 & 0 & \alpha_6 \end{bmatrix}.$$

From Equation (18), the design target for the controlled USV's collision-free trajectory tracking problem can be described as a robust performance as follows [14–16]:

$$\min_{\mathbf{R}_u(t) \in L_2[0,t_f]} \min_{\mathbf{d}(t) \in L_2[0,t_f]} \frac{\left\| \left[\mathbf{Q}^{\frac{1}{2}} \mathbf{E}(t) + \mathbf{O}^{\frac{1}{2}} \mathbf{R}_u(t) \right] \right\|_{L_2[0,t_f]}}{\|\mathbf{d}(t)\|_{L_2[0,t_f]}} \leq \rho \tag{19}$$

where ρ is a designable attenuation level, and $\mathbf{Q}$ and $\mathbf{O} > 0$ are the weighting matrices as well.

The results disclosed in Theorem 1 below indicate the fact that the design objective in Equation (19) can be achieved with the derived robust compensator $\mathbf{R}_u$ and the adaptive law for optimally searching the parameter vector $\mathbf{\Theta}_w$ of the fuzzy approximator $\hat{\Xi}$.

Theorem 1. *The precise trajectory tracking problem of unmanned surface vessels can be tackled well with the robust fuzzy control law* τ_E *which integrates a robust compensator* $\mathbf{R}_u$ *and an adaptive law* $\dot{\mathbf{\Theta}}_w$ *expressed below.*

$$\tau_E = \overline{\mathbf{M}_E(\eta)} \left\{ -\mathbf{\Gamma}_2 \mathbf{e} + \left(\overline{\mathbf{C}_E(\mathbf{B},\eta)} \dot{\eta} + \overline{\mathbf{D}_E(\eta)} \dot{\eta} \right) - \ddot{\eta}_d + \hat{\Xi} + \mathbf{R}_u \right\} \tag{20}$$

$$\mathbf{R}_u(t) = -\mathbf{R}^{-1} \mathbf{B}^T \mathbf{P} \mathbf{E}(t) \tag{21}$$

and $\mathbf{P} = \mathbf{P}^T > 0$ is one of the solutions to the following equation:

$$\mathbf{AP} + \mathbf{PA}^T + \mathbf{PB}\left(\frac{1}{\rho^2}\mathbf{I} - \mathbf{O}^{-1}\right)\mathbf{B}^T \mathbf{P} + \mathbf{Q} = 0 \tag{22}$$

The adaptive law for optimally searching the parameter vector Θ_w is derived as:

$$\dot{\Theta}_w = -\gamma_f \lambda_W^T B^T PE(t) \tag{23}$$

where γ_f is the designable learning rate.

Proof of Theorem 1 can be obtained in Appendix A.

2.5. Summary of the Proposed Fuzzy-Based Control System

STEP 1. Set up key parameters DCPA, TCPA, and total length D of the fuzzy decision maker to generate the fuzzy collision risk index μ_{CRI} and the fuzzy collision avoidance acting timing index μ_{CA}.

STEP 2. Specify A in Equation (18) with design eigenvalues $\alpha_I > 0$, for $I = 1, \ldots, 6$.

STEP 3. Select the weight matrices $Q > 0$, the desired attenuation level ρ, and the weighting factor O such that $\rho^2 I - O$ must be a positive definite matrix.

STEP 4. Solve Equation (22) to obtain P.

STEP 5. Construct the fuzzy approximator $\hat{\Xi}(t) = \Theta_w^T(t)\lambda_w$ and $\dot{\Theta}_w(t) = -\gamma_f \lambda_W^T B^T PE(t)$ for mimicking the overall disturbance $\Xi(t)$.

STEP 6. Construct the robust compensator $R_u(t) = -R^{-1}B^T PE(t)$ and the nonlinear fuzzy robust control law $\tau_E = \overline{M_E(\eta)}\left\{-\Gamma_2 e + \left(\overline{C_E(B,\eta)}\dot{\eta} + \overline{D_E(\eta)}\dot{\eta}\right) - \ddot{\eta}_d + \hat{\Xi} + R_u\right\}$ in Equation (13) for the collision-free and precise trajectory tracking problem of the controlled USV.

3. Simulation Results

3.1. System and Control Parameters of the Controlled USV

The controlled USV utilized for simulation in this investigation had a length of 1.72 m, as shown in Figure 5. The related hydrodynamic parameters ($X_{\dot{u}}$, $Y_{\dot{v}}$, $Y_{\dot{r}}$, $N_{\dot{r}}$, X_u, Y_v, Y_r, N_v, and N_r) of this USV were measured by using a towing tank experiment, and the detailed parameters of this USV are stated in Table 1.

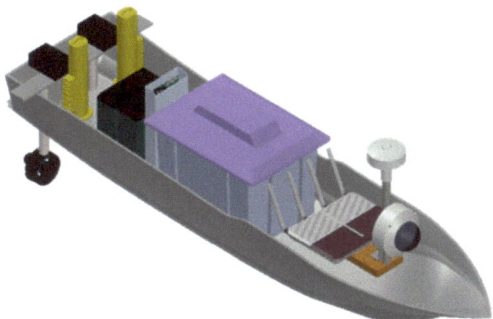

Figure 5. The controlled USV of this investigation.

Table 1. Detail system parameters of the controlled USV.

Length L	1.72 m
Width B	0.4 m
Draft T	0.3 m
Mass m	41 kg
I_z	6.522 kg·m
x_g	0 m
$X_{\dot{u}}$	−1.291 kg
$Y_{\dot{v}}$	−40.326 kg
$Y_{\dot{r}}$	−39.04525 N·s^2/m^2
$N_{\dot{r}}$	200.79808 N·m·s
X_u	−0.98 N·s^2/m^2
Y_v	−38.808 N·s^2/m^2
Y_r	−16.43778 N·s
N_v	−14.340 N·s^2/m^2
N_r	−236.5 N·m·s

3.2. Collision Avoidance Simulation Results of the Proposed Control System

One collision avoidance scenario was simulated in Yongxin Fish Harbor of Kaohsiung City, Taiwan, for the validation of the collision avoidance performance of this proposed control system under the influences of ocean disturbances and modeling uncertainties. The modeling uncertainties of the controlled USV were considered 10% of the nominal values of the system parameters in Table 1, and the ocean environmental disturbance τ_{dE} was created by referring to the published paper [17]. To verify the collision avoidance performance of the proposed control system, a crossing situation was arranged in this scenario. As displayed in Figure 6 and according to rule 15 of the COLREGs, the controlled USV was a give-way ship, and the target ship was a stand-on ship for this crossing situation. Following rule 15, it was suggested that the stand-on ship sail straight forward, and the give-way ship perform a give-way action along a collision-free trajectory.

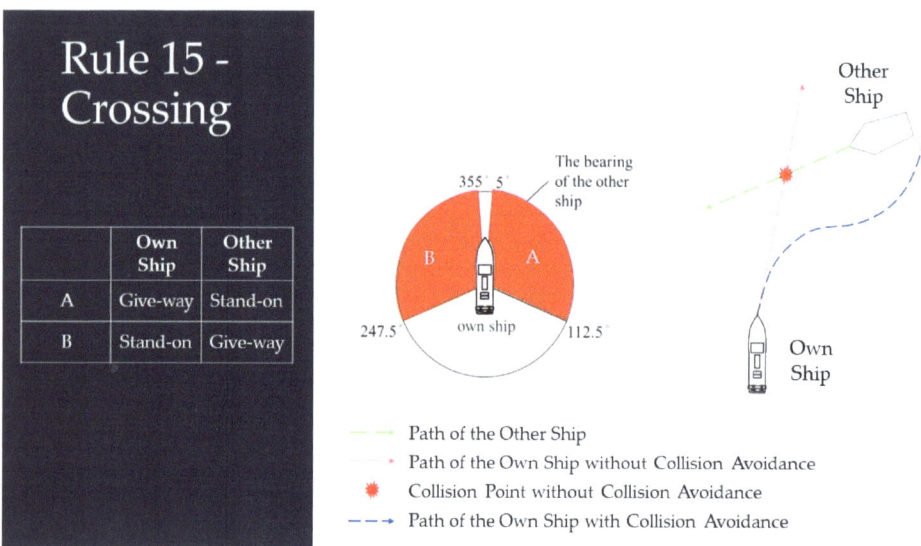

Figure 6. Collision avoidance strategy for a two-ship crossing situation based on rule 15 of the COLREGs.

In this scenario, the corresponding settings of the controlled USV (own ship) and the target ship are listed in Tables 2 and 3.

Table 2. Setting of the controlled USV for the simulation.

Starting Point	(2400 m, 800 m)
Goal Point	(6300 m, 1280 m)
Desired Velocity	1 m/s
Initial Condition of the Controlled USV	$\eta = \begin{bmatrix} 2399.95 \text{ m} & 799.95 \text{ m} & 0 \end{bmatrix}$

Table 3. Setting of target ship for the simulation.

Starting Point	(3586 m, 559 m)
Goal Point	(0, 2700 m)
Desired Velocity	0.663 m/s

Figure 7 shows the collision avoidance simulation result for two sailing ships. In this scenario, a target ship sails straight from the coast (southeast) to the ocean (northwest), and the controlled USV sails from the ocean (west) to the internal river. From Figure 8, it is obvious that these two ships have a very high probability of colliding at point 4; hence, the controlled USV should take evasive action according to rule 15 of the COLREGs because it is its own ship.

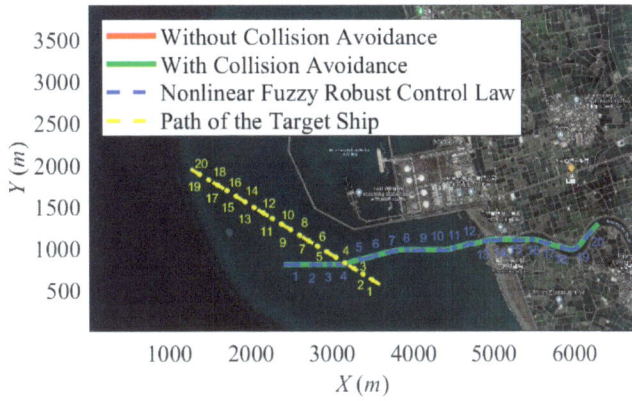

Figure 7. Collision avoidance simulation in Yongxin Fishing Harbor: the yellow line is the trajectory of the target ship, the blue line is the trajectory of the controlled USV, and the green line is the desired collision-free trajectory.

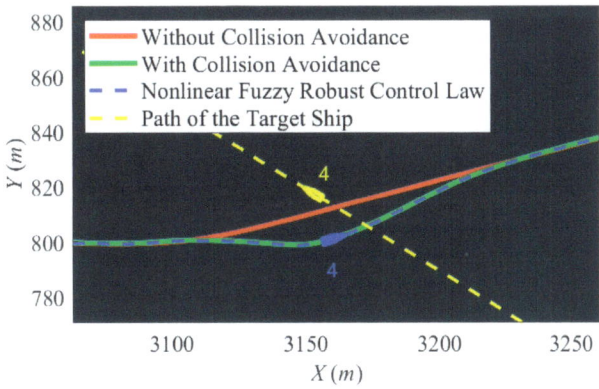

Figure 8. Magnifying the collision part of Figure 7.

The enlarged figure around point 4 of Figure 8 details the relative actions taken by the target ship and the controlled USV.

This figure shows that a collision will occur at point 4 if the controlled USV sails along the original predefined trajectory (red line). To avoid this unexpected collision situation, a decision was made by the proposed control system: "the proposed control system rearranges a collision-free trajectory (blue line) once a ship-ship collision is estimated by the proposed fuzzy collision risk evaluator, and the fuzzy robust control law then robustly guide the USV to precisely follow the collision-free trajectory under influences of modelling uncertainties and ocean environmental disturbances". Figures 9a–c and 10a–c show that the proposed fuzzy robust control law has very promising robustness in terms of modeling uncertainties and ocean disturbances and can guide the USV to precisely follow the collision-free trajectory not only in position but also in attitude. Figure 9d indicates the sailing velocity, and it was well-maintained at 1 m/s by the trajectory generator.

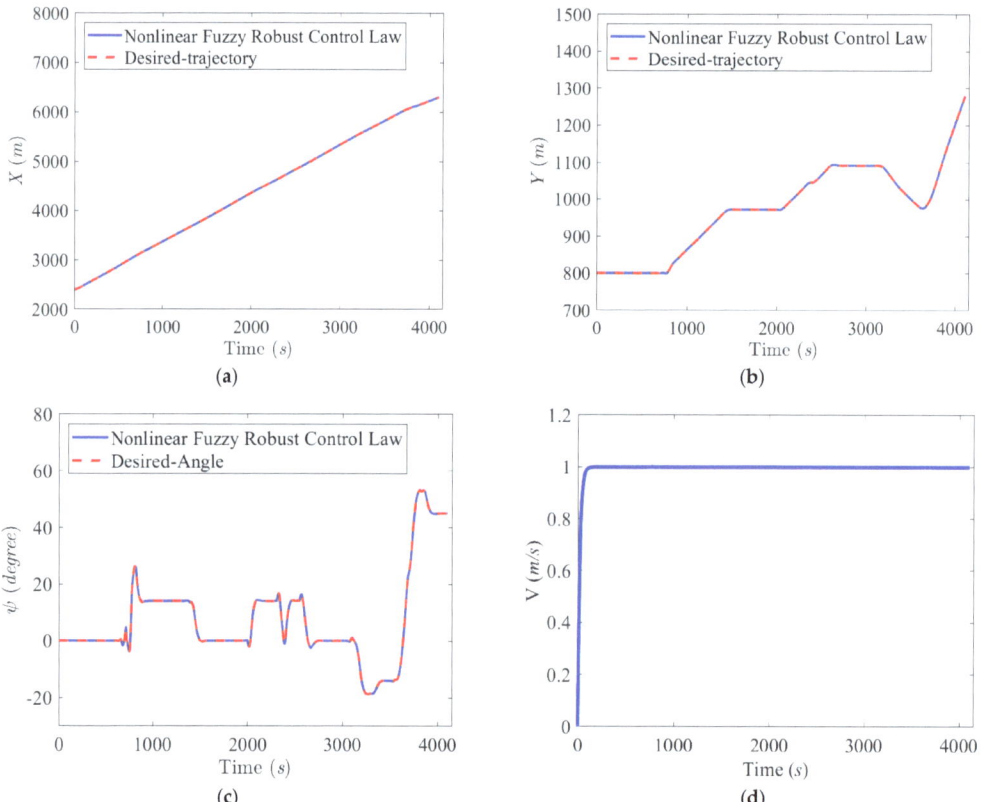

Figure 9. Collision-free trajectory tracking histories in *X-axis* (**a**) and *Y-axis* (**b**), tracking history of the heading angle ψ (**c**), and (**d**) the sailing velocity V with respect to Scenario 1.

The control forces and torque of this scenario are illustrated in Figure 11. From these control command histories, bigger control forces and torque can be seen in the time interval [600 s, 800 s]. This is because collision risks were detected by the fuzzy decision maker at about 600 s, and a right-hand side turn was made by the proposed fuzzy robust control law for the controlled USV to avoid a collision with the target ship. The collision avoidance response of this proposed control system certainly follows rule 15 of the COLREGs: "In crossing situation, the own ship must take a give-way action". From the simulation results of this scenario, we can conclude that this proposed control system delivers very promising collision avoidance performance for USVs carrying out tasks in an ocean environment full of various sailing surface vessels and random disturbances, such as waves, winds, and currents.

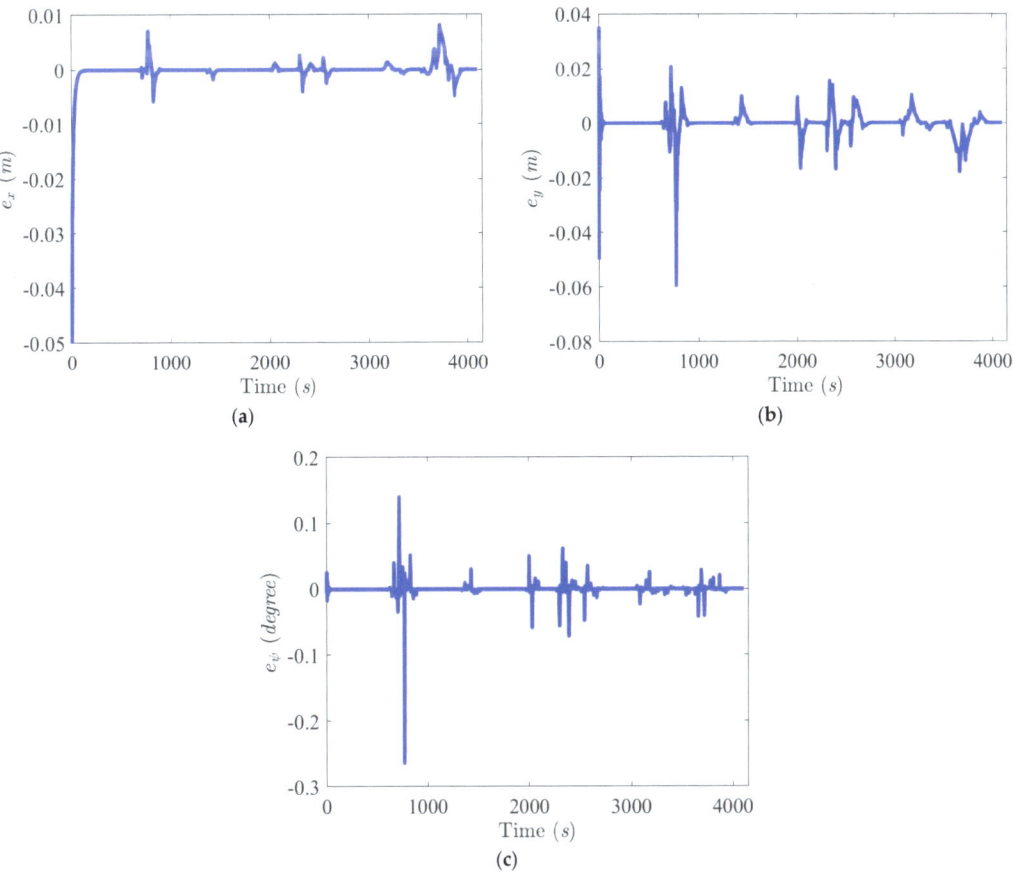

Figure 10. Collision-free trajectory tracking error histories in *X-axis* (**a**) and *Y-axis* (**b**), and tracking error history of heading angle ψ (**c**) with respect to Scenario 1.

From the trajectory tracking error histories in the *X-axis* (a) and *Y-axis* (b) and the tracking error history of the heading angle ψ, we can determine that the mean square errors in positions ($MSEe_P$) and in the heading angle ($MSEe_\psi$) under the influences of 10% modeling uncertainties and random environmental disturbances are $MSEe_P \leq 0.04$m and $MSEe_\psi \leq 0.1°$, respectively.

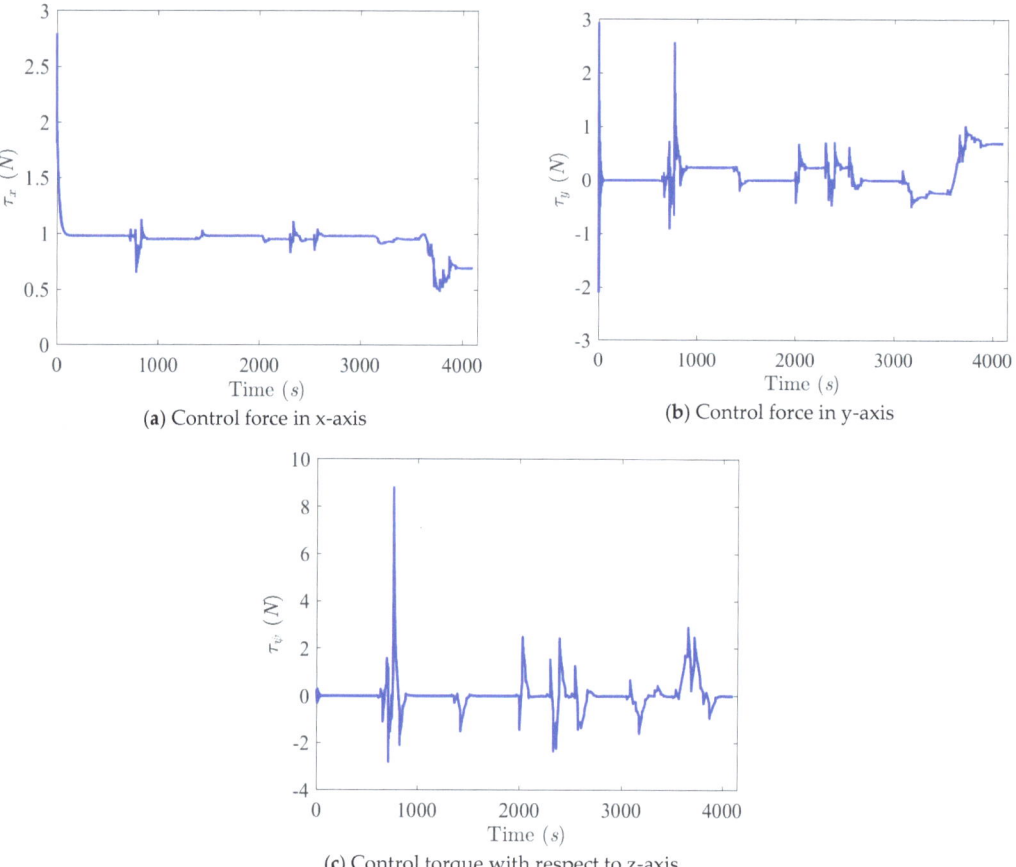

Figure 11. Histories of the control commands, including the forces τ_x, τ_y, and the torque τ_ψ with respect to Scenario 1.

4. Conclusions

An integrated fuzzy-based control system with collision-free trajectory and precise trajectory tracking properties was tested in the real-time collision avoidance sailing operation of a controlled USV in this investigation. The trajectory tracking problem of intelligent USVs with a collision-free property comprises developments in data sensing, decision making, collision-free trajectory generation, and robust control; hence, the complexity of this problem is higher than that of the conventional control design of USVs. This proposed fuzzy-based control system consists of four major subsystems: a fuzzy collision risk evaluator, a fuzzy collision avoidance acting timing indicator, a collision-free trajectory generator, and a nonlinear adaptive fuzzy robust control law. The first two functions provide the controlled USVs with a decision-making function to determine when to take evasive action. Based on the pre-alarm of the first two functions, one new collision-free trajectory can be generated by using the cubic spline method in real-time. Finally, the nonlinear adaptive fuzzy control law plays the role of precisely guiding the USV to sail along the new collision-free trajectory. To realistically examine the performance of this proposed method, a crossing situation scenario that frequently occurs in the encounter situation of ships was simulated in the area of the Yongxin Fish Harbor of Kaohsiung City, Taiwan. From the simulation results, transparently, this proposed control system could make the correct evasion decisions to guide the USV to sail along the rearranged collision-free trajectory precisely and robustly by following the COLREG rules under the effects of modeling uncertainties and ocean environmental disturbances. The mean-square errors could be controlled to levels of $MSEe_P \leq 0.04$m for the position and $MSEe_\psi \leq 0.1°$ for the heading angle, respectively. Although this proposed control system of intelligent USVs integrates four subsystems and can deliver satisfactory collision-free and precise trajectory tracking performance, merging actuator models, such as rudders and thrusters, etc., are inevitably required for real applications. How to analytically convert actuator models' inputs into the desired control law (τ_x, τ_y, and τ_ψ) will be the next research challenge due to the high nonlinearity of the input and output relationship of actuator models.

Author Contributions: Conceptualization, Y.-Y.C.; methodology, Y.-Y.C.; software, M.-Z.E.-T.; validation, Y.-Y.C. and M.-Z.E.-T.; formal analysis, M.-Z.E.-T.; investigation, Y.-Y.C.; re-sources, Y.-Y.C.; data curation, M.-Z.E.-T.; writing—original draft preparation, Y.-Y.C.; writing—review and editing, M.-Z.E.-T.; visualization, M.-Z.E.-T.; supervision, Y.-Y.C.; project administration, Y.-Y.C.; funding acquisition, Y.-Y.C. All authors have read and agreed to the published version of the manuscript.

Funding: This research was funded by the MOST (Ministry of Science and Technology of Taiwan, project number is NSTC112-2221-E-006-152-.

Data Availability Statement: Not applicable.

Conflicts of Interest: The authors declare no conflict of interest.

Appendix A

We defined the robust performance index J for the controlled USV's collision-free trajectory tracking problem as:

$$J(\mathbf{E}(t), \mathbf{R_u}(t), \mathbf{d}(t)) = \int_0^{t_f} \left(\mathbf{E}(t)^T \mathbf{Q} \mathbf{E}(t) + \mathbf{R_u}(t)^T \mathbf{O} \mathbf{R_u}(t) - \rho^2 \mathbf{d}(t)^T \mathbf{d}(t) \right) dt \quad (A1)$$

Equation (A1) can be further reformulated as below:

$$\begin{aligned} J(\mathbf{E}(t), \mathbf{R_u}(t), \mathbf{d}(t)) &= \mathbf{E}(0)^T \mathbf{P} \mathbf{E}(0) - \mathbf{E}(t_f)^T \mathbf{P} \mathbf{E}(t_f) + \tfrac{1}{\gamma_f} \tilde{\mathbf{\Theta}}_\mathbf{w}(0)^T \tilde{\mathbf{\Theta}}_\mathbf{w}(0) \\ &\quad - \tfrac{1}{\gamma_f} \tilde{\mathbf{\Theta}}_\mathbf{w}(t_f)^T \tilde{\mathbf{\Theta}}_\mathbf{w}(t_f) + \int_0^{t_f} \Big[\mathbf{E}(t)^T \big(\mathbf{AP} + \mathbf{PA}^T \\ &\quad + \mathbf{PB} \big(\tfrac{1}{\rho^2} \mathbf{I} - \mathbf{O}^{-1} \big) \mathbf{B}^T \mathbf{P} + \mathbf{Q} \big) \mathbf{E}(t) + \mathbf{R_u}(t)^T \mathbf{O} \mathbf{R_u}(t) \\ &\quad + \mathbf{R_u}(t)^T \mathbf{B}^T \mathbf{P} \mathbf{E}(t) + \mathbf{E}(t)^T \mathbf{PB} \mathbf{R_u}(t) \\ &\quad + \Big(\mathbf{E}(t)^T \mathbf{PB} \lambda_\mathbf{w} + \tfrac{1}{\gamma_f} \dot{\tilde{\mathbf{\Theta}}}_\mathbf{w}(t)^T \Big) \tilde{\mathbf{\Theta}}_\mathbf{w}(t) \\ &\quad + \tilde{\mathbf{\Theta}}_\mathbf{w}(t)^T \Big(\lambda_\mathbf{w}^T \mathbf{B}^T \mathbf{P} \mathbf{E}(t) + \tfrac{1}{\gamma_f} \dot{\tilde{\mathbf{\Theta}}}_\mathbf{w}(t) \Big) \\ &\quad + \mathbf{d}(t)^T \mathbf{B}^T \mathbf{P} \mathbf{E}(t) + \mathbf{E}(t)^T \mathbf{PB} \mathbf{d}(t) + \mathbf{d}(t)^T \mathbf{d}(t) \Big] dt \end{aligned} \quad (A2)$$

Equation (A2) can be expressed as the following result based on the selections of $\dot{\tilde{\mathbf{\Theta}}}_\mathbf{w}(t) = -\gamma_f \lambda_\mathbf{w}^T \mathbf{B}^T \mathbf{P} \mathbf{E}(t)$ and $\mathbf{A}^T \mathbf{P} + \mathbf{PA} + \mathbf{Q} + \mathbf{PB} \big(\tfrac{1}{\rho^2} \mathbf{I} - \mathbf{O}^{-1} \big) \mathbf{B}^T \mathbf{P} = 0$:

$$\begin{aligned} J(\mathbf{E}(t), \mathbf{R_u}(t), \mathbf{d}(t)) &= \mathbf{E}(0)^T \mathbf{P} \mathbf{E}(0) - \mathbf{E}(t_f)^T \mathbf{P} \mathbf{E}(t_f) + \tfrac{1}{\gamma_f} \tilde{\mathbf{\Theta}}_\mathbf{w}(0)^T \tilde{\mathbf{\Theta}}_\mathbf{w}(0) \\ &\quad - \tfrac{1}{\gamma_f} \tilde{\mathbf{\Theta}}_\mathbf{w}(t_f)^T \tilde{\mathbf{\Theta}}_\mathbf{w}(t_f) + \int_0^{t_f} \Big[\mathbf{R_u}(t)^T \mathbf{O} \mathbf{R_u}(t) + \mathbf{R_u}(t)^T \mathbf{B}^T \mathbf{P} \mathbf{E}(t) \\ &\quad + \mathbf{E}(t)^T \mathbf{PB} \mathbf{R_u}(t) + \mathbf{d}(t)^T \mathbf{B}^T \mathbf{P} \mathbf{E}(t) + \mathbf{E}(t)^T \mathbf{PB} \mathbf{d}(t) + \mathbf{d}(t)^T \mathbf{d}(t) \Big] dt \end{aligned} \quad (A3)$$

By completing the square, Equation (A3) can be described as a more concise form:

$$\begin{aligned}J(\mathbf{E}(t),\mathbf{R_u}(t),\mathbf{d}(t)) &= \mathbf{E}(0)^T\mathbf{PE}(0) - \mathbf{E}(t_f)^T\mathbf{PE}(t_f) \\&+ \frac{1}{\gamma_f}\tilde{\mathbf{\Theta}}_\mathbf{w}(0)^T\tilde{\mathbf{\Theta}}_\mathbf{w}(0) - \frac{1}{\gamma_f}\tilde{\mathbf{\Theta}}_\mathbf{w}(t_f)^T\tilde{\mathbf{\Theta}}_\mathbf{w}(t_f) \\&+ \int_0^{t_f}\left[\left[(\mathbf{OR_u}(t) + \mathbf{B}^T\mathbf{PE}(t))^T\mathbf{O}^{-1}(\mathbf{OR_u}(t) + \mathbf{B}^T\mathbf{PE}(t))\right]\right. \\&+ \left.\left(\mathbf{d}(t) - \frac{1}{\rho}\mathbf{B^TPE}(t)\right)^T\left(\mathbf{d}(t) - \frac{1}{\rho}\mathbf{B^TPE}(t)\right) + \mathbf{d}(t)^T\mathbf{d}(t)\right]dt\end{aligned} \quad (A4)$$

For the purpose of minimizing Equation (A4), we selected the robust compensator $\mathbf{R_u}(t)$ and the worst-case modeling uncertainty $\mathbf{d}(t)$ as the following:

$$\mathbf{R_u}(t) = -\mathbf{R}^{-1}\mathbf{B}^T\mathbf{PE}(t) \quad (A5)$$

$$\mathbf{d}(t) = \frac{1}{\rho}\mathbf{B^TPE(t)} \quad (A6)$$

After choosing $\mathbf{R_u}(t)$ and $\mathbf{d}(t)$ as Equations (A5) and (A6), the minimum value of the robust performance index J can be obtained as follows:

$$J(\mathbf{E}(t),\mathbf{R_u}(t),\mathbf{d}(t)) = \mathbf{E}(0)^T\mathbf{PE}(0) + \frac{1}{\gamma_f}\tilde{\mathbf{\Theta}}_\mathbf{w}(0)^T\tilde{\mathbf{\Theta}}_\mathbf{w}(0) \quad (A7)$$

If $\mathbf{E}(0) = \tilde{\mathbf{\Theta}}_\mathbf{w}(0) = \mathbf{0}$, Equations (A7) and (19) are equivalent. Then, Theorem 1 is proven.

References

1. Autonomous Shipping Is Making Waves. International Telecommunication Union. Available online: https://www.itu.int/hub/2020/04/autonomous-shipping-is-making-waves/ (accessed on 14 July 2020).
2. Autonomous Ships Market Expected to Reach US$ 235.73 Bn by 2028. Acute Market Reports. Available online: https://www.acutemarketreports.com/press/global-autonomous-ships-market (accessed on 15 March 2017).
3. Hyundai Heavy Industries (HHI) Group. *HD Hyundai's Avikus Successfully Conducts the World's First Transoceanic Voyage of a Large Merchant Ship Relying on Autonomous Navigation Technologies*; HD Hyundai: Seoul, Republic of Korea, 2022.
4. Goerlandt, F.; Montewka, J.; Kuzmin, V.; Kujala, P. A Risk-Informed Ship Collision Alert System: Framework and Application. *Saf. Sci.* **2015**, *77*, 182–204. [CrossRef]
5. Beser, F.; Yildirim, T. COLREGS Based Path Planning and Bearing only Obstacle Avoidance for Autonomous Unmanned Surface Vehicles. *Procedia Comput. Sci.* **2018**, *131*, 633–640. [CrossRef]
6. Sedova, N.A.; Sedov, V.A.; Bazhenov, R.I.; Alutina, E.F.; Arkhipova, Z.V.; Mendel, V.V. Intelligent Collision Danger Assessment of Autonomous Unmanned Sea-Going Vessels. In Proceedings of the 2022 International Conference on Quality Management, Transport and Information Security, Information Technologies (IT&QM&IS), Saint Petersburg, Russia, 26–30 September 2022; pp. 197–201.
7. Chiang, H.T.L.; Tapia, L. COLREG-RRT: An RRT-Based COLREGS-Compliant Motion Planner for Surface Vehicle Navigation. *IEEE Robot. Autom. Lett.* **2018**, *3*, 2024–2031. [CrossRef]
8. Hu, L.; Naeem, W.; Rajabally, E.; Watson, G.; Mills, T.; Bhuiyan, Z.; Raeburn, C.; Salter, I.; Pekcan, C. A Multiobjective Optimization Approach for COLREGs-Compliant Path Planning of Autonomous Surface Vehicles Verified on Networked Bridge Simulators. *IEEE Trans. Intell. Transp. Syst.* **2020**, *21*, 1167–1179. [CrossRef]
9. Zhao, L.; Roh, M.-I. COLREGs-Compliant Multiship Collision Avoidance Based on Deep Reinforcement Learning. *Ocean. Eng.* **2019**, *191*, 106436. [CrossRef]
10. Chen, Y.-Y.; Ellis-Tiew, M.-Z.; Chen, W.-C.; Wang, C.-Z. Fuzzy Risk Evaluation and Collision Avoidance Control of Unmanned Surface Vessels. *Appl. Sci.* **2021**, *11*, 6338. [CrossRef]
11. Llama, M.; Flores, A.; Garcia-Hernandez, R.; Santibañez, V. Heuristic Global Optimization of an Adaptive Fuzzy Controller for the Inverted Pendulum System: Experimental Comparison. *Appl. Sci.* **2020**, *10*, 6158. [CrossRef]
12. Ruiyun, Q.; Gang, T.; Bin, J. *Fuzzy System Identification and Adaptive Control*; Springer International Publishing: Cham Switzerland, 2019. [CrossRef]
13. Chen, Y.-Y.; Chang, Y.-T.; Chen, B. Fuzzy Solutions to Partial Differential Equations: Adaptive Approach. *IEEE Trans. Fuzzy Syst.* **2009**, *17*, 116–127. [CrossRef]
14. Wang, A.; Liu, L.; Qiu, J.; Feng, G. Event-Triggered Robust Adaptive Fuzzy Control for a Class of Nonlinear Systems. *IEEE Trans. Fuzzy Syst.* **2019**, *27*, 1648–1658. [CrossRef]

15. Wu, J.L. Robust H∞ Control for polytopic Nonlinear Control Systems. *IEEE Trans. Autom. Control* **2013**, *58*, 2957–2962. [CrossRef]
16. Chen, Y.-Y.; Lin, L.-K.; Hung, M.-H. Controllable Micromseter Positioning Design of Piezoelectric Actuators Using a Robust Fuzzy Eliminator. *Microelectron. Reliab.* **2019**, *103*, 113497. [CrossRef]
17. Fossen, T. *Handbook of Marine Craft Hydrodynamics and Motion Control*; John Wiley & Sons: Hoboken, NJ, USA, 2021.

Disclaimer/Publisher's Note: The statements, opinions and data contained in all publications are solely those of the individual author(s) and contributor(s) and not of MDPI and/or the editor(s). MDPI and/or the editor(s) disclaim responsibility for any injury to people or property resulting from any ideas, methods, instructions or products referred to in the content.

Article

Medical Diagnosis under Effective Bipolar-Valued Multi-Fuzzy Soft Settings

Hanan H. Sakr [1,*], Salem A. Alyami [2] and Mohamed A. Abd Elgawad [2,3]

1. Mathematics Department, Faculty of Education, Ain Shams University, Cairo 11341, Egypt
2. Department of Mathematics and Statistics, Faculty of Science, Imam Mohammad Ibn Saud Islamic University (IMSIU), Riyadh 11432, Saudi Arabia
3. Department of Mathematics, Faculty of Science, Benha University, Benha 13518, Egypt
* Correspondence: hananhassan@edu.asu.edu.eg

Citation: Sakr, H.H.; Alyami, S.A.; Abd Elgawad, M.A. Medical Diagnosis under Effective Bipolar-Valued Multi-Fuzzy Soft Settings. *Mathematics* **2023**, *11*, 3747. https://doi.org/10.3390/math11173747

Academic Editors: Himansu Das, Sy-Ming Guu and Mahendra Kumar Gourisaria

Received: 7 June 2023
Revised: 30 July 2023
Accepted: 31 July 2023
Published: 31 August 2023

Copyright: © 2023 by the authors. Licensee MDPI, Basel, Switzerland. This article is an open access article distributed under the terms and conditions of the Creative Commons Attribution (CC BY) license (https://creativecommons.org/licenses/by/4.0/).

Abstract: The Molodtsov-initiated soft set theory plays an important role as a powerful mathematical tool for handling uncertainty. As an extension of the soft set, the fuzzy soft set can be seen to be more generic and flexible than utilizing the soft set only that fails to represent problem parameters fuzziness. Through this progress, the fuzzy soft set theory cannot deal with decision-making problems involving multi-attribute sets, bipolarity, or some effective considered parameters. Therefore, the goal of this article is to adapt effectiveness and bipolarity concepts with the multi-fuzzy soft set of order n. One can see that this approach generates a novel, extended, effective decision-making environment that is more applicable than any previously introduced one. In addition, types, concepts, and operations of effective bipolar-valued multi-fuzzy soft sets of dimension n are provided, each with an example. Furthermore, properties like absorption, associative, distributive, commutative, and De Morgan's laws of those new sets are investigated. Moreover, a decision-making methodology under effective bipolar-valued multi-fuzzy soft settings is established. This technique facilitates reaching the final decision that this student is qualified to take a certain education level, or this patient is suffering from a certain disease, etc. In addition, a case study represented in a medical diagnosis example is discussed in detail to make the proposed algorithm clearer. Applying matrix techniques in this example as well as using MATLAB®, not only makes it easier and faster in doing calculations, but also gives more accurate, optimal, and effective decisions. Finally, the sensitivity analysis, as well as a comparison with the existing methods, are conducted in detail and are summarized in a chart to show the difference between them and the current one.

Keywords: bipolarity; effective fuzzy soft set; medical diagnosis; multi-set

MSC: 92C50; 03E05; 03E72

1. Introduction

In real life, ambiguity and uncertainty are the most typical contributing factors to complexity when generating judgments. Uncertain data are basic and common in many vital fields, including environmental research, corporate management, engineering, economics, medical science, sociology, and numerous others. This uncertainty is produced by missing data updates, inadequate information, data randomness, measurement device barriers, and so on.

Because of the huge quantity of uncertain data that is being gathered and accumulated, as well as the significance of these applications, research on effective methods for illustrating uncertain data and handling uncertainties has sparked plenty of interest in recent years, but it continues to be difficult. As a result, we always have numerous complex challenges in these and other fields. We cannot solve the challenges that arise from uncertainties in those cases using normal mathematical methods.

Decision-making is a process employed at the managerial level of any company to identify and pick alternatives based on individual preferences. Every decision context can be defined as a collection of data, replacement possibilities, choices, and values that are readily accessible at the time of the decision. Because the work and time necessary to obtain statistics or locate alternatives limit both knowledge and its replacements, any conclusions reached must be made within such a constrained framework.

Decision-making has become one of the most important aspects of life and work in recent years, owing to its tight relationship to success and effectiveness. Successful people achieve their life and work goals through effective and efficient decision-making. Individual perspectives, values, attitudes, and concepts, as well as ideas, are commonly utilized to guide decision-making. While a person can arrive at decisions based on a range of principles, they should exercise extreme caution in selecting one that is productive and contributes to significant performance. However, these theories exist in order to help people become better decision-makers in the world. The decision-making issue in an uncertain environment has attracted attention in recent years.

There are a lot of research studies, as well as applications in the literature, about many special mathematical tools, like probability theory, fuzzy sets [1], intuitionistic fuzzy set theory [2], soft set theory [3], and other mathematical methods, which are helpful ways for modeling uncertain data and making successful and useful decisions. Nevertheless, each of them faces particular difficulties while handling uncertainty. The probability theory is an old and useful strategy for tackling uncertainty, but it is only capable of being applied to circumstances involving random processes, or processes in which the occurrence of events is purely determined by chances.

In 1965, Zadeh [1] introduced a very important extension of the well-known crisp set to represent and overcome appearing uncertainty, which is the fuzzy concept approach. In fuzzy set theory, one can measure the degree of membership of an element by the element's membership (indicator, or characteristic) function from the domain X to the interval $[0,1]$.

A well-known crisp set on the initial universe X can be measured by the element's membership (indicator, or characteristic) function from X to $\{0,1\}$. Despite the fact that the fuzzy set has been recognized as a viable mathematical method of handling uncertainty, it has the following drawback: this particular number tells us almost nothing concerning how precise it is. The specific number (membership percent) involves reasoning both in favor of as well as against an object belonging, with no detail about exactly how much more of each there actually is. To overcome this limitation, an extended or generalized new concept of the term "fuzzy set" was provided by Atanassov [2] and was cleared by an example, which is the "intuitionistic fuzzy set". The new concept represented in the soft set idea was first formulated, in 1999, by Molodtsov [3]. There has been a claim that made them introduce the soft set theory. The claim was that the inadequate parametrization tools of the previously introduced theories might be one of the important reasons for the issues and difficulties.

The novel-introduced softness concept or the soft set concept is a new practical mathematical tool, which is free from the above difficulties. Then, it was used to facilitate dealing with uncertainties for a long time. After that, in 2002, Maji et al. ([4,5]) examined and analyzed the Molodtsov-proposed soft set theory. They looked into many soft set-related ideas, developed an in-depth theoretical outline of the discipline, and then implemented it in a decision-making situation.

The bipolarity in information when dealing with decision-making issues, on the other hand, seemed to be an essential factor to take into account. That is because it is a very helpful component when building the mathematical structure for the majority of cases in problems with decision-making. According to bipolarity theory, bipolar sensibility beliefs cover a range of different decision-making processes. Love versus hate, advantages versus drawbacks, sweet versus salty, and finally, starvation versus satisfaction, are a few examples of different analyses of decision approaches.

By way of example, if we have an effective drug, this cannot prevent it from resulting in probable serious side effects. On the other hand, if it is an ineffective drug, it can have no dangerous side effects. As an innovative generalization or extension of the fuzzy set concept, Lee [6] developed the bipolar-valued fuzzy idea in 2000. In this scenario, the membership range that defines the element's belonging was expanded from the interval $[0,1]$ to the interval $[-1,1]$.

Later, Maji et al. [7] created, in 2001, the novel concept of the fuzzy soft set theory by integrating the principles of fuzzy sets into the softness concept. Additionally, Roy and Maji [8] generated a decision-making method based on a fuzzy soft set to choose the ideal (best) item to purchase out of a variety of options. Furthermore, Yang et al. [9] provided the fuzzy soft set matrix formulation depending on the fuzzy soft set notion.

Moreover, ağman et al. [10] examined fuzzy soft matrixes and various algebraic operations, and performed a theoretical investigation in fuzzy soft contexts. In their studies of fuzzy soft matrixes, Basu et al. [11] and Kumar and Kaur [12] developed novel concepts and operations. For more novel information about the fuzzy soft extension and its properties, one can refer to [13–20] to obtain many more theorems, results, and examples.

After that, Maji et al. [21] constructed, in 2004, the new notion of the intuitionistic fuzzy soft sets being an original extension of the soft sets. A few more operations were also offered on intuitionistic fuzzy soft sets and several their properties were recognized. A straightforward example was also provided to illustrate how to use this mathematical tool. The intuitionistic fuzzy soft matrixes idea was then developed by Chetia et al. [22] in order to readily express intuitionistic fuzzy soft sets and facilitate operations on them. They also detailed their higher functional operations in order to conduct theoretical research in the intuitionistic fuzzy soft set environment and produce some conclusions.

Moreover, Abdullah et al. [23] presented, in 2014, the idea of the bipolar fuzzy soft set and provided its fundamental properties. Further, the fundamental principles of the bipolar fuzzy soft sets were discovered. In addition, they overcame problems that occurred in decision-making by using the bipolar fuzzy soft set. In fact, the bipolar fuzzy soft sets and intuitionistic fuzzy soft sets are different from each other, contrary to their appearances. Following that, Sebastian and Ramakrishnan [24] suggested the idea of the multi-fuzzy set concept by employing the multi-characteristic function, which is an ordered sequence of the aforementioned characteristic functions.

Actually, the multi-fuzzy sets can solve some particular issues which are exceedingly challenging for other fuzzy set extensions to describe. For example, the three-dimensional characteristic function, whose components are the characteristic functions representing the three primary known colors; red, green, and blue, can describe the color of pixels in a two-dimensional image in a way that the characteristic function of the regular fuzzy set cannot. As a result, any image may be generally represented as a set of arranged pixels with a multi-characteristic function. Moreover, Yang et al. [25] introduced the multi-fuzzy soft sets and proposed many applications using decision-making techniques based on those new sets.

Santhi and Shyamala [26] also described the bipolar-valued multi-fuzzy set and provided some observations on the bipolar-valued multi-fuzzy subgroups of a group. Furthermore, Yang et al. [27] offered various decision-making applications based on their concept of the bipolar-valued multi-fuzzy soft set. In addition, Sakr et al. ([28,29]) have introduced the bipolar-valued vague soft sets, the bipolar-valued multi-vague soft sets and their applications. The vague set is a generalization for a fuzzy set, in which any membership value is an interval subset from $[0,1]$, not only a specific single membership value lying within the range of 0 to 1 as known in fuzzy sets. Furthermore, for additional knowledge on those topics and many more interesting related topics, refer to [30–33].

In addition, using well-known techniques, Chakraborty et al. [34] have constructed the sense of de-bipolarization for a triangular bipolar neutrosophic number, such that any bipolar neutrosophic fuzzy number of any type can be smoothly turned into a real number quickly. Using bipolar neutrosophic perception to create an issue is a more accurate, reliable and trusted way than others. They have also considered a multi-criteria decision-making problem (MCDM) for several users in the bipolar neutrosophic area.

Moreover, Haque et al. [35] have investigated a novel scheme to detect the best cloud service provider using logarithmic operational law in the generalized spherical fuzzy environment. Furthermore, for more information about other decision-making techniques, one can refer to [36,37].

Moreover, Xiao [38] introduced the complex evidential distance (CED), which is a strict distance metric with the properties of nonnegativity, nondegeneracy, symmetry and triangle inequality that satisfies the axioms of a distance. For a long time, evidence theory has been an effective methodology for modeling and processing uncertainty that has been widely applied in various fields. In evidence theory, several distance measures have been presented, which play an important role in representing the degree of difference between pieces of evidence. The complex evidential distance (CED) has been considered to be a generalization of the traditional evidential distance.

Furthermore, Alkhazaleh [39] recently noticed that in the fuzzy soft set theory, the final decision in the given decision-making problems depends only on the usual parameters without considering the effect of any other external parameters. To overcome this limitation, he proposed a new concept to represent those external parameters which is the effective parameter set. In addition, he defined the effective fuzzy soft set concept built on the effective set definition. He also established the operations of the effective fuzzy soft sets and studied some of their properties. Moreover, he gave an application of the effective fuzzy soft set in decision-making problems. Finally, he introduced an application of this novel theory to medical diagnosis and exhibited the technique with a hypothetical case study.

Work Motivation

As stated above, we have the fuzzy set, the soft set, the bipolarity, the effective set, and the multi-attribute concepts. If we have all those concepts in one decision-making problem as its circumstances are described, then any one, two, or even more combined sets of those stated above will fail to handle this issue. Then, there is a need to have a new extension that collects all those concepts in one combined set to deal easily with this type of problem.

In other words, the idea of this research comes from a need to generalize the multi-fuzzy soft set, the bipolar-valued fuzzy soft set, and the multipolar fuzzy soft set. This is necessary when we have multi attributes and bipolar attributes together with fuzzy soft information and effective needed parameters. The effective bipolar-valued multi-fuzzy soft set of dimension n is the best one to satisfy this need by combining all needed circumstances in one novel generalized definition. Therefore, in this paper, we define the effective bipolar-valued multi-fuzzy soft sets of dimension n along with their types, properties, operations, and real-life medical applications. The rest of this paper is organized as follows:

Section 2 is nominated to state the needed preliminary definitions and concepts. In Section 3, the effective bipolar-valued multi-fuzzy soft set, its types and some novel associated concepts are inferred. Moreover, their operations, like union and intersection, are presented in Section 4. After that, Section 5 concludes some related properties, for example, commutative properties, absorption properties, associative properties, De Morgan's laws, and distributive laws.

Moreover, the purpose of Section 6 is to derive a decision-making algorithm based on the effective bipolar-valued multi-fuzzy soft sets. This helps us to conduct the decision that this patient is suffering from this disease or this student is qualified or accepted to take or study at this education level, . . . The technique steps are introduced using matrixes to make it easier to do computations.

Furthermore, the MATLAB® program is used to do the addition and multiplication operations of matrixes, to obtain effective sets, or to make any calculations quickly, accurately, and easily. In addition, we give the sensitivity analysis as well as the comparative analysis at the end of Section 6. This detailed comparison between the existing methodologies and the current one is presented to highlight the distinctions between them. The results of this comparison are also summarized in a chart. Finally, Section 7 is set up for concluding remarks and some predicted future works. The structure of the paper content is given by a graphical tree diagram shown below in Figure 1.

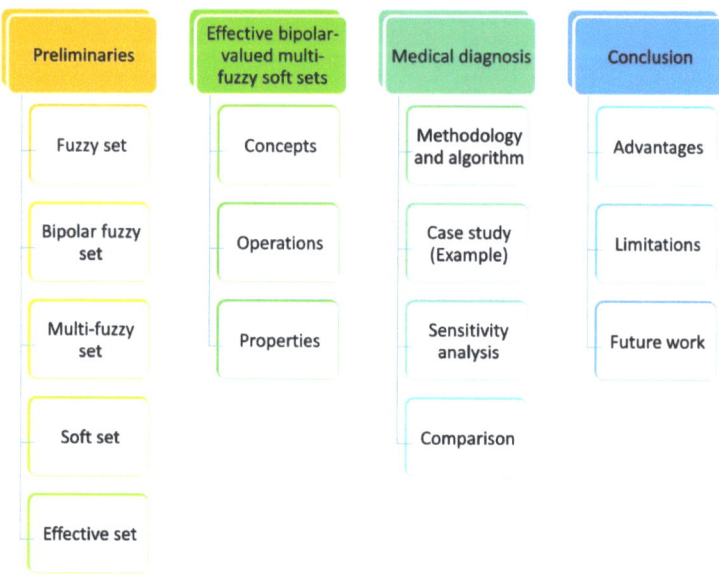

Figure 1. Paper content diagram.

2. Preliminaries

The fundamental preliminary definitions, required in the subsequent results, are discussed in this section. These definitions are about the fuzzy set, bipolar-valued fuzzy set, multi-fuzzy set, bipolar-valued multi-fuzzy set, soft set, effective set, and effective fuzzy soft set. One can refer to [1,3,6,24,26,39] to find more detailed results and examples about those above concepts.

Definition 1 ((Fuzzy set) [1]). *Assume that Ξ is an initial universe. Then, we can define the fuzzy class (set) F over Ξ as a set characterized by a characteristic function $\eta_F : \Xi \to [0,1]$. We can call η_F the indicator function, or the membership function of the fuzzy set F. In addition, $\eta_F(u)$ is called the degree of membership, or the membership grade value of $\xi \in \Xi$ in F. We can represent the fuzzy set F over an initial universe Ξ by one of the following two formulas:*

$$F = \{(\eta_F(\xi)/\xi) : \xi \in \Xi, \, \eta_F(\xi) \in [0,1]\}, \text{ or}$$

$$F = \{(\xi, \eta_F(\xi)) : \xi \in \Xi, \, \eta_F(\xi) \in [0,1]\}.$$

Definition 2 ((Bipolar-valued fuzzy set) [6]). *For the positive characteristic function $\eta_{\mathcal{A}}^+ : \Xi \to [0,1]$ and the negative characteristic function $\eta_{\mathcal{A}}^- : \Xi \to [-1,0]$, the formula*

$$\mathcal{A} = \{(\xi, \eta_{\mathcal{A}}^+(\xi), \eta_{\mathcal{A}}^-(\xi)) : \xi \in \Xi\}$$

represents the bipolar-valued fuzzy set $\mathcal{A}$ on Ξ. $\eta_{\mathcal{A}}^+ : \Xi \to [0,1]$ can describe the satisfaction degree of ξ to the property corresponding to $\mathcal{A}$ and $\eta_{\mathcal{A}}^- : \Xi \to [-1,0]$ can describe the satisfaction degree of ξ to the counter-property of $\mathcal{A}$.

Definition 3 ((Multi-fuzzy set) [24]). *A multi-fuzzy set $\mathcal{N}$ of dimension n over Ξ is characterized by a set of ordered sequences in the following structure:*

$$\mathcal{N} = \{(\xi, \eta_{1\mathcal{N}}(\xi), \eta_{2\mathcal{N}}(\xi), \ldots, \eta_{n\mathcal{N}}(\xi)) : \xi \in \Xi\},$$

taking into account that, for $i = 1, 2, \cdots, n$, $\eta_{i\mathcal{N}} : \Xi \to [0, 1]$ represent the characteristic or the membership functions. We can call the function $\eta_{\mathcal{N}} = (\eta_{1\mathcal{N}}, \eta_{2\mathcal{N}}, \ldots, \eta_{n\mathcal{N}})$, the fuzzy multi-membership function of a multi-fuzzy set $\mathcal{N}$ of dimension n.

Definition 4 ((Bipolar-valued multi-fuzzy set) [26]). *The following formula represents the bipolar-valued multi-fuzzy set $\mathcal{B}$ of dimension n over an initial universe Ξ:*

$$\mathcal{B} = \{(\xi, \eta_{1\mathcal{B}}^+(\xi), \eta_{2\mathcal{B}}^+(\xi), \ldots, \eta_{n\mathcal{B}}^+(\xi), \eta_{1\mathcal{B}}^-(\xi), \eta_{2\mathcal{B}}^-(\xi), \ldots, \eta_{n\mathcal{B}}^-(\xi)) : \xi \in \Xi\},$$

taking into account that, for $i = 1, 2, \cdots, n$, $\eta_{i\mathcal{B}}^+ : \Xi \to [0, 1]$ represent the positive characteristic (or membership) functions indicating the satisfaction degrees of ξ to some properties corresponding to $\mathcal{B}$ and $\eta_{i\mathcal{B}}^- : \Xi \to [-1, 0]$ represent the negative characteristic (or membership) functions indicating the satisfaction degrees of ξ to some implicit counter-properties of $\mathcal{B}$.

Definition 5 ((Soft set) [3]). *Let Ξ be an initial universe, Y be a set of parameters (or attributes), and $\Lambda \subseteq Y$. The power set of Ξ is obtained from $P(\Xi) = 2^\Xi$. A pair (Γ, Λ) or Γ_Λ is called a soft set over Ξ, taking into account that Γ is a mapping represented by $\Gamma : \Lambda \to P(\Xi)$. In addition, we can formulate Γ_Λ as a set of ordered pairs $\Gamma_\Lambda = \{(\lambda, \Gamma_\Lambda(\lambda)) : \lambda \in \Lambda, \Gamma_\Lambda(\lambda) \in P(\Xi)\}$. Λ is said to be the support of Γ_Λ, as well as $\Gamma_\Lambda(\lambda) \neq \phi$, for any $\lambda \in \Lambda$ and $\Gamma_\Lambda(\lambda) = \phi$ for any $\lambda \notin \Lambda$. That is to say that a soft set (Γ, Λ) over Ξ can be considered to be a parameterized family of subsets of Ξ.*

Definition 6 ((Effective set) [39]). *An effective set is defined as a fuzzy set $\daleth$ over the universal set Δ, in which $\daleth$ is given by the mapping $\daleth : \Delta \to [0, 1]$. We can say that Δ is the set of all effective attributes or parameters that can affect the value of membership of every element. It has a positive effect on the membership values of the elements after applying it to them. Note that, in some cases, some membership values remain as is, even after implementation. One can define $\daleth$ by the following formula: $\daleth = \{(\delta, \varrho_\daleth(\delta)), \delta \in \Delta\}$.*

Definition 7 ((Effective fuzzy soft set) [39]). *For a given initial universal set Ξ, we can indicate the set of all fuzzy subsets of Ξ by $\mathfrak{F}(\Xi)$. Suppose that $v_i \in Y$ are the usual parameters, Δ is the effective parameter set and $\daleth$ is the effective set over Δ. Then, we call the pair $(\Psi_\daleth, Y)$ an effective fuzzy soft set over Ξ, taking into account that the mapping $\Psi : \Xi \to \mathfrak{F}(\Xi)$ is given by the following formula: $\Psi(\delta_i)_\daleth = \{(\xi_j, \eta_\Psi(\xi_j)_\daleth), \xi_j \in \Xi, \delta_i \in \Delta\}$, where, for all $\delta_k \in \Delta$, we have:*

$$\eta_\Psi(\xi_j, v_i)_\daleth = \begin{cases} \eta_\Psi(\xi_j, v_i) + \dfrac{(1 - \eta_\Psi(\xi_j, v_i))\sum_k \varrho_{\daleth_{\xi_j}}(\delta_k)}{|\Delta|}, & \text{if } \eta_\Psi(\xi_j, v_i) \in (0, 1), \\ \eta_\Psi(\xi_j), & \text{otherwise.} \end{cases} \quad (1)$$

where $|\Delta|$ is the number of elements in the given effective parameter set Δ, $\eta_\Psi(\xi_j, v_i)$ is the membership degree value of the item ξ_j for the parameter v_i and $\sum_k \varrho_{\daleth_{\xi_j}}(\delta_k)$ is the summation of all effective parameters values of ξ_j.

Example 1. *If we have an initial universal set $\Xi = \{\xi_1, \xi_2, \xi_3\}$ and the set of parameters $Y = \{v_1, v_2, v_3\}$. Let the fuzzy soft set for the parameter v_1 be*

$$(\Psi, Y)(v_1) = \{(\xi_1, 0.3), (\xi_2, 0.7), (\xi_3, 0.5)\}.$$

Then, to compute the effective membership value for the first item ξ_1 with a membership value 0.3 for the first parameter v_1 and the following given effective set $\daleth$ for ξ_1:

$$\daleth(\xi_1) = \{(\delta_1, 0.8), (\delta_2, 1), (\delta_3, 0), (\delta_4, 0.2)\},$$

where δ_1, δ_2, δ_3 and δ_4 are the given effective parameters, we do the following computation according to Formula (1) from Definition 7:

$$\eta_\Psi(\xi_1, v_1)_\daleth = 0.3 + \frac{(1-0.3)[0.8+1+0+0.2]}{4} = 0.3 + \frac{0.7 \times 2}{4} = 0.3 + 0.35 = 0.65.$$

Similarly, we can calculate the effective membership values for the remaining membership values of ξ_1 for the last two parameters v_2 and v_3 and also for the other two items ξ_2 and ξ_3. The reader can refer to [39] page 3 to find the full illustrative example to understand this definition well.

Remark 1. *For simplicity, instead of writing the full complex Formula (1) from Definition 7, one can write the effective membership value $\eta_\Psi(\xi_j, v_i)_\daleth$ corresponding to the membership value $\eta_\Psi(\xi_j, v_i)$ of a specific item ξ_j for a certain parameter v_i as $\eta_\daleth$, when we know that Ψ is the only fuzzy soft set we talking about. In case we have two fuzzy soft sets Ψ_1 and Ψ_2 or more, we must write the full formulas $\eta_{\Psi_1}(\xi_j, v_i)$ and $\eta_{\Psi_2}(\xi_j, v_i)$, respectively, to distinguish between them.*

3. Effective Bipolar-Valued Multi-Fuzzy Soft Sets

The major goal of the current section is to formulate the definition of the effective bipolar-valued fuzzy soft set and the effective multi-fuzzy soft set. Furthermore, the definition of the effective bipolar-valued multi-fuzzy soft set of dimension n is derived and reflected by an illustrative example. In addition, their kinds and some associated concepts are conducted.

Definition 8 (Effective bipolar-valued fuzzy soft set). *For a given initial universal set Ξ, we can indicate the set of all bipolar-valued fuzzy subsets of Ξ by $\mathfrak{BF}(\Xi)$. Suppose that Y is the parameter set, Δ is the effective parameter set, and $\daleth$ is the effective set over Δ. Then, we call the pair $(\Psi_\daleth, Y)$ an effective bipolar-valued fuzzy soft set over Ξ, taking into account that the mapping $\Psi : \Xi \to \mathfrak{BF}(\Xi)$ is given by the following formula:*

$$\Psi(\delta_i)_\daleth = \{(\xi_j, \eta_\Psi^+(\xi_j)_\daleth, \eta_\Psi^-(\xi_j)_\daleth), \xi_j \in \Psi, \delta_i \in \Delta\},$$

where, for all $\delta_k \in \Delta$, we have the positive and negative effective membership values $\eta_\daleth^+$ and $\eta_\daleth^-$ corresponding to the positive and negative membership values $\eta^+ \in (0,1)$ and $\eta^- \in (-1,0)$ of the item ξ_j for the parameter v_l given, respectively, by the following two formulas:

$$\eta_\daleth^+ = \eta^+ + \frac{(1-\eta^+)\sum_k \varrho_\daleth(\delta_k)}{|\Delta|}, \quad (2)$$

and

$$\eta_\daleth^- = \eta^- + \frac{(-1-\eta^+)\sum_k \varrho_\daleth(\delta_k)}{|\Delta|}, \quad (3)$$

where $|\Delta|$ is the number of elements in the given effective parameter set Δ.

In case that $\eta^+ = 0$ or 1, then $\eta_\daleth^+ = \eta^+$. Similarly, if $\eta^- = 0$ or -1, then $\eta_\daleth^- = \eta^-$.

Remark 2. *Formulas (2) and (3), stated in Definition 8, can be combined into one formula as follows:*

$$\eta\daleth = \begin{cases} \eta + \frac{(1-\eta)\sum_k \varrho_{\daleth_{\xi_j}}(\delta_k)}{|\Delta|}, & \text{if } \eta \in (0,1), \\ \eta + \frac{(-1-\eta)\sum_k \varrho_{\daleth_{\xi_j}}(\delta_k)}{|\Delta|}, & \text{if } \eta \in (-1,0), \\ \eta, & \text{otherwise.} \end{cases} \quad (4)$$

regarding that

$$\eta\daleth = \begin{cases} \eta\daleth^+, & \text{if } \eta \in [0,1], \\ \eta\daleth^-, & \text{if } \eta \in [-1,0], \end{cases}$$

where $|\Delta|$ is the number of elements in the given effective parameter set Δ.

Definition 9 (Effective multi-fuzzy soft set of order n). *For a given initial universal set Ξ, we can indicate the set of all multi-fuzzy subsets of order n on Ξ by $\mathfrak{MF}(\Xi)$. Suppose that Y is the parameter set, Δ is the effective parameter set, and $\daleth$ is the effective set over Δ. Then, we call the pair $(\Psi\daleth, Y)$ an effective multi-fuzzy soft set of order n over Ξ, taking into account that the mapping $\Psi : \Xi \to \mathfrak{MF}(\Xi)$ is given by the following formula:*

$$\Psi(\delta_i)\daleth = \{(\xi_j, \eta_{1\Psi}(\xi_j)\daleth, \eta_{2\Psi}(\xi_j)\daleth, \cdots, \eta_{n\Psi}(\xi_j)\daleth), \xi_j \in \Xi, \delta_i \in \Delta\},$$

where, for all $\delta_k \in \Delta$, we have:

$$\eta_r\daleth = \begin{cases} \eta_r + \frac{(1-\eta_r)\sum_k \varrho_{\daleth_{\xi_j}}(\delta_k)}{|\Delta|}, & \text{if } \eta_r \in (0,1), \\ \eta_r, & \text{otherwise.} \end{cases} \quad (5)$$

regarding that $r : 1, 2, \cdots, n$ and $|\Delta|$ is the number of elements in the given effective parameter set Δ.

Definition 10 (Effective bipolar-valued multi-fuzzy soft set of order n). *For a given initial universal set Ξ, we can indicate the set of all bipolar-valued multi-fuzzy subsets of order n on Ξ by $\mathfrak{BMF}(\Xi)$. Suppose that Y is the parameter set, Δ is the effective parameter set, and $\daleth$ is the effective set over Δ. Then, we call the pair $(\Psi\daleth, Y)$ an effective bipolar-valued multi-fuzzy soft set of order n over Ξ, taking into account that the mapping $\Psi : \Xi \to \mathfrak{BMF}(\Xi)$ is given by the following formula:*

$$\Psi(\delta_i)\daleth = \{(\xi_j, \eta_{1\Psi}^+(\xi_j)\daleth, \eta_{2\Psi}^+(\xi_j)\daleth, \cdots, \eta_{n\Psi}^+(\xi_j)\daleth, \eta_{1\Psi}^-(\xi_j)\daleth, \eta_{2\Psi}^-(\xi_j)\daleth, \cdots, \eta_{n\Psi}^-(\xi_j)\daleth),$$
$$\xi_j \in \Xi, \delta_i \in \Delta\},$$

where, for all $\delta_k \in \Delta$, we have:

$$\eta_r\daleth = \begin{cases} \eta_r + \frac{(1-\eta_r)\sum_k \varrho_{\daleth_{\xi_j}}(\delta_k)}{|\Delta|}, & \text{if } \eta_r \in (0,1), \\ \eta_r + \frac{(-1-\eta_r)\sum_k \varrho_{\daleth_{\xi_j}}(\delta_k)}{|\Delta|}, & \text{if } \eta_r \in (-1,0), \\ \eta_r, & \text{otherwise,} \end{cases} \quad (6)$$

where

$$\eta_{r\daleth} = \begin{cases} \eta_{r\daleth}^+, & \text{if } \eta_r \in [0,1], \\ \eta_{r\daleth}^-, & \text{if } \eta_r \in [-1,0], \end{cases}$$

taking into account that $r : 1, 2, \cdots, n$ and $|\Delta|$ are the number of elements in the given effective parameter set Δ.

Example 2. Consider a universal set of houses $\Xi = \{\xi_1, \xi_2, \xi_3\}$ which are considered to be bought. Let the two major sets of parameters (attributes) that describe their features be $Y = \{v_1, v_2, v_3\}$, $v_i(i = 1,2,3)$ and its opposite set $-Y = \{-v_1, -v_2, -v_3\}$, $-v_i(i = 1,2,3)$ stand for the features and the opposite-features, respectively. These features can be classified into the following three main types of parameters: Location affairs, financial affairs, and design affairs, respectively. Location affairs and their opposite features are as follows: ("near the main road" and "far from the main road"), ("close to the city center" and "far from the city center"), ("in a green surrounding" and "in an industrial surrounding"). Financial affairs and their opposite features are as follows: ("expensive" and "cheap"), ("cash payment" and "payment facilities"), ("long-term installment" and "short-term installment"). Design affairs and their opposite features are as follows: ("large house" and "small house"), ("within stacked apartments" and "within unstacked apartments"), ("luxurious design" and "poor design"). In addition, suppose that $\Delta = \{\delta_1, \delta_2, \delta_3, \delta_4\}$ is a set of effective attributes, where $\delta_1 = $ the house has not been licensed yet, $\delta_2 = $ there have been people living in this house before, $\delta_3 = $ there is no an elevator and $\delta_4 = $ there is a broker fee. Let the effective set over Δ, for $\xi_i, i = 1,2,3$, be as follows according to experts' evaluation:

$$\daleth(\xi_1) = \{(\delta_1, 0.7), (\delta_2, 0.2), (\delta_3, 0.5), (\delta_4, 0.4)\},$$

$$\daleth(\xi_2) = \{(\delta_1, 0.5), (\delta_2, 0.1), (\delta_3, 0), (\delta_4, 0.8)\},$$

$$\daleth(\xi_3) = \{(\delta_1, 1), (\delta_2, 0.6), (\delta_3, 0.3), (\delta_4, 0.9)\}.$$

Furthermore, the attractiveness of the given houses according to the purchaser's preferences can be described by a bipolar-valued multi-fuzzy soft set (Ψ, Y) of order 3 over a universal set Ξ as follows:

$$(\Psi, Y) = \{(v_1, \{(\xi_1, 0.4, 0.8, 0.6, -0.3, -0.9, -0.2), (\xi_2, 0.1, 0.5, 0.3, -0.7, -0.6, -0.4),$$
$$(\xi_3, 0.9, 0.4, 0.5, -0.7, -0.2, -0.3)\}), (v_2, \{(\xi_1, 0.6, 0.3, 1, -0.7, -0.5, -0.3),$$
$$(\xi_2, 0.5, 1, 0.9, -0.2, -1, -0.4), (\xi_3, 0.2, 0.4, 0.6, -0.3, -0.8, -0.1)\}),$$
$$(v_3, \{(\xi_1, 1, 0.6, 0.3, -0.2, -0.5, -0.4), (\xi_2, 0.7, 0.9, 0.1, -0.9, -1, -0.3),$$
$$(\xi_3, 0.1, 0.7, 0.2, -0.2, -0.5, -0.8)\})\}.$$

Then, using Formula (6) from Definition 10, we have the effective bipolar-valued multi-fuzzy soft set $(\Psi\daleth, Y)$ of order 3 over a universal set Ξ that describes the attractiveness of the of above houses, effectively, as the following:

$$(\Psi\daleth, Y) = \{(v_1, \{(\xi_1, 0.67, 0.89, 0.78, -0.61, -0.94, -0.56),$$
$$(\xi_2, 0.41, 0.67, 0.54, -0.8, -0.74, -0.61),$$
$$(\xi_3, 0.97, 0.82, 0.85, -0.91, -0.76, -0.79)\}),$$
$$(v_2, \{(\xi_1, 0.78, 0.61, 1, -0.83, -0.72, -0.61),$$
$$(\xi_2, 0.67, 1, 0.93, -0.48, -1, -0.61), \quad (7)$$
$$(\xi_3, 0.76, 0.82, 0.88, -0.79, -0.94, -0.73)\}),$$
$$(v_3, \{(\xi_1, 1, 0.78, 0.61, -0.56, -0.72, -0.67),$$
$$(\xi_2, 0.8, 0.93, 0.41, -0.93, -1, -0.54),$$
$$(\xi_3, 0.73, 0.91, 0.76, -0.76, -0.85, -0.94)\})\}.$$

($\Psi_\daleth$, Y) description can help the purchaser decide which house is the best choice for him/her. This decision-making technique comes from extracting the matrix corresponding to every positive pole and every negative pole of the effective bipolar-valued multi-fuzzy soft set that contains the membership values of the given items. After that, by doing some matrix operations like multiplication and addition, one can easily obtain the final decision from the final resulting matrix.

Remark 3. *The above effective bipolar-valued multi-fuzzy soft set ($\Psi_\daleth$, Y) of order 3 (7) from Example 2 can be represented in a matrix form to be easy to deal with. It can be divided into two matrixes; one represents the positive poles, say A^+ and the other represents the negative poles, say A^-, as follows:*

$$A^+ = \begin{array}{c} \\ \xi_1 \\ \xi_2 \\ \xi_3 \end{array} \begin{pmatrix} v_1' & v_2' & v_3' & v_1'' & v_2'' & v_3'' & v_1''' & v_2''' & v_3''' \\ 0.67 & 0.78 & 1 & 0.89 & 0.61 & 0.78 & 0.78 & 1 & 0.61 \\ 0.41 & 0.67 & 0.8 & 0.67 & 1 & 0.93 & 0.54 & 0.93 & 0.41 \\ 0.97 & 0.76 & 0.73 & 0.82 & 0.82 & 0.91 & 0.85 & 0.88 & 0.76 \end{pmatrix},$$

$$A^- = \begin{array}{c} \\ \xi_1 \\ \xi_2 \\ \xi_3 \end{array} \begin{pmatrix} -v_1' & -v_2' & -v_3' & -v_1'' & -v_2'' & -v_3'' & -v_1''' & -v_2''' & -v_3''' \\ -0.61 & -0.83 & -0.56 & -0.94 & -0.72 & -0.72 & -0.56 & -0.61 & -0.67 \\ -0.8 & -0.48 & -0.93 & -0.74 & -1 & -1 & -0.61 & -0.61 & -0.54 \\ -0.91 & -0.79 & -0.76 & -0.76 & -0.94 & -0.85 & -0.79 & -0.73 & -0.94 \end{pmatrix}.$$

We can call (A^+, A^-) the effective bipolar-valued multi-fuzzy soft matrix corresponding to the effective bipolar-valued multi-fuzzy soft set ($\Psi_\daleth$, Y).

Definition 11 (Complete effective bipolar-valued multi-fuzzy soft set). *Assume that Ξ is an initial universe. Suppose that Y is a parameter set. Then, any effective bipolar-valued multi-fuzzy soft set ($\Psi_\daleth$, Y) of dimension n on an initial universe Ξ, constructed by an effective set $\daleth$, is called absolute (or complete), stand for ($C_\daleth$, Y), if for all $v \in Y$, we have $\Psi_Y(v)_\daleth = \mathfrak{BMF}(\Xi)$. That is to say that, for $i = 1, 2, \ldots, n$, we have $\eta^+_{i\Psi_Y(v)}(\xi)_\daleth = 1$ and $\eta^-_{i\Psi_Y(v)}(\xi)_\daleth = -1$, for all $v \in Y$ and for all $\xi \in \Xi$. i.e.,*

$$(C_\daleth, Y) = \{(v, \{(\xi, 1, \overset{n-times}{\ldots}, 1, -1, \overset{n-times}{\ldots}, -1)\}) : v \in Y, \xi \in \Xi\}.$$

Definition 12 (Null effective bipolar-valued multi-fuzzy soft set). *Given that, Ξ is an initial universe. Assume that Y is a parameter set. Then, any effective bipolar-valued multi-fuzzy soft set ($\Psi_\daleth$, Y) of dimension n on an initial universe Ξ, constructed by an effective set $\daleth$, is called empty (or null), stand for ($\phi_\daleth$, Y), if for all $v \in Y$, we have $\Psi_Y(v)_\daleth = \phi$. That is to say that, for $i = 1, 2, \ldots, n$, we have $\eta^+_{i\Psi_Y(v)}(\xi)_\daleth = 0$ and $\eta^-_{i\Psi_Y(v)}(\xi)_\daleth = 0$, for all $v \in Y$ and for all $\xi \in \Xi$. i.e.,*

$$(\phi_\daleth, Y) = \{(v, \{(\xi, 0, \overset{2n-times}{\ldots}, 0)\}) : v \in Y, \xi \in \Xi\}.$$

4. Operations on Effective Bipolar-Valued Multi-Fuzzy Soft Sets

The basic objective of this section is to propose the operations on effective bipolar-valued multi-fuzzy soft sets. Operations like the union, the intersection, the complement, the subset, and many more are established. Furthermore, an example for each operation is given to illustrate how this operation can be.

Definition 13 (Union of two effective bipolar-valued multi-fuzzy soft sets). *Assume that Ξ is an initial universe. Suppose that Y_1 and Y_2 are two parameter sets. Let $\daleth_1$ and $\daleth_2$ be two effective parameter sets over Δ. Then, the operation of the union of two effective bipolar-valued multi-fuzzy* soft sets $(\Psi_{1\daleth_1}, Y_1)$ and $(\Psi_{2\daleth_2}, Y_2)$ of dimension n on an initial universe Ξ is defined as a new effective bipolar-valued multi-fuzzy soft set $(\Psi_{\daleth^U}^U, Y^U)$ of dimension n, where $\daleth^U : \Delta \to [0,1]$ is a mapping characterized by $\daleth^U = \daleth_1 \widetilde{\cup} \daleth_2$, as well as, $(\Psi, Y)^U = (\Psi^U, Y^U) = (\Psi_1, Y_1)\widetilde{\cup}(\Psi_2, Y_2)$, taking into account that $Y^U = Y_1 \cup Y_2$.

The two formulas that compute $\daleth^U = \daleth_1 \widetilde{\cup} \daleth_2$ and $(\Psi^U, Y^U) = (\Psi_1, Y_1)\widetilde{\cup}(\Psi_2, Y_2)$, respectively, can be determined, for each $\xi \in \Xi$, as follows:

$$\varrho_{\daleth_\xi^U}(\delta) = \begin{cases} \varrho_{\daleth_{1\xi}}(\delta), & \text{if } e \in \daleth_1 - \daleth_2, \\ \varrho_{\daleth_{2\xi}}(\delta), & \text{if } e \in \daleth_2 - \daleth_1, \\ \max\{\varrho_{\daleth_{1\xi}}(\delta), \varrho_{\daleth_{2\xi}}(\delta)\}, & \text{if } e \in \daleth_1 \cap \daleth_2, \end{cases} \quad (8)$$

for each $\delta \in \Delta$ and

$$(\Psi^U, Y^U) = \begin{cases} = \{(v, \{(\xi, \eta^+_{1\Psi_1(v)}(\xi)\daleth, \eta^+_{2\Psi_1(v)}(\xi)\daleth, \ldots, \eta^+_{n\Psi_1(v)}(\xi)\daleth, \\ \eta^-_{1\Psi_1(v)}(\xi)\daleth, \eta^-_{2\Psi_1(v)}(\xi)\daleth, \ldots, \eta^-_{n\Psi_1(v)}(\xi)\daleth)\}, \xi \in \Xi\}, \text{ if } v \in Y_1 - Y_2, \\ = \{(v, \{(\xi, \eta^+_{1\Psi_2(v)}(\xi)\daleth, \eta^+_{2\Psi_2(v)}(\xi)\daleth, \ldots, \eta^+_{n\Psi_2(v)}(\xi)\daleth, \\ \eta^-_{1\Psi_2(v)}(\xi)\daleth, \eta^-_{2\Psi_2(v)}(\xi)\daleth, \ldots, \eta^-_{n\Psi_2(v)}(\xi)\daleth)\}, \xi \in \Xi\}, \text{ if } v \in Y_2 - Y_1, \\ = \{(v, \{(\xi, \max\{\eta^+_{1\Psi_1(v)}(\xi), \eta^+_{1\Psi_2(v)}(\xi)\}\daleth, \max\{\eta^+_{2\Psi_1(v)}(\xi), \eta^+_{2\Psi_2(v)}(\xi)\}\daleth, \ldots, \\ \max\{\eta^+_{n\Psi_1(v)}(\xi), \eta^+_{n\Psi_2(v)}(\xi)\}\daleth, \min\{\eta^-_{1\Psi_1(v)}(\xi), \eta^-_{1\Psi_2(v)}(\xi)\}\daleth, \\ \min\{\eta^-_{2\Psi_1(v)}(\xi), \eta^-_{2\Psi_2(v)}(\xi)\}\daleth, \ldots, \min\{\eta^-_{n\Psi_1(v)}(\xi), \eta^-_{n\Psi_2(v)}(\xi)\}\daleth)\}, \xi \in \Xi\}, \\ \text{if } v \in Y_1 \cap Y_2, \end{cases} \quad (9)$$

for each $v \in Y^U$.

Example 3. *Under assumptions of Example 2, one can define two effective sets $\daleth_1$ and $\daleth_2$ over $\Delta = \{\delta_1, \delta_2, \delta_3, \delta_4\}$, for h_1 and h_2, as follows:*

$$\daleth_1(\xi_1) = \{(\delta_1, 0.35), (\delta_2, 0), (\delta_3, 0.91), (\delta_4, 0.46)\},$$

$$\daleth_1(\xi_2) = \{(\delta_1, 0.75), (\delta_2, 0.52), (\delta_3, 1), (\delta_4, 0.29)\},$$

$$\daleth_2(\xi_1) = \{(\delta_1, 0.62), (\delta_2, 0.13), (\delta_3, 0.22), (\delta_4, 0.38)\},$$

$$\daleth_2(\xi_2) = \{(\delta_1, 0.57), (\delta_2, 0.88), (\delta_3, 0), (\delta_4, 1)\},$$

respectively, associated with the following two bipolar-valued multi-fuzzy soft sets (Ψ_1, Y_1) and (Ψ_2, Y_2), each of order 3, over a universal set Ξ:

$$(\Psi_1, Y_1) = \{(v_1, \{(\xi_1, 0.27, 0, 0.11, -0.8, -0.55, -0.4), (\xi_2, 0.62, 0.2, 0.47, -0.19, -1, -0.72),$$
$$(v_2, \{(\xi_1, 0.76, 1, 0.5, -0.67, -0.45, -0.33), (\xi_2, 0.15, 1, 0.29, 0, -0.7, -0.44),$$
$$(v_3, \{(\xi_1, 0, 0.36, 0.3, -0.24, -0.85, -1), (\xi_2, 0.97, 0.19, 0.1, -0.69, 0, -0.1)\})\},$$

$$(\Psi_2, Y_2) = \{(v_1, \{(\xi_1, 0.34, 0, 0.1, -0.51, -0.15, -0.94), (\xi_2, 0.23, 0.76, 0.73, -0.09, -0.35, 0),$$
$$(v_2, \{(\xi_1, 0.9, 0.74, 0.6, -0.34, -0.54, -0.3), (\xi_2, 0.5, 0.65, 0.32, -0.2, -0.9, -0.4),$$
$$(v_3, \{(\xi_1, 0.3, 0.6, 0.53, -0.28, -0.75, 0), (\xi_2, 0.77, 0.11, 0.51, -0.43, -1, -0.66)\})\}.$$

Then, compute the union of the two effective sets, namely $\daleth^U = \daleth_1 \widetilde{\cup} \daleth_2$, applying Formula (8) from Definition 13, as follows:

$$\daleth^U(\xi_1) = \{(\delta_1, 0.62), (\delta_2, 0.13), (\delta_3, 0.91), (\delta_4, 0.46)\},$$

$$\daleth^U(\xi_2) = \{(\delta_1, 0.75), (\delta_2, 0.88), (\delta_3, 1), (\delta_4, 1)\}.$$

In addition, compute the union of the two bipolar-valued multi-fuzzy soft sets (Ψ_1, Y_1) *and* (Ψ_2, Y_2) *of order 3, namely* $(\Psi, Y)^U = (\Psi^U, Y^U) = (\Psi_1, Y_1)\widetilde{\cup}(\Psi_2, Y_2)$, *where* $Y^U = Y_1 \cup Y_2$, *applying Formula (9) from Definition 13, as follows:*

$$(\Psi^U, Y^U) = \{(v_1, \{(\xi_1, 0.34, 0, 0.11, -0.8, -0.55, -0.94), (\xi_2, 0.62, 0.76, 0.73, -0.19, -1, 0),$$
$$(v_2, \{(\xi_1, 0.9, 1, 0.6, -0.67, -0.54, -0.33), (\xi_2, 0.5, 1, 0.32, -0.2, -0.9, -0.44),$$
$$(v_3, \{(\xi_1, 0.3, 0.6, 0.53, -0.28, -0.85, -1), (\xi_2, 0.97, 0.19, 0.51, -0.69, -1, -0.66)\})\}.$$

Finally, computing effective union of bipolar-valued multi-fuzzy soft sets $(\Psi^U_{\daleth U}, Y^U)$ *of order 3, using Formula (6) from Definition 10, results the following:*

$$(\Psi^U_{\daleth U}, Y^U) = \{(v_1, \{(\xi_1, 0.6898, 0, 0.5817, -0.906, -0.7885, -0.9718),$$
$$(\xi_2, 0.96485, 0.9778, 0.975025, -0.925075, -1, 0),$$
$$(v_2, \{(\xi_1, 0.953, 1, 0.812, -0.8449, -0.7838, -0.6851),$$
$$(\xi_2, 0.95375, 1, 0.9371, -0.926, -0.99075, -0.9482),$$
$$(v_3, \{(\xi_1, 0.671, 0.812, 0.7791, -0.6616, -0.9295, -1),$$
$$(\xi_2, 0.997225, 0.925075, 0.954675, -0.971325, -1, -0.96855)\})\}.$$

Definition 14 (Restricted union of two effective bipolar-valued multi-fuzzy soft sets). *Assume that Ξ is an initial universe. Suppose that Y_1 and Y_2 are two parameter sets. Let $\daleth_1$ and $\daleth_2$ be two effective parameter sets over Δ. Then, the restricted union of two effective bipolar-valued multi-fuzzy soft sets $(\Psi_{1\daleth_1}, Y_1)$ and $(\Psi_{2\daleth_2}, Y_2)$ of dimension n on an initial universe Ξ is defined as a new effective bipolar-valued multi-fuzzy soft set $(\Psi^{U_R}_{\daleth U_R}, Y^{U_R})$ of dimension n, where $\daleth^{U_R} : \Delta \to [0, 1]$ is a mapping characterized by $\daleth^{U_R} = \daleth_1 \widetilde{\cup}_R \daleth_2$, as well as, $(\Psi, Y)^{U_R} = (\Psi^{U_R}, Y^{U_R}) = (\Psi_1, Y_1)\widetilde{\cup}_R(\Psi_2, Y_2)$, taking into account that $Y^{U_R} = Y_1 \cap Y_2 \neq \phi$ and $\daleth_1 \cap \daleth_2 \neq \phi$. The two formulas that compute $\daleth^{U_R} = \daleth_1 \widetilde{\cup}_R \daleth_2$ and $(\Psi^{U_R}, Y^{U_R}) = (\Psi_1, Y_1)\widetilde{\cup}_R(\Psi_2, Y_2)$, respectively, can be determined, for each $\xi \in \Xi$, as $\varrho_{\daleth^{U_R}_\xi}(\delta) = \max\{\varrho_{\daleth_{1\xi}}(\delta), \varrho_{\daleth_{2\xi}}(\delta)\}$, for each $\delta \in \Delta$ and*

$$(\Psi^{U_R}, Y^{U_R}) = \{(v, \{(\xi, \max\{\eta^+_{1\Psi_1(v)}(\xi), \eta^+_{1\Psi_2(v)}(\xi)\}_{\daleth}, \max\{\eta^+_{2\Psi_1(v)}(\xi), \eta^+_{2\Psi_2(v)}(\xi)\}_{\daleth}, \dots,$$
$$\max\{\eta^+_{n\Psi_1(v)}(\xi), \eta^+_{n\Psi_2(v)}(\xi)\}_{\daleth}, \min\{\eta^-_{1\Psi_1(v)}(\xi), \eta^-_{1\Psi_2(v)}(\xi)\}_{\daleth},$$
$$\min\{\eta^-_{2\Psi_1(v)}(\xi), \eta^-_{2\Psi_2(v)}(\xi)\}_{\daleth}, \dots, \min\{\eta^-_{n\Psi_1(v)}(\xi), \eta^-_{n\Psi_2(v)}(\xi)\}_{\daleth}\}), \xi \in \Xi\},$$

for each $v \in Y^{U_R}$.

Definition 15 (Intersection of two effective bipolar-valued multi-fuzzy soft sets). *Assume that Ξ is an initial universe. Suppose that Y_1 and Y_2 are two parameter sets. Let $\daleth_1$ and $\daleth_2$ be two effective parameter sets over Δ. Then, the operation of the intersection of two effective bipolar-valued multi-fuzzy soft sets $(\Psi_{1\daleth_1}, Y_1)$ and $(\Psi_{2\daleth_2}, Y_2)$ of dimension n on an initial universe Ξ is defined as a new effective bipolar-valued multi-fuzzy soft set $(\Psi^I_{\daleth^I}, Y^I)$ of dimension n, where $\daleth^I : \Delta \to [0, 1]$ is a mapping characterized by $\daleth^I = \daleth_1 \widetilde{\cap} \daleth_2$, as well as, $(\Psi, Y)^I = (\Psi^I, Y^I) = (\Psi_1, Y_1)\widetilde{\cap}(\Psi_2, Y_2)$, taking into account that $Y^I = Y_1 \cup Y_2$.*

The two formulas that compute $\daleth^I = \daleth_1 \widetilde{\cap} \daleth_2$ and $(\Psi^I, Y^I) = (\Psi_1, Y_1)\widetilde{\cap}(\Psi_2, Y_2)$, respectively, can be determined, for each $\xi \in \Xi$, as follows:

$$\varrho_{\daleth^I_\xi}(\delta) = \begin{cases} \varrho_{\daleth_{1\xi}}(\delta), & \text{if } e \in \daleth_1 - \daleth_2, \\ \varrho_{\daleth_{2\xi}}(\delta), & \text{if } e \in \daleth_2 - \daleth_1, \\ \min\{\varrho_{\daleth_{1\xi}}(\delta), \varrho_{\daleth_{2\xi}}(\delta)\}, & \text{if } e \in \daleth_1 \cap \daleth_2, \end{cases} \quad (10)$$

for each $\delta \in \Delta$ and

$$(\Psi^I, Y^I) = \begin{cases} = \{(v, \{(\xi, \eta^+_{1\Psi_1(v)}(\xi)\urcorner, \eta^+_{2\Psi_1(v)}(\xi)\urcorner, \ldots, \eta^+_{n\Psi_1(v)}(\xi)\urcorner, \\ \quad \eta^-_{1\Psi_1(v)}(\xi)\urcorner, \eta^-_{2\Psi_1(v)}(\xi)\urcorner, \ldots, \eta^-_{n\Psi_1(v)}(\xi)\urcorner)\}, \xi \in \Xi\}, \text{ if } v \in Y_1 - Y_2, \\ = \{(v, \{(\xi, \eta^+_{1\Psi_2(v)}(\xi)\urcorner, \eta^+_{2\Psi_2(v)}(\xi)\urcorner, \ldots, \eta^+_{n\Psi_2(v)}(\xi)\urcorner, \\ \quad \eta^-_{1\Psi_2(v)}(\xi)\urcorner, \eta^-_{2\Psi_2(v)}(\xi)\urcorner, \ldots, \eta^-_{n\Psi_2(v)}(\xi)\urcorner)\}, \xi \in \Xi\}, \text{ if } v \in Y_2 - Y_1, \\ = \{(v, \{(\xi, \min\{\eta^+_{1\Psi_1(v)}(\xi), \eta^+_{1\Psi_2(v)}(\xi)\}\urcorner, \min\{\eta^+_{2\Psi_1(v)}(\xi), \eta^+_{2\Psi_2(v)}(\xi)\}\urcorner, \ldots, \\ \quad \min\{\eta^+_{n\Psi_1(v)}(\xi), \eta^+_{n\Psi_2(v)}(\xi)\}\urcorner, \max\{\eta^-_{1\Psi_1(v)}(\xi), \eta^-_{1\Psi_2(v)}(\xi)\}\urcorner, \\ \quad \max\{\eta^-_{2\Psi_1(v)}(\xi), \eta^-_{2\Psi_2(v)}(\xi)\}\urcorner, \ldots, \max\{\eta^-_{n\Psi_1(v)}(\xi), \eta^-_{n\Psi_2(v)}(\xi)\}\urcorner)\}, \xi \in \Xi\}, \\ \text{if } v \in Y_1 \cap Y_2, \end{cases} \quad (11)$$

for each $v \in Y^I$.

Example 4. *Compute the intersection of the two effective sets stated in Example 3, say $\urcorner^I = \urcorner_1 \widetilde{\cap} \urcorner_2$, applying Formula (10) from Definition 15, as the following:*

$$\urcorner^I(\xi_1) = \{(\delta_1, 0.35), (\delta_2, 0), (\delta_3, 0.22), (\delta_4, 0.38)\},$$

$$\urcorner^I(\xi_2) = \{(\delta_1, 0.57), (\delta_2, 0.52), (\delta_3, 0), (\delta_4, 0.29)\}.$$

Also, compute the intersection of the two bipolar-valued multi-fuzzy soft sets (Ψ_1, Y_1) and (Ψ_2, Y_2) of order 3 stated in Example 3, say $(\Psi, Y)^I = (\Psi^I, Y^I) = (\Psi_1, Y_1) \widetilde{\cap} (\Psi_2, Y_2)$, where $Y^I = Y_1 \cup Y_2$, applying Formula (11) from Definition 15, as follows:

$$(\Psi^I, Y^I) = \{(v_1, \{(\xi_1, 0.27, 0, 0.1, -0.51, -0.15, -0.4), (\xi_2, 0.23, 0.2, 0.47, -0.09, -0.35, 0),$$
$$(v_2, \{(\xi_1, 0.76, 0.74, 0.5, -0.34, -0.45, -0.3), (\xi_2, 0.15, 0.65, 0.29, 0, -0.7, -0.4),$$
$$(v_3, \{(\xi_1, 0, 0.36, 0.3, -0.24, -0.75, 0), (\xi_2, 0.77, 0.11, 0.1, -0.43, 0, -0.1)\})\}.$$

Then, computing effective intersection of bipolar-valued multi-fuzzy soft sets $(\Psi^I_{\urcorner^I}, Y^I)$ of order 3, using Formula (6) from Definition 10; the results are as follows:

$$(\Psi^I_{\urcorner^I}, Y^I) = \{(v_1, \{(\xi_1, 0.443375, 0, 0.31375, -0.626375, -0.351875, -0.5425),$$
$$(\xi_2, 0.49565, 0.476, 0.65285, -0.40395, -0.57425, 0),$$
$$(v_2, \{(\xi_1, 0.817, 0.80175, 0.61875, -0.49675, -0.580625, -0.46625),$$
$$(\xi_2, 0.44325, 0.77075, 0.53495, 0, -0.8035, -0.607),$$
$$(v_3, \{(\xi_1, 0, 0.512, 0.46625, -0.4205, -0.809375, 0),$$
$$(\xi_2, 0.84935, 0.41705, 0.4105, -0.62665, 0, -0.4105)\})\}.$$

Definition 16 (Restricted intersection of two effective bipolar-valued multi-fuzzy soft sets). *Assume that Ξ is an initial universe. Suppose that Y_1 and Y_2 are two parameter sets. Let $\urcorner_1$ and $\urcorner_2$ be two effective parameter sets over Δ. Then, the restricted intersection of two effective bipolar-valued multi-fuzzy soft sets $(\Psi_{1\urcorner_1}, Y_1)$ and $(\Psi_{2\urcorner_2}, Y_2)$ of dimension n on an initial universe Ξ is defined as a new effective bipolar-valued multi-fuzzy soft set $(\Psi^{I_R}_{\urcorner^{I_R}}, Y^{I_R})$ of dimension n, where $\urcorner^{I_R} : \Delta \to [0,1]$ is a mapping characterized by $\urcorner^{I_R} = \urcorner_1 \widetilde{\cap}_R \urcorner_2$, as well as, $(\Psi, Y)^{I_R} = (\Psi^{I_R}, Y^{I_R}) = (\Psi_1, Y_1) \widetilde{\cap}_R (\Psi_2, Y_2)$, taking into account that $Y^{I_R} = Y_1 \cap Y_2 \neq \phi$ and $\urcorner_1 \cap \urcorner_2 \neq \phi$. The two formulas that compute $\urcorner^{I_R} = \urcorner_1 \widetilde{\cap}_R \urcorner_2$ and $(\Psi^{I_R}, Y^{I_R}) = (\Psi_1, Y_1) \widetilde{\cap}_R (\Psi_2, Y_2)$, respectively, can be determined, for each $\xi \in \Xi$, as $\varrho_{\urcorner^{I_R}_{\xi}}(\delta) = \min\{\varrho_{\urcorner_{1\xi}}(\delta), \varrho_{\urcorner_{2\xi}}(\delta)\}$, for each $\delta \in \Delta$ and*

$$(\Psi^{I_R}, Y^{I_R}) = \{(v, \{(\xi, \min\{\eta^+_{1\Psi_1(v)}(\xi), \eta^+_{1\Psi_2(v)}(\xi)\}\urcorner, \min\{\eta^+_{2\Psi_1(v)}(\xi), \eta^+_{2\Psi_2(v)}(\xi)\}\urcorner, \ldots,$$
$$\min\{\eta^+_{n\Psi_1(v)}(\xi), \eta^+_{n\Psi_2(v)}(\xi)\}\urcorner, \max\{\eta^-_{1\Psi_1(v)}(\xi), \eta^-_{1\Psi_2(v)}(\xi)\}\urcorner,$$
$$\max\{\eta^-_{2\Psi_1(v)}(\xi), \eta^-_{2\Psi_2(v)}(\xi)\}\urcorner, \ldots, \max\{\eta^-_{n\Psi_1(v)}(\xi), \eta^-_{n\Psi_2(v)}(\xi)\}\urcorner)\}, \xi \in \Xi\},$$

for each $v \in Y^{I_R}$.

Definition 17 (Subset of effective bipolar-valued multi-fuzzy soft set). *Suppose that Ξ is an initial universe. Assume that Y_1 and Y_2 are two parameter sets. Given that $\daleth_1$ and $\daleth_2$ are two effective parameter sets over Δ. Let (Ψ_1, Y_1) and (Ψ_2, Y_2) are two effective bipolar-valued multi-fuzzy soft sets of dimension n on a universal set Ξ. Then, (Ψ_1, Y_1) is called an effective bipolar-valued multi-fuzzy soft subset of (Ψ_2, Y_2) if the following are satisfied:*

1. $\daleth_1 \subseteq \daleth_2$,
2. $Y_1 \subseteq Y_2$ and
3. $\Psi_1(v) \subseteq \Psi_2(v)$, for all $v \in Y_1$.

(1) means that, for $\xi \in \Xi$ and each $\delta \in \Delta$, we have $\varrho_{\daleth_{1\xi}}(\delta) \leq \varrho_{\daleth_{2\xi}}(\delta)$.

(2) means ordinary inclusion (usual subset).

(3) means that, for $i = 1, 2, \ldots, n$, $\eta^+_{i\Psi_1(v)}(\xi) \leq \eta^+_{i\Psi_2(v)}(\xi)$ and $\eta^-_{i\Psi_1(v)}(\xi) \geq \eta^-_{i\Psi_2(v)}(\xi)$,

i.e., $\eta^+_{i\Psi_1(v)}(\xi) \leq \eta^+_{i\Psi_2(v)}(\xi)$ and $\eta^-_{i\Psi_1(v)}(\xi) \geq \eta^-_{i\Psi_2(v)}(\xi)$, for each $v \in Y_1$ and for each $\xi \in \Xi$

One can write $(\Psi_1, Y_1) \widetilde{\subseteq} (\Psi_2, Y_2)$. In this case, (Ψ_2, Y_2) is called an effective bipolar-valued multi-fuzzy soft superset of (Ψ_1, Y_1), denoted by $(\Psi_2, Y_2) \widetilde{\supseteq} (\Psi_1, Y_1)$.

Definition 18 (Equality of two effective bipolar-valued multi-fuzzy soft sets). *Given that Ξ is an initial universe, suppose that Y_1 and Y_2 are two parameter sets. Assume that $\daleth_1$ and $\daleth_2$ are two effective parameter sets over Δ. Then, two effective bipolar-valued multi-fuzzy soft sets (Ψ_1, Y_1) and (Ψ_2, Y_2) of dimension n on an initial universe Ξ are called effective bipolar-valued multi-fuzzy soft equal if they are effective bipolar-valued multi-fuzzy soft subsets of each other as stated in Definition 17, i.e., $(\Psi_1, Y_1) \widetilde{\subseteq} (\Psi_2, Y_2)$ and $(\Psi_2, Y_2) \widetilde{\subseteq} (\Psi_1, Y_1)$.*

Definition 19 (Complement of effective bipolar-valued multi-fuzzy soft set). *For a parameter set Y and an effective parameter set Δ, the operation of the complement of an effective bipolar-valued multi-fuzzy soft set $(\Psi_\daleth, Y)$ of dimension n on an initial universe Ξ is defined by $(\Psi_\daleth, Y)^c = (\Psi^c_{\daleth^c}, Y)$. We have $\daleth^c : \Delta \to [0,1]$ is characterized by $\varrho_{\daleth^c_\xi}(\delta) = 1 - \varrho_{\daleth_\xi}(\delta)$, for each $\xi \in \Xi$ and for each $\delta \in \Delta$. In addition, we have $\Psi^c : Y \to \mathfrak{BMF}(\Xi)$ is described, for $i = 1, 2, \cdots, n$, as follows: $\eta^+_{i\Psi^c(v)}(\xi) = 1 - \eta^+_{i\Psi(v)}(\xi)$ and $\eta^-_{i\Psi^c(v)}(\xi) = 1 - \eta^-_{i\Psi(v)}(\xi)$, for each $\xi \in \Xi$ and for each $v \in Y$. That is to say that we have the following:*

$$(\Psi_\daleth, Y)^c = \{(v, \{(\xi, 1 - \eta^+_{1\Psi_Y(v)}(\xi)_{\daleth^c}, 1 - \eta^+_{2\Psi_Y(v)}(\xi)_{\daleth^c}, \ldots, 1 - \eta^+_{n\Psi_Y(v)}(\xi)_{\daleth^c}, \\ 1 - \eta^-_{1\Psi_Y(v)}(\xi)_{\daleth^c}, 1 - \eta^-_{2\Psi_Y(v)}(\xi)_{\daleth^c}, \ldots, 1 - \eta^-_{n\Psi_Y(v)}(\xi)_{\daleth^c})\}) : v \in Y, \xi \in \Xi\}. \tag{12}$$

Example 5. *The complement of $(\Psi_\daleth, Y)$ in Example 2 can be calculated as follows:*

$$(\Psi_\daleth, Y)^c = (\Psi^c_{\daleth^c}, Y) = \{(v_1, \{(\xi_1, 0.82, 0.64, 0.73, -0.865, -0.595, -0.91),$$
$$(\xi_2, 0.965, 0.825, 0.895, -0.755, -0.79, -0.86),$$
$$(\xi_3, 0.37, 0.72, 0.65, -0.51, -0.86, -0.79)\}),$$
$$(v_2, \{(\xi_1, 0.73, 0.865, 0, -0.685, -0.775, -0.82),$$
$$(\xi_2, 0.825, 0, 0.685, -0.93, 0, -0.86),$$
$$(\xi_3, 0.86, 0.72, 0.58, -0.79, -0.44, -0.93)\}),$$
$$(v_3, \{(\xi_1, 0, 0.73, 0.865, -0.91, -0.775, -0.82),$$
$$(\xi_2, 0.755, 0.685, 0.965, -0.685, 0, -0.895),$$
$$(\xi_3, 0.93, 0.51, 0.86, -0.86, -0.65, -0.44)\})\}.$$

Remark 4. *The above definitions can be extended from the case of just two sets to the case of a family of sets. One can easily infer the formulas that describe those definitions and can give an example for each one.*

5. Properties of Effective Bipolar-Valued Multi-Fuzzy Soft Sets

In this section, we give many significant properties for effective bipolar-valued multi-fuzzy soft sets of dimension n like associative, commutative, distributive, absorption, and De Morgan's properties. Using Definitions 11–13, 15–17 and 19 of Section 4 makes the following theorems hold. By applying formulas and operations stated in those definitions, one can easily prove these theorems directly.

Theorem 1. *Given that Ξ is an initial universe, assume that Y is a parameter set. Suppose that $(\Psi_\daleth, Y)$ is an effective bipolar-valued multi-fuzzy soft set of dimension n on an initial universe Ξ, constructed by an effective set $\daleth$. Let $(\phi_\daleth, Y)$ and $(\mathcal{C}_\daleth, Y)$ be, respectively, the null and the absolute effective bipolar-valued multi-fuzzy soft set of dimension n on a common initial universe Ξ. Then, we have the following satisfied for them:*

1. $(\Psi_\daleth, Y) \tilde{\cup} (\Psi_\daleth, Y) = (\Psi_\daleth, Y) \tilde{\cap} (\Psi_\daleth, Y) = (\Psi_\daleth, Y)$.
2. $(\Psi_\daleth, Y) \tilde{\cap} (\mathcal{C}_\daleth, Y) = (\Psi_\daleth, Y) \tilde{\cup} (\phi_\daleth, Y) = (\Psi_\daleth, Y)$.
3. $(\Psi_\daleth, Y) \tilde{\cup} (\mathcal{C}_\daleth, Y) = (\mathcal{C}_\daleth, Y) \tilde{\cup} (\phi_\daleth, Y) = (\mathcal{C}_\daleth, Y)$.
4. $(\Psi_\daleth, Y) \tilde{\cap} (\phi_\daleth, Y) = (\mathcal{C}_\daleth, Y) \tilde{\cap} (\phi_\daleth, Y) = (\phi_\daleth, Y)$.

Proof. We prove (4). Similarly, (1), (2) and (3) can be proved by using the same technique. For (4), we prove that $(\mathcal{C}_\daleth, Y) \tilde{\cap} (\phi_\daleth, Y) = (\phi_\daleth, Y)$ and by following the same method $(\Psi_\daleth, Y) \tilde{\cap} (\phi_\daleth, Y) = (\phi_\daleth, Y)$ can be proved. From Definitions 11 and 12, $(\mathcal{C}_\daleth, Y) = \{(v, \{(\xi, 1, \overset{n-times}{\ldots}, 1, -1, \overset{n-times}{\ldots}, -1)\}) : v \in Y, \xi \in \Xi\}$ and $(\phi_\daleth, Y) = \{(v, \{(\xi, 0, \overset{2n-times}{\ldots}, 0)\}) : v \in Y, \xi \in \Xi\}$, respectively. Assume, for $Y = Y \cup Y = Y$, that

$(\mathcal{C}_\daleth, Y) \tilde{\cap} (\phi_\daleth, Y)$
$= (\Psi_\daleth, Y)$
$= \{(v, \{(\xi, \eta^+_{1\Psi(v)}(\xi)_\daleth, \eta^+_{2\Psi(v)}(\xi)_\daleth, \ldots, \eta^+_{n\Psi(v)}(\xi)_\daleth, \eta^-_{1\Psi(v)}(\xi)_\daleth, \eta^-_{2\Psi(v)}(\xi)_\daleth, \ldots, \eta^-_{n\Psi(v)}(\xi)_\daleth)\}) :$
$\quad v \in Y, \xi \in \Xi\}$
$= \{(v, \{(\xi, \min\{1, 0\}_\daleth, \overset{n-times}{\ldots}, \min\{1, 0\}_\daleth, \max\{-1, 0\}_\daleth, \overset{n-times}{\ldots}, \max\{-1, 0\}_\daleth)\}) :$
$\quad v \in Y, \xi \in \Xi\}$
$= \{(v, \{(\xi, (0, \overset{n-times}{\ldots}, 0), (0, \overset{n-times}{\ldots}, 0))\}) : v \in Y, \xi \in \Xi\}$
$= \{(v, \{(\xi, 0, \overset{2n-times}{\ldots}, 0)\}) : v \in Y, \xi \in \Xi\} = (\phi_\daleth, Y).$

Then, this is true for $v \in Y \cap Y = Y$, which is the third case in Definition 15. But, we have no parameters for the first and second cases since $v \in Y - Y = \phi$. □

Theorem 2. *Let Ξ be an initial universe. Suppose that Y_1 and Y_2 are two parameter sets. For a common effective set $\daleth$, let $(\Psi_{1\daleth}, Y_1)$ and $(\Psi_{2\daleth}, Y_2)$ be two effective bipolar-valued multi-fuzzy soft sets of dimension n on a universal set Ξ. Then, we have the following absorption properties are true:*

1. $(\Psi_{1\daleth}, Y_1) \tilde{\cup} ((\Psi_{1\daleth}, Y_1) \tilde{\cap}_R (\Psi_{2\daleth}, Y_2)) = (\Psi_{1\daleth}, Y_1)$.
2. $(\Psi_{1\daleth}, Y_1) \tilde{\cap}_R ((\Psi_{1\daleth}, Y_1) \tilde{\cup} (\Psi_{2\daleth}, Y_2)) = (\Psi_{1\daleth}, Y_1)$.

Proof. To prove (1), assume that

$(\Psi_{2\daleth}, Y_2) = \{(v, \{(\xi, \eta^+_{1\Psi_2(v)}(\xi)_\daleth, \eta^+_{2\Psi_2(v)}(\xi)_\daleth, \ldots, \eta^+_{n\Psi_2(v)}(\xi)_\daleth,$
$\eta^-_{1\Psi_2(v)}(\xi)_\daleth, \eta^-_{2\Psi_2(v)}(\xi)_\daleth, \ldots, \eta^-_{n\Psi_2(v)}(\xi)_\daleth)\}) : v \in Y_2, \xi \in \Xi\},$

$(\Psi_{1\daleth}, Y_1) = \{(v, \{(\xi, \eta^+_{1\Psi_1(v)}(\xi)_\daleth, \eta^+_{2\Psi_1(v)}(\xi)_\daleth, \ldots, \eta^+_{n\Psi_1(v)}(\xi)_\daleth,$
$\eta^-_{1\Psi_1(v)}(\xi)_\daleth, \eta^-_{2\Psi_1(v)}(\xi)_\daleth, \ldots, \eta^-_{n\Psi_1(v)}(\xi)_\daleth)\}) : v \in Y_1, \xi \in \Xi\},$

$$(\Psi_3\neg, Y_3) = (\Psi_1\neg, Y_1) \tilde{\cap}_R (\Psi_2\neg, Y_2), \ Y_3 = Y_1 \cap Y_2,$$
$$= \{(v, \{(\xi, \eta^+_{1\Psi_3(v)}(\xi)\neg, \eta^+_{2\Psi_3(v)}(\xi)\neg, \ldots, \eta^+_{n\Psi_3(v)}(\xi)\neg,$$
$$\eta^-_{1\Psi_3(v)}(\xi)\neg, \eta^-_{2\Psi_3(v)}(\xi)\neg, \ldots, \eta^-_{n\Psi_3(v)}(\xi)\neg\}\}) : v \in Y_3, \xi \in \Xi\},$$

and

$$(\Psi_4\neg, Y_4) = (\Psi_1\neg, Y_1) \tilde{\cup} (\Psi_3\neg, Y_3), \ Y_4 = Y_1 \cup Y_3,$$
$$= \{(v, \{(\xi, \eta^+_{1\Psi_4(v)}(\xi)\neg, \eta^+_{2\Psi_4(v)}(\xi)\neg, \ldots, \eta^+_{n\Psi_4(v)}(\xi)\neg,$$
$$\eta^-_{1\Psi_4(v)}(\xi)\neg, \eta^-_{2\Psi_4(v)}(\xi)\neg, \ldots, \eta^-_{n\Psi_4(v)}(\xi)\neg\}\}) : v \in Y_4, \xi \in \Xi\}.$$

We must prove that (1) is true for all following three cases, according to Definition 13:

(i) If $v \in Y_1 - Y_2$, therefore, from Definition 16, we have:

$$(\Psi_3\neg, Y_3) = (\Psi_1\neg, Y_1) \tilde{\cap}_R (\Psi_2\neg, Y_2)$$
$$= \{(v, \{(\xi, \eta^+_{1\Psi_3(v)}(\xi)\neg, \eta^+_{2\Psi_3(v)}(\xi)\neg, \ldots, \eta^+_{n\Psi_3(v)}(\xi)\neg,$$
$$\eta^-_{1\Psi_3(v)}(\xi)\neg, \eta^-_{2\Psi_3(v)}(\xi)\neg, \ldots, \eta^-_{n\Psi_3(v)}(\xi)\neg\}\}) : v \in Y_1 - Y_2, \xi \in \Xi\} = \phi.$$

Then, by using (3) from Theorem 1, we have:

$$(\Psi_4\neg, Y_4) = (\Psi_1\neg, Y_1) \tilde{\cup} (\Psi_3\neg, Y_3) = (\Psi_1\neg, Y_1) \tilde{\cup} \phi = (\Psi_1\neg, Y_1).$$

(ii) If $v \in Y_2 - Y_1$, then we obtain from Definition 16 that:

$$(\Psi_3\neg, Y_3) = (\Psi_1\neg, Y_1) \tilde{\cap}_R (\Psi_2\neg, Y_2)$$
$$= \{(v, \{(\xi, \eta^+_{1\Psi_3(v)}(\xi)\neg, \eta^+_{2\Psi_3(v)}(\xi)\neg, \ldots, \eta^+_{n\Psi_3(v)}(\xi)\neg,$$
$$\eta^-_{1\Psi_3(v)}(\xi)\neg, \eta^-_{2\Psi_3(v)}(\xi)\neg, \ldots, \eta^-_{n\Psi_3(v)}(\xi)\neg\}\}) : v \in Y_2 - Y_1, \xi \in \Xi\} = \phi.$$

Then, by using (3) from Theorem 1, we have:

$$(\Psi_4\neg, Y_4) = (\Psi_1\neg, Y_1) \tilde{\cup} (\Psi_3\neg, Y_3) = (\Psi_1\neg, Y_1) \tilde{\cup} \phi = (\Psi_1\neg, Y_1).$$

(iii) If $v \in Y_1 \cap Y_2$, then we obtain from Definition 16 that:

$$(\Psi_3\neg, Y_3) = (\Psi_1\neg, Y_1) \tilde{\cap}_R (\Psi_2\neg, Y_2)$$
$$= \{(v, \{(\xi, \eta^+_{1\Psi_3(v)}(\xi)\neg, \eta^+_{2\Psi_3(v)}(\xi)\neg, \ldots, \eta^+_{n\Psi_3(v)}(\xi)\neg,$$
$$\eta^-_{1\Psi_3(v)}(\xi)\neg, \eta^-_{2\Psi_3(v)}(\xi)\neg, \ldots, \eta^-_{n\Psi_3(v)}(\xi)\neg\}\}) : v \in Y_1 \cap Y_2, \xi \in \Xi\}$$
$$= \{(v, \{(\xi, \min\{\eta^+_{1\Psi_1(v)}(\xi)\neg, \eta^+_{1\Psi_2(v)}(\xi)\neg\}, \min\{\eta^+_{2\Psi_1(v)}(\xi)\neg, \eta^+_{2\Psi_2(v)}(\xi)\neg\}, \ldots,$$
$$\min\{\eta^+_{n\Psi_1(v)}(\xi)\neg, \eta^+_{n\Psi_2(v)}(\xi)\neg\}, \max\{\eta^-_{1\Psi_1(v)}(\xi)\neg, \eta^-_{1\Psi_2(v)}(\xi)\neg\},$$
$$\max\{\eta^-_{2\Psi_1(v)}(\xi)\neg, \eta^-_{2\Psi_2(v)}(\xi)\neg\}, \ldots, \max\{\eta^-_{n\Psi_1(v)}(\xi)\neg, \eta^-_{n\Psi_2(v)}(\xi)\neg\}\}) :$$
$$v \in Y_1 \cap Y_2, \xi \in \Xi\}.$$

Since,

$$(\Psi_4\neg, Y_4) = (\Psi_1\neg, Y_1) \tilde{\cup} (\Psi_3\neg, Y_3)$$
$$= \{(v, \{(\xi, \eta^+_{1\Psi_4(v)}(\xi)\neg, \eta^+_{2\Psi_4(v)}(\xi)\neg, \ldots, \eta^+_{n\Psi_4(v)}(\xi)\neg,$$
$$\eta^-_{1\Psi_4(v)}(\xi)\neg, \eta^-_{2\Psi_4(v)}(\xi)\neg, \ldots, \eta^-_{n\Psi_4(v)}(\xi)\neg\}\}) : v \in Y_1 \cap Y_2, \xi \in \Xi\}.$$

Therefore, we have from Definition 13 that:

$$(\Psi_4\daleth, Y_4) = \{(v, \{(\xi, \max\{\eta^+_{1\Psi_1(v)}(\xi)\daleth, \min\{\eta^+_{1\Psi_1(v)}(\xi)\daleth, \eta^+_{1\Psi_2(v)}(\xi)\daleth\}\},$$
$$\max\{\eta^+_{2\Psi_1(v)}(\xi)\daleth, \min\{\eta^+_{2\Psi_1(v)}(\xi)\daleth, \eta^+_{2\Psi_2(v)}(\xi)\daleth\}\}, \ldots,$$
$$\max\{\eta^+_{n\Psi_1(v)}(\xi)\daleth, \min\{\eta^+_{n\Psi_1(v)}(\xi)\daleth, \eta^+_{n\Psi_2(v)}(\xi)\daleth\}\},$$
$$\min\{\eta^-_{1\Psi_1(v)}(\xi)\daleth, \max\{\eta^-_{1\Psi_1(v)}(\xi)\daleth, \eta^-_{1\Psi_2(v)}(\xi)\daleth\}\},$$
$$\min\{\eta^-_{2\Psi_1(v)}(\xi)\daleth, \max\{\eta^-_{2\Psi_1(v)}(\xi)\daleth, \eta^-_{2\Psi_2(v)}(\xi)\daleth\}\}, \ldots,$$
$$\min\{\eta^-_{n\Psi_1(v)}(\xi)\daleth, \max\{\eta^-_{n\Psi_1(v)}(\xi)\daleth, \eta^-_{n\Psi_2(v)}(\xi)\daleth\}\}\}) : v \in Y_1 \cap Y_2, \xi \in \Xi\}$$
$$= \{(v, \{(\xi, \eta^+_{1\Psi_1(v)}(\xi)\daleth, \eta^+_{2\Psi_1(v)}(\xi)\daleth, \ldots, \eta^+_{n\Psi_1(v)}(\xi)\daleth,$$
$$\eta^-_{1\Psi_1(v)}(\xi)\daleth, \eta^-_{2\Psi_1(v)}(\xi)\daleth, \ldots, \eta^-_{n\Psi_1(v)}(\xi)\daleth\}) : v \in Y_1 \cap Y_2, \xi \in \Xi\}$$
$$= (\Psi_1\daleth, Y_1).$$

To prove (2), one can follow the same steps as (1). □

Corollary 1. *Given that, Ξ is an initial universe. Let Y_1 and Y_2 be two parameter sets. For two effective bipolar-valued multi-fuzzy soft sets of dimension n on a common initial universe $(\Psi_1\daleth, Y_1)$ and $(\Psi_2\daleth, Y_2)$, generated by a common effective set $\daleth$, we obtain that:*

$$(\Psi_1\daleth, Y_1)\tilde{\cup}((\Psi_1\daleth, Y_1)\tilde{\cap}_R(\Psi_2\daleth, Y_2)) = (\Psi_1\daleth, Y_1)\tilde{\cap}_R((\Psi_1\daleth, Y_1)\tilde{\cup}(\Psi_2\daleth, Y_2)) = (\Psi_1\daleth, Y_1).$$

Proof. This corollary can be proved directly as the above Theorem 2. □

Theorem 3. *Let Ξ be an initial universe. Assume that Y_1 and Y_2 are two parameter sets. Suppose that we have a common effective set $\daleth$, associated with two effective bipolar-valued multi-fuzzy soft sets of dimension n, namely $(\Psi_1\daleth, Y_1)$ and $(\Psi_2\daleth, Y_2)$. Then, we obtain that the abelian (commutative) property hold as below:*
1. $(\Psi_1\daleth, Y_1)\tilde{\cap}(\Psi_2\daleth, Y_2) = (\Psi_2\daleth, Y_2)\tilde{\cap}(\Psi_1\daleth, Y_1)$.
2. $(\Psi_1\daleth, Y_1)\tilde{\cup}(\Psi_2\daleth, Y_2) = (\Psi_2\daleth, Y_2)\tilde{\cup}(\Psi_1\daleth, Y_1)$.

Proof. Applying the same technique stated in Theorem 2, one can easily prove this result using Definitions 13 and 15. □

Proposition 1. *Suppose that Ξ is an initial universe. Given that Y_1 and Y_2 are two parameter sets, assume that we have a common effective set $\daleth$, associated with two effective bipolar-valued multi-fuzzy soft sets of dimension n, namely $(\Psi_1\daleth, Y_1)$ and $(\Psi_2\daleth, Y_2)$. If $(\Psi_1\daleth, Y_1)\tilde{\subseteq}(\Psi_2\daleth, Y_2)$, then*
1. $(\Psi_1\daleth, Y_1)\tilde{\cap}_R(\Psi_2\daleth, Y_2) = (\Psi_1\daleth, Y_1)$.
2. $(\Psi_1\daleth, Y_1)\tilde{\cup}(\Psi_2\daleth, Y_2) = (\Psi_2\daleth, Y_2)$.

Proof. This proposition can be proved directly like Theorem 2, applying Definitions 14 and 16. □

Theorem 4. *Let Ξ be an initial universe and Y_1, Y_2 and Y_3 be three parameter sets. For a common effective set $\daleth$, suppose that $(\Psi_1\daleth, Y_1)$, $(\Psi_2\daleth, Y_2)$ and $(\Psi_3\daleth, Y_3)$ are effective bipolar-valued multi-fuzzy soft sets of dimension n on a common initial universe Ξ. Then, we have the associative and distributive laws, respectively, satisfied as the following:*
1. $(\Psi_1\daleth, Y_1)\tilde{\cap}((\Psi_2\daleth, Y_2)\tilde{\cap}(\Psi_3\daleth, Y_3)) = ((\Psi_1\daleth, Y_1)\tilde{\cap}(\Psi_2\daleth, Y_2))\tilde{\cap}(\Psi_3\daleth, Y_3)$.
2. $(\Psi_1\daleth, Y_1)\tilde{\cup}((\Psi_2\daleth, Y_2)\tilde{\cup}(\Psi_3\daleth, Y_3)) = ((\Psi_1\daleth, Y_1)\tilde{\cup}(\Psi_2\daleth, Y_2))\tilde{\cup}(\Psi_3\daleth, Y_3)$.
3. $(\Psi_1\daleth, Y_1)\tilde{\cap}((\Psi_2\daleth, Y_2)\tilde{\cup}(\Psi_3\daleth, Y_3)) = ((\Psi_1\daleth, Y_1)\tilde{\cap}(\Psi_2\daleth, Y_2))\tilde{\cup}((\Psi_1\daleth, Y_1)\tilde{\cap}(\Psi_3\daleth, Y_3))$.
4. $(\Psi_1\daleth, Y_1)\tilde{\cup}((\Psi_2\daleth, Y_2)\tilde{\cap}(\Psi_3\daleth, Y_3)) = ((\Psi_1\daleth, Y_1)\tilde{\cup}(\Psi_2\daleth, Y_2))\tilde{\cap}((\Psi_1\daleth, Y_1)\tilde{\cup}(\Psi_3\daleth, Y_3))$.

Proof. Using Definitions 13 and 15 and applying the same technique stated in Theorem 2, we can prove this theorem. □

Theorem 5. *Assume that Ξ is an initial universe. Suppose that Y_1 and Y_2 are two parameter sets. For a common effective set $\daleth$, we have the following De Morgan's laws hold for any two effective bipolar-valued multi-fuzzy soft sets $(\Psi_{1\daleth}, Y_1)$ and $(\Psi_{2\daleth}, Y_2)$ of dimension n on a common initial universe Ξ:*

1. $((\Psi_{1\daleth}, Y_1) \tilde{\cup} (\Psi_{2\daleth}, Y_2))^c = (\Psi_{1\daleth}, Y_1)^c \tilde{\cap} (\Psi_{2\daleth}, Y_2)^c$.
2. $((\Psi_{1\daleth}, Y_1) \tilde{\cap} (\Psi_{2\daleth}, Y_2))^c = (\Psi_{1\daleth}, Y_1)^c \tilde{\cup} (\Psi_{2\daleth}, Y_2)^c$.

Proof. One can easily prove this theorem with the help of Theorem 2's technique by using Definitions 13, 15 and 19. □

6. Medical Diagnosis

The aim of this section is to focus on a real-life issue of diagnosis. An algorithm for medical diagnosis, or educational evaluation, ..., using the effective bipolar-valued multi-fuzzy soft set of dimension n is introduced. One can apply this technique using matrixes operations and properties to diagnose the case. This diagnosis includes determining what student, or what patient, ..., respectively, is succeeding in taking which education level, or is suffering from which disease, ...

Furthermore, a case study example of medical diagnosis is discussed in detail. The steps of the initiated method are framed under matrix operations to facilitate doing computations. Moreover, the addition and the multiplication of matrixes, as well as calculations of effective memberships, are made with the help of the MATLAB® program to make them faster, more accurate, and easy to do.

6.1. Methodology and Algorithm

Suppose that there is a set of n students or patients, ... $\Pi = \{\pi_1, \pi_2, \ldots, \pi_n\}$, say. In addition, assume that we have two sets of m exams or symptoms, ... and their opposites $Y = \{v_1, v_2, \ldots, v_m\}$ and $-Y = \{-v_1, -v_2, \ldots, -v_m\}$, respectively. Furthermore, let those sets be related to a set of k levels or diseases, ... $\Xi = \{\xi_1, \xi_2, \ldots, \xi_k\}$. Moreover, consider $\Delta = \{\delta_1, \delta_2, \ldots, \delta_r\}$ is a set of r effective parameters or attributes proposed according to the problem.

The effective set $\daleth$ can be constructed according to the students' says or the patients' says. In addition, the bipolar-valued multi-fuzzy soft set (Ψ, Y) can be obtained by asking every student or patient many questions and subjecting him/her to some tests or analyses by experts. Moreover, the multi-fuzzy soft set (Γ, Y) that indicates an approximate description of the given levels or diseases and their exams or symptoms, respectively, can be built from expert documentation.

Then, under these given assumptions, we can start the algorithm's steps to determine what student, or what patient, ..., respectively, is succeeding in taking which education level, or is suffering from which disease, ... The first step is to compute the effective bipolar-valued multi-fuzzy soft set $(\Psi_\daleth, Y)$ from the given bipolar-valued multi-fuzzy soft set (Ψ, Y) and the given effective set $\daleth$ for the given students or patients by using Formula (6) from Definition 10. After that, the second step is to extract the matrix corresponding to every positive pole of the effective bipolar-valued multi-fuzzy soft set that contains the membership values of the given items, say A_i. Again, similarly, the third step is to extract the matrix corresponding to every negative pole of the effective bipolar-valued multi-fuzzy soft set that contains the membership values of the given items, say B_i.

Also, similarly, the fourth step is to extract the matrix corresponding to every pole of the given multi-fuzzy soft set, say C_j, where $j = 2i$. Then, the fifth step is to multiply every A_i and B_i matrix by its C_j corresponding matrix (or multiply it by the transpose of its C_j corresponding matrix, if necessary according to the problem conditions). Finally, the sixth step is to add all resulting matrixes, say D_j, to obtain the final diagnosis matrix, say

D, in which the diagnosis for each student or patient is regarded as the maximum value in their row. For simplicity, Figure 2 briefly represents the proposed algorithm's steps as a simple flowchart.

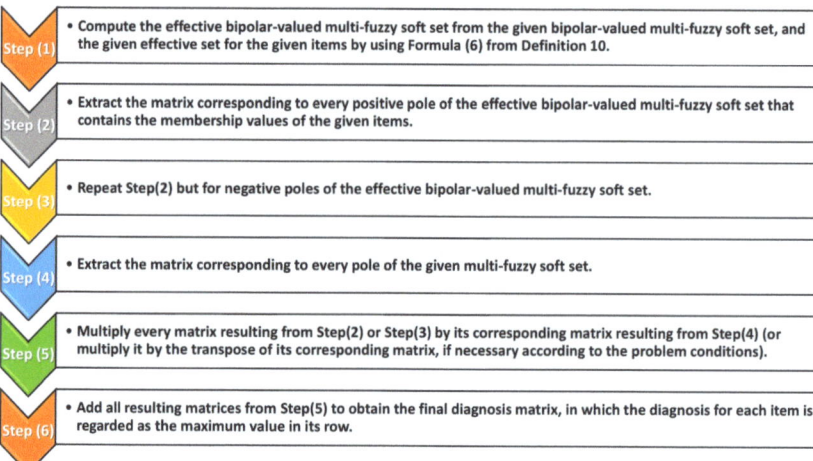

Figure 2. Steps of the proposed algorithm.

6.2. Case Study

This section is devoted to discussing a medical example, in which we follow the above algorithm steps to determine the best diagnosis for every patient who has some known symptoms by a specific degree. In every step that needs calculations, we use the MATLAB® program to perform any computations like calculating effective values, the matrix addition operation, and the matrix multiplication operation.

Example 6. *Consider a universal set of patients* $\Pi = \{\pi_1, \pi_2, \pi_3\}$ *who are predicted to be possibly suffering from one of four proposed diseases according to their symptoms and circumstances.*

Let the two major sets of parameters (attributes) that describe the symptoms be $Y = \{v_1, v_2, v_3\}$, $v_i (i = 1, 2, 3)$ and its opposite set $-Y = \{-v_1, -v_2, -v_3\}$, $-v_i (i = 1, 2, 3)$ stand for the symptoms and the opposite-symptoms, respectively. These symptoms can be classified, according to their association with different human systems, into the following three main types of parameters:

1. Respiratory symptoms, digestive symptoms, and neurological symptoms, respectively. Respiratory symptoms and their opposite symptoms are as follows:
   ("difficult and slow breath" and "easy and fast breath"), ("runny nose" and "stuffy nose"), ("difficult swallow" and "easy swallow").
2. Digestive symptoms and their opposite symptoms are as follows:
   ("diarrhea" and "constipation"), ("nausea" and "appetite"), ("abdominal pain" and "abdominal relax").
3. Neurological symptoms and their opposite symptoms are as follows:
   ("headache" and "head relax"), ("increased sweating" and "decreased sweating"), ("fatigue and pain" and "ability and well-being").

In addition, let the universal set $\Xi = \{\xi_1, \xi_2, \xi_3, \xi_4\}$ be a set of possible proposed diseases, where $\xi_1 =$ Malaria, $\xi_2 =$ Dengue fever, $\xi_3 =$ Corona virus $(COVID - 19)$. and $\xi_4 =$ respiratory syncytial virus (RSV).

Furthermore, suppose that $\Delta = \{\delta_1, \delta_2, \delta_3, \delta_4\}$ is a set of effective attributes, where $\delta_1 =$ the patient has closely contacted with anyone who was suffering from COVID-19, $\delta_2 =$ the patient has used to sleep without a mosquito net, or any other cover $\delta_3 =$ the patient works in a hospital, or a medical center and $\delta_4 =$ the patient has closely contacted with anyone who was suffering from

RSV. After talking to the patients, we can construct the effective set $\daleth$ over Δ, for $\pi_i, i = 1, 2, 3$, as follows according to the patient's words and an expert medical evaluation:

$$\daleth(\pi_1) = \{(\delta_1, 0.7), (\delta_2, 0.2), (\delta_3, 0.5), (\delta_4, 0.4)\},$$

$$\daleth(\pi_2) = \{(\delta_1, 0.5), (\delta_2, 0.1), (\delta_3, 0), (\delta_4, 0.8)\},$$

$$\daleth(\pi_3) = \{(\delta_1, 1), (\delta_2, 0.6), (\delta_3, 0.3), (\delta_4, 0.9)\}.$$

Moreover, after asking every patient many questions as well as subjecting him/her to some medical tests by a medical committee, we have the following bipolar-valued multi-fuzzy soft set (Ψ, Y) of order 3:

$$(\Psi, Y) = \{(v_1, \{(\pi_1, 0.4, 0.8, 0.6, -0.3, -0.9, -0.2), (\pi_2, 0.1, 0.5, 0.3, -0.7, -0.6, -0.4),$$
$$(\pi_3, 0.9, 0.4, 0.5, -0.7, -0.2, -0.3)\}), (v_2, \{(\pi_1, 0.6, 0.3, 1, -0.7, -0.5, -0.3),$$
$$(\pi_2, 0.5, 1, 0.9, -0.2, -1, -0.4), (\pi_3, 0.2, 0.4, 0.6, -0.3, -0.8, -0.1)\}),$$
$$(v_3, \{(\pi_1, 1, 0.6, 0.3, -0.2, -0.5, -0.4), (\pi_2, 0.7, 0.9, 0.1, -0.9, -1, -0.3),$$
$$(\pi_3, 0.1, 0.7, 0.2, -0.2, -0.5, -0.8)\})\}.$$

Furthermore, from expert medical documentation, we have a multi-fuzzy soft set (Γ, Y) of order 6 indicating an approximate description of the four diseases and their symptoms.

$$(\Gamma, Y) = \{(v_1, \{(\xi_1, 0.1, 0.2, 0.3, 0.8, 0.3, 0.2), (\xi_2, 0.2, 0.3, 0.1, 0.1, 0.2, 0.1),$$
$$(\xi_3, 0.4, 0.5, 0.7, 0.4, 0.5, 0.1), (\xi_4, 1, 0.8, 0.6, 0, 0.2, 0.1)\}),$$
$$(v_2, \{(\xi_1, 0.7, 0.8, 0.9, 0.1, 0.2, 0.1), (\xi_2, 0.1, 0.9, 0.9, 0.1, 0.1, 0.1),$$
$$(\xi_3, 0.9, 0.6, 0.7, 0.8, 0.1, 0.1)\}), (\xi_4, 0.6, 0.5, 0.2, 0.1, 0.1, 0.2)\}),$$
$$(v_3, \{(\xi_1, 0.9, 0.1, 1, 0.2, 0.1, 0.1), (\xi_2, 0.8, 0.3, 0.7, 0.1, 0.3, 0.2),$$
$$(\xi_3, 0.7, 0.9, 0.8, 0.2, 0.1, 0.2), (\xi_4, 0.7, 0.1, 0.6, 0.1, 0, 0.2)\})\}.$$

What is the best medical diagnosis for all patients?

Solution.

- *Step* (1): Compute the effective bipolar-valued multi-fuzzy soft set $(\Psi_\daleth, Y)$ of order 3, that describes the above patients' cases, by using Formula (6) from Definition 10, as follows:

$$(\Psi_\daleth, Y) = \{(v_1, \{(\pi_1, 0.67, 0.89, 0.78, -0.61, -0.94, -0.56),$$
$$(\pi_2, 0.41, 0.67, 0.54, -0.8, -0.74, -0.61),$$
$$(\pi_3, 0.97, 0.82, 0.85, -0.91, -0.76, -0.79)\}),$$
$$(v_2, \{(\pi_1, 0.78, 0.61, 1, -0.83, -0.72, -0.61),$$
$$(\pi_2, 0.67, 1, 0.93, -0.48, -1, -0.61),$$
$$(\pi_3, 0.76, 0.82, 0.88, -0.79, -0.94, -0.73)\}),$$
$$(v_3, \{(\pi_1, 1, 0.78, 0.61, -0.56, -0.72, -0.67),$$
$$(\pi_2, 0.8, 0.93, 0.41, -0.93, -1, -0.54),$$
$$(\pi_3, 0.73, 0.91, 0.76, -0.76, -0.85, -0.94)\})\}.$$

- *Step* (2): Extract the matrixes A_1, A_2 and A_3 representing the patient-symptom $(+ve)$ relations from the membership values of the first, second and third positive poles of the effective bipolar-valued multi-fuzzy soft set $(\Psi_\daleth, Y)$ of order 3, respectively, as the following:

$$A_1 = \begin{array}{c} \\ \pi_1 \\ \pi_2 \\ \pi_3 \end{array} \begin{pmatrix} v'_1 & v'_2 & v'_3 \\ 0.67 & 0.78 & 1 \\ 0.41 & 0.67 & 0.8 \\ 0.97 & 0.76 & 0.73 \end{pmatrix},$$

$$A_2 = \begin{array}{c} \\ \pi_1 \\ \pi_2 \\ \pi_3 \end{array} \begin{pmatrix} v''_1 & v''_2 & v''_3 \\ 0.89 & 0.61 & 0.78 \\ 0.67 & 1 & 0.93 \\ 0.82 & 0.82 & 0.91 \end{pmatrix},$$

$$A_3 = \begin{array}{c} \\ \pi_1 \\ \pi_2 \\ \pi_3 \end{array} \begin{pmatrix} v'''_1 & v'''_2 & v'''_3 \\ 0.78 & 1 & 0.61 \\ 0.54 & 0.93 & 0.41 \\ 0.85 & 0.88 & 0.76 \end{pmatrix}.$$

- *Step (3)*: Similarly, extract the matrixes B_1, B_2 and B_3 representing the patient-symptom $(-ve)$ relations from the membership values of the first, second and third negative poles of the effective bipolar-valued multi-fuzzy soft set $(\Psi_\neg, Y)$ of order 3, respectively, as the following:

$$B_1 = \begin{array}{c} \\ \pi_1 \\ \pi_2 \\ \pi_3 \end{array} \begin{pmatrix} -v'_1 & -v'_2 & -v'_3 \\ -0.61 & -0.83 & -0.56 \\ -0.8 & -0.48 & -0.93 \\ -0.91 & -0.79 & -0.76 \end{pmatrix},$$

$$B_2 = \begin{array}{c} \\ \pi_1 \\ \pi_2 \\ \pi_3 \end{array} \begin{pmatrix} -v''_1 & -v''_2 & -v''_3 \\ -0.94 & -0.72 & -0.72 \\ -0.74 & -1 & -1 \\ -0.76 & -0.94 & -0.85 \end{pmatrix},$$

$$B_3 = \begin{array}{c} \\ \pi_1 \\ \pi_2 \\ \pi_3 \end{array} \begin{pmatrix} -v'''_1 & -v'''_2 & -v'''_3 \\ -0.56 & -0.61 & -0.67 \\ -0.61 & -0.61 & -0.54 \\ -0.79 & -0.73 & -0.94 \end{pmatrix}.$$

- *Step (4)*: In addition, extract the matrixes C_1, C_2, C_3, C_4, C_5, and C_6, representing the symptom-disease relations from the membership values of the six poles of the multi-fuzzy soft set (Γ, Y) of order 6, respectively, as the following:

$$C_1 = \begin{array}{c} \\ \xi_1 \\ \xi_2 \\ \xi_3 \\ \xi_4 \end{array} \begin{pmatrix} v'_1 & v'_2 & v'_3 \\ 0.1 & 0.7 & 0.9 \\ 0.2 & 0.1 & 0.8 \\ 0.4 & 0.9 & 0.7 \\ 1 & 0.6 & 0.7 \end{pmatrix},$$

$$C_2 = \begin{array}{c} \\ \xi_1 \\ \xi_2 \\ \xi_3 \\ \xi_4 \end{array} \begin{pmatrix} v''_1 & v''_2 & v''_3 \\ 0.2 & 0.8 & 0.1 \\ 0.3 & 0.9 & 0.3 \\ 0.5 & 0.6 & 0.9 \\ 0.8 & 0.5 & 0.1 \end{pmatrix},$$

$$C_3 = \begin{array}{c} \\ \xi_1 \\ \xi_2 \\ \xi_3 \\ \xi_4 \end{array} \begin{pmatrix} v'''_1 & v'''_2 & v'''_3 \\ 0.3 & 0.9 & 1 \\ 0.1 & 0.9 & 0.7 \\ 0.7 & 0.7 & 0.8 \\ 0.6 & 0.2 & 0.6 \end{pmatrix},$$

$$C_4 = \begin{array}{c} \\ \xi_1 \\ \xi_2 \\ \xi_3 \\ \xi_4 \end{array} \begin{pmatrix} -v'_1 & -v'_2 & -v'_3 \\ 0.8 & 0.1 & 0.2 \\ 0.1 & 0.1 & 0.1 \\ 0.4 & 0.8 & 0.2 \\ 0 & 0.1 & 0.1 \end{pmatrix},$$

$$C_5 = \begin{array}{c} \\ \xi_1 \\ \xi_2 \\ \xi_3 \\ \xi_4 \end{array} \begin{pmatrix} -v''_1 & -v''_2 & -v''_3 \\ 0.3 & 0.2 & 0.1 \\ 0.2 & 0.1 & 0.3 \\ 0.5 & 0.1 & 0.1 \\ 0.2 & 0.1 & 0 \end{pmatrix},$$

$$C_6 = \begin{array}{c} \\ \tilde{\varsigma}_1 \\ \tilde{\varsigma}_2 \\ \tilde{\varsigma}_3 \\ \tilde{\varsigma}_4 \end{array} \begin{pmatrix} -v_1''' & -v_2''' & -v_3''' \\ 0.2 & 0.1 & 0.1 \\ 0.1 & 0.1 & 0.2 \\ 0.1 & 0.1 & 0.2 \\ 0.1 & 0.2 & 0.2 \end{pmatrix}.$$

- *Step* (5): To obtain the patient-disease matrixes (patient-diagnosis matrixes) D_1, D_2, D_3, D_4, D_5 and D_6, we take the transpose for C_1, C_2, C_3, C_4, C_5 and C_6, then find the products $D_1 = A_1 \times C_1^T$, $D_2 = A_2 \times C_2^T$, $D_3 = A_3 \times C_3^T$, $D_4 = B_1 \times C_4^T$, $D_5 = B_2 \times C_5^T$ and $D_6 = B_3 \times C_6^T$, respectively, as follows:

$$D_1 = A_1 \times C_1^T = \begin{array}{c} \\ \pi_1 \\ \pi_2 \\ \pi_3 \end{array} \begin{pmatrix} \tilde{\varsigma}_1 & \tilde{\varsigma}_2 & \tilde{\varsigma}_3 & \tilde{\varsigma}_4 \\ 1.513 & 1.012 & 1.67 & 1.838 \\ 1.23 & 0.789 & 1.327 & 1.372 \\ 1.286 & 0.854 & 1.583 & 1.937 \end{pmatrix},$$

$$D_2 = A_2 \times C_2^T = \begin{array}{c} \\ \pi_1 \\ \pi_2 \\ \pi_3 \end{array} \begin{pmatrix} \tilde{\varsigma}_1 & \tilde{\varsigma}_2 & \tilde{\varsigma}_3 & \tilde{\varsigma}_4 \\ 0.744 & 1.05 & 1.513 & 1.095 \\ 0.997 & 1.29 & 1.502 & 1.099 \\ 0.911 & 1.257 & 1.721 & 1.157 \end{pmatrix},$$

$$D_3 = A_3 \times C_3^T = \begin{array}{c} \\ \pi_1 \\ \pi_2 \\ \pi_3 \end{array} \begin{pmatrix} \tilde{\varsigma}_1 & \tilde{\varsigma}_2 & \tilde{\varsigma}_3 & \tilde{\varsigma}_4 \\ 1.744 & 1.405 & 1.734 & 1.034 \\ 1.409 & 1.178 & 1.357 & 0.756 \\ 1.807 & 1.409 & 1.819 & 1.142 \end{pmatrix},$$

$$D_4 = B_1 \times C_4^T = \begin{array}{c} \\ \pi_1 \\ \pi_2 \\ \pi_3 \end{array} \begin{pmatrix} \tilde{\varsigma}_1 & \tilde{\varsigma}_2 & \tilde{\varsigma}_3 & \tilde{\varsigma}_4 \\ -0.683 & -0.2 & -1.02 & -0.139 \\ -0.874 & -0.221 & -0.89 & -0.141 \\ -0.959 & -0.246 & -1.148 & -0.155 \end{pmatrix},$$

$$D_5 = B_2 \times C_5^T = \begin{array}{c} \\ \pi_1 \\ \pi_2 \\ \pi_3 \end{array} \begin{pmatrix} \tilde{\varsigma}_1 & \tilde{\varsigma}_2 & \tilde{\varsigma}_3 & \tilde{\varsigma}_4 \\ -0.498 & -0.476 & -0.614 & -0.26 \\ -0.522 & -0.548 & -0.57 & -0.248 \\ -0.501 & -0.501 & -0.559 & -0.246 \end{pmatrix},$$

$$D_6 = B_3 \times C_6^T = \begin{array}{c} \\ \pi_1 \\ \pi_2 \\ \pi_3 \end{array} \begin{pmatrix} \tilde{\zeta}_1 & \tilde{\zeta}_2 & \tilde{\zeta}_3 & \tilde{\zeta}_4 \\ -0.24 & -0.251 & -0.251 & -0.312 \\ -0.237 & -0.23 & -0.23 & -0.291 \\ -0.325 & -0.34 & -0.34 & -0.413 \end{pmatrix}.$$

- *Step* (6): Finally, to obtain the final diagnosis matrix D, we calculate the summation of $D_i, i = 1, 2, \cdots, 6$ as the following:

$$D = D_1 + D_2 + D_3 + D_4 + D_5 + D_6 =$$

$$\begin{array}{c} \\ \pi_1 \\ \pi_2 \\ \pi_3 \end{array} \begin{pmatrix} \tilde{\zeta}_1 & \tilde{\zeta}_2 & \tilde{\zeta}_3 & \tilde{\zeta}_4 \\ 2.58 & 2.54 & 3.032 & 3.256 \\ 2.003 & 2.258 & 2.496 & 2.547 \\ 2.219 & 2.433 & 3.076 & 3.422 \end{pmatrix}.$$

It is clear from the above final diagnosis matrix D that the maximum value in each row is the fourth one. That is, the values 3.256, 2.547 and 3.422, respectively, are the maximum values for the patients π_1, π_2 and π_3 corresponding to the disease $\tilde{\zeta}_4$.
Consequently, we conclude that the patients π_1, π_2 and π_3 are suffering from the disease $\tilde{\zeta}_4$, which is RSV. Then, the best medical diagnosis for all those patients is RSV.

If more than one patient is suffering from the same disease, as occurred in the current example, one can determine which patient is in the most need of treatment. According to the above final diagnosis matrix D, the order of alternatives (patients) is as follows: $\pi_3 > \pi_1 > \pi_2$.

This shows that the third patient must be the first one to be treated, followed by the first patient and finally, the second patient. Normally, we give the necessary treatment to every needing patient, but in case of a lack of treatments or medical devices (like ventilators needed to treat RSV), we follow that priority.

6.3. Sensitivity Analysis

In the above Example 6, the computation of the effective bipolar-valued multi-fuzzy soft set $(\Psi_\neg, Y)$ depends on the given effective set $\daleth$, which arises from the patients' words and the expert medical evaluation. This means that if the experts evaluate parameters satisfying by different values, then the effective set $\daleth$ values will be different.

Consequently, this leads to different values for parameters considered in the effective bipolar-valued multi-fuzzy soft set $(\Psi_\neg, Y)$. Then, the final decisions and the ranking will also be different. On the one hand, to avoid this problem, we can consider the evaluations of more than one expert who take the patient's words and then calculate the arithmetic mean to be more accurate.

On the other hand, if we notice that one of the nominated experts usually gives us inordinate evaluations like 0 or 1, we can cancel their opinion and not refer to them again in any future evaluations. For example, if all values of the effective set are zeros, then all values of the effective bipolar-valued multi-fuzzy soft set $(\Psi_\neg, Y)$ remain the same. Therefore, the final diagnosis matrix D becomes as the following:

$$D = \begin{array}{c} \\ \pi_1 \\ \pi_2 \\ \pi_3 \end{array} \begin{pmatrix} \tilde{\zeta}_1 & \tilde{\zeta}_2 & \tilde{\zeta}_3 & \tilde{\zeta}_4 \\ 2.32 & 2.17 & 2.48 & 2.57 \\ 1.59 & 2.02 & 2.3 & 1.79 \\ 0.63 & 1.11 & 1.62 & 1.84 \end{pmatrix}.$$

Consequently, the patients π_1 and π_3 are suffering from the disease ξ_4 (RSV) and the patient π_2 is suffering from the disease ξ_3 (COVID-19). In addition, the alternatives' order according to treatment need is $\pi_1 > \pi_2 > \pi_3$. Furthermore, if all values of the effective set are ones, then the values of the effective bipolar-valued multi-fuzzy soft set $(\Psi_\neg, Y)$ are 1 for positive poles and -1 for negative poles. Therefore, the final diagnosis matrix D becomes the following:

$$D = \begin{array}{c} \\ \pi_1 \\ \pi_2 \\ \pi_3 \end{array} \begin{array}{cccc} \xi_1 & \xi_2 & \xi_3 & \xi_4 \\ \begin{pmatrix} 2.9 & 3 & 3.7 & 4.1 \\ 2.9 & 3 & 3.7 & 4.1 \\ 2.9 & 3 & 3.7 & 4.1 \end{pmatrix} \end{array}.$$

Hence, the diagnosis remains the same, but the ranking order of the three patients (alternatives) becomes $\pi_1 = \pi_2 = \pi_3$.

Similarly, the evaluation of how much each patient suffers from each symptom is represented in the two major sets of parameters that describe the symptoms. This means that if the medical devices that measure some symptoms have any problem, then the values of the membership will vary. This also can affect the final decision because we will have a different initial bipolar-valued multi-fuzzy soft set (Ψ, Y). To overcome this issue, we must be sure that all medical devices work properly before starting the decision-making process.

Finally, proposing the parameters that can serve as effective parameters or as the parameters representing the symptoms can also affect the decision. This arises from the fact that these proposed parameters may not represent a true measure for the proposed diseases. In addition, the connection between every symptom and every disease is represented in a multi-fuzzy soft set (Γ, Y). Then, if the values of membership in (Γ, Y) vary according to different expert medical documentation, it will affect the final decision again. Therefore, the process of choosing suitable experts for the medical problem is very important first of all.

6.4. Comparison

A comparative analysis is conducted to compare decision-making under the effective bipolar-valued multi-fuzzy soft set of dimension n environment with previous existing different settings or models. We solve the same Example 6 under those previous existing different settings. The results of this comparative analysis are outlined as the following:

1. If we make the final decision under the multi-fuzzy soft set, offered by Yang et al. [25] using algorithm steps, then the results are given as follows. The final diagnosis matrix D is provided as the following:

$$D = \begin{array}{c} \\ \pi_1 \\ \pi_2 \\ \pi_3 \end{array} \begin{array}{cccc} \xi_1 & \xi_2 & \xi_3 & \xi_4 \\ \begin{pmatrix} 3.2 & 2.8 & 3.88 & 3.05 \\ 2.98 & 2.86 & 3.56 & 2.3 \\ 1.68 & 1.7 & 2.61 & 2.22 \end{pmatrix} \end{array}.$$

Therefore, from the final obtained diagnosis matrix D, the maximum value for all patients is the third one in each row, which is 3.88, 3.56, and 2.61, for patients π_1, π_2, and π_3, respectively. That is to say that all patients are diagnosed with ξ_3, which is COVID-19. In addition, the patients' order as alternatives according to the need of treatment is as follows: $\pi_1 > \pi_2 > \pi_3$. Finally, we notice that those three patients are diagnosed with *RSV* under our proposed model. On the other hand, they are diagnosed with COVID-19 under this model of Yang et al. [25]. This may occur because these two diseases have many similar symptoms. Therefore, the effectiveness of our model is to distinguish between those similar diseases.

2. when one makes the final decision under the bipolar-valued fuzzy soft set, presented by Abdullah et al. [23] using method steps, then we have the results as the following. The final diagnosis matrix D is given by

$$D = \begin{array}{c} \\ \pi_1 \\ \pi_2 \\ \pi_3 \end{array} \begin{pmatrix} \tilde{\zeta}_1 & \tilde{\zeta}_2 & \tilde{\zeta}_3 & \tilde{\zeta}_4 \\ 1.01 & 0.82 & 0.68 & \mathbf{1.37} \\ 0.23 & 0.45 & 0.36 & \mathbf{0.78} \\ -0.31 & 0.16 & 0.05 & \mathbf{1.04} \end{pmatrix}.$$

Then, from the above final diagnosis matrix D, one can find that the maximum value for all patients π_1, π_2, and π_3 is the fourth one in each row, which is, respectively, as follows: 1.37, 0.78, and 1.04. That is to say that all patients are diagnosed with $\tilde{\zeta}_4$, which is RSV. In addition, the alternatives' order according to treatment need is as the following: $\pi_1 > \pi_3 > \pi_2$.

3. If the final decision is made under the bipolar-valued multi-fuzzy soft set, introduced by Yang et al. [27] using process steps, then the results are obtained as below. We obtain the final diagnosis matrix D as follows:

$$D = \begin{array}{c} \\ \pi_1 \\ \pi_2 \\ \pi_3 \end{array} \begin{pmatrix} \tilde{\zeta}_1 & \tilde{\zeta}_2 & \tilde{\zeta}_3 & \tilde{\zeta}_4 \\ 2.32 & 2.17 & 2.48 & \mathbf{2.57} \\ 1.59 & 2.02 & \mathbf{2.3} & 1.79 \\ 0.63 & 1.11 & 1.62 & \mathbf{1.84} \end{pmatrix}.$$

Hence, from this final diagnosis matrix D, we have the maximum value for the first patient π_1 is 2.57, occurred by the fourth disease $\tilde{\zeta}_4$. Then, the patient π_1 is suffering from the disease $\tilde{\zeta}_4$, which is RSV. In addition, the maximum value in the second patient's row π_2 is 2.3, obtained by the fourth disease $\tilde{\zeta}_4$. Therefore, the patient π_2 is suffering from the disease $\tilde{\zeta}_3$, which is COVID-19. Moreover, the maximum value for the third patient π_3 is 1.84, scored by the fourth disease $\tilde{\zeta}_4$. Then, the patient π_3 is also suffering from RSV. Furthermore, the order of alternatives (patients) according to their need of treatment is as follows: $\pi_1 > \pi_2 > \pi_3$.

Finally, we can summarize the final medical decisions and the ranking order of the three patients in the following comparative table, namely Table 1, as well as one can find a chart that shows different models' comparative results below in Figure 3:

Table 1. Decisions and ranking of alternatives using different models on Example 6.

Models	π_1	π_2	π_3	Ranking Order
Yang et al. [25]	3.88 → $\tilde{\zeta}_3$	3.56 → $\tilde{\zeta}_3$	2.61 → $\tilde{\zeta}_3$	$\pi_1 > \pi_2 > \pi_3$
Abdullah et al. [23]	1.37 → $\tilde{\zeta}_4$	0.78 → $\tilde{\zeta}_4$	1.04 → $\tilde{\zeta}_4$	$\pi_1 > \pi_3 > \pi_2$
Yang et al. [27]	2.57 → $\tilde{\zeta}_4$	2.3 → $\tilde{\zeta}_3$	1.84 → $\tilde{\zeta}_4$	$\pi_1 > \pi_2 > \pi_3$
Proposed model	3.256 → $\tilde{\zeta}_4$	2.547 → $\tilde{\zeta}_4$	3.422 → $\tilde{\zeta}_4$	$\pi_3 > \pi_1 > \pi_2$

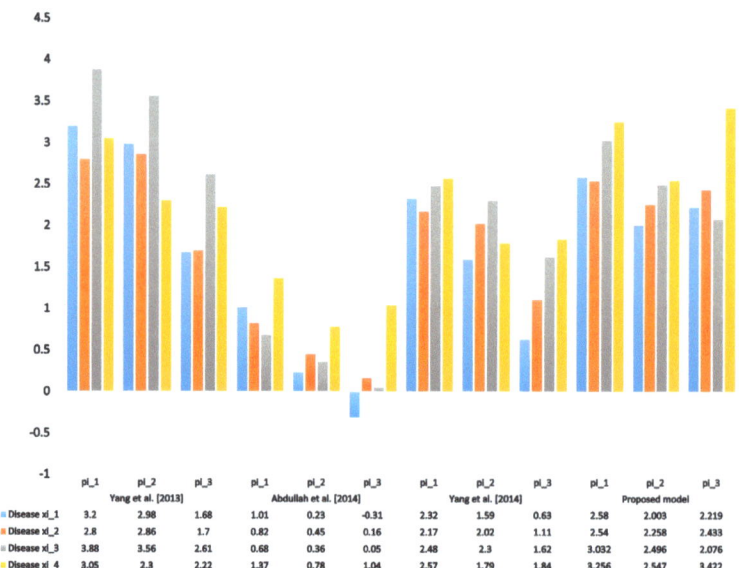

Figure 3. Different models' comparative results [23–25].

7. Concluding Notes and Future Researches

The aim of this article is to derive a new hybrid extension of the ordinary or the crisp set, which is the effective bipolar-valued multi-fuzzy soft set of dimension n. The types and the related novel important concepts and operations, have been discussed. Furthermore, De Morgan's laws and distributive laws, as well as associative properties, absorption properties, and commutative properties, have been conducted. Moreover, a decision-making approach has been provided based on the effective bipolar-valued multi-fuzzy soft sets of dimension n.

In addition, a real example of medical diagnosis has been illustrated to show how to use the proposed technique. To reach the best diagnosis easily, we have formulated the technique steps using matrices instead of set extensions to be easier to deal with. Furthermore, to reach more accurate and faster results, we have used MATLAB® to add and multiply matrices through the paper, as well as to compute the effective values or any other calculations. This method facilitates obtaining the optimal decision that this patient is suffering from this disease or this student is accepted to take this education level, ... In addition, the sensitivity analysis on parameters has been conducted. Finally, a comparison with other existing algorithms in terms of application to better demonstrate the advantages of the proposed algorithm has been established.

One of the advantages of the suggested model is that it is a generalization of many previous models like multi-fuzzy soft, bipolar-valued fuzzy soft, and multipolar fuzzy soft set. That is to say that either the multi-fuzzy soft set, the bipolar-valued fuzzy soft set, or the multipolar fuzzy soft set is a special case of the effective bipolar-valued multi-fuzzy soft set. This implies that using any one of them in decision-making applications may face limitations when the problem contains more complicated circumstances like bipolar attributes and/or multi attributes. Therefore, combining bipolarity and multi-set with fuzzy soft and effectiveness concepts increases the decision's accuracy and uniqueness.

In certain cases, the suggested approach, like any other technique or framework, may have inherent restrictions, limitations, or drawbacks. In particular, one of those limitations happens if there are a significant number of attributes (parameters) or/and items (patients or students), resulting in a huge number of computations when using the method being proposed. In order to overcome this restriction, several mathematical programs, such as MATLAB® or Wolfram Mathematica®, which are capable of processing massive amounts of data quickly and efficiently, can be used.

Furthermore, another limitation is that the effective bipolar-valued multi-fuzzy soft model works effectively when combining bipolarity with multi-fuzzy soft data, but it cannot be effective when combining bipolarity with multi-vague soft data noticed in a variety of situations in the real world. That is to say that the effective bipolar-valued multi-fuzzy soft set definition alone is unable to communicate the vagueness, which is a generalization of the fuzziness.

Therefore, as a future idea, authors can define the effective bipolar-valued multi-vague soft set and use it in applications to overcome this limitation. In addition, applying either the effective bipolar-valued multi-fuzzy soft set or the effective bipolar-valued multi-vague soft set to real data and comparing the two results also may be an interesting future work because it will clarify the effectiveness of the two methods in reality. Moreover, in future research, authors can extend the ideas to picture effective bipolar-valued multi-fuzzy soft sets of dimension n, spherical effective bipolar-valued multi-fuzzy soft sets of dimension n, and Pythagorean effective bipolar-valued multi-fuzzy soft sets of dimension n.

Author Contributions: The authors contributed equally to the paper. All authors have read and agreed to the published version of the manuscript.

Funding: The authors extend their appreciation to the Deputyship for Research & Innovation, Ministry of Education in Saudi Arabia for funding this research through the project number IFP-IMSIU-2023136. The authors also appreciate the Deanship of Scientific Research at Imam Mohamed Ibn Saud Islamic University (IMSIU) for supporting and supervising this project.

Data Availability Statement: All the data sets are provided within the main body of the paper.

Conflicts of Interest: The authors declare having no conflict of interest.

References

1. Zadeh, L.A. Fuzzy sets. *Inf. Control* **1965**, *8*, 338–353. [CrossRef]
2. Atanassov, K. Intuitionistic fuzzy sets. *Fuzzy Set Syst.* **1986**, *20*, 87–96. [CrossRef]
3. Molodtsov, D. Soft set theory-First results. *Comput. Math. Appl.* **1999**, *37*, 19–31. [CrossRef]
4. Maji, P.K.; Biswas, R.; Roy, A.R. Soft set theory. *Comput. Math. Appl.* **2003**, *45*, 555–562. [CrossRef]
5. Maji, P.K.; Roy, A.R.; Biswas, R. An application of soft sets in a decision-making problem. *Comput. Math. Appl.* **2002**, *44*, 1077–1083. [CrossRef]
6. Lee, K.M. Bipolar-valued fuzzy sets and their operations. In Proceedings of the International Conference on Intelligent Technologies, Bangkok, Thailand, 13–15 December 2000; pp. 307–312.
7. Maji, P.K.; Biswas, R.; Roy, A.R. Fuzzy soft set. *J. Fuzzy Math.* **2001**, *9*, 677–692.
8. Roy, A.R.; Maji, P.K. A fuzzy soft set theoretic approach to decision making problems. *J. Comput. Appl. Math.* **2007**, *203*, 412–418. [CrossRef]
9. Yang, Y.; Ji, C. Fuzzy soft matrices and their applications. *Art. Intell. Comput. Intell.* **2011**, *7002*, 618–627. [CrossRef]
10. Çağman, N.; Enginoğlu, S. Fuzzy soft matrix theory and its application in decision making. *Iran. J. Fuzzy Syst.* **2012**, *9*, 109–119. [CrossRef]
11. Basu, T.M.; Mahapatra, N.K.; Mondal, S.K. Different types of matrices in fuzzy soft set theory and their application in decision-making problems. *Eng. Sci. Technol.* **2012**, *2*, 389–398.
12. Kumar, A.; Kaur, M. A new algorithm for solving network flow problems with fuzzy arc lengths. *Turk. J. Fuzzy Syst.* **2011**, *2*, 1–13.
13. Faried, N.; Ali, M.S.S.; Sakr, H.H. Fuzzy soft inner product spaces. *Appl. Math. Inf. Sci.* **2020**, *14*, 709–720. [CrossRef]
14. Faried, N.; Ali, M.S.S.; Sakr, H.H. Fuzzy soft Hilbert spaces. *J. Math. Comp. Sci.* **2020**, *22*, 142–157. [CrossRef]
15. Faried, N.; Ali, M.S.S.; Sakr, H.H. On fuzzy soft linear operators in fuzzy soft Hilbert spaces. *Abstr. Appl. Anal.* **2020**, *2020*, 5804957. [CrossRef]
16. Faried, N.; Ali, M.S.S.; Sakr, H.H. Fuzzy soft symmetric operators. *Ann. Fuzzy Math. Inform.* **2020**, *19*, 275–280. [CrossRef]
17. Faried, N.; Ali, M.S.S.; Sakr, H.H. Fuzzy soft hermitian operators. *Adv. Math. Sci. J.* **2020**, *9*, 73–82. [CrossRef]
18. Faried, N.; Ali, M.; Sakr, H. A note on FS isometry operators. *Math. Sci. Lett.* **2021**, *10*, 1–3. [CrossRef]
19. Faried, N.; Ali, M.; Sakr, H. On FS normal operators. *Math. Sci. Lett.* **2021**, *10*, 41–46. [CrossRef]
20. Faried, N.; Ali, M.; Sakr, H. A theoretical approach on unitary operators in fuzzy soft settings. *Math. Sci. Lett.* **2022**, *11*, 45–49. [CrossRef]
21. Maji, P.K.; Roy, A.R.; Biswas, R. On intuitionistic fuzzy soft sets. *J. Fuzzy Math.* **2004**, *12*, 669–683.

22. Chetia, B.; Das, P.K. Some results of intuitionistic fuzzy matrix theory. *Adv. Appl. Sci. Res.* **2012**, *3*, 421–423.
23. Abdullah, S.; Aslam, M.; Ullah, K. Bipolar fuzzy soft sets and its applications in decision-making problem. *J. Intell. Fuzzy Syst.* **2014**, *27*, 729–742. [CrossRef]
24. Sebastian, S.; Ramakrishnan, T.V. Multi-fuzzy sets: An extension of fuzzy sets. *Fuzzy Inform. Engin.* **2011**, *3*, 35–43. [CrossRef]
25. Yang, Y.; Tan, X.; Meng, C. The multi-fuzzy soft set and its application in decision making. *Appl. Math. Model.* **2013**, *37*, 4915–4923. [CrossRef]
26. Santhi, V.K.; Shyamala, G. Notes on bipolar-valued multi-fuzzy subgroups of a group. *Int. J. Math. Arch.* **2015**, *6*, 234–238.
27. Yang, Y.; Peng, X.; Chen, H.; Zeng, L. A decision making approach based on bipolar multi-fuzzy soft set theory. *J. Intell. Fuzzy Syst.* **2014**, *27*, 1861–1872. [CrossRef]
28. Sakr, H.H.; Muse, A.H.; Aldallal, R. A generalized decision-making technique based on bipolar-valued multi-vague soft sets. *J. Funct. Spaces* **2022**, *2022*, 9453172. [CrossRef]
29. Sakr, H.H.; Muse, A.H.; Mohamed, M.S.; Ateya, S.F. Applications on bipolar vague soft sets. *J. Math.* **2023**, *2023*, 5467353. [CrossRef]
30. Faried, N.; Ali, M.S.S.; Sakr, H.H. On generalized fractional order difference sequence spaces defined by a sequence of modulus functions. *Math. Sci. Lett.* **2017**, *6*, 163–168. [CrossRef]
31. Faried, N.; Ali, M.S.S.; Sakr, H.H. Vague soft matrix-based decision making. *Glob. J. Pure Appl. Math.* **2019**, *15*, 755–780.
32. Faried, N.; Ali, M.; Sakr, H. Generalized difference sequence spaces of fractional-order via Orlicz-functions sequence. *Math. Sci. Lett.* **2021**, *10*, 101–107. [CrossRef]
33. Faried, N.; Ali, M.; Sakr, H. Modulus functions sequence-based operator ideal. *Math. Sci. Lett.* **2022**, *11*, 65–71. [CrossRef]
34. Chakraborty, A.; Mondal, S.P.; Alam, S.; Ahmadian, A.; Senu, N.; De, D.; Salahshour, S. Disjunctive representation of triangular bipolar neutrosophic numbers, de-bipolarization technique and application in multi-criteria decision-making problems. *Symmetry* **2019**, *11*, 932. [CrossRef]
35. Haque, T.S.; Chakraborty, A.; Alam, S. A novel scheme to detect the best cloud service provider using logarithmic operational law in generalized spherical fuzzy environment. *Knowl. Inf. Syst.* **2023**, *65*, 3695–3724. [CrossRef]
36. Haque, T.S.; Chakraborty, A.; Alrabaiah, H.; Alam, S. Multiattribute decision-making by logarithmic operational laws in interval neutrosophic environments. *Granul. Comput.* **2022**, *7*, 837–860. [CrossRef]
37. Haque, T.S.; Chakraborty, A.; Mondal, S.P.; Alam, S. New exponential operational law for measuring pollution attributes in mega-cities based on MCGDM problem with trapezoidal neutrosophic data. *J. Ambient. Intell. Humaniz. Comput.* **2022**, *13*, 5591–5608. [CrossRef]
38. Xiao, F. CED: A distance for complex mass functions. *IEEE Trans. Neural Netw. Learn. Syst.* **2023**, *32*, 1525–1535. [CrossRef]
39. Alkhazaleh, S. Effective fuzzy soft set theory and its applications. *Appl. Comput. Intell. Soft Comput.* **2022**, *2020*, 6469745. [CrossRef]

Disclaimer/Publisher's Note: The statements, opinions and data contained in all publications are solely those of the individual author(s) and contributor(s) and not of MDPI and/or the editor(s). MDPI and/or the editor(s) disclaim responsibility for any injury to people or property resulting from any ideas, methods, instructions or products referred to in the content.

Article

Advancing Disability Management in Information Systems: A Novel Approach through Bidirectional Federated Learning-Based Gradient Optimization

Surbhi Bhatia Khan [1,*], Mohammed Alojail [2] and Moteeb Al Moteri [2]

[1] Department of Data Science, School of Science, Engineering and Environment, University of Salford, Manchester M5 4WT, UK

[2] Department of Management Information Systems, College of Business Administration, King Saud University, P.O. Box 28095, Riyadh 11437, Saudi Arabia; malojail@ksu.edu.sa (M.A.)

* Correspondence: s.khan138@salford.ac.uk

Citation: Khan, S.B.; Alojail, M.; Al Moteri, M. Advancing Disability Management in Information Systems: A Novel Approach through Bidirectional Federated Learning-Based Gradient Optimization. *Mathematics* **2024**, *12*, 119. https://doi.org/10.3390/math12010119

Academic Editors: Himansu Das and Mahendra Kumar Gourisaria

Received: 10 November 2023
Revised: 7 December 2023
Accepted: 8 December 2023
Published: 29 December 2023

Copyright: © 2023 by the authors. Licensee MDPI, Basel, Switzerland. This article is an open access article distributed under the terms and conditions of the Creative Commons Attribution (CC BY) license (https://creativecommons.org/licenses/by/4.0/).

Abstract: Disability management in information systems refers to the process of ensuring that digital technologies and applications are designed to be accessible and usable by individuals with disabilities. Traditional methods face several challenges such as privacy concerns, high cost, and accessibility issues. To overcome these issues, this paper proposed a novel method named bidirectional federated learning-based Gradient Optimization (BFL-GO) for disability management in information systems. In this study, bidirectional long short-term memory (Bi-LSTM) was utilized to capture sequential disability data, and federated learning was employed to enable training in the BFL-GO method. Also, gradient-based optimization was used to adjust the proposed BFL-GO method's parameters during the process of hyperparameter tuning. In this work, the experiments were conducted on the Disability Statistics United States 2018 dataset. The performance evaluation of the BFL-GO method involves analyzing its effectiveness based on evaluation metrics, namely, specificity, F1-score, recall, precision, AUC-ROC, computational time, and accuracy and comparing its performance against existing methods to assess its effectiveness. The experimental results illustrate the effectiveness of the BFL-GO method for disability management in information systems.

Keywords: disability management; information systems; federated learning; bidirectional long short-term memory; gradient-based optimization

MSC: 68T04

1. Introduction

According to the *Global Burden of Disease* survey, disability is the fastest-growing global burden as the population ages worldwide. Similarly, disability-related healthcare costs are increasing, which requires the development of sustainable policies and approaches to avert and minimize functional impairment [1]. Environmental factors exert an important influence on human health conditions with evidence recommending that many physical, biological, chemical, and social factors can serve as potential goals to execute effective approaches to improve human health [2]. Disability management is referred to as a constructive and systematic technique of ensuring job retention in competitive employment for individuals with disabilities. In the 1980s, DM was initially developed in northern Europe and America but is still poorly applied in Italy. Disability management is broadly utilized in the public sector, namely to manage and prevent unavailability to work because of injury, with tools like planning of benefits and sick leave and adjustments of duties when people return to work [3]. Additionally, the attention of physicians, researchers, and program developers in several fields in terms of possible transformation for treating human diseases has grown. Artificial intelligence supports diagnosis, treatment, and operation, and some people consider that in the future medical practitioners will become outdated [4]. Despite that, to investigate challenges and opportunities related to AI applications in the healthcare sector, it is important to assess the contribution of AI. AI has broad potential related to real-world applications in the most sophisticated treatment of emergency patients ranging from simple operational process interventions [5]. In addition, there has been discussion of the contribution of advancements in machine learning and artificial intelligence to those concerned with disability, therapeutic and non-therapeutic users, knowledge consumers, producers, and victims [6]. To participate in governance discussions, disabled people face specific obstacles like knowledge production and consumption.

Federated learning (FL) is one of the methods that can preserve the privacy of the patient, and it also resolves the issue in the deep learning model's training process of federated medical data [7]. With a coordinated central aggregate server, the FL method offers decentralized machine learning model training, and for this, it does not send medical data. Medical institutions sometimes transmit deep learning models to the aggregate server; before this, they train the model and work as client nodes [8]. To generate a global model, the central server combines the local models between the nodes, and afterward, this global model is distributed, and other nodes receive this model. FL proves that it can improve efficiency in development processes and medicine discovery [9]. Currently, many large companies, ten pharmaceutical companies, and academic research labs have developed industry-scale FL models in drug discovery. To generate this model, there is no need to share confidential datasets. The reliability of the patient data is secured and to acquire the identification of prediction of drug efficacy, targets, and optimization of treatment protocols, assorted patient data can be trained on the federated learning models [10]. Multiple methods of applying machine and deep learning are introduced for the enhancement of disability management, and these methods have advantages and disadvantages. These methods struggle to produce better efficiency and have some issues like low accuracy, high cost, and lack of datasets. By permitting organizations to keep control and ownership of data, FL can assist in controlling data, and thus the risks of data can be decreased. So, motivated by this reason, this paper uses the federated learning method and is combined with bidirectional long short-term memory for efficient results in disability management. This study contributes to disability management in information systems by using various techniques. The major contribution of the proposed BFL-GO method is explained below.

Novel method: This paper concerns a novel approach that combines a Bi-LSTM with federated learning, along with the integration of the gradient-based optimizer algorithm with local search strategy. This unique combination of techniques offers a new perspective on disability management in information systems.

Real-time application: By incorporating multiple layers of LSTM, the system can capture complex dependencies in the data and also manage real-time disabilities based on sensor inputs, ensuring timely control of the people's disabilities conditions.

Efficient hyperparameter optimization: The incorporation of an improved GBO algorithm efficiently optimizes the parameters and enhances the BFL-GO method performance for disability management in information systems.

Enhanced disability management: The composition of the gradient-based optimizer algorithm executes augmented performance for disability management in information systems. The symbiotic assimilation of these methods improves the parameters.

The organization of this work is arranged as follows: A survey of the literature on AI with federated learning is discussed in Section 2, which includes various existing techniques associated with disability management, the drawbacks and challenges of the existing techniques, and the research gaps. Section 3 depicts the proposed methodology that includes different methods to achieve better performance. The results section is shown in Section 4, and the experimental evaluations were conducted by using graphical representations, performance evaluations, and comparison studies. Section 5 concludes the work with future directions.

2. Literature Review

Cheng et al. [11] introduced AI in work disability management using a smart work injury management system (SWIM). SWIM was an established, safe cloud platform with some operational devices for data storage and machine learning. Starting from the Jjob damage folder to every other folders, considering static as well as dynamic information, the text mining method was analyzed by using AI, and RTW (return to work) prediction was also utilized. This method contains three levels, as the first is to find the basis of enablers and impediments in regard to detecting the human factor, RTW face meetings, and conversation with various RTW shareholders to gather the information to enablers. Second is to improve the ML. Finally, ML connects long- and short-term memory (LSTM). In summary, these methods predict the price of work injuries. Garcia et al. [12] presented a sustainability-based conception for an urban pavement management system (PMS) using deep learning techniques. This method of PMS was improved in the urban area networks and the geographic information system (GIS) was utilized to examine and handle the information in these area networks. Further, the analyzed information that was found by creating the automated materials, a webcam was placed in the automobile, and pictures were evaluated using DL-CNN. As a result, it helped urban areas provide exact information, but this method does not detect different global states and also poorly handles optimization.

Bolanos et al. [13] discussed fleet management and control systems (FMCS) for improving countries' implementation using intelligent transportation systems (ITS) services. FMCS observes the automobile in the present time and also aids in checking the agenda. Furthermore, FMCS faces some issues like communication, expenses, interactivity, etc. To overcome these issues, this method developed a ITS framework that was only made for the FMCS. Further high-speed conversation, ITS, using this service developing states for FMCS was created. In addition, the test of FMCS utilized transport vehicles in the urban areas along with finding the one path employed in the test. As a result, the merit of this method was improved communication, reduced cost, and more security. Also, this method's data set was extremely small. Sprunt et al. [14] discussed a combination of child functioning data-based learning and support needs data to produce a disability identification method in Fiji's education management information system (FEMIS). Most of the separated FEMIS by disease occurred in low states and needed more accuracy. This method demonstrated that domain-based certain illness findings for disablement disaggregate FEMIS were possible when action data from the CFM were merged with information on environmental factors following procedures. Further, a LSN was utilized for handicapped infants and Fiji's policy provides charitable funds for schools. As a result, this method does not handle or collect information from all the countries.

Kim et al. [15] established the protection offered by the recent accessibility act and guidelines to people with disabilities utilizing information technology devices. Currently, the population has increased, so IT is utilized in worldwide environments. However, handicapped people face some challenges in using IT. To avoid this problem, a method was developed called the 179 Information Technology Devices. On the other hand, IT interaction disability (ITID) is a method that makes it easy to converse in the virtual world and also plays a role in perceiving disordered patients. The instructions from the UX give new methods to information technology creators. As a result, this method is not relevant to aging people. Alshammari et al. [16] presented online training to help caretakers of children with intellectual and developmental disabilities manage issues at home. Caretakers face many challenges in taking care of disabled children and the parents of the children also face strain. This method was developed online for the caretakers to easily handle the disordered children. Furthermore, caretakers mainly focus on providing care, maintenance, daily tasks, and support to those in need. However, they receive information in the house using online techniques. As a result, this reduces stress and makes it easy to interact with children, as a drawback of online learning is limited access to informational resources.

Chiscano et al. [17] developed a model of the urban transport experience for people with disabilities. This method aims to provide a service for disabled people within city transport. Further, this method contains two stages; thirty-seven members were involved in Stages 1 and 2, which focused on designing an experience based on humans with disorders. In addition, target groups, contributors during the transit experience, and post-experience questionnaires with semi-structured questions comprising establishing sufficient participant communication encounters before the experience ensured a good design of the urban transportation experience. As a result, this method does not use smart technology for the people's experience. Elfakki et al. [18] implemented effective methods based on experimental laboratories in three 3-dimensional virtual infrastructures for students with learning disabilities. Virtual reality can improve the quality of life and education of students with learning difficulties. In this method, three-dimensional items of various colors easily draw the attention of children. Further, the simulator was 3D VLE, with the incorporation of the altered Moodle training tool, and also aids children with different disorders. In addition, these methods help disabled students improve their reading skills; however, the limitation of three-dimensional methods is that they are more expensive, as well as cause health issues.

The current progress in federated learning, as emphasized in the cited publications, tackles significant obstacles in the area, improving efficiency and efficacy. The emergence of Federated Adaptive Gradient Methods (Federated AGMs) represents a notable advancement in enhancing the generalization of models, specifically in situations involving non-IID (independent and identically distributed) and imbalanced data [19]. These strategies efficiently utilize first-order and second-order momenta to adapt to the intricacies of real-world data distributions. The authors of [20] suggest a hierarchical federated learning system that optimizes edge assignment to tackle the non-IID dilemma. This approach aims to reduce discrepancies in class distribution among nodes, leading to improved model performance and data representation. The distributed quantized gradient strategy developed by the researchers in [21] effectively enhances communication efficiency by prioritizing the transmission of more relevant gradient updates, which is critical in large-scale distributed learning environments. The authors in [22] propose an auction-based method for cloud-edge systems in federated learning that effectively manages energy usage while maintaining the high accuracy of AI models. This approach not only enhances the allocation of resources, but also corresponds to the increasing demand for sustainable and efficient AI solutions. Together, these progressions demonstrate a deliberate endeavor to enhance the resilience, effectiveness, and flexibility of federated learning in various complex data settings.

Research Gap

Because of disabilities, organizations and individuals encounter considerable difficulties. Via the use of the AI-based recommendation system [23] and federated learning, this paper focuses on providing reasonable output in disability management. Therefore, many methods introduced in this domain offer the best effectiveness in disability management; here, the existing methods are not able to generate a model for the improvement of disability management and have challenges such as computational cost, required amount of data, weight optimizations, etc. These issues require increased model complexity in order to provide a better output [24]. So, to solve these issues, this work proposes a Bidirectional Federated-Learning-based Gradient Optimization (BFL-GO) model. The research gap this work addresses is as follows:

Enhanced accessibility and inclusivity: The Bi-LSTM with Federated Learning was employed because this method can improve the accessibility and inclusivity of information systems for people who have disabilities.

Hyperparameter tuning: The existing methods have difficulty tuning the parameters to enhance efficiency. The gradient-based optimization algorithm can tune the parameters of the model effectively, so this algorithm was combined with the proposed method for hyperparameter tuning.

3. Proposed Methodology

This paper proposes a novel method named the Bidirectional Federated-Learning-based Gradient Optimization (BFL-GO) algorithm to accurately predict diseases in the healthcare system. In this study, a gradient optimization algorithm was employed with Bi-LSTM with a federated learning method to enhance disability management. The Disability Statistics-United States-2018 dataset was given as the input to the developed model. Figure 1 shows the overall structure of the BFL-GO model. It contains 4 phases, namely data collection, data pre-processing, the disability management phase, and the predicted output.

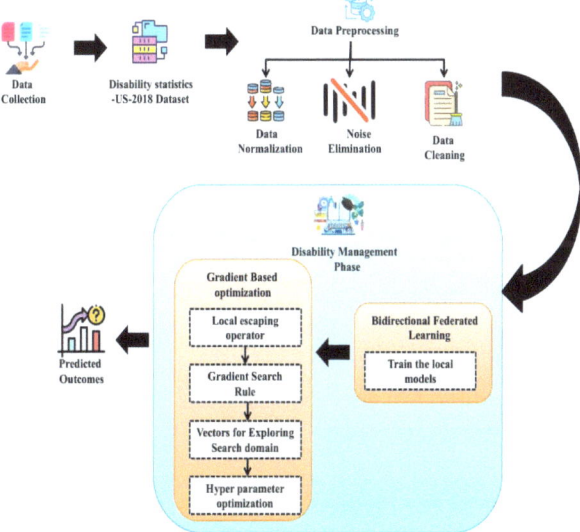

Figure 1. Overall structure of the BFL-GO model.

3.1. Pre-Processing

Data preprocessing performs a main role in federated learning algorithms; suitable preprocessing is mandatory for obtaining good performance [25]. In terms of the signal, it clears unnecessary effects, prevents issues, and improves accuracy. In this stage, the dataset Disability Statistics-United States-2018 and three types of operations, namely, data normalization, noise elimination, and data cleaning, were performed for disability management in the information systems.

3.1.1. Data Normalization

To eliminate the influence of dissimilar scale features, a process was executed to reduce the training model's implementation time [26]. By applying the min-max normalization procedure, the numerical features captured from the outlier elimination process were normalized, and the mathematical expression is provided below:

$$M_{scale} = M_T * (MAXI - MINI) + MINI$$
$$M_T = \frac{M - M_{MINI}}{M_{MAXI} - M_{MINI}} \quad (1)$$

where the $MINI$ and $MAXI$ values were assumed to be 0 and 1.

3.1.2. Noise Elimination

Noise is a vital piece used in most edge detection calculations. In the detection cycle, noise is a significant impediment. The method we used removed or reduced data without affecting the original data [26].

3.1.3. Data Cleaning

Data cleaning is the process of cleaning and removing missing data, duplicate data, and resolving data inconsistencies from the dataset. This results in an improved quality of data and usefulness of data [27].

3.2. Disability Management Phase

Disability management is a dedicated domain for managing the victims of accidents, reducing disabilities, and also returning to the work persons who are affected by incidents. So, for this, the Bidirectional Federated-based Gradient Optimization (BFL-GO) model was applied in this work.

3.2.1. Bidirectional Long Short-Term Memory

The classifier LSTM has 4 major elements, namely, input gate, memory cell, output gate, and forget gate [28].The memory cell in the LSTM saves data for long or short durations. To manage the retention of information and hold the amount of information, the input gate and the LSTM cell are utilized with a forget gate. To format and evaluate the output activation for the output gate, the information on the LSTM layer cell can be managed. These networks are an unusual class of RNN and are presented to overcome the difficulties of long-term vanishing and bursting gradients in RNN [29,30]. Due to the preparation of back-proliferation through time, obtaining long successions from standard RNN is hard, which causes the problem of vanishing or exploding gradients. To overcome these problems, the RNN is transformed into a Bi-LSTM cell with an input cell. The initial gate to select which data to discard from a cell state is an ignore gate, as mentioned in the following equation; this decision is made by a sigmoid layer

$$e_s = \sigma(X_e \cdot [g_{s-1}, w_s] + a_e) \quad (2)$$

To select the updated values, the input gate is next door with a sigmoid layer, and as shown in the below equations, the tan g layer generates new updated vector values

$$j_s = \sigma(X_j \cdot [g_{s-1}, w_s] + a_j) \quad (3)$$

$$\underline{D_s} = \tan g(X_d \cdot [g_{s-1}, w_s] + a_d) \quad (4)$$

From the above Equations (2)–(4), the updated cell state is

$$D_s = e_s \cdot D_{s-1} + j_s \cdot \underline{D_s} \quad (5)$$

Depending on the updated cell state, the present state's output is determined, and the sigmoid layer selects the regions of the cell state that are the final specified output.

$$p_s = \sigma(X_p \cdot [g_{s-1}, w_s] + a_p) \quad (6)$$

$$g_s = p_s * \tan g(D_s) \quad (7)$$

where σ, X, $\tan g$, g_{s-1}, w_s denotes the sigmoid activation function, weight metrics, tangent activation function, last hidden state, and input vector. a_e, a_d, a_j, and a_p are biased. The Bi-LSTM-based learning algorithm feeds the input sequence in a normal time sequence to a network and the reverse order to an alternate network. The stacked Bik-LSTM layer allows for obtaining both background and forward information about the sequence at every time step, which yields exact maximum categorization. The Bi-LSTM classifier manages the back-to-forward transmission of data.

$$\overrightarrow{g_s} = e(x_1\ w_s + x_2 \overrightarrow{g_{s-1}}) \quad (8)$$

$$\overleftarrow{g_s} = e(x_3\ w_s + x_5 \overleftarrow{g_{s+1}}) \quad (9)$$

$$P_{\vec{s}} = h(x_4\ w_{\vec{s}} + x_6 g_{\underset{s}{\leftarrow}}) \tag{10}$$

Bi-LSTM is a slower model and requires additional time for training. To address this issue, federated learning mechanisms are utilized. FL is a model of distributed learning that trains and aggregates the local models on the user side and central manager. The information that each user uploads to the server is not original data, but a sub-model trained on FL [31]. Despite that, the FL grants asynchronous transmission and approximately reduces the communication cost. Depending on this, the formulation of federated ML can be updated given below:

$$\underset{x}{\operatorname{argmin}} iK(w, z, x) = \sum_{l} o_l K_l(w, z, x) \tag{11}$$

where l represents the number of clients, o_l is the lth client's weight value, and the structure of federated learning is the decentralized several users $\{E_1, E_2, \ldots E_l\}$. Each client user has the data set of the present user $\{C_1, C_2, \ldots, C_l\}$. These data are scheduled into a dataset $C = V_1 \cup V_2 \cup \ldots \cup V_l$ in deep learning methods. We consider the global model next to the accomplishment of federal modeling N_{fdr} and N_{sum} the training model after aggregation. In particular, N_{fdr} is the functioning of the global model because of the parameter interchange and collection operation. At the time of completing the training process, the models lose accuracy, and the performance of the global model N_{fdr} is as poor as the performance of the aggregate model N_{sum}. To calculate this deviation, the efficiency of the aggregate model N_{sum} and the global model N_{fdr} on the test set U_{sum} is determined. The χ loss in accuracy is expressed as

$$\left| U_{fdr} - U_{sum} \right| < \chi \tag{12}$$

where χ denotes a non-negative number. However, as the fundamental need of federated learning is privacy protection, at the end of the actual scenario, the aggregation model N_{sum} cannot be attained. Bidirectional federated learning is presented in Algorithm 1.

Algorithm 1: Bidirectional Federated Learning

Input: number of clients l, weight value of client o_l, global model N_{fdr}, federal modeling N_{sum}
Output: Obtain global value $(Y_{maxi} - Y_{mini})$

1. Initialize local data
2. Obtain as sub-model of FL from the original data

$$\underset{x}{\operatorname{argmin}} iK(w, z, x) = \sum_{l} o_l K_l(w, z, x)$$

3. Generate federated ML as
4. If $\{E_1, E_2, \ldots E_l\}$ is determined with current user $\{C_1, C_2, \ldots, C_l\}$
5. Validate learning method as $C = V_1 \cup V_2 \cup \ldots \cup V_l$
6. Perform training of aggregate as well as federated learning by N_{fdr} and N_{sum}
7. Else
8. Vary the parameter with test data U_{sum}
9. End if
10. Loss accuracy χ evaluation
11. Predict the total fundamental loss
12. If $\left| U_{fdr} - U_{sum} \right| < \chi$
13. Diminished information loss
14. End if
15. End

3.2.2. Gradient-Based Optimizer (GBO)

Through Newton's method, the search direction is indicated, the GBO utilizes the local escaping operator, gradient search rule, and set of vectors for exploring the search domain, and this algorithm integrates population-based methods and gradient methods [32]. Concerning optimization issues, the minimization of the objective function is determined.

Initialization: In GBO, the parameters that have probability rates and changes between exploration and exploitation β exist, and an optimization issue possesses an objective function, decision variables, and constraints. For balancing the switching in the exploration and exploitation, these probability β and control parameters are employed. According to the problem complexity, the population size and the number of iterations are considered. Here, the number of the population of the GBO algorithm is represented as a vector, hence, among d-dimensional search space, the GBO algorithm has M vectors. In the d-dimensional search space, the initial parameters of the algorithm are produced at random.

$$Y_m = Y_{mini} + r_d(0,1) \times (Y_{maxi} - Y_{mini}) \tag{13}$$

The decision variables are represented as Y; its bounds are denoted as Y_{mini} and Y_{maxi}. r_d is specified as a random number having the range of $[0, 1]$.

Gradient search rule (GSR): The important factor ω attains global points and near-optimum points and is employed for attaining balanced exploration in the important search space regions. The following equations specify the usage of the ω:

$$\omega_1 = 2 \times r_d \times \beta - \beta \tag{14}$$

$$\beta = \left| \alpha \times \sin\left(\frac{3\pi}{2} + \sin\left(\alpha \times \frac{2\pi}{2}\right)\right) \right| \tag{15}$$

$$\alpha = \alpha_{mini} + (\alpha_{maxi} - \alpha_{mini}) \times \left(1 - \left(\frac{n}{N}\right)^3\right)^2 \tag{16}$$

Here, α_{maxi} and α_{mini} are specified as constants with values of 1.2 and 0.2, the total number of iterations is indicated as N, and the current iteration number is denoted as n. For balancing exploration and exploitation, ω_1 is viable in terms of the sine function. In the optimization iterations, the ω_1 parameter value varies, and for expediting convergence, it reduces in the iterations. In a range, the iterations that define the ω_1 parameter are increased, and as a result, the diversity is raised. The following equation represents the GSR computation:

$$GSR = r_d m \times \omega_1 \times \frac{2\Delta y \times y_m}{(y_{ws} - y_{bs} + \rho)} \tag{17}$$

For generating the randomized exploration mechanism, which has local optima, a random behavior is deployed, and iterations alter the Δy of the variables because of Equation (20).

$$\Delta y = r_d(1:M) \times |step| \tag{18}$$

$$step = \frac{(y_{bs} - y_{o1}^n) + \gamma}{2} \tag{19}$$

$$\gamma = 2 \times r_d \times \left(\left| \frac{y_{o1}^n + y_{o2}^n + y_{o3}^n + y_{o4}^n}{4} \right| - y_m^n \right) \tag{20}$$

In this, the M element's random vector is represented $r_d(1:M)$ with a range of $\in [0,1]$. step indicates the phase scale, and $o1$, $o2$, $o3$, and $o4$ are the four integers that are chosen randomly. From the candidate vectors, directional movement employs the best vector for presenting a significant local search. At the direction of the best vector $(y_{bs} - y_m)$, it changes the current vector (y_m).

$$DM = r_d \times \omega \times (y_{bs} - y_m) \qquad (21)$$

In this, the random number has a range of $[0,1]$. For the adjustment of every vector agent's phase size, the random parameter ω_2 is utilized. The computation of the ω_2 parameter is presented in the below equation:

$$\omega_2 = 2 \times r_d \times \beta - \beta \qquad (22)$$

In terms of the current vector (y_m^n), Equations (23) and (24) can be altered.

$$Y1_m^n = y_m^n - GSR\_DM \qquad (23)$$

$$Y1_m^n = y_m^n - r_d m \times \omega \times \frac{2\Delta y \times y_m^n}{(xq_m^n - xp_m^n + \rho)} + r_d m \times \omega_2 \times (y_{bs} - y_m^n) \qquad (24)$$

This shows that xq_m^n, $xp_{nm} = x_m + \Delta y$, and x_m is equivalent to the average of w_{m+1} and y_m.

$$w_{m+1} = y_m - r_d m \times \frac{2\Delta y \times y_m}{(y_{ws} - y_{bs} + \rho)} \qquad (25)$$

where the current solution is denoted as y_m, the best and worst solutions are indicated as y_{ws} and y_{bs}, and the random solution vector with dimension is indicated as $r_d m$.

$$Y2_m^n = y_{bs} - r_d m \times \omega_1 \times \frac{2\Delta y \times y_m^n}{(xq_m^n - xp_m^n + \rho)} + r_d m \times (y_{o1}^n - y_{o2}^n) \qquad (26)$$

Enhancing exploitation and detection is the major objective of the GBO algorithm; for increasing the process of exploitation of the local search, Equation (26) is employed. Below Equation (28) is the calculation for $Y3_m^n$, where o_i and o_j are the denoted as random numbers that have a range of $[0,1]$.

$$y_m^{n+1} = o_i \times \left(o_2 \times Y1_m^n + (1 - o_j \times Y2_m^n)\right) + (1 - o_i) \times Y3_m^n \qquad (27)$$

$$Y3_m^n = Y_m^{n+1} - \omega_2 \times (Y2_m^n - Y1_m^n) \qquad (28)$$

Local search escaping operator (LEO): For changing local optima points to boost the convergence of the GBO algorithm, this LEO operator is employed. Here, the LEO operator uses several solutions for generating new solutions that have efficiency and this is specified as the following equation:

$$Y_{LEO}^n = \begin{cases} Y_m^{n+1} + g_1(v_1 y_{bs} - v_2 y_k^n) + g_2 \omega_1(v_3(Y2_m^n - Y1_m^n)) + v_2\left(y_{o1}^n - y_{o2}^n\right)/2 & \text{if } rand < 0.5 \\ Y_m^{n+1} + g_1(v_1 y_{bs} - v_2 y_k^m) + g_2 \omega_1(v_3(Y2_m^n - Y1_m^n)) + v_2\left(y_{o2}^n - y_{o2}^n\right)/2 & \text{otherwise} \end{cases} \qquad (29)$$

where, g_1 and g_2 are specified as the uniform distribution with $\in [-1,1]$, qr is represented as the probability value, and here the random values are denoted as v_1, v_2, v_3.

$$v_1 = \begin{cases} 2 \times r_d & \text{if } \mu_1 < 0.5 \\ 1 & \text{otherwise} \end{cases} \qquad (30)$$

$$v_2 = \begin{cases} r_d & \text{if } \mu_1 < 0.5 \\ 1 & \text{otherwise} \end{cases} \qquad (31)$$

$$v_3 = \begin{cases} r_d & \text{if } \mu_1 < 0.5 \\ 1 & \text{otherwise} \end{cases} \qquad (32)$$

The below equation B_1 is represented as the binary parameter with a range of $[0,1]$. The value of the binary parameter is equal to one when $\mu_1 < 0.5$; otherwise, the binary parameter is zero.

$$v_1 = B_1 \times 2 \times r_d + (1 - B_1) \tag{33}$$

$$v_2 = B_1 \times r_d + (1 - B_1) \tag{34}$$

$$v_3 = B_1 \times r_d + (1 - B_2) \tag{35}$$

$$y_k^n = \begin{cases} y_{r_d} & if\ \mu_2 < 0.5 \\ y_q^n & otherwise \end{cases} \tag{36}$$

$$y_{r_d} = Y_{mini} + r_d(0,1) \times (Y_{maxi} - Y_{mini}) \tag{37}$$

From Equation (36), the variable y_{r_d} is indicated as the solution that is generated randomly based on the following equation. μ_2 is referred to as a random number $\in [0,1]$. The algorithm to perform the secure data transmission is presented in Algorithm 2.

Algorithm 2: The algorithm to perform the secure data transmission
---
Input: Set the optimal threshold value
Output: Perform secure data transmission
1. Initialize the parameters to address the optimization problems
2. Load exploration and exploitation phase
3. Balance the control parameters to extract the secured data with probability β
4. Determine the privacy enhanced data individually
5. Randomly select the parameters $Y_m = Y_{mini} + r_d(0,1) \times (Y_{maxi} - Y_{mini})$
6. Validate maximum and minimum value
7. Attain global data point ω
8. If $\omega_1 = 2 \times r_d \times \beta - \beta$ then gradient optimization is achieved by
   $GSR = r_d m \times \omega_1 \times \frac{2\Delta y \times y_m}{(y_{ws} - y_{bs} + \rho)}$
9. End if
10. Validate the random behavior of the obtained iteration by $\Delta y = r_d(1:M) \times |step|$
11. If $r_d(1:M)$ with $\in [0,1]$
12. Obtain best vector $(y_{bs} - y_m)$
13. Else
14. Vary current vector by (y_m)
15. Estimate the accurate threshold value to distinguish best and worst data
16. Validate the data features based on provided information
17. Generate a warning signal to secure the data
18. End if
19. End

3.2.3. Hyperparameter Tuning Using Gradient-Based Optimization Algorithm

In the development of an efficient and reliable model for disability management, hyperparameter tuning is a significant process. Therefore, for this process of hyperparameter tuning, a Gradient-Based Optimizer algorithm was deployed. This algorithm efficiently tunes the parameters of the proposed Bi-directional with Federated Learning model; thereby, the efficiency of the proposed BFL-GO model is enhanced. Therefore, the proposed BFL-GO method expertly enhances and resolves the requirements of disability management. Applying a gradient-based optimization algorithm to tune hyperparameters substantially improves the field of advancing disability management in data networks; within this context, the process entails utilizing a gradient-based optimization algorithm. The algorithm refines model hyperparameters by iteratively following gradients related to a specific performance metric. It updates hyperparameters to minimize the metric, aiming for the optimal configuration. This method helps in customizing algorithms for specific disability management needs, enhancing information systems. Gradient-based optimization, like gradient descent, iteratively adjusts hyperparameters based on computed gradients to optimize functions like accuracy. This process refines a model's hyperparameters to improve its work. Gradients, indicating the function's slope, are used to guide the adjustments to the model's hyperparameters. These algorithms search hyperparameter options for optimal model performance. Fine-tuning with gradient-based optimization upgrades precision, combination speed, and speculation to new information. This is essential for tailoring machine learning algorithms to specific tasks and datasets, resulting in more effective and reliable models.

The flowchart of the BFL-GO model is presented in Figure 2. In the Figure, we can see the working of the hyperparameter tuning of the developed model.

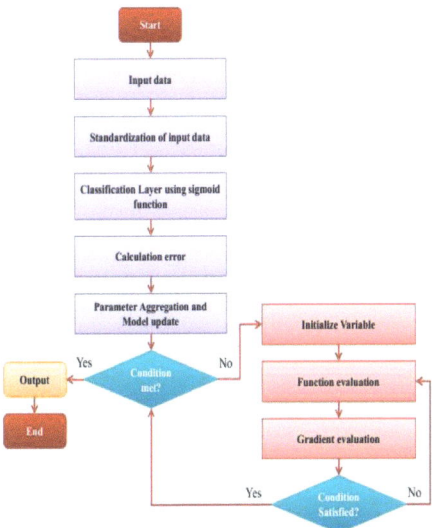

Figure 2. Flowchart of the BFL-GO Model.

The significant research contributions of the proposed model can be described as follows:

The initial section introduces the Bidirectional Federated Learning-based Gradient Optimization (BFL-GO) model. This novel approach combines the strengths of Bidirectional Long Short-Term Memory (Bi-LSTM) and federated learning to address the specific challenges of disability management in information systems. This model aims to enhance privacy, reduce computational costs, and improve accessibility in processing disability data.

The choice of utilizing Bi-LSTM is strategic for capturing the intricacies of sequential and time-series disability data. This section emphasizes how Bi-LSTM layers are configured and integrated to effectively process and interpret disability-related information over time, capturing both forward and backward dependencies in the data. The methodology further elaborates on the integration of federated learning. This section explains how federated learning is employed to distribute the data processing across multiple nodes, thereby ensuring data privacy and security. It describes the federated learning process, including data distribution, local model training, and aggregation of learning, highlighting how this approach mitigates privacy concerns common in centralized data processing methods. Gradient-based optimization for hyperparameter tuning in the methodology focuses on the application of gradient-based optimization techniques for hyperparameter tuning. Moreover, the inclusion of federated learning distributes the data processing across multiple nodes, thereby ensuring data privacy and security.

4. Experimental Results and Discussions

The effectiveness of the BFL-GO method for disability management in information systems and the results achieved from the study are demonstrated in this section. The

BFL-GO method was evaluated with various evaluation measures, namely specificity, recall, F1-score, accuracy, and precision, and the results were compared with existing methods such as SWIM [11], UM-PMS [12], FMCS [13], and FEMIS [14].

4.1. Experimental Setup

In this work, the BFL-GO method was implemented in Python; the system used was an Intel Core I7-9700 with 64 GB RAM operating at a clock speed of 3.60 GHz. Furthermore, the computing platform met minimum software and hardware requirements including sufficient storage capacity, computational power, and compatibility with Bi-LSTM with federated learning frameworks. Considering these system requirements and platform specifications, this study ensures the reliable and efficient implementation of the SMGR-BS method for the development of an AAL for aging and disabled people.

4.2. Parameter Settings

The performance of the BFL-GO method was enhanced by implementing parameter settings, and Table 1 depicts the parameter settings of the study. In this process, optimal parameter values were created to improve the performance of the BFL-GO method.

Table 1. Parameter settings.

Hyperparameter	Specifications
Number of LSTM Layers	3 layers
LSTM Units per Layer	64 units per layer
Activation Function	ReLU (for hidden layers), Softmax (for output layers)
Dropout Rate	0.5
Federated Learning Rounds	20 rounds
Clients in Federated Learning	10 clients
Learning Rate	0.01
Optimizer	Adam
Batch Size	64
Training Epochs	50 epochs
Training Time	2 h
Loss Function	Mean squared error (MSE)
Gradient Optimization Method	Stochastic gradient descent (SGD)
Regularization Technique	L2 regularization
Data Augmentation Techniques	None used
Early Stopping Criteria	Yes, with a patience of 5 epochs

In this study, MSE and ReLu were utilized as the loss function and the activation function, respectively. Also, the learning rate was 0.01, the batch size was 64, and the dropout rate was 0.5. In this work, a gradient-based optimizer was utilized for hyperparameter optimization to improve the performance of the BFL-GO method. This study ensures reliable and efficient implementation of the BFL-GO method for disability management in information systems.

4.3. Dataset Description

In this work, the Disability Statistics-United States-2018 dataset [33] was utilized to implement the BFL-GO method for disability management in information systems. In this study, 8000 observations were collected from the dataset, and these observations included various types of disabilities. The observations were categorized in terms of sex, age, and the severity of disability and divided into training and testing in the ratio of 80:20 to enhance the performance of the BFL-GO method for disability management in the information system.

4.4. Evaluation Measures

The performance of the BFL-GO method for disability management in information systems was evaluated through evaluation measures, namely specificity, recall, F1-score, accuracy, and precision [34,35]. The performance evaluation of these metrics was based on the mathematical expressions mentioned below.

Accuracy: Accuracy (A_C) is the measurement of correctly classified instances to the total number of instances. The accuracy can be expressed as

$$A_C = \frac{true^{pos} + true^{neg}}{true^{pos} + true^{neg} + false^{pos} + false^{neg}} \quad (38)$$

Precision: Precision (P_R) is the proportion of correctly predicted positive events to all events predicted as positive. The precision can be represented as

$$P_R = \frac{true^{pos}}{true^{pos} + false^{pos}} \quad (39)$$

Recall: Recall (R_E) is the proportion of correctly predicted positive instances out of all actual positive instances. It can be formulated as

$$R_E = \frac{true^{pos}}{true^{pos} + false^{neg}} \quad (40)$$

F1-score: F1-score ($F1 - sco$) is the harmonic mean of recall and precision and during the precision–recall tradeoff, if the precision increases, recall decreases. The F1-score can be expressed as

$$F_{1-sco} = 2 \times \frac{(P_R \times R_E)}{(P_R + R_E)} \quad (41)$$

Specificity: Specificity (S_P) is the ratio of correctly predicted negative events out of all actual negative events. The specificity can be represented as

$$S_P = \frac{true^{neg}}{true^{neg} + false^{pos}} \quad (42)$$

In Equations (38)–(42), $true^{pos}$, $true^{neg}$, $false^{pos}$ and $false^{neg}$ represent the true positive, true negative, false positive, and false negative, respectively.

4.5. Performance Analysis

The performance analysis of the BFL-GO method for disability management in information systems using the specified performance metrics, namely specificity, F1-score, recall, precision, and accuracy, provides a comprehensive evaluation of its effectiveness [36]. The performance was evaluated by comparing the BFL-GO method with the existing methods such as SWIM, UM-PMS, FMCS, and FEMIS. Figures 3–7 depicts the comparative graphical representation of the BFL-GO method and the existing methods for different evaluation metrics based on disability management in the information system.

The accuracy of the BFL-GO method and the existing methods is demonstrated by the graphical analysis shown in Figure 3. The BFL-GO method achieved a high accuracy of 98.65%, while the existing methods such as SWIM, UM-PMS, FMCS, and FEMIS obtained low accuracies of 97.52%, 96.43%, 95.38%, and 94.26%, respectively. Figure 4 illustrates the graphical analysis depicting the precision of the BFL-GO method and the existing methods. The BFL-GO method achieved a high precision of 97.91% while the existing methods such as SWIM, UM-PMS, FMCS, and FEMIS obtained low precisions of 96.89%, 96.17%, 95.34%, and 94.73%, respectively.

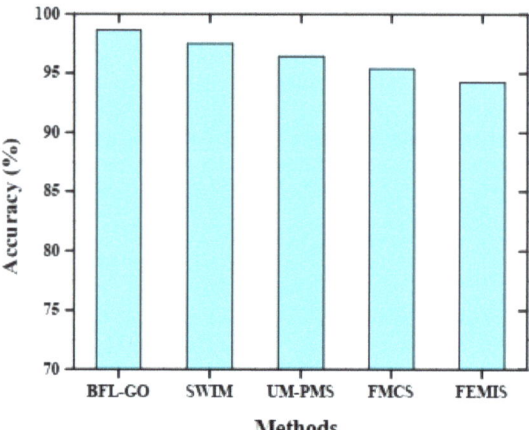

Figure 3. Performance validation based on accuracy.

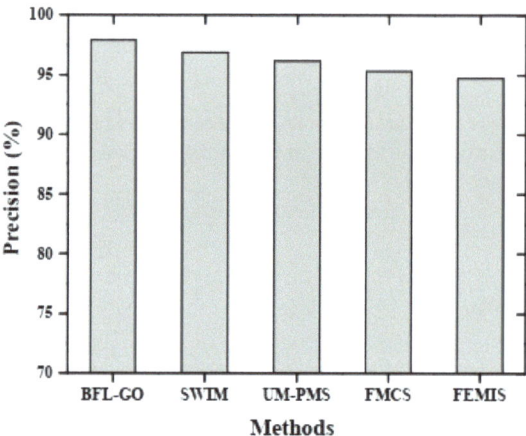

Figure 4. Graphical representation of precision analysis.

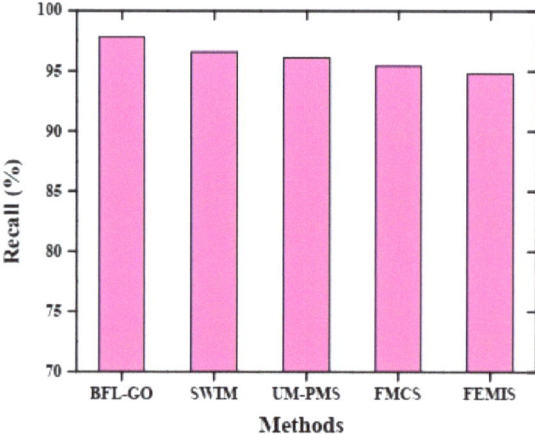

Figure 5. Recall analysis for performance evaluation.

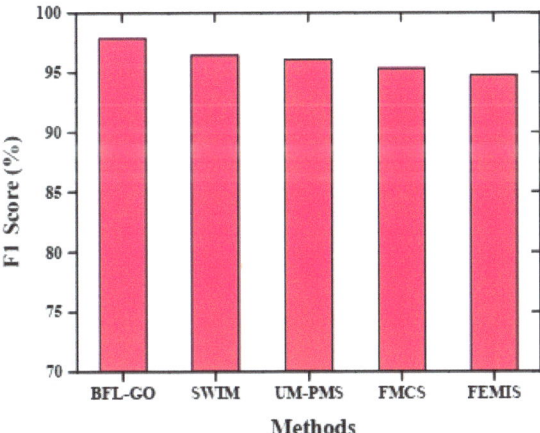

Figure 6. Performance validation based on F1-score.

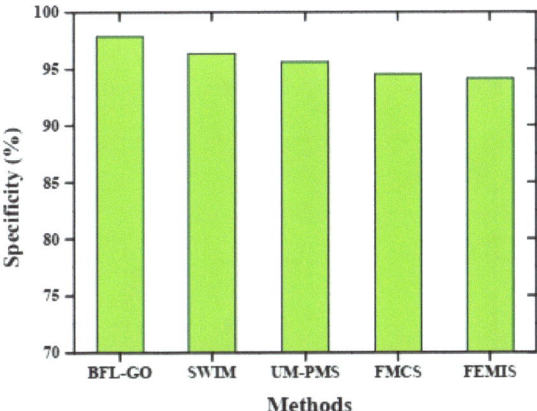

Figure 7. Graphical representation of specificity analysis.

In Figure 5, the recall of the BFL-GO method and the existing methods is illustrated by the graphical analysis. The BFL-GO method achieved a high recall of 97.82% while the existing methods such as SWIM, UM-PMS, FMCS, and FEMIS obtained the low recalls of 96.58%, 96.13%, 95.41%, and 94.79%, respectively. Figure 6 represents a graphical analysis illustrating the F1-score of the BFL-GO method and the existing methods. The BFL-GO method attained a high F1-score of 97.86% while the existing methods such as SWIM, UM-PMS, FMCS, and FEMIS obtained low F1-scores of 96.42%, 96.07%, 95.34%, and 94.73%, respectively.

The specificity of the BFL-GO method and the existing methods is represented by the graphical analysis shown in Figure 7. The BFL-GO method achieved a high specificity of 97.85% while the existing methods such as SWIM, UM-PMS, FMCS, and FEMIS obtained low specificities of 96.37%, 95.61%, 94.53%, and 94.16%, respectively. The performance analyses evaluate the effectiveness of the BFL-GO method for disability management in information systems. The results show that the BFL-GO method achieved high precision, recall, accuracy, specificity, and F1-score compared to existing methods.

In Figure 8, the AUC-ROC of the BFL-GO method and the existing methods are illustrated by the graphical analysis. The BFL-GO method achieved a high AUC-ROC of 0.9812 while the existing methods such as SWIM, UM-PMS, FMCS, and FEMIS obtained low AUC-ROCs of 0.9721, 0.9632, 0.9574 and 0.9526, respectively. Figure 9 represents the graphical analysis illustrating the computational time of the BFL-GO method and the existing methods. The BFL-GO method achieved a low computation time of 16 s, while the existing methods such as SWIM, UM-PMS, FMCS, and FEMIS obtained high computation times of 19 s, 22 s, 27 s, and 33 s, respectively.

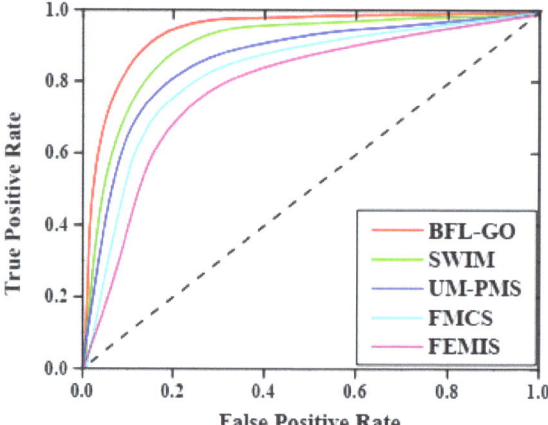

Figure 8. Performance evaluation based on AUC-ROC.

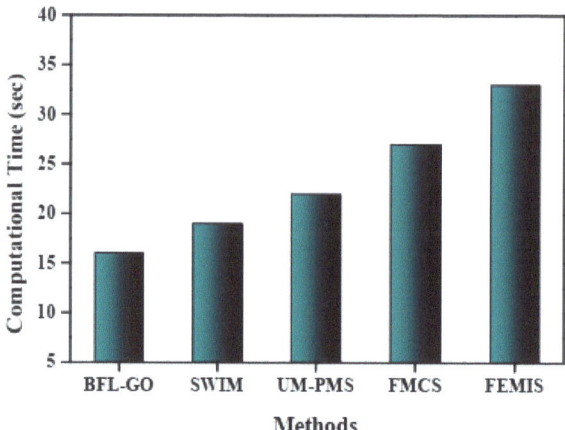

Figure 9. Graphical analysis based on computational time.

Figure 10 depicts the validation of detection rate. The evaluation determines the ratio of true positive values from the obtained samples. The accurate information was determined by validating with test cases. The evaluation was performed with the proposed BFL-GO and existing SWIM, UM-PMS, FMCS as well as FEMIS techniques. Compared to existing methods, the method proposed attained a better performance by attaining the value of 85.6%.

The false rate analysis for the proposed and existing methods is delineated in Figure 11. It is highly utilized to detect the faults of information systems in real-world applications. The proposed model's superior performance is evidenced by its lower results. In this validation, the achieved range of existing methods were 72.6%, 78.5%, 75.4%, and 74.9%, respectively. Meanwhile, the proposed method minimized the false rate at 68.2% and had enhanced performance.

Figure 12 depicts the MSE evaluation to predict the obtained errors in the model. The error validation is performed with the actual as well as the estimated values. We measured the average squares of the error and found that the MSE was equal to zero. However, in the evaluation process, the proposed method diminished the total error by 0.34.

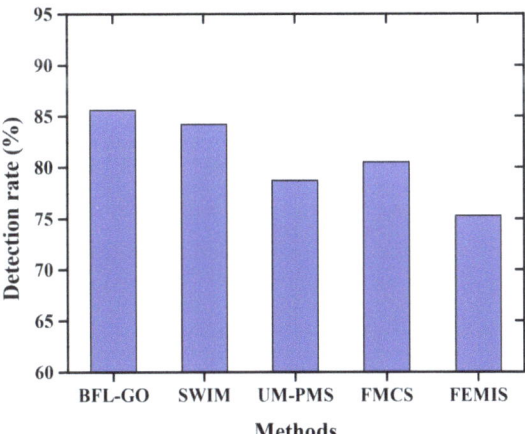

Figure 10. Validation of detection rate.

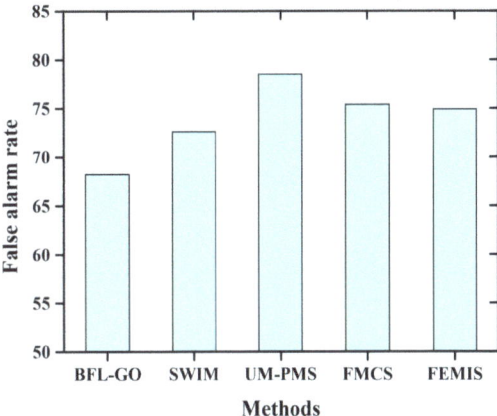

Figure 11. False alarm rate analysis.

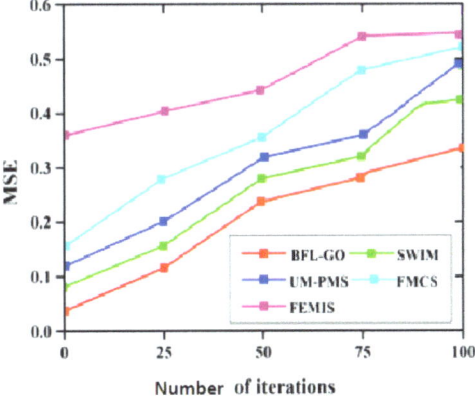

Figure 12. Evaluation of MSE.

Table 2 depicts the comparison of the BFL-GO method and the existing methods such as SWIM, UM-PMS, FMCS, and FEMIS. The BFL-GO method attained high accuracy, recall, precision, specificity, F1-score, and an AUC-ROC of 98.65%, 97.82%, 97.91%, 97.85%, 97.86%, and 0.9812, respectively. Also, the BFL-GO method achieved a low computation time of 16 s for disability management in information systems.

Table 2. Comparison of the proposed method with state-of-the-art methods.

Methods	Accuracy (%)	Precision (%)	Recall (%)	F1-Score (%)	Specificity (%)	AUC-ROC	Computational Time (s)
BFL-GO	98.65	97.91	97.82	97.86	97.85	0.9812	16
SWIM	97.52	96.89	96.58	96.42	96.37	0.9721	19
UM-PMS	96.43	96.17	96.13	96.07	95.61	0.9632	22
FMCS	95.38	95.34	95.41	95.34	94.53	0.9574	27
FEMIS	94.26	94.73	94.79	94.73	94.16	0.9526	33

The SWIM method obtained accuracy, recall, precision, specificity, F1-score, and AUC-ROC values of 97.52%, 96.58%, 96.89%, 96.37%, 96.42%, and 0.9721, respectively. Also, the SWIM method obtained a high computation time of 19 s compared to the BFL-GO method for disability management in information systems. The UM-PMS method obtained accuracy, recall, precision, specificity, F1-score, and AUC-ROC values of 96.43%, 96.13%, 96.17%, 95.61%, 96.07%, and 0.9632, respectively. Also, the UM-PMS method obtained a high computation time of 22 s compared to the BFL-GO method for disability management in information systems. The FMCS method attained accuracy, recall, precision, specificity, F1-score, and AUC-ROC values of 95.38%, 95.41%, 95.34%, 94.53%, 95.34%, and 0.9574, respectively. Also, the FMCS method obtained a high computation time of 27 s compared to the BFL-GO method for disability management in information systems. The FEMIS method obtained accuracy, recall, precision, specificity, F1-score, and AUC-ROC values of 94.26%, 94.79%, 94.73%, 94.16%, 94.73%, and 0.9526, respectively. Also, the FEMIS method attained a high computation time of 33 s compared to the BFL-GO method for disability management in information systems.

5. Conclusions

This paper proposes a novel method named Bidirectional Federated Learning-based Gradient Optimization (BFL-GO) for disability management in information systems, and it holds significant advantages. In this study, Bi-LSTM was utilized to capture sequential disability data, and federated learning was employed to enable training the BFL-GO method across decentralized and distributed data sources while keeping the data localized and without the need to centralize it. A gradient-based optimizer is used to adjust the proposed BFL-GO method's parameters during the training process to minimize its loss function. The utilization of the Disability Statistics-United States-2018 dataset, with its diverse and extensive disability data, enhances the BFL-GO method to make informed decisions. The performance of the proposed BFL-GO method was evaluated using different evaluation measures, namely specificity, accuracy, precision, recall, and F1-score, and these results were compared with existing methods such as SWIM, UM-PMS, FMCS, and FEMIS. The BFL-GO method achieved a high accuracy of 98.65%, precision of 97.91%, recall of 97.82%, F1-score of 97.86%, specificity of 97.85%, AUC-ROC of 0.9812, and computational time of 16 s. The results illustrate that the BFL-GO method achieves better results in improving disability management in information systems.

Limitation and Future Scope

A drawback of the suggested method is the complexity of Bidirectional Federated Learning-based Gradient Optimization. This complexity may demand significant computational resources and strong network connections. The method's effectiveness depends on dataset diversity and size, affecting its applicability in specific contexts. Future advancements in computational power and communication technology may enhance accessibility and efficiency. Exploring the integration of emerging technologies like blockchain or edge computing could improve the methodology's versatility and dependability. This could open avenues for more extensive applications in disability boards inside data frameworks. Additionally, real-world case studies and user feedback analysis can give significant experiences into the strategy's ease of use and viability, leading to continuous improvements.

Author Contributions: Conceptualization, S.B.K. and M.A.; Methodology, S.B.K.; Software, M.A.; Validation, M.A.; Formal analysis, S.B.K. and M.A.M.; Data curation, S.B.K.; Writing—original draft, S.B.K.; Writing—review & editing, M.A. and M.A.M.; Visualization, M.A.; Project administration, M.A.M. All authors have read and agreed to the published version of the manuscript.

Funding: The authors extend their appreciation to the King Salman center For Disability Research for funding this work through Research Group no KSRG-2023-394.

Data Availability Statement: The datasets used during the current study are available from the corresponding author on reasonable request.

Conflicts of Interest: The authors declare no conflict of interest.

References

1. Lippi, L.; de Sire, A.; Folli, A.; Turco, A.; Moalli, S.; Ammendolia, A.; Maconi, A.; Invernizzi, M. Environmental Factors in the Rehabilitation Framework: Role of the One Health Approach to Improve the Complex Management of Disability. *Int. J. Environ. Res. Public Health* **2022**, *19*, 15186. [CrossRef] [PubMed]
2. Camisa, V.; Gilardi, F.; Di Brino, E.; Santoro, A.; Vinci, M.R.; Sannino, S.; Bianchi, N.; Mesolella, V.; Macina, N.; Focarelli, M.; et al. Return on Investment (ROI) and Development of a Workplace Disability Management Program in a Hospital—A Pilot Evaluation Study. *Int. J. Environ. Res. Public Health* **2020**, *17*, 8084. [CrossRef] [PubMed]
3. Wang, Q.; Dai, W.; Zhang, C.; Zhu, J.; Ma, X. A Compact Constraint Incremental Method for Random Weight Networks and Its Application. *IEEE Trans. Neural Netw. Learn. Syst.* **2023**. [CrossRef] [PubMed]
4. Jain, A.; Hassard, J.; Leka, S.; Di Tecco, C.; Iavicoli, S. The role of occupational health services in psychosocial risk management and the promotion of mental health and well-being at work. *Int. J. Environ. Res. Public Health* **2021**, *18*, 3632. [CrossRef] [PubMed]
5. Li, T.; Li, Y.; Hoque, M.A.; Xia, T.; Tarkoma, S.; Hui, P. To What Extent We Repeat Ourselves? Discovering Daily Activity Patterns Across Mobile App Usage. *IEEE Trans. Mob. Comput.* **2022**, *21*, 1492–1507. [CrossRef]
6. Zhou, X.; Liu, X.; Zhang, G.; Jia, L.; Wang, X.; Zhao, Z. An Iterative Threshold Algorithm of Log-Sum Regularization for Sparse Problem. *IEEE Trans. Circuits Syst. Video Technol.* **2023**, *33*, 4728–4740. [CrossRef]
7. Magrin, M.E.; Marini, E.; Nicolotti, M. Employability of disabled graduates: Resources for a sustainable employment. *Sustainability* **2019**, *11*, 1542. [CrossRef]
8. Li, C.; Dong, M.; Xin, X.; Li, J.; Chen, X.; Ota, K. Efficient Privacy-preserving in IoMT with Blockchain and Lightweight Secret Sharing. *IEEE Internet Things J.* **2023**, *10*, 22051–22064. [CrossRef]
9. Prayitno; Shyu, C.R.; Putra, K.T.; Chen, H.C.; Tsai, Y.Y.; Hossain, K.T.; Jiang, W.; Shae, Z.Y. A systematic review of federated learning in the healthcare area: From the perspective of data properties and applications. *Appl. Sci.* **2021**, *11*, 11191. [CrossRef]
10. Gu, X.; Sabrina, F.; Fan, Z.; Sohail, S. A Review of Privacy Enhancement Methods for Federated Learning in Healthcare Systems. *Int. J. Environ. Res. Public Health* **2023**, *20*, 6539. [CrossRef]
11. Cheng, A.S.; Ng, P.H.; Sin, Z.P.; Lai, S.H.; Law, S.W. Smart work injury management (swim) system: Artificial intelligence in work disability management. *J. Occup. Rehabil.* **2020**, *30*, 354–361. [CrossRef] [PubMed]
12. García-Segura, T.; Montalbán-Domingo, L.; Llopis-Castelló, D.; Sanz-Benlloch, A.; Pellicer, E. Integration of Deep Learning Techniques and Sustainability-Based Concepts into an Urban Pavement Management System. *Expert Syst. Appl.* **2023**, *231*, 120851. [CrossRef]
13. Bolaños, C.; Rojas, B.; Salazar-Cabrera, R.; Ramírez-González, G.; de la Cruz, Á.P.; Molina, J.M.M. Fleet management and control systems for developing countries implemented with Intelligent Transportation Systems (ITS) services. *Transp. Res. Interdiscip. Perspect.* **2022**, *16*, 100694. [CrossRef]
14. Sprunt, B.; Marella, M. Combining child functioning data with learning and support needs data to create disability-identification algorithms in Fiji's Education Management Information System. *Int. J. Environ. Res. Public Health* **2021**, *18*, 9413. [CrossRef] [PubMed]
15. Kim, H.K.; Park, J. Examination of the protection offered by current accessibility acts and guidelines to people with disabilities in using information technology devices. *Electronics* **2020**, *9*, 742. [CrossRef]
16. Alshammari, M.; Doody, O.; Richardson, I. Software Engineering Issues: An exploratory study into the development of Health Information Systems for people with Mild Intellectual and Developmental Disability. In Proceedings of the 2020 IEEE First International Workshop on Requirements Engineering for Well-Being, Aging, and Health (REWBAH), Zurich, Switzerland, 31 August 2020; pp. 67–76.

17. Chiscano, M.C. Improving the design of urban transport experience with people with disabilities. *Res. Transp. Bus. Manag.* **2021**, *41*, 100596. [CrossRef]
18. Elfakki, A.O.; Sghaier, S.; Alotaibi, A.A. An Efficient System Based on Experimental Laboratory in 3D Virtual Environment for Students with Learning Disabilities. *Electronics* **2023**, *12*, 989. [CrossRef]
19. Algarni, M.; Saeed, F.; Al-Hadhrami, T.; Ghabban, F.; Al-Sarem, M. Deep learning-based approach for emotion recognition using electroencephalography (EEG) signals using bi-directional long short-term memory (Bi-LSTM). *Sensors* **2022**, *22*, 2976. [CrossRef]
20. Hu, K.; Li, Y.; Xia, M.; Wu, J.; Lu, M.; Zhang, S.; Weng, L. Federated learning: A distributed shared machine learning method. *Complexity* **2021**, *2021*, 8261663. [CrossRef]
21. Deb, S.; Abdelminaam, D.S.; Said, M.; Houssein, E.H. Recent methodology-based gradient-based optimizer for economic load dispatch problem. *IEEE Access* **2021**, *9*, 44322–44338. [CrossRef]
22. Available online: https://www.kaggle.com/datasets/michaelacorley/disability-statistics-united-states-2018 (accessed on 1 August 2023).
23. Chen, M.; Xu, Y.; Xu, H.; Huang, L. Enhancing Decentralized Federated Learning for Non-IID Data on Heterogeneous Devices. In Proceedings of the 2023 IEEE 39th International Conference on Data Engineering (ICDE), Anaheim, CA, USA, 3–7 April 2023. [CrossRef]
24. Mhaisen, N.; Awad, A.; Mohamed, A.M.; Erbad, A.; Guizani, M. Analysis and Optimal Edge Assignment for Hierarchical Federated Learning on Non-IID Data. *arXiv* **2020**, arXiv:2012.05622.
25. Sun, J.; Chen, T.; Giannakis, G.B.; Yang, Q.; Yang, Z. Lazily Aggregated Quantized Gradient Innovation for Communication-Efficient Federated Learning. *IEEE Trans. Pattern Anal. Mach. Intell.* **2022**, *44*, 2031–2044. [CrossRef] [PubMed]
26. Wang, F.; Jiao, L.; Zhu, K.; Lin, X.; Li, L. Toward Sustainable AI: Federated Learning Demand Response in Cloud-Edge Systems via Auctions. In Proceedings of the IEEE INFOCOM 2023—IEEE Conference on Computer Communications, New York City, NY, USA, 17–20 May 2023; pp. 1–10. [CrossRef]
27. Gerges, F.; Shih, F.; Azar, D. Automated diagnosis of acne and rosacea using convolution neural networks. In Proceedings of the 2021 4th International Conference on Artificial Intelligence and Pattern Recognition, Xiamen, China, 20–21 September 2023. [CrossRef]
28. Lian, Z.; Zeng, Q.; Wang, W.; Gadekallu, T.R.; Su, C. Blockchain-based two-stage federated learning with non-IID data in IoMT system. *IEEE Trans. Comput. Soc. Syst.* **2022**, *10*, 1701–1710. [CrossRef]
29. Rani, S.; Babbar, H.; Srivastava, G.; Gadekallu, T.R.; Dhiman, G. Security Framework for Internet of Things based Software Defined Networks using Blockchain. *IEEE Internet Things J.* **2022**, *10*, 6074–6081. [CrossRef]
30. Chahoud, M.; Sami, H.; Mourad, A.; Otoum, S.; Otrok, H.; Bentahar, J.; Guizani, M. ON-DEMAND-FL: A Dynamic and Efficient Multi-Criteria Federated Learning Client Deployment Scheme. *IEEE Internet Things J.* **2023**, *10*, 15822–15834. [CrossRef]
31. Sirine, T.; Abbas, N. Hybrid Machine Learning Classification and Inference of Stalling Events in Mobile Videos. In Proceedings of the 2022 4th IEEE Middle East and North Africa COMMunications Conference, Amman, Jordan, 6–8 December 2022; pp. 209–214. [CrossRef]
32. Wehbi, O.; Arisdakessian, S.; Wahab, O.A.; Otrok, H.; Otoum, S.; Mourad, A.; Guizani, M. FedMint: Intelligent Bilateral Client Selection in Federated Learning with Newcomer IoT Devices. *IEEE Internet Things J.* **2023**, *1*, 20884–20898. [CrossRef]
33. Ibrahim, J.N.; Audi, L. Anxiety Symptoms among Lebanese Health-care Students: Prevalence, Risk Factors, And Relationship With Vitamin D Status. *J. Health Sci.* **2021**, *11*, 29–36. [CrossRef]
34. Khouloud, S.; El Akoum, F.; Tekli, J. Unsupervised knowledge representation of panoramic dental X-ray images using SVG image-and-object clustering. *Multimed. Syst.* **2023**, *29*, 2293–2322. [CrossRef]
35. Hassan, H.F.; Koaik, L.; Khoury, A.E.; Atoui, A.; El Obeid, T.; Karam, L. Dietary exposure and risk assessment of mycotoxins in thyme and thyme-based products marketed in Lebanon. *Toxins* **2022**, *14*, 331. [CrossRef]
36. Judith, A.M.; Priya, S.B.; Mahendran, R.K.; Gadekallu, T.R.; Ambati, L.S. Two-phase classification: ANN and A-SVM classifiers on motor imagery BCI. *Asian J. Control* **2022**, *25*, 3318–3329.

Disclaimer/Publisher's Note: The statements, opinions and data contained in all publications are solely those of the individual author(s) and contributor(s) and not of MDPI and/or the editor(s). MDPI and/or the editor(s) disclaim responsibility for any injury to people or property resulting from any ideas, methods, instructions or products referred to in the content.

Article

Trends and Extremes in Time Series Based on Fuzzy Logic

Sergey Agayan [1], Shamil Bogoutdinov [1,2], Dmitriy Kamaev [3], Boris Dzeboev [1,*] and Michael Dobrovolsky [1]

[1] Geophysical Center of the Russian Academy of Sciences, Moscow 119296, Russia; s.agayan@gcras.ru (S.A.); shm@gcras.ru (S.B.); m.dobrovolsky@gcras.ru (M.D.)
[2] Schmidt Institute of Physics of the Earth of the Russian Academy of Sciences, Moscow 123995, Russia
[3] Research and Production Association "Typhoon", Obninsk 249038, Russia; post@typhoon.obninsk.ru
* Correspondence: b.dzeboev@gcras.ru

Abstract: The authors develop the theory of discrete differentiation and, on its basis, solve the problem of detecting trends in records, using the idea of the connection between trends and derivatives in classical analysis but implementing it using fuzzy logic methods. The solution to this problem is carried out by constructing fuzzy measures of the trend and extremum for a recording. The theoretical justification of the regression approach to classical differentiation in the continuous case given in this work provides an answer to the question of what discrete differentiation is, which is used in constructing fuzzy measures of the trend and extremum. The detection of trends using trend and extremum measures is more stable and of higher quality than using traditional data analysis methods, which consist in studying the intervals of constant sign of the derivative for a piecewise smooth approximation of the original record. The approach proposed by the authors, due to its implementation within the framework of fuzzy logic, is largely focused on the researcher analyzing the record and at the same time uses the idea of multiscale. The latter circumstance provides a more complete and in-depth understanding of the process behind the recording.

Keywords: trend problem; discrete regression derivatives; trend measures; extremum measures; multiscale; extremum migration

MSC: 26E50

1. Introduction

Research on data and methods of their analysis using fuzzy mathematics has now taken shape as an independent direction, which includes methods of fuzzy regression and the analysis of fuzzy time series [1–7]. We can highlight the main stages of development of this direction.

In the initial stage, studies of the fuzzy regression model were carried out. The second stage was the development of soft-computing methods, within which a huge number of studies have been carried out on the effectiveness of soft computing for time series analysis. The third stage consisted in the transition from the analysis of time series using fuzzy mathematics methods to the analysis of fuzzy time series. The development of fuzzy database methods has made it possible to move to the stage of extracting rules from fuzzy (granular) time series.

Within each of the listed stages, a significant part consists of methods for identifying trends and, more broadly, a morphological analysis of time series. The proposed work should be attributed to the use of fuzzy mathematics methods for the analysis of discrete time series.

1.1. Trends and Fuzzy Principles for Their Modeling

Trends in a time series are its fundamental characteristic and therefore can tell a lot about the nature of the process behind it. The identification of trends is a significant part of what is traditionally considered to be the morphological analysis of time series [8–11], including:

- The decomposition of the time series into trend and seasonal components, as well as the remainder: the trend shows the general direction of changes over time, seasonality reflects repeating patterns associated with certain periods of time, and the remainder reflects random fluctuations within the time series;
- An autocorrelation analysis, which helps identify periodic fluctuations associated with seasonality;
- A spectral analysis, which allows one to analyze the cyclicity in a time series and the most important time periods for it.

Currently, a broader understanding of morphological analysis as the study of the manifestation of one or another geometric property in a graphical representation of the dynamics of a time series is gaining momentum [12]. A morphological analysis of time series is useful for a better understanding of their dynamics and more accurate forecasting.

There are several methods for constructing and identifying time series trends. Here are the main ones [8,11,13–18]: smoothing with a kernel (in particular, the moving average method, exponential smoothing), regression and autoregressive (AR) methods, wavelet analysis, nonlinear methods (in particular, machine learning and neural networks).

Real trends are stochastic and are not at all similar to ideal mathematical ones, since they have glitches. This does not confuse the researcher, who perceives the trend adaptively and understands when a violation is insignificant and the trend continues, and when a violation interrupts the trend.

Thus, if mathematical trends are strict and unambiguous segments in each subsequent node for which the value of the record is greater than, or equal to (less than, or equal to) the value of the record in the present node, then stochastic ones depend on the point of view of the researcher and therefore can differ.

Let us call the formalization and search for trends and extrema in a function the trend problem. Its solution, according to the authors, consists of a sequence of answers to the following questions:

- What is the trend of a function at a point?
- Which parts of the function should be considered definitely trendy?
- How do these fragments form a general trend?
- What is an extremum of a function?

The solution to the trend problem, according to the authors, should be fuzzy, multiparameter and multiscale in the spirit of wavelets and fractals. By changing the parameters and scale, the researcher gets a complete picture of the trends and selects the ones they need. In addition, a multiscale trend analysis is very useful, objective and can tell a lot about the function as a whole.

The above is fully consistent with the principles of fuzzy modeling, on the basis of which it is supposed to approach stochastic trends. In this regard, we quote Zadeh [19]: "All we need to solve most practical problems is a parameterized family of definitions that, if necessary, would allow a non-standard choice of operators that reflect the characteristic features of a particular application. The advantage of this approach is that by avoiding fixed, concrete-independent definitions, fuzzy set theory and fuzzy logic achieve a pluralism that increases their flexibility and expressive capabilities".

In this work, such operators will be regression differentiation, regression smoothing, fuzzy trend measure and fuzzy extremum measure.

It should be noted that regression derivatives were used earlier, in a simpler form than in this work, for the classification of time series, which made it possible to determine groups of series similar in morphology using various similarity measures [20–24]. In such problems, the choice of similarity measure affects the classification accuracy to a greater extent than the choice of classification method.

The advantage of similarity measures constructed using regression derivatives is the ability to take into account both positive dependencies, when time series simultaneously increase or decrease values, and negative dependencies, when the values of one time series decrease and another increase, and vice versa [23]. Similar results based on the fuzzy correlation measure constructed by the authors are given in the conclusion.

1.2. Solution of the Problem of Trends and on the Basis of Discrete Mathematical Analysis

The problem of trends (see Section 1.1) in this work is solved within the framework of discrete mathematical analysis (DMA)—a new approach to data analysis, researcher-oriented and occupying an intermediate position between hard mathematical methods and soft intellectual ones [25–29].

The solution to the problem within the framework of DMA consists of two parts. The first is informal: it explains the researcher's logic, introduces the necessary concepts, and explains the scheme and principles of the solution. The second is of a formal nature: with the help of the DMA apparatus, all concepts receive strict definitions within the framework of fuzzy mathematics and fuzzy logic, and the scheme and principles become algorithms.

We call the first, informal part of solving the trend problem within the framework of DMA the logic of the researcher's trends (RTL) and formulate it in the form of the following provisions:

- There is a record f on a finite uniform set of nodes T. At each node, the researcher vaguely but unambiguously sees a positive, negative or neutral trend f.
- The researcher considers positive (negative) trends for f to be segments in T consisting of positive and neutral (negative and neutral) nodes from T.
- Opposite trends intersect at neutral nodes, among which the researcher can choose an extremum for f.

The further, main part of the work is devoted to the transformation of RTL into algorithms (the second part of solving the problem of trends within the framework of DMA): fuzzy measures of the trend and extremum are constructed, expressing the researcher's opinion about the presence of a trend and extremum in a record in a particular node. The combined use of these measures makes it possible in a discrete situation to repeat the classical results of mathematical analysis regarding trends and extrema for piecewise smooth functions.

The measures are based on discrete regression derivatives. Their definition, study and rationale for use are given below. Having a discrete derivative, there is a natural desire to repeat on its basis, in a discrete situation, the scheme of the approach of classical mathematical analysis to trends and extremes. This determines both the motivation and goals of this work.

1.3. Regression Approach to Derivatives (Continuous Case)

Let the function f be integrable on an interval I containing zero internally. Then, for a sufficiently small $\Delta > 0$, the segment $[-\Delta, \Delta]$ is contained in I. Let us denote by f_Δ the restriction of f to the segment $[-\Delta, \Delta]$: $f_\Delta = f_{[-\Delta,\Delta]}$ and calculate the projection pr f_Δ of the function f_Δ in space $L^2[-\Delta, \Delta]$ into the two-dimensional subspace of linear functions $\text{Lin}^2[-\Delta, \Delta]$.

Statement 1. *If a function f has a tangent at zero, then, as $\Delta \to 0$, the linear projection pr f_Δ tends to it.*

Proof. Let $e_1 = e_1(\Delta)$, $e_2 = e_2(\Delta)$ be an orthonormal basis in $\text{Lin}^2[-\Delta, \Delta]$, obtained from the natural basis $(1, x)$ by a Gram–Schmidt orthogonalization [30], then:

$$\text{pr } f_\Delta = (f_\Delta, e_1)_\Delta e_1 + (f_\Delta, e_2)_\Delta e_2.$$

Let us put $e_1 = c$, $e_2 = ax + b$. Three conditions arise on a, b and c:

$$\begin{aligned} \|e_1\|_\Delta = 1 &\longleftrightarrow \int_{-\Delta}^{\Delta} c^2 dt = 1 &\longleftrightarrow c^2 = \tfrac{1}{2\Delta}, \\ (e_1, e_2)_\Delta = 0 &\longleftrightarrow \int_{-\Delta}^{\Delta} c(at + b) dt = 0 &\longleftrightarrow b = 0, \\ \|e_2\|_\Delta = 1 &\longleftrightarrow \int_{-\Delta}^{\Delta} a^2 t^2 dt = 1 &\longleftrightarrow a^2 = \tfrac{3}{2\Delta^3}. \end{aligned}$$

Thus,
$$\operatorname{pr} f_\Delta(x) = \frac{1}{2\Delta} \int_{-\Delta}^{\Delta} f(t) dt + \left(\frac{3}{2\Delta^3} \int_{-\Delta}^{\Delta} t f(t) dt \right) x.$$

Additionally, the function f is differentiable at zero:
$$f(x) = f(0) + f'(0)x + \alpha(x)x,$$
where $\alpha(x) \to 0$ when $x \to 0$.

The limit
$$\frac{1}{2\Delta} \int_{-\Delta}^{\Delta} f(x) dx \to f(0)$$
in the free term of the projection $\operatorname{pr} f_\Delta$ is explained by the mean value theorem [31].

Let us analyze the expansion coefficient $\operatorname{pr} f_\Delta$ at x:

$$\frac{3}{2\Delta^3} \int_{-\Delta}^{\Delta} t f(t) dt = \frac{3}{2\Delta^3} \int_{-\Delta}^{\Delta} t(f(0) + f'(0)x + \alpha(t)t) dt =$$
$$\frac{3}{2\Delta^3} \int_{-\Delta}^{\Delta} t f(0) dt + \frac{3}{2\Delta^3} \int_{-\Delta}^{\Delta} t^2 f'(0) dt + \frac{3}{2\Delta^3} \int_{-\Delta}^{\Delta} t^2 \alpha(t) dt =$$
$$0 + f'(0) + \frac{3}{2\Delta^3} \int_{-\Delta}^{\Delta} t^2 \alpha(t) dt.$$

The last integral tends to zero as $\Delta \to 0$:
$$\forall \varepsilon > 0 \ \exists \Delta(\varepsilon) : \forall \Delta < \Delta(\varepsilon) |\alpha|\big|_{[-\Delta, \Delta]} < \varepsilon \Rightarrow$$
$$\Rightarrow \left| \frac{3}{2\Delta^3} \int_{-\Delta}^{\Delta} t^2 \alpha(t) dt \right| \leq \frac{3}{2\Delta^3} \left| \int_{-\Delta}^{\Delta} \varepsilon t^2 dt \right| = \varepsilon.$$

□

1.4. Regression Approach to Derivatives (Discrete Case)

We postpone the consequences of the proven statement and its further development in the continuous case until the Appendix A, and now we discuss its significance mainly for the analysis of data in a discrete situation.

Replacing the tangent to f with the projection $\operatorname{pr} f_\Delta$ for small Δ makes it possible to determine the tangent for discrete functions, since the projection $\operatorname{pr} f_\Delta$ is nothing more than a linear regression for f on $[-\Delta, \Delta]$ and can be generalized to the discrete case.

The limit transition $\bar{t} \to t$ in the discrete case is replaced by a fuzzy weight structure $\delta_t(\bar{t}) \in [0, 1]$ of proximity to node t in a finite set of nodes T, the domain of definition of the function f.

The proven statement gives grounds to consider the linear regression of the function f with respect to the weight structure δ_t on T as a tangent for f at t, and its slope as the derivative of f at t.

Having a derivative for f, there is a natural desire to repeat on its basis in a discrete situation the classical approach to trends and extrema from mathematical analysis.

2. Discrete Regression Derivatives

Statement 1 proved above allows us to conclude that for a function f that is differentiable at zero, its linear continuous regressions on the segments $[-\Delta, \Delta]$ tend to the tangent as $\Delta \to 0$.

This approach to differentiation in the continuous case allows a continuation to the discrete case, since discrete regressions are just as efficient and fundamental as continuous ones.

Let $T = [a, b]$ be a finite discrete segment with equal nodes $t = t_i : T = \{t\} = \{t_i|_{i=1}^N\}$, $t_i = a + (i-1)h$, $h = \frac{b-a}{N-1}$.

Let us call a segment τ in T a piece in T without gaps: $\tau = [t_i, t_j] = \{t_i < \cdots < t_j\}$ for some $1 \leq i \leq j \leq N$. In addition, we call the beginning (end) τ and denote by $b\tau$ ($e\tau$) the first and last nodes t_i and t_j, respectively.

We consider any real function on T to be a time series (record) f; $F(T)$ is the space of such functions.

The analysis by a researcher of the behavior of a time series involves considering its values not only in a separate node but also simultaneously taking into account the values in some of its vicinity. This is precisely why the segment T needs to be localized at each of its nodes. It can be implemented using the fuzzy structure δ_t on T, which plays the role of a neighborhood of node t and expresses the proximity to it of individual nodes $\bar{t}$ normalized in t: δ_t is a measure of the proximity of $\bar{t}$ to t.

$$(\delta_t(t) = 1) \wedge \left(|\bar{t} - t| \leq |\bar{\bar{t}} - t| \to \delta_t(\bar{\bar{t}}) \leq \delta_t(\bar{t}) \right). \tag{1}$$

We consider the proximity measure δ on T to be a set of fuzzy structures δ_t: $\delta = \{\delta_t : t \in T\}$, $\delta_t \in$ Fuzzy T.

The measure δ is the only parameter in the theory of trends and extrema constructed below and is therefore very important. Its choice is entirely determined by the researcher. The authors' choice is the family $\delta = \delta(p, r)$.

Definition 1. $\delta = \delta(p, r)$, p—scale parameter, r—viewing radius (Figure 1).

$$\delta_t(\bar{t}) = \delta_t(\bar{t}|p, r) = \begin{cases} \left(1 - \frac{|\bar{t}-t|}{r}\right)^p, & \text{if } |\bar{t} - t| \leq r \\ 0, & \text{if } |\bar{t} - t| > r \end{cases}. \tag{2}$$

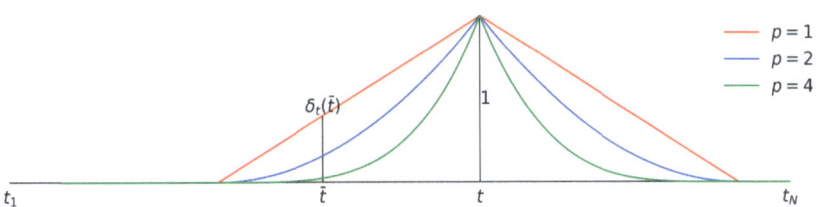

Figure 1. Proximity of $\delta_t(p, r)$ to node t for different p's.

The family $\delta(p, r)$ expresses the authors' point of view on localization: a researcher analyzing a record f at node t first selects the boundary of the view (parameter r) and then its thoroughness (scale, parameter p). The required localization can be achieved using the family $\delta(p, r)$ in two ways: either by the parameter r tending to zero, or by the parameter p tending to infinity. In this paper, the authors chose the second path: in the measure $\delta(p, r)$, there is an interesting dependence on the scale parameter p, which allows you to "look at the record from a different height".

The parameters p and r are chosen by the researcher. In this work, the measure $\delta(p, r)$ is used for trend analysis, which can be simple (p and r are fixed) and multiscale (p changes, r is fixed). The work focuses on multiscale analysis. For its objectivity and completeness, the radius r is assumed to be equal to a quarter of the length of the segment T. Figure 1 shows the dependence of the proximity $\delta_t(\bar{t}|p,r)$ to node t on p for r equal to a quarter of the length of the segment T.

The limit transition $\bar{t} \to t$ to T performs a proximity measure δ_t by distributing weights on T: $\bar{t} \to t \leftrightarrow T = \{\bar{t}\} \to T_\delta(t) = \{(\bar{t}, \delta_t(\bar{t}))\}$. With that said, we should consider a linear regression based on the fuzzy image $\text{Im}_\delta f(t) = \{(f(\bar{t}), \delta_t(\bar{t})), \bar{t} \in T\}$ at the beginning of the tangent $l_\delta f(t) = l_\delta f(t)(\bar{t}) = a_t \bar{t} + b_t$ to the function f at node t. Associated with the image $\text{Im}_\delta, f(t)$ is the functional

$$J(a,b) = \sum_{\bar{t} \in T} \delta_t(\bar{t})(f(\bar{t}) - a\bar{t} - b)^2.$$

The values (a_t, b_t) of the parameters of the tangent $l_\delta f(t)$ are the minimum point of $J(a,b)$. Therefore, a_t and b_t satisfy the system of equations

$$a_t \sum_{\bar{t} \in T} \delta_t(\bar{t})\bar{t}^2 + b_t \sum_{\bar{t} \in T} \delta_t(\bar{t})\bar{t} = \sum_{\bar{t} \in T} \delta_t(\bar{t}) f(\bar{t})\bar{t},$$

$$a_t \sum_{\bar{t} \in T} \delta_t(\bar{t})\bar{t} + b_t \sum_{\bar{t} \in T} \delta_t(\bar{t}) = \sum_{\bar{t} \in T} \delta_t(\bar{t}) f(\bar{t}).$$

Hence,

$$a_t = \frac{\begin{vmatrix} \sum_{\bar{t} \in T} \bar{t}\delta_t(\bar{t})f(\bar{t}) & \sum_{\bar{t} \in T} \bar{t}\delta_t(\bar{t}) \\ \sum_{\bar{t} \in T} \delta_t(\bar{t})f(\bar{t}) & \sum_{\bar{t} \in T} \delta_t(\bar{t}) \end{vmatrix}}{\begin{vmatrix} \sum_{\bar{t} \in T} \bar{t}^2\delta_t(\bar{t}) & \sum_{\bar{t} \in T} \bar{t}\delta_t(\bar{t}) \\ \sum_{\bar{t} \in T} \bar{t}\delta_t(\bar{t}) & \sum_{\bar{t} \in T} \delta_t(\bar{t}) \end{vmatrix}},$$

$$b_t = \frac{\begin{vmatrix} \sum_{\bar{t} \in T} \bar{t}^2\delta_t(\bar{t}) & \sum_{\bar{t} \in T} \bar{t}\delta_t(\bar{t})f(\bar{t}) \\ \sum_{\bar{t} \in T} \bar{t}\delta_t(\bar{t}) & \sum_{\bar{t} \in T} \delta_t(\bar{t})f(\bar{t}) \end{vmatrix}}{\begin{vmatrix} \sum_{\bar{t} \in T} \bar{t}^2\delta_t(\bar{t}) & \sum_{\bar{t} \in T} \bar{t}\delta_t(\bar{t}) \\ \sum_{\bar{t} \in T} \bar{t}\delta_t(\bar{t}) & \sum_{\bar{t} \in T} \delta_t(\bar{t}) \end{vmatrix}}. \quad (3)$$

To build trends, the formulas in (3) are used. A simpler expression for a_t and b_t is used in Appendix A.1.

Definition 2. *The slope coefficient a_t is called the regression derivative of f at t and is denoted by $D_\delta f(t)$. The function $t \to a_t$ is called the regression derivative of f and is denoted by $D_\delta f \in F(T)$. The functional correspondence $f \to D_\delta f$ is a linear operator on $F(T)$, called regression differentiation and denoted by D_δ.*

Definition 3. *The value $l_\delta f(t)(t) = a_t t + b_t$ of the regression tangent $l_\delta f(t)$ of the function f at t is called the regression value of f at t and is denoted $R_\delta f(t)$. The function $t \to R_\delta f(t)$ is called regression smoothing of f and is denoted by $R_\delta f \in F(T)$. The functional correspondence $f \to R_\delta f$ is a linear operator on $F(T)$, called regression smoothing and denoted by R_δ.*

A special notation for differentiation and smoothing in the case of a measure $\delta = \delta(p,r)$ is:

$$D_{\delta(p,r)} = D(p,r); \quad R_{\delta(p,r)} = R(p,r). \quad (4)$$

The theoretical justification for the regression approach to differentiation presented in this work finds additional empirical confirmation in the form of the good performance of regression smoothing: with the same review (parameter p) on smooth functions, regression smoothing works better than conventional averaging. In Figure 2, regression smoothing is shown with a solid line, and conventional averaging is shown with a dotted line. The visual comparison is supported by the quadratic discrepancy with the ideal. The advantage of regression smoothing over conventional smoothing is especially visible at the ends of both the synthetic smooth recording (Figure 2) and the real one (Figure 3). Until the end of this paper, these records participate in the game and serve as a testing ground for the trends and extremes proposed in this work.

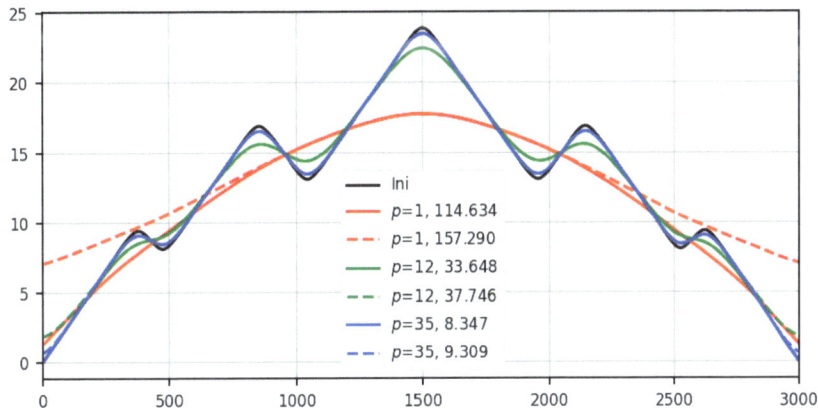

Figure 2. Results of smoothing $R(p,r)$ (solid line) and averaging $M(p,r)$ (dotted line) for smooth records (black line) at different scales p with quadratic residuals deviations: $p = 1$ (red lines), $p = 12$ (green) and $p = 35$ (blue).

Figure 3 shows the performance of the regression smoothing $R(p,r)$ on the real magnetic storm record in the same p-scale parameters as in Figure 2 for the synthetic one. The above figures confirm the convergence proved in Appendix A.1 to the record f of its regression smoothing $R(p,r)$ at $p \to \infty$.

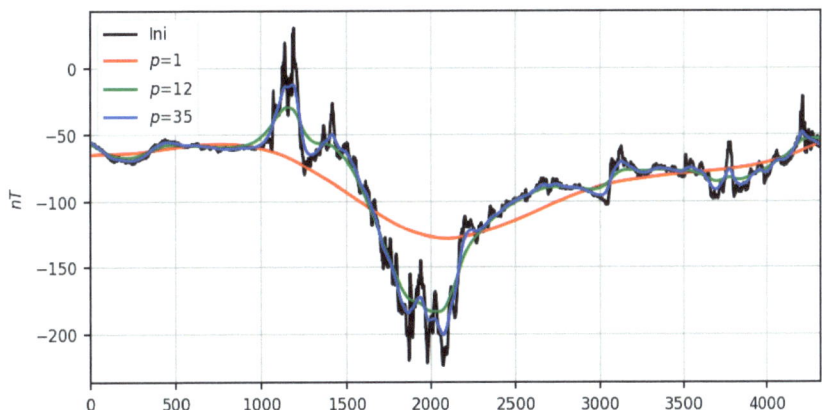

Figure 3. Results of smoothing $R(p,r)$ on a real recording (black line) at different scales p: $p = 1$ (red line), $p = 12$ (green line) and $p = 35$ (blue line).

3. Trend Measure: Preliminary Solution to the Trend Problem

The assumption that a researcher looking at a record f can determine its trend at any node $t \in T$ is central to the researcher's trend logic. Based on it, we construct its implementation using a fuzzy trend measure.

The researcher's view of the record f is formalized by its regression smoothing $f_\delta = R_\delta f$ based on the proximity (localization) measure δ on T chosen by the researcher. Next, the researcher is not interested in the smoothing f_δ itself, but in the result f'_δ of its differentiation by the operator $D(0,h)$: $f'_\delta = D(0,h)f_\delta$ (4). The value of $f'_\delta(t)$ is called the elementary dynamics of the entry f at node t based on the localization of δ. Their totality, that is, the image $\text{Im}\, f'_\delta$, serves as the basis for constructing a fuzzy trend measure $\tau r_\delta f$. The value $\tau r_\delta f(t)$ in the fuzzy scale $[0,1]$ expresses the degree of confidence of the researcher (the measure of their reason) to consider the trend of the record f at node t to be positive.

It is constructed as follows: the researcher gives the weight $|f'_\delta(t)|\delta_t(\bar{t})$ to the elementary dynamics $f'_\delta(\bar{t})$ at node $\bar{t}$. The argument for a positive trend f at node t is all positive dynamics $f'_\delta(\bar{t}) > 0$, and against, all negative dynamics $f'_\delta(\bar{t}) < 0$ with their weights.

The measure of trend $\tau r_\delta f(t)$ is considered the ratio of the sum of the weights of positive dynamics (the argument "for" the positive trend f at node t) to the total sum of weights:

$$\tau r_\delta f(t) = \frac{\sum \delta_t(\bar{t}) f'_\delta(\bar{t}) : f'_\delta(\bar{t}) > 0}{\sum \delta_t(\bar{t})|f'_\delta(\bar{t})| : \bar{t} \in T}. \tag{5}$$

If $\tau r_\delta f(t) > 1/2$, then the total argument of the weights of increasing dynamics is greater than the total argument of the weights of decreasing dynamics; therefore, the researcher considers node t to be positive according to the trend for f, and the degree of conditionality of its solution is $\tau r_\delta f(t)$.

Similarly, if $\tau r_\delta f(t) < 1/2$, then node t is considered negative according to the trend for f with a base of $1 - \tau r_\delta f(t)$ and neutral in the case of equality $\tau r_\delta f(t) = 1/2$.

Let us summarize the intermediate result: based on the measure $\tau r_\delta f$, the answer to the first question formulated in the introduction was obtained: "What is a trend at a point?".

Next, partitioning $T = T^+_\delta f \vee T^-_\delta f \vee T^0_\delta f$ into positive, negative, and trend-neutral nodes

$$\begin{aligned} T^+_\delta f &= \{t \in T : \tau r_\delta f(t) > 1/2\} \\ T^-_\delta f &= \{t \in T : \tau r_\delta f(t) < 1/2\} \\ T^0_\delta f &= \{t \in T : \tau r_\delta f(t) = 1/2\} \end{aligned}$$

allows one to simultaneously answer the following two questions of the trend problem: "Which fragments of the record should be considered unconditionally trendy?" and "How do these add up to overall final trends?"

The fact is that in real conditions, there are very few neutral trends from $T^0_\delta f$, or none at all. Therefore, it seems natural to consider segments of the record f entirely consisting of positive and neutral (negative and neutral) nodes, respectively, as positive and negative trends τr^+ (τr^-) for f: τr^+ (τr^-), a set of nodes without gaps in $T^+_\delta f \vee T^0_\delta f$ ($T^-_\delta f \vee T^0_\delta f$).

Definition 4. *We denote an arbitrary trend by τr: $\tau r = \tau r^+ \vee \tau r^-$. Trends τr replace each other and can intersect only at neutral nodes, forming an almost disjunct covering T, which we denote as $Tr_\delta f = \{\tau\}$.*

We call the partition $Tr_\delta f$ a preliminary solution to the trend problem for recording f based on the proximity measure δ. An explanation of its preliminary nature is given below, but now, we note that strongly depending on δ, in the case $\delta = \delta(p,r)$, turns out to be very effective and gives good results at different scales p on difficult real recordings with, in our opinion, a large radius review r. It was this circumstance that served as the reason for writing this work.

The proof is presented in the form of a complete display of the solution to trends $Tr_\delta f$: record $f \to$ smoothing $f_\delta \to$ trend measure $\tau r_\delta f$ with a partition $Tr_\delta f$ applied to it $\to$ partition $Tr_\delta f$ on smoothing $f_\delta \to$ partitioning $Tr_\delta f$ into records f. The obvious presence of scale p requires additional effort. Continuing (4) for $\delta = \delta(p,r)$ and omitting the viewing radius r, we introduce the following notation:

- smoothing $f_{\delta(p,r)} \leftrightarrow f_p$,
- elementary dynamics $f'_{\delta(p,r)} \leftrightarrow f'_p$,
- trend measure $\tau r_{\delta(p,r)} \leftrightarrow \tau r_p$,

- partition $Tr_{\delta(p,r)} \leftrightarrow Tr_p$.

In order not to confuse the trend measure τr_p with the trend segments τr obtained on its basis, in the latter, we agree to indicate the dependence on the scale p in the form of an argument:

- $\tau r \leftrightarrow \tau r(p)$,
- $Tr_p f = \{\tau r(p)\}$.

In Figures 4–6, the complete scenario for solving $Tr_p f$ is given for a smooth function on three scales, and for a real record on two scales in Figures 7 and 8.

The effectiveness of working in difficult real-world conditions is the main criterion in data analysis, a largely empirical discipline. According to the authors, success in the problem of trends based on the tr_p measure lies in two reasons: stability and adequacy.

Stability is a general property of the construction of the measure $tr_p f$. Figure 9 illustrates this; Figure 9b,c shows the trend solution on a scale $p = 35$ for a smooth record and its disturbance, indicated in Figure 9a in black and green, respectively.

Adequacy: Trends $\tau r(p)$ obtained on the basis of the measure $\tau r_p f$ are consistent with the "p" scale: there are no small dynamics in modulus p on smoothing f_p among them. As noted above, it was precisely this circumstance that served as the reason for this work. The explanation of adequacy at the moment is semiempirical: according to the apologetics of regression differential calculus given at the beginning of the work and Appendix A.1, regression derivatives and values inherit the fundamental properties of linear regression, and the measure of trend very naturally depends on them. Therefore, if the effect for trends through regression derivatives exists, then it must necessarily manifest itself through the trend measure. This is illustrated in Figure 10, whose detailed story is given below.

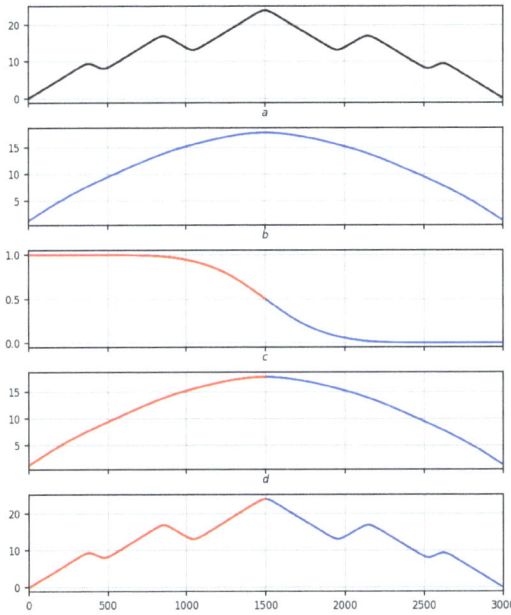

Figure 4. Preliminary solution of the problem of trends on a smooth record on a scale $p = 1$. Red lines are positive trends, blue lines are negative ones. (**a**) Original record f. (**b**) Regression smoothing f_1. (**c**) Measure of trend $\tau r_1 f$ with red–blue partition $Tr_1 f$. (**d**) Partition $Tr_1 f$ on smoothing f_1. (**e**) Partitioning $Tr_1 f$ into records f.

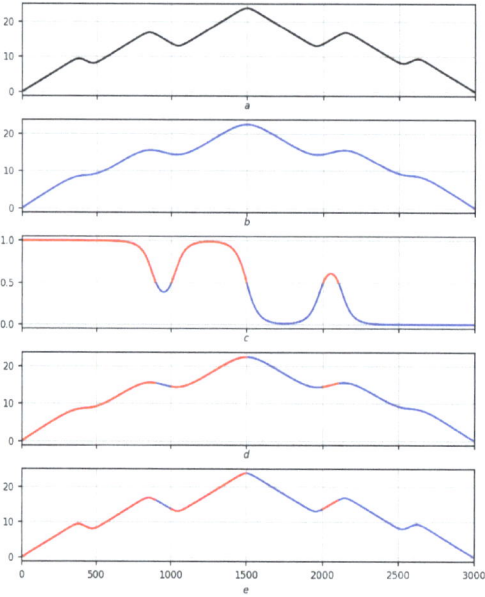

Figure 5. Preliminary solution of the problem of trends on a smooth record on a scale $p = 12$. Red lines are positive trends, blue lines are negative ones. (**a**) Original record f. (**b**) Regression smoothing f_{12}. (**c**) Measure of trend $\tau r_{12} f$ with red–blue partition $Tr_{12} f$. (**d**) Partition $Tr_{12} f$ on smoothing f_{12}. (**e**) Partitioning $Tr_{12} f$ into records f.

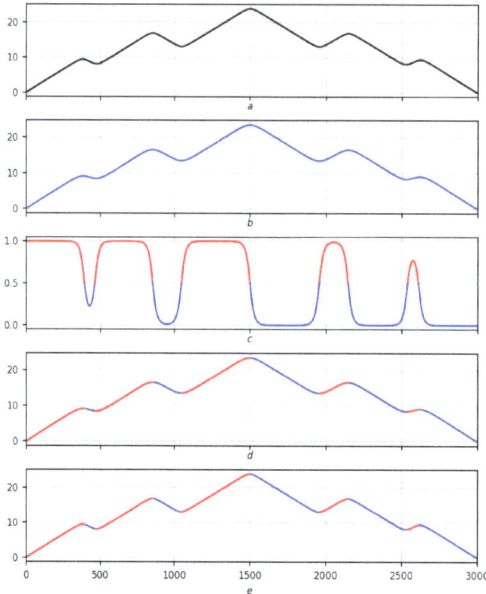

Figure 6. Preliminary solution of the problem of trends on a smooth record on a scale $p = 35$. Red lines are positive trends, blue lines are negative ones. (**a**) Original record f. (**b**) Regression smoothing f_{35}. (**c**) Measure of trend $\tau r_{35} f$ with red–blue partition $Tr_{35} f$. (**d**) Partition $Tr_{35} f$ on smoothing f_{35}. (**e**) Partitioning $Tr_{35} f$ into records f.

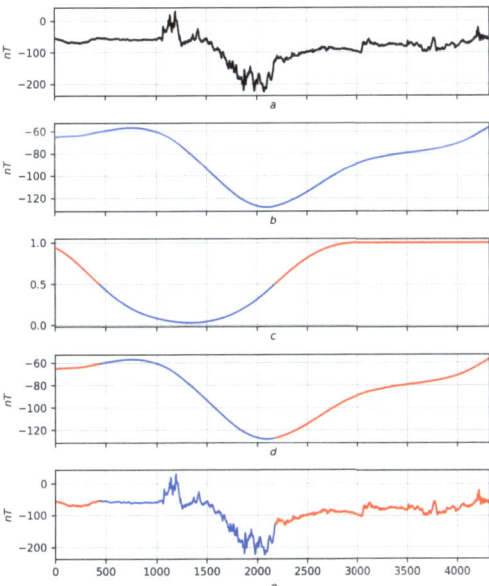

Figure 7. Preliminary solution of the problem of trends on a real record on a scale $p = 1$. Red lines are positive trends, blue lines are negative ones. (**a**) Original record f. (**b**) Regression smoothing f_1. (**c**) Measure of trend $\tau r_1 f$ with red–blue partition $Tr_1 f$. (**d**) Partition $Tr_1 f$ on smoothing f_1. (**e**) Partitioning $Tr_1 f$ into records f.

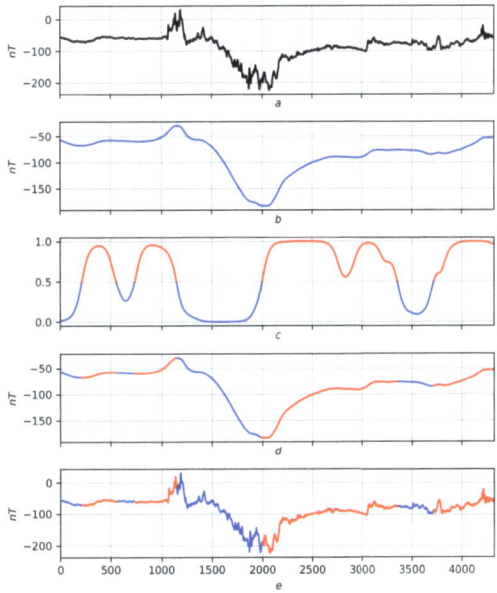

Figure 8. Preliminary solution of the problem of trends on a real record on a scale $p = 12$. Red lines are positive trends, blue lines are negative ones. (**a**) Original record f. (**b**) Regression smoothing f_{12}. (**c**) Measure of trend $\tau r_{12} f$ with red–blue partition $Tr_{12} f$. (**d**) Partition $Tr_{12} f$ on smoothing f_{12}. (**e**) Partitioning $Tr_{12} f$ into records f.

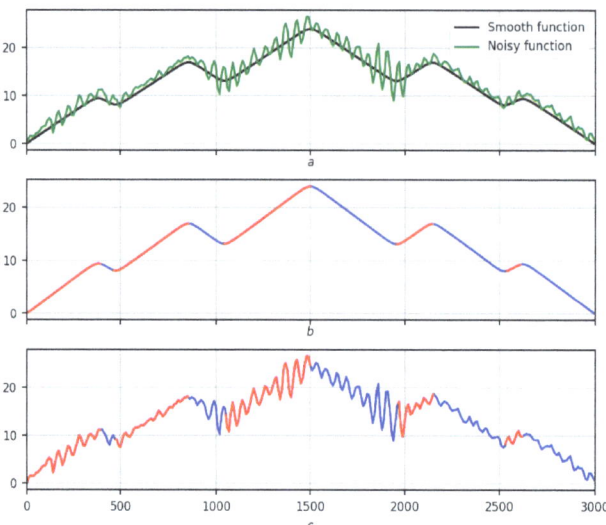

Figure 9. Stability of the preliminary solution to the trend problem. Red lines are positive trends, blue lines are negative ones. (**a**) Smooth notation (black) and its disturbance (green). (**b**) Solution for the smooth recording. (**c**) Solution to its disturbance.

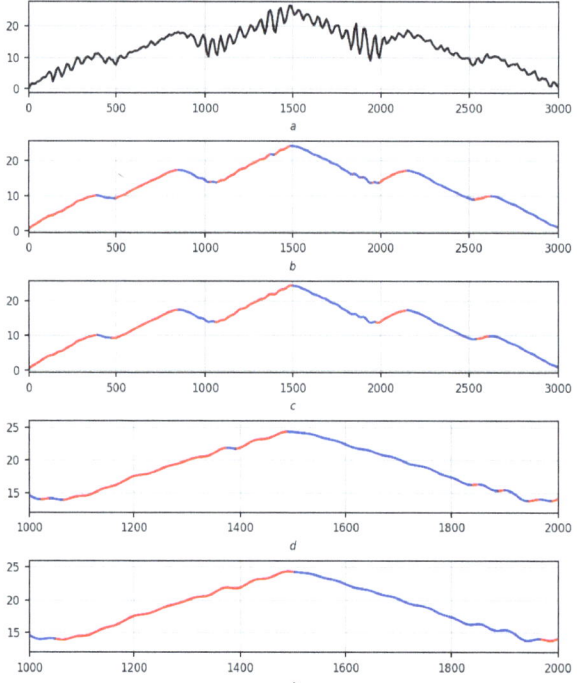

Figure 10. Adequacy of the preliminary solution to the trend problem. Red lines are positive trends, blue lines are negative ones. (**a**) Initial recording. (**b**) Mathematical solution to the trend problem. (**c**) Preliminary solution to the trend problem. (**d**) Mathematical solution to the trend problem (fragment). (**e**) Preliminary solution to the trend problem (fragment).

The stability and adequacy of the solution to the trend problem made it possible to answer the second and third questions relatively simply, i.e., construct final (currently) versions of trend sections $\tau r(p)$ of record f at scale p.

This does not always happen. The traditional solution to the trend problem based on smoothing, for example, polynomial, uses a standard mathematical understanding of trends: trends in a record are considered to be mathematical trends in its smoothing. In this solution, the problem of small dynamics remains: on the one hand, smoothing must sufficiently scan the record, on the other hand, the stochastic nature of the record leads to the appearance of small dynamics in the smoothing (short segments of increase/decrease), which a mathematical understanding of the trend in smoothing will highlight as separate trends on the recording.

Let us turn to Figure 10: the classic solution to trends for recording f based on smoothing f_δ is shown in Figure 10b, and the solution currently proposed by the authors is in Figure 10c. Selected fragment in Figure 10d,e illustrates the above and shows a greater stability of the $Tr_\delta f$ solution compared to the classical one. The solution $Tr_\delta f$ is also better in comparison with the previous solution of the authors, where the trend was obtained in several stages and for this, it was necessary to solve the difficult problem of combining fragments of the f record into a single trend.

However, the solution $Tr_p f$, despite all the advantages mentioned above, has some inaccuracy that does not allow it to be considered the final solution to the trend problem (Figure 11). To do this, we need a measure of extremity that eliminates the inaccuracy in the solution $Tr_p f$ and adds stability and adequacy to it.

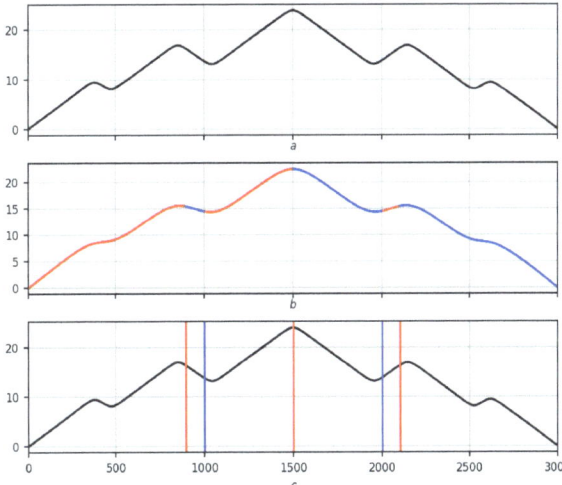

Figure 11. Partition inaccuracy $Tr_p f$. (**a**) Original record. (**b**) Preliminarily solving the trend problem on a scale $p = 12$. (**c**) Extrema partition $Tr_{12} f$ (highs are red, lows are blue, black is the original record).

4. Extremum Measure: The Final Solution to the Trend Problem

In the trend problem, there is one last question about extrema. Of course, the first answer to this question is similar to the classical one: extrema are the boundaries between opposite trends in $Tr_\delta f$. On this path, the problem of their existence arises: as noted above, there are few or no neutral nodes from $Tr_\delta^0 f$ (namely, the extrema should lie within them) due to the stochasticity of f and discreteness of T. The second option, the most natural of the nonempty ones, is as follows: if the positive trend τr^+ is replaced by a negative τr^-, then the maximum should be considered the choice from the end $e(\tau r^+)$ and the beginning $b(\tau r^-)$, where the entry f is maximum, and, conversely, if the negative trend

τr^- is replaced by a positive τr^+, then the minimum should be considered the choice from the end $e(\tau r^-)$ and the beginning $b(\tau r^+)$, where the entry f is minimal.

But even after this, some problems remain: the global nature of the trend measure $\tau r_\delta f$ makes the partition $Tr_\delta f$ stable and quite satisfactory (at least in the case $\delta = \delta(r, p)$) on the one hand, and on the other hand, it entails some inaccuracy.

We construct a fuzzy extremum measure $ex_\delta f$, similar to the trend measure $\tau r_\delta f$: the value $ex_\delta f$ in the fuzzy scale of the segment $[0, 1]$ expresses the degree of confidence of the researcher (the measure of their basis) to consider node t the maximum for the function f. Together, the measures $\tau r_\delta f$ and $ex_\delta f$ solve the problem of trends: they finally determine the trends and extrema of the record f.

The construction of the measure $ex_\delta f$ begins in the same way as the measure $\tau r_\delta f$: the researcher gives the elementary dynamics $f'_\delta(\bar{t})$ at node $\bar{t}$ the weight $\delta_t(\bar{t})|f'_\delta(\bar{t})|$. If node $\bar{t}$ lies to the left of t ($\bar{t} < t$), then the weight $\delta_t(\bar{t})|f'_\delta(\bar{t})|$ speaks in favor of a maximum at t for f with $f'_\delta(\bar{t}) > 0$ (climbing an imaginary mountain with a peak at t), and against, all $\delta_t(\bar{t})|f'_\delta(\bar{t})|$ with $f'_\delta(\bar{t}) < 0$. To the right of t ($\bar{t} > t$), everything is the other way around: the weights $\delta_t(\bar{t})|f'_\delta(\bar{t})|$ with $f'_\delta(\bar{t}) < 0$ (descent from an imaginary mountain with a top at t), and against, all $\delta_t(\bar{t})|f'_\delta(\bar{t})|$ with $f'_\delta(\bar{t}) > 0$. The measure of the extremum $ex_\delta f$ is considered the sum of the pros to the total sum of weights:

$$ex_\delta f = \frac{\left(\sum_{\bar{t}<t} \delta_t(\bar{t})f'_\delta(\bar{t}) : f'_\delta(\bar{t}) > 0\right) - \left(\sum_{\bar{t}>t} \delta_t(\bar{t})f'_\delta(\bar{t}) : f'_\delta(\bar{t}) < 0\right)}{\sum \delta_t(\bar{t})|f'_\delta(\bar{t})| : \bar{t} \neq t}. \tag{6}$$

By analogy with the partition $Tr_\delta f$, we introduce and denote by $Ex_\delta f$ the partition by alternating segments ex^+ (ex^-) obtained by switching $ex_\delta f \lessgtr 1/2$: $ex^+ \leftrightarrow ex_\delta f \geq 1/2$, $ex^- \leftrightarrow ex_\delta f \leq 1/2$ (Figures 12–16). $Ex(t)$ denotes the segment of this partition containing node t.

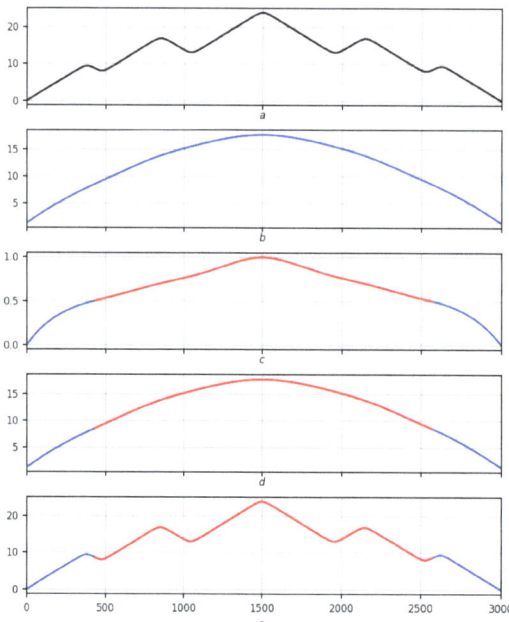

Figure 12. Partition of $Ex_p f$ on a smooth record on a scale $p = 1$. Red lines are positive trends, blue lines are negative ones. (**a**) Original record f. (**b**) Regression smoothing f_1. (**c**) Measure of extremum $ex_1 f$ with red–blue partition $Ex_1 f$. (**d**) Partition of $ex_1 f$ on smoothing f_1. (**e**) Partition of $Ex_1 f$ into records f.

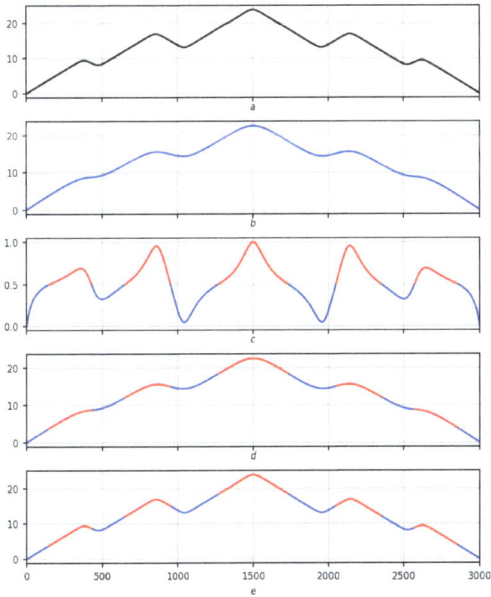

Figure 13. Partition of $Ex_p f$ on a smooth record on a scale $p = 12$. Red lines are positive trends, blue lines are negative ones. (**a**) Original record f. (**b**) Regression smoothing f_{12}. (**c**) Measure of extremum $ex_{12}f$ with red–blue partition $Ex_{12}f$. (**d**) Partition of $ex_{12}f$ on smoothing f_{12}. (**e**) Partition of $Ex_{12}f$ into records f.

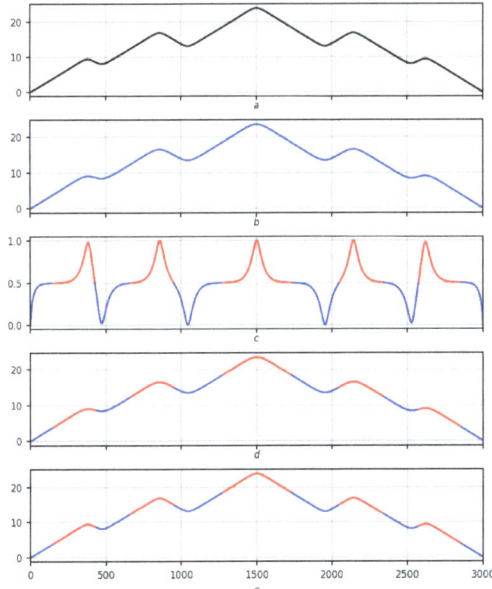

Figure 14. Partition of $Ex_p f$ on a smooth record on a scale $p = 35$. Red lines are positive trends, blue lines are negative ones. (**a**) Original record f. (**b**) Regression smoothing f_{35}. (**c**) Measure of extremum $ex_{35}f$ with red–blue partition $Ex_{35}f$. (**d**) Partition of $ex_{35}f$ on smoothing f_{35}. (**e**) Partition of $Ex_{35}f$ into records f.

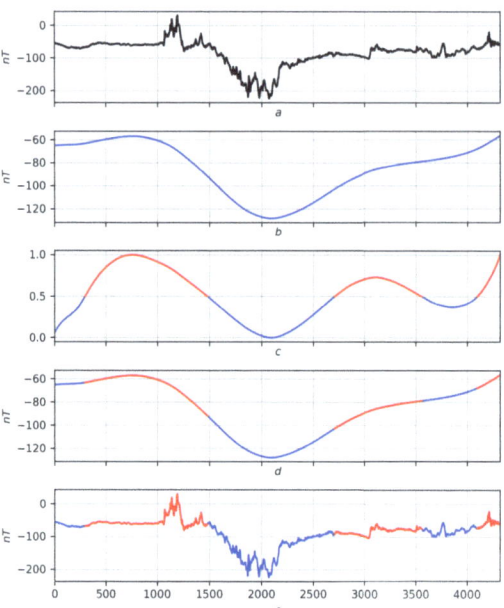

Figure 15. Partition of $Ex_p f$ on a real record on a scale $p = 1$. Red lines are positive trends, blue lines are negative ones. (**a**) Original record f. (**b**) Regression smoothing f_1. (**c**) Measure of extremum $ex_1 f$ with red–blue partition $Ex_1 f$. (**d**) Partition of $ex_1 f$ on smoothing f_1. (**e**) Partition of $Ex_1 f$ into records f.

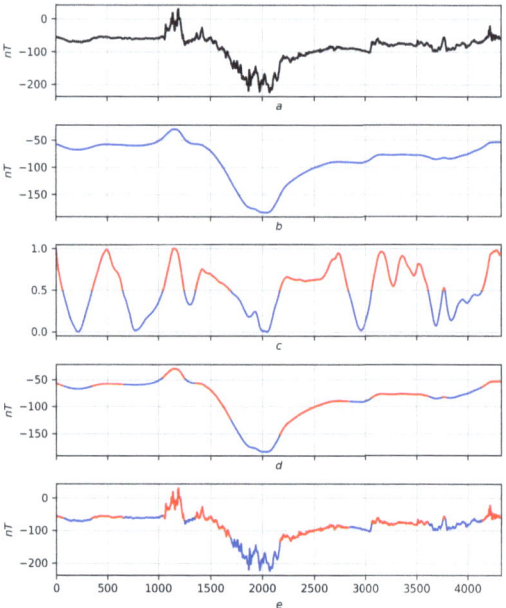

Figure 16. Partition of $Ex_p f$ on a real record on a scale $p = 12$. Red lines are positive trends, blue lines are negative ones. (**a**) Original record f. (**b**) Regression smoothing f_{12}. (**c**) Measure of extremum $ex_{12} f$ with red–blue partition $Ex_{12} f$. (**d**) Partition of $ex_{12} f$ on smoothing f_{12}. (**e**) Partition of $Ex_{12} f$ into records f.

The scheme for displaying the partition $Ex_\delta f$ is exactly the same as for the partition $Tr_\delta f$: record $f \to$ smoothing $f_\delta \to$ extremum measure $ex_\delta f$ with the partition $Ex_\delta f$ applied to it $\to$ partition $Ex_\delta f$ on smoothing $f_\delta \to$ partition $Ex_\delta f$ on records f. Taking into account the notations $ex_{\delta(p,r)} \leftrightarrow ex_p$ and $Ex_{\delta(p,r)} \leftrightarrow Ex_p$, in Figures 12–14, the full scenario $Ex_p f$ is shown for a smooth function on three scales $p = 1, 12, 35$, and in Figures 15 and 16, for a real recording on a scale $p = 1, 12$.

Let e^+ be the version of the maximum obtained above based on $\tau r_\delta f$. Let us say that it allows a correction if $ex_\delta f(e^+) > 1/2$, and the correction itself consists in the transition of e^+ to the nearest maximum of the measure $ex_\delta f$ on the segment $Ex(e^+)$. Similarly, if e^- is a version of the minimum obtained above on the basis of $\tau r_\delta f$, then it allows a correction if $ex_\delta f(e^-) < 1/2$, and the correction itself consists in the transition of e^- to the nearest minimum of the measure $ex_\delta f$ on the segment $Ex(e^-)$. Extrema based on the measure $\tau r_\delta f$ that do not allow corrections are preserved. This can happen in two situations.

- First, the extremum e is already in the correct position $\leftrightarrow$ no correction is needed (it is zero); this happens often, for example, for $\delta = \delta(r, p)$, and confirms the high efficiency of the measure $\tau r_\delta f$, as well as solving the problem of trends $Tr_p f$ on its basis.
- Second, the extremum e is not consistent with the measure $ex_\delta f$: $ex_\delta f(e^+) < 1/2$ or $ex_\delta f(e^-) > 1/2$. This means that the measure $ex_\delta f$ at the extremum e shows the opposite of its essence: the maximum seems to the researcher to lie in the lowlands, and the minimum on the hills.

Let us look at this in more detail, assuming that the maximum e^+ is the extremum. Let $L_\delta^+ f(e^+)$, $L_\delta^- f(e^+)$ be the arguments for (against) the maximum of f in e^+ to the left of it; in notation (5) and (6),

$$L_\delta^+ f(e^+) = \sum_{t \leq e^+} \delta_{e^+}(t) f'_\delta(t) : \quad f'_\delta(t) > 0,$$
$$L_\delta^- f(e^+) = \sum_{t \leq e^+} \delta_{e^+}(t) |f'_\delta(t)| : \quad f'_\delta(t) < 0.$$

Similarly, we define arguments $R_\delta^+ f(e^+)$, $R_\delta^- f(e^+)$ for (against) the maximum of f in e^+ to the right of it:

$$R_\delta^+ f(e^+) = \sum_{t \geq e^+} \delta_{e^+}(t) f'_\delta(t) : \quad f'_\delta(t) > 0,$$
$$R_\delta^- f(e^+) = \sum_{t \geq e^+} \delta_{e^+}(t) |f'_\delta(t)| : \quad f'_\delta(t) < 0.$$

In e^+, there is an equilibrium

$$\tau r_\delta f(e^+) = 1/2 \leftrightarrow L_\delta^+ f(e^+) + R_\delta^- f(e^+) = L_\delta^- f(e^+) + R_\delta^+ f(e^+).$$

It allows us to conclude that one-sided extremalities are equivalent for e^+: e^+ is the left maximum for $f \leftrightarrow L_\delta^+ f(e^+) > L_\delta^- f(e^+) \leftrightarrow R_\delta^+ f(e^+) > R_\delta^- f(e^+) \leftrightarrow e^+$—the maximum on the right for f.

Further, it follows that $L_\delta^+ f(e^+) + R_\delta^+ f(e^+) > L_\delta^- f(e^+) + R_\delta^- f(e^+) \leftrightarrow ex_\delta f(e^+) > 1/2$. Hence, if the maximum e^+ does not allow any correction due to an inconsistency with the measure of extremity ($ex_\delta f(e^+) < 1/2$), then e^+ is not a maximum on any side. It is probably possible to construct an artificial example of this situation; however, the authors have never encountered this on real recordings. They are calm about the possible appearance of this kind of extrema, since they consider them unstable and, with increasing scale p, either disappearing or turning into normal extrema.

- Third, the extremum e can be consistent with the extremum measure $ex_\delta f$ but not unique on the segment $Ex(e)$. In this case, its trace will necessarily be an extremum that does not allow any correction for the second reason.

Let us summarize: the extremes obtained after correction are considered final, and the segments between them are considered the final trends of the f record. Let us retain their previous designations e, τr, $Tr_\delta f$, noting that after correction, they are the result of the joint activity of the measures $\tau r_\delta f$ and $ex_\delta f$ (Figure 17).

The correction of extrema for a smooth recording is shown in Figure 17, and for a real recording, in Figure 18, according to the scheme: recording $f \to$ smoothing $f_\delta \to$ trend measure $\tau r_\delta f$ with preliminary extrema in strokes $\to$ extrema measure $ex_\delta f$ with preliminary extrema in strokes and their continuous correction $\to$ final solution to the trend problem on smoothing $f_\delta \to$ preliminary solution to the trend problem for comparison on smoothing $f_\delta \to$ final solution to the trend problem on record f.

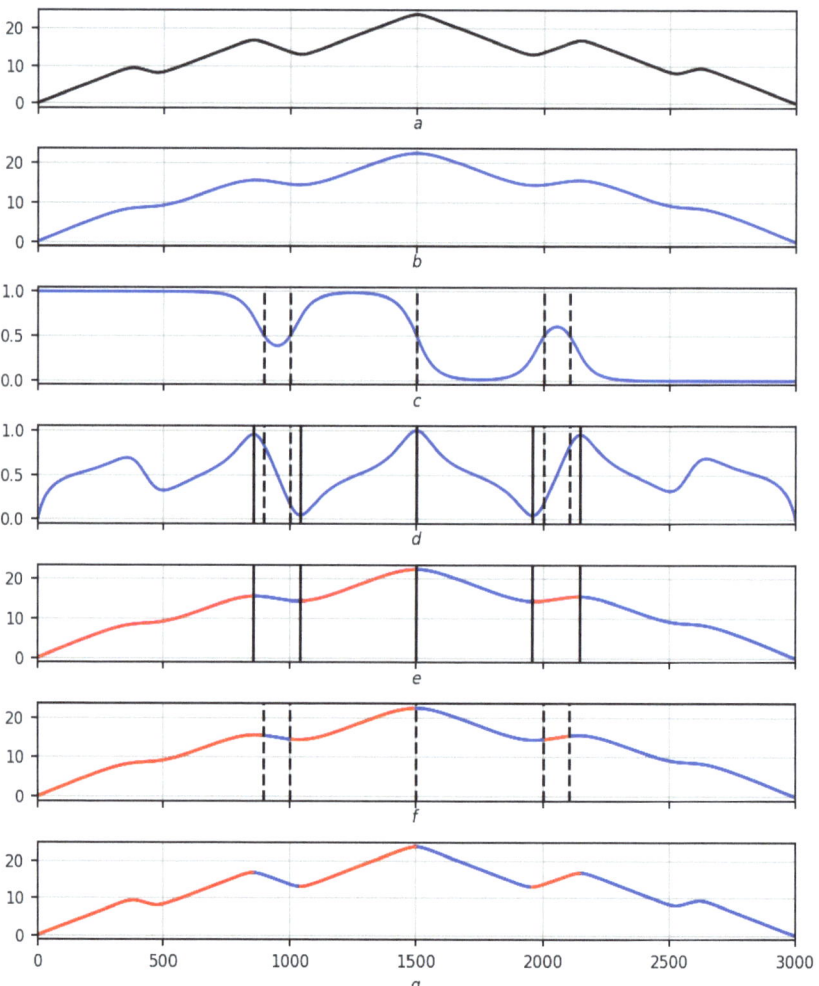

Figure 17. The final solution of trends for a smooth record on a scale $p = 12$. Red lines are positive trends, blue lines are negative ones. (**a**) Original record f. (**b**) Smoothing f_{12}. (**c**) Dashed extrema of a preliminary nature on the trend measure $\tau r_{12} f$. (**d**) Dashed extrema of a preliminary nature on the trend measure $ex_{12} f$ and their solid corrections. (**e**) Final solution of trends using smoothing f_{12}. (**f**) Preliminary solution of trends using smoothing f_{12}. (**g**) Final solution of trends on record f.

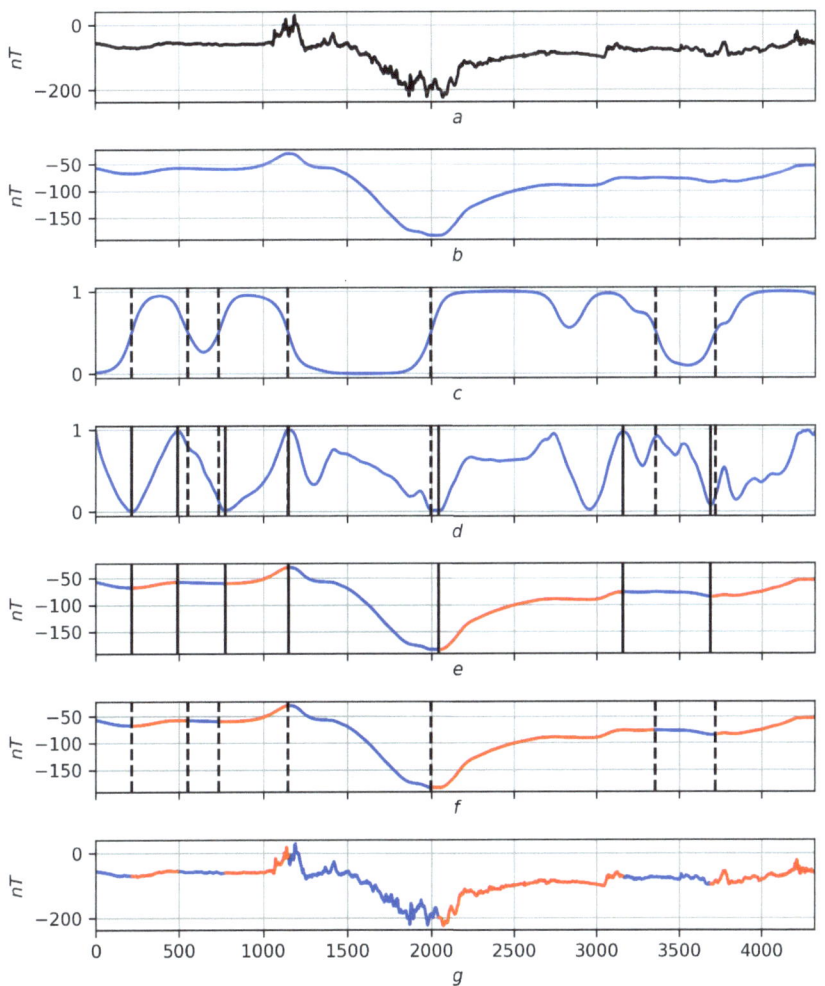

Figure 18. The final solution of trends for a real record on a scale $p = 12$. Red lines are positive trends, blue lines are negative ones. (**a**) Original record f. (**b**) Smoothing f_{12}. (**c**) Dashed extrema of a preliminary nature on the trend measure $\tau r_{12} f$. (**d**) Dashed extrema of a preliminary nature on the trend measure $ex_{12} f$ and their solid corrections. (**e**) Final solution of trends using smoothing f_{12}. (**f**) Preliminary solution of trends using smoothing f_{12}. (**g**) Final solution of trends on record f.

5. Various Scales

As mentioned above, there are two dynamic scenarios for tending to node t from the position of the family $\delta(p, r)$: the first is $r \to 0$ for a fixed p^*, the second is $p \to \infty$ for a fixed r^*. In this article, the authors chose the second path, considering that the behavior of $\delta(p, r^*)$, $p \to \infty$ for a large radius r^* gives a more objective dynamic picture of localization at t, since a large number of nodes $\bar{t}$ take a nontrivial part in it $\bar{t} : |\bar{t} - t| < r^*$ (see Definition 1 and the text after Figure 1).

The stability and adequacy of the solution to the problem of trends $Tr_p f$, the convergence of smoothings f_p to f as $p \to \infty$, established in Appendix A.1, give reason to believe that a simultaneous analysis of partitions $Tr_p f$, measures $\tau r_p f$ and $ex_p f$ for different p's can be useful and allow us to gain knowledge about f at a new level.

The scale parameter p is assumed to be from some discrete uniform segment $P = [p_1, p_M]$; $p = p_i, i = 1, \ldots, M$. The initial scale $p_1 = p_b$ is usually equal to zero, and the final scale p_M plays the role of infinity $p_M = p_\infty$. The choice of P is up to the researcher.

The parametric families $(t, p) \to \tau r_p f(t)$ and $(t, p) \to ex_p f(t)$, like the wavelet spectrum, characterize the trendiness and extremity of f on a two-dimensional grid $P \times T$ at different nodes and scales. Let us use them to determine the hierarchy of extrema on f. The very ability to see the hierarchy of extremes suggests a different scale of the researcher's view of the record. First, one looks at the recording from the greatest height $\leftrightarrow$ at the largest scale. Then, it gradually descends lower, making the viewing scale smaller. Along this path, extrema appear, forming chains. The latter express the migration dependence of the extremum on the scale and generate a hierarchy of extrema: the earlier the chains appear, the more significant the corresponding extremum for the record f.

What was said above according to the scheme "record $f \to$ different-scale partitioning $Tr_p f \to$ migration of extrema to $Tr_p f \to$ hierarchy of extrema on record f" is illustrated for a noisy smooth record in Figure 19, and for a real recording in Figure 20.

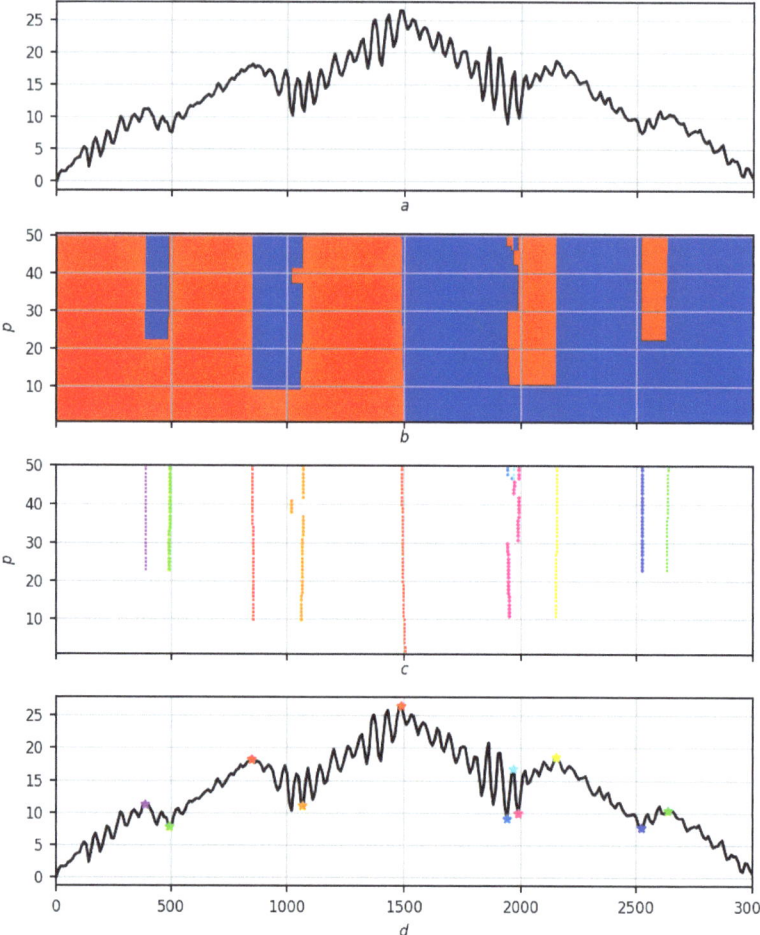

Figure 19. Multiscale solution of the trend problem on a synthetic record. (**a**) Original entry f. (**b**) Partition $Tr_p f$. Red areas are positive trends, blue areas are negative ones. (**c**) Migration of extrema to $Tr_p f$. Different colors correspond to different extrema. (**d**) Hierarchy of extrema on record f. Asterisks in different colors correspond to extrema on a scale $p = 50$.

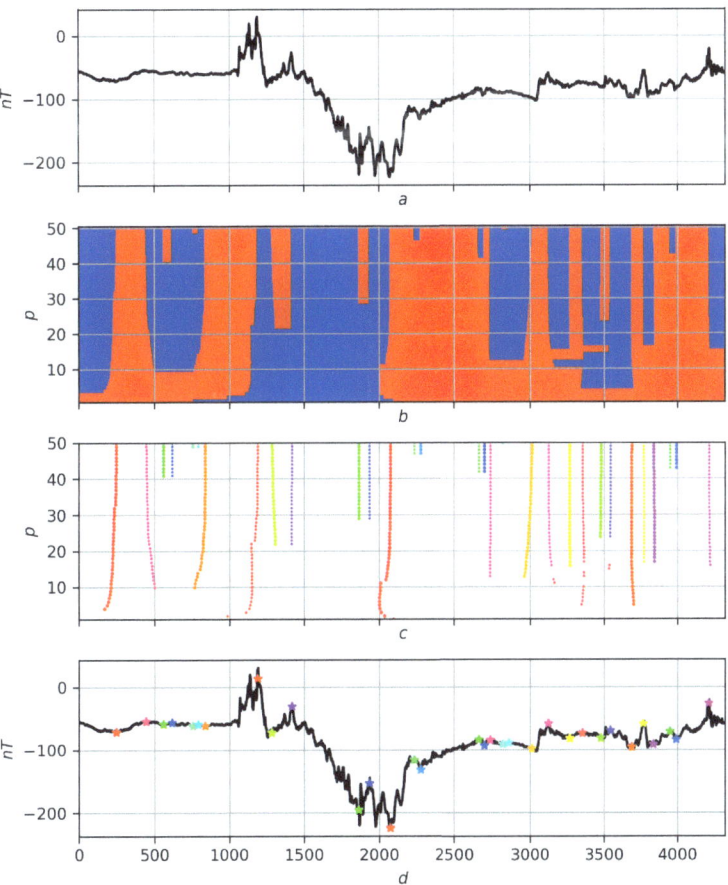

Figure 20. Multiscale solution of the trend problem on a real record. (**a**) Original entry f. (**b**) Partition $Tr_p f$. Red areas are positive trends, blue areas are negative ones. (**c**) Migration of extrema to $Tr_p f$. Different colors correspond to different extrema. (**d**) Hierarchy of extrema on record f. Asterisks in different colors correspond to extrema on a scale $p = 50$.

Definition 5. *Let $Tr_{p+1}(e(p))$ be a segment in the final solution of trends at level $p+1$, which contains the extremum $e(p)$. Let us call the migration $e(p+1)$: $e(p) \to e(p+1)$ the same oriented end of the segment $Tr_{p+1}(e(p))$.*

The maximal chains $CEx = \{e(p) \to e(p+2) \to \cdots \to e(p+k)\}$ are migration scenarios of the extremum $e(p_1)$ on the $P \times T$ grid for record f. For any extremum $e = e(p)$, let $CEx(e)$ denote the chain passing through it. Note that the extremum $e = e(p)$ can be internal in it: $p_1 < p < p_k$.

Definition 6. *The weight $\omega(e)$ of extremum e is the exponent p_1 of the chain $CEx(e)$ containing it.*

Next, we take the last level of the scale p_∞ and all its extrema for f: $Exf(p_\infty)$. Let us order $Exf(p_\infty)$ by weights: $e_i < e_j \leftrightarrow \omega(e_j) < \omega(e_i)$; thus, the most fundamental for f is the extremum with the minimum weight.

The identification of trends using trend and extremum measures is stable, and therefore, a multiscale analysis based on these measures is stable and informative. The algorithm for migrating extrema (constructing their chains) proposed in this work is effective only if the quality of their determination is high. The classical approach to trends based on smoothing, for example, polynomial, and using a standard mathematical understanding of trends, is unstable and is not suitable for such an algorithm: a continuation of a really important extremum at one scale level can become a weak (unreasonable) extremum at the next level, which will lead to a migration (chain) of extrema in the wrong direction. As confirmation of what was said earlier, Figures 21 and 22 present a different-scale solution of trends based on a strict mathematical relationship to them for the same records f and on the same scales p as the solutions $Tr_p f$ in Figures 19 and 20. Omitting the details of their comparison, let us pay attention only to the narrow red wedge in Figure 21 slightly to the right of $t = 1000$. It is associated with the appearance of unreasonable highs of high rank, while in fact, there should be only one significant minimum, and it is this one that is shown in Figure 19d, and the corresponding chain of migrations is shown in yellow in Figure 19c.

Note that replacing $p \to \infty$ by $r \to 0$ and r^* by p^* leads to another dynamic implementation of the above scenario with partitioning $Tr_r f$ by measures $\tau r_r f$ and $ex_r f$.

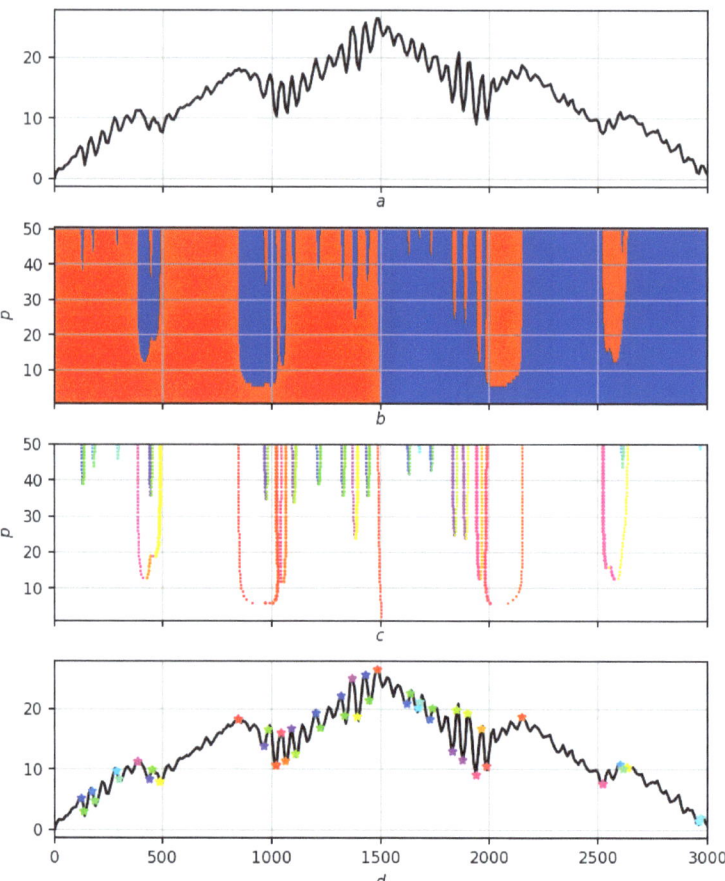

Figure 21. Multiscale rigorous mathematical solution to the problem of trends on a synthetic record. (**a**) Original record f. (**b**) Partition $Tr_p f$. Red areas are positive trends, blue areas are negative ones. (**c**) Migration of extrema to $Tr_p f$. Different colors correspond to different extrema. (**d**) Hierarchy of extrema on record f. Asterisks in different colors correspond to extrema on a scale $p = 50$.

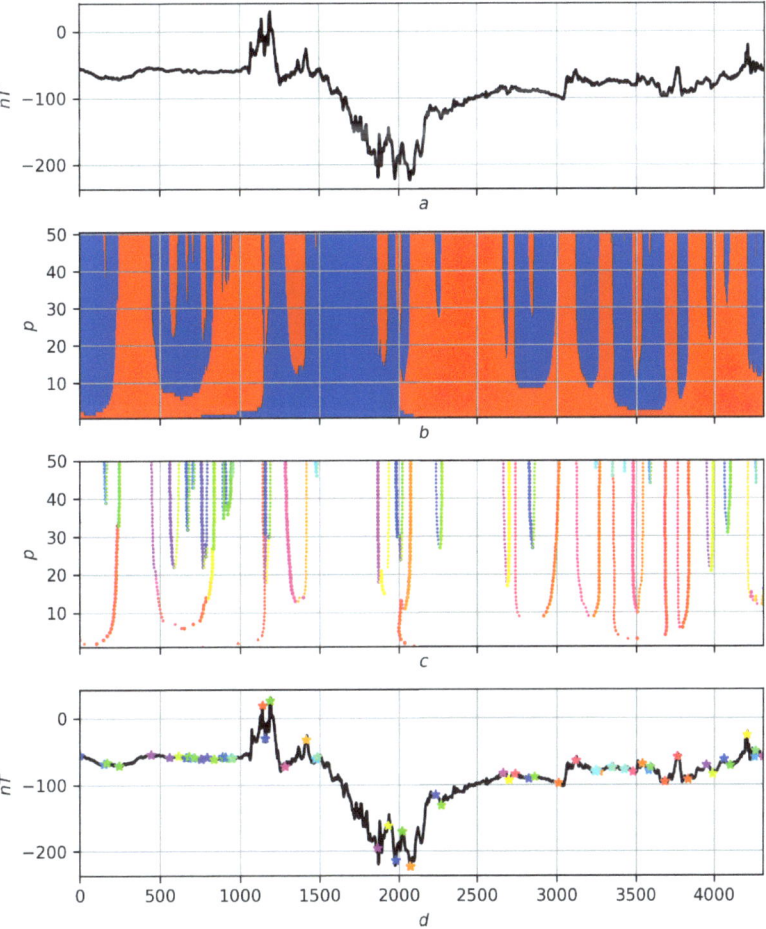

Figure 22. Multiscale rigorous mathematical solution to the problem of trends on a real record. (**a**) Original record f. (**b**) Partition $Tr_p f$. Red areas are positive trends, blue areas are negative ones. (**c**) Migration of extrema to $Tr_p f$. Different colors correspond to different extrema. (**d**) Hierarchy of extrema on record f. Asterisks in different colors correspond to extrema on a scale $p = 50$.

6. Trends and Fuzzy Logic

The measures $tr_\delta f$ and $ex_\delta f$ make it possible to use fuzzy logic in a further study of the record f. The authors plan this in the future, and in this work, we provide two announcements of our research.

- In addition to the measures $tr_\delta f$ and $ex_\delta f$, we take into consideration their fuzzy negations $\neg tr_\delta f$ and $\neg ex_\delta f$. According to (5) and (6), the measures $tr_\delta f$ and $ex_\delta f$ are responsible for the increase and maximum of f; therefore, their negations $\neg tr_\delta f$ and $\neg ex_\delta f$ are responsible for the decrease and minimum of f, respectively. Let us denote their fuzzy disjunction by $\mu_\delta f$:

$$\mu_\delta f(t) = \max\{tr_\delta f(t), \neg tr_\delta f(t), ex_\delta f(t), \neg ex_\delta f(t)\}$$

We display the manifestation of the measure $\mu_\delta f$ on the record f in a color scale (Figure 23):

Cyan ↔ manifestation through an increase: $\mu_\delta f(t) = tr_\delta f$;
Violet ↔ manifestation through a decrease: $\mu_\delta f(t) = \neg tr_\delta f$;
Red ↔ manifestation through a maximum: $\mu_\delta f(t) = ex_\delta f$;
Blue ↔ manifestation through minimality: $\mu_\delta f(t) = \neg ex_\delta f$.

Such an encoding of the record by the measure $\mu_\delta f$, together with the final solution to the problem of trends for f in the form of a partition $Tr_\delta f = \{\tau r\}$, allows us to move further in understanding the behavior of the record through trends.

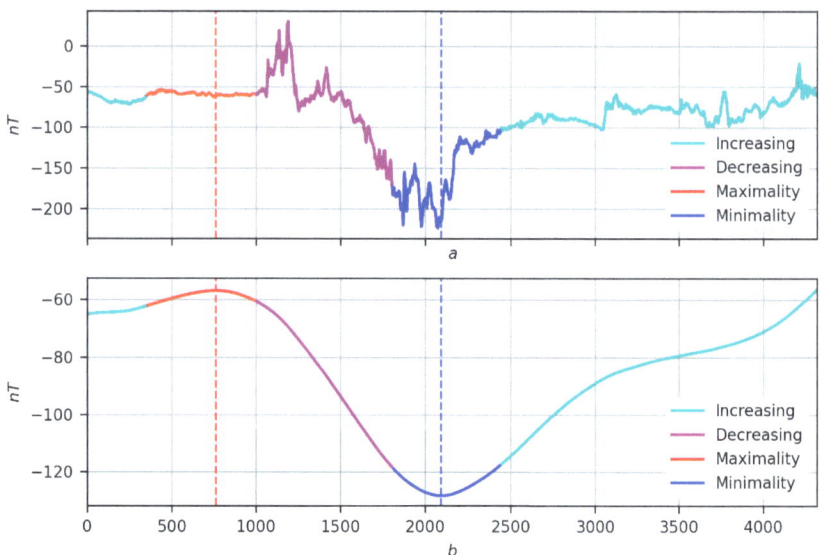

Figure 23. Coding a record by measure $\mu_\delta f$. (**a**) original record f. (**b**) Its smoothing at $p = 1$ with the manifestation of the measure $\mu_\delta f$.

A few first observations: to be specific, the trend is $\tau r = \tau r^+$. In the regular case, the increasing trend τr^+ is a sequential alternation of blue, green and red sections (minimality, growth and maximum). Similarly, a decreasing trend τr^- will be an alternation of red, lilac and blue sections (maximum, decrease and minimum). The relationships between the parts indicate both the nature of the extrema (trend boundaries) and the trend itself: the relatively larger the central part, the more singular the extrema, and the more pronounced the trend (Figure 24, $p = 5$, increasing trend containing node 3000 and decreasing trend containing node 3500).

In addition, red or blue inclusions may appear in the central phase: they are outliers in the τr^+ trend and indicate its stochastic nature (Figure 25, $p = 10$, increasing trend containing node 3000).

- Considering Boolean logic to be part of fuzzy logic, we present a second direction of further research related to it. It concerns the dynamic correlation of records f and g on T in the form of a fuzzy measure $\text{cor}_\delta(f,g)$. It is constructed similarly to the measures $tr_\delta f$ and $ex_\delta f$: the researcher selects a node t and a point of view δ_t on T, then each joint elementary dynamics $(f'_\delta(\bar{t}), g'_\delta(\bar{t}))$ is assigned weight $\delta_t(\bar{t})|f'_\delta(\bar{t})g'_\delta(\bar{t})|$. The argument for the correlation of f and g at t are all equally oriented elementary dynamics, $\text{sgn}\, f'_\delta(\bar{t}) \cdot \text{sgn}\, g'_\delta(\bar{t}) = 1$, and against, oppositely oriented elementary dynamics, $\text{sgn}\, f'_\delta(\bar{t}) \cdot \text{sgn}\, g'_\delta(\bar{t}) = -1$, with its weights. The correlation measure $\text{cor}_\delta(f,g)(t)$ is considered the ratio of the sums of weights "for" to the total sum of weights

$$\text{cor}_\delta(f,g)(t) = \frac{\sum \left[\delta_t(\bar{t})|f'_\delta(\bar{t})g'_\delta(\bar{t})| : \text{sgn}\, f'_\delta(\bar{t}) \cdot \text{sgn}\, g'_\delta(\bar{t}) = 1\right]}{\sum \left[\delta_t(\bar{t})|f'_\delta(\bar{t})g'_\delta(\bar{t})| : t \in T\right]}.$$

Fuzzy negation $\neg\mathrm{cor}_\delta(f,g)$ is a measure of anticorrelation (multidirectionality) of records f and g. The correlation of functions f (Figure 26a) and g (Figure 26b) for proximity $\delta(p,r)$ on three scales $p = 1, 5, 10$ is shown in Figures 27–29: the areas where $\mathrm{cor}_{\delta(p,r)}(f,g) > 0.5$ (<0.5) are shown on the regression smoothings f_p and g_p in red and blue, respectively.

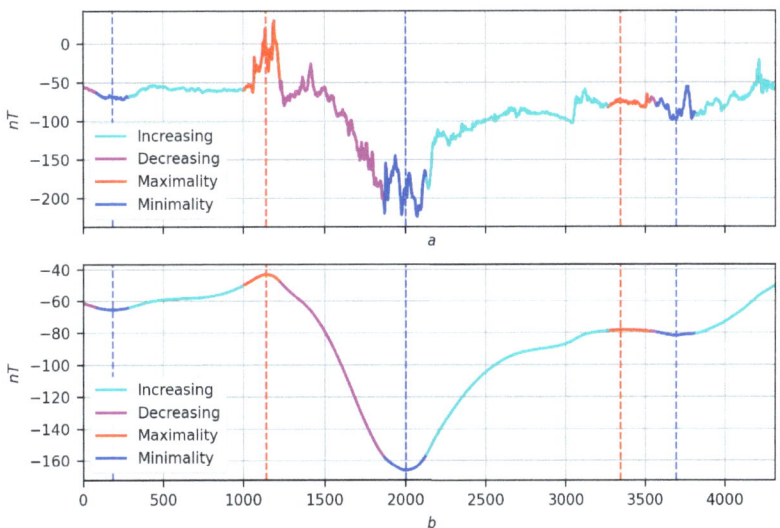

Figure 24. Coding a record by measure $\mu_\delta f$: (**a**) original record f; (**b**) its smoothing at $p = 5$ with the manifestation of the measure $\mu_\delta f$.

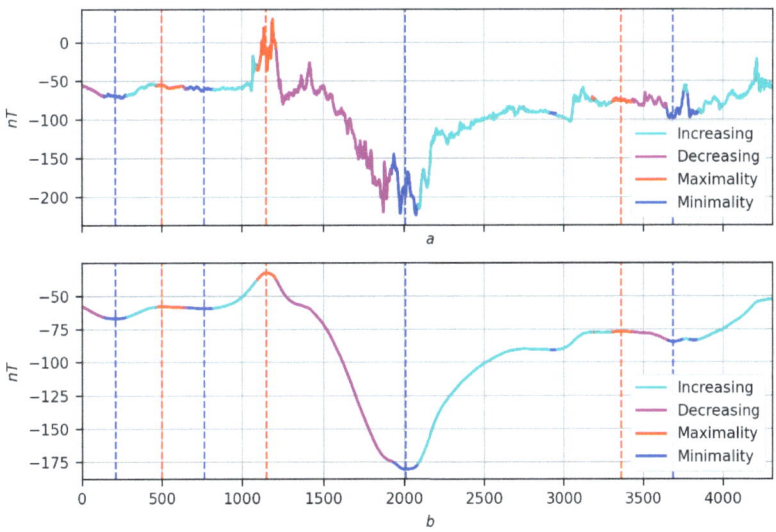

Figure 25. Coding a record by measure $\mu_\delta f$: (**a**) original record f; (**b**) its smoothing at $p = 10$ with the manifestation of the measure $\mu_\delta f$.

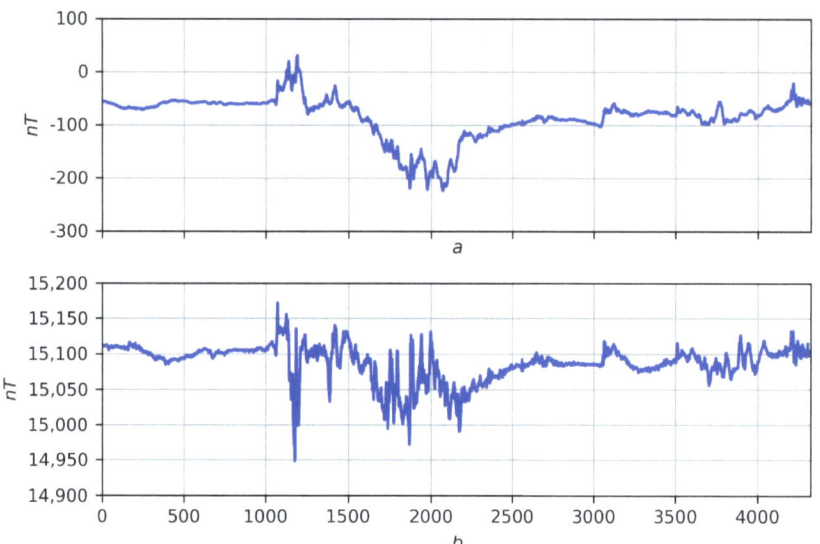

Figure 26. (**a**) Record f. (**b**) Record g.

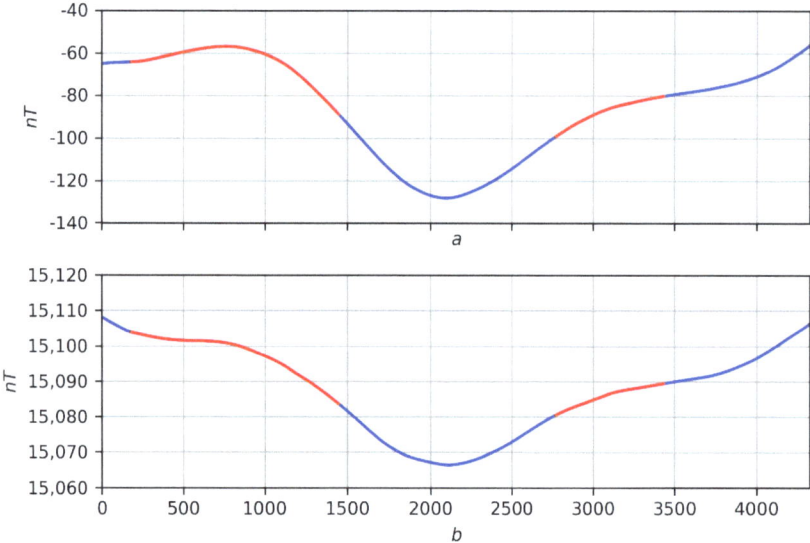

Figure 27. Smoothing functions f and g at $p = 1$ with selected areas' correlations (red is where functions correlate). (**a**) f_1. (**b**) g_1.

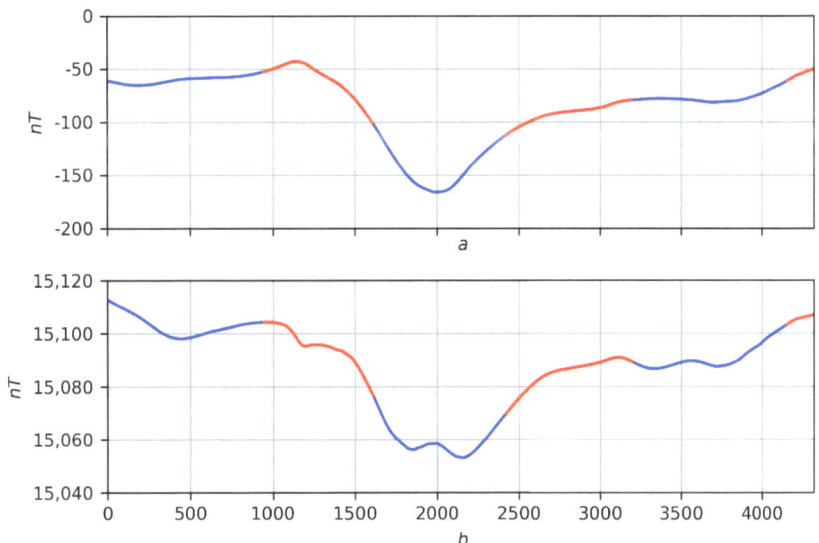

Figure 28. Smoothing functions f and g at $p = 5$ with selected areas' correlations (red is where functions correlate). (**a**) f_5. (**b**) g_5.

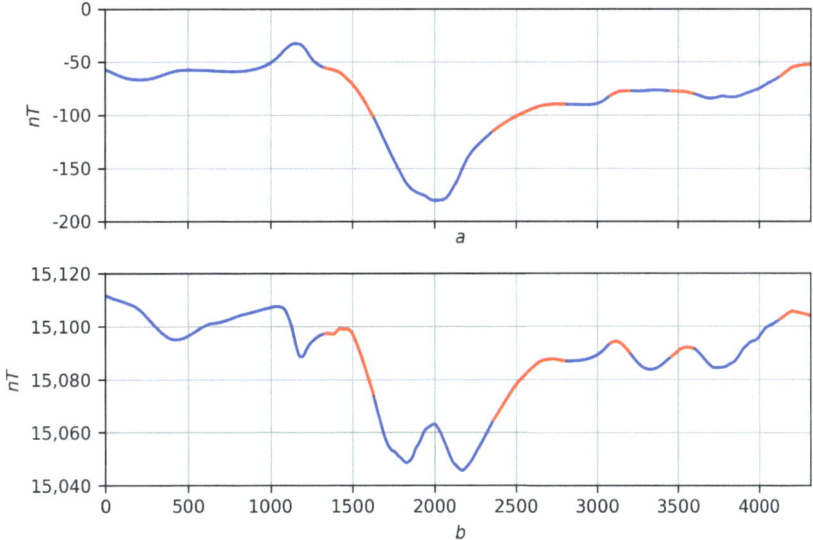

Figure 29. Smoothing functions f and g at $p = 10$ with selected areas' correlations (red is where functions correlate). (**a**) f_{10}. (**b**) g_{10}.

7. Conclusions

In classical mathematical analysis, the concept of locality is based on a passage to the limit and thus has an infinitesimal character. For this reason, solving the problem of finding trends for piecewise smooth functions is reduced to determining segments of constant sign of the derivative.

In a discrete case, within the framework of DMA, a comparative, fuzzy, multiscale perception of locality is natural and important. It is this perception of locality that is important for analyzing discrete data and understanding the dynamics of the processes that these data express.

Solving the problem of determining trends in discrete time series provides only a preliminary fragmentation of the process. Without identifying the relationship between trends, a deep understanding of the dynamics of the process, which is obtained by constructing a hierarchy of trends and extremes, is impossible.

The theoretical justification of the regression approach to differentiation presented in the work allows, firstly, to give an answer to the question: "What is discrete differentiation", and secondly, outlines a path for solving the problem of trends at different scales within the framework of the classical approach. It consists in transferring to the continuous case the discrete solution of the trend problem proposed in this work based on measures of trend and extremum by replacing the sum in constructions (5) and (6) with an integral. The efficiency of the discrete solution allows us to hope for success in the continuous case.

About future plans for our research announced in Section 6, we add the following

- A comparative analysis of the solution to the trend problem $Tr_p f$ based on the scale parameter p at a fixed viewing radius r^* with the solution to the trend problem $Tr_r f$ based on the viewing radius r at a fixed scale parameter p^*.
- The trend measures $\tau r_p f$ and $\tau r_p \bar{f}$ are very convenient for comparing records f and $\bar{f}$ on scales p and $\bar{p}$: such a comparison $\text{cor}_{(p,\bar{p})}(f,\bar{f})$ can be any functional distance between fuzzy measures $\tau r_p f$ and $\tau r_p \bar{f}$ on the general domain of their definition T. The fuzzy weight $\sigma(p,\bar{p})$ of the comparison depends on the researcher. The general conclusion for the set $\{f, \bar{f}, \sigma(p, \bar{p}), p \in P, \bar{p} \in \bar{P}\}$ will give a final comparison of a new type $\text{cor}(f, \bar{f})$ between records f and $\bar{f}$, which is a measure of similarity that can serve as the basis for clustering on records.
- The last direction of further research by the authors, similar to the study of wavelet spectra, is related to the migration of extrema [18,32,33]. It involves two stages: the construction of chains of migration of extrema and their subsequent multifractal analysis (Gibbs sums, scaling exponent, Hölder index). The stage of constructing chains of migration of extremes is described in the proposed article.

In conclusion, we note the following. Regression motives in the analysis of discrete series are present, in particular, in the form of F-transformations (more precisely, f^1-transformations for differentiating a series). Following Zadeh's principle of incompatibility, they are focused on data analysis for the purpose of decision making. Thus, F-transformations during localization do not deal with the entire family of proximity measures $\{\delta_t, t \in T\}$ but only with a certain sample $\{\delta_{t_k}, t_k \in T, k = 1, \ldots, K\}$, where $k \ll |T|$ to effectively simplify calculations [34].

Author Contributions: Conceptualization and original draft preparation, S.A. and D.K.; conceptualization, methodology, review and editing and validation, S.B. and B.D.; material preparation, formal analysis, data curation and algorithm development, S.B. and M.D. All authors contributed to the study conception and design. All authors have read and agreed to the published version of the manuscript.

Funding: This work was conducted in the framework of budgetary funding of the Geophysical Center of RAS, adopted by the Ministry of Science and Higher Education of the Russian Federation (grant number 075-01349-23-00).

Data Availability Statement: No new data were created or analyzed in this study. Data sharing is not applicable to this article.

Conflicts of Interest: The authors declare no conflicts of interest.

Appendix A

Appendix A.1

For the proximity measure δ on T and its nodes $t_i, t_j; i,j = 1,\ldots,N$, by $a_{ij} = a_{ij}(\delta)$, we denote the fraction $\delta_{t_i}(t_j)\left(\sum_{j=1}^{N}\delta_{t_i}(t_j)\right)^{-1}$. For each i, the set $\left\{a_{ij}|_{j=1}^{N}\right\}$ is a probability distribution on T: $\sum_{j=1}^{N}a_{ij} = 1$.

Let us denote by $M_i(x)$ the functional of the mathematical expectation relative to this distribution on $F(T)$: $M_i(x) = \sum_{j=1}^{N}a_{ij}x_j$, $x \in F(T)$ and use it to express the regression value $f_\delta(t_i)$:

$$f_\delta(t_i) = M_i(f) - \frac{M_i(t) - t_i}{M_i(t^2) - M_i(t)^2}(M_i(tf) - M_i(t)M_i(f)), \tag{A1}$$

where tf is the series $(t_1 f_1,\ldots,t_N f_N)$, and t^2 is the series $(t_1^2,\ldots,t_N^2)$.

We are interested in the convergence of $f_{\delta^p}(t_i) \to f(t_i)$ as $p \to \infty$. To achieve this, we require the measure δ to satisfy two conditions: symmetry $\delta_{t_i}(t_j) = \delta_{t_j}(t_i)$ and nontrivial strict monotonicity

$$\left(|t_j - t_i| < |t_{\bar{j}} - t_i|\right) \wedge \left(\delta_{t_i}(t_j)\delta_{t_i}(t_{\bar{j}}) \neq 0\right) \to \delta_{t_i}(t_{\bar{j}}) < \delta_{t_i}(t_j).$$

Let us put $a_{ij}(\delta^p) = a_{ij}(p)$. Then, $\lim_{p\to\infty}a_{ii}(p) = 1$, and for $i \neq j$, $\lim_{p\to\infty}a_{ij}(p) = 0$. Let us consider node t_i internal in T: $i > 1$; then, due to the conditions on δ, in the distribution $\left\{a_{ij}(p)|_{j=1}^{N}\right\}$, for any $p \geq 0$, there are three main actors: a_{ii} and $a_{i\,i+1} = a_{i+1\,i}$, which we denote by $a_i(p)$.

Let us reveal the uncertainty of the relation $(M_i(t) - t_i)(M_i(t^2) - M_i(t)^2)^{-1}$ in (A1) by expanding the numerator and denominator modulo $a_i(p)$:

$$1 - a_{ii} = 2a_i + o(a_i),$$
$$M_i(t) = a_{ii}t_i + a_i(t_{i-1} + t_{i+1}) + o(a_i) = t_i(a_{ii} + 2a_i) + o(a_i),$$
$$M_i(t)^2 = t_i^2(a_{ii} + 2a_i)^2 + o(a_i) = t_i^2(a_{ii}^2 + 4a_{ii}a_i + 4a_i^2) + o(a_i),$$
$$M_i(t^2) = a_{ii}t_i^2 + a_i(t_{i-1}^2 + t_{i+1}^2) + o(a_i) = t_i^2 + a_i(2t_i^2 + 2h^2) + o(a_i).$$

Numerator:

$$\begin{aligned}M_i(t) - t_i &= t_i(a_{ii} + 2a_i) - t_i + o(a_i) = \\ &= t_i(a_{ii} - 1) + 2a_i t_i + o(a_i) = -2a_i t_i + 2a_i t_i + o(a_i) = o(a_i).\end{aligned}$$

Denominator:

$$\begin{aligned}M_i(t^2) - M_i(t)^2 &= t_i^2 + a_i(2t_i^2 + 2h^2) - t_i^2(a_{ii}^2 + 4a_{ii}a_i + 4a_i^2) + o(a_i) = \\ &= a_{ii}(1 - a_{ii})t_i^2 - 4a_{ii}a_i t_i^2 + 2a_i t_i^2 - 4a_i^2 t_i^2 + 2h^2 a_i + o(a_i) = \\ &= 2a_i(1 - a_{ii})t_i^2 - 4a_{ii}a_i t_i^2 + 2h^2 a_i + o(a_i) = \\ &= 4a_{ii}a_i t_i^2 - 4a_{ii}a_i t_i^2 + 2h^2 a_i + o(a_i) = 2h^2 a_i + o(a_i).\end{aligned}$$

Thus, as $p \to \infty$, the fraction $(M_i(t) - t_i)(M_i(t^2) - M_i(t)^2)^{-1}$ tends to zero, and the regression values $f_{\delta^p}(t_i)$ tends to $f(t_i)$.

Appendix A.2

The regression approach to derivatives continues into higher dimensions.

Let $f(x)$ be a function on the segment $[-1, 1]$ having on it continuous derivatives $f^i(x)$, $i = 1, \ldots, n + 1$ up to and including order $n + 1$. Under these assumptions, the McLaren decomposition of nth order takes place for $f(x)$:

$$f(x) = f(0) + \frac{f'(0)}{1!}x + \cdots + \frac{f^{(n)}(0)}{n!}x^n + r_n(x), \qquad (A2)$$

where $r_n(x)$ is the remainder term in Lagrange form

$$r_n(x) = \frac{f^{(n+1)}(\theta(x))}{(n+1)!}x^{n+1}, \ \theta(x) \in [0, x].$$

Let us denote by $T_n f(x)$ the Taylor polynomial for $f(x)$ [31,35–38], so that

$$\begin{array}{c} f(x) = T_n f(x) + r_n(x), \ r_n(x) = c(x)x^{(n+1)} \\ \text{and } |c(x)| < M \text{ evenly on } [-1, 1] \end{array}. \qquad (A3)$$

We fix $\Delta \in (0, 1)$. Let us denote by $\mathrm{pr}_n f_\Delta$ the projection of the restriction $f|_{[-\Delta,\Delta]}$ onto the $(n+1)$th subspace $\mathcal{P}_n[-\Delta, \Delta]$ of polynomials of degree $\leq n$ in the space $L^2[-\Delta, \Delta]$: $\mathrm{pr}_n f_\Delta = \sum_{j=0}^n b_j(f, \Delta) x^j$ is nth order quadratic regression of f on $[-\Delta, \Delta]$.

Statement A1. $\lim_{\Delta \to 0} b_j(f, \Delta) = \frac{f^{(j)}(0)}{j!}, \ j = 0, \ldots, n$.

The proof follows from the tendency to zero as $\Delta \to 0$ of the regression $\mathrm{pr}_n(r_n)_\Delta \leftrightarrow a_0^*(\Delta) + a_1^*(\Delta)x + \cdots + a_n^*(\Delta)x^n$.

For simplicity of presentation, let us temporarily omit the dependence on Δ in the coefficients of the polynomials, setting $a_i = a_i(\Delta)$. The regression functional $\mathcal{P}(a_0, \ldots, a_n)$ is the distance from $r_n(x)$ to the polynomial $P(x) = a_0 + a_1 x + \cdots + a_n x^n$ in the space $L^2[-\Delta, \Delta]$:

$$\mathcal{P}(a_0, \ldots, a_n) = \int_{-\Delta}^{\Delta} (a_0 + a_1 x + \cdots + a_n x^n - r_n(x))^2 dx$$

and the set $a_0^*, \ldots, a_n^*$ gives its minimum.

The following equations arise

$$\begin{array}{c} \frac{\partial \mathcal{P}}{\partial a_i} = 0 \leftrightarrow \int_{-\Delta}^{\Delta} x^i (a_0 + a_1 x + \cdots + a_n x^n - r_n(x)) = 0 \leftrightarrow \\ \sum_{j=0}^n \left(\int_{-\Delta}^{\Delta} x^{i+j} dx \right) a_j^* = \int_{-\Delta}^{\Delta} x^i r_n(x) dx; \quad i = 0, \ldots, n \end{array} \qquad (A4)$$

and the integral

$$\int_{-\Delta}^{\Delta} x^{i+j} dx = \begin{cases} \frac{2}{i+j+1} \Delta^{i+j+1} & \text{even} \\ 0 & \text{, if } i+j \text{ odd} \end{cases}.$$

Therefore, the matrix $M = M(\Delta)$ of system (A4) has the form

$$M = \begin{Vmatrix} 2\Delta & 0 & \frac{2}{3}\Delta^3 & 0 & \frac{2}{5}\Delta^5 & \ldots & \ldots & \ldots \\ 0 & \frac{2}{3}\Delta^3 & 0 & \frac{2}{5}\Delta^5 & \ldots & \ldots & \ldots & \ldots \\ \frac{2}{3}\Delta^3 & 0 & \frac{2}{5}\Delta^5 & \ldots & \ldots & \ldots & \ldots & \ldots \\ 0 & \frac{2}{5}\Delta^5 & \ldots & \ldots & \ldots & \ldots & \ldots & \ldots \\ \frac{2}{5}\Delta^5 & \ldots & \ldots & \ldots & \ldots & \ldots & \ldots & \ldots \\ \ldots & \ldots & \ldots & \ldots & \ldots & \ldots & \ldots & \ldots \\ \ldots & \ldots & \ldots & \ldots & \ldots & \ldots & \ldots & \ldots \end{Vmatrix}. \qquad (A5)$$

A nontrivial contribution to the determinant of det M is made only by even strategies $\sigma = (j, \sigma(j))$, going along M from left to right: strategy σ is even $\leftrightarrow$ the sum $j + \sigma(j)$ is even in j.

If σ is an even strategy, then the product $\Pi(\sigma)$ of its corresponding matrix elements satisfies the equality

$$\Pi(\sigma) = \Pi_{j=0}^{n} \frac{2\Delta^{j+\sigma(j)+1}}{j + \sigma(j) + 1} = 2^{n+1} K(\sigma) \Delta^{(n+1)^2},$$

where $K(\sigma) = \Pi_{j=0}^{n}(j + \sigma(j) + 1)^{-1}$.

Because of

$$\sum_{j=0}^{n} j = \sum_{j=0}^{n} \sigma(j) = \frac{n(n+1)}{2},$$

then

$$\sum_{j=0}^{n}(j + \sigma(j) + 1) = \sum_{j=0}^{n} j + \sum_{j=0}^{n} \sigma(j) + \sum_{j=0}^{n} 1 = \frac{2n(n+1)}{2} + n + 1 = (n+1)^2.$$

Thus,

$$\det M = \det M(\Delta) = \left(\sum (-1)^{\operatorname{sgn}\sigma} K(\sigma)\right) 2^{n+1} \Delta^{(n+1)^2}, \tag{A6}$$

where σ are even strategies and sgn σ is the signature of the permutation σ.

The alternative sum K in (A6) is necessarily nontrivial. This is a consequence of Euclidean geometry and linear algebra: the projection $r_n(x)$ in the space $L^2[-\Delta, \Delta]$ onto any of its subspaces always exists and is unique, which, in turn, is equivalent to the nontriviality of $\det M(\Delta)$. Thus, the order of smallness of the determinant $\det M(\Delta)$ as $\Delta \to 0$ is equal to $(n+1)^2$.

The next step is to analyze the determinants $\det M_{j^*}$ of the auxiliary matrices M_{j^*} of system (A4), obtained from the main M by replacing the j^*th column with a column of free terms:

$$M_{j^*} = M_{j^*}(\Delta) = \begin{Vmatrix} 2\Delta & 0 & \frac{2}{3}\Delta^3 & 0 & \frac{2}{5}\Delta^5 & \ldots & \int_{-\Delta}^{\Delta} r_n(x)dx & \ldots \\ 0 & \frac{2}{3}\Delta^3 & 0 & \frac{2}{5}\Delta^5 & \ldots & \ldots & \int_{-\Delta}^{\Delta} x r_n(x)dx & \ldots \\ \frac{2}{3}\Delta^3 & 0 & \frac{2}{5}\Delta^5 & \ldots & \ldots & \ldots & \int_{-\Delta}^{\Delta} x^2 r_n(x)dx & \ldots \\ 0 & \frac{2}{5}\Delta^5 & \ldots & \ldots & \ldots & \ldots & \int_{-\Delta}^{\Delta} x^3 r_n(x)dx & \ldots \\ \frac{2}{5}\Delta^5 & \ldots & \ldots & \ldots & \ldots & \ldots & \int_{-\Delta}^{\Delta} x^4 r_n(x)dx & \ldots \\ \ldots & \ldots & \ldots & \ldots & \ldots & & \ldots & \ldots \\ \ldots & \ldots & \ldots & \ldots & \ldots & & \ldots & \ldots \end{Vmatrix}.$$

A nontrivial contribution to $\det M_{j^*}$ is also made only by even strategies: such σ must necessarily be even for $j \neq j^*$, but always $\sum_{j=0}^{n}(j + \sigma(j)) = n(n+1)$, and therefore, the sum $j^* + \sigma(j^*)$ is also even.

Let σ be any even strategy; then, the product $\Pi(\sigma, j^*)$ associated with it in $\det M_{j^*}$ is equal to

$$\Pi(\sigma, j^*) = 2^n \left(\Pi_{j \neq j^*} \frac{1}{j + \sigma(j) + 1}\right) \Delta^{(n+1)^2 - (j^* + \sigma(j^*) + 1)} \int_{-\Delta}^{\Delta} x^{\sigma(j^*)} r_n(x)dx.$$

According to assumption (A3) on f,

$$\left|\int_{-\Delta}^{\Delta} x^{\sigma(j^*)} r_n(x)dx\right| \leq \int_{-\Delta}^{\Delta} |x|^{\sigma(j^*)} |r_n(x)|dx \leq M \int_{-\Delta}^{\Delta} |x|^{\sigma(j^*) + n + 1} dx \leq \tilde{M} \Delta^{\sigma(j^*) + n + 2};$$

therefore, the product $\Pi(\sigma, j^*)$ is $o\left(\Delta^{(n+1)^2}\right)$, since $n + 1 - j^* > 0$:

$$|\Pi(\sigma, j^*)| \leq \widetilde{\widetilde{M}} \Delta^{(n+1)^2 - (j^* + \sigma(j^*) + 1)} \Delta^{\sigma(j^*) + n + 2} = \widetilde{\widetilde{M}} \Delta^{(n+1)^2 n + 1 - j^*}.$$

The determinant $\det M_j = \det M_j(\Delta)$ is an alternative sum of the products $\Pi(\sigma, j^*)$ and therefore is $o\left(\Delta^{(n+1)^2}\right)$ and also relative to $\det M(\Delta)$. The equality $a_j^* = a_j^*(\Delta) = \det M_j(\Delta)$ $(\det M)^{-1}$ completes the proof.

References

1. Tanaka, H.; Uejima, S.; Asai, K. Linear regression analysis with fuzzy model. *IEEE Trans. Syst. Man Cybern.* **1982**, *12*, 903–907.
2. Kacprzyk, J.; Wilbik, A.; Zadrożny, S. Linguistic summarization of time series by using the choquet integral. In *Lecture Notes in Computer Science*; Springer: Berlin/Heidelberg, Germany, 2007; pp. 284–294.
3. Pedrycz, W.; Smith, M.H. Granular correlation analysis in data mining. In Proceedings of the UZZ-IEEE'99, 1999 IEEE International Fuzzy Systems, Conference Proceedings (Cat. No.99CH36315), Seoul, Republic of Korea, 22–25 August 1999.
4. Batyrshin, I.Z.; Nedosekin, A.O.; Stetsko, A.A. *Fuzzy Hybrid Systems. Theory and Practice*; Fizmatlit: Moscow, Russia, 2007.
5. Yarushkina, N.G. *Fundamentals of the Theory of Fuzzy and Hybrid Systems*; Finance and Statistics: Moscow, Russia, 2004.
6. Kovalev, S.M. Hybrid fuzzy-temporal models of time series in problems of analysis and identification of weakly formalized processes. In *Integrated Models and Soft Computing in Artificial Intelligence, Proceedings of the IVth International Scientific and Practical Conference, Kolomna, Russia, 28–30 May 2007*; Fizmatlit: Moscow, Russia, 2007; Volume 1, pp. 26–41.
7. Yarushkina, N.G.; Yunusov, T.R.; Afanasyeva, T.V. Terminal-server traffic modeling based on fuzzy time series trend analysis. *Softw. Prod. Syst.* **2007**, *4*, 15–19.
8. Shumway, R.H.; Stoffer, D.S. *Time Series Analysis and Its Applications*; Springer International Publishing: Berlin/Heidelberg, Germany, 2017.
9. Brockwell, P.J.; Davis, R.A. *Introduction to Time Series and Forecasting*; Springer International Publishing: Berlin/Heidelberg, Germany, 2016.
10. Brockwell, P.J.; Davis, R.A. *Time Series: Theory and Methods*; Springer: New York, NY, USA, 1987.
11. Hyndman, R.J.; Athanasopoulos, G. *Forecasting: Principles and Practice*; OTexts: Melbourne, Australia, 2018.
12. Agayan, S.M.; Kamaev, D.A.; Bogoutdinov, S.R.; Aleksanyan, A.O.; Dzeranov, B.V. Time series analysis by fuzzy logic methods. *Algorithms* **2023**, *16*, 238. [CrossRef]
13. Montgomery, D.C.; Jennings, C.L.; Kulahci, M. *Introduction to Time Series Analysis and Forecasting*, 2nd ed.; Wiley: Hoboken, NJ, USA, 2015.
14. Cryer, J.D.; Chan, K.-S. *Time Series Analysis*; Springer: New York, NY, USA, 2008.
15. Tsay, R.S. *Analysis of Financial Time Series*; Wiley: Hoboken, NJ, USA, 2005.
16. Greene, W.H. *Econometric Analysis*; Prentice Hall: Hoboken, NJ, USA, 2003.
17. Percival, D.B.; Walden, A.T. *Wavelet Methods for Time Series Analysis*; Cambridge University Press: Cambridge, UK, 2000.
18. Mallat, S. *A Wavelet Tour of Signal Processing*; Elsevier: Amsterdam, The Netherlands, 2009.
19. Yager, R.R. *Fuzzy Sets and Possibility Theory*; Radio and communications; Pergamon Press: Oxford, UK, 1986.
20. Zhu, Q.; Batista, G.; Rakthanmanon, T.; Keogh, E. A novel approximation to dynamic time warping allows anytime clustering of massive time series datasets. In Proceedings of the 2012 SIAM International Conference on Data Mining; Society for Industrial and Applied Mathematics, Anaheim, CA, USA, 26–28 April 2012.
21. Giusti, R.; Batista, G.E. An empirical comparison of dissimilarity measures for time series classification. In Proceedings of the 2013 Brazilian Conference on Intelligent Systems, Fortaleza, Brazil, 19–24 October 2013; IEEE: Piscataway, NJ, USA, 2013.
22. Ding, H.; Trajcevski, G.; Scheuermann, P.; Wang, X.; Keogh, E. Querying and mining of time series data: Experimental comparison of representations and distance measures. *Proc. VLDB Endow.* **2008**, *1*, 1542–1552. [CrossRef]
23. Batyrshin, I.; Herrera-Avelar, R.; Sheremetov, L.; Panova, A. Moving approximation transform and local trend associations in time series data bases. In *Perception-Based Data Mining and Decision Making in Economics and Finance*; Springer: Berlin/Heidelberg, Germany, 2007; pp. 55–83.
24. Almanza, V.; Batyrshin, I. On trend association analysis of time series of atmospheric pollutants and meteorological variables in mexico city metropolitan area. In *Lecture Notes in Computer Science*; Springer: Berlin/Heidelberg, Germany, 2011; pp. 95–102.
25. Agayan, S.M.; Bogoutdinov, S.R.; Dobrovolsky, M.N. Discrete perfect sets and their application in cluster analysis. *Cybern. Syst. Anal.* **2014**, *50*, 176–190. [CrossRef]
26. Agayan, S.; Bogoutdinov, S.; Soloviev, A.; Sidorov, R. The study of time series using the DMA methods and geophysical applications. *Data Sci. J.* **2016**, *15*, 16. [CrossRef]
27. Agayan, S.M.; Bogoutdinov, S.R.; Krasnoperov, R.I. Short introduction into DMA. *Russ. J. Earth Sci.* **2018**, *18*, 1–10. [CrossRef]
28. Agayan, S.M.; Bogoutdinov, S.R.; Krasnoperov, R.I.; Efremova, O.V.; Kamaev, D.A. Fuzzy logic methods in the analysis of tsunami wave dynamics based on sea level data. *Pure Appl. Geophys.* **2022**, *179*, 4053–4062. [CrossRef]

29. Agayan, S.M.; Bogoutdinov, S.R.; Dzeboev, B.A.; Dzeranov, B.V.; Kamaev, D.A.; Osipov, M.O. DPS clustering: New results. *Appl. Sci.* **2022**, *12*, 9335. [CrossRef]
30. Kolmogorov, A.N.; Fomin, S.V. *Elements of Function Theory and Functional Analysis*; Nauka: Moscow, Russia, 1976.
31. Fichtenholtz, G.M. *Differential and Integral Calculus Course*; Nauka: Moscow, Russia, 1969.
32. Muzy, J.F.; Bacry, E.; Arneodo, A. Wavelets and multifractal formalism for singular signals: Application to turbulence data. *Phys. Rev. Lett.* **1991**, *67*, 3515–3518. [CrossRef] [PubMed]
33. Muzy, J.F.; Bacry, E.; Arneodo, A. Multifractal formalism for fractal signals: The structure-function approach versus the wavelet-transform modulus-maxima method. *Phys. Rev. E* **1993**, *47*, 875–884. [CrossRef] [PubMed]
34. Perfilieva, I.; Daňková, M.; Bede, B. Towards a higher degree f-transform. *Fuzzy Sets Syst.* **2011**, *180*, 3–19. [CrossRef]
35. Rudin, U. *Principles of Mathematical Analysis*; McGraw-Hill: New York, NY, USA, 1976.
36. Dieudonne, J. *Foundations of Modern Analysis*; Academic Press, Inc.: Cambridge, MA, USA, 1969.
37. Schwartz, L. *Analysis*; Mir: Moscow, Russia, 1972.
38. Shilov, G.E. *Mathematical Analysis*; GIFML: Moscow, Russia, 1961.

Disclaimer/Publisher's Note: The statements, opinions and data contained in all publications are solely those of the individual author(s) and contributor(s) and not of MDPI and/or the editor(s). MDPI and/or the editor(s) disclaim responsibility for any injury to people or property resulting from any ideas, methods, instructions or products referred to in the content.

Article

A Fuzzy Logic Inference Model for the Evaluation of the Effect of Extrinsic Factors on the Transmission of Infectious Diseases

Antonios Kalampakas [1], Sovan Samanta [2,3,*], Jayanta Bera [4] and Kinkar Chandra Das [4]

1. College of Engineering and Technology, American University of the Middle East, Egaila 54200, Kuwait; antonios.kalampakas@aum.edu.kw
2. Department of Mathematics, Tamralipta Mahavidyalaya, Tamluk 721636, West Bengal, India
3. Research Center of Performance and Productivity Analysis, Istinye University, 34010 Istanbul, Türkiye
4. Department of Mathematics, Sungkyunkwan University, Suwon 16419, Gyeonggi-do, Republic of Korea; jayantabera@g.skku.edu (J.B.); kinkardas2003@gmail.com (K.C.D.)
* Correspondence: ssamantavu@gmail.com

Abstract: COVID-19 is a contagious disease that poses a serious risk to public health worldwide. To reduce its spread, people need to adopt preventive behaviours such as wearing masks, maintaining physical distance, and isolating themselves if they are infected. However, the effectiveness of these measures may depend on various factors that differ across countries. This paper investigates how some factors, namely outsiders' effect, life expectancy, population density, smoker percentage, and temperature, influence the transmission and death rate of COVID-19 in ninety-five top-affected countries. We collect and analyse the data of COVID-19 cases and deaths using statistical tests. We also use fuzzy logic to model the chances of COVID-19 based on the results of the statistical tests. Unlike the conventional uniform weighting of the rule base in fuzzy logic, we propose a novel method to calculate the weights of the rule base according to the significance of the factors. This study aims to provide a comprehensive and comparative analysis of the factors of COVID-19 transmission and death rates among different countries.

Keywords: COVID-19; statistical tests; rule-based weighting; fuzzy logic

MSC: 03B52

1. Introduction

Infectious agents such as COVID-19 are a major threat to global health and security, especially in the context of increasing population mobility, urbanisation, and climate change [1]. However, the transmission and mortality of infectious agents are not uniform across different countries or regions, as they depend on various factors that affect the susceptibility, exposure, and response of human populations and pathogens [2]. Understanding these factors and their interactions can help design effective prevention and control strategies and estimate the infection risk based on a fuzzy logic model [3].

Some of the factors that may influence the transmission and mortality of infectious agents are temperature, population density, life expectancy, smoking index, and outsiders' effect. Temperature can affect the survival and replication of pathogens, as well as the behaviour and immunity of hosts [2]. Population density can reflect the frequency and intensity of contact among individuals, which can facilitate or hinder the spread of infectious agents [1]. Life expectancy can indicate the overall health status and quality of life of a population, which can affect their vulnerability and resilience to infectious agents [4]. The smoking index can measure the prevalence and intensity of tobacco use among a population, which can impair the respiratory and immune systems and increase the risk of chronic diseases that may complicate the infection [5]. Outsiders' effect can measure the exposure to foreign visitors or products that may introduce or disseminate pathogens [1].

Previous studies have explored some of these factors individually or in relation to specific regions or illnesses. For example, Liu et al. [6] talked about how COVID-19 spreads differently depending on the season. They found that the virus spreads more in colder weather. Lian et al. [7] talked about a surprising increase in COVID-19 cases in the summer of 2022, saying it happened because of really hot weather. They found that almost 70% of those cases might not have happened if there were not heat waves. Several studies [8–11] analysed the correlation between temperature and infection rate for COVID-19. Kjerulff et al. [12] examined the association of smoking with the risk of infections in a large cohort of healthy blood donors. Few other studies [13,14] found a positive association between the smoking index and the infection rate or death rate for COVID-19. Hamidi et al. [15] found no significant effect of population density on disease transmission or death rates in 913 cities in the USA. Trias-Llimós & Bilal [4] showed that the COVID-19 pandemic severely impacted life expectancy in Madrid, the most affected region in Spain. In another article, Trias-Llimós et al. [16] estimated the impact of the first wave of the COVID-19 pandemic by estimating both weekly and annual life expectancies in Spain and its 17 regions. Cevik et al. [17] analysed the role of age and comorbidities in COVID-19 death rate. Few other studies on COVID-19 can be found in [18–20]. However, none of these studies considered all the factors we suggest in this paper or applied a fuzzy logic model with weights derived from statistical tests.

Fuzzy logic models can provide a flexible and intuitive way to model and analyse the factors of infectious agent transmission by incorporating linguistic variables, fuzzy sets, fuzzy rules, and fuzzy inference systems [3]. Fuzzy logic models can handle the vagueness and imprecision of these factors and the non-linearity and uncertainty of their relationships by using fuzzy membership functions, fuzzy operators, and fuzzy reasoning [3]. Fuzzy logic models can also incorporate expert knowledge or empirical data to assign different weights or values to the input parameters or output variables and adjust or optimise the model performance [3]. Several studies applied fuzzy logic models to diagnose or predict infectious agents based on various factors or parameters. For example, Dhiman & Sharma [21] introduced a fuzzy logic technique to assess the risk of COVID-19 based on six parameters such as breathing difficulty, atmospheric temperature, body temperature, etc. Şimşek & Yangın [22] created a fuzzy logic system to swiftly detect COVID-19 risks, using three subsystems for common and rare symptoms and personal information. Shatnawi et al. [23] proposed a smart fuzzy inference system to diagnose COVID-19 based on the symptoms that appear in the patient. A few more related topics are referred to in [24–31].

In this paper, we aim to fill this gap by conducting a comprehensive analysis of the factors that influence the transmission and death rates of COVID-19 across 95 top-affected countries. We collect data from multiple sources and perform statistical tests to validate our assumptions. We then calculate the weights of the input parameters for the fuzzy logic model based on the results of the statistical tests. Based on these weights and input parameters, we design a fuzzy inference system (FIS) that can estimate the chance of transmitting COVID-19 in a region/state.

Motivation: This study is motivated by the need to understand the factors that affect the spread and severity of infectious agents, especially COVID-19, which pose a serious threat to global health and security. By applying a fuzzy logic model with weights based on statistical tests, we aim to provide a flexible and intuitive way to analyse the factors of infectious disease transmission and to estimate the infection risk in different settings. This can help design effective prevention and control strategies and contribute to the existing knowledge in the field.

Objective: The objective of this study is to develop and apply a fuzzy logic model that can estimate the transmission and death rates of COVID-19 based on five factors: temperature, population density, life expectancy, smoking index, and outsiders' effect. The model is intended to be generalisable to any country or region, using data from 95 top-affected countries as a sample.

The expected results of this study are

- A fuzzy logic model that can estimate the transmission and death rates of COVID-19 based on five factors: temperature, population density, life expectancy, smoking index, and outsiders' effect.
- A fuzzy inference system (FIS) that can apply the fuzzy logic model to any country or region, using data from 95 top-affected countries as a sample.
- An analysis of the significance and limitations of the fuzzy logic model and the FIS.

This study will help the health authorities to vanish or control the disease by

- Providing a flexible and intuitive way to model and analyse the factors of infectious disease transmission and to estimate the infection risk in different settings.
- Identifying the most influential factors and their interactions that affect the spread and severity of COVID-19.
- Suggesting effective prevention and control strategies based on the estimated transmission and death rates and the implications of the fuzzy logic model.

The rest of the paper is organised as follows. Section 2 describes Data Collection, Processing, and Analysis. Section 3 explains the calculation of input weights for the fuzzy logic model. Section 4 presents the design and implementation of the FIS. Section 5 discourses the results and findings. Section 6 analyses the results. Section 7 concludes the paper and suggests future work.

2. Data Collection, Processing, and Analysis

2.1. Data Collection

We assume that visitor/export–import data, temperature, population density, smoking, and life expectancy are a few factors that may affect the transmission of the disease and also the death rate due to COVID-19. We collected the mentioned data of the top 95 countries as per the numbers of affected cases from https://www.worldometers.info, https://en.wikipedia.org/wiki/Prevalence_of_tobacco_use, and https://www.timeanddate.com/weather/?sort=1&low=c, accessed on 2 July 2020. The collected data are shown in Appendix A.

2.2. Data Processing and Analysis

In this section, we aim to examine the factors that affect the transmission and death rates of COVID-19 across 95 top-affected countries. We used life expectancy, smoking level, population density, and outsiders' effect (tourism and global export indicators) as the independent variables and total cases, total cases per million, death rate, and death rate per million as the dependent variables. We used t-tests to compare the means of the dependent variables between two groups of countries based on the median values of the independent variables. We also used fuzzy logic to model the chance of transmitting COVID-19 based on the weights of the independent variables derived from the statistical results.

2.2.1. Data Processing

We collected the data from various sources, such as the World Health Organisation, the World Bank, and the United Nations. The data were collected as of 30 June 2020. We cleaned the data by removing any missing, duplicate, or erroneous values. We also checked the data for outliers and normality. We sorted the data according to the independent variables in ascending order. We then divided the data into two groups based on the median values of the independent variables. For example, for life expectancy, we divided the data into a low life expectancy group (less than or equal to 76.65 years) and a high life expectancy group (greater than 76.65 years). We performed the same for smoking level, population density, and outsiders' effect.

2.2.2. Data Analysis

We performed t-tests to test the null hypothesis that there are no significant differences in the means of the dependent variables between the two groups of countries for each independent variable. We used a significance level of 0.05. We reported the mean, variance, observations, pooled variance, degrees of freedom, t-statistic, p-value (one-tail and two-tail), and t-critical value (one-tail and two-tail) for each t-test. We also presented the results in tables for each independent variable. We rejected the null hypotheses if the p-value (two-tail) was less than 0.05 and accepted them otherwise.

We found that life expectancy and outsiders' effect had significant effects on the death rate and the total cases of COVID-19, respectively. We also found that smoking level, population density, and temperature had no significant effects on any of the dependent variables. We concluded that life expectancy and outsiders' effect were the most important factors for the transmission and mortality of COVID-19, while smoking level, population density, and temperature were less relevant.

We also used fuzzy logic to create a model that can estimate the chance of transmitting COVID-19 in a region/state based on the four independent variables. We used the following steps to create the model:

Step 1: We selected the independent variables that had significant effects on the dependent variables based on the t-tests. We chose life expectancy and outsiders' effect as the input variables for the fuzzy logic model.

Step 2: We calculated the weights of the input variables based on the p-values of the t-tests. We used the following formula: Weight percentage = $(1 - p\text{-value}) * 100/2.15788$, where 2.15788 is the sum of the $1 - p$-values of all the independent variables. We rounded the weight percentages to the nearest integer. We obtained the following weights: outsiders' effect: 46%, life expectancy: 21%, temperature: 10%, and others: 23%.

Step 3: We defined the fuzzy sets and the membership functions for the input and output variables. We used three fuzzy sets for each variable: low, medium, and high. We used triangular membership functions for the input variables and trapezoidal membership functions for the output variable. We used the median values of the input variables to define the breakpoints of the membership functions. We used the following ranges for the output variable: low: [10, 12.5], medium: (12.5, 16.5), and high: [16.5, 20].

Step 4: We defined the fuzzy rules for the inference process by a specific fuzzy rule base.

Step 5: We applied the fuzzy inference system to the input data and obtained the output values. We used the Mamdani method for the inference process and the centroid method for the defuzzification process. We presented the output values in graphs and tables.

Case 1 (Life expectancy): Life expectancy is a statistical indicator of how long an individual is predicted to live on average based on their birth year, current age, and other demographic variables such as biological sex. It is different in different regions and periods. The death rate due to COVID-19 is higher in countries where life expectancy is higher. In this section, the analysis is performed.

H_0-Null Hypothesis. *There are no significant differences in death rate when comparing low (less than or equal to 76.65 years) to high values (greater than 76.65 years) of life expectancy of COVID-19-affected countries.*

H_1-Alternative Hypothesis. *There are significant differences in death rate when comparing low (less than or equal to 76.65 years) to high values (greater than 76.65 years) of life expectancy in COVID-19-affected countries.*

First, data from the countries were sorted as per life expectancy in increasing order. Then, we divided the list into two groups: a country list whose life expectancy is low, less than or equal to 76.65 years, and a list whose life expectancy is high, greater than 76.65 years. Then, we compared the death rates between the two groups. As per the results of the t-test for equal variances, the mean was 0.023584419 for low values and 0.050352366 for high values of life expectancy, and variances are shown in Table 1. The p-value (two tails) was 0.000284975, which was less than 0.05. Thus, the null hypothesis can not be accepted.

Hence, there are significant differences in death rate when comparing low to high values of life expectancy of COVID-19-affected countries. This concludes that life expectancy has a high impact on death chances. Older persons having COVID-19 have death chances almost double those compared to younger people.

Table 1. Significant differences in death rate.

	Death Rate of Low Life Expectancy Countries	Death Rate of High Life Expectancy Countries
Mean	0.023584419	0.050352366
Variance	0.000448951	0.001959616
Observations	48	47
Pooled Variance	0.001196161	
Hypothesised Mean Difference	0	
Degrees of Freedom	93	
t Stat	−3.771620183	
$p(T \leq t)$ one-tail	0.000142487	
t Critical one-tail	1.661403674	
$p(T \leq t)$ two-tail	0.000284975	
t Critical two-tail	1.985801814	

[While comparing low (less than or equal to 76.65 years) to high values (greater than 76.65 years) of life expectancy].

Case 2 (Smoking):

H_0-Null Hypothesis. *There are no significant differences in death rate while comparing low (less than or equal to 0.226 indexes) to high values (greater than 0.226 indexes) of smoking levels of COVID-19-affected countries.*

H_1-Alternative Hypothesis. *There are significant differences in death rate while comparing low (less than or equal to 0.226 indexes) to high values (greater than 0.226 indexes) of smoking levels of COVID-19-affected countries.*

Data were sorted as per smoking levels in increasing order. Then, we divided the list into two groups: a country list whose smoking level was low (less than or equal to 0.226 indexes) and a list whose smoking level was high (greater than 0.226 indexes). Then, we compared the two groups. As per the results of the *t*-test for equal variances, the mean was 0.031749961 for low values and 0.042013 for high values of smoking level, and variances are shown in Table 2. The *p*-value (two tails) was 0.177094358, which was higher than 0.05. Thus, the null hypothesis is accepted. Hence, there are no significant differences in death rates when comparing low (less than or equal to 0.226 indexes) to high values (greater than 0.226 indexes) of smoking levels in COVID-19-affected countries. This concludes that the smoking level of a person has a minor impact on death. Highly smoking persons having COVID-19 have death chances larger (but not significantly) compared to non-smoking people.

Table 2. Differences in death rate.

	Death Rates of Low-Smoking-Index Countries	Death Rate of High-Smoking-Index Countries
Mean	0.031749961	0.042013
Variance	0.000926522	0.001787
Observations	48	47
Pooled Variance	0.001352228	
Hypothesised Mean Difference	0	
Degrees of Freedom	93	
t Stat	−1.360074066	
$p(T \leq t)$ one-tail	0.088547179	
t Critical one-tail	1.661403674	
$p(T \leq t)$ two-tail	0.177094358	
t Critical two-tail	1.985801814	

[While comparing low (less than or equal to 0.226 indexes) to high values (greater than 0.226 indexes) of smoking levels in countries].

Case 3 (Population density):

H_0-Null Hypothesis. *There are no significant differences in affected cases (affected cases/million) while comparing low (less than or equal to 92/sqkm) to high values (higher than 92/sqkm) of population density of COVID-19-affected countries.*

H_1-Alternative Hypothesis. *There are significant differences in affected cases (affected cases/million) while comparing low (less than or equal to 92/sqkm) to high values (higher than 92/sqkm) of population density of COVID-19-affected countries.*

Data were sorted as per population density in increasing order. Then, we divided the list into two groups: a country list whose population density was low (less than or equal to 92/sqkm) and a list whose population density was high (higher than 92/sqkm). Then, we separately compared the two groups for affected cases and affected cases/million. In Table 3, the results of affected cases are shown, and in Table 4, affected cases/million are shown. p-value (two tails) was 0.186759117 for Table 3 and 0.933317888 for Table 4; these were large values (greater than 0.05). Thus, the null hypothesis is accepted for both cases. Hence, there are no significant differences in affected cases while comparing low to high values of population density of COVID-19-affected countries. This concludes that the population density of a country has no impact on COVID-19 transmissions.

Table 3. Differences in affected cases of COVID-19 due to population density.

	Affected Cases in Low Density	Affected Cases in High Density
Mean	157,615.1458	67,599.87234
Variance	2.03787×10^{11}	11,693,419,305
Observations	48	47
Pooled Variance	1.08773×10^{11}	
Hypothesised Mean Difference	0	
Degrees of Freedom	93	
t Stat	1.330035917	
$p(T \leq t)$ one-tail	0.093379558	
t Critical one-tail	1.661403674	
$p(T \leq t)$ two-tail	0.186759117	
t Critical two-tail	1.985801814	

Table 4. Population density (low and high).

	Total Cases/1 M in Low Density	Total Cases/1 M in High Density
Mean	3595.5	3507.297872
Variance	16,493,772.38	36,211,163.34
Observations	48	47
Pooled Variance	26,246,460.39	
Hypothesised Mean Difference	0	
Degrees of Freedom	93	
t Stat	0.083897967	
$p(T \leq t)$ one-tail	0.466658944	
t Critical one-tail	1.661403674	
$p(T \leq t)$ two-tail	0.933317888	
t Critical two-tail	1.985801814	

Case 4 (Outsiders' effect):

H_0-Null Hypothesis. *There are no significant differences in affected cases (or affected cases/million) while comparing low (less than or equal to 0.2 global sharing) to high values (greater than 0.2 global sharing) of percentages of outsiders (tourism and global export indicators) of COVID-19-affected countries.*

H_1-Alternative Hypothesis. *There are significant differences in affected cases (or affected cases/million) while comparing low (less than or equal to 0.2 global sharing) to high values (greater than 0.2 global sharing) of percentages of outsiders (tourism and global export indicators) of COVID-19-affected countries.*

Data were sorted as per sharing percentages of outsiders (tourism/global export indicators) in increasing order. Then, we divided the list into two groups: a country list whose sharing percentages of outsiders (tourism/global export indicators) was low (less than or equal to 0.2 sharing) and a list whose sharing percentages of outsiders (tourism/global export indicators) was high (greater than 0.2 sharing). Then, we compared the two groups for affected cases and affected cases/million separately. In Table 5, the results of affected cases are shown, and in Table 6, affected cases/million are shown. p-value (two tails) was 0.012169463 for Table 5, which was less than 0.05, and was 0.249465449 (greater than 0.05) for Table 6. Thus, the null hypothesis is not accepted for Table 5 and accepted for Table 6. Hence, there are significant differences in affected cases while comparing low to high values of sharing percentages of outsiders (tourism/global export indicators) of COVID-19-affected countries. This concludes that sharing percentages of outsiders (tourism/global export indicators) of a country has a significant impact on the transmission of COVID-19.

Table 5. Tourists/export–import indicators.

	Affected Cases in Low Outsiders' Effect	Affected Cases in High Outsiders' Effect
Mean	31,275.59	200,222.11
Variance	2,965,654,152	2.10861×10^{11}
Observations	49	46
Pooled Variance	1.0356×10^{11}	
Hypothesised Mean Difference	0	

Table 5. *Cont.*

	Affected Cases in Low Outsiders' Effect	Affected Cases in High Outsiders' Effect
Degrees of Freedom	93	
t Stat	−2.557220227	
$p(T \leq t)$ one-tail	0.006084732	
t Critical one-tail	1.661403674	
$p(T \leq t)$ two-tail	0.012169463	
t Critical two-tail	1.985801814	

Table 6. Tourists/export–import indicators have no significant differences in affected cases/million.

	Total Cases/1 M for Low Indicators Value	Total Cases/1 M for High Indicators Value
Mean	2965.86	4176.09
Variance	17,914,825.92	34,365,400.48
Observations	49	46
Pooled Variance	25,874,781.35	
Hypothesised Mean Difference	0	
Degrees of Freedom	93	
t Stat	−1.158896514	
$p(T \leq t)$ one-tail	0.124732725	
t Critical one-tail	1.661403674	
$p(T \leq t)$ two-tail	0.249465449	
t Critical two-tail	1.985801814	

Other cases:

A few other cases were also analysed in this section. In Table 7, it is observed that life expectancy has no significant effect on transmission of COVID-19 as the *p*-value is higher than the 0.05 significance level. In Table 8, we find that temperature is also a non-significant factor for the transfer of COVID-19. Table 9 shows that the smoking level of countries has some impact on the transmission of COVID-19. However, these factors are not significant to spread such a deadly disease.

Table 7. Differences in affected cases of COVID-19 due to life expectancy.

	Affected Cases of Low Life Expectancy	Affected Cases of High Life Expectancy
Mean	92,724.85	133,870.81
Variance	57,743,028,575	1.64221×10^{11}
Observations	48	47
Pooled Variance	1.1041×10^{11}	
Hypothesised Mean Difference	0	
Degrees of Freedom	93	
t Stat	−0.603435983	
$p(T \leq t)$ one-tail	0.273843824	
t Critical one-tail	1.661403674	
$p(T \leq t)$ two-tail	0.547687647	
t Critical two-tail	1.985801814	

Table 8. Differences in affected cases of COVID-19 due to temperature.

	Effected Cases for Low Temperature	Effected Cases for High Temperature
Mean	103,716.69	122,645.11
Variance	54,089,839,644	1.68643×10^{11}
Observations	48	47
Pooled Variance	1.10751×10^{11}	
Hypothesised Mean Difference	0	
Degrees of Freedom	93	
t Stat	−0.277171863	
$p(T \leq t)$ one-tail	0.391131648	
t Critical one-tail	1.661403674	
$p(T \leq t)$ two-tail	0.782263295	
t Critical two-tail	1.985801814	

Table 9. Differences in affected cases of COVID-19 due to smoking.

	Affected Cases in Low-Smoking Countries	Affected Cases in High-Smoking Countries
Mean	157,971.35	67,236.09
Variance	2.02246×10^{11}	13,200,648,298
Observations	48	47
Pooled Variance	1.0874×10^{11}	
Hypothesised Mean Difference	0	
Degrees of Freedom	93	
t Stat	1.340879173	
$p(T \leq t)$ one-tail	0.091612808	
t Critical one-tail	1.661403674	
$p(T \leq t)$ two-tail	0.183225616	
t Critical two-tail	1.985801814	

3. Creating Input Weights for Fuzzy Logic Based on Statistical Results and Fuzzy Inference System (FIS)

To define fuzzy logic [32], input variables are to be selected first. In this study, the variables, whose impact of spreading COVID-19 were recorded as per our statistical analysis, are to be considered. To find the weight percentages, we followed the steps below.

Step 1: Check the mean ratio of the two considered groups (low and high) for each factor. If the mean of the first group (lower values) is greater than or equal to the mean of the second group (higher values), that variable will not be considered. Otherwise, go to step 2. For example, the mean of the first group is higher than the mean of the second group in Table 3. Hence, the variable population density is not considered here.

Step 2: The p-values (two tails) of t-test for each selected variable are taken, and the '$1 - p$ values' are recorded. These values are put in Table 10. For example, the p-values (two tails) of outsiders' effect (tourism/global export indicators) are considered from Table 5. It is tabulated as outsiders' effect in Table 10. Similarly, the values of other variables are tabulated in Table 10.

Step 3: It is almost well known that a few factors of the spreading of COVID-19 are still unknown. In our proposed model, we take a variable named 'others', and its taken

p-value as 0.5 for the default case. Then, all the values of the second column of Table 10 are added, and the sum is 2.15788.

Step 4: The final weight percentage is obtained as follows. Weight percentage = $(1 - p \text{ value}) * 100/2.15788$. Based on this formula, the nearest integer values are taken. To simplify the process, we take weight ratio as the outsiders' effect/life expectancy index/temperature/others = 5:2:1:2.

Table 10. Weight percentages.

Influencing Factors	$1 - p$-Value	Weight Percentages
Outsiders' effect	0.987831	46
Life expectancy index	0.452312	21
Temperature	0.217737	10
Others	0.5	23

4. Fuzzy Inference System (FIS) to Find the Chance of Transmission of Some Infectious Agents in a Region/State

Fuzzy inference system [33] grips the imprecise and vagueness data. Fuzzy logic has been used in many areas like automatic control, banks, hospitals, and academic institutions.

The factors associated with affectedness of COVID-19 are taken as outsiders' effect/life expectancy index/temperature/others = 5:2:1:2. It is implemented in Table 11. To combine these factors, the fuzzy logic inference system is perfect to represent as the factors are imprecise. Hence, to find the chance of affectedness of COVID-19, an FIS is modelled here (see Appendix A for details).

Table 11. The rule base weights.

	Outsiders' Index	Life Expectancy	Temperature	Others	Chances of Transmission
low	5	2	1	2	[10,12.5]
medium	7.5	3	1.5	3	(12.5, 16.5)
high	10	4	2	4	[16.5,20]

5. Results Analysis

This study concludes that the death rate significantly increases in countries with a life expectancy higher than 77 years of age.

This study also highlights that population density has no major impact either on transmission or death rate increase in countries globally.

Another important result of this study is to capture the outsiders' impact on the transmission of COVID-19. The data were captured based on the export-sharing index globally and the amount of tourism. We have a significant result that the country whose global export-sharing index is more than or equal to 0.3 has significant chances of disease transmission.

The proposed FIS concludes with a satisfactory result. Two instances are given here. In Figure 1, the input values are 0.1, 0.1, 0.8, and 0.5. The output value is 0.153, which indicates the low chances of transmission. Again, in Figure 2, it is found that if the input values are 0.9, 0.8, 0.8, and 0.5, the output value is 0.847. Thus, based on four input parameters, the chances of transmission can be found.

Figure 1 shows that low outsiders' effect, low life expectancy, and high temperature are kept, and other parameters are kept neutral. It indicates low chances of transmission. Also, in Figure 2, outsiders' effect is set high along with life expectancy. But, the result is different. It indicates a high chance of transmission. Thus, life expectancy and outsiders' effect play a significant role in transmission of infectious disease. In Figures 3 and 4, 3D images are shown corresponding to Figures 1 and 2, respectively. In the 3D images, the X and Y axes are represented as 'lifeExpectancy' and 'outsiders' effect. The other combinations can be similarly found.

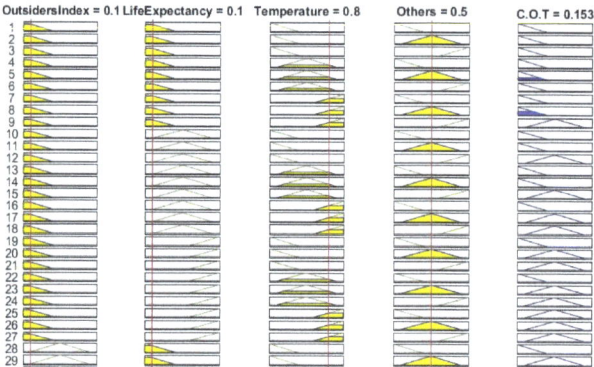

Figure 1. Low outsiders' effect indicating low chances of transmission.

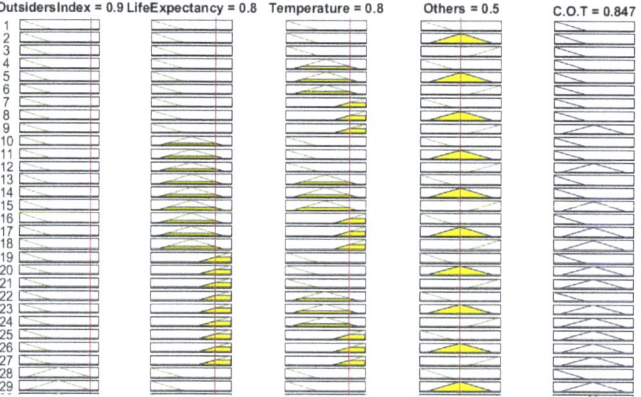

Figure 2. High outsiders' effect indicating high chances of transmission.

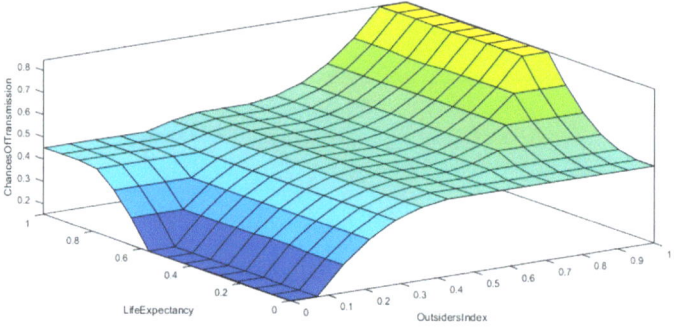

Figure 3. Three-dimensional image of outsiders' index life expectancy to chances of transmission of COVID-19.

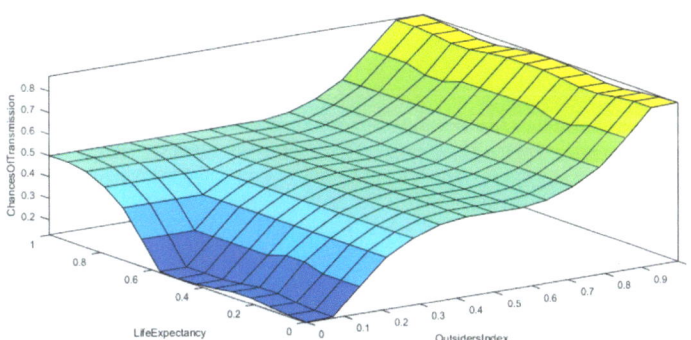

Figure 4. Three-dimensional image of outsiders' index 'Life Expectancy' to chances of transmission of COVID-19.

6. Discussion

In this paper, we investigated the factors that influence the transmission and death rates of COVID-19 across 95 top-affected countries. We used a fuzzy logic model to estimate the chance of transmitting COVID-19 in a region/state based on four input parameters: outsiders' effect, life expectancy, temperature, and others. We also performed statistical tests to validate our assumptions and to calculate the weights of the input parameters for the fuzzy logic model.

Our results show that the death rate significantly increases for countries with a life expectancy higher than 77 years of age. This is consistent with previous studies that have found that older age groups and males are more vulnerable to COVID-19 and have higher mortality rates [4,17,34,35]. This may be due to the higher prevalence of comorbidities, lower immune response, and lower access to healthcare resources among older populations [17,36]. Therefore, our study suggests that life expectancy is an important factor to consider when designing and implementing public health measures and policies to prevent and control COVID-19.

Our results also highlight that population density has no major impact either on transmission or death rate increase in countries globally. This is contrary to the common assumption that higher population density facilitates the spread of infectious agents by increasing the contact and exposure of individuals [1]. However, this finding is in line with some recent studies that have found no significant effect of population density on disease transmission or death rates for COVID-19 [15,37,38]. This may be explained by the confounding effects of other factors, such as mobility patterns, social distancing measures, testing capacities, and healthcare resources [37]. Moreover, population density may not capture the heterogeneity and complexity of human interactions within and between different groups and settings [1]. Therefore, our study suggests that population density is not a reliable indicator of COVID-19 transmission or mortality and that more nuanced models are needed to account for the diversity and uncertainty of this factor.

Another important result of this study is to capture the outsiders' impact on the transmission of COVID-19. The data were captured based on the export-sharing index globally and the amount of tourism. We have a significant result that the country whose global export-sharing index is more than or equal to 0.3 has significant chances of disease transmission. This is consistent with previous studies that have found a positive correlation between international travel or trade and infection rate for COVID-19 [39,40]. This may be due to the increased contact and mixing of different populations or sources of infection [1]. However, this finding is not conclusive, as some studies have found no significant effect or a negative effect of outsiders' effect on disease transmission [41–43]. Moreover, outsiders' effects may not capture the variation and uncertainty of different modes or routes of transmission, such as air, land, sea, or animal [1,41,42]. Therefore, our study suggests that outsiders' effect is a relevant but not sufficient predictor of COVID-19 transmission and that more detailed models are needed to account for the diversity and uncertainty of this factor.

Our FIS model is based on the fuzzy logic theory, which can handle the vagueness and imprecision of the factors and the non-linearity and uncertainty of their relationships by using fuzzy membership functions, fuzzy operators, and fuzzy reasoning [3]. Fuzzy logic has been used in many areas like automatic control, banks, hospitals, and academic institutions [3]. Our study is one of the first to apply a fuzzy logic model with weights derived from statistical tests to estimate the chance of transmitting COVID-19 in a region/state based on four input parameters: outsiders' effect, life expectancy, temperature, and others. Our study contributes to the existing literature on the factors of infectious agent transmission and the applications of fuzzy logic models to diagnose or predict infectious agents.

7. Conclusions

This study explored the factors that influence the transmission of COVID-19 across 95 top-affected countries. We found that the global export index, which reflects the exposure to foreign visitors or products, was positively associated with the infection rate. On the other hand, the population density, which reflects the contact frequency and intensity among individuals, was not a significant factor. Based on these findings, we developed a fuzzy inference system that can estimate the transmission rate of COVID-19 based on five input parameters: temperature, population density, life expectancy, smoking index, and outsiders' effect. Our fuzzy inference system can provide a flexible and intuitive way to model and analyse the factors of infectious agent transmission and to estimate the infection risk in different settings.

Future Work

This study has some limitations that can be addressed in future research. First, we used the global export index and tourism index as proxies for the outsiders' effect, but there may be other indicators that can better capture the exposure to foreign sources of infection. Second, we included an unknown variable 'others' in our fuzzy inference system, which represents the uncertainty and complexity of the infection process. The nature and impact of this variable need to be further investigated and clarified. Future research can also extend our fuzzy inference system to other infectious agents or regions and compare its performance with other models or methods.

Author Contributions: Conceptualisation, S.S.; methodology, S.S. and A.K.; software, S.S. and J.B.; validation, A.K., S.S., and K.C.D.; formal analysis, S.S.; investigation, A.K.; resources, K.C.D.; data curation, S.S.; writing—original draft preparation, S.S.; writing—review and editing, S.S. and J.B.; visualisation, S.S. and J.B.; supervision, K.C.D.; project administration, A.K.; funding acquisition, A.K. All authors have read and agreed to the published version of the manuscript.

Funding: This research received no external funding.

Data Availability Statement: Data sharing is not applicable to this article as no datasets were generated or analysed during the current study.

Conflicts of Interest: The authors declare that they have no competing interests.

Abbreviations

M	Mean
V	Variance
O	Observation
PV	Pooled Variance
HMD	Hypothesised Mean Difference
df	Degrees of Freedom

tS	t Stat
P1	$p(T \leq t)$ one-tail
tC1	t Critical one-tail
P2	$p(T \leq t)$ two-tail
tC2	t Critical two-tail

Appendix A

Table A1. Collection of data for 95 countries. (Data were collected on 2 July 2020).

Sl. No.	Country	Affected Cases	Total Cases/1 M	Death	Density (per sqkm)	Life Expectancy	Temperature (°C)	Smoking	Global Export Sharing
1	USA	2,781,085	9545	130,813	35	79.11	27	0.137	8.6
2	Brazil	1,456,969	8073	60,813	25	76.57	24	0.153	1.9
12	Russia	661,165	4847	9683	9	72.99	22	0.409	2.3
8	India	606,907	559	17,860	420	70.42	39	0.1115	1.7
3	UK	313,483	4227	43,906	279	78.46	10	0.147	2.5
7	Spain	296,739	6408	28,363	92	83.99	32	0.292	1.7
10	Peru	288,477	9488	9860	26	77.44	16	0.054	0.2
16	Chile	282,043	15,852	5753	25	80.74	3	0.38	0.4
4	Italy	240,760	4005	34,788	201	84.01	33	0.24	2.8
9	Iran	232,863	2981	11,106	51	77.33	33	0.111	0.5
6	Mexico	231,770	2132	28,510	66	75.41	16	0.137	2.3
21	Pakistan	217,809	1090	4473	250	67.79	31	0.2245	0.1
18	Turkey	201,098	2477	5150	108	78.45	31	0.2595	0.9
29	Saudi Arabia	197,608	6322	1752	16	68.87	26	0.154	1.5
13	Germany	196,372	2373	9061	235	81.88	24	0.3035	8.1
5	France	165,719	2596	29,861	118	83.13	21	0.277	3
25	South Africa	159,333	3787	2749	49	83.5	21	0.1895	0.5
28	Bangladesh	153,277	1065	1926	1116	73.57	33	0.2025	0.2
14	Canada	104,271	2820	8615	4	82.96	26	0.1495	2.3
22	Colombia	102,009	2528	3470	45	77.87	14	0.111	0.2
73	Qatar	97,897	36,168	118	249	80.73	36	0.206	0.4
19	China	83,537	58	4634	148	77.47	27	0.247	12.9
23	Egypt	69,814	765	3034	102	72.54	36	0.251	0
17	Sweden	69,692	7312	5370	22	83.33	17	0.206	0.9
34	Argentina	67,197	1925	1351	16	77.17	8	0.2395	0.3
52	Belarus	62,698	6797	405	46	75.2	26	0.284	0.2
11	Belgium	61,598	5367	9761	380	82.17	20	0.2325	2.4
24	Indonesia	59,394	259	2987	144	72.32	27	0.399	0.9
20	Ecuador	58,257	3584	4576	64	77.71	9	0.0865	0.1
26	Iraq	51,524	1676	2050	92	71.08	44	0.31	0.5
15	Netherlands	50,335	2961	6113	409	82.78	19	0.2505	3
57	UAE	49,069	5416	316	118	72.5	28	0.24	1.6
53	Kuwait	47,859	12,370	359	240	75.85	43	0.225	0.4
37	Ukraine	45,887	1171	1185	72	81.77	31	0.317	0.2
92	Singapore	44,310	7763	26	8240	58.34	29	0.165	2.1
68	Kazakhstan	42,574	2823	188	7	73.9	21	0.266	0.3
69	Oman	42,555	10,126	188	16	78.58	33	0.11	0.2
32	Portugal	42,454	4400	1579	111	82.65	24	0.226	0.4

Table A1. Cont.

Sl. No.	Country	Affected Cases	Total Cases/1 M	Death	Density (per sqkm)	Life Expectancy	Temperature (°C)	Smoking	Global Export Sharing
35	Philippines	38,805	472	1274	320	71.66	30	0.2575	0.3
33	Poland	35,146	976	1492	121	79.27	26	0.2805	1.4
44	Panama	34,463	9558	645	57	73.74	26	0.066	0
36	Bolivia	34,227	3681	1201	11	72.35	22	0.238	0
42	Dominican Republic	33,387	3649	754	223	74.65	26	0.141	0
41	Afghanistan	32,022	871	807	60	65.98	20	0.352	0
27	Switzerland	31,967	3765	1965	210	84.25	23	0.233	1.6
31	Romania	27,746	1601	1687	81	76.5	33	0.298	0.4
80	Bahrain	27,414	18,174	93	2224	77.73	36	0.282	0
51	Armenia	26,658	10,240	459	100	75.55	26	0.269	0
46	Nigeria	26,484	147	603	223	55.75	21	0.0925	0.3
56	Israel	26,452	3691	324	417	83.49	30	0.3025	0.3
30	Ireland	25,477	5172	1738	70	82.81	17	0.2215	0.9
50	Honduras	20,262	2622	542	88	75.87	24	0.177	0
40	Guatemala	19,011	1418	817	165	75.05	18	0.239	0
38	Japan	18,723	160	974	335	85.03	25	0.2215	3.8
74	Ghana	18,134	734	117	130	64.94	28	0.0675	0.1
64	Azerbaijan	18,112	2161	220	117	73.33	26	0.2345	0
43	Austria	17,941	2055	705	107	82.05	28	0.3515	0.9
49	Moldova	16,898	4579	549	119	72.3	33	0.2555	0
59	Serbia	15,195	1955	287	99	84.07	32	0.4165	0.1
90	Nepal	14,519	567	31	198	71.74	25	0.241	0
39	Algeria	14,272	396	920	18	77.5	28	0.156	0
60	S. Korea	12,904	259	282	512	75.69	12	0.45	3.1
63	Morocco	12,854	405	228	83	77.43	24	0.234	0.2
45	Denmark	12,815	2230	606	134	81.4	20	0.17	0.6
58	Cameroon	12,592	562	313	56	60.32	28	0.2235	0
54	Czechia	12,046	1197	349	136	79.85	21	0.383	0
82	Ivory Coast	9702	436	68	82	57.02	26	0.237	0.1
47	Sudan	9573	230	602	23	66.09	41	0.203	0
91	Uzbekistan	8996	336	27	75	72.04	30	0.131	0.1
61	Norway	8902	1651	251	17	82.94	13	0.2225	0.6
72	Malaysia	8643	268	121	98	76.65	30	0.222	1.3
78	Australia	8001	355	104	3	83.94	5	0.149	1.3
55	Finland	7241	1313	328	16	82.48	19	0.2085	0.4
71	Senegal	7054	465	121	85	76.47	29	0.1205	0
66	El Salvador	7000	1363	191	308	74.06	22	0.17	0
70	Kenya	6941	159	149	93	67.47	22	0.1335	0
83	Kyrgyzstan	6261	1356	66	33	71.95	28	0.27	0
86	Venezuela	6062	282	54	31	72.34	23	0.167	0.2
77	Haiti	6040	569	107	411	64.99	28	0.123	0
87	Tajikistan	6005	667	52	67	71.76	33	0.17	0
79	Ethiopia	5846	59	103	104	67.81	20	0.047	0
88	Gabon	5513	2637	42	8	67.03	28	0.147	0
89	Guinea	5404	434	33	53	62.64	26	0.069	0
62	Bulgaria	5154	913	232	63	75.49	31	0.353	0.2
67	Bosnia and Herzegovina	4788	1855	189	64	77.93	18	0.386	0

Table A1. Cont.

Sl. No.	Country	Affected Cases	Total Cases/1 M	Death	Density (per sqkm)	Life Expectancy	Temperature (°C)	Smoking	Global Export Sharing
85	Djibouti	4704	4947	55	43	67.87	37	0.245	0
76	Luxembourg	4345	7426	110	242	82.79	20	0.236	0.1
94	French Guiana	4268	18,272	16	4	80.53	23	0.356	0
48	Hungary	4166	437	587	104	77.31	29	0.284	0.6
93	Costa Rica	3753	1145	17	100	80.94	25	0.134	0.1
65	Greece	3432	348	192	79	82.8	34	0.4265	0.2
84	Thailand	3179	46	58	136	77.74	28	0.2185	1.3
95	Palestine	2978	1023	8	820	79.1	20	0.22	0
81	Somalia	2924	190	90	25	64.88	29	0.24	0
75	Croatia	2912	832	110	73	79.02	29	0.3645	0.1

Pseudo-Codes of proposed FIS
Output='Chances of transmission.'
Matlab type='Mamdani'
Number of inputs=4
Number of outputs=1
And Method=' min.'
Or Method='max'
Imp Method=' min.'
Agg Method='max'
Defuzzyfy Method='centroid.'
[First input]
Name='Outsiders_Index'
Range= [0 1]
Number of Membership Functions (MF) =3
First MF='low':'trimf',[-0.4 0 0.4]
Second MF ='med':'trimf',[0.1 0.5 0.9]
Third MF ='high':'trimf',[0.6 1 1.4]
[Second input]
Name='Life_Expectancy'
Range=[0 1]
Number of Membership Functions (MF) =3
First MF='low':'trimf',[-0.4 0 0.4]
Second MF ='med':'trimf',[0.1 0.5 0.9]
Third MF ='high':'trimf',[0.6 1 1.4]
[Third input]
Name='Temperature'
Range=[0 1]
Number of Membership Functions (MF) =3
First MF='low':'trimf',[-0.4 0 0.4]
Second MF ='med':'trimf',[0.1 0.5 0.9]
Third MF ='high':'trimf',[0.6 1 1.4]
[Fourth input]
Name='Others'
Range=[0 1]
Number of Membership Functions (MF) =3
First MF='low':'trimf',[-0.4 0 0.4]
Second MF ='med':'trimf',[0.1 0.5 0.9]
Third MF ='high':'trimf',[0.6 1 1.4]

[Output function]
Name='Chances_of_Transmission_of_COVID19'
Range=[0 1]
Number of Membership Functions (MF) =3
First MF='low':'trimf',[-0.4 0 0.4]
Second MF ='med':'trimf',[0.1 0.5 0.9]
Third MF ='high':'trimf',[0.6 1 1.4]
[Rules]
The rule base is modelled with the following weights

References

1. Ganasegeran, K.; Jamil, M.F.A.; Ch'ng, A.S.H.; Looi, I.; Peariasamy, K.M. Influence of population density for COVID-19 spread in Malaysia: An ecological study. *Int. J. Environ. Res. Public Health* **2021**, *18*, 9866. [CrossRef] [PubMed]
2. Bukhari, Q.; Jameel, Y. Will coronavirus pandemic diminish by summer? *SSRN Electron. J.* **2020**, 3556998. [CrossRef]
3. Arji, G.; Ahmadi, H.; Nilashi, M.; Rashid, T.A.; Ahmed, O.H.; Aljojo, N.; Zainol, A. Fuzzy logic approach for infectious disease diagnosis: A methodical evaluation, literature and classification. *Biocybern. Biomed. Eng.* **2019**, *39*, 937–955. [CrossRef] [PubMed]
4. Trias-Llimós, S.; Bilal, U. Impact of the COVID-19 pandemic on life expectancy in Madrid (Spain). *J. Public Health* **2020**, *42*, 635–636. [CrossRef] [PubMed]
5. Arcavi, L.; Benowitz, N.L. Cigarette smoking and infection. *Arch. Intern. Med.* **2004**, *164*, 2206–2216. [CrossRef] [PubMed]
6. Liu, X.; Huang, J.; Li, C.; Zhao, Y.; Wang, D.; Huang, Z.; Yang, K. The role of seasonality in the spread of COVID-19 pandemic. *Environ. Res.* **2021**, *195*, 110874. [CrossRef] [PubMed]
7. Lian, X.; Huang, J.; Li, H.; He, Y.; Ouyang, Z.; Fu, S.; Zhao, Y.; Wang, D.; Wang, R.; Guan, X. Heat waves accelerate the spread of infectious diseases. *Environ. Res.* **2023**, *231*, 116090. [CrossRef] [PubMed]
8. Wang, M.; Jiang, A.; Gong, L.; Lu, L.; Guo, W.; Li, C.; Zheng, J.; Li, C.; Yang, B.; Zeng, J.; et al. Temperature significantly change COVID-19 transmission in 429 cities. *medRxiv* **2020**. [CrossRef]
9. Palialol, B.; Pereda, P.; Azzoni, C. Does weather influence COVID-19 transmission? *Reg. Sci. Policy Pract.* **2020**, *12*, 981–1004. [CrossRef]
10. Prata, D.N.; Rodrigues, W.; Bermejo, P.H. Temperature significantly changes COVID-19 transmission in (sub) tropical cities of Brazil. *Sci. Total Environ.* **2020**, *729*, 138862. [CrossRef]
11. Xie, J.; Zhu, Y. Association between ambient temperature and COVID-19 infection in 122 cities from China. *Sci. Total Environ.* **2020**, *724*, 138201. [CrossRef] [PubMed]
12. Kjerulff, B.; Kaspersen, K.A.; Dinh, K.M.; Boldsen, J.; Mikkelsen, S.; Erikstrup, L.T.; Sørensen, E.; Nielsen, K.R.; Bruun, M.T.; Hjalgrim, H.; et al. Smoking is associated with infection risk in healthy blood donors. *Clin. Microbiol. Infect.* **2020**, *29*, 506–514. [CrossRef] [PubMed]
13. Alqahtani, J.S.; Oyelade, T.; Aldhahir, A.M.; Alghamdi, S.M.; Almehmadi, M.; Alqahtani, A.S.; Quaderi, S.; Mandal, S.; Hurst, J.R. Prevalence, severity and mortality associated with COPD and smoking in patients with COVID-19: A rapid systematic review and meta-analysis. *PLoS ONE* **2020**, *15*, e0233147. [CrossRef] [PubMed]
14. Patanavanich, R.; Glantz, S.A. Smoking is associated with COVID-19 progression: A meta-analysis. *Nicotine Tob. Res.* **2020**, *22*, 1653–1656. [CrossRef]
15. Hamidi, S.; Sabouri, S.; Ewing, R. Does density aggravate the COVID-19 pandemic? Early findings and lessons for planners. *J. Am. Plan. Assoc.* **2020**, *86*, 495–509. [CrossRef]
16. Trias-Llimós, S.; Riffe, T.; Bilal, U. Monitoring life expectancy levels during the COVID-19 pandemic: Example of the unequal impact of the first wave on Spanish regions. *PLoS ONE* **2020**, *15*, e0241952. [CrossRef] [PubMed]
17. Cevik, M.; Tate, M.; Lloyd, O.; Maraolo, A.E.; Schafers, J.; Ho, A. SARS-CoV-2, SARS-CoV, and MERS-CoV viral load dynamics, duration of viral shedding, and infectiousness: A systematic review and meta-analysis. *Lancet Microbe* **2021**, *2*, e13–e22. [CrossRef] [PubMed]
18. Samanta, S.; Dubey, V.K.; Das, K. Coopetition bunch graphs: Competition and cooperation on COVID-19 research. *Inf. Sci.* **2022**, *589*, 1–33. [CrossRef]
19. Mahapatra, R.; Samanta, S.; Pal, M.; Lee, J.G.; Khan, S.K.; Naseem, U.; Bhadoria, R.S. Colouring of COVID-19 affected region based on fuzzy directed graphs. *Comput. Mater. Contin.* **2021**, *68*, 1219–1233. [CrossRef]
20. Das, K.; Naseem, U.; Samanta, S.; Khan, S.K.; De, K. Fuzzy mixed graphs and its application to identification of COVID-19 affected central regions in India. *J. Intell. Fuzzy Syst.* **2021**, *40*, 1051–1064. [CrossRef]
21. Dhiman, N.; Sharma, M.K. Fuzzy logic inference system for identification and prevention of Coronavirus (COVID-19). *Int. J. Innov. Technol. Explor. Eng.* **2020**, *9*, 2278–3075.
22. Şimşek, H.; Yangın, E. An alternative approach to determination of COVID-19 personal risk index by using fuzzy logic. *Health Technol.* **2022**, *12*, 569–582. [CrossRef]
23. Shatnawi, M.; Shatnawi, A.; AlShara, Z.; Husari, G. Symptoms-based fuzzy-logic approach for COVID-19 diagnosis. *Int. J. Adv. Comput. Sci. Appl.* **2021**, *12*, 444–452. [CrossRef]

24. Ahmad, Z.; El-Kafrawy, S.A.; Alandijany, T.A.; Giannino, F.; Mirza, A.A.; El-Daly, M.M.; Faizo, A.A.; Bajrai, L.H.; Kamal, M.A.; Azhar, E.I. A global report on the dynamics of COVID-19 with quarantine and hospitalization: A fractional order model with non-local kernel. *Comput. Biol. Chem.* **2022**, *98*, 107645. [CrossRef] [PubMed]
25. Okposo, N.I.; Adewole, M.O.; Okposo, E.N.; Ojarikre, H.I.; Abdullah, F.A. A mathematical study on a fractional COVID-19 transmission model within the framework of nonsingular and nonlocal kernel. *Chaos Solitons Fractals* **2021**, *152*, 111427. [CrossRef] [PubMed]
26. Lu, H.; Giannino, F.; Tartakovsky, D.M. Parsimonious models of in-host viral dynamics and immune response. *Appl. Math. Lett.* **2023**, *145*, 108781. [CrossRef]
27. Malik, A.; Alkholief, M.; Aldakhee, F.M.; Khan, A.A.; Ahmad, Z.; Kamal, W.; Gatasheh, M.K.; Alshamsan, A. Sensitivity analysis of COVID-19 with quarantine and vaccination: A fractal-fractional model. *Alex. Eng. J.* **2022**, *61*, 8859–8874. [CrossRef]
28. Liu, P.; Huang, X.; Zarin, R.; Cui, T.; Din, A. Modeling and numerical analysis of a fractional order model for dual variants of SARS-CoV-2. *Alex. Eng. J.* **2023**, *65*, 427–442. [CrossRef]
29. Trisilowati; Darti, I.; Musafir, R.R.; Rayungsari, M.; Suryanto, A. Dynamics of a Fractional-Order COVID-19 Epidemic Model with Quarantine and Standard Incidence Rate. *Axioms* **2023**, *12*, 591. [CrossRef]
30. Das, K.; Samanta, S.; Naseem, U.; Khalid Khan, S.; De, K. Application of fuzzy logic in the ranking of academic institutions. *Fuzzy Inf. Eng.* **2019**, *11*, 295–306. [CrossRef]
31. Das, K.; Samanta, S.; De, K.; Encarnacion, X.; Das, C.B. Ranking of educational institutions using fuzzy logic: A mathematical approach. *Afr. Mat.* **2020**, *31*, 1295–1310. [CrossRef]
32. Zadeh, L.A. Fuzzy algorithms. *Inf. Control* **1968**, *12*, 94–102. [CrossRef]
33. Mamdani, E.H.; Assilian, S. An experiment in linguistic synthesis with a fuzzy logic controller. *Int. J. Man-Mach. Stud.* **1975**, *7*, 1–13. [CrossRef]
34. Aburto, J.M.; Schöley, J.; Kashnitsky, I.; Zhang, L.; Rahal, C.; Missov, T.I.; Mills, M.C.; Dowd, J.B.; Kashyap, R. Quantifying impacts of the COVID-19 pandemic through life-expectancy losses: A population-level study of 29 countries. *Int. J. Epidemiol.* **2022**, *51*, 63–74. [CrossRef]
35. Muniyandi, M.; Singh, P.K.; Aanandh, Y.; Karikalan, N.; Padmapriyadarsini, C. A national-level analysis of life expectancy associated with the COVID-19 pandemic in India. *Front. Public Health* **2022**, *10*, 1000933. [CrossRef]
36. Vasishtha, G.; Mohanty, S.K.; Mishra, U.S.; Dubey, M.; Sahoo, U. Impact of COVID-19 infection on life expectancy, premature mortality, and DALY in Maharashtra, India. *BMC Infect. Dis.* **2021**, *21*, 343. [CrossRef] [PubMed]
37. Carozzi, F.; Provenzano, S.; Roth, S. *Urban Density and COVID-19 (No. 108484)*; London School of Economics and Political Science, LSE Library: London, UK, 2020.
38. Hsu, J. Population density does not doom cities to pandemic dangers. *Scientific American*, 16 September 2020.
39. Chinazzi, M.; Davis, J.T.; Ajelli, M.; Gioannini, C.; Litvinova, M.; Merler, S.; Pastore y Piontti, A.; Mu, K.; Rossi, L.; Sun, K.; et al. The effect of travel restrictions on the spread of the 2019 novel coronavirus (COVID-19) outbreak. *Science* **2020**, *368*, 395–400. [CrossRef] [PubMed]
40. Pullano, G.; Pinotti, F.; Valdano, E.; Boëlle, P.Y.; Poletto, C.; Colizza, V. Novel coronavirus (2019-nCoV) early-stage importation risk to Europe, January 2020. *Eurosurveillance* **2020**, *25*, 2000057. [CrossRef] [PubMed]
41. Brockmann, D.; Helbing, D. The hidden geometry of complex, network-driven contagion phenomena. *Science* **2013**, *342*, 1337–1342. [CrossRef] [PubMed]
42. Kraemer, M.U.G.; Yang, C.H.; Gutierrez, B.; Wu, C.H.; Klein, B.; Pigott, D.M.; Plessis, L.; Faria, N.R.; Li, R.; Hanage, W.P.; et al. The effect of human mobility and control measures on the COVID-19 epidemic in China. *Science* **2020**, *368*, 493–497. [CrossRef] [PubMed]
43. Ruktanonchai, N.W.; Floyd, J.R.; Lai, S.; Ruktanonchai, C.W.; Sadilek, A.; Rente-Lourenco, P.; Ben, X.; Carioli, A.; Gwinn, J.; Steele, J.E.; et al. Assessing the impact of coordinated COVID-19 exit strategies across Europe. *Science* **2020**, *369*, 1465–1470. [CrossRef] [PubMed]

Disclaimer/Publisher's Note: The statements, opinions and data contained in all publications are solely those of the individual author(s) and contributor(s) and not of MDPI and/or the editor(s). MDPI and/or the editor(s) disclaim responsibility for any injury to people or property resulting from any ideas, methods, instructions or products referred to in the content.

Article

Integrating Fuzzy MCDM Methods and ARDL Approach for Circular Economy Strategy Analysis in Romania

Camelia Delcea, Ionuț Nica *, Irina Georgescu, Nora Chiriță and Cristian Ciurea

Department of Economic Informatics and Cybernetics, Bucharest University of Economic Studies, 010552 Bucharest, Romania; camelia.delcea@csie.ase.ro (C.D.); irina.georgescu@csie.ase.ro (I.G.); nora.chirita@csie.ase.ro (N.C.); cristian.ciurea@ie.ase.ro (C.C.)
* Correspondence: ionut.nica@csie.ase.ro; Tel.: +40-728111808

Abstract: This study investigates the factors influencing CO_2 emissions in Romania from 1990 to 2023 using the Autoregressive Distributed Lag (ARDL) model. Before the ARDL model, we identified a set of six policies that were ranked using Fuzzy Electre, Topsis, DEMATEL, and Vikor. The multi-criteria decision-making (MCDM) methods have highlighted the importance of a circular policy on CO_2 emission reduction, which should be a central focus for policymakers. The results of the ARDL model indicate that, in the long term, renewable energy production reduces CO_2 emissions, showing a negative relationship. Conversely, an increase in patent applications and urbanization contributes to higher CO_2 emissions, reflecting a positive impact. In total, five key factors were analyzed: CO_2 emissions per capita, patent applications, gross domestic product, share of energy production from renewables, and urbanization. Notably, GDP does not significantly explain CO_2 emissions in the long run, suggesting that economic growth alone is not a direct driver of CO_2 emission levels in Romania. This decoupling might result from improvements in energy efficiency, shifts towards less carbon-intensive industries, and the increased adoption of renewable energy sources. Romania has implemented effective environmental regulations and policies that mitigate the impact of economic growth on CO_2 emissions.

Keywords: circular economy; Fuzzy Electre; Fuzzy Topsis; Fuzzy Vikor; fuzzy DEMATEL; ARDL

MSC: 03B52; 03E72; 28E10; 47S40

Citation: Delcea, C.; Nica, I.; Georgescu, I.; Chiriță, N.; Ciurea, C. Integrating Fuzzy MCDM Methods and ARDL Approach for Circular Economy Strategy Analysis in Romania. *Mathematics* **2024**, *12*, 2997. https://doi.org/10.3390/math12192997

Academic Editor: James Liou

Received: 6 August 2024
Revised: 14 September 2024
Accepted: 24 September 2024
Published: 26 September 2024

Copyright: © 2024 by the authors. Licensee MDPI, Basel, Switzerland. This article is an open access article distributed under the terms and conditions of the Creative Commons Attribution (CC BY) license (https://creativecommons.org/licenses/by/4.0/).

1. Introduction

Considered as an innovative economic model, the Circular Economy (CE) promotes the main policy of using resources in an efficient way coupled with a waste minimization objective. The CE model, as opposed to a traditional, linear economic model, as it is currently in Romania, offers sustainable solutions taking into account the current global challenges of climate change and environmental protection.

In the Romanian context, the implementation of CE strategies becomes essential to support sustainable development and improve the economic and environmental performance. The present study uses a fuzzy multi-criteria approach and an ARDL econometric model to analyze and prioritize CE strategies relevant for Romania. By integrating these methods, the research provides a detailed understanding of the critical factors influencing the transition to a CE, helping to inform strategic and operational decisions for the country's sustainable development. This comprehensive approach enables the assessment of the dynamic interdependencies between CO_2 emissions and economic and social factors, providing a holistic perspective on the impact of circular policies.

According to the National Strategy for the CE (NSCE) [1], Romania needs a long-term framework and strategic direction to overcome the challenges in the transition from a linear to a CE. The overall objective of the NSCE is to provide this framework, and decoupling economic development from the use of natural resources and environmental degradation is considered as a metric of success for this transition.

CE means responsible consumption and production, and the National Strategy proposes [1], among other things, to increase resource productivity, reduce waste generation, and increase recycling.

According to the European Parliament [2], CE is a production and consumption model that focuses on maximizing the use of resources through sharing, renting, reuse, repair, refurbishment, and recycling. This model extends the life of products, thereby reducing waste and the consumption of new resources. This approach contributes to sustainable development by providing solutions to protect the environment and make efficient use of the available resources.

Currently, the most impactful factor in addressing global climate change is technological advancement [3]. By Chen and Lee [4], the enhancement of environmental legislation has led to a consistent increase in environmental technologies having the goal to reduce CO_2 emissions. These advancements foster the rapid expansion of new technological applications, boosting energy efficiency and reducing energy consumption [5]. Technological innovation is important in economic restructuring and optimization, shifting traditional economic development from a production-driven approach to an innovation-driven model, lowering CO_2 emissions associated with industrialization [6].

The main goal of our study is to assess how to set clear priorities in the implementation of CE strategies using multi-criteria fuzzy decision-making methods. Prioritizing these strategies is important given the limited resources and the urgent need for effective solutions to reduce CO_2 emissions. Additionally, based on the established priorities, we assess how CE contributes to CO_2 emissions reduction and long-term economic sustainability.

Our research makes an innovative contribution by integrating fuzzy MCDM methods (Fuzzy Electre, Topsis, DEMATEL, and Vikor) with the ARDL model for the evaluation and prioritization of the factors that influence CO_2 emissions within the circular economy strategies in Romania. Although the methods used are well known in the literature, the originality of this study lies in their application in a specific context, related to the circular economy and emission reduction strategies in Romania, a field little explored until now. The integration of these methods enables a complex analysis of influencing factors, providing a unique insight into the interdependencies between these factors and their impact on CO_2 emissions.

Our study can contribute to the development of a framework for prioritizing specific CE policies that contribute to the transition towards a CE. By integrating multi-criteria fuzzy methodologies and a quantitative model, our approach allows an in-depth and detailed analysis of the impact of different CE policies on CO_2 emissions, economic productivity, and sustainability. The benefits include identifying the most effective policies to reduce emissions and stimulate economic growth, as well as providing a framework for informed decision making by policymakers. This model offers a valuable new perspective on how to effectively implement CE strategies. Also, prioritization is important because it allows policymakers to focus on the most significant contributors to CO_2 emissions, enabling more targeted and efficient mitigation strategies. Without understanding which factors have the greatest impact, whether positive or negative, it is challenging to allocate resources and develop policies that maximize environmental and economic benefits.

The structure of this research is as follows: In Section 2 we explore the relevant literature on the relationships between technological innovations and CO_2 emissions, between GDP and CO_2 emissions, between renewable energy and CO_2 emissions, as well as some current research applying fuzzy MCDM in specific CE studies. Section 3 is dedicated to describing the methodological flow as well as the data collection phase. The Fuzzy Electre, Topsis, Vikor, and DEMATEL methods will be described, together with the ARDL model. Section 4 presents the empirical results obtained from the application of fuzzy MCDM methods, as well as the relationships established by the ARDL model both in the long and short term between CO_2 emissions and patent application, GDP, share of energy production from renewables, and urbanization. Section 5 is dedicated to presenting the main conclusions, policy recommendations, and to describing the limitations of our study, as well as future research directions.

2. Literature Review

2.1. The Relationship between Technological Innovation and CO_2 Emissions

The study by Liu et al. [7] tests China's fast-tracking green patent applications (FGPA) system by studying the effect of green innovation incentive-based policies (GIIPs) on CO_2 emissions in Chinese cities. The findings indicate that cities in the treatment group experienced a significant reduction in CO_2 emissions by approximately 1.6% following the implementation of the FGPA. Wang et al. [8] examine the long-term and short-term effects of green invention patents and green utility model patents on CO_2 emissions using an ARDL model for China for the period 1993–2020. Green invention patents help reduce the carbon emission intensity in the short term but become a hindrance in the long term. In contrast, green utility model patents consistently suppress the carbon emission intensity in both the short and long terms.

Extreme weather events have increased in frequency and intensity, causing significant damage in Europe, particularly in 2023, which recorded the highest temperatures in history. Dunyo et al. [9] examine, in their study, economic and policy uncertainty on CO_2 emissions using the environmental Kuznets curve. The results of the study point to a direct negative impact of uncertainty on averages. Technologies also reduce CO_2 emissions. Another study by Zhao et al. [10] evaluates the level of technological innovation and carbon efficiency in China using panel data from 30 provinces. They also apply the Panel Vector Error Correction Model to explore differences across regions in the impact of technological innovation on CO_2 emissions. The results highlighted that although the trend of technological innovation is still growing, the overall level is relatively low.

Raihan et al. [5] found for Malaysia that a 1% increase in the number of patent applications is linked to a 0.05% reduction in CO_2 emissions. These findings reveal that increased renewable energy use and technological innovation can reduce Malaysia's carbon emissions while economic growth deteriorates the environmental quality. The study by Hu et al. [11] examines the status, spatial network, and determining factors of low-carbon patent applications in China since 2001 using social network analysis.

2.2. The Relationship between GDP and CO_2 Emissions

Georgescu and Kinnunen [12] studied the determinants of CO_2 emissions for Finland during 1990–2021. The authors obtained a negative long-term influence of productivity on CO_2 emissions. Higher productivity often results from technological advancements that improve the energy efficiency. In Finland, industries may adopt more efficient machinery and processes, reducing the energy required for production and, consequently, lowering CO_2 emissions. Increased productivity can also stem from better management practices and optimized production processes, which minimize waste and reduce energy consumption. Georgescu and Kinnunen [13] explored the impact of GDP per capita, FDI, and energy use on the ecological footprint in Finland during 1990–2021 using the ARDL model. A result of the paper is that GDP negatively influences the ecological footprint. A higher GDP often correlates with a greater investment in technology and innovation. Finland, known for its technological advancements, has developed and adopted energy-efficient technologies across various sectors, reducing the ecological footprint despite economic growth. Finland's advancements in clean energy technologies, such as bioenergy and wind power, contribute to a lower ecological footprint. The paper by Onofrei et al. [14] examines the dynamics of the relationship between GDP and CO_2 emissions in the 27 EU member states from 2000 to 2017 using a panel data approach. The DOLS method indicates that, on average, a 1% increase in GDP results in a 0.072% increase in CO_2 emissions. If energy efficiency improvements are not achieved, rising GDP per capita will lead to increased CO_2

emissions, meaning that as an economy becomes wealthier, its per capita CO_2 emissions will also rise [15].

2.3. The Relationship between Urbanization and CO_2 Emissions

Luqman et al. [16] measure urban CO_2 emissions across 91 cities. A cluster analysis indicates that in developing countries, rapid increases in both urban areas and per capita CO_2 emissions are prevalent. Cities in the developed countries exhibit slower growth in both urban areas and per capita CO_2 emissions. The study by Muñoz et al. [17] examines the carbon footprints of over 8000 Austrian households across three urbanization levels: urban, semi-urban, and rural. The findings indicate that urban residents in Austria have the lowest carbon footprint among the three groups, followed by rural residents, with semi-urban residents having the highest. Overall, the study suggests that urbanization in Austria could lead to a relative reduction in emissions in the future due to more compact city structures. Chen et al. [18] use panel data from OECD countries spanning from 1996 to 2018. The study employs the Feasible Generalized Least Squares (FGLS) method and reveals an inverted U-shaped curve between urbanization and carbon emissions. The average urbanization level in OECD countries falls on the left side of this curve, suggesting that increased urbanization leads to higher carbon emissions in most OECD countries. Zhang et al. [19] argued that urbanization creates an economy of scale effect, becoming the primary driver for the development of non-fossil energy sources, which significantly aids in reducing carbon emissions.

2.4. The Relationship between Renewable Energy and CO_2 Emissions

Szetela et al. [20] apply two-step GMM and Generalized Least Squares (GLS) methods for 43 countries heavily reliant on natural resources from 2000 to 2015. They obtain that renewable energy significantly reduces per capita CO_2 emissions, with a 1 percentage point increase in renewable energy consumption resulting in a 1.25% decrease in CO_2 emissions per capita. Bilan et al. [21] investigates the impact of renewable energy and GDP growth on CO_2 emissions in EU member states from 1995 to 2015. Through the use of cointegration and other empirical methods, including the Vector Error Correction Model (VECM), the study demonstrates that the adoption of renewable energy leads to enhanced environmental quality by reducing CO_2 emissions. Feng [22] uses FMOLS and the Markov switching regression model to investigate the long-term impact of green finance, green energy, openness, and R&D expenditures on carbon emissions for China. It follows that these variables enhance the environmental quality. Petruška et al. [23] analyze the relationship between CO_2 emissions and other factors including energy from renewable sources across 22 European countries from 1992 to 2019. By means of FMOLS and DOLS, it was proved that the energy produced from renewable sources leads to a reduction in CO_2 emissions per capita.

2.5. Application of Fuzzy MCDM in Circular Economy Assessment

CE is a concept of converting waste materials and energy into capital for other purposes, according to the study by Petković et al. [24]. The authors used an adaptive neuro fuzzy inference system (ANFIS) in their study to analyze the effect of waste generation, recycling, renewable energy, biomass, and soil pollution on GDP.

Gou et al. [25], in their study, consider that CE is even more important as it has attracted the attention of specialists, especially due to the evolution of industry to Industry 4.0. The authors conducted a bibliometric analysis in their study to identify the fuzzy techniques used in CE. Among the MCDM methods identified by the authors are Fuzzy Topsis, Fuzzy DEMATEL, Fuzzy Analytic Hierarchy Process (ANP), Fuzzy Vikor, Fuzzy Electre, and other fuzzy MCDM.

Given the difficulties in managerial and policy choices, CE remains a still-contested concept in essence, given that circularity has not been systematically adopted, according to the study by Bai et al. [26]. The authors propose a set of measures specific to circularity and utilize the double hesitation fuzzy sets (DHFS) method for the evaluation and selection of CE providers.

Another study focuses on the fashion industry, as the authors Abdelmeguid et al. [27] consider that this industry generates a large amount of pollution. In their study, the authors use Fuzzy Total Interpretive Structural Modeling (Fuzzy-TISM) to determine how decisions should be made regarding the main challenges in the successful implementation of CE in the fashion industry.

Table 1 presents a synthesis of relevant studies addressing topics related to the circular economy and renewable energy, using various fuzzy multi-criteria decision-making methods (Fuzzy MCDM) and other similar techniques. The selected studies cover a wide range of topics, from the classification of business models for the successful adoption of the circular economy to the identification and evaluation of optimal renewable energy sources.

Table 1. Overview of Key Studies on Circular Economy and Renewable Energy Using Fuzzy MCDM Methods.

Authors, Year, References	Scope	Technique	Criteria
Husain et al., 2021, [28]	Classification of business models for the successful adoption of the CE	Fuzzy Topsis	Partnership; Activities; Resources; Value proposition; Customer Relationships; Distribution Channels; Client Segments; Cost structure; Revenue flows;
Damgaci et al., 2017, [29]	Evaluation of Turkey's Renewable Energy	Intuitionistic Fuzzy Topsis	Technical; Economical; Environmental; Social;
Öztayşi and Kahraman, 2015, [30]	Evaluation of Renewable Energies Alternatives	Interval Type-2 Fuzzy AHP; Hesitant Fuzzy Topsis	Renewable energy factors; uncertainty; linguistic preference;
Khan and Haleem, 2020, [31]	Identifying and evaluating key strategies for adopting circular economy practices	Fuzzy DEMATEL	11 strategies for adopting the CE, including involving management, creating a vision and goals;
Boran et al., 2012, [32]	Assessment of renewable energy technologies for electricity generation in Turkey	Intuitionistic Fuzzy Topsis	Renewable Energy Technologies: Photovoltaic, Hydro, Wind, Geothermal
Kaya and Kahraman, 2010, [33]	Determining the best renewable energy alternative and optimal location for production in Istanbul	Integrated Fuzzy VIKOR-AHP	Criteria for the selection of renewable energy and location: technical, economic, geographical, social
Li et al., 2024, [34]	Identifying the most suitable renewable energy source for Malaysia's sustainable development	Fuzzy Multi-Criteria Decision Making (MCDM) based on cumulative prospect theory	Technology, economy, society, environment; Efficiency, payback period, job creation, CO_2 emissions
Riaz et al., 2023, [35]	Application of cubic bipolar fuzzy sets for the selection of the best renewable energy source	Cubic Bipolar Fuzzy Set (CBFS), CBF-VIKOR, Einstein averaging aggregation operators	Selection of renewable energy sources
Simmhan et al., 2009, [36]	Evaluation of the development of the circular economy in the coal mining industry	Membership transformation algorithm, fuzzy evaluation	Developing the circular economy in coal mining, dynamic assessment
Govindan et al., 2022, [37]	Prioritizing barriers to circular economy adoption in the cable and wire industry	Fuzzy Best-Worst Method (BWM), Fuzzy DEMATEL, Super matrix	Barriers to circular economy adoption: installation costs, financial limitations, lack of public awareness, etc.

Table 1. Cont.

Authors, Year, References	Scope	Technique	Criteria
Ayçin and Kayapinar Kaya, 2021, [38]	Identification of barriers to the implementation of the zero-waste strategy in Turkey in the context of the circular economy	Fuzzy DEMATEL	12 key barriers to zero waste implementation: uncertainty of goals, lack of financial aid, etc.
Turgut and Tolga, 2018, [39]	Evaluation and selection of the best sustainable and/or renewable energy alternative	Fuzzy VIKOR, Fuzzy TODIM, Sensitivity Analysis	Renewable Energy: Solar, Wind, Hydroelectric, Storage Gas (LFG)
Rejeb et al., 2022, [40]	Identifying and prioritizing barriers in the adoption of blockchain technology in the circular economy	Fuzzy Delphi, Best-Worst Method (BWM)	16 barriers to blockchain adoption in the CE: lack of knowledge, reluctance to change, technological immaturity
Khan and Ali, 2022, [41]	Creating a framework for the adoption of smart waste management in the context of the circular economy for Pakistan	Fuzzy SWARA, Fuzzy VIKOR	16 critical enablers for the adoption of smart waste management, including regulations, industry responsibility, digitalization (ICT and IoT)
Poonia et al., 2024, [42]	Development of a multi-objective mathematical model for the circular economy, integrating leasing and other strategies	Multi-objective Fuzzy Mixed Integer Linear Programming	Economic, environmental and social objectives; the concept of leasing, reuse, refurbishment, primary and secondary recycling

The main methodologies used include Fuzzy Topsis, Fuzzy DEMATEL, Fuzzy Vikor, Fuzzy Delphi, as well as integrated approaches such as combinations of AHP, BWM, and other methods. Each study focused on criteria ranging from technical, economic, social, and environmental to assessing barriers to the adoption of the circular economy and innovative technologies such as blockchain.

3. Methodology and Data Collection

3.1. Fuzzy Multi-Criteria Decision-Making Methods

Since the introduction of fuzzy set theory by Zadeh [43] and the subsequent development of decision-making methods in fuzzy environments by Bellman and Zadeh [44], there has been a growing body of research addressing uncertain and fuzzy problems using this theoretical framework. Building on these foundational works, this study employs fuzzy decision-making theory to account for the potential subjective and imprecise judgments of evaluators in assessing some economic policies according to various criteria.

Fuzzy decision making is particularly effective when the information available is uncertain or incomplete. It allows for the incorporation of subjective judgments and expert opinions, which are often expressed in qualitative terms. This approach frequently uses linguistic variables, which are variables whose values are not numbers but words or sentences in natural language. Fuzzy decision making is widely used in MCDM, where multiple conflicting criteria need to be evaluated to make a decision. It provides a framework for aggregating different criteria, each potentially expressed in fuzzy terms, into a final decision. In this section we will discuss three fuzzy decision-making techniques: fuzzy ELECTRE, fuzzy TOPSIS, and fuzzy VIKOR. These methods were chosen due to their robustness in handling complex decision-making scenarios with multiple conflicting criteria [45–49], which makes them suitable for evaluating priorities in the implementation of CE strategies to reduce CO_2 emissions.

3.1.1. Fuzzy Electre

Fuzzy ELECTRE (Elimination and Choice Translating Reality) is an extension of the traditional ELECTRE method by Roy and Bertier [50]. Fuzzy Electre is a MCDM that uses fuzzy set theory to address uncertainty and ambiguity in the assessment process. It is used to evaluate and prioritize alternatives by assessing several criteria, facilitating a more sophisticated analysis of complex decision-making scenarios. There have been several fuzzy versions of the ELECTRE method proposed: Akram et al. [51], Rouyendegh and Erol [52], Komsiyah et al. (2019), etc. We briefly present a well-known fuzzy ELECTRE version in line with Dubois and Prade [53], Komsiyah et al. [54], and Kahraman [55]:

➤ Step 1: Defining the problem and identifying the set of criteria.

We identify m criteria $C_1, C_2, \ldots, C_m$.

➤ Step 2: Defining the set of alternatives.

We define n alternatives $A_1, A_2, \ldots, A_n$.

➤ Step 3: Building the fuzzy decision matrix $X = (x_{ij})$, $i = 1, \ldots, n$, $j = 1, \ldots, m$.

The element x_{ij} represents the evaluation of the alternative i according to the criterion j. These values can be fuzzy numbers, sometimes represented by the triangular fuzzy numbers $A = (a, b, c)$. The membership function of the triangular fuzzy number A is given in relation (1), according to [53]:

$$A(x) = \begin{cases} 0, \text{ if } x < a \text{ and } x > c \\ \frac{x-a}{b-a}, \text{ if } a \leq x \leq b \\ \frac{c-x}{c-b}, \text{ if } b \leq x \leq c \end{cases} \quad (1)$$

➤ Step 4: Normalization of the fuzzy decision matrix: $R = (r_{ij})$, $i = 1, \ldots, n$, $j = 1, \ldots, m$.

For a maximization criterion, the normalization of triangular fuzzy numbers $A = (a, b, c)$ is generally carried out with respect to the maximum possible value across all alternatives for that criterion. Let us denote the maximum possible value as c_{max}. The normalized triangular fuzzy number A' for maximization can be given by relation (2):

$$A' = \left(\frac{a}{c_{max}}, \frac{b}{c_{max}}, \frac{c}{c_{max}} \right) \quad (2)$$

For a minimization criterion, we invert the original numbers so that lower values correspond to higher normalized values, indicating a better preference. Let a_{min} denote the minimum possible value across all alternatives for that criterion. The normalized triangular fuzzy number A' for minimization can be given by relation (3):

$$A' = \left(\frac{1}{c}, \frac{1}{b}, \frac{1}{a} \right) \text{ or equivalently } A' = \left(\frac{1}{c} \times \frac{1}{a_{min}}, \frac{1}{b} \times \frac{1}{a_{min}}, \frac{1}{a} \times \frac{1}{a_{min}} \right) \quad (3)$$

This approach inverts the values, making larger original values less preferable after normalization.

➤ Step 5: Determination of the weights of the criteria.

The fuzzy weights $w = (w_1, w_2, \ldots, w_m)$ are established for the m criteria, sometimes as triangular fuzzy numbers.

➤ Step 6: The calculation of the weighted matrix $V = (w_{ij})$, $i = 1, \ldots, n$, $j = 1, \ldots, m$, where w_{ij} is calculated according to relation (4):

$$w_{ij} = r_{ij} \times w_j \quad (4)$$

➢ Step 7: Calculation of the Concordance Matrix C.

The concordance matrix C is determined by computing the concordance indexes C_{kl} between the alternatives A_k and A_l as follows (relation (5)):

$$C_{kl} = \sum_{j \in J_{kl}} w_j \qquad (5)$$

where J_{kl} is the set of criteria for which A_k is at least as good as A_l. The concordance matrix is constructed by repeating this calculation for all pairs of alternatives.

➢ Step 8: Calculation of the Discordance Matrix D.

For each pair of alternatives A_k and A_l, we identify the set of criteria D_{kl} where A_k is not at least as good as A_l. This involves comparing the fuzzy evaluations of both alternatives for each criterion. We compute the discordance index D_{kl}. For two triangular fuzzy numbers and the criterion j, $A_k = \left(a_k^j, b_k^j, c_k^j\right)$ and $A_l = \left(a_l^j, b_l^j, c_l^j\right)$, the discordance index D_{kl}^j is computed according to relation (6):

$$D_{kl}^j = \frac{\max\left[0, \left(a_l^j - c_k^j\right), \left(b_l^j - b_k^j\right), \left(c_l^j - a_k^j\right)\right]}{\max\left[\left(\left(c_l^j - a_l^j\right), \left(c_k^j - a_k^j\right)\right]} \qquad (6)$$

The overall discordance index D_{kl} between the alternatives A_k and A_l is the maximum discordance index across all criteria, which is given in relation (7):

$$D_{kl} = max_{j \in \{1,...,m\}} D_{kl}^j \qquad (7)$$

The discordance matrix is constructed by repeating this calculation for all pairs of alternatives.

➢ Step 9: Construction of the Concordance Dominance Matrix.

This step involves determining whether the concordance index C_{kl} for the pair of alternatives (A_k, A_l) exceeds a predetermined concordance threshold c. The concordance dominance matrix S is obtained as follows (relation (8)):

$$S_{kl} = \begin{cases} 1, & if\ C_{kl} \geq c \\ 0, & if\ C_{kl} < c \end{cases} \qquad (8)$$

The concordance threshold c is often set based on the decision maker's preference or statistical considerations.

➢ Step 10: Construction of the Discordance Dominance Matrix.

Similarly, the discordance dominance matrix T is constructed by comparing the discordance index D_{kl} with a discordance threshold d, such that $c + d = 1$. Its elements are given in relation (9):

$$T_{kl} = \begin{cases} 1, & if\ D_{kl} \geq d \\ 0, & if\ D_{kl} < d \end{cases} \qquad (9)$$

The lower the discordance index, the more preferable the alternative.

➢ Step 11: Construction of the Aggregate Dominance Matrix.

The aggregate dominance matrix F indicates the overall dominance of one alternative over another. Its elements are given in relation (10):

$$F_{kl} = S_{kl} T_{kl} \qquad (10)$$

The values in the matrix are binary, where 1 indicates that alternative A_k dominates alternative A_l, considering both concordance and discordance, and 0 indicates otherwise.

➤ Step 12: Determination of Outranking Relations.

An alternative A_k is the said outrank alternative A_l if $F_{kl} = 1$ and $F_{lk} = 0$. This means A_k is preferred over A_l under the given criteria and thresholds.

This methodological flow was implemented in Python using the basic functions: *fuzzy_min*, *fuzzy_max*, *fuzzy_multiple*, and *fuzzy_compare*. The first two functions are used to calculate the minimum and maximum elements of the fuzzy intervals, and the function *fuzzy_multiple* was used to calculate the product of the elements of the fuzzy intervals and the function *fuzzy_compare* to determine if all the elements in one interval are greater than or equal to the elements in another interval (concordance), but also to check if at least one element in an interval is smaller than the elements in another interval (discordance). The final scores for each policy will be determined by aggregating measures of concordance and discordance, thereby providing an assessment of the relative performance of each alternative. Based on these scores, policies will be ranked to identify the most effective solutions. We will also use graphical representations to clearly visualize these scores and the final ranking, making it easier to interpret the results.

3.1.2. Fuzzy Topsis

Fuzzy Topsis is a method used to identify the best alternative by calculating the geometric distance from an ideal and an anti-ideal solution [56,57]. This technique assumes that the chosen alternatives should have the smallest distance from the ideal solution and the largest distance from the anti-ideal solution, facilitating a direct comparative analysis [58,59].

According to Chen [60], Awasthi et al. [61], and Nădăban et al. [62], the methodological flow for fuzzy Topsis is:

➤ Step 1: Determination of Decision Matrix.

The decision matrix is $X = (x_{ij})$, $i = 1, \ldots, n$, $j = 1, \ldots, m$, where n is the number of alternatives and m is the number of criteria. The elements of X are fuzzy numbers representing the evaluation of alternative i with respect to criterion j.

➤ Step 2: Determine the Fuzzy Positive Ideal Solution (FPIS) and Fuzzy Negative Ideal Solutions (FNIS).

FPIS is denoted A^+ and is computed as $A^+ = (v_1^+, \ldots, v_n^+)$, where $v_j^+ = max_i x_{ij}$ for the benefit criteria and $v_j^+ = min_i x_{ij}$ for the cost criteria.

FNIS is denoted A^- and is computed as $A^- = (v_1^-, \ldots, v_n^-)$, where $v_j^- = min_i x_{ij}$ for the benefit criteria and $v_j^- = max_i x_{ij}$ for the cost criteria.

➤ Step 3: Calculate the Distance from FPIS and FNIS.

The distance from FPIS is calculated as follows (relation (11)):

$$d_i^+ = \sqrt{\sum_{j=1}^{n} d\left(x_{ij}, v_j^+\right)^2} \tag{11}$$

The distance from FNIS is calculated according to Equation (12):

$$d_i^- = \sqrt{\sum_{j=1}^{n} d\left(x_{ij}, v_j^-\right)^2} \tag{12}$$

➤ Step 4: Compute the Closeness Coefficient *(CC)*.

The closeness coefficient for each alternative i is calculated according to relation (13):

$$CC_i = \frac{d_i^-}{d_i^- + d_i^+} \tag{13}$$

The alternatives are ranked based on closeness coefficients CC_i. The alternative with the highest CC_i value is considered the best option.

The Fuzzy Topsis algorithm was implemented in Python starting from the mathematical flow described above. Considering the decision matrix and fuzzy weights already defined, the first step performed in Python to apply the algorithm is to normalize the decision matrix to bring the values to a common scale. For normalization, I used the *normalize_fuzzy* function. After normalization, we will apply the previously defined fuzzy weights to each criterion to obtain the normalized weighted matrix. For each element in the normalized matrix, we will use the function *fuzzy_multiply* to multiply the fuzzy values with the corresponding weights. The next step is to determine the positive and negative ideal solutions that we will use to calculate the proximity coefficient. Later, we will graphically represent the results to visualize the appropriation coefficients of each policy.

3.1.3. Fuzzy Vikor

The VIKOR method was developed by Opricovic and Tzeng [48] and discussed by Opricovic and Tzeng [63]. It was introduced as a multi-criteria decision-making technique designed to identify a compromise solution when dealing with conflicting criteria. The method's name, VIKOR, stands for "VIseKriterijumska Optimizacija i Kompromisno Resenje" [64], which translates to a multi-criteria optimization and compromise solution. Vikor is a multi-criteria optimization technique aimed at ranking and choosing an alternative from a collection of possibilities. It highlights compromise solutions by evaluating the closeness of alternatives to the optimal solution and addressing conflicting criteria to obtain a conclusion that maximizes the social benefit and minimizes individual regret.

A fuzzy version of the VIKOR method was developed by Opricovic and Tzeng [63] and Kizielewicz and Bączkiewicz [65]. We present briefly its steps:

➤ Step 1: Determination of Decision Matrix.

The decision matrix is $X = (x_{ij})$, $i = 1, \ldots, n$, $j = 1, \ldots, m$, where n is the number of alternatives and m is the number of criteria. The elements of X are fuzzy numbers representing the evaluation of alternative i with respect to criterion j. Let $x = (l, m, u)$ be a triangular fuzzy number, where l is the lower limit, m is the most probable value, and u is the upper limit.

➤ Step 2: Determine Fuzzy Positive Ideal Solution (FPIS) and Fuzzy Negative Ideal Solution (FNIS).

FPIS is denoted A^+ and is computed as $A^+ = (v_1^+, \ldots, v_n^+)$, where $v_j^+ = max_i x_{ij}$ for the benefit criteria and $v_j^+ = min_i x_{ij}$ for the cost criteria.

FNIS is denoted A^- and is computed as $A^- = (v_1^-, \ldots, v_n^-)$, where $v_j^- = min_i x_{ij}$ for the benefit criteria and $v_j^- = max_i x_{ij}$ for the cost criteria.

➤ Step 3: Compute the Distance from FPIS and FNIS.

Calculate the distance between each alternative and the FPIS and FNIS using the fuzzy distance metric. For triangular fuzzy numbers, the distance $d(x_i, x_j)$ can be computed according to relation (14):

$$d(x_i, x_j) = \sqrt{\left[(l_i - l_j)^2 + (m_i - m_j)^2 + (u_i - u_j)\right]^2 \times \frac{1}{3}} \tag{14}$$

➤ Step 4: Calculate S_i, R_i, Q_i.

S_i is the sum of distances to FPIS and is calculated according to relation (15).

$$S_i = \sum_{j=1}^{n} [w_j \frac{d(x_{ij}, A^+)}{d(A^-, A^+)}] \tag{15}$$

where w_j is the weight of the j criterion.

R_i is the maximum regret (distance) for the worst-performing criterion and is calculated according to relation (16).

$$R_i = max_j [w_j \frac{d(x_{ij}, A^+)}{d(A^-, A^+)}] \qquad (16)$$

Q_i is the compromise ranking index (relation (17)).

$$Q_i = v \left(\frac{S_i - S^+}{S^- - S^+} \right) + (1 - v) \left(\frac{R_i - R^+}{R^- - R^+} \right) \qquad (17)$$

where S^+ and R^+ are the minimum S_i and R_i, S^- and R^- are the maximum S_i and R_i, and v is the weight of the strategy of most criteria.

➢ Step 5: Rank the Alternatives.

The alternatives are ranked based on their Q_i values, with the lowest Q_i indicating the best compromise solution.

3.1.4. Fuzzy DEMATEL

The Fuzzy DEMATEL (Decision-Making Trial and Evaluation Laboratory) method has been popularized quite recently in Japan as a practical way to visually express complex causal relationships. Basically, this method separates the established indicators into cause classes and effect classes; it succeeds in converting the relationship between cause-effect factors into an unintelligible structural model [66]. DEMATEL facilitates the identification of critical elements and their inter-relations, offering insight into the impacts and interactions among the criteria. Steps for making fuzzy DEMATEL are presented in the following:

➢ Step 1: Define the problem and identify criteria.

We convert variables into triangular fuzzy numbers $x_{ij} = (l, m, n)$, where l is the lower limit, m is the most likely value, and u is the upper limit.

➢ Step 2: Construct the Direct-Relation Matrix.

The decision matrix is $X = (x_{ij})$, where each element x_{ij} is the fuzzy number representing the direct influence of criterion i on criterion j.

➢ Step 3: Normalize the Direct-Relation Matrix.

We compute the normalization factor λ using Formula (18):

$$\lambda = \max \left(\max_i \sum_{j=1}^n u_{ij}, \max_j \sum_{i=1}^n u_{ij} \right) \qquad (18)$$

We normalize the matrix by dividing each element by λ, according to relation (19):

$$N = \frac{X}{\lambda} \qquad (19)$$

➢ Step 4: Calculate the Total-Relation Matrix.

We compute the total-relation matrix (T) using the following Formula (20):

$$T = N(I - N)^{-1} \qquad (20)$$

where I is the identity matrix and $N^k \to 0$ as $k \to \infty$, so we compute $(I - N)^{-1}$ as the fuzzy inverse.

➢ Step 5: Defuzzification.

We convert the fuzzy total-relation matrix into a crisp matrix T' using a defuzzification method, such as the centroid method, according to relation (21):

$$t_{ij} = \frac{l_{ij} + m_{ij} + u_{ij}}{3} \tag{21}$$

➢ Step 6: Calculate Prominence and Relation.

We calculate the prominence $D_i + R_i$ and $D_i - R_i$ for each criterion i:

$$D_i = \sum_{j=1}^{n} t_{ij}, \; R_i = \sum_{j=1}^{n} t_{ij} \tag{22}$$

where $D_i + R_i$ represents centrality and $D_i - R_i$ is causality. Centrality indicates the overall importance of each criterion in the network, being the sum of influences exerted and received. Causality shows the cause or effect role of the criteria.

➢ Step 7: Plot the Network Relationship Map (NRM)

We use the values of $D_i + R_i$ and $D_i - R_i$ to plot the causal relationship and visualize the prominence and net influence of each criterion.

3.2. Autoregressive Distributed Lag Model

The five variables are in a linear relationship, according to Equation (23):

$$\Delta CO_{2_t} = a_0 + \sum_{k=1}^{n} a_1 \Delta CO_{2_{t-k}} + \sum_{k=1}^{p} a_2 \Delta GDP_{t-k} + \sum_{k=1}^{q} a_3 \Delta PA_{t-k} + \\ + \sum_{k=1}^{r} a_4 \Delta URB_{t-k} + \sum_{k=1}^{s} a_5 EPREN_{t-k} \tag{23}$$

The time series data were converted to natural logarithms to reduce abrupt fluctuations in the series [67]. Equation (23) becomes an ARDL (n, p, q, r, s) regression (Equation (24)):

$$\Delta CO_{2_t} = a_0 + \sum_{k=1}^{n} a_1 \Delta CO_{2_{t-k}} + \sum_{k=1}^{p} a_2 \Delta GDP_{t-k} + \sum_{k=1}^{q} a_3 \Delta PA_{t-k} + \\ + \sum_{k=1}^{r} a_4 \Delta URB_{t-k} + \sum_{k=1}^{s} a_5 EPREN_{t-k} + \lambda_1 CO_{2_{t-1}} + \lambda_2 GDP_{t-1} + \lambda_3 PA_{t-1} + \\ \lambda_4 URB_{t-1} + \lambda_5 EPREN_{t-1} + \varepsilon_t \tag{24}$$

Δ is the first difference and n, p, q, r, and s are the lag orders. The Bayer and Hanck [68] cointegration test provides robust results by integrating four distinct cointegration techniques: Engle and Granger [69]—EG, Johansen [70]—J, Boswijk [71]—BO, and Banerjee et al. [72]—BA. It utilizes Fisher F-statistics to prove cointegration. The formulations of the test, following the Fisher method, are given by (25) and (26):

$$EG - J = -[ln(PEG) + ln(PJ)] \tag{25}$$

$$EG - J - BO - BA = -2[ln(PEG) + ln(PJ) + ln(PBO) + ln(PA)] \tag{26}$$

PEG, PJ, PBO, and PA represent the test probabilities for the EG, J, BO, and BA tests, respectively. If the computed Fisher statistic exceeds the critical value established by Bayer and Hanck [68], the null hypothesis of no cointegration is rejected. The study's findings are further validated using the ARDL bounds testing approach from Pesaran et al. [73]. When cointegration is present, the Error Correction Model (ECM) is specified as follows, according to relation (27):

$$\Delta CO_{2_t} = a_0 + \sum_{k=1}^{n} a_1 \Delta CO_{2_{t-k}} + \sum_{k=1}^{p} a_2 \Delta GDP_{t-k} + \sum_{k=1}^{q} a_3 \Delta PA_{t-k} + \\ + \sum_{k=1}^{r} a_4 \Delta URB_{t-k} + \sum_{k=1}^{s} a_5 \Delta EPREN_{t-k} + \Gamma ECM_{t-1} + \varepsilon_t \tag{27}$$

The Error Correction Term (ECT) represents the adjustment term that corrects deviations from the long-term equilibrium. ECT should be statistically significant and between

−2 and 0. In an ARDL framework, once the cointegration relationship is established, ECT quantifies the speed at which the dependent variable adjusts to restore the equilibrium after a disturbance. Finally, the normality test, the GLEJSER heteroskedasticity test, the Breusch–Godfrey serial correlation test, the LM test, and the Ramsey-Reset test were performed. The cumulative sum (CUSUM) and cumulative sum of squares (CUSUMSQ) tests proved the model's stability.

3.3. Data Collection

Table 2 describes the variables and their sources for the period 1990–2023. This study investigates the impact of PA, GDP, URB, and EPREN on CO_2 emissions in Romania during 1990–2023. The number of patent applications was computed as the sum of resident and non-resident patent applications. We will use it as a proxy for the level of innovation and technological advancement in an economy. It reflects the creation and dissemination of new technologies, processes, and products. In the context of CO_2 emissions, PA related to green technologies, such as renewable energy, energy efficiency, and pollution control, are representative. These innovations can directly contribute to reducing CO_2 emissions. Innovations can lead to the development of more energy-efficient technologies, which reduce the amount of energy required for industrial processes, transportation, and residential use. Patents in renewable energy technologies (e.g., solar, wind, hydro, and bioenergy) can facilitate the transition from fossil fuel-based energy sources to cleaner, renewable sources. Innovations in Carbon Capture and Storage (CCS) technologies allow for the capture of CO_2 emissions from industrial processes and their storage underground, preventing them from entering the atmosphere. Patents in CCS technologies can significantly mitigate emissions from heavy industries and power plants. For a clearer understanding of all the acronyms used in our study, see Abbreviations, which describes these acronyms.

Table 2. Variables specification.

Variable	Acronym	Measurement Unit	Source
CO_2 emissions per capita	CO_2	Tons	Our World in Data [74]
Patent applications	PA	Number	World Bank [75,76]
Gross domestic product	GDP	Constant 2015 $USD	World Bank [77]
Share of energy production from renewables	EPREN	%	Our World in Data [78]
Urbanization	URB	%	World Bank [79]

4. Empirical Results

4.1. Fuzzy Electre

Table 3 summarizes how different policies influence various criteria related to the CE and sustainability. It highlights the role of specific policies such as waste management and energy efficiency in increasing the recycling rates and renewable energy capacity. The table also highlights the importance of innovation for advancing CE technologies and how sustainable consumption can reduce material use. In addition, the table shows how CE practices can boost GDP growth and how policies to reduce CO_2 emissions improve carbon efficiency.

In Table 4, the fuzzy linguistic scale used for pairwise comparisons was created. This scale defines the relative importance of the criteria by means of linguistic terms, which are expressed in the form of intervals of triangular fuzzy numbers. The linguistic scale was created based on the way it was defined in the study by Arantes et al. [58].

Table 3. Policy impacts on CE.

Criteria	Policy
Waste recycling rate	Waste management policy (P1): Studies show that effective waste management policies can significantly increase recycling rates. Implementation of these policies leads to more efficient waste management and reduced environmental impacts [80–83].
Installed capacity of renewable energy	Energy efficiency policy (P2): There is a direct link between energy efficiency policies and the increase in installed renewable energy capacity. This is due to investments in more efficient technologies and the transition to more sustainable energy sources [84–87].
Investments in CE technologies	Innovation and development (P3): Investments in innovation and development are essential to advance circular technologies. They enable the development of more efficient processes and products, thereby reducing the impact on resources [88–92].
Materials consumption per capita	Sustainable production and consumption (P4): By implementing policies that promote responsible consumption, per capita material consumption can be significantly reduced [93–97]. This includes consumer education and regulations that encourage resource efficiency [98,99].
GDP from circular activities	GDP growth through the CE (P5): studies show that economies that adopt circular models can see an increase in GDP due to innovation and the creation of new markets and jobs [100–106].
CO_2 emissions per capita of GDP	Reducing CO_2 emissions (P6): Policies to reduce CO_2 emissions are fundamental to improving the carbon efficiency of the economy [107–109]. This is achieved by promoting green energy and optimizing industrial processes.

Table 4. Linguistic fuzzy scales for pairwise comparisons.

Fuzzy Linguistic Terms	Triangular Fuzzy Number Interval
Very High Importance (VHI)	[0.8, 0.9, 1.0]
High Importance (HI)	[0.7, 0.8, 0.9]
Moderately High Importance (MHI)	[0.6, 0.7, 0.8]
Medium Importance (MI)	[0.5, 0.6, 0.7]
Moderately Low Importance (MLI)	[0.4, 0.5, 0.6]
Low Importance (LI)	[0.3, 0.4, 0.5]
Very Low Importance (VLI)	[0.2, 0.3, 0.4]

In Table 5, the decision matrix has been constructed for the fuzzy MCDM to be applied in the following. The matrix shows the weights for each policy and the key indicator set in the context of the CE. These were established based on expert judgment, a literature review, and on empirical data, using variables such as CO_2 emissions, patent applications, GDP, renewable energy production, and urbanization. The fuzzy values associated with each policy were determined by analyzing these variables, providing an objective and evidence-based perspective on how the policies influence the circular economy. This approach eliminates the subjectivity that can occur in the evaluation by expert opinions or surveys and allows for a more precise analysis based on the relationships between the historical data and the selected evaluation criteria. Thus, for the waste management policy (P1) and the waste recycling rate, we have set revised weights, considering the importance of recycling in waste management. Regarding the installed capacity of renewable energy, we set average values considering that renewable energy contributes to P1, although it is not the main focus in waste management. For investments in CE technologies, the moderate values of the weights reflect the significant but not the most important impact on P1. Material consumption per capita is not a priority for P1; therefore, the weights set are low. A high relevance was considered for GDP from circular activities, emphasizing the close link between efficient waste management and circular economic activities. Concerning CO_2 emissions per capita of GDP, the weights set are moderate, indicating the concern to reduce CO_2 emissions. In terms of the energy efficiency policy (P2), the highest weight in the decision matrix was set for the installed capacity of renewable energy, illustrating a high importance in the policy set. CO_2 emissions per capita of GDP also received higher weights, like GDP from circular activities emphasizing both the economic link and the objective to reduce CO_2 emissions. For the policy on increasing innovation and development (P3), major importance was given to investments in technologies for the CE, emphasizing the major role of technological innovation. High weights were also set for GDP from circular activities. Of major importance for policy P4 was sustainable production and consumption, for which a high weight was set for the criterion material consumption per capita, emphasizing the need for sustainability. In order to emphasize the economic dependence on circular activities for the GDP growth policy (P5), a high weight has been assigned to the criterion GDP from circular activities, but also to the increase in investments in CE technologies. As for P6, we considered that the CO_2 emission reduction policy is directly linked to the installed capacity of renewable energy, and this criterion is important for emission reduction.

Table 5. Fuzzy decision matrix.

Policy	Waste Recycling Rate	Installed Capacity of Renewable Energy	Investments in Circular Economy Technologies	Materials Consumption per Capita	GDP from Circular Activities	CO_2 Emissions per Capita of GDP
Waste management (P1)	[0.7, 0.8, 0.9] (HI)	[0.3, 0.4, 0.5] (LI)	[0.4, 0.5, 0.6] (MLI)	[0.2, 0.3, 0.4] (VLI)	[0.6, 0.7, 0.8] (MHI)	[0.4, 0.5, 0.6] (MLI)
Energy efficiency (P2)	[0.5, 0.6, 0.7] (MI)	[0.7, 0.8, 0.9] (HI)	[0.3, 0.4, 0.5] (LI)	[0.3, 0.4, 0.5] (LI)	[0.5, 0.6, 0.7] (MI)	[0.5, 0.6, 0.7] (MI)
Innovation and development (P3)	[0.6, 0.7, 0.8] (MHI)	[0.5, 0.6, 0.7] (MI)	[0.8, 0.9, 1.00] (VHI)	[0.4, 0.5, 0.6] (MLI)	[0.6, 0.7, 0.8] (MHI)	[0.3, 0.4, 0.5] (LI)
Sustainable production and consumption (P4)	[0.3, 0.4, 0.5] (LI)	[0.4, 0.5, 0.6] (MLI)	[0.5, 0.6, 0.7] (MI)	[0.7, 0.8, 0.9] (HI)	[0.4, 0.5, 0.6] (MLI)	[0.6, 0.7, 0.8] (MHI)
GDP growth through CE (P5)	[0.4, 0.5, 0.6] (MLI)	[0.6, 0.7, 0.8] (MHI)	[0.7, 0.8, 0.9] (HI)	[0.5, 0.6, 0.7] (MI)	[0.8, 0.9, 1.00] (VHI)	[0.2, 0.3, 0.4] (VLI)
Reducing CO_2 emissions (P6)	[0.5, 0.6, 0.7] (MI)	[0.8, 0.9, 1.00] (VHI)	[0.6, 0.7, 0.8] (MHI)	[0.6, 0.7, 0.8] (MHI)	[0.7, 0.8, 0.9] (HI)	[0.4, 0.5, 0.6] (MLI)

Triangular fuzzy numbers have been set in Table 6. For the waste recycling rate, the weights [0.1, 0.2, and 0.3] were set, indicating a moderate importance of waste recycling in the CE. Recycling contributes to the reduction of resources needed for production and less waste with a semi-significant impact on sustainability. In terms of the installed renewable energy capacity, higher weights have been set in view of the importance of the transition to renewable energy sources, which is important in reducing CO_2 emissions and increasing long-term economic sustainability. The third criterion considered is material consumption per capita. The established weights underline the importance of controlling resource consumption to minimize the impact on the environment and to promote sustainable consumption practices. GDP from circular activities received higher triangular fuzzy values which emphasizes the significant contribution of the CE to economic growth, indicating that circular activities not only protect the environment, but also stimulate economic development. CO_2 emissions per capita of GDP have also been given higher weights, reflecting the need to reduce CO_2 emissions to meet environmental objectives and to support the transition to a low-carbon economy. These values were based on both professional judgment and a literature review.

The next step before applying Fuzzy MCDM was to calculate the concordance and discordance matrix. The concordance matrix was calculated in Table 7. This evaluates the extent to which one policy is better or equal to another based on the previously established criteria. We observe that the policy on CO_2 emission reduction (P6) has the highest level of concordance, being considered superior to the other policies in several comparisons, indicating strong support for this policy in reducing CO_2 emissions. Also, policies P1 and P3 have a high level of agreement with the other policies, suggesting that they can also be considered effective in the CE analysis.

Table 6. Fuzzy weight for each criterion.

Criteria	Fuzzy Weights	Linguistic Term
Waste recycling rate	[0.1, 0.2, 0.3]	Moderate importance
Installed capacity of renewable energy	[0.2, 0.3, 0.4]	Higher importance
Investments in CE technologies	[0.15, 0.25, 0.35]	Medium importance
Materials consumption per capita	[0.1, 0.2, 0.3]	Moderate importance
GDP from circular activities	[0.25, 0.35, 0.45]	Higher importance
CO_2 emissions per capita of GDP	[0.2, 0.3, 0.4]	Higher importance

Table 7. Concordance Matrix.

	P1	P2	P3	P4	P5	P6
P1	0.00	0.50	0.50	0.33	0.33	0.33
P2	0.50	0.00	0.33	0.50	0.50	0.33
P3	0.67	0.67	0.00	0.67	0.50	0.33
P4	0.67	0.50	0.33	0.00	0.33	0.33
P5	0.67	0.50	0.50	0.67	0.00	0.33
P6	0.83	0.83	0.67	0.67	0.67	0.00

The discordance matrix measures the difference between the performance of two policies on a given criterion when one is worse. We note in Table 8 that policy P6 has the lowest discordance, indicating that in comparison, the differences between it and the other policies are minimal, strengthening the support for its effectiveness. Policies P4 and P5 have higher discordances, suggesting significant variations in the efficiency relative to other policies.

Table 8. Discordance matrix.

	P1	P2	P3	P4	P5	P6
P1	0.00	0.50	0.50	0.67	0.67	0.67
P2	0.50	0.00	0.67	0.50	0.50	0.67
P3	0.33	0.33	0.00	0.33	0.50	0.67
P4	0.33	0.50	0.67	0.00	0.67	0.67
P5	0.33	0.50	0.50	0.33	0.00	0.67
P6	0.17	0.17	0.33	0.33	0.33	0.00

Having computed the concordance and discordance matrices, we determine the final scores for each alternative using the Fuzzy Electre method and plot the scores and ranking of the alternatives. In Figure 1, the final score for each policy was plotted in python using the libraries "matplotlib" and "seaborn", and in Figure 2, the ranking of the policies resulting from the Fuzzy Electre method was plotted.

We observe in Figure 1 that the CO_2 emission reduction policy has the highest score of 2.33, indicating that policy P6 is considered the most efficient and successful policy in the context of the evaluated criteria. This may mean that the CO_2 emission reduction strategy has a strong positive impact and should be prioritized in policy decisions. Policy P5 on GDP growth through circular activities scores 0.33 and rank 2, being the second most prioritized policy, suggesting that the CE can contribute significantly to GDP growth. Investing in circular technologies and creating new markets and jobs could have a positive impact. Energy efficiency (P2) in the case of Romania scores -0.66 and rank 3. Although this policy is also important, it may need further improvements or better integration with other strategies to have a greater impact. Policy P4 has the same score as policy P2, as seen in Figure 2, indicating that promoting responsible consumption and reducing material consumption per capita has a moderate impact. The innovation and development policy (P3) is a lower priority, suggesting that while it has a positive impact, it may not be implemented effectively or receive sufficient resources. Policy P1 has the lowest score, suggesting that waste management could be substantially improved. New strategies or additional resources may be needed to improve the waste recycling rates.

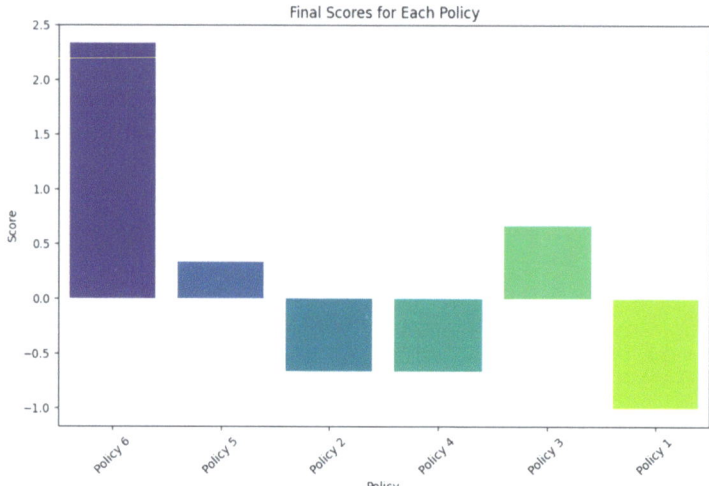

Figure 1. Final Score Plot for Fuzzy Electre.

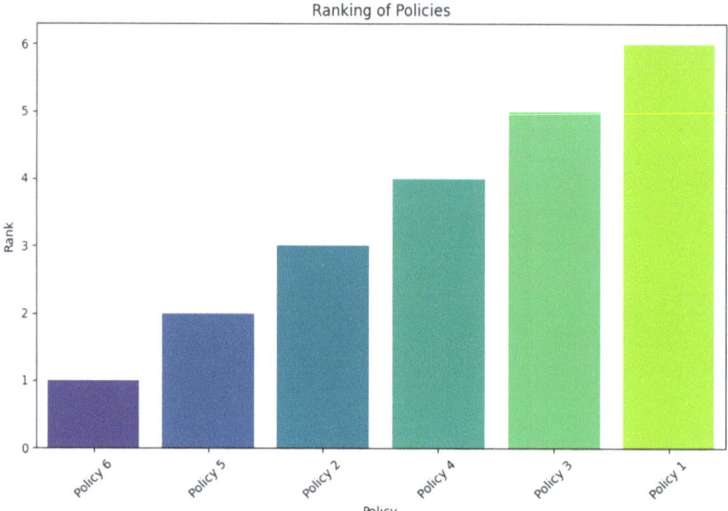

Figure 2. Policy ranking using Fuzzy Electre.

4.2. Fuzzy Topsis

Based on the fuzzy decision matrix and the fuzzy weights previously established, we used the 'normalize_fuzzy' function in Python to prepare the flow of using the Fuzzy Topsis method. We computed the function to compute the positive and negative ideal solution. Next, we used the closeness coefficient computation function 'closeness_coefficient' to compute this coefficient, which is a measure of how close each policy is to the positive ideal solution and how far it is from the negative ideal solution.

Table 9 shows the results and rank stability for each policy based on the CC.

Table 9. Results of the Fuzzy Topsis multi-criteria method.

Criteria	Closeness Coefficient (CC)	Rank
P1	0.35	6
P2	0.42	5
P3	0.53	3
P4	0.41	2
P5	0.56	4
P6	0.70	1

The results of the Fuzzy Topsis method can be visualized in Figure 3. With a CC of 0.70, P6 approaches the ideal solution. It suggests that the policy related to CO_2 emission reduction is the most effective in the analyzed context. With a coefficient of 0.56, P5 ranks second, indicating that the policy of increasing the GDP through the CE is also effective. P3 has a coefficient of 0.53, showing that the innovation and development policy is important to achieve the desired objectives. P4, with a CC of 0.41, and P2, with a CC of 0.42, respectively, suggest that the two policies have a moderate impact, being related to sustainable production and consumption and energy efficiency. The furthest from the ideal solution is P1, which indicates that the waste management policy in Romania needs improvement in order to be more effective.

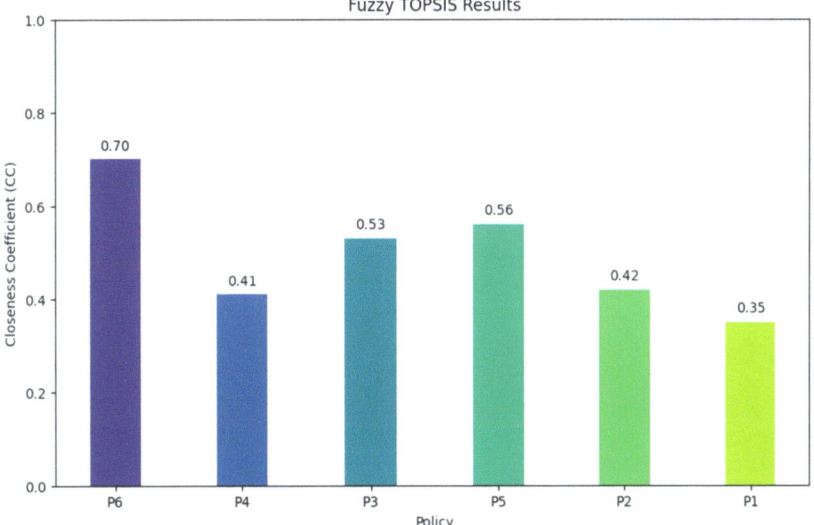

Figure 3. Policy ranking using Fuzzy Topsis.

4.3. Fuzzy DEMATEL

As for the Fuzzy DEMATEL method, centrality and causality are the two most important metrics that we calculated to prioritize the policies. In Table 10, we observe that P1, P2, P3, and P5 have positive values from a causality perspective, indicating that they are causes rather than effects, having a greater impact on the other criteria. P4 and P6, having negative values, suggest that they can be considered effects, being influenced by other criteria.

In Figure 4, we observe that although policy P1 has a negative centrality value, the causality is positive which indicates that, although it is not very central, it has a causal impact on the other policies. Policy P2 shows negative centrality and positive causality, showing that it influences other policies, but is not significantly influenced. With the lowest centrality, policy P3 indicates a moderate impact on other policies, having positive causality. With negative centrality and negative causality, policy P4 can be considered an effect rather than a cause, being influenced by other policies. Although it has negative centrality, the positive causality value for policy P5 suggests that it is influential in the policy network. Policy P6 can also be considered an effect, with less influence on other policies.

Table 10. Results of the Fuzzy DEMATEL multi-criteria method.

Criteria	Centrality (D + R)	Causality (D − R)
P1	−2.61	0.24
P2	−2.73	0.18
P3	−2.97	0.14
P4	−2.56	−0.27
P5	−3.11	0.24
P6	−2.61	−0.54

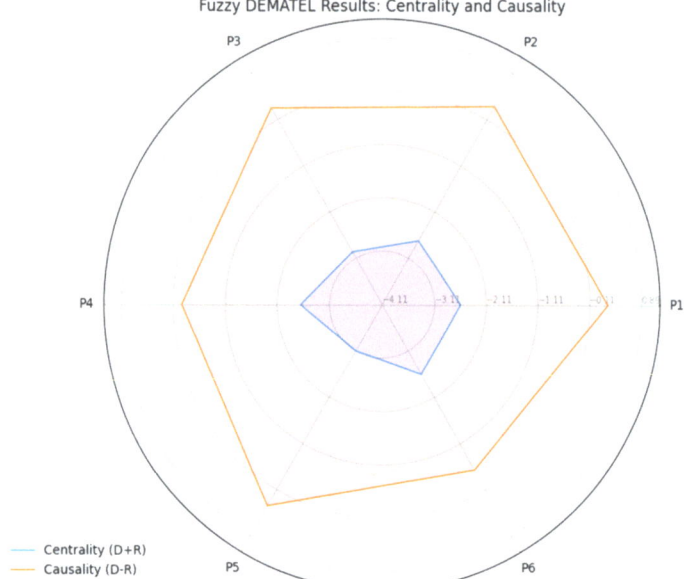

Figure 4. Policy ranking using Fuzzy DEMATEL.

4.4. Fuzzy Vikor

The last method applied is Fuzzy Vikor, being a multi-criteria decision-making technique. We computed in python the positive and negative ideal solutions based on normalized values and computed the performance metrics S, R, and Q. S is the total distance from the ideal solution, R is the maximum distance from an ideal criterion and Q is the trade-off coefficient combining S and R. Finally, the rank was stability, as shown in Table 11, based on the alternatives as a function of Q.

Table 11. Results of the Fuzzy Vikor multi-criteria method.

Policy	S	R	Q	Rank
P1	1.02	0.30	0.87	5
P2	0.90	0.35	0.67	4
P3	0.75	0.26	0.43	2
P4	0.94	0.15	0.92	6
P5	0.70	0.22	0.57	3
P6	0.47	0.30	0.00	1

Figure 5 plots the performance metrics for the Fuzzy Vikor methód. We observe that policy P6 has the lowest Q score, indicating that it is the best option according to the defined criteria and weights. Also, policies P3 and P5 have a lower Q score than the rest of the policies, being important alternatives in policy setting.

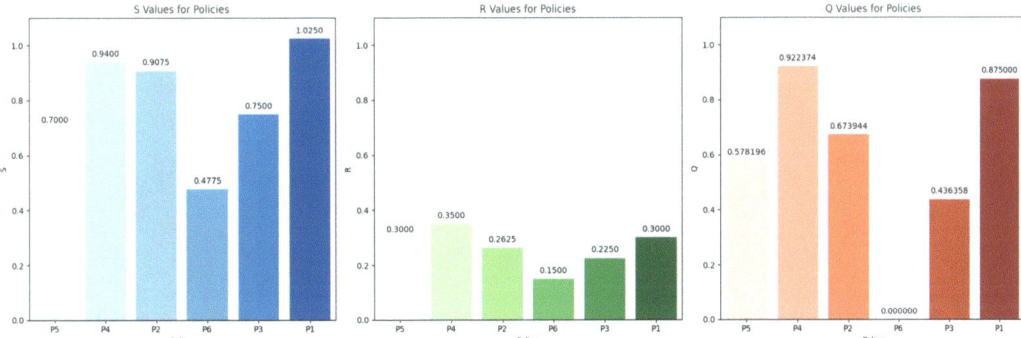

Figure 5. Policy ranking using Fuzzy Vikor.

In Figure 6, the policy prioritizations for each applied fuzzy method have been centralized. Its results will be useful in establishing the quantitative ARDL model that we will apply in the next section. We observe that in all fuzzy MCDM methods, CO_2 emissions per capita (P6) was identified as the prioritized policy (rank 1 in Fuzzy Electre, Topsis, and Vikor and an important effect factor in Fuzzy DEMATEL). Thus, it will be selected as a dependent variable in the ARDL model, associated with P1. For policy P3, we have selected in the ARDL model the variable Patent Applications (PA). Technological innovation, measured by the number of patent applications, can indicate the efficiency in developing solutions to reduce CO_2 emissions. This policy ranked 2nd with the Fuzzy Vikor method and 3rd with the Fuzzy Topsis method. Since economic growth can influence CO_2 emissions, including GDP, as a dependent variable in the ARDL model, it allows one to assess the impact of economic development on the environment. In Fuzzy DEMATEL, P5 (GDP growth through CE) was a causal factor even though its rank is 6. However, Fuzzy Electre ranks P5 at rank 2, Fuzzy Vikor at rank 3, and Fuzzy Topsis at rank 4, suggesting that economic growth through CE can influence emissions. Policies P2 and P3 ranked 3rd according to Fuzzy Electre, respectively, Fuzzy Topsis, and P3 according to Fuzzy Vikor ranked 2nd. Thus, in the ARDL model, we have selected the independent variable Share of Energy Production from Renewables (EPREN), indicating the importance of renewable energy in the context of CO_2 emission reduction. Urbanization affects both the energy demand and consumption patterns, which can have a direct impact on CO_2 emissions. Thus, the last independent variable in the model was urbanization (URB), being related to the P4 policy on sustainable production and consumption which, according to Fuzzy DEMATEL, ranks 1st.

4.5. Sensitivity Analysis of Fuzzy Results

The application of four different fuzzy methods to prioritize the same circular policies provides an image of the consistency of the results between the methods in different methodological contexts. As a complementary method, the sensitivity analysis examines the stability of the obtained results in the face of the addition of a disturbance factor, that is, it shows the robustness of the obtained results.

This section presents a sensitivity analysis of the results obtained by Fuzzy MCDM to assess their robustness and sensitivity to variations in the approximation coefficients. Sensitivity analysis is essential to understand the stability of the results and to assess whether they are reliable in the presence of possible uncertainties in the data. Regarding Fuzzy MCDM, to simulate the uncertainty and variability inherent in the data, we applied a disturbance factor between [−10%, +10%] on each coefficient. This variance was generated using a uniform distribution to reflect possible variations in the data. Basically, each CC was multiplied by an aleatory factor generated from the disturbance interval.

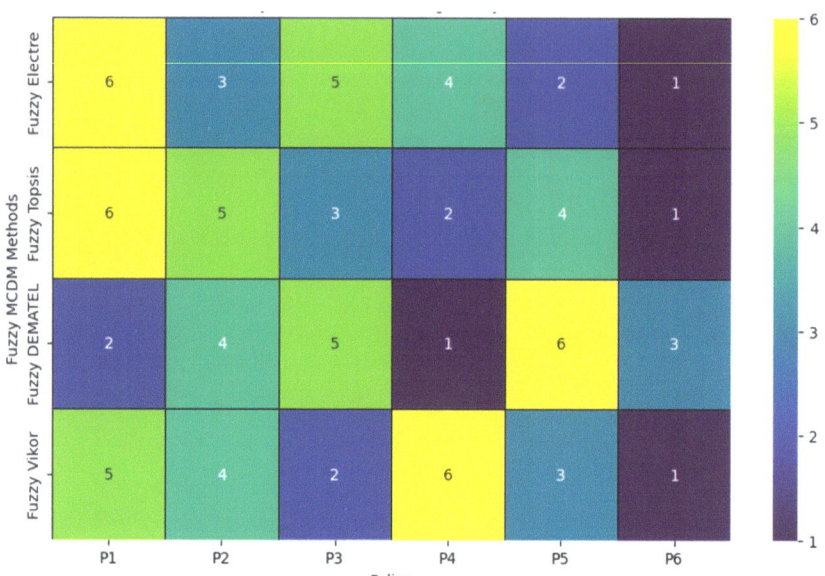

Figure 6. Policy prioritization using Fuzzy MCDM.

Thus, in Figure 7, a comparison was made between the results initially obtained with the Fuzzy Electre method and the results obtained by applying the disturbance factor. We notice that the changes in the scores of the policies are relatively small. The biggest change is observed in policy P1, from -1.00 to -0.92, and in policy P6, from 2.33 to 2.27. However, we can say that the overall ranking of the policies remains robust, with the P6 policy remaining the best alternative.

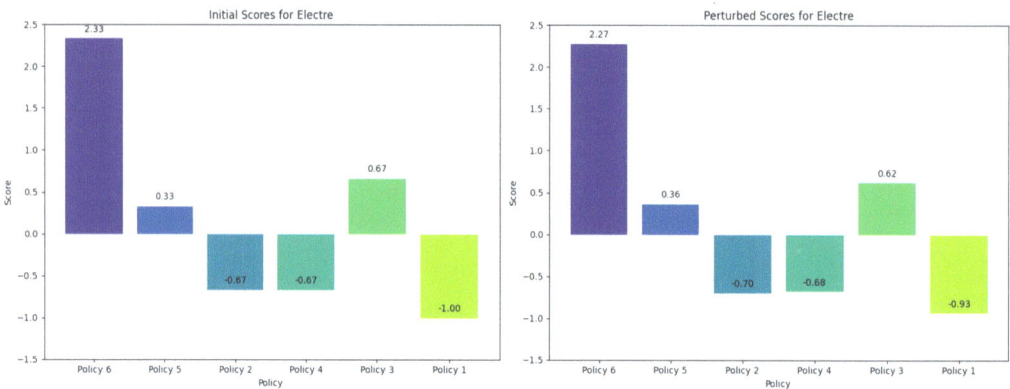

Figure 7. Sensitivity analysis for Fuzzy Electre.

Regarding the sensitivity analysis for Fuzzy Topsis, we can see in Figure 8 that after the application of the disturbance factor, the scores of the policies underwent slight changes. For example, for policy P2, the score increased from 0.42 to 0.46, and for policy P6, it decreased from 0.70 to 0.65. However, the P6 policy remains the best alternative, even after applying the disturbance factor, an aspect that underlines the robustness of the results.

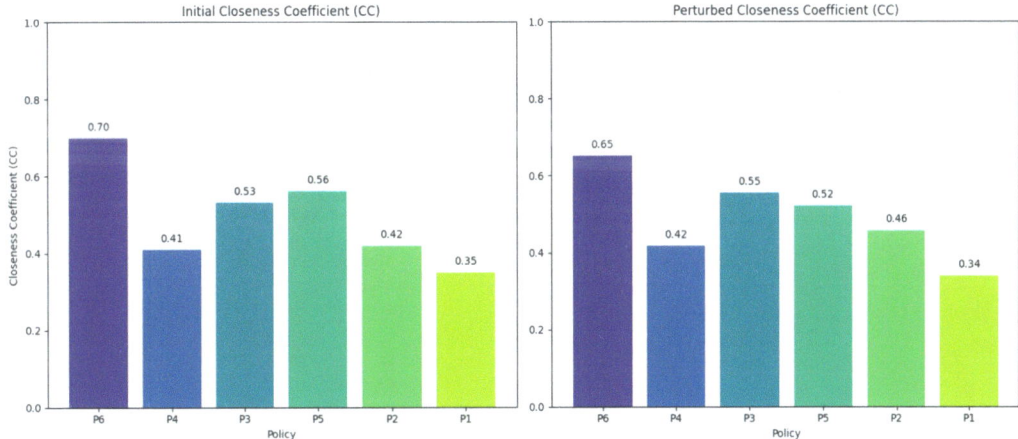

Figure 8. Sensitivity analysis for Fuzzy Topsis.

In Figure 9, the sensitivity analysis was performed for the Fuzzy DEMATEL method. We observe that the centrality and causality for the policies, when we add the disturbance factor, undergo small changes. For example, policy P2 decreases from −2.73 to −2.97 and policy P6 increases from −2.62 to −2.43. Therefore, the application of the disturbance factor did not significantly change the relations between policies, the results obtained through Fuzzy DEMATEL remained quite robust in the face of disturbances.

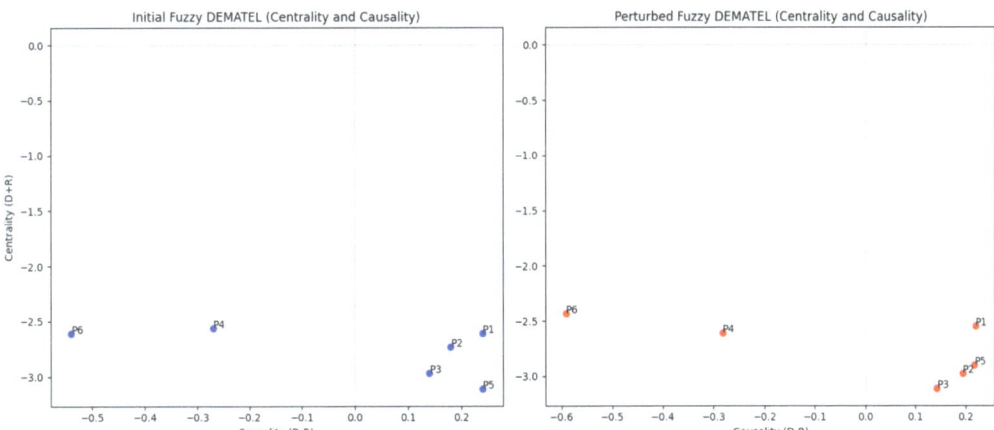

Figure 9. Sensitivity analysis for Fuzzy DEMATEL.

From the perspective of the sensitivity analysis for the Fuzzy Vikor method, in Figure 10, we can see the comparison of the score after applying the disturbance factor. It produced small variations in the scores, the largest being for policy P1 from 0.87 to 0.93 and for policy P4 from 0.92 to 0.86. However, policy P6 remains the alternative with the lowest score, further suggesting that it is the best choice according to Vikor's criteria.

Figure 11 shows the comparison of the global results of the four fuzzy MCDM methods and the results obtained after the application of the disturbance factor. We note that from the perspective of robustness and sensitivity, the Fuzzy Electre and Fuzzy Vikor methods prove to be the most robust to disturbances, maintaining the initial rankings. Fuzzy Topsis shows a moderate sensitivity, with minor changes in the ranking, while Fuzzy DEMATEL shows the highest sensitivity to disturbances.

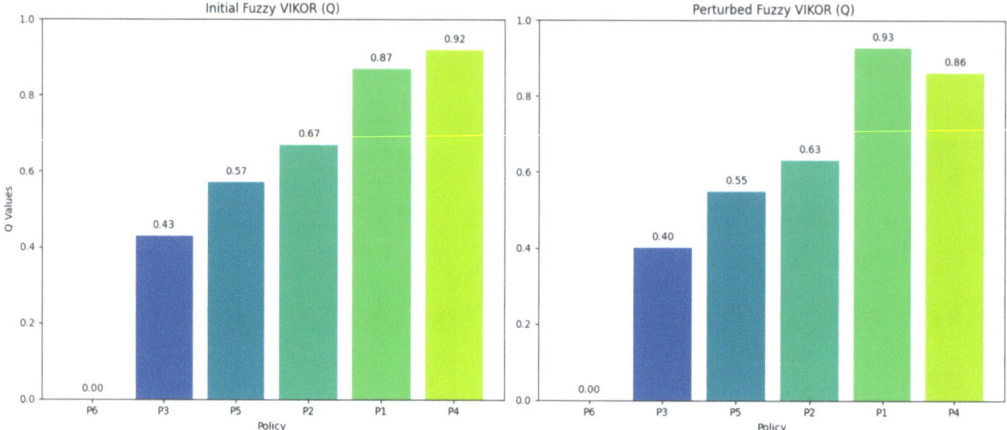

Figure 10. Sensitivity analysis for Fuzzy Vikor.

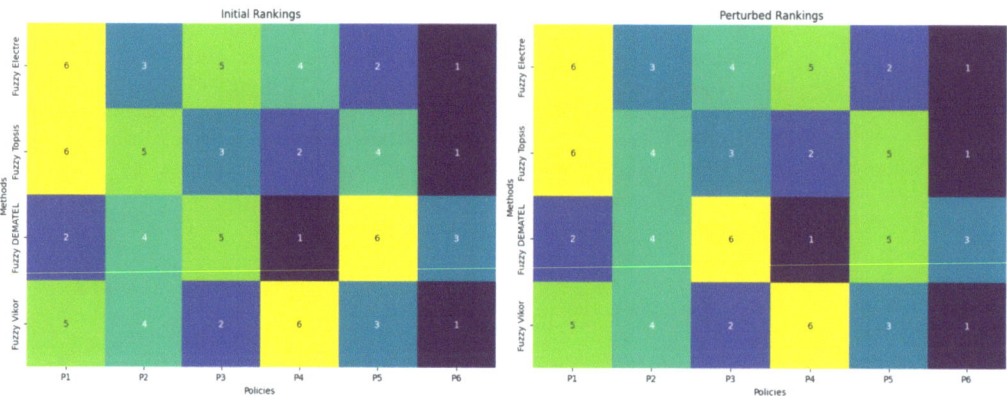

Figure 11. Comparison of Initial and Perturbed Rankings Across Fuzzy MCDM Methods.

4.6. Autoregressive Distributed Lag Model

The plots in Figure 12 show the time series for the five economic and environmental indicators in Romania. There is a clear downward trend in CO_2 emissions over the period, especially noticeable in the early years and stabilizing somewhat in the later years. Some fluctuations can be observed, but the general trend is a reduction in CO_2 emissions, indicating potential improvements in environmental policies or shifts in industrial activities. A consistent upward trend of GDP is observed, indicating economic growth over the period. This trend is relatively smooth with only minor fluctuations. The sharp increase in the GDP after around year 10 indicates periods of accelerated economic growth, possibly due to policy changes, increased investments, or integration into global markets. A downward trend for the PA is noticeable and especially pronounced in the first half of the period. This suggests a decline in innovation activities or changes in the patent system. The PA series shows significant fluctuations, indicating volatility in patent applications, which could be due to economic cycles, policy changes, or shifts in the research and development focus. The URB series shows a general upward trend, indicating increasing urbanization. There is a dip around the middle of the period followed by a recovery. The initial rapid urbanization could be due to rural-to-urban migration, economic development, and modernization, while the mid-period dip might reflect economic slowdowns or population stabilization. There is a clear upward trend if EPREN is evident, indicating an increasing share of renewable energy in electricity production. The EPREN series exhibits fluctuations, but the overall direction is positive, reflecting a shift towards sustainable energy sources, likely driven by environmental policies and technological advancements.

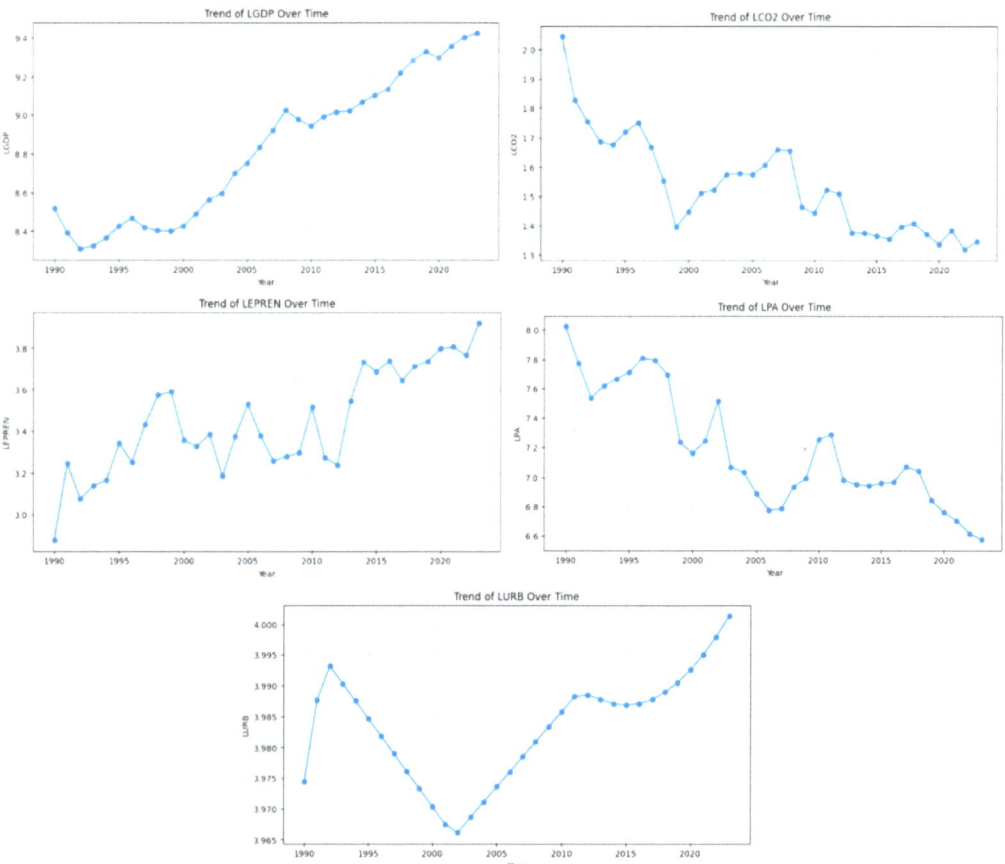

Figure 12. The evolution of CO_2, GDP, PA, URB, and EPREN for Romania (1990–2023).

Table 12 reports descriptive statistics for the variables following logarithmic transformation.

Table 12. Summary Statistics.

	CO_2	GDP	PA	URB	EPREN
Mean	1.53	8.82	7.18	3.98	3.44
Median	1.51	8.87	7.05	3.98	3.38
Maximum	2.04	9.42	8.02	4.00	3.92
Minimum	1.31	8.30	6.57	3.96	2.87
Std. Dev.	0.16	0.36	0.39	0.01	0.24
Skewness	0.88	0.10	0.48	−0.21	−0.01
Kurtosis	3.60	1.58	2.10	2.24	2.26
Jarque–Bera	4.96	2.90	2.48	1.06	0.77
Probability	0.08	0.23	0.28	0.58	0.68

In Table 12, CO_2 and PA show some positive skewness and moderate deviation from normality, suggesting that while most values are centered around the mean, there are occasionally higher values. GDP, URB, and EPREN are relatively symmetric, with mean and median values close to each other. The standard deviations indicate moderate variation except for URB, which shows minimal variation. Most variables are reasonably close to a normal distribution, as indicated by the Jarque–Bera test probabilities, which generally do not reject the null hypothesis of normality. These statistics provide insights into the behavior and trends of key economic and environmental indicators in Romania over the given period, highlighting the overall stability and variation in these measures.

The application of the Augmented Dickey Fuller [110] unit root test leads to the conclusion that CO_2 is stationary at the level and variables are integrated in order 1 (see Table 13).

Table 13. ADF Unit Root Test Results.

Variables	Level T-Statistics	First Difference T-Statistics	Order of Integration
CO_2	−3.31 ** (0.02)	−4.88 *** (0.00)	I (0)
GDP	0.88 (0.99)	−4.50 *** (0.00)	I (1)
PA	−1.76 (0.39)	−5.16 *** (0.00)	I (1)
URB	0.00 (0.95)	−3.92 ** (0.02)	I (1)
EPREN	−2.13 (0.23)	−5.52 *** (0.00)	I (1)

, * indicate the significance of variables at 5% and 1% levels, respectively.

According to Table 14, four of the five criteria indicate that a lag order of 3 is the optimal choice for the Vector Autoregression (VAR) model.

Table 14. VAR Lag order selection criteria.

Lag	LogL	LR	FPE	AIC	SC	HQ
0	163.43	N/A	2.50×10^{-11}	−10.22	−9.99	−10.14
1	333.27	273.92	2.24×10^{-15}	−19.56	−18.17 *	−19.11
2	365.60	41.71	1.60×10^{-15}	−20.03	−17.49	−19.20
3	411.86	44.77 *	5.99×10^{-16} *	−21.41 *	−17.71	−20.20 *

* indicates the lag order selected by the criterion; LR: sequential modified LR test statistic (each test at 5% level); FPE: Final prediction error; AIC: Akaike information criterion; SC: Schwarz information criterion; HQ: Hannan–Quinn information criterion.

The obtained model is ARDL (3, 3, 3, 3, 3). Table 15 shows that the F-statistic values from the EG-J and EG-J-BA-BO methods surpass the critical values at the 5% significance level. This result supports rejecting the null hypothesis of no cointegration at the 5% level.

Table 15. Bayer–Hank cointegration test.

Tests	Engle–Granger (EG)	Johansen (J)	Banerjee (BA)	Boswijk (BO)
Test statistic	−3.47	66.72	−7.69	98.99
p-value	0.32	0.00	0.00	0.00
EG-J	57.50		5% critical value, 10.57	
EG-J-BA-BO	168.02		5% critical value, 20.14	

Table 16 presents the results of the ARDL cointegration bounds test. This result indicates that the calculated F-statistic is 8.66, which exceeds the upper critical bound for I (1). Also, this result confirms the existence of cointegration among the variables.

The corresponding long-term coefficients are presented in Table 17.

From Table 17, it follows that GDP does not have a long-term influence on CO_2. Typically, economic growth can lead to increased industrial activity, higher energy consumption, and more emissions. Conversely, it can also lead to more resources for cleaner technologies and environmental regulations. The non-significant relationship here suggests that these effects might be balancing each other out in Romania, leading to no clear long-term trend.

Table 16. Results of ARDL cointegration bounds test.

Test Statistic	Value	K (Number of Regressors)
F-statistic	8.66	4
	Critical value bounds	
Significance	I (0)	I (1)
10%	2.20	3.09
5%	2.56	3.49
1%	3.29	4.37

Table 17. Long-run estimated results.

Variables	Coefficient	T-Statistics	Prob.
GDP	−0.14	−0.91	0.38
PA	0.35	2.48	0.03 **
URB	9.23	3.70	0.00 ***
EPREN	−0.42	−3.24	0.00 ***
C	−35.21	−3.89	0.00 ***

, * indicate the significance of variables at 5% and 1% levels, respectively.

During 1990–2023, Romania may have experienced shifts from heavy industry to service-based sectors, which typically emit less CO_2. This structural change could mitigate the impact of GDP growth on emissions, contributing to the lack of a significant relationship. Advances in energy efficiency and technology might reduce emissions even as the GDP grows. If Romania has adopted such measures, the expected increase in emissions from economic growth could be offset, resulting in an insignificant relationship. The implementation of environmental policies and regulations can play a crucial role in reducing emissions. If Romania has strengthened its environmental policies over time, these measures could counteract the potential emission increases associated with GDP growth.

A 1% increase in PA exerts a long-term 0.35% increase in CO_2. A 1% increase in PA exerts a long-term 0.35% increase in CO_2. The positive relationship suggests that the types of innovations being patented may be energy-intensive or not necessarily focused on reducing emissions. For example, advancements in heavy industries, transportation, or other high-emission sectors could lead to increased CO_2 emissions despite technological progress. Patent applications are often correlated with economic growth and increased industrial activity. As industries expand and new technologies are implemented, energy consumption and emissions can rise, reflecting the positive correlation between patents and CO_2. During Romania's transition period from a centrally planned to a market economy, there could have been a surge in industrial activity and associated emissions, even as the country pursued technological advancements. This finding underscores the importance of directing innovation towards sustainable and environmentally friendly technologies. Policymakers might need to incentivize green technologies and sustainable practices to decouple technological progress from CO_2 emissions.

A 1% increase in URB exerts a long-term 9.23% increase in CO_2. The substantial coefficient indicates that urbanization has a very large impact on CO_2 emissions in Romania. As more people move to urban areas, there is a significant increase in activities that contribute to emissions. Urban areas often require substantial energy to support residential, commercial, and industrial activities. A 1% increase in urbanization could mean more buildings, factories, vehicles, and overall energy demand, particularly from fossil fuels. In Romania, this leads to a disproportionate increase in CO_2 emissions, indicated by the 9.23% rise, reflecting inefficient energy use or heavy reliance on carbon-intensive energy sources. The expansion of urban infrastructure such as roads, bridges, and public transportation systems involves significant construction activities, which are typically carbon intensive. Additionally, the increase in the urban population heightens the demand for housing and commercial spaces, further boosting CO_2 emissions.

A 1% increase in EPREN leads to a 0.42% long-term decrease in CO_2. Shifting to renewable energy sources reduces the reliance on fossil fuels, which are major contributors to CO_2 emissions. This transition involves significant economic activities, including investments in renewable energy technologies, infrastructure development, and grid modernization. Renewable energy sources, particularly when scaled up, often have lower operating costs compared to fossil fuels. Over time, these cost savings can contribute to economic efficiency and reduce the overall carbon footprint of electricity production. The reduction in CO_2 emissions directly correlates with improvements in air quality, public health, and environmental sustainability. These benefits, while not always directly quantified in economic terms, contribute to a more sustainable economy and reduce the social costs associated with pollution and climate change. Increasing the share of renewables enhances energy security by diversifying the energy supply and reducing dependence on imported fossil fuels. This can lead to greater economic stability and resilience against global energy market fluctuations. The renewable energy sector fosters innovation and can create new jobs in manufacturing, installation, maintenance, and research and development. This economic activity can stimulate growth and provide new employment opportunities.

As seen in Table 18, D(CO_2(-2)) is significant at the 5% level, indicating that emissions from two periods ago have a positive and significant effect on current emissions. The GDP has a complex impact on CO_2 emissions.

Table 18. ARDL-ECM model for short-run estimated results.

Variables	Coefficient	T-Statistics	Prob.
D(CO_2(-1))	0.005	0.04	0.962
D(CO_2(-2))	0.28	2.33	0.039 **
D(GDP)	0.91	−6.91	0.000 ***
D(GDP(-1))	0.05	0.35	0.728
D(GDP(-2))	0.56	3.14	0.009 ***
D(PA)	0.15	4.83	0.005 ***
D(PA(-1))	−0.09	−2.36	0.037 **
D(PA(-2))	−0.26	−6.91	0.000 ***
D(URB)	28.79	4.65	0.000 ***
D(URB(-1))	3.07	0.38	0.704
D(URB(-2))	−8.12	−2.20	0.049 **
D(EPREN)	−0.30	−6.75	0.000 ***
D(EPREN(-1))	0.01	0.274	0.788
D(EPREN(-2))	0.18	3.85	0.002 ***
CointEq(-1)	−0.72	−8.62	0.000 ***
R-squared		0.93	
Adjusted R-squared		0.87	

, * indicate the significance of variables at 5% and 1% levels, respectively.

Current GDP growth significantly increases emissions (coefficient 0.91, significant at 1%). The second lag of GDP (D(GDP(-2))) also shows a positive and significant effect, implying that economic activities two periods ago continue to influence emissions. PA positively influences CO_2 emissions in the short term, suggesting that innovative activities or new technologies may initially increase emissions. The negative coefficients for D(PA(-1)) and D(PA(-2)) indicate that over time, these innovations likely lead to efficiency improvements or cleaner technologies, which then reduce emissions. The immediate increase could be due to the energy-intensive nature of research and development or initial deployment phases. URB has a significant immediate positive effect on emissions, suggesting that rapid urban growth drives up emissions. The second lag of URB shows a negative effect, indicating that earlier urbanization efforts might have led to infrastructural or policy changes, reducing emissions later. Increasing EPREN significantly reduces CO_2 emissions in the short term. The immediate impact is strongly negative, showing the effectiveness of renewable energy in lowering emissions. However, the second lag of EPREN has a positive effect, suggesting some delayed impact or transitional effects might temporarily offset reductions.

ECT is highly significant and negative, indicating a strong tendency to revert to the long-run equilibrium. The speed of adjustment is 72%, suggesting that deviations from the long-run equilibrium level of CO_2 emissions are corrected relatively quickly. Table 19 presents the null hypotheses for the diagnostic and stability tests.

Table 19. Results of diagnostic and stability tests.

Diagnostic Test	H_0	Decision Statistic [p-Value]
Serial Correlation	There is no serial correlation in the residuals	Accept H_0 0.39 [0.54]
Heteroscedasticity (GLEJSER)	There is no autoregressive conditional heteroscedasticity	Accept H_0 0.96 [0.54]
Jarque–Bera	Normal distribution	Accept H_0 1.15 [0.56]
Ramsey Reset	Absence of model misspecification	Accept H_0 0.56 [0.58]

The CUSUM and CUSUM of the Squares paths stay within the 5% significance level, as depicted by the red dashed line in Figures 13 and 14. This indicates that the model's parameters are stable.

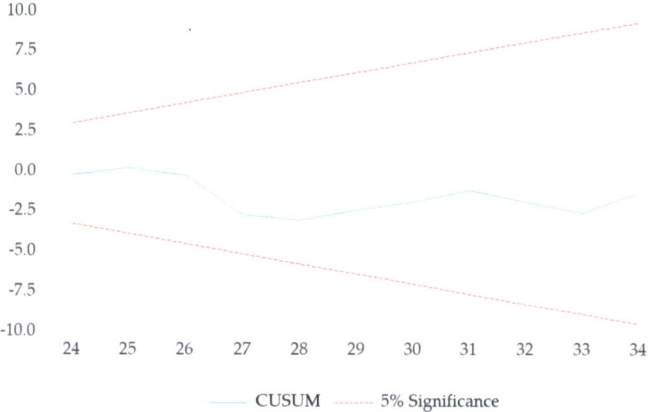

Figure 13. Plot of CUSUM for coefficients' stability of ARDL model at 5% level of significance.

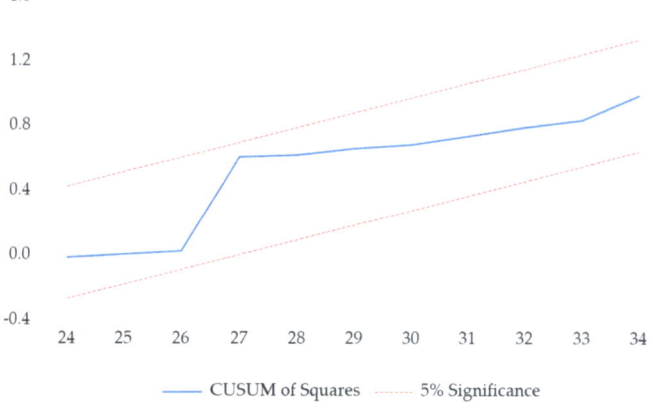

Figure 14. Plot of CUSUMSQ for coefficients' stability of ARDL model at 5% level of significance.

5. Conclusions and Policy Recommendations

Romania is in a process of transition towards a CE model, in the context of the growing need for sustainability and environmental protection. This transition entails adopting practices that reduce the dependence on finite resources and minimize negative environmental impacts. To this end, the country has implemented various policies and strategies to promote recycling, energy efficiency, and the use of renewable resources. However, challenges remain, including the need for adequate infrastructure and a sustainability mindset to ensure a sustainable future.

This study demonstrates that the implementation of CE strategies in Romania has the potential to significantly reduce CO_2 emissions, thus contributing to combating climate change.

The use of fuzzy MCDM has allowed the identification and prioritization of specific CE policies, ensuring a more efficient and targeted approach in their implementation. The six established policies focus on waste management, energy efficiency, innovation and development, sustainable production and consumption, GDP growth, and reducing CO_2 emissions. From the four fuzzy MCDM, Electre, Topsis, and Vikor prioritize for Romania the policy of CO_2 emission reduction, which was addressed in the ARDL quantitative model.

In the context of a CE, patent applications play a critical role in driving innovations that reduce CO_2 emissions. By focusing on resource efficiency, product lifecycle extension, industrial symbiosis, renewable resources, and circular supply chains, innovations can significantly contribute to sustainability and emission reduction. In Romania, fostering CE innovations and supporting green patents can enhance environmental outcomes and support the transition to a more sustainable economic model.

The strong correlation between urbanization and CO_2 emissions suggests that current economic policies and regulations in Romania may not effectively mitigate the environmental impact of urban growth. This could indicate a need for stronger policies aimed at promoting energy efficiency, renewable energy adoption, and sustainable urban planning. The findings highlight a potential trade-off between urbanization and environmental sustainability. Policymakers need to balance economic growth driven by urbanization with the environmental goal of reducing CO_2 emissions. This might involve investing in green technologies, enhancing public transportation, implementing stricter building codes for energy efficiency, and incentivizing low-carbon innovations.

While GDP growth leads to increased CO_2 emissions in the short run, indicating the carbon-intensive nature of economic activities, policy interventions and sustainable practices are needed to mitigate this impact. Rapid urbanization significantly raises emissions, highlighting the need for sustainable urban planning and development practices to balance growth with environmental concerns. EPREN has a significant short-term effect in reducing emissions. This supports policies aimed at boosting renewable energy investment as a key strategy for emission reduction. The initial increase in CO_2 emissions following an increase in PA suggests that innovation and the development of new technologies may have short-term environmental costs. However, the longer-term reduction in emissions indicates that these innovations are likely to lead to more efficient or cleaner technologies over time. Overall, these results emphasize the need for a balanced approach to economic growth, urban development, innovation, and energy policy to achieve sustainable environmental outcomes in Romania.

The result of this study offers valuable insights into the long-term factors that influence CO_2 emissions in Romania, with a particular emphasis on economic growth, urbanization, patent applications, and renewable energy. Although these findings provide significant theoretical contributions, their practical applicability necessitates meticulous consideration, particularly in the context of the practical obstacles that Romania encounters when implementing effective CO_2 reduction policies. Also, this study underlines a substantial contribution of renewable energy to the reduction of CO_2 emissions, showing a negative correlation between the production of renewable energy and emissions. This is in line with Romania's continued initiatives to boost its proportion of renewable energy in the national energy mix. It is essential to implement additional policy incentives in order to expedite the adoption of renewable energy sources. The study's identification of a positive correlation between patent applications and CO_2 emissions suggests that innovation, while advantageous, may result in higher emissions in specific sectors. This creates a challenge for policymakers. To ensure that the increase in patent applications contributes to environmental sustainability rather than increased emissions, Romania should consider devising industrial policies that stimulate research and development in low-carbon technologies. The environmental pressures that are associated with accelerated urban development are underscored by the positive relationship between urbanization and CO_2 emissions. The demand for energy increases, transportation becomes more intensive, and waste management becomes more difficult as cities expand. The real-world applicability of this discovery indicates that there are numerous areas that policymakers should concentrate on. Romania must advocate for sustainable urban development practices, including the adoption of energy-efficient transportation systems, the implementation of green construction codes, and the improvement of refuse management infrastructure.

Our results are in line with the fundamental principles of the National Strategy for the CE in Romania [1]. The first principle of stability in the NSCE is to reduce pollution by phasing out non-recyclable waste, the second to use products and materials at their highest utilization value for as long as possible, and the last one focuses on the regeneration of natural and eco-systems.

As in any scientific study, it is important to recognize its limitations. The first limitation refers to the fuzzy MCDMs used, which, as is well known, are also based on professional judgment and on certain estimates that may vary depending on the context analyzed. Also, the results are specific to the Romanian context and may not be applicable in other countries without additional adaptations. Another limitation could be represented by the fact that there are many external factors that could influence CO_2 emissions and the effectiveness of CE strategies that cannot be captured in a single study, such as global economic trends, international policies, or the impact of climate change. Future research directions can focus on monitoring these factors in order to ensure a holistic understanding of the dynamics of these changes.

In future research, we plan to integrate more variables or indicators that may influence the CE and CO_2 emissions, such as governmental policies and consumer behaviors. Also, another research direction can be in the direction of conducting comparative studies between Romania and other countries to assess the effectiveness of different CE strategies.

Author Contributions: Conceptualization, C.D., I.N., I.G., N.C. and C.C.; Data curation, C.D., I.N., I.G., N.C. and C.C.; Formal analysis, I.N. and I.G.; Funding acquisition, C.D.; Investigation, C.D., I.N., I.G. and N.C.; Methodology, I.N. and I.G.; Project administration, C.D.; Resources, C.D., N.C. and C.C.; Software, I.N., I.G. and C.C.; Validation, I.N., I.G., N.C. and C.C.; Visualization, I.N., I.G., N.C. and C.C.; Writing—original draft, I.N. and I.G.; Writing—review and editing, C.D., N.C. and C.C. All authors have read and agreed to the published version of the manuscript.

Funding: This research received no external funding.

Data Availability Statement: The data presented in this study are available on request from the corresponding author.

Acknowledgments: This work was funded by Bucharest University of Economic Studies under the project "Modeling and Analysis the Circular Economy in the Context of Sustainable Development using Emerging Technologies—2024".

Conflicts of Interest: The authors declare no conflicts of interest.

Abbreviations

Acronym	Definition
CE	Circular Economy
NSCE	National Strategy for the Circular Economy

MCDM	Multi-criteria decision making
ELECTRE	Elimination and Choice Translating Reality
TOPSIS	Technique for Order Preference by Similarity to Ideal Solution
Vikor	Multi-criteria optimization and compromise solution
DEMATEL	Decision-Making Trial and Evaluation Laboratory
FPIS	Fuzzy Positive Ideal Solution
FNIS	Fuzzy Negative Ideal Solution
CC	Closeness Coefficient
ARDL	Autoregressive Distributed Lag
ECM	Error correction model
ECT	Error correction term
ADF	Augmented Dickey–Fuller
VAR	Vector Autoregression
FPE	Final prediction error
AIC	Akaike information criterion
SC	Schwarz information criterion
HQ	Hannan–Quinn information criterion
GDP	Gross domestic product
PA	Patent Applications
EPREN	Share of energy production from renewables
URB	Urbanization

References

1. European Union National Strategy for the Circular Economy in Romania. Available online: https://circulareconomy.europa.eu/platform/en/strategies/national-strategy-circular-economy-romania (accessed on 8 April 2024).
2. European Parliament Circular Economy: Definition, Importance and Benefits. Available online: https://www.europarl.europa.eu/topics/en/article/20151201STO05603/circular-economy-definition-importance-and-benefits (accessed on 8 April 2024).
3. Yang, L.; Li, Z. Technology Advance and the Carbon Dioxide Emission in China—Empirical Research Based on the Rebound Effect. *Energy Policy* **2017**, *101*, 150–161. [CrossRef]
4. Chen, Y.; Lee, C.-C. Does Technological Innovation Reduce CO_2 Emissions? Cross-Country Evidence. *J. Clean. Prod.* **2020**, *263*, 121550. [CrossRef]
5. Raihan, A.; Begum, R.A.; Said, M.N.M.; Pereira, J.J. Relationship between Economic Growth, Renewable Energy Use, Technological Innovation, and Carbon Emission toward Achieving Malaysia's Paris Agreement. *Env. Syst. Decis.* **2022**, *42*, 586–607. [CrossRef]
6. Sohag, K.; Begum, R.A.; Abdullah, S.M.S.; Jaafar, M. Dynamics of Energy Use, Technological Innovation, Economic Growth and Trade Openness in Malaysia. *Energy* **2015**, *90*, 1497–1507. [CrossRef]
7. Liu, R.; Zhu, X.; Zhang, M.; Hu, C. Innovation Incentives and Urban Carbon Dioxide Emissions: A Quasi-Natural Experiment Based on Fast-Tracking Green Patent Applications in China. *J. Clean. Prod.* **2023**, *382*, 135444. [CrossRef]
8. Wang, N.; Yu, H.; Shu, Y.; Chen, Z.; Li, T. Can Green Patents Reduce Carbon Emission Intensity?—An Empirical Analysis Based on China's Experience. *Front. Environ. Sci.* **2022**, *10*, 1084977. [CrossRef]
9. Dunyo, S.K.; Odei, S.A.; Chaiwet, W. Relationship between CO_2 Emissions, Technological Innovation, and Energy Intensity: Moderating Effects of Economic and Political Uncertainty. *J. Clean. Prod.* **2024**, *440*, 140904. [CrossRef]
10. Zhao, X.; Long, L.; Yin, S.; Zhou, Y. How Technological Innovation Influences Carbon Emission Efficiency for Sustainable Development? Evidence from China. *Resour. Environ. Sustain.* **2023**, *14*, 100135. [CrossRef]
11. Hu, F.; Qiu, L.; Xiang, Y.; Wei, S.; Sun, H.; Hu, H.; Weng, X.; Mao, L.; Zeng, M. Spatial Network and Driving Factors of Low-Carbon Patent Applications in China from a Public Health Perspective. *Front. Public. Health* **2023**, *11*, 1121860. [CrossRef]
12. Georgescu, I.; Kinnunen, J. The Role of Foreign Direct Investments, Urbanization, Productivity, and Energy Consumption in Finland's Carbon Emissions: An ARDL Approach. *Env. Sci. Pollut. Res.* **2023**, *30*, 87685–87694. [CrossRef]
13. Georgescu, I.; Kinnunen, J. Effects of FDI, GDP and Energy Use on Ecological Footprint in Finland: An ARDL Approach. *World Dev. Sustain.* **2024**, *4*, 100157. [CrossRef]
14. Onofrei, M.; Vatamanu, A.F.; Cigu, E. The Relationship Between Economic Growth and CO_2 Emissions in EU Countries: A Cointegration Analysis. *Front. Environ. Sci.* **2022**, *10*, 934885. [CrossRef]
15. Mitić, P.; Fedajev, A.; Radulescu, M.; Rehman, A. The Relationship between CO_2 Emissions, Economic Growth, Available Energy, and Employment in SEE Countries. *Env. Sci. Pollut. Res.* **2022**, *30*, 16140–16155. [CrossRef] [PubMed]
16. Luqman, M.; Rayner, P.J.; Gurney, K.R. On the Impact of Urbanisation on CO_2 Emissions. *npj Urban. Sustain.* **2023**, *3*, 6. [CrossRef]
17. Muñoz, P.; Zwick, S.; Mirzabaev, A. The Impact of Urbanization on Austria's Carbon Footprint. *J. Clean. Prod.* **2020**, *263*, 121326. [CrossRef]
18. Chen, F.; Liu, A.; Lu, X.; Zhe, R.; Tong, J.; Akram, R. Evaluation of the Effects of Urbanization on Carbon Emissions: The Transformative Role of Government Effectiveness. *Front. Energy Res.* **2022**, *10*, 848800. [CrossRef]

19. Zhang, X.; Geng, Y.; Shao, S.; Wilson, J.; Song, X.; You, W. China's Non-Fossil Energy Development and Its 2030 CO_2 Reduction Targets: The Role of Urbanization. *Appl. Energy* **2020**, *261*, 114353. [CrossRef]
20. Szetela, B.; Majewska, A.; Jamroz, P.; Djalilov, B.; Salahodjaev, R. Renewable Energy and CO_2 Emissions in Top Natural Resource Rents Depending Countries: The Role of Governance. *Front. Energy Res.* **2022**, *10*, 872841. [CrossRef]
21. Bilan, Y.; Streimikiene, D.; Vasylieva, T.; Lyulyov, O.; Pimonenko, T.; Pavlyk, A. Linking between Renewable Energy, CO_2 Emissions, and Economic Growth: Challenges for Candidates and Potential Candidates for the EU Membership. *Sustainability* **2019**, *11*, 1528. [CrossRef]
22. Feng, H. The Impact of Renewable Energy on Carbon Neutrality for the Sustainable Environment: Role of Green Finance and Technology Innovations. *Front. Environ. Sci.* **2022**, *10*, 924857. [CrossRef]
23. Petruška, I.; Litavcová, E.; Chovancová, J. Impact of Renewable Energy Sources and Nuclear Energy on CO_2 Emissions Reductions—The Case of the EU Countries. *Energies* **2022**, *15*, 9563. [CrossRef]
24. Petković, B.; Agdas, A.S.; Zandi, Y.; Nikolić, I.; Denić, N.; Radenkovic, S.D.; Almojil, S.F.; Roco-Videla, A.; Kojić, N.; Zlatković, D.; et al. Neuro Fuzzy Evaluation of Circular Economy Based on Waste Generation, Recycling, Renewable Energy, Biomass and Soil Pollution. *Rhizosphere* **2021**, *19*, 100418. [CrossRef]
25. Gou, X.; Xu, X.; Xu, Z.; Skare, M. Circular Economy and Fuzzy Set Theory: A Bibliometric and Systematic Review Based on Industry 4.0 Technologies Perspective. *Technol. Econ. Dev. Econ.* **2024**, *30*, 489–526. [CrossRef]
26. Bai, C.; Zhu, Q.; Sarkis, J. Circular Economy and Circularity Supplier Selection: A Fuzzy Group Decision Approach. *Int. J. Prod. Res.* **2024**, *62*, 2307–2330. [CrossRef]
27. Abdelmeguid, A.; Afy-Shararah, M.; Salonitis, K. Mapping of the Circular Economy Implementation Challenges in the Fashion Industry: A Fuzzy-TISM Analysis. *Circ. Econ. Sust.* **2024**, *4*, 585–617. [CrossRef]
28. Husain, Z.; Maqbool, A.; Haleem, A.; Pathak, R.D.; Samson, D. Analyzing the Business Models for Circular Economy Implementation: A Fuzzy TOPSIS Approach. *Oper. Manag. Res.* **2021**, *14*, 256–271. [CrossRef]
29. Damgaci, E.; Boran, K.; Boran, F.E. Evaluation of Turkey's Renewable Energy Using Intuitionistic Fuzzy Topsis Method. *J. Polytech.-Politek. Derg.* **2017**, *20*, 629–637.
30. *Soft Computing Applications for Renewable Energy and Energy Efficiency*; Cascales, M.D.S.G.; Lozano, J.M.S.; Arredondo, A.D.M.; Corona, C.C. (Eds.) Advances in Environmental Engineering and Green Technologies; IGI Global: Hershey, PA, USA, 2015; ISBN 978-1-4666-6631-3.
31. Khan, S.; Haleem, A. Strategies to Implement Circular Economy Practices: A Fuzzy DEMATEL Approach. *J. Ind. Intg. Mgmt.* **2020**, *05*, 253–269. [CrossRef]
32. Boran, F.E.; Boran, K.; Menlik, T. The Evaluation of Renewable Energy Technologies for Electricity Generation in Turkey Using Intuitionistic Fuzzy TOPSIS. *Energy Sources Part B Econ. Plan. Policy* **2012**, *7*, 81–90. [CrossRef]
33. Kaya, T.; Kahraman, C. Multicriteria Renewable Energy Planning Using an Integrated Fuzzy VIKOR & AHP Methodology: The Case of Istanbul. *Energy* **2010**, *35*, 2517–2527. [CrossRef]
34. Li, T.; Wang, H.; Lin, Y. Selection of Renewable Energy Development Path for Sustainable Development Using a Fuzzy MCDM Based on Cumulative Prospect Theory: The Case of Malaysia. *Sci. Rep.* **2024**, *14*, 15082. [CrossRef] [PubMed]
35. Riaz, M.; Habib, A.; Saqlain, M.; Yang, M.-S. Cubic Bipolar Fuzzy-VIKOR Method Using New Distance and Entropy Measures and Einstein Averaging Aggregation Operators with Application to Renewable Energy. *Int. J. Fuzzy Syst.* **2023**, *25*, 510–543. [CrossRef]
36. Simmhan, Y.; Ingen, C.V.; Szalay, A.; Barga, R.; Heasley, J. Building Reliable Data Pipelines for Managing Community Data Using Scientific Workflows. In Proceedings of the 2009 Fifth IEEE International Conference on e-Science, Oxford, UK, 9–11 December 2009; IEEE: Oxford, UK, 2009; pp. 321–328.
37. Govindan, K.; Nasr, A.K.; Karimi, F.; Mina, H. Circular Economy Adoption Barriers: An Extended Fuzzy Best–Worst Method Using Fuzzy DEMATEL and Supermatrix Structure. *Bus. Strat. Env.* **2022**, *31*, 1566–1586. [CrossRef]
38. Ayçin, E.; Kayapinar Kaya, S. Towards the Circular Economy: Analysis of Barriers to Implementation of Turkey's Zero Waste Management Using the Fuzzy DEMATEL Method. *Waste Manag. Res.* **2021**, *39*, 1078–1089. [CrossRef]
39. Turgut, Z.K.; Tolga, A.Ç. Fuzzy MCDM Methods in Sustainable and Renewable Energy Alternative Selection: Fuzzy VIKOR and Fuzzy TODIM. In *Energy Management—Collective and Computational Intelligence with Theory and Applications*; Kahraman, C., Kayakutlu, G., Eds.; Studies in Systems, Decision and Control; Springer International Publishing: Cham, Switzerland, 2018; Volume 149, pp. 277–314, ISBN 978-3-319-75689-9.
40. Rejeb, A.; Rejeb, K.; Keogh, J.G.; Zailani, S. Barriers to Blockchain Adoption in the Circular Economy: A Fuzzy Delphi and Best-Worst Approach. *Sustainability* **2022**, *14*, 3611. [CrossRef]
41. Khan, F.; Ali, Y. A Facilitating Framework for a Developing Country to Adopt Smart Waste Management in the Context of Circular Economy. *Env. Sci. Pollut. Res.* **2022**, *29*, 26336–26351. [CrossRef]
42. Poonia, V.; Kulshrestha, R.; Sangwan, K.S.; Sharma, S. A Multi-Objective Fuzzy Mathematical Model for Circular Economy with Leasing as a Strategy. *MEQ* **2024**. [CrossRef]
43. Zadeh, L.A. Fuzzy Sets. *Inf. Control* **1965**, *8*, 338–353. [CrossRef]
44. Bellman, R.E.; Zadeh, L.A. Decision-Making in a Fuzzy Environment. *Manag. Sci.* **1970**, *17*, 141–164. [CrossRef]
45. Wang, T.-C.; Chang, T.-H. Application of TOPSIS in Evaluating Initial Training Aircraft under a Fuzzy Environment. *Expert. Syst. Appl.* **2007**, *33*, 870–880. [CrossRef]

46. Awasthi, A.; Chauhan, S.S.; Goyal, S.K. A Fuzzy Multicriteria Approach for Evaluating Environmental Performance of Suppliers. *Int. J. Prod. Econ.* **2010**, *126*, 370–378. [CrossRef]
47. Wu, W.-W.; Lee, Y.-T. Developing Global Managers' Competencies Using the Fuzzy DEMATEL Method. *Expert. Syst. Appl.* **2007**, *32*, 499–507. [CrossRef]
48. Opricovic, S.; Tzeng, G.-H. Compromise Solution by MCDM Methods: A Comparative Analysis of VIKOR and TOPSIS. *Eur. J. Oper. Res.* **2004**, *156*, 445–455. [CrossRef]
49. Mardani, A.; Zavadskas, E.; Govindan, K.; Amat Senin, A.; Jusoh, A. VIKOR Technique: A Systematic Review of the State of the Art Literature on Methodologies and Applications. *Sustainability* **2016**, *8*, 37. [CrossRef]
50. Roy, B.; Bertier, P. La Méthode Electre II—Une Methode Au Media-Planning. *Oper. Res.* **1973**, 291–302.
51. Akram, M.; Zahid, K.; Kahraman, C. A New ELECTRE-Based Decision-Making Framework with Spherical Fuzzy Information for the Implementation of Autonomous Vehicles Project in Istanbul. *Knowl. Based Syst.* **2024**, *283*, 111207. [CrossRef]
52. Daneshvar Rouyendegh, B.; Erol, S. Selecting the Best Project Using the Fuzzy ELECTRE Method. *Math. Probl. Eng.* **2012**, *2012*, 790142. [CrossRef]
53. Dubois, D.; Prade, H. *Fuzzy Sets and Systems: Theory and Applications*, 1st ed.; Elsevier Science: New York, NY, USA, 1980; Volume 144, ISBN 978-0-12-399465-3.
54. Komsiyah, S.; Wongso, R.; Pratiwi, S.W. Applications of the Fuzzy ELECTRE Method for Decision Support Systems of Cement Vendor Selection. *Procedia Comput. Sci.* **2019**, *157*, 479–488. [CrossRef]
55. *Fuzzy Multi-Criteria Decision Making*; Kahraman, C. (Ed.) Springer Optimization and Its Applications; Springer: Boston, MA, USA, 2008; Volume 16, ISBN 978-0-387-76812-0.
56. Montanari, R.; Micale, R.; Bottani, E.; Volpi, A.; La Scalia, G. Evaluation of Routing Policies Using an Interval-Valued TOPSIS Approach for the Allocation Rules. *Comput. Ind. Eng.* **2021**, *156*, 107256. [CrossRef]
57. Wanke, P.; Pestana Barros, C.; Chen, Z. An Analysis of Asian Airlines Efficiency with Two-Stage TOPSIS and MCMC Generalized Linear Mixed Models. *Int. J. Prod. Econ.* **2015**, *169*, 110–126. [CrossRef]
58. Arantes, R.F.M.; Zanon, L.G.; Calache, L.D.D.R.; Bertassini, A.C.; Carpinetti, L.C.R. A Fuzzy Multicriteria Group Decision Approach for Circular Business Models Prioritization. *Production* **2022**, *32*, e20220019. [CrossRef]
59. Haleem, A.; Khan, S.; Luthra, S.; Varshney, H.; Alam, M.; Khan, M.I. Supplier Evaluation in the Context of Circular Economy: A Forward Step for Resilient Business and Environment Concern. *Bus. Strat. Env.* **2021**, *30*, 2119–2146. [CrossRef]
60. Chen, C.-T. Extensions of the TOPSIS for Group Decision-Making under Fuzzy Environment. *Fuzzy Sets Syst.* **2000**, *114*, 1–9. [CrossRef]
61. Awasthi, A.; Chauhan, S.S.; Goyal, S.K. A Multi-Criteria Decision Making Approach for Location Planning for Urban Distribution Centers under Uncertainty. *Math. Comput. Model.* **2011**, *53*, 98–109. [CrossRef]
62. Nădăban, S.; Dzitac, S.; Dzitac, I. Fuzzy TOPSIS: A General View. *Procedia Comput. Sci.* **2016**, *91*, 823–831. [CrossRef]
63. Opricovic, S.; Tzeng, G.-H. Extended VIKOR Method in Comparison with Outranking Methods. *Eur. J. Oper. Res.* **2007**, *178*, 514–529. [CrossRef]
64. Yazdani, M.; Graeml, F.R. VIKOR and its Applications: A State-of-the-Art Survey. *Int. J. Strateg. Decis. Sci.* **2014**, *5*, 56–83. [CrossRef]
65. Kizielewicz, B.; Bączkiewicz, A. Comparison of Fuzzy TOPSIS, Fuzzy VIKOR, Fuzzy WASPAS and Fuzzy MMOORA Methods in the Housing Selection Problem. *Procedia Comput. Sci.* **2021**, *192*, 4578–4591. [CrossRef]
66. Chang, B.; Chang, C.-W.; Wu, C.-H. Fuzzy DEMATEL Method for Developing Supplier Selection Criteria. *Expert. Syst. Appl.* **2011**, *38*, 1850–1858. [CrossRef]
67. Lütkepohl, H.; Xu, F. The Role of the Log Transformation in Forecasting Economic Variables. *Empir. Econ.* **2012**, *42*, 619–638. [CrossRef]
68. Bayer, C.; Hanck, C. Combining Non-cointegration Tests. *J. Time Ser. Anal.* **2013**, *34*, 83–95. [CrossRef]
69. Engle, R.F.; Granger, C.W.J. Co-Integration and Error Correction: Representation, Estimation, and Testing. *Econometrica* **1987**, *55*, 251. [CrossRef]
70. Johansen, S. Statistical Analysis of Cointegration Vectors. *J. Econ. Dyn. Control* **1988**, *12*, 231–254. [CrossRef]
71. Peter Boswijk, H. Testing for an Unstable Root in Conditional and Structural Error Correction Models. *J. Econom.* **1994**, *63*, 37–60. [CrossRef]
72. Banerjee, A.; Dolado, J.; Mestre, R. Error-correction Mechanism Tests for Cointegration in a Single-equation Framework. *J. Time Ser. Anal.* **1998**, *19*, 267–283. [CrossRef]
73. Pesaran, M.H.; Shin, Y.; Smith, R.J. Bounds Testing Approaches to the Analysis of Level Relationships. *J. Appl. Econom.* **2001**, *16*, 289–326. [CrossRef]
74. Our World in Data Per Capital CO2 Emissions (Tonnes). Available online: https://ourworldindata.org/co2-and-greenhouse-gas-emissions (accessed on 7 September 2024).
75. World Bank Patent Applications, Residents. Available online: https://data.worldbank.org/indicator/IP.PAT.RESD (accessed on 7 September 2024).
76. World Bank Patent Applications, Nonresidents. Available online: https://data.worldbank.org/indicator/IP.PAT.NRES (accessed on 7 September 2024).

77. World Bank GDP per Capita (Constant 2015 US$). Available online: https://data.worldbank.org/indicator/NY.GDP.PCAP.KD (accessed on 7 September 2024).
78. Our World in Data Share of Electricity Production from Renewables 2023.
79. World Bank Urban Population (% of Total Population). Available online: https://data.worldbank.org/indicator/SP.URB.TOTL.IN.ZS (accessed on 7 September 2024).
80. Giovanis, E. Relationship between Recycling Rate and Air Pollution: Waste Management in the State of Massachusetts. *Waste Manag.* **2015**, *40*, 192–203. [CrossRef]
81. Sidique, S.F.; Joshi, S.V.; Lupi, F. Factors Influencing the Rate of Recycling: An Analysis of Minnesota Counties. *Resour. Conserv. Recycl.* **2010**, *54*, 242–249. [CrossRef]
82. Nastase, C.; Chașovschi, C.E.; State, M.; Scutariu, A.-L. Municipal Waste Management in Romania in The context of the EU. A Stakeholders' Perspective. *Technol. Econ. Dev. Econ.* **2019**, *25*, 850–876. [CrossRef]
83. Delcea, C.; Crăciun, L.; Ioanăș, C.; Ferruzzi, G.; Cotfas, L.-A. Determinants of Individuals' E-Waste Recycling Decision: A Case Study from Romania. *Sustainability* **2020**, *12*, 2753. [CrossRef]
84. Aceleanu, M.I.; Șerban, A.C.; Pociovălișteanu, D.M.; Dimian, G.C. Renewable Energy: A Way for a Sustainable Development in Romania. *Energy Sources Part B Econ. Plan. Policy* **2017**, *12*, 958–963. [CrossRef]
85. Vanegas Cantarero, M.M. Of Renewable Energy, Energy Democracy, and Sustainable Development: A Roadmap to Accelerate the Energy Transition in Developing Countries. *Energy Res. Soc. Sci.* **2020**, *70*, 101716. [CrossRef]
86. Jefferson, M. Accelerating the Transition to Sustainable Energy Systems. *Energy Policy* **2008**, *36*, 4116–4125. [CrossRef]
87. Prăvălie, R.; Sîrodoev, I.; Ruiz-Arias, J.; Dumitrașcu, M. Using Renewable (Solar) Energy as a Sustainable Management Pathway of Lands Highly Sensitive to Degradation in Romania. A Countrywide Analysis Based on Exploring the Geographical and Technical Solar Potentials. *Renew. Energy* **2022**, *193*, 976–990. [CrossRef]
88. Dobre-Baron, O.; Nițescu, A.; Niță, D.; Mitran, C. Romania's Perspectives on the Transition to the Circular Economy in an EU Context. *Sustainability* **2022**, *14*, 5324. [CrossRef]
89. Topliceanu, L.; Puiu, P.G.; Drob, C.; Topliceanu, V.V. Analysis Regarding the Implementation of the Circular Economy in Romania. *Sustainability* **2022**, *15*, 333. [CrossRef]
90. Botezat, E.A.; Dodescu, A.O.; Văduva, S.; Fotea, S.L. An Exploration of Circular Economy Practices and Performance Among Romanian Producers. *Sustainability* **2018**, *10*, 3191. [CrossRef]
91. Aceleanu, M.I.; Serban, A.C.; Suciu, M.-C.; Bitoiu, T.I. The Management of Municipal Waste through Circular Economy in the Context of Smart Cities Development. *IEEE Access* **2019**, *7*, 133602–133614. [CrossRef]
92. Platon, V.; Pavelescu, F.M.; Antonescu, D.; Frone, S.; Constantinescu, A.; Popa, F. Innovation and Recycling—Drivers of Circular Economy in EU. *Front. Environ. Sci.* **2022**, *10*, 902651. [CrossRef]
93. Lakatos, E.; Cioca, L.-I.; Dan, V.; Ciomos, A.; Crisan, O.; Barsan, G. Studies and Investigation about the Attitude towards Sustainable Production, Consumption and Waste Generation in Line with Circular Economy in Romania. *Sustainability* **2018**, *10*, 865. [CrossRef]
94. Dinu, M.; Pătărlăgeanu, S.R.; Petrariu, R.; Constantin, M.; Potcovaru, A.-M. Empowering Sustainable Consumer Behavior in the EU by Consolidating the Roles of Waste Recycling and Energy Productivity. *Sustainability* **2020**, *12*, 9794. [CrossRef]
95. Liobikienė, G.; Dagiliūtė, R. The Relationship between Economic and Carbon Footprint Changes in EU: The Achievements of the EU Sustainable Consumption and Production Policy Implementation. *Environ. Sci. Policy* **2016**, *61*, 204–211. [CrossRef]
96. Firoiu, D.; Ionescu, G.H.; Băndoi, A.; Florea, N.M.; Jianu, E. Achieving Sustainable Development Goals (SDG): Implementation of the 2030 Agenda in Romania. *Sustainability* **2019**, *11*, 2156. [CrossRef]
97. Oroian, C.; Safirescu, C.; Harun, R.; Chiciudean, G.; Arion, F.; Muresan, I.; Bordeanu, B. Consumers' Attitudes towards Organic Products and Sustainable Development: A Case Study of Romania. *Sustainability* **2017**, *9*, 1559. [CrossRef]
98. OECD Resource Efficiency and Circular Economy. Available online: https://www.oecd.org/en/topics/policy-issues/resource-efficiency-and-circular-economy.html (accessed on 8 April 2024).
99. Mocanu, A.A.; Brătucu, G.; Ciobanu, E.; Chițu, I.B.; Szakal, A.C. Can the Circular Economy Unlock Sustainable Business Growth? Insights from Qualitative Research with Specialists in Romania. *Sustainability* **2024**, *16*, 2031. [CrossRef]
100. Andrei, J.; Mieila, M.; Popescu, G.; Nica, E.; Cristina, M. The Impact and Determinants of Environmental Taxation on Economic Growth Communities in Romania. *Energies* **2016**, *9*, 902. [CrossRef]
101. Busu, M. Adopting Circular Economy at the European Union Level and Its Impact on Economic Growth. *Soc. Sci.* **2019**, *8*, 159. [CrossRef]
102. Mihaela Cristina, D.; Maria-Floriana, P.; Jean Vasile, A.; Mihai, M. Developments of the Circular Economy in Romania under the New Sustainability Paradigm. *Econ. Comput. Econ. Cybern. Stud. Res.* **2018**, *52*, 125–138. [CrossRef]
103. Trica, C.L.; Banacu, C.S.; Busu, M. Environmental Factors and Sustainability of the Circular Economy Model at the European Union Level. *Sustainability* **2019**, *11*, 1114. [CrossRef]
104. Nica, I.; Chiriță, N.; Delcea, C. Towards a Sustainable Future: Economic Cybernetics in Analyzing Romania's Circular Economy. *Sustainability* **2023**, *15*, 14433. [CrossRef]
105. Nica, I.; Ciocan, M.-L. Mapping Circular Pathways: A Bibliometric Exploration and Multilinear Regression Model of Romania's Circular Economy. *Theor. Appl. Econ.* **2023**, *30*, 17–34.

106. Chiriță, N.; Georgescu, I. Cybernetics Analysis of the Circular Economy from Romania. In *Proceedings of 22nd International Conference on Informatics in Economy (IE 2023)*; Ciurea, C., Pocatilu, P., Filip, F.G., Eds.; Smart Innovation, Systems and Technologies; Springer Nature: Singapore, 2024; Volume 367, pp. 319–330, ISBN 978-981-9969-59-3.
107. Cioca, L.-I.; Ivascu, L.; Rada, E.; Torretta, V.; Ionescu, G. Sustainable Development and Technological Impact on CO_2 Reducing Conditions in Romania. *Sustainability* **2015**, *7*, 1637–1650. [CrossRef]
108. Hatmanu, M.; Cautisanu, C.; Iacobuta, A.O. On the Relationships between CO_2 Emissions and Their Determinants in Romania and Bulgaria. An ARDL Approach. *Appl. Econ.* **2022**, *54*, 2582–2595. [CrossRef]
109. Busu, M. Measuring the Renewable Energy Efficiency at the European Union Level and Its Impact on CO_2 Emissions. *Processes* **2019**, *7*, 923. [CrossRef]
110. Dickey, D.A.; Fuller, W.A. Distribution of the Estimators for Autoregressive Time Series with a Unit Root. *J. Am. Stat. Assoc.* **1979**, *74*, 427–431. [CrossRef]

Disclaimer/Publisher's Note: The statements, opinions and data contained in all publications are solely those of the individual author(s) and contributor(s) and not of MDPI and/or the editor(s). MDPI and/or the editor(s) disclaim responsibility for any injury to people or property resulting from any ideas, methods, instructions or products referred to in the content.

MDPI AG
Grosspeteranlage 5
4052 Basel
Switzerland
Tel.: +41 61 683 77 34

Mathematics Editorial Office
E-mail: mathematics@mdpi.com
www.mdpi.com/journal/mathematics

Disclaimer/Publisher's Note: The title and front matter of this reprint are at the discretion of the Guest Editors. The publisher is not responsible for their content or any associated concerns. The statements, opinions and data contained in all individual articles are solely those of the individual Editors and contributors and not of MDPI. MDPI disclaims responsibility for any injury to people or property resulting from any ideas, methods, instructions or products referred to in the content.

www.ingramcontent.com/pod-product-compliance
Lightning Source LLC
LaVergne TN
LVHW072321090526
838202LV00019B/2327